6TH EDITION

LOOKING AT MOVIES

6TH EDITION

LOOKING AT MOVIES
AN INTRODUCTION TO FILM

RICHARD BARSAM & DAVE MONAHAN

W. W. NORTON & COMPANY
NEW YORK • LONDON

W. W. Norton & Company has been independent since its founding in 1923, when William Warder Norton and Mary D. Herter Norton first published lectures delivered at the People's Institute, the adult education division of New York City's Cooper Union. The firm soon expanded its program beyond the Institute, publishing books by celebrated academics from America and abroad. By midcentury, the two major pillars of Norton's publishing program—trade books and college texts—were firmly established. In the 1950s, the Norton family transferred control of the company to its employees, and today—with a staff of four hundred and a comparable number of trade, college, and professional titles published each year—W. W. Norton & Company stands as the largest and oldest publishing house owned wholly by its employees.

Editor: Peter Simon
Senior project editor: Thomas Foley
Associate director, college production: Benjamin Reynolds
Copy editor: Chris Curioli
Editorial assistant: Katie Pak
Media editor: Carly Fraser Doria
ebook manager: Danielle Lehmann
Media editorial assistant: Alexander Lee
Digital media project editor: Cooper Wilhelm
Marketing manager: Kimberly Bowers
Managing editor, college: Marian Johnson
Managing editor, college digital media: Kim Yi
Design director: Rubina Yeh
Book designer: Lissi Sigillo
Cover designer: Jillian Burr
Photo editor: Agnieszka Czapski
Composition: Achorn International, Inc.
Digital art file manipulation: Jay's Publishers Services, Inc.
Manufacturing: LSC Communications—Willard, OH
Development editor for the First Edition: Kurt Wildermuth

ISBN: 978-0-393-64499-9
W. W. Norton & Company, Inc., 500 Fifth Avenue, New York, NY 10110
wwnorton.com

W. W. Norton & Company Ltd., 15 Carlisle Street, London W1D 3BS

4 5 6 7 8 9 0

ABOUT THE AUTHORS

RICHARD BARSAM is Professor Emeritus of Film Studies at Hunter College, City University of New York. He is the author of *Nonfiction Film: A Critical History* (rev. and exp. ed., 1992), *The Vision of Robert Flaherty: The Artist as Myth and Filmmaker* (1988), *In the Dark: A Primer for the Movies* (1977), and *Filmguide to Triumph of the Will* (1975); editor of *Nonfiction Film: Theory and Criticism* (1976); and contributing author to Paul Monaco's *The Sixties: 1960–1969* (Vol. 8 in the History of the American Cinema series, 2001) and *Filming Robert Flaherty's Louisiana Story: The Helen van Dongen Diary* (ed. Eva Orbanz, 1998). His articles and book reviews have appeared in *Cinema Journal, Quarterly Review of Film Studies, Film Comment, Studies in Visual Communication*, and *Harper's*. He has been a member of the Executive Council of the Society for Cinema and Media Studies and the Editorial Board of *Cinema Journal*, and he cofounded the journal *Persistence of Vision*.

DAVE MONAHAN is a Professor of Film Studies at the University of North Carolina, Wilmington. His work as a writer, director, and editor includes narrative, documentary, and experimental films, among them: *Face Age* (2016), *Things Grow* (2011), *Ringo* (2005), *Monkey Junction* (2004), *Prime Time* (1996), and *Angels Watching Over Me* (1993). His work has been screened internationally in over seventy film festivals and has earned numerous awards, including the New Line Cinema Award for Most Original Film (*Prime Time*) and the Seattle International Film Festival Grand Jury Prize for Best Animated Short Film (*Ringo*)

CONTENTS

CHAPTER 4
Elements of Narrative   115

CHAPTER 5
Mise-en-Scène   153

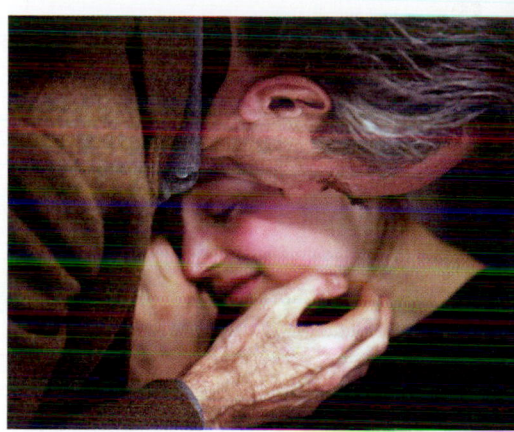

CHAPTER 7
ACTING   235

CHAPTER 8
EDITING   281

CHAPTER 9
SOUND   319

CHAPTER 10
FILM HISTORY 357

PREFACE

Students in an introductory film course who read *Looking at Movies* carefully and take full advantage of its media program will finish the course with a solid grounding in the major principles of film form as well as a more perceptive and analytic eye. A short description of the book's main features follows.

An Accessible and Comprehensive Overview of Film

Recognized from its first publication as an accessible introductory text, *Looking at Movies* covers key concepts in films studies as comprehensively as possible. In addition to its clear and inviting presentation of the fundamentals of film form, the text discusses film genres, film history, and the relationships between film and culture in an extensive but characteristically accessible way, thus providing students with a thorough introduction to the major subject areas in film studies. In the Sixth Edition three chapters in particular—Chapter 5: Mise-en-Scène, Chapter 6: Cinematography, and Chapter 8: Editing—arguably the "core" of the text, have been thoroughly revised by Dave Monahan to be even clearer, more accessible, and more enlightening than ever before.

Film Examples Chosen with Undergraduates in Mind

From its very first chapter, which features sustained analyses and examples from the Star Wars series and Jason Reitman's *Juno* (2009), *Looking at Movies* invites students into the serious study of cinema via films that they are probably familiar with and that they have, in all likelihood, seen outside the classroom prior to taking the course. Major films from the entire history of cinema are also generously represented, but always with an eye to helping students see enjoyment and serious study as complementary experiences.

A Focus on Analytic Skills

A good introductory film book needs to help students make the transition from the natural enjoyment of movies to a critical understanding of the form, content, and meanings of movies. *Looking at Movies* accomplishes this task in several different ways:

Model Analyses

Hundreds of illustrative examples and analytic readings of films throughout the book provide students with concrete models for their own analytic work. The sustained analyses in Chapter 1 of *Juno* and the Star Wars saga—films that most undergraduates will have seen and enjoyed but perhaps not viewed with a critical eye—discuss not only the formal structures and techniques of these films, but also their social and cultural meanings. These analyses offer students an accessible and jargon-free introduction to most of the major themes and goals of an introductory film course, and show students that looking at movies analytically can start immediately, even before they learn the specialized vocabulary of film study. Each chapter also concludes with an in-depth "Looking at . . ." analysis that offers a sustained look at a single film through the lens of that chapter's particular focus. A new analysis of *Moonlight* in Chapter 6 and significantly revised analyses of *Stagecoach* (Chapter 4) and *City of God* (Chapter 8) join existing analyses to provide clear models for students' own analyses and interpretations of films.

Interactives

Interactives developed with Dave Monahan provide students with hands-on practice manipulating key concepts of filmmaking and formal analysis. Students can work at their own pace to see how elements such as lighting, sound, editing, composition, and color function within a film. A new interactive for the Sixth Edition features a 3D rendering of the set for the famous cabin scene from Charlie Chaplin's *The Gold Rush*. Students are able to move freely around the virtual space with their "camera" to attempt different shot set-ups and compositions.

Available in the ebook and on the *Looking at Movies* student website, these features can be accessed at **digital .wwnorton.com/movies6**.

Video Tutorials

A series of video tutorials—written, directed, and hosted by Dave Monahan—complement and expand on the book's analyses. Ranging from 2 to 15 minutes in length, these tutorials show students via moving-image media what the book describes and illustrates in still images. The Sixth Edition offers one new tutorial on the Star Wars series that expands on the in-text analysis. Helpful as a quick review of core concepts in the text, these tutorials also provide useful models for film analysis, thus helping students further develop their analytical skills. Available in the ebook and on the *Looking at Movies* student website, these tutorials can be found at **digital.wwnorton.com/movies6**.

Screening Checklists

Each chapter ends with an Analyzing section that includes a Screening Checklist feature. This series of leading questions prompts students to apply what they've learned in the chapter to their own critical viewing, in class or at home.

The Most Visually Dynamic Text Available

Looking at Movies was written with one goal in mind: to prepare students for a lifetime of intelligent and perceptive viewing of motion pictures. In recognition of the central role visuals play in the film-studies classroom, *Looking at Movies* includes an illustration program that is both visually appealing and pedagogically focused, as well as accompanying moving-image media that are second to none.

Hundreds of In-Text Illustrations

The text is illustrated by over 750 illustrations in color and in black-and-white. Nearly all the still pictures were captured from digital or analog film sources, thus ensuring that the images directly reflect the textual discussions and the films from which they're taken. Unlike publicity stills, which are attractive as photographs but less useful as teaching aids, the captured stills throughout this book provide visual information that will help students learn as they read and—because they are re-

produced in the aspect ratio of the original source—will serve as accurate reference points for students' analyses.

Five Hours of Moving-Image Media

The ebook and student website that accompany *Looking at Movies* offer five hours of video content:

- The twenty-eight video tutorials described above were specifically created to complement *Looking at Movies* and are exclusive to this text. Because they are viewable in full-screen, they are suitable for presentation in class as well as for students' self-study. In addition to the longer video tutorials, there are also over fifty short-form animations based on illustrations in the print text.

- A mini-anthology of thirteen complete short films, ranging from 5 to 30 minutes in length, provides a curated selection of accomplished and entertaining examples of short-form cinema, as well as useful material for short in-class activities or for students' analyses. Most of the films are also accompanied by optional audio commentary from the filmmakers. This commentary was recorded specifically for *Looking at Movies* and is exclusive to this text.

Accessible Presentation; Effective Pedagogy

Among the reasons that *Looking at Movies* is considered the most accessible introductory film text available is its clear and direct presentation of key concepts and unique pedagogical organization. The first three chapters of the book—"Looking at Movies," "Principles of Film Form," and "Types of Movies"—provide a comprehensive yet truly introductory overview of the major topics and themes of any film course, giving students a solid grounding in the basics before they move on to study those topics in greater depth in later chapters.

In addition, pedagogical features throughout provide a structure that clearly identifies the main ideas and primary goals of each chapter for students:

Learning Objectives

A checklist at the beginning of every chapter provides a brief summary of the core concepts to be covered in the chapter.

Extensive Captions

Each illustration is accompanied by a caption that elaborates on a key concept or that guides students to look at elements of the film more analytically. These captions expand on the in-text presentation and reinforce students' retention of key terms and ideas.

Analyzing Sections

At the end of each chapter is a section that ties the terms, concepts, and ideas of the chapter to the primary goal of the book: honing students' own analytical skills. This short overview makes explicit how the knowledge students have gained in the chapter can move their own analytical work forward. A short Screening Checklist provides leading questions that students can ponder as they screen a film or scene.

Questions for Review

A section at the end of each chapter tests students' knowledge of the concepts first mentioned in the Learning Objectives at the beginning of the chapter.

Beyond the in-text pedagogy, the abundant resources that accompany *Looking at Movies* are designed to help students succeed.

InQuizitive: A game-like, media-rich, interactive quizzing tool

Students in an introductory film course are already motivated to watch movies and discuss them with their classmates. But they sometimes struggle to learn the essential terms and concepts that make those conversations more analytical and interesting. InQuizitive is an engaging, adaptive quizzing tool that helps students master important concepts and gives them support where they need it most.

Enhanced Ebook

Looking at Movies is also available as an enhanced ebook free with every new copy of the print book. This ebook works on all computers and mobile devices, and embeds all the rich media—video tutorials, animations, interactives, and more—into one seamless experience. Instructors can focus student reading by sharing notes in the ebook, as well as embed images and other videos. Reports on student and class-wide access and time on task also enable instructors to monitor student reading and engagement.

Writing About Movies

Written by Karen Gocsik (University of California, San Diego) and the authors of *Looking at Movies*, this book is a clear and practical overview of the process of writing papers for film-studies courses. In addition to providing helpful information about the writing process, the new *Writing About Movies,* Fifth Edition, offers a substantial introduction-in-brief to the major topics in film studies, including an overview of the major film theories and their potential application to student writing, practical advice about note-taking during screenings and private viewings, information about the study of genre and film history, and an illustrated glossary of essential film terms. This inexpensive text is available separately or in a significantly discounted package with *Looking at Movies*.

Resources for Instructors

All of the following resources are free to adopters of *Looking at Movies* and can be found at wwnorton.com/instructors or by clicking the Instructor Resources tile at digital.wwnorton.com/movies6. Contact your local sales representative for access.

Interactive Instructors Guide

This searchable, sortable site for instructors contains over 1,000 resources for class preparation and presentation, including all of the video content from the student site, hundreds of downloadable images, Lecture Power-Points, suggestions for in-class activities, clip suggestions from the popular Clip Guide, and more.

Clip Guide

An invaluable class-prep tool, the Clip Guide suggests a wide range of clips for illustrating film concepts covered in the text. Each entry in the Clip Guide offers a quick overview of the scene, the idea, and crucially, time-stamp information on exactly where to find each clip. The *Looking at Movies* Clip Guide includes suggestions from not just the authors but from a wide range of teachers, offering a broad perspective of insightful teaching tips that can inspire and save valuable prep time.

Test Bank

Each chapter of the Test Bank includes 60–65 multiple-choice and 10–15 essay questions (with sample answer guides). Questions are labeled by concept, difficulty, and Bloom's Taxonomy.

Coursepacks for Learning Management Systems

Ready-to-use coursepacks for Blackboard and other learning management systems are available free of charge to instructors who adopt *Looking at Movies*. These coursepacks offer customizable quizzes, chapter overviews and learning objectives, and links to media.

***

Looking at Movies is not just a book that is supplemented by media. *Looking at Movies* is _made_ of media. For more information about how to make the most out of *Looking at Movies*, see "Five Steps to Getting the Most Out of the *Looking at Movies* Digital Resources" on the following page.

Five steps to getting the most out of the
LOOKING AT MOVIES DIGITAL RESOURCES

Looking at Movies offers a wealth of resources for students and instructors. This one-page guide is intended to help instructors incorporate these resources into their course.

❭ **INQUIZITIVE** New to the Sixth Edition, InQuizitive is Norton's game-like quizzing tool. InQuizitive uses interactive question types and rich media to help students understand key film terms and concepts from the book. InQuizitive is adaptive, so students receive extra help on the concepts they might be struggling with, and it integrates seamlessly with your learning management system, making it easy to track student progress. A code to access InQuizitive is found in every new copy of *Looking at Movies*, Sixth Edition, or students can purchase access at DIGITAL.WWNORTON.COM/MOVIES6.

❭ **Make sure your students know about the ebook.** Students can get all of the great content of the print book enhanced with animations, video tutorials, and links to interactives with the *Looking at Movies*, Sixth Edition ebook. All students who purchase a new print book get automatic access to the ebook. Students can purchase the ebook at DIGITAL.WWNORTON.COM/MOVIES6 as a standalone product for just a fraction of the cost of the print text. For instructor access to the ebook, contact your Norton sales representative.

❭ **Incorporate exclusive *Looking at Movies* video content into your course.** Students can find over five hours of video content at DIGITAL.WWNORTON.COM/MOVIES6, including twenty-eight 5-to-30-minute video tutorials on key concepts in the book, written, directed, and narrated by Dave Monahan. These videos are ideal for in-class presentation or for assigning to students for at-home viewing. In addition to the video tutorials, the site also offers over fifty short animations and a collection of thirteen compete short films.

❭ **Use interactives to help students understand filmmaking decisions.** Six interactives found at DIGITAL.WWNORTON.COM/MOVIES6 provide students with hands-on practice manipulating key concepts of filmmaking and formal analysis. Students can work at their own pace to see how elements such as lighting, sound, editing, composition, and color function within a film. A new interactive for the Sixth Edition features a 3D rendering of the set for the famous cabin scene from Charlie Chaplin's *The Gold Rush*. Students are able to move freely around the virtual space with their "camera" to attempt different shot set-ups and compositions.

❭ **Use the Interactive Instructor's Guide (IIG) and Norton Coursepacks to plan and prep your course.** This searchable, sortable site for instructors contains over 1,000 resources for class prep and presentation, including all of the video content from the student site, hundreds of downloadable images, Lecture PowerPoints, suggestions for in-class activities, clip suggestions from the popular Clip Guide, a 700+ question test bank, and more. Finally, Norton Coursepacks for Blackboard and other learning management systems are available free of charge to instructors who adopt *Looking at Movies*. Norton Coursepacks allow you to plug customizable quizzes, chapter overviews, and links to media right into your existing online course. For access to the IIG and Norton Coursepacks, contact your Norton sales representative or request access at WWNORTON.COM/INSTRUCTORS.

ACKNOWLEDGMENTS

Writing a book seems very much at times like the collaborative effort involved in making movies. In writing this Sixth Edition of *Looking at Movies,* I am grateful to my generous partners at W. W. Norton & Company. Chief among them is my editor, Pete Simon, who has thoughtfully guided and improved every edition. Other collaborators at Norton were Thom Foley, senior project editor; Benjamin Reynolds, associate production director; Carly Fraser Doria, media editor; Alex Lee, media editorial assistant; Cooper Wilhelm, media project editor; Rachel Truong and Pat Cartelli, media designers; Kimberly Bowers, marketing manager; Gerra Goff, associate editor; and Katie Pak, editorial assistant. It has been a pleasure to work with such a responsive, creative, and supportive team.

My sincere thanks to my longtime mentor Richard Barsam, who wrote the first two editions of *Looking at Movies* before I joined him as co-author for the three editions that followed. Richard's knowledge and love of cinema permeate every chapter in this book. Each new word I write is in service to his original vision.

I would also like to thank the faculty, staff, and students of the Film Studies Department at the University of North Carolina, Wilmington. My colleagues Todd Berliner, Glenn Pack, Sue Richardson, Mariana Johnson, Elizabeth Rawitsch, Shannon Silva, Andre Silva, Tim Palmer, Carlos Kase, Chip Hackler, Terry Linehan, Georg Koszulinski, Lexi Cavazos, Alex Markowski, and David Kreutzer contributed expertise and advice, as did university colleagues Dale Cohen, Richard Blaylock, and Myke Holmes. Film Studies students Christian Wheeler, Greg Guidry, Shanik Ramirez, Austin Chesnutt, Connor Lummert, Alexis Dickerson, Garrett Farrington, and Brendan Murphy—as well as alumni Charles Riggs and Kevin Bahr—served as research assistants. Charles Riggs contributed invaluable research and ideas to the revision of chapter 11. My colleague Aaron Cavazos deserves special thanks for his postproduction contributions to this edition's new media additions, including the new Star Wars formal analysis tutorial. Aaron created the animation and motion graphics and supervised the sound recording and design. A number of talented university and community friends helped create the new *Camera as Moderator* module that re-creates a scene from Charlie Chaplin's *The Gold Rush.* Mark Eaton modeled the set, furnishings, and props; Mark Sorenson designed the costumes; Michael Rosander and Anthony Lawson played 'The Lone Prospector' and 'Big Jim McKay'; Stephanie Galbraith did make-up; and Boston Dao set the lights. Brittany Morago scanned the actors, assembled the various digital components, and developed the software for the interactive.

Thanks, too, to Melissa Lenos (Donnelly College), who authored the questions and feedback for the exciting new InQuizitive feature and who produced the lecture PowerPoints for this edition; to Kevin Sandler (Arizona State University), author of the instructors' Test Bank and Coursepack supplements; and Richard Wiebe (University of Iowa), who authored the Clip Guide.

Love and thanks to my family: Julie, for her patience and support; Iris, for teaching me about narrative gaming and contributing an illustration to the new Star Wars tutorial; and Rae, for helping me to look at all movies with fresh eyes.

Reviewers

I would like to join the publisher in thanking all the professors and students who provided valuable guidance as I planned this revision. *Looking at Movies* is their book, too, and I am grateful to both students and faculty who have cared enough about this text to help make it better.

Thoughtful and substantive reviews from the following colleagues and fellow instructors helped shape both the book and its media program for this Sixth Edition: Drew Ayers (Eastern Washington University), Claudia Calhoun (New York University), Kathleen Coate (Normandale Community College), Laurene DeBord-Foulk (University of Nevada, Las Vegas), Ryan Friedman (Ohio State University), Anna Froula (East Carolina University), Robert S. Goald (University of Nevada, Las Vegas),

Sarah Hamblin (University of Massachusetts, Boston), Matthew Hanson (Eastern Michigan University), Peter Lester (Brock University), Shellie Michael (Volunteer State University), William Molloy (Brookdale Community College), Matthew Montemorano (Brookdale Community College), Kensil Bradford Owen (California State University, San Bernadino), Jennifer Proctor (University of Michigan), Paul N. Reinsch (Texas Tech University), Jared Saltzman (Bergen Community College), Kevin Sandler (Arizona State University), Mark von Schlemmer (University of Central Missouri), Phillip Sipiora (University of South Florida), and Katherine Spring (Wilfred Laurier University).

Since the First Edition's publication in 2004, the publisher and authors of *Looking at Movies* have depended on constructive criticism and good advice from the hundreds of scholars and teachers who have used the book in their courses over the years. The following people all had a hand in shaping previous editions of *Looking at Movies*: Rebecca Alvin, Sandra Annett, Edwin Arnold, Antje Ascheid, Dyrk Ashton, Tony Avruch, Peter Bailey, Scott Baugh, Harry Benshoff, Mark Berrettini, Yifen Beus, Mike Birch, Robin Blaetz, Richard Blake, Ellen Bland, Carroll Blue, James Bogan, Laura Bouza, Katrina Boyd, Aaron Braun, Karen Budra, Don Bullens, Gerald Burgess, Derek Burrill, James B. Bush, Jeremy Butler, Gary Byrd, Ed Cameron, Jose Cardenas, Jerry Carlson, Emily Carman, Diane Carson, Donna Casella, Robert Castaldo, Beth Clary, Darcy Cohn, Megan Condis, Marie Connelly, Roger Cook, John G. Cooper, Robert Coscarelli, Bob Cousins, Angela Dancy, Donna Davidson, Rebecca Dean, Marshall Deutelbaum, Kent DeYoung, Michael DiRaimo, Carol Dole, Rodney Donahue, Dan Dootson, John Ernst, James Fairchild, Adam Fischer, Craig Fischer, Tay Fizdale, Dawn Marie Fratini, Isabelle Freda, Karen Fulton, Paul Gaustad, Christopher Gittings, Barry Goldfarb, Neil Goldstein, Daryl Gonder, Patrick Gonder, Cynthia Gottshall, Curtis Green, Michael Green, William Green, Tracy Greene, Michael Griffin, Peter Hadorn, William Hagerty, Mickey Hall, Stefan Hall, Cable Hardin, John Harrigan, Catherine Hastings, Sherri Hill, Glenn Hopp, Tamra Horton, Alan Hutchison, Mike Hypio, Tom Isbell, Christopher Jacobs, Delmar Jacobs, Mitchell Jarosz, John Lee Jellicorse, Jennifer Jenkins, Robert S. Jones, Matthew Judd, Charles Keil, Joyce Kessel, Mark Kessler, Garland Kimmer, Tammy A. Kinsey, Lynn Kirby, David Kranz, James Kreul, David Kreutzer, Mikael Kreuzriegler, Andrew Kunka, Nee Lam, G. S. Larke-Walsh, Cory Lash, Elizabeth Lathrop, Melissa Lenos, Leon Lewis, Mildred Lewis, Vincent LoBrutto, Jane Long, John Long, Albert Lopez, Jay Loughrin, Daniel Machon, Yuri Makino, Travis Malone, Todd McGowan, Casey McKittrick, Maria Mendoza-Enright, Andrea Mensch, Sharon Mitchler, Mary Alice Molgard, John Moses, Sheila Nayar, Sarah Nilsen, Stephanie O'Brien, Jun Okada, Ian Olney, Hank Ottinger, Dan Pal, Mitchell Parry, Frances Perkins, Christina Petersen, Gary Peterson, Klaus Phillips, W. D. Phillips, Alexander Pitofsky, Lisa Plinski, Leland Poague, Walter Renaud, Patricia Roby, Carole Rodgers, George Rodman, Stuart Rosenberg, Michael Rowin, Ben Russell, Kevin Sandler, Bennet Schaber, Mike Schoenecke, Hertha Schulze, David Seitz, Matthew Sewell, Timothy Shary, Robert Sheppard, Rosalind Sibielski, Robert Sickels, Nicholas Sigman, Charles Silet, Eric Smoodin, Jason Spangler, Michael Stinson, Ken Stofferahn, Bill Swanson, Molly Swiger, Joe Tarantowski, Susan Tavernetti, Edwin Thompson, Frank Tomasulo, Deborah Tudor, Bill Vincent, Richard Vincent, Ken White, Mark Williams, Deborah Wilson, Elizabeth Wright, Suzie Young, and Michael Zryd.

Thank you all.

Dave Monahan

6TH EDITION

LOOKING AT MOVIES

Star Wars: The Last Jedi (2017). Rian Johnson, director. Pictured: Kelly Marie Tran and John Boyega.

LOOKING AT MOVIES

[1]

[2]

Movies shape the way we see the world

By presenting a gay relationship in the context of the archetypal American West and casting popular leading men (Heath Ledger, Jake Gyllenhaal) in starring roles that embodied traditional notions of masculinity, *Brokeback Mountain* (2005; director Ang Lee) [1] influenced the way many Americans perceived same-sex relationships and gay rights. In the 13 years since the film's release, LGBT characters and story lines have become increasingly commonplace, and the U.S. Supreme Court legalized same-sex marriage. Recently, even popular horror films have contributed to the cultural conversation on a number of social issues. Jordan Peele's *Get Out* (2017) [2] confronts racism and privilege; *The Purge* (2013; director James DeMonaco) and its three (so far) sequels examine America's gun culture; and *Don't Breathe* (2016; director Fede Alvarez) is a critical portrait of urban and social decay.

Looking at Movies

In just over a hundred years, movies have evolved into a complex form of artistic representation and communication: they are at once a hugely influential, wildly profitable global industry and a modern art—the most popular art form today. Popular may be an understatement. This art form has permeated our lives in ways that extend far beyond the multiplex. We watch movies on hundreds of cable and satellite channels. We buy movies online or from big-box retailers. We rent movies through the mail and from Redbox machines at the supermarket. We TiVo movies, stream movies, and download movies to watch on our televisions, our computers, and our smartphones.

Unless you were raised by wolves—and possibly even if you were—you have likely devoted thousands of hours to absorbing the motion-picture medium. With so much experience, no one could blame you for wondering why you need a course or this book to tell you how to look at movies.

After all, you might say, "It's just a movie." For most of us most of the time, movies are a break from our daily obligations—a form of escape, entertainment, and pleasure. Motion pictures had been popular for 50 years before even most filmmakers, much less scholars, considered movies worthy of serious study. But motion pictures are much more than entertainment. The movies we see shape the way we view the world around us and our place in that world. Moreover, a close analysis of any particular movie can tell us a great deal about the artist, society, or industry that created it. Surely any art form with that kind of influence and insight is worth understanding on the deepest possible level.

Movies involve much more than meets the casual eye . . . or ear, for that matter. Cinema is a subtle—some might even say sneaky—medium. Because most movies seek to engage viewers' emotions and transport them inside the world presented on-screen, the visual vocabulary of film is designed to play upon those same instincts that we use to navigate and interpret the visual and aural information of our "real life." This often imperceptible **cinematic language**, composed not of words but of myriad integrated techniques and concepts, connects us to the story while deliberately concealing the means by which it does so.

Yet behind this mask, all movies, even the most blatantly commercial ones, contain layers of complexity and meaning that can be studied, analyzed, and appreciated. This book is devoted to that task—to actively *looking at* movies rather than just passively watching them. It will teach you to recognize the many tools and principles that filmmakers employ to tell stories, convey information and meaning, and influence our emotions and ideas.

Once you learn to speak this cinematic language, you'll be equipped to understand the movies that pervade our world on multiple levels: as narrative, as artistic expression, and as a reflection of the cultures that produce and consume them.

What Is a Movie?

Now that we've established what we mean by looking at movies, the next step is to attempt to answer the deceptively simple question, What is a movie? As this book will repeatedly illustrate, when it comes to movies, nothing is as straightforward as it appears.

Let's start, for example, with the word *movies*. If the course that you are taking while reading this book is "Introduction to Film" or "Cinema Studies 101," does that mean that your course and this book focus on two different things? What's the difference between a movie and a *film*? And where does the word *cinema* fit in?

For whatever reason, the designation *film* is often applied to a motion picture that critics and scholars consider to be more serious or challenging than the *movies* that entertain the masses at the multiplex. The still loftier designation of *cinema* seems reserved for groups of films that are considered works of art (e.g., "French cinema"). The truth is, the three terms are essentially interchangeable. *Cinema*, from the Greek *kinesis* ("move-

ment"), originates from the name that filmmaking pioneers Auguste and Louis Lumière coined for the hall where they exhibited their invention; *film* derives from the celluloid strip on which the images that make up motion pictures were originally captured, cut, and projected; and *movies* is simply short for motion pictures. Because we consider all cinema worthy of study, acknowledge that films are increasingly shot on formats other than film stock, and believe motion to be the essence of the movie medium, this book favors the term used in our title. That said, we'll mix all three terms into these pages (as evidenced in the preceding sentence) for the sake of variety, if nothing else.

To most people, a movie is a popular entertainment, a product produced and marketed by a large commercial studio. Regardless of the subject matter, this movie is pretty to look at—every image is well polished by an army of skilled artists and technicians. The finished product, which is about 2 hours long, screens initially in movie theaters; is eventually released to DVD and Blu-ray, streaming, download, or pay-per-view; and ultimately winds up on television. This common expectation is certainly understandable: most movies that reach most English-speaking audiences have followed a good part of this model for three-quarters of a century. Of course, in this century, that distribution chain is evolving. Increasingly, movies are released simultaneously to the theatrical and home-video markets. Companies such as Amazon and Netflix produce original films for both theatrical release and their streaming services. In 2017, Netflix produced two big-budget feature films that were released directly to its streaming subscribers: *Bright* (director David Ayer) and *Okja* (director Bong Joon-ho).

Regardless of their point of origin, almost all of these ubiquitous commercial, feature-length movies share another basic characteristic: narrative. When it comes to categorizing movies, the narrative designation simply means that these movies tell fictional (or at least fictionalized) stories. Of course, if you think of narrative in its broadest sense, *every* movie that selects and arranges subject matter in a cause-and-effect sequence of events is employing a narrative structure. For all their creative flexibility, movies by their very nature must travel a straight line. A conventional motion picture is essentially one very long strip of images. This linear quality makes movies perfectly suited to develop subject matter in a sequential progression. When a medium so compatible with narrative is introduced to a culture with an already well-established storytelling tradition, it's easy to

Are video games movies?

For the purposes of this introduction to cinema, the answer is no. But video games employ cause-and-effect narrative structure, characterization, and a cinematic approach to images and sounds in ways that are beginning to blur the line between movies and gaming. Titles such as *The Last of Us* (2013) feature complex stories and incorporate noninteractive movie-like scenes (known as *cutscenes*). Of course, unlike a conventional movie, the story in a video game can be shaped by its audience: the player. But viewers can also choose to watch a video game in the same way they watch a film. Some players record their journey through the game's story, then post the linear viewing experience on YouTube as a "walk-through" that in many ways resembles a narrative movie. But is a walk-through a movie? If not, what is it? If so, is the recording gamer a character, a director, or simply a surrogate?

understand how popular cinema came to be dominated by those movies devoted to telling fictional stories. Because these fiction films are so central to most readers' experience and so vital to the development of cinema as an art form and cultural force, we've made narrative movies the focus of this introductory textbook.

But keep in mind that commercial, feature-length narrative films represent only a fraction of the expressive potential of this versatile medium. Cinema and narrative are both very flexible concepts. Documentary films strive for objective, observed veracity, of course, but that doesn't mean they don't tell stories. These movies often arrange and present factual information and images in the form of a narrative, whether it be a predator's attempts to track and kill its prey, an activist's quest to free a wrongfully convicted innocent, or a rookie athlete's struggle to make the big leagues. While virtually every movie, regardless of category, employs narrative

in some form, cultural differences often affect exactly how these stories are presented. Narrative films made in Africa, Asia, and Latin America reflect storytelling traditions very different from the story structure we expect from films produced in North America and Western Europe. The unscripted, minimalist films by Iranian director Abbas Kiarostami, for example, often intentionally lacked dramatic resolution, inviting viewers to imagine their own ending.[1] Sanskrit dramatic traditions have inspired "Bollywood" Indian cinema to feature staging that breaks the illusion of reality favored by Hollywood movies, such as actors that consistently face, and even directly address, the audience.[2] This practice, known as *breaking the fourth wall*, refers to the imaginary, invisible "wall" between the movie and the audience watching it.

The growing influence of these and other even less familiar approaches, combined with emerging technologies that make filmmaking more accessible and affordable, have made possible an ever-expanding range of independent movies created by crews as small as a single filmmaker and shot on any one of a variety of film and digital formats. The Irish director John Carney shot his musical love story *Once* (2006) on the streets of Dublin with a cast of mostly nonactors and a small crew using consumer-grade video cameras. American Oren Peli's homemade horror movie *Paranormal Activity* (2007) was produced on a minuscule $15,000 budget and was shot entirely from the point of view of its characters' camcorder. *Once* received critical acclaim and an Academy Award for Best Original Song; *Paranormal Activity* eventually earned almost $200 million at the box office, making it one of the most profitable movies in the history of cinema. Even further out on the fringes of popular culture, an expanding universe of alternative cinematic creativity continues to flourish. These noncommercial movies innovate styles and aesthetics, can be of any length, and exploit an array of exhibition options—from independent theaters to cable television to film festivals to Netflix streaming to YouTube.

And let's not forget the narrative motion pictures classified broadly as television. Cable networks and streaming services now produce high-quality cinematic programs that tell extended stories over multiple episodes. The only things that distinguish a movie from series such

1. Laura Mulvey, "Kiarostami's Uncertainty Principle," *Sight and Sound* 8, no. 6 (June 1998): 24–27.
2. Philip Lutgendorf, "Is There an Indian Way of Filmmaking?" *International Journal of Hindu Studies* 10, no. 3 (December 2006): 227–256.

as Hulu's *The Handmaid's Tale* and Netflix's *Stranger Things* are the length of the narrative and the original intended viewing device. These longer narratives are serialized over the course of many episodes, but those episodes can be binge-watched sequentially like a very long movie. The quality of the writing, acting, cinematography, and editing rivals—and sometimes exceeds—that found in theatrically released feature-length movies.

No matter what you call it, no matter the approach, no matter the format, and no matter the ultimate duration, every movie is a motion picture: a series of still images that, when viewed in rapid succession (usually 24 images per second), the human eye and brain see as fluid movement. In other words, movies *move*. That essential quality is what separates movies from all other two-dimensional pictorial art forms. Each image in every motion picture draws upon basic compositional principles developed by these older cousins (photography, painting, drawing, etc.), including the arrangement of visual elements and the interaction of light and shadow. But unlike photography or painting, films are constructed from individual **shots**—an unbroken span of action captured by an uninterrupted run of a motion-picture camera—that allow visual elements to rearrange themselves and the viewer's perspective itself to shift within any composition.

And this movie movement extends beyond any single shot because movies are constructed of multiple individ-

Is virtual reality a movie?

The answer to that question is no, but it is certainly *something*. Virtual reality (sometimes abbreviated as VR) immerses viewers in a simulated three-dimensional environment. Instead of watching a linear series of moving images on a separate and finite two-dimensional screen, the VR viewer wears a special headset that makes it appear as if she is surrounded by a digitally animated environment or a space captured in 360 degrees by a specialized camera. Like a movie, a VR experience can be curated by technicians and artists: they can provide us engaging and spectacular things to look at. But virtual reality cannot control exactly when and how we see those things. For example, a movie can choose to show us a close-up detail in a character's expression at a particular moment and in a precise way that conveys specific meaning and elicits a particular emotional response. A viewer shown the same thing as part of a VR experience would not necessarily be close enough to see the detail and could even be looking the other way at something else at the moment that particular detail emerged. Innovative filmmakers and artists are already finding exciting new ways to tell stories using the immersive qualities of virtual reality. Those VR experiences will employ many cinematic elements, and they will certainly make for fascinating viewing, but they won't be movies—at least not the kind we are examining in this textbook.

Cultural narrative traditions

The influence of Sanskrit dramatic traditions on Indian cinema can be seen in the prominence of staging that breaks the illusion of reality favored by Hollywood movies, such as actors that consistently face, and even directly address, the audience. In this image from the opening minutes of Rohit Shetty's *Chennai Express* (2013), the lonely bachelor Rahul (Shah Rukh Khan) interrupts his own voice-over narration to complain to viewers about attractive female customers who consider him only a "brother."

ual shots joined to one another in an extended sequence. With each transition from one shot to another, a movie is able to move the viewer through time and space. This joining together of discrete shots, or **editing**, gives movies the power to choose what the viewer sees and how that viewer sees it at any given moment.

To understand better how movies control what audiences see, we can compare cinema to another, closely related medium: live theater. A stage play, which confines the viewer to a single wide-angle view of the action, might display a group of actors, one of whom holds a small object in her hand. The audience sees every cast member at once and continually from the same angle and in the same relative size. The object in one performer's hand is too small to see clearly, even for those few viewers lucky enough to have front-row seats. The playwright, director, and actors have very few practical options to convey the object's physical properties, much less its narrative significance or its emotional meaning to the character. In contrast, a movie version of the same story can establish the dramatic situation and spatial relationships of its subjects from the same wide-angle viewpoint, then instantaneously jump to a composition isolating the actions of the character holding the object, then **cut** to a **close-up** view revealing the object to be a charm bracelet, move up to feature the character's face as she contemplates the bracelet, then leap 30 years into the past to a depiction of the character as a young girl receiving the jewelry as a gift. Editing's capacity to isolate details and juxtapose images and sounds within and between shots gives movies an expressive agility impossible in any other dramatic art or visual medium.

The Movie Director

Throughout this book, we give primary credit to the movie's director; you'll see references, for example, to Patty Jenkins's *Wonder Woman* (2017) or to Guillermo del Toro's *The Shape of Water* (2017). You may not know anything about the directorial style of Ms. Jenkins or Mr. del Toro, but if you enjoy these movies, you might seek out their work in the future.

Still, all moviegoers know—if only from seeing the seemingly endless credits at the end of most movies—that today's movies represent not the work of a single artist, but a collaboration between a group of creative contributors. In this collaboration, the director's role is basically that of a coordinating lead artist. He or she is the vital link between creative, production, and technical teams. The bigger the movie, the larger the crew, and the more complex and challenging the collaboration. Though different directors bring varying levels of foresight, pre-planning, and control to a project, every director must have a vision for the story and style to inform the initial instructions to collaborators and to apply in the continual decision-making process necessary in every stage of production. In short, the director must be a strong leader with a passion for filmmaking and a gift for collaboration.

The other primary collaborators on the creative team—screenwriter, actors, director of photography, production designer, editor, and sound designer—all work with the director to develop their contributions, and the director must approve their decisions as they progress. The director is at the top of the creative hierarchy, responsible for choosing (or at least approving) each of those primary collaborators. A possible exception is the screenwriter, though even then the director often contributes to revisions and assigns additional writers to provide revised or additional material.

The director's primary responsibilities are performance and camera—and the coordination of the two. The director selects actors for each role, works with those actors to develop their characters, leads rehearsals, blocks performances in relationship with the camera on set, and modulates those performances from take to take and shot to shot as necessary throughout the shoot. He or she works with the director of photography to design an overall cinematic look for the movie and to visualize the framing and composition of each shot before and during shooting. Along the way, as inspiration or obstacles necessitate, changes are made to everything from the script to **storyboards** to **blocking** to edits. The director is the one making or approving each adjustment—sometimes after careful deliberation, sometimes on the fly.

On the set, the director does more than call "action" and "cut" and give direction to the actors and cinematographer. He or she must review the footage if necessary, decide when a shot or scene is satisfactory, and say that it's time to move on to the next task. In the editing room, the director sometimes works directly with the editor throughout the process but more often reviews successive "cuts" of scenes and provides the editor with feedback to use in revision.

Ways of Looking at Movies

Every movie is a complex synthesis—a combination of many separate, interrelated elements that form a coherent whole. A quick scan of this book's table of contents will give you an idea of just how many elements get mixed together to make a movie. Anyone attempting to comprehend a complex synthesis must rely on analysis—the act of taking apart something complicated to figure out what it is made of and how it all fits together.

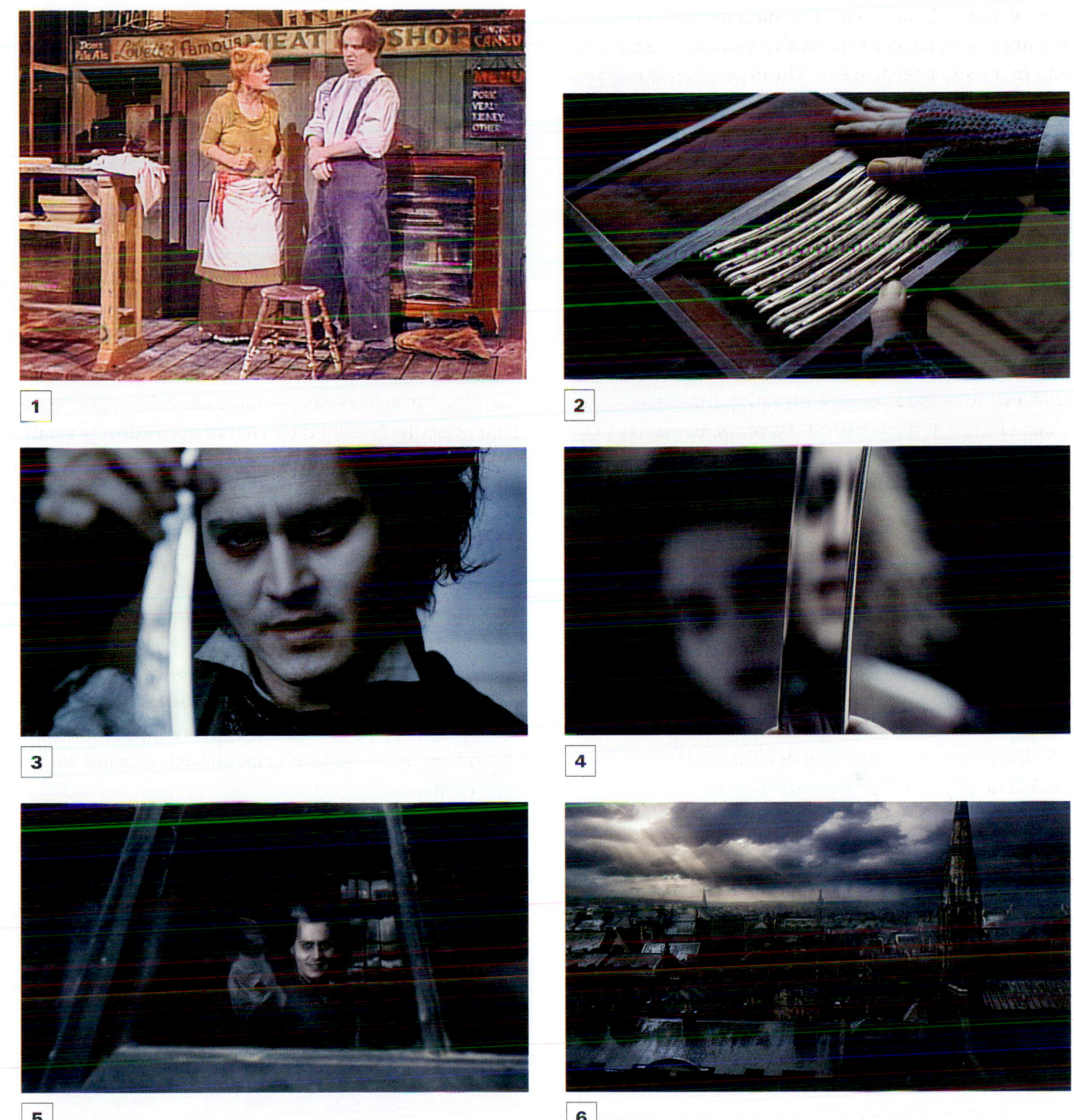

The expressive agility of movies

Even the best seats in the house offer a viewer of a theatrical production like Stephen Sondheim's *Sweeney Todd: The Demon Barber of Fleet Street* only one unchanging view of the action. The stage provides the audience a single wide-angle view of the scene in which the title character is reintroduced to the set of razors he will use in his bloody quest for revenge [1]. In contrast, cinema's spatial dexterity allows viewers of Tim Burton's 2007 film adaptation to experience the same scene as a sequence of fifty-nine viewpoints. Each one isolates and emphasizes distinct meanings and perspectives, including Sweeney Todd's (Johnny Depp) point of view as he gets his first glimpse of his long-lost tools of the trade [2]; his emotional reaction as he contemplates righteous murder [3]; the razor replacing Mrs. Lovett (Helena Bonham Carter) as the focus of his attention [4]; and a dizzying simulated camera move that starts with the vengeful antihero [5], then pulls back to reveal the morally corrupt city he (and his razors) will soon terrorize [6].

A chemist breaks down a compound substance into its constituent parts to learn more than just a list of ingredients. The goal usually extends to determining how the identified individual components work together toward some sort of outcome: What is it about this particular mixture that makes it taste like strawberries, or grow hair, or kill cockroaches? Likewise, film analysis involves more than breaking down a sequence, a scene, or an entire movie to identify the tools and techniques that compose it; the investigation is also concerned with the function and potential effect of that combination: Why does it make you laugh, or prompt you to tell your friend to see it, or incite you to join the Peace Corps? The search for answers to these sorts of questions boils down to one essential inquiry: What does it mean? For the rest of the chapter, we'll explore film analysis by applying that question to some very different movies: first, and most extensively, the 2007 independent film *Juno*, and then the perennial blockbuster Star Wars film series.

Unfortunately, or perhaps intriguingly, not all movie meaning is easy to see. As we mentioned earlier, movies have a way of hiding their methods and meaning. So before we dive into specific approaches to analysis, let's wade a little deeper into this whole notion of hidden, or "invisible," meaning.

Invisibility and Cinematic Language

The moving aspect of moving pictures is one reason for this invisibility. Movies simply move too fast for even the most diligent viewers to consciously consider everything they've seen. When we read a book, we can pause to ponder the meaning or significance of any word, sentence, or passage. Our eyes often flit back to review something we've already read in order to further comprehend its meaning or to place a new passage in context. Similarly, we can stand and study a painting or sculpture or photograph for as long as we require to absorb whatever meaning we need or want from it. But until very recently, the moviegoer's relationship with every cinematic composition has been transitory. We experience a movie shot, which is capable of delivering multiple layers of visual and auditory information, for the briefest of moments before it is taken away and replaced with another moving image and another and another. If you are watching a movie the way it is designed to be experienced, there is little time to contemplate the various potential meanings of any single movie moment.

Recognizing a viewer's tendency (especially when sitting in a dark theater, staring at a large screen) to identify subconsciously with the camera's viewpoint, early filmmaking pioneers created a film grammar (or cinematic language) that draws upon the way we automatically interpret visual information in our real lives, thus allowing audiences to absorb movie meaning intuitively—and instantly.

The **fade-out/fade-in** is one of the most straightforward examples of this phenomenon. When such a transition is meant to convey a passage of time between scenes, the last shot of a scene grows gradually darker (fades out) until the screen is rendered black for a moment. The first shot of the subsequent scene then fades in out of the darkness. Viewers don't have to think about what this means; our daily experience of time's passage marked by the setting and rising of the sun lets us understand intuitively that significant story time has elapsed over that very brief moment of screen darkness.

A **low-angle shot** communicates in a similarly hidden fashion. When, near the end of *Juno* (2007; director Jason Reitman), we see the title character happily transformed back into a "normal" teenager, our sense of her newfound empowerment is heightened by the low angle from which this (and the next) shot is captured. Viewers' shared experience of literally looking up at powerful figures—people on stages, at podiums, memorialized in statues, or simply bigger than them—sparks an automatic interpretation of movie subjects seen from

Cinematic invisibility: low angle

When it views a subject from a low camera angle, cinematic language taps our instinctive association of figures who we must literally "look up to" with figurative or literal power. In this case, the penultimate scene in *Juno* emphasizes the newfound freedom and resultant empowerment the title character feels by presenting her from a low angle for the first time in the film.

Invisible editing: cutting on action in *Juno*
Juno and Leah's playful wrestling continues over the cut between two shots, smoothing and hiding the instantaneous switch from one camera viewpoint to the next. Overlapping sound and the matching hairstyles, wardrobe, and lighting further obscure the audience's awareness that these two separate shots were filmed minutes or even hours apart and from different camera positions.

this angle. Depending on context, we see these figures as strong, noble, or threatening.

This is all very well; the immediacy of cinematic language is what makes movies one of the most visceral experiences that art has to offer. The problem is that it also makes it all too easy to take movie meaning for granted.

The relatively seamless presentation of visual and narrative information found in most movies can also cloud our search for movie meaning. To exploit cinema's capacity for transporting audiences into the world of the story, the commercial filmmaking process stresses polished continuity of lighting, performance, costume, makeup, and movement to smooth transitions between shots and scenes, thus minimizing any distractions that might remind viewers that they're watching a highly manipulated, and manipulative, artificial reality.

Cutting on action is one of the most common editing techniques designed to hide the instantaneous and potentially jarring shift from one camera viewpoint to another. When connecting one shot to the next, a film editor often ends the first shot in the middle of a continuing action and starts the connecting shot at some point in the same action. As a result, the action flows so continuously over the cut between different moving images that most viewers fail to register the switch.

As with all things cinematic, invisibility has its exceptions. From the earliest days of moviemaking, innovative filmmakers have rebelled against the notion of hidden structures and meaning. The pioneering Soviet filmmaker and theorist Sergei Eisenstein believed that

every edit, far from being invisible, should be very noticeable—a clash or collision of contiguous shots, rather than a seamless transition from one shot to the next. Filmmakers whose work is labeled "experimental"— inspired by Eisenstein and other predecessors—embrace self-reflexive styles that confront and confound conventional notions of continuity. Even some commercial films use techniques that undermine invisibility: in *The Limey* (1999), for example, Hollywood filmmaker Steven Soderbergh deliberately jumbles spatial and chronological continuity, forcing viewers to actively scrutinize the cinematic structures on-screen in order to assemble, and thus comprehend, the story. But most scenes in most films that most of us watch rely heavily on largely invisible techniques that convey meaning intuitively. It's not that cinematic language is impossible to spot; you simply have to know what you're looking for. And soon, you will. The rest of this book is dedicated to helping you identify and appreciate each of the many different secret ingredients that movies blend to convey meaning.

Luckily for you, motion pictures have been liberated from the imposed impermanence that helped create all this cinematic invisibility in the first place. Thanks to DVDs, Blu-rays, digital files, and streaming video, you can now watch a movie in much the same way you read a book: pausing to scrutinize, ponder, or review as necessary. This relatively new relationship between movies and viewers will surely spark new approaches to cinematic language and attitudes toward invisibility. That's for future filmmakers, maybe including you, to decide.

Invisible editing: continuity of screen direction

Juno's opening-credits sequence uses the title character's continuous walking movement to present the twenty-two different shots that compose the scene as one continuous action. In every shot featuring lateral movement, Juno strolls consistently toward the left side of the screen, adding continuity of screen direction to the seamless presentation of the otherwise stylized animated sequence.

For now, these viewing technologies allow students of film like yourself to study movies with a lucidity and precision that was impossible for your predecessors.

But not even repeated viewings can reveal those movie messages hidden by our own preconceptions and belief systems. Before we can detect and interpret these meanings, we must first be aware of the ways that expectations and cultural traditions obscure what movies have to say.

Cultural Invisibility

The same commercial instinct that inspires filmmakers to use seamless continuity also compels them to favor stories and themes that reinforce viewers' shared belief systems. After all, the film industry, for the most part, seeks to entertain, not to provoke, its customers. A key to entertaining the customers is to give them what they want—to tap into and reinforce their most fundamental desires and beliefs. Even movies deemed controversial or provocative can be popular if they trigger emotional responses from their viewers that reinforce yearnings or beliefs that lie deep within. And because so much of this occurs on an unconscious, emotional level, the casual viewer may be blind to the implied political, cultural, and ideological messages that help make the movie so appealing.

Of course, this cultural invisibility is not always a calculated decision by the filmmakers. Directors, screenwriters, and producers are, after all, products of the same society inhabited by their intended audience. Frequently, the people making the movies may be just as oblivious of the cultural attitudes shaping their cinematic stories as the people who watch them.

Juno's filmmakers are certainly aware that their film, which addresses issues of abortion and pregnancy, di-

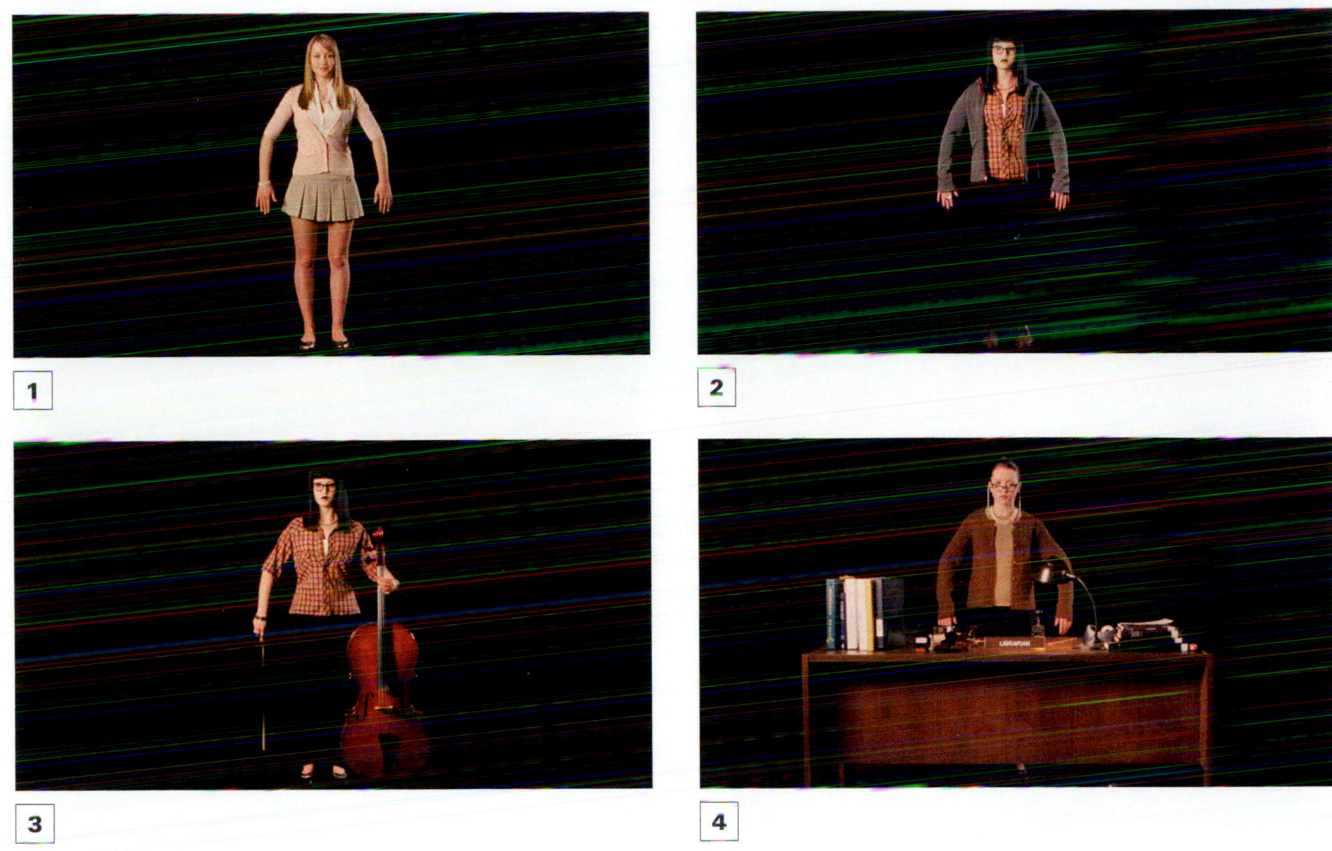

Exceptions to invisibility

Even *Juno* deviates from conventional invisibility in a stylized sequence illustrating a high-school jock's secret lust for "freaky girls." As Juno's voice-over aside detailing Steve Rendazo's fetish begins, the movie suddenly abandons conventional continuity to launch into a series of abrupt juxtapositions that dress a generic girl posed like a paper doll in a rapid-fire succession of eccentric accessories. The moment Juno's diatribe ends, the film returns to a smooth visual flow of events and images. While this sequence is far from realistic, its ostentatious style effectively illustrates the trappings of teenage conformity and the ways that young women are objectified.

verges from the ways that movies traditionally represent family structures and teenage girls. In this sense, the movie might be seen as resisting common cultural values. But these filmmakers may not be as conscious of the way their **protagonist** (main character) reinforces our culture's celebration of the individual. Her promiscuous, forceful, and charming persona is familiar because it displays traits we often associate with Hollywood's male-dominant view of the rogue hero. Like Sam Spade, the Ringo Kid, Dirty Harry, and countless other classic American characters, Juno rejects convention yet ultimately upholds the very institutions she seemingly scorns. Yes, she's a smart-ass who cheats on homework, sleeps with her best friend, and pukes in her stepmother's decorative urn, yet in the end she does everything in her power to create the traditional nuclear family she

never had. So even as the movie seems to call into question some of contemporary America's attitudes about family, its appeal to an arguably more fundamental American value (namely, robust individualism) explains in part why, despite its controversial subject matter, *Juno* was so popular with audiences.

Implicit and Explicit Meaning

As you attempt to become more skilled at looking at movies, try to be alert to the cultural values, shared ideals, and other ideas that lie just below the surface of the movie you're looking at. Being more alert to these things will make you sensitive to, and appreciative of, the many layers of meaning that any single movie contains. Of course, all this talk of layers and the notion that much of

Cultural invisibility in *Juno*

An unrepentant former stripper (Diablo Cody) writes a script about an unrepentantly pregnant sixteen-year-old, her blithely accepting parents, and the dysfunctional couple to whom she relinquishes her newborn child. The resulting film goes on to become one of the biggest critical and box-office hits of 2007, attracting viewers from virtually every consumer demographic. How did a movie based on such seemingly provocative subject matter appeal to such a broad audience? One reason is that, beneath its veneer of controversy, *Juno* repeatedly reinforces mainstream, even conservative, societal attitudes toward pregnancy, family, and marriage. Although Juno initially decides to abort the pregnancy, she quickly changes her mind. Her parents may seem relatively complacent when she confesses her condition, but they support, protect, and advise her throughout her pregnancy. When we first meet Mark and Vanessa, the prosperous young couple Juno has chosen to adopt her baby, it is with the youthful Mark [1] that we (and Juno) initially sympathize. He plays guitar and appreciates alternative music and vintage slasher movies. Vanessa, in comparison, comes off as a shallow and judgmental yuppie. But ultimately, both the movie and its protagonist side with the traditional values of motherhood and responsibility embodied by Vanessa [2] and reject Mark's rock-star ambitions as immature and self-centered.

a movie's meaning lies below the surface may make the entire process of looking at movies seem unnecessarily complex and intimidating. But you'll find that the process of observing, identifying, and interpreting movie meaning will become considerably less mysterious and complicated once you grow accustomed to actively looking at movies rather than just watching them. It might help to keep in mind that, no matter how many different layers of meaning a movie may have, each layer is either implicit or explicit.

An **implicit meaning**, which lies below the surface of a movie's story and presentation, is closest to our everyday sense of the word *meaning*. It is an association, connection, or inference that a viewer makes on the basis of the **explicit meanings** available on the surface of the movie.

To get a sense of the difference between these two levels of meaning, let's look at two statements about *Juno*. First, let's imagine that a friend who hasn't seen the movie asks you what the film is *about*. Your friend doesn't want a detailed plot summary; she simply wants to know what she'll see if she decides to attend the movie. In other words, she is asking for a statement about *Juno*'s

explicit meaning. You might respond to her question by explaining:

> The movie's about a rebellious but smart sixteen-year-old girl who gets pregnant and resolves to tackle the problem head-on. At first, she decides to get an abortion; but after she backs off that choice, she gets the idea to find a couple to adopt the kid after it's born. She spends the rest of the movie dealing with the implications of that choice.

It's not that this is the *only* explicit meaning in the film, but we can see that it is a fairly accurate statement about one meaning that the movie explicitly conveys to viewers, right there on its surface.

Now what if your friend hears this statement of explicit meaning and asks, "Okay, sure, but what do you think the movie is trying to say? What does it *mean*?" In a case like this, when someone is asking in general about an entire film, he or she is seeking something like an overall message or a point. In essence, your friend is asking you to *interpret* the movie—to say something arguable about it—not simply to make a statement of obvious surface meaning that everyone can agree on, as we did when we presented its explicit meaning. In other words, she is asking for your sense of the movie's implicit meaning. Here is one possible response: "A teenager faced with a difficult decision makes a bold leap toward adulthood but, in doing so, discovers that the world of adults is no less uncertain or overwhelming than adolescence." At first glance, this statement might seem to have a lot in common with your summary of the movie's explicit meaning, as, of course, it does—after all, even though a meaning is under the surface, it still has to relate to the surface, and your interpretation needs to be grounded in the explicitly presented details of that surface. But if you compare the two statements more closely, you can see that the second one is more interpretive than the first, more concerned with what the movie means.

Explicit and implicit meanings need not pertain to the movie as a whole, and not all implicit meaning is tied to broad messages or themes. Movies convey and imply smaller, more specific doses of both kinds of meaning in virtually every scene. Juno's application of lipstick before she visits the adoptive father, Mark, is explicit information. The implications of this action—that her admiration for Mark is beginning to develop into something approaching a crush—are implicit. Later, Mark's announcement that he is leaving his wife and does not want to be a father sends Juno into a panicked retreat. On her drive home, a crying jag forces the disillusioned

Explicit detail and implied meaning in *Juno*
Vanessa is the earnest yuppie mommy-wannabe to whom Juno has promised her baby. In contrast to the formal business attire she usually sports, Vanessa wears an Alice in Chains T-shirt to paint the nursery. This small explicit detail conveys important implicit meaning about her relationship with her husband, Mark, a middle-aged man reluctant to let go of his rock-band youth. The paint-spattered condition of the old shirt implies that she no longer values this symbol of the 1990s grunge-rock scene and, by extension, her past association with it.

Juno to pull off the highway. She skids to a stop beside a rotting boat abandoned in the ditch. The discarded boat's decayed condition and the incongruity of a watercraft adrift in an expanse of grass are explicit details that convey implicit meaning about Juno's isolation and alienation.

It's easy to accept that recognizing and interpreting implicit meaning requires some extra effort, but keep in mind that explicit meaning cannot be taken for granted simply because it is by definition obvious. Although explicit meaning is on the surface of a film for all to observe, viewers or writers likely will not remember and acknowledge every part of that meaning. Because movies are rich in plot detail, a good analysis must begin by taking into account the breadth and diversity of what has been explicitly presented. For example, we cannot fully appreciate the significance of Juno's defiant dumping of a blue slushy into her stepmother's beloved urn unless we have noticed and noted her dishonest denial when accused earlier of vomiting a similar substance into the same precious vessel. Our ability to discern a movie's explicit meanings directly depends on our ability to notice such associations and relationships.

Viewer Expectations

The discerning analyst must also be aware of the role expectations play in how movies are made, marketed, and received. Our experience of nearly every movie we see is shaped by what we have been told about that movie beforehand by previews, commercials, reviews, interviews, and word of mouth. After hearing your friends rave endlessly about *Juno*, you may have been underwhelmed by the actual movie. Or you might have been surprised and charmed by a film you entered with low expectations, based on the inevitable backlash that followed the movie's surprise success. Even the most general knowledge affects how we react to any given film. We go to see blockbusters because we crave an elaborate special effects extravaganza. We can still appreciate a summer movie's relatively simpleminded storytelling, as long as it delivers the promised spectacle. On the other hand, you might revile a high-quality tragedy if you bought your ticket expecting a lighthearted comedy.

Of course, the influence of expectation extends beyond the kind of anticipation generated by a movie's promotion. As we discussed earlier, we all harbor essential expectations concerning a film's form and organization.

1

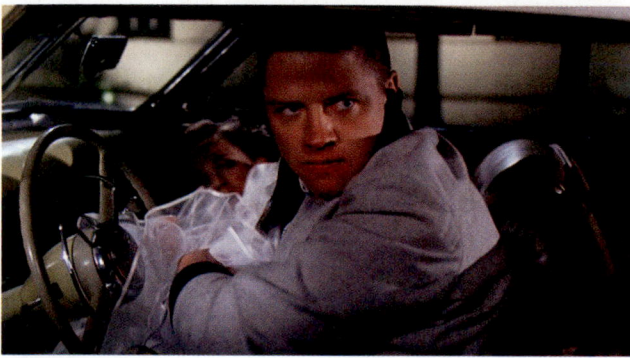

2

Expectations and character in *Juno*

Audience reactions to Michael Cera's characterization of Juno's sort-of boyfriend, Paulie Bleeker, are colored by expectations that are based on the actor's perpetually embarrassed persona established in previous roles in the television series *Arrested Development* and films like *Superbad* [1]. We don't need the movie to tell us much of anything about Paulie—we form an almost instant affection for the character based on our familiarity with Cera's earlier performances. But while the character Paulie meets our expectations of Michael Cera, he defies our expectations of his character type. Repeated portrayals of high-school jocks as vain bullies, such as Thomas F. Wilson's iconic Biff in Robert Zemeckis's *Back to the Future* (1985) [2], have conditioned viewers to expect such characters to look and behave very differently than Paulie Bleeker.

And most filmmakers give us what we expect: a relatively standardized cinematic language, seamless continuity, and a narrative organized like virtually every other fiction film we've ever seen. For example, years of watching movies has taught us to expect a clearly motivated protagonist to pursue a goal, confronting obstacles and

antagonists along the way toward a clear (and usually satisfying) resolution. Sure enough, that's what we get in most commercial films.

We'll delve more deeply into narrative in the chapters that follow. For now, what's important is that you understand how your experience—and thus your interpretation—of any movie is affected by how the particular film manipulates these expected patterns. An analysis might note a film's failure to successfully exploit the standard structures or another movie's masterful subversion of expectations to surprise or mislead its audience. A more experimental approach might deliberately confound our presumption of continuity or narrative. Viewers must be aware of the expected patterns in order to fully appreciate the significance of that deviation.

Expectations specific to a particular performer or filmmaker can also alter the way we perceive a movie. For example, any fan of actor Michael Cera's previous performances as an endearingly awkward adolescent in the film *Superbad* (2007; director Greg Mottola) and television series *Arrested Development* (2003–2006) will watch *Juno* with a built-in affection for Paulie Bleeker, Juno's sort-of boyfriend. This predetermined fondness does more than help us like the movie; it dramatically changes the way we approach a character type (the high-school athlete who impregnates his teenage classmate) that our expectations might otherwise lead us to distrust. Ironically, audience expectations of Cera's sweetness may have contributed to the disappointing box-office performance of *Scott Pilgrim vs. the World* (2010; director Edgar Wright). Some critics proposed that viewers were uncomfortable seeing Cera play the somewhat vain and self-centered title character.

Viewers who know director Guillermo del Toro's commercial action/horror movies *Mimic* (1997), *Blade II* (2002), *Hellboy* (2004), *Pacific Rim* (2013), and *Crimson Peak* (2015) might be surprised by the sophisticated political and philosophical metaphor of *Pan's Labyrinth* (2006), *The Devil's Backbone* (2001), and *The Shape of Water* (2017). Yet all eight films feature fantastic and macabre creatures as well as social commentary. An active awareness of an audience's various expectations of del Toro's films would inform an analysis of the elements common to the filmmaker's seemingly schizophrenic body of work. Such an analysis could focus on his visual style in terms of production design, lighting, or special effects, or it might instead examine recurring themes such as oppression, childhood trauma, or the role of the outcast.

As you can see, cinematic invisibility is not necessarily an impediment; once you know enough to acknowledge their existence, these potential blind spots also offer opportunities for insight and analysis. There are many ways to look at movies and many possible types of film analysis. We'll spend the rest of this chapter discussing the most common analytical approaches to movies.

Because this book considers an understanding of how film grammar conveys meaning, mood, and information as the essential foundation for any further study of cinema, we'll turn now to **formal analysis**—that analytical approach primarily concerned with film **form**, or the means by which a subject is expressed. Don't worry if you don't fully understand the function of the techniques discussed; that's what the rest of this book is for.

Formal Analysis

Formal analysis dissects the complex synthesis of cinematography, sound, composition, design, movement, performance, and editing orchestrated by creative artists such as screenwriters, directors, cinematographers, actors, editors, sound designers, and art directors as well as the many craftspeople who implement their vision. The movie meaning expressed through form ranges from narrative information as straightforward as where and when a particular scene takes place to more subtle implied meaning, such as mood, tone, significance, or what a character is thinking or feeling.

While the overeager analyst certainly can read more meaning into a particular visual or audio component than the filmmaker intended, you should realize that cinematic storytellers exploit every tool at their disposal and that, therefore, every element in every frame is there for a reason. It's the analyst's job to carefully consider the narrative intent of the moment, scene, or sequence before attempting any interpretation of the formal elements used to communicate that intended meaning to the spectator.

For example, the simple awareness that *Juno*'s opening shot [1] is the first image of the movie informs us of the moment's most basic and explicit intent: to convey setting (contemporary middle-class suburbia) and time of day (dawn). But only after we have determined that

1

2

the story opens with its title character overwhelmed by the prospect of her own teenage pregnancy are we prepared to deduce how this implicit meaning (her state of mind) is conveyed by the composition: Juno is at the far left of the frame and is tiny in relationship to the rest of the wide-angle composition. In fact, we may be well into the 4-second shot before we even spot her. Her vulnerability is conveyed by the fact that she is dwarfed by her surroundings. Even when the scene cuts to a closer viewpoint [2], she, as the subject of a movie composition, is much smaller in frame than we are used to seeing, especially in the first shots used to introduce a protagonist. She is standing in a front yard contemplating an empty stuffed chair from a safe distance, as if the inanimate object might attack at any moment. Her pose adds to our implicit impression of Juno as alienated or off-balance.

Our command of the film's explicit details alerts us to another function of the scene: to introduce the recurring **theme** (or **motif**) of the empty chair that frames—and in some ways defines—the story. In this opening scene, accompanied by Juno's voice-over explanation, "It started with a chair," the empty, displaced object represents

Juno's status and emotional state and foreshadows the unconventional setting for the sexual act that got her into this mess. By the story's conclusion, when Juno announces, "It ended with a chair," the motif—in the form of an adoptive mother's rocking chair—has been transformed, like Juno herself, to embody hope and potential.

All that meaning was packed into two shots spanning about 12 seconds of screen time. Let's see what we can learn from a formal analysis of a more extended sequence from the same film: Juno's visit to the Women Now clinic. To do so, we'll first want to consider what information the filmmaker needs this scene to communicate for viewers to understand and appreciate this pivotal piece of the movie's story in relation to the rest of the narrative. As we delve into material that deals with *Juno*'s sensitive subject matter, keep in mind that you don't have to agree with the meaning or values projected by the object of your analysis; you can learn even from a movie you dislike. Personal values and beliefs will undoubtedly influence your analysis of any movie. And personal views provide a legitimate perspective, as long as we recognize and acknowledge how they may color our interpretation.

Throughout *Juno*'s previous 18 minutes, all information concerning its protagonist's attitude toward her condition has explicitly enforced our expectation that she will end her unplanned pregnancy with an abortion. She pantomimes suicide once she's forced to admit her condition; she calmly discusses abortion facilities with her friend Leah; she displays no ambivalence when scheduling the procedure. As she approaches the clinic, Juno's nonchalant reaction to the comically morose pro-life demonstrator Su-Chin reinforces our expectations. Juno treats Su-Chin's assertion that the fetus has fingernails as more of an interesting bit of trivia than a concept worthy of serious consideration.

The subsequent waiting-room sequence is about Juno making an unexpected decision that propels the story in an entirely new direction. A formal analysis will tell us how the filmmakers orchestrated multiple formal elements, including sound, composition, moving camera, and editing, to convey in 13 shots and 30 seconds of screen time how the seemingly insignificant fingernail factoid infiltrates Juno's thoughts and ultimately drives her from the clinic. By the time you have completed your course (and have read the book), you should be prepared to apply this same sort of formal analysis to any scene you choose.

VIDEO In this tutorial, Dave Monahan analyzes the "waiting room" scene from *Juno* and covers other key concepts of film analysis.

The waiting-room sequence's opening shot [1] **dollies in** (the camera moves slowly toward the subject), which gradually enlarges Juno in frame, increasing her visual significance as she fills out the clinic admittance form on the clipboard in her hand [2]. The shot reestablishes her casual acceptance of the impending procedure, providing context for the events to come. Its relatively long 10-second **duration** sets up a relaxed rhythm that will shift later along with her state of mind. As the camera reaches its closest point, a loud sound invades the low hum of the previously hushed waiting room.

This obtrusive drumming sound motivates a somewhat startling cut to a new shot that plunges our viewpoint right up into Juno's face [3]. The sudden spatial shift gives the moment resonance and conveys Juno's thought process as she instantly shifts her concentration from the admittance form to this strange new sound. She turns her head in search of the sound's source, and the camera adjusts to adopt her **point of view** of a mother and daughter sitting beside her [4]. The mother's fingernails drumming on her own clipboard is revealed as the source of the tapping sound. The sound's abnormally loud level signals the audience that we're not hearing at a natural volume level—we've begun to experience Juno's psychological perceptions. The little girl's stare into Juno's (and our) eyes helps to establish the association between the fingernail sound and Juno's latent guilt.

The sequence cuts back to the already troubled-looking Juno [5]. The juxtaposition connects her anxious expression to both the drumming mother and the little girl's gaze. The camera creeps in on her again. This time, the resulting enlargement initiates our intuitive association of this gradual intensification with a character's moment of realization. Within half a second, another noise joins the mix, and Juno's head turns in response [6].

The juxtaposition marks the next shot as Juno's point of view, but it is much too close to be her literal point of view. Like the unusually loud sound, the unrealistically close viewpoint of a woman picking her thumbnail reflects not an actual spatial relationship but the sight's significance to Juno [7]. When we cut back to Juno about a second later, the camera continues to close in on her, and her gaze shifts again to follow yet another sound as it joins the rising clamor [8].

A new shot of another set of hands, again from a close-up, psychological point of view, shows a woman applying fingernail polish [9]. What would normally be a silent action emits a distinct, abrasive sound.

When we cut back to Juno half a second later, she is much larger in the frame than the last few times we saw her [10]. This break in pattern conveys a sudden intensification; this is really starting to get to her. Editing often establishes patterns and rhythms, only to break them for dramatic impact. Our appreciation of Juno's situation is

enhanced by the way editing connects her reactions to the altered sights and sounds around her, as well as by her implied isolation—she appears to be the only one who notices the increasingly boisterous symphony of fingernails. Of course, Juno's not entirely alone—the audience is with her. At this point in the sequence, we have begun to associate the waiting-room fingernails with Su-Chin's attempt to humanize Juno's condition.

Juno's head jerks as yet another, even more invasive sound enters the fray [11]. We cut to another close-up

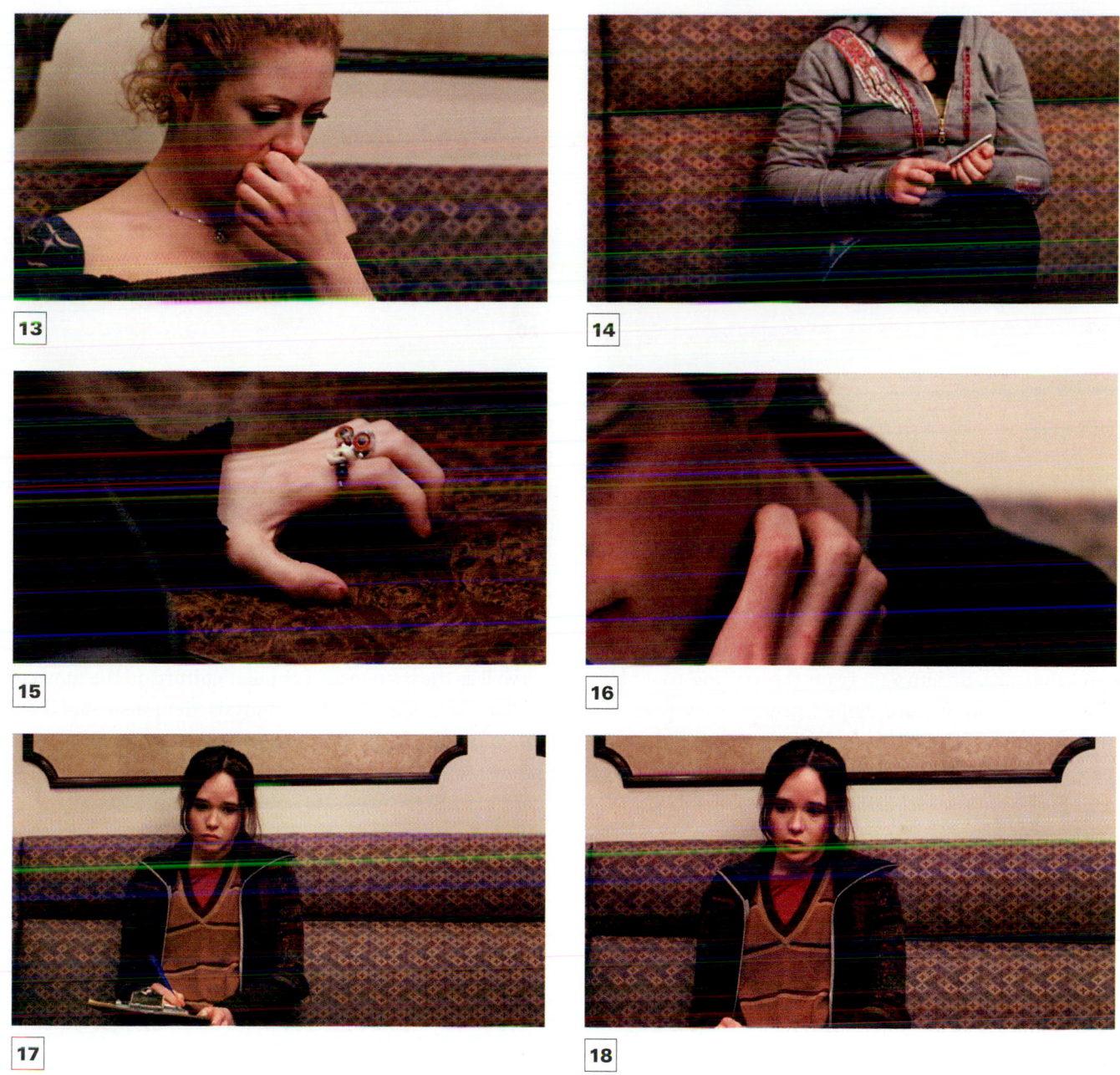

point-of-view shot, this time of a young man scratching his arm [12]. At this point, another pattern is broken, initiating the scene's formal and dramatic climax. Up until now, the sequence alternated between shots of Juno and shots of the fingernails as they caught her attention. Each juxtaposition caused us to identify with both Juno's reaction and her point of view. But now, the sequence shifts gears; instead of the expected switch back to Juno, we are subjected to an accelerating succession of fingernail shots, each one shorter and louder

than the last. A woman bites her fingernails [13]; another files her nails [14]; a woman's hand drums her fingernails nervously [15]; a man scratches his neck [16]. With every new shot, another noise is added to the sound mix.

This pattern is itself broken in several ways by the scene's final shot. We've grown accustomed to seeing Juno look around every time we see her, but this time, she stares blankly ahead, immersed in thought [17]. A cacophony of fingernail sounds rings in her (and our) ears as the camera glides toward her for 3½ very long

19

20

seconds—a duration six times longer than any of the previous nine shots. These pattern shifts signal the scene's climax, which is further emphasized by the moving camera's enlargement of Juno's figure [18], a visual action that cinematic language has trained viewers to associate with a subject's moment of realization or decision.

But the shot doesn't show us Juno acting on that decision. We don't see her cover her ears, throw down her clipboard, or jump up from the waiting-room banquette. Instead, we are ripped prematurely from this final waiting-room image and plunged into a shot that drops us into a different space and at least several moments ahead in time—back to Su-Chin chanting in the parking lot [19]. This jarring spatial, temporal, and visual shift helps us feel Juno's own instability at this crucial narrative moment. Before we can get our bearings, the camera has pivoted right to reveal Juno bursting out of the clinic door in the background [20]. She races past Su-Chin without a word. She does not have to say anything. Cinematic language—film form—has already told us what she decided and why.

Anyone watching this scene would sense the narrative and emotional meaning revealed by this analysis, but only a viewer actively analyzing the film form used to construct it can fully comprehend how the sophisticated machinery of cinematic language shapes and conveys that meaning. Formal analysis is fundamental to all approaches to understanding and engaging cinema—whether you're making, studying, or simply appreciating movies—which is why the elements and grammar of film form are the primary focus of *Looking at Movies*.

Alternative Approaches to Analysis

Although we'll be looking at movies primarily to learn the forms they take and the nuts and bolts they are constructed from, any serious student of film should be aware that there are many other legitimate frameworks for analysis. These alternative approaches analyze movies more as cultural artifacts than as traditional works of art. They search beneath a movie's form and content to expose implicit and hidden meanings that inform our understanding of cinema's function within popular culture as well as the influence of popular culture on the movies.

The preceding formal analysis demonstrated how *Juno* used cinematic language to convey meaning and tell a story. Given the right interpretive scrutiny, our case study film may also speak eloquently about social conditions and attitudes. For example, considering that the protagonist is the daughter of an air-conditioner repairman and a manicurist, and that the couple she selects to adopt her baby are white-collar professionals living in an oversized McMansion, a cultural analysis of *Juno* could explore the movie's treatment of class.

An analysis from a feminist perspective could concentrate on, among other elements, the movie's depiction of women and childbirth, not to mention Juno's father, the father of her baby, and the prospective adoptive father. Such an analysis might also consider the creative and ideological contributions of the movie's female screenwriter, Diablo Cody, an outspoken former stripper and sex blogger.

A linguistic analysis might explore the historical, cultural, or imaginary origins of the highly stylized slang spouted by Juno, her friends, even the mini-mart clerk who sells her a pregnancy test. A thesis could be (and probably has been) written about the implications of the T-shirt messages displayed by the film's characters or the implicit meaning of the movie's track-team motif.

Some analyses place movies within the stylistic or political context of a director's career. *Juno*'s director, Jason Reitman, has made only five other feature films. But even that relatively short filmography provides opportunity for comparative analysis: most of Reitman's movies take provocative political stances, gradually generate empathy for initially unsympathetic characters, and favor fast-paced expositional montages featuring expressive juxtapositions, graphic compositions, and first-person voice-over narration. *Labor Day* (2013), his first film to diverge from that established style, disappointed expectations and failed with critics and audiences.

Another comparative analysis could investigate society's evolving (or perhaps fixed) attitudes toward "illegitimate" pregnancy by placing *Juno* in context with the long history of films about the subject. These movies range from D. W. Griffith's 1920 silent drama *Way Down East*, which banished its unwed mother and drove her to attempted suicide, to Preston Sturges's irreverent 1944 comedy *The Miracle of Morgan's Creek* and its mysteriously pregnant protagonist, Trudy Kockenlocker (whose character name alone says a great deal about its era's attitudes toward women), to another mysterious but ultimately far more terrifying pregnancy in Roman Polanski's 1968 horror masterpiece *Rosemary's Baby*.

Juno is only one in a small stampede of recent popular films dealing with this ever-timely issue. A cultural analysis might compare and contrast *Juno* with its American contemporaries *Knocked Up* (2007; director Judd Apatow) and *Waitress* (2007; director Adrienne Shelly). Both movies share *Juno*'s blend of comedy and drama as well as a pronounced ambivalence concerning abortion but depict decidedly different characters, settings, and stories. What might such an analysis of these movies (and their critical and popular success) tell us about that particular era's attitudes toward women, pregnancy, and motherhood? Seven years later, in 2014, *Obvious Child* was initially marketed as an "abortion comedy." When the protagonist Donna finds herself pregnant after a one-night stand, her decision to get an abortion is immediate and matter of fact. Unlike all of its 2007 predecessors, *Obvious Child* does not deliver a baby in the end. Was director Gillian Robespierre reacting to those earlier films, influenced by evolving attitudes, or simply offering her own perspective on the subject? *Knocked Up* was written and directed by a man, *Juno* was written by a woman and directed by a man, and *Waitress* and *Obvious Child* were written and directed by women. Does the relative gender of each film's creator affect stance and story? If this comparative analysis incorporated Romanian filmmaker Cristian Mungiu's stark abortion drama *4 Months, 3 Weeks and 2 Days* (2007) or Mike Leigh's nuanced portrayal of an abortionist, *Vera Drake* (2004), the result might inform a deeper understanding of the differences between European and American sensibilities.

An unwanted pregnancy is a potentially controversial subject for any film, especially when the central character is a teenager. Any extensive analysis focused on *Juno*'s cultural meaning would have to address what this particular film's content implies about the hot-button issue of abortion. To illustrate, let's return to the clinic waiting room. An analysis that asserts *Juno* espouses a "pro-life" (i.e., antiabortion) message could point to several explicit details in this sequence and to those preceding and following it. In contrast to the relatively welcoming suburban settings that dominate the rest of the story, the ironically named Women Now abortion clinic is an unattractive stone structure squatting at one end of an urban asphalt parking lot. Juno is confronted by clearly stated and compelling arguments against abortion via Su-Chin's dialogue: the "baby" has a beating heart, can feel pain, . . . and has fingernails. The clinic receptionist, the sole on-screen representative of the pro-choice alternative, is a sneering cynic with multiple piercings and a declared taste for fruit-flavored condoms. The idea of the fetus as a human being, stressed by Su-Chin's earnest admonishments, is driven home by the scene's formal presentation analyzed earlier.

On the other hand, a counterargument maintaining that *Juno* implies a pro-choice stance could state that the lone on-screen representation of the pro-life position is portrayed just as negatively (and extremely) as the clinic receptionist. Su-Chin is presented as an infantile simpleton who wields a homemade sign stating, rather clumsily, "No Babies Like Murdering," shouts "All babies want to get borned!" and is bundled in an oversized stocking cap and pink quilted coat as if dressed by an overprotective mother. Juno's choice can hardly be labeled a righteous conversion. Even after fleeing the clinic, the clearly ambivalent mother-to-be struggles to rationalize her decision, which she announces not as "I'm having this baby" but as "I'm staying pregnant." Some analysts may conclude that the filmmakers, mindful of audience demographics, were trying to have it both ways. Others could argue that the movie is understandably

Comparative cultural analysis

A comparison of *Juno*'s treatment of unwanted pregnancy with other films featuring the same subject matter is but one of many analytical approaches that could be used to explore cinema's function within culture, as well as the influence of culture on the movies. Such an analysis could compare *Juno* with American films produced in earlier eras, from D. W. Griffith's dramatic *Way Down East* (1920) [1] to Preston Sturges's 1944 screwball comedy *The Miracle of Morgan's Creek* [2] to Roman Polanski's paranoid horror film *Rosemary's Baby* (1968) [3]. An alternate analysis might compare *Juno* with the other American films released in 2007 that approached the subject with a similar blend of comedy and drama: Judd Apatow's *Knocked Up* [4] and Adrienne Shelly's *Waitress* [5]. A comparative analysis of the independent film *Obvious Child* (2014; director Gillian Robespierre) [6] might reveal evolving cultural attitudes toward abortion 7 years after *Juno*, *Knocked Up*, and *Waitress* all concluded with a birth scene.

more concerned with narrative considerations than a precise political stance. The negative aspects of every alternative are consistent with a story world that offers its young protagonist little comfort and no easy choices.

Cultural and Formal Analysis in the Star Wars Series

When the film *Star Wars* (director George Lucas) was released in 1977, few—including the actors and technicians who helped make it—expected it to reach large audiences. To almost everyone's surprise, *Star Wars* quickly became what was then the highest grossing film in history. The unexpected hit launched a franchise consisting of (so far) four sequels and five prequels that together have earned well over $8 billion in worldwide box office. That staggering figure doesn't adjust decades-old receipts for inflation or include the additional exposure and revenue generated by DVD and Blu-ray sales, digital downloads, video on demand, and television broadcasts. Before it was eclipsed by the last two installments of the *Avengers* series, the $247 million opening weekend earnings posted by *Star Wars: The Force Awakens* (2015; director J. J. Abrams) was the biggest in American history. Its successor, *Star Wars: The Last Jedi* (2017; director Rian Johnson), is fourth in that all-time ranking, with opening weekend earnings topping $220 million.[3] Clearly, the Star Wars series was, is, and continues to be an influential and important cultural phenomenon. But how can we even begin to explain its popularity?

To start with, the sheer scope of the series provides viewers a particular brand of narrative development unavailable in most other movies or film series. Most people enjoy recognizing and tracking progression; this tendency is largely responsible for the sequential nature of traditional storytelling. The Star Wars films offer the rare opportunity to experience familiar characters' physical and emotional development over an extended period of time; the stories chronicled in the multiple episodes span generations, as do the release dates of the films themselves. If we stop to consider other well-known film series, few (with the notable exception of Harry Potter) feature any significant figurative or literal character growth. Although they accomplish extraordi-

1

2

Familiarity and progression

The extraordinary longevity of the Star Wars series offers the rare opportunity to experience familiar characters' physical and emotional development over an extended period of time. For fans who grew up knowing Luke Skywalker as an awkward and earnest apprentice [1], his return as a world-weary cynic [2]—and his old master versus young upstart showdown with Kylo Ren—was especially meaningful.

nary feats in spectacular adventures, Frodo Baggins in The Lord of the Rings, Captain Jack Sparrow in Pirates of the Caribbean, and even Katniss Everdeen from The Hunger Games all act and look much the same from the first movie to the final installment. In contrast, the young, inexperienced upstarts in the original Star Wars trilogy have now evolved into grizzled leaders and mentors for the next fresh wave of adventurous protagonists. Old Luke is the grumpy new Yoda who reluctantly trains his Jedi-prodigy replacement, Rey. The gray-haired Han Solo (briefly) mentors Rey and Finn, and he and Princess Leia are the divorced parents of Rey's nemesis/soulmate Kylo Ren, an aspiring Darth Vader.

The longevity of the series ensures that most of us have been (at least periodically) immersed in its universe since childhood. We know the players, the politics, and the rules of engagement. The character types,

What genre is Star Wars?

How a narrative film applies character types, story formulas, settings, and themes can place it in a particular genre. It seems logical to assume the Star Wars films belong in the science-fiction genre because they all take place across multiple planets in a universe filled with aliens, spaceships, robots, and other futuristic technology. But science-fiction films are speculative; their stories explore the implications of unfettered science and technology that may threaten as much as enable humanity. In contrast, Star Wars is made up of multiple references to past cultures and traditions—it doesn't presume to forecast our future. After all, the stories take place "a long time ago in a galaxy far, far away." The series does have its clone armies and death stars, but the films' conflicts and themes are more concerned with human nature and spirituality than with science or technology. One could argue that the films blend multiple genres, just as they blend other cultural elements. For example, the story of *Rogue One: A Star Wars Story* (2016) is structured like a plot from an old-fashioned war movie.

story formulas, settings, and themes are repeated from episode to episode in ways that fulfill most expectations but surprise others. This satisfying combination of the comfortably predictable and the thrillingly unexpected is the same formula that keeps viewers returning to similarly convention-driven film genres such as horror and science fiction. A scholarly analysis might explore if and how the Star Wars films engage genre—or even if they constitute their own genre.

But the stories at the heart of Star Wars are more deeply rooted in our culture than those of any single film genre. The quests led by the series' chosen ones—first Luke Skywalker, and now Rey—have their narrative origins in a basic pattern found in the folktales, myths, and religions of multiple cultures. In his influential book *The Hero with a Thousand Faces*, mythologist Joseph Campbell called this fundamental story structure the "monomyth" or "hero's journey." Like the archetypal hero in the ancient myths and folktales Campbell describes, Luke and Rey start out as seemingly ordinary people in their own normal worlds who receive an unexpected call to adventure, which they initially resist. Eventually, events compel them to heed the call, which leads them to cross into an unknown world. They each meet mentors, gather allies, receive supernatural aid, and are given a talisman (notably, in each case, that talisman is the same lightsaber). Rey and Luke undergo training and are initiated with a series of increasingly dangerous challenges that reveal previously hidden strengths or powers. The heroes each ultimately win a decisive victory over a seemingly invincible opponent, then return from the mysterious journey with the power to bestow boons to his (or her) fellow man.[4] Of course, the precise application of this ancient formula differs from character to character and trilogy to trilogy, and our current heroes' journey is not yet completed. A narrative analysis of the Star Wars films and their resonance with audiences might explore the different (and similar) ways each protagonist's story fits this classical storytelling tradition.

Other cultural sources that influenced the Star Wars universe might also provide insight into the franchise's international popularity. Indeed, the franchise seems

---

4. Joseph Campbell, *The Hero with a Thousand Faces*, 2nd ed. (Princeton, NJ: Princeton University Press, 1949), p. 30.

to have been engineered for universal appeal. George Lucas, the filmmaker who wrote and directed the prototypical 1977 *Star Wars* (later renamed *Star Wars: Episode IV—A New Hope*) and remained the dominant creative force behind the first six films, drew upon a number of world religions and philosophies for the spirituality (including the interdependence of positive and negative forces) that underlies and informs the action-packed stories. For the Jedi knights, Lucas blended the traditions of knighthood and chivalry found in medieval Europe with those of the Japanese samurai. He borrowed other stylistic, character, and narrative elements from disparate twentieth-century sources: swashbuckler films beginning in the silent era (e.g., boisterous swordplay and roguish protagonists); space-based action-adventure comics and serialized movies of the 1930s; and *The Hidden Fortress*, Akira Kurosawa's 1958 adventure film set in feudal Japan. All these different influences resulted in a sort of timeless cultural collage that may help explain the enduring international appeal of the Star Wars movies. The helmets and layered armor worn by villains such as Darth Vader, Kylo Ren, and Captain Phasma evoke both samurai and medieval warriors. The Jedis may be knights, but their flowing outfits look more like a mix of traditional Japanese garments and the humble robes worn by self-denying monks found in multiple world religions. Other characters dress (and act) like cowboys, or gangsters, or World War II fighter pilots, or decadent European aristocrats. All of these people fly around with robots in spaceships, but many of them live in adobe or stone dwellings, and some of them fight with swords. In fact, the lightsaber—a powerful laser used exclusively for hand-to-hand combat—might be the ultimate demonstration of Star Wars' successful marriage between the futuristic and the classical.

Viewers don't just recognize the cultural ingredients of the Star Wars universe: we see ourselves reflected in the archetypical conflicts and characters the stories present. The Resistance is courageous, resourceful, and resilient, but also overmatched. The Empire and the First Order that seek to squash the righteous rebels are both overwhelmingly powerful, greedy, heartless—and seemingly indestructible. This binary good-versus-evil struggle allows working-class and middle-class ticket buyers to vicariously identify with plucky protagonists who endure crushing odds in a never-ending struggle against an overwhelming force. The First Order serves as a symbolic stand-in for any number of oppressive overlords, from international enemies to one's own government

1

2

A meaningful weapon

This blue laser blade [1, 2] used by the successive Jedi protagonists in every Star Wars trilogy serves the film franchise in a number of important ways. As a high-tech version of an ancient and universal weapon, the lightsaber epitomizes the amalgam of diverse cultural and historical references that creator George Lucas blended to form the eclectic Star Wars universe. The lightsaber also functions as a talisman (a special item that serves heroes on a quest), which is central to the films' application of the universal story structure known as the monomyth. Its blue blade signals it as a force for good in a binary good versus evil conflict in which the villains wield red—until the lightsaber is literally torn between the light side and the dark side in *The Last Jedi* (2017).

or opposing political party. The well-equipped tyrannical organization may even be equated with the kind of modern mega-corporation that makes and markets Star Wars itself. Of course, representations of oppression and resistance have deep roots in our culture. The imagery and actions of the Empire and First Order also reference authoritarian movements bent on world domination that shaped recent world history, including and especially the infamous Nazis that launched World War II.

The latest wave of Star Wars films is decidedly forward looking in one significant way. The cast portraying "the good guys" is multiethnic—and not even necessarily "guys." The primary protagonists in *The Last Jedi* include a white woman, a black man, a Latino man, and a woman of Asian descent. Even one of the seemingly cruel masked antagonists is female. The 2016 prequel

The new faces of Star Wars

The directors of the most recent Star Wars films have approached casting and character in ways that break with expectations established in the previous trilogies. Finn (John Boyega) is not just the franchise's first black major character, he's also a charismatic and free-thinking Stormtrooper. Rose Tico (Kelly Marie Tran) is similarly a common worker who proves capable of greatness. Costume and hairstyle help this first non-princess female supporting character transcend the usual standards of beauty assigned to women in Hollywood blockbusters. In another reversal of action movie expectations, Rose saves Finn from needlessly sacrificing himself and then declares, "We're going to win this war not by fighting what we hate, but saving what we love." Star Wars may have changed the world, but it appears that the world is changing Star Wars, too.

spin-off *Rogue One: A Star Wars Story* (director Gareth Edwards) also features a female protagonist fighting alongside a band of Latino, Asian, and African American fellow-revolutionaries. These casts, and the characters they play, represent a departure from the previous films, which were dominated by white, male characters. Perhaps the biggest change—one that upset some Star Wars traditionalists—was making the latest and greatest Jedi hero a woman. In fact, one could argue that Rey and the other female characters in *The Last Jedi* are rational leaders saddled with male counterparts who are incapable of facing their own emotions or learning from their mistakes. While these new Star Wars women understand the power of self-examination and strategic restraint, their male counterparts either run away from their problems or charge into conflict without considering the inevitable consequences. As Leia—the former mostly helpless princess who has risen to the position of general leading the Resistance—says to the swashbuckling pilot Poe: "Not every problem can be solved by jumping in an X-wing and blowing stuff up."

Perhaps motivated by these changes, some of the same female viewers that drove the success of The Hun-ger Games series may have contributed to the popularity of *The Last Jedi*. According to Box Office Mojo, the website that tracks movie industry ticket sales, women made up 43 percent of the movie's audience over opening weekend, a significant showing in what is typically a male-dominated market. A cultural analysis of the most recent Star Wars films might ask if the saga's heroine and fan base qualify the movies as feminist. Unlike a surprising number of Hollywood movies, these Star Wars films do seem to pass the Bechdel test. This test is an evaluative tool—credited to feminist cartoonist and author Alison Bechdel—that qualifies films as woman-friendly only if they (a) have at least two women characters who (b) talk to each other (c) about something besides a man.

Rey doesn't get many chances to talk to other women at all in *The Force Awakens*; the closest she gets is a quick exchange with the female alien Maz Kanata, and much (but not all) of that conversation is about Luke and his lightsaber. Later in the same film, Rey comes face to face with Leia, but their communication is nonverbal. Instead, the women share an emotional embrace that may be more meaningful than any conversation, regardless of the topic. Near the end of the film, Leia's "may the force be with you," spoken as Rey prepares to board the Millennium Falcon in search of Luke, are the only words exchanged between these two principal characters. *The Last Jedi* adds several additional female characters, but because they are all paired with male partners and/or adversaries, they almost never get to talk to one another. The touching final farewell between Leia and Vice Admiral Holdo, the two women leading what's left of the Resistance, provides a rare opportunity. Once again, the opening topic is a man (the impulsive fighter pilot Poe this time), but the discussion quickly turns more personal, and Bechdel-worthy, when the old friends reconcile Holdo's looming sacrifice and exchange the traditional Star Wars force-be-with-you farewell. A critical analysis may ask if brief exchanges like these are enough to pass the Bechdel test or if the test is a fair indicator of feminist intent in films featuring multiple strong, active female characters pursuing goals once reserved for male protagonists. One could at least argue that the series has progressed in terms of Bechdel's feminist standard. The original Star Wars saga featured a female character who was just as brave, and arguably smarter, than her male counterparts, but she had very little company. In those

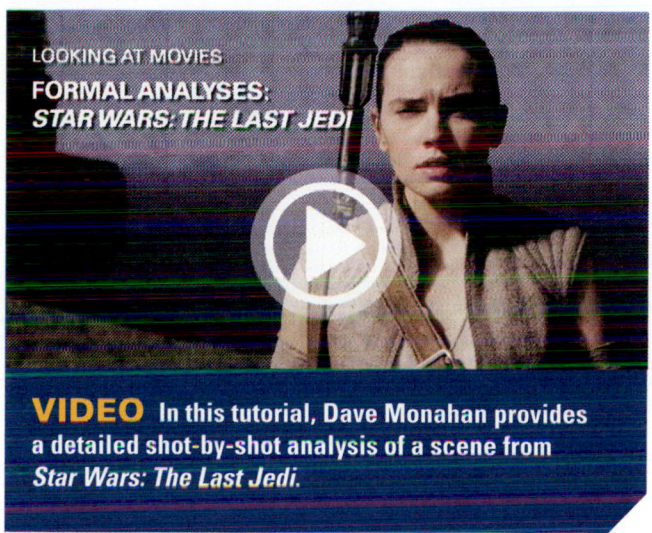

LOOKING AT MOVIES
FORMAL ANALYSES:
STAR WARS: THE LAST JEDI

VIDEO In this tutorial, Dave Monahan provides a detailed shot-by-shot analysis of a scene from *Star Wars: The Last Jedi*.

first three films, only four women have any lines at all, and they never speak to one another at all.

As you read the preceding paragraphs, you probably thought of still more ways you might examine the Star Wars phenomenon. The examples presented in our brief analysis illustrate only a few of the virtually limitless

An evolved and empathetic Jedi heroine

Any examination of the evolution and reception of Star Wars must include Rey, the character at the center of the most recent trilogy. The differences between her and her Jedi protagonist predecessors are significant. The abandoned daughter of common paupers, Rey is neither of (secret) royal birth like Luke Skywalker nor a prophesied messiah like Luke's father, Anakin (the future Darth Vader), who was birthed by a mortal but conceived by the force itself. Rey tries to understand and redeem her enemy, Kylo Ren, not destroy him; she seeks balance and reconciliation, not glory or vengeance. This approach is reflected in her no-nonsense wardrobe. Instead of the brooding browns and blacks favored by Anakin in the prequel trilogy or Luke's good-guy white from the original installments, Rey's modest outfit is made up of neutral grays.

approaches available to advanced students and scholars interested in interpreting the relationship between culture and cinema. But before we can effectively interpret a movie as a cultural artifact, we must first understand how that artifact functions. To begin that process, let's return our focus to the building blocks of film form, starting with the tutorial film analyzing some of the cinematic language used in *Star Wars: The Last Jedi*. In the next chapter, we'll expand the exploration of the principles of film form that is begun here.

ANALYZING LOOKING AT MOVIES

As we said at the beginning of the chapter, the primary goal of *Looking at Movies* is to help you graduate from being a spectator of movies—from merely *watching* them—to actively and analytically *looking* at them. The chapters that follow provide specific information about each of the major formal components of film, information that you can use to write and talk intelligently about the films you view in class and elsewhere. Once you've read the chapter on cinematography, for example, you will have at hand the basic vocabulary to describe accurately the lighting and camera work you see on-screen.

As you read the subsequent chapters of this book, you will acquire a specialized vocabulary for describing, analyzing, discussing, and writing about the movies you see. But now, as a beginning student of film and armed only with the general knowledge that you've acquired in this first chapter, you can begin looking at movies more analytically and perceptively. You can easily say more than "I liked" or "I didn't like" the movie, because you can enumerate and understand the cinematic techniques and concepts the filmmakers employed to convey story, character state of mind, and other meanings. What's more, by cultivating an active awareness of the meanings and structures hidden under every movie's surface, you will become increasingly capable of recognizing the film's implicit meanings and interpreting what they reveal about the culture that produced and consumed it.

The following checklist provides a few ideas about how to start.

SCREENING CHECKLIST: LOOKING AT MOVIES

✔ Be aware that there are many ways to look at movies. Are you primarily interested in interpreting the ways in which the movie manipulates formal elements such as composition, editing, and sound to tell its story moment to moment or are you concerned with what the movie has to say in broader cultural terms, such as a political message?

✔ Whenever you prepare a formal analysis of a scene's use of film grammar, start by considering the filmmakers' intent. Remember that filmmakers use every cinematic tool at their disposal: very little in any movie moment is left to chance. So before analyzing any scene, first ask yourself some basic questions: What is this scene about? After watching this scene, what do I understand about the character's thoughts and emotions? How did the scene make me feel? Once you determine what information and mood the scene conveyed, you'll be better prepared to figure out how cinematic tools and

techniques were used to communicate the scene's intended meaning.

✔ Do your best to see beyond cinematic invisibility. Remember that a great deal of a movie's machinery is designed to make you forget you are experiencing a highly manipulated, and manipulative, artificial reality. One of the best ways to combat cinema's seamless presentation is to watch a movie more than once. You may allow yourself to be transported into the world of the story on your first viewing. Repeated viewings will give you the distance required for critical observation.

✔ On a related note, be aware that you may be initially blind to a movie's political, cultural, and ideological meaning, especially if that meaning reinforces ideas and values you already hold. The greater your awareness of your own belief systems (and those you share with your culture in general), the easier it will be to recognize and interpret a movie's implicit meaning.

✔ Ask yourself how expectations shaped your reaction to this movie. Does it conform to the ways you've come to expect a movie to function? How did what you'd heard about this movie beforehand—through the media, your friends, or your professor—affect your attitude toward the film? Did your previous experience of the director or star inform your prior understanding of what to expect from this particular film? In each case, did the movie fulfill, disappoint, or confound your expectations?

✔ Before and after you see a movie, think about the direct meanings, as well as the implications, of its title. The title of Roman Polanski's *Chinatown* (1974) is a specific geographic reference, but once you've seen the movie, you'll understand that it functions as a metaphor for a larger body of meaning. Richard Kelly's *Donnie Darko* (2001) makes us wonder if Darko is a real name (it is) or if it is a not-so-subtle clue that Donnie has a dark side (he does). Try to explain the title's meaning if it isn't self-evident.

Questions for Review

1. What do you think of when you hear the word *movie*? Has your perception changed since reading this chapter? In what ways?

2. How is the experience of seeing a movie different from watching a play? Reading a book? Viewing a painting or photograph?

3. Why has the grammar of film evolved to allow audiences to absorb movie meaning intuitively?

4. In what ways do movies minimize viewers' awareness that they are experiencing a highly manipulated, artificial reality?

5. What do we mean by *cultural invisibility*? How is this different from *cinematic invisibility*?

6. What is the difference between *implicit* and *explicit* meaning?

7. How might your previous experiences of a particular actor influence your reaction to a new movie featuring the same performer?

8. What are some of the other expectations that can affect the way viewers react to a movie?

9. What are you looking for when you do a formal analysis of a movie scene? What are some other alternative approaches to analysis, and what sorts of meaning might they uncover?

10. At this point, would you say that learning what a movie is all about is more challenging than you first thought? If so, why?

The Shape of Water (2017). Guillermo del Toro, director. Pictured: Doug Jones and Sally Hawkins.

PRINCIPLES OF FILM FORM

Film Form

Chapter 1's analyses of scenes from *Juno* and the Star Wars series provided us with a small taste of how the various elements of movies work. We saw how the filmmakers coordinated performance, composition, sound, and editing to create meaning and tell a story. All of these elements were carefully chosen and controlled by the filmmakers to produce each movie's form.

If we've learned nothing else so far, we can at least now say with confidence that very little in any movie is left to chance. Each of the multiple systems that together become the "complex synthesis" that we know as a movie is highly organized and deliberately assembled and sculpted by filmmakers. For example, **mise-en-scène**, one elemental system of film, comprises design elements such as lighting, setting, props, costumes, and makeup within individual shots. **Sound**, another elemental system, is organized into a series of dialogue, music, ambience, and effects tracks. **Narrative** is structured into acts that establish, develop, and resolve character conflict. **Editing** juxtaposes individual **shots** to create **sequences** (a series of shots unified by theme or purpose), arranges these sequences into **scenes** (complete units of plot action), and from these scenes builds a movie. The synthesis of all of these elemental systems (and others not mentioned above) constitutes the over-

all form that the movie takes. We'll spend some time with each of these elemental formal systems in later chapters, but first let's take a closer look at the concept of form itself, beginning with the correlation between form and the content it shapes and communicates.

Form and Content

The terms *form* and *content* crop up in almost any scholarly discussion of the arts, but what do they mean, and why are they so often paired? To start with, we can define **content** as the subject of an artwork (what the work is about) and **form** as the means by which that subject is expressed and experienced. The two terms are often paired because works of art need them both. Content provides something to express; form supplies the methods and techniques necessary to present it to the audience.

And form doesn't just allow us to *see* the subject/content; it lets us see that content *in a particular way*. Form enables the artist to shape our particular experience *and interpretation* of that content. In the world of movies, form is **cinematic language:** the tools and techniques that filmmakers use to convey meaning and mood to the viewer, including lighting, mise-en-scène, cinematography, performance, editing, and sound—in other words, the content of most of this textbook.

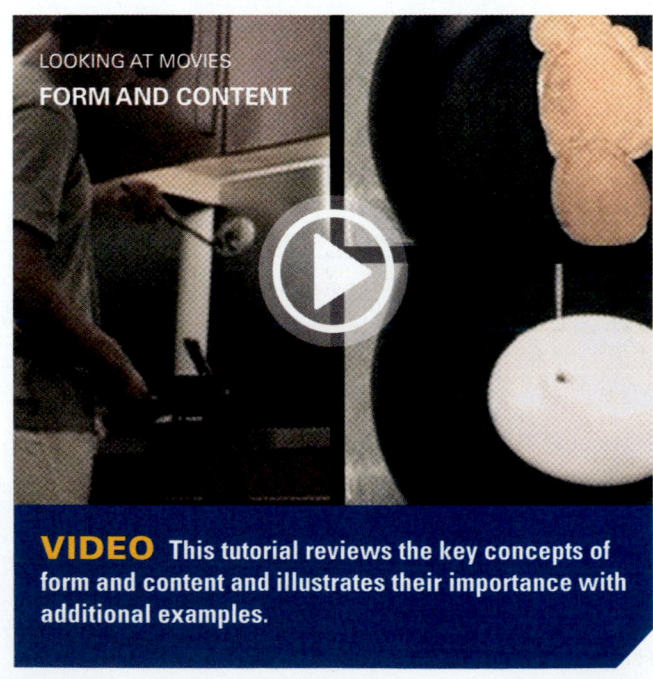

LOOKING AT MOVIES
FORM AND CONTENT

VIDEO This tutorial reviews the key concepts of form and content and illustrates their importance with additional examples.

Form and content

The *content* of the *Juno* "waiting room" scene analyzed in Chapter 1 is Juno thinking about fingernails and changing her mind. As we saw in that analysis, a great deal of *form* was employed to shape our experience and interpretation of that content, including sound, juxtaposition, pattern, point of view, and the relative size of the subject in each frame.

If we consider the *Juno* scene analyzed in Chapter 1, the content is: *Juno in the waiting room.* We could be more specific and say that the content is *Juno thinking about fingernails and changing her mind.* The form used to express that subject and meaning includes decor, patterns, implied proximity, point of view, moving camera, and sound.

The relationship between form and content is central not just to our study of movies; it is an underlying concern in all art. An understanding of the two intersecting concepts can help us to distinguish one work of art from another or to compare the styles and visions of different artists approaching the same subject.

If we look at three sculptures of a male figure, for example—by Praxiteles, Alberto Giacometti, and Keith Haring, artists spanning history from ancient Greece to the present—we can see crucial differences in vision, style, and meaning (see the illustrations on p. 34). Each sculpture can be said to express the same subject, the

male body, but they clearly differ in form. Of the three, Praxiteles's sculpture, *Hermes Carrying the Infant Dionysus*, comes closest to resembling a flesh-and-blood body. Giacometti's *Walking Man II* (1960) elongates and exaggerates anatomical features, but the figure remains recognizable as a male human. Haring's *Self Portrait* (1989) smooths out and simplifies the contours of the human body to create an even more abstract rendering.

Once we recognize the formal differences and similarities among these three sculptures, we can ask questions about how the respective forms shape our emotional and intellectual responses to the subject matter. Look again at the ancient Greek sculpture. Although there might once have been a living man whose body looked like this, very few bodies do. The sculpture is an idealization— less a matter of recording the way a particular man actually looked than of visually describing an ideal male form. As such, it is as much an interpretation of the subject matter as—and thus no more "real" than—the other two

1

2

3

Form and content

Compare these sculptures: [1] *Hermes Carrying the Infant Dionysus*, by Praxiteles, who lived in Greece during the fourth century BCE; [2] *Walking Man II,* by Alberto Giacometti (1901–1966), a Swiss artist; and [3] *Self Portrait*, by Keith Haring (1958–1990), an American. Although all three works depict the male figure, their forms are so different that their meanings, too, must be different. What, then, is the relationship between the form of an artwork and its content?

sculptures. Giacometti's version, because of its exaggerated form, conveys a sense of isolation and nervousness, perhaps even anguish. Haring's sculpture, relying on stylized and almost cartoon-like form, seems more playful and mischievous than the other two. Suddenly, because of the different form each sculpture takes, we realize that the content of each has changed: they are no longer *about* the same subject. Praxiteles's sculpture is somehow about defining an ideal; Giacometti's

Form serves content

Anomalisa (2015) is about a man unable to find any meaningful or lasting connections to other human beings. When writer and co-director Charlie Kaufman was searching for a cinematic form that served his dramatic content, he and fellow codirector Duke Johnson chose stop-motion animation. That particular form allowed them to create their protagonist's skewed perspective, in which everyone he encounters looks and sounds exactly the same. Experiencing this very adult story of alienation and self-absorption in a form we associate with comedic children's stories forces viewers to feel the same sense of disconnect experienced by the marginalized protagonist.

seems to reach for something that lies beneath the surface of human life and the human form; and Haring's appears to celebrate the body as a source of joy. As we become more attentive to their formal differences, these sculptures become more unlike each other in their content, too.

Thus form and content—rather than being separate things that come together to produce art—are instead two aspects of the entire formal system of a work of art. They are interrelated, interdependent, and interactive.

Form and Expectations

As we discussed in Chapter 1, our decision to see a particular movie is almost always based on certain expectations. Perhaps we have enjoyed previous work by the director, the screenwriter, or the actors; or publicity, advertisements, friends, or reviews have attracted us; or the genre is appealing; or we're curious about the techniques used to make the movie.

Even if we have no such preconceptions before stepping into a movie theater, we will form impressions very quickly once the movie begins, sometimes even from the moment the opening credits roll. (In Hollywood, producers and screenwriters assume that audiences de-

cide whether they like or dislike a movie within its first 10 minutes.) As the movie continues, we experience a more complex web of expectations. Many of them may be tied to the narrative—the formal arrangement of the events that make up the story—and specifically to our sense that certain events produce likely actions or outcomes.

We've learned to expect that most movies start with a "normal" world that is altered by a particular incident, which in turn compels the characters to pursue a goal. And once the narrative begins, those expectations provoke us to ask predictive questions about the story's outcome, questions we will be asking ourselves repeatedly and waiting to have answered over the course of the film.

The nineteenth-century Russian playwright Anton Chekhov famously said that when a theater audience sees a character produce a gun in the first act, they expect that gun to be used before the play ends. Movie audiences have similar expectations. In the Coen brothers' 2010 version of *True Grit*, the villain Tom Chaney threatens the young protagonist Mattie Ross: "That pit is one hundred feet deep and I will throw you in it." From that moment on, our interpretation of events is colored by the suggestion that Mattie is destined for the abyss. Later, when her would-be rescuer LeBoeuf says in passing, "Mind your footing, there is a pit here," our expectations are reinforced. We can't help but suppose that somebody is going down that hole. Screenwriters often organize a film's narrative structure around the viewer's desire to learn the answers to such central questions as, "Will Dorothy get back to Kansas?" or "Will Frodo destroy the ring?"

Fede Alvarez's *Don't Breathe* (2016) is a horror thriller about what happens to three young people who break into a blind man's home to steal his hidden fortune. The three characters are already in conflict with one another and are about to take on an unexpectedly formidable antagonist. In the first scene inside the dark house, the camera glides along with the protagonists as they silently search the creepy premises. Along the way, the camera strays to linger on items the thieves don't initially notice, including a heavy hammer hung over a tool bench and a pistol taped under their victim's bed. By clearly pointing out the existence of these weapons, the camera is setting up an explicit expectation that each will be used at some point in the story; we just don't know by who or on whom.

Expectations in *Bonnie and Clyde*

Much of the development and ultimate impact of Arthur Penn's *Bonnie and Clyde* (1967) depends on the sexual chemistry between the title characters [1], established through physical expression, dialogue, and overt symbolism. Early in the film, Clyde, ruthless and handsome, brandishes his gun threateningly and phallically [2]. Attracted by this display and others, the beautiful Bonnie is as surprised as we are when Clyde later rebuffs her obvious sexual attraction to him (at one point, he demurs, "I ain't much of a lover boy"). We may not like this contradiction, but it is established early in the film and quickly teaches us that our expectations will not always be satisfied.

In each of the cases described, the general expectation is ultimately fulfilled, but none of the situations play out exactly as we initially predict. Making, processing, and revising expectations is part of what makes watching movies a compelling participatory experience.

Director Alfred Hitchcock treated his audiences' expectations in ironic, even playful, ways—sometimes using the gun, so to speak, and sometimes not—and this became one of his major stylistic traits. Hitchcock used the otherwise meaningless term *MacGuffin* to refer to an object, document, or secret within a story that is vitally important to the characters, and thus motivates their actions and the conflict, but that turns out to be less significant to the overall narrative than we might at first expect. In *Psycho* (1960), for example, Marion Crane believes that the $40,000 she steals from her employer will help her start a new life. Instead, her flight with the money leads to the Bates Motel, the resident psychopath, and Marion's death. The money plays no role in motivating her murderer; in fact, the killer doesn't seem to know it exists. Once the murder has occurred, the money—a classic MacGuffin—is of no real importance to the rest of the movie. With the death of our assumed protagonist, Hitchcock sends our expectations in a new and unanticipated direction. The question that drew us into the narrative—"Will Marion get away with embezzlement?"—suddenly switches to "Who will stop this murderously overprotective mother?" As anyone who has seen *Psycho* knows, this narrative about-face isn't the end of the director's manipulation of audience expectations.

Even as the narrative form of a movie is shaping and sometimes confounding our expectations, other formal qualities may perform similar functions. Seemingly insignificant and abstract elements of film such as color schemes, sounds, shot length, and camera movement often cooperate with dramatic elements to either heighten or confuse our expectations. One way they do this is by establishing patterns.

Patterns

Instinctively, we search for patterns and progressions in all art forms. The more these meet our expectations (or contradict them in interesting ways), the more likely we are to enjoy, analyze, and interpret the work.

The penultimate scene in D. W. Griffith's *Way Down East* (1920), one of the most famous chase scenes in movie history, illustrates how the movies depend on our recognition of patterns. Banished from a "respectable" family's house because of her scandalous past, Anna Moore tries to walk through a blizzard but quickly becomes disoriented and wanders onto a partially frozen river. She faints on an ice floe and, after much suspense, is rescued by David Bartlett just as she is about

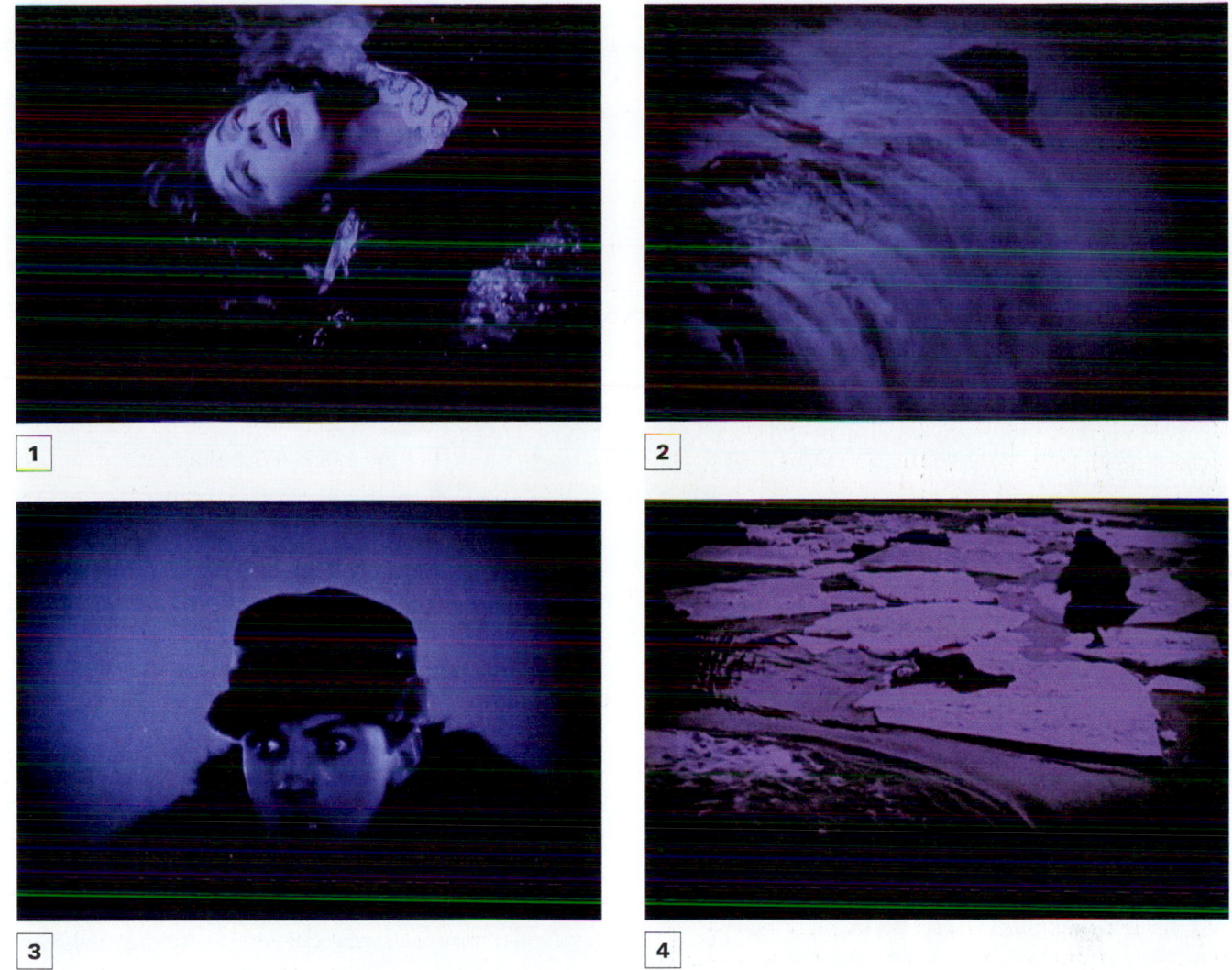

Parallel editing in *Way Down East*

Pioneering director D. W. Griffith risked the lives of actors Lillian Gish and Richard Barthelmess to film *Way Down East*'s now classic "ice break" scene—a scene that builds suspense by exposing us to a pattern of different shots called *parallel editing*. Griffith shot much of the blizzard and ice-floe footage along the Connecticut River, then edited it together with studio shots and scenes of Niagara Falls. Gish, thinly dressed, was freezing on the ice and was periodically revived with hot tea. Although the dangers during filming were real enough, the "reality" portrayed in the final scene—a rescue from the certain death that would result from a plunge over Niagara Falls—is wholly the result of Griffith's use of a pattern of editing that has by now become a standard technique in narrative filmmaking.

to go over a huge waterfall to what clearly would have been her death.

To heighten the drama of his characters' predicament, Griffith employs **parallel editing**—a technique that makes different lines of action appear to be occurring simultaneously. Griffith shows us Anna on the ice, Niagara Falls, and David jumping from one floe to another as he tries to catch up with her. As we watch these three lines of action edited together (in a general pattern of ABCACBCABCACBC), they appear simultaneous. We assume that the river flows over Niagara Falls and that the ice floe Anna is on is heading down that river. It doesn't matter that the actors weren't literally in danger of going over the falls or that David's actions did not occur simultaneously with Anna's progress downriver. The form of the scene, established by the pattern of parallel editing, has created an illusion of connections among these various shots, leaving us

Patterns and suspense

Filmmakers can use patterns to catch us unawares. In *The Silence of the Lambs* (1991), Jonathan Demme exploits our sense that when shots are juxtaposed, they must share a logical connection. After FBI agents surround a house, an agent disguised as a deliveryman rings the doorbell [1]; a bell rings in the serial killer Buffalo Bill's basement [2]; Bill reacts to that ring [3], leaves behind the prisoner he was about to harm, goes upstairs, and answers his front door, revealing not the deliveryman we expect to see but Clarice Starling [4]. As agents storm the house they've been staking out [5], Clarice and Bill continue to talk [6]. The agents have entered the wrong house, Clarice is now alone with a psychopath, and our anxiety rises as a result of the surprise.

with an impression of a continuous, anxiety-producing drama.

The editing in one scene of Jonathan Demme's *The Silence of the Lambs* (1991) takes advantage of our nat-ural interpretation of parallel action to achieve a disori-enting effect. Earlier in the movie, Demme has already shown us countless versions of a formal pattern in which two elements seen in separation are alternated

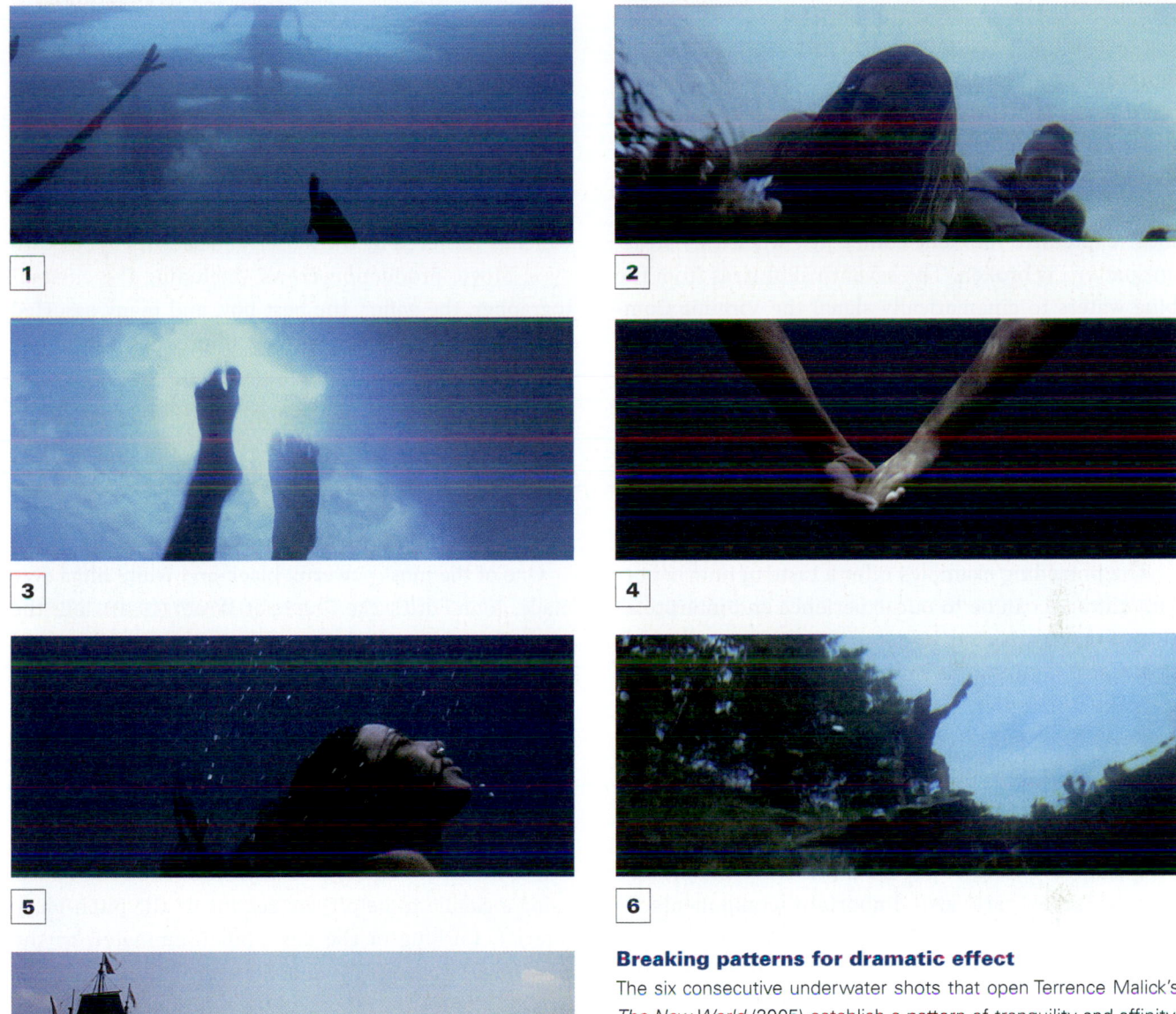

Breaking patterns for dramatic effect

The six consecutive underwater shots that open Terrence Malick's *The New World* (2005) establish a pattern of tranquility and affinity. Each shot conveys a harmonious fusion of indigenous people and their natural environment. The seventh shot rises from the blue waters to break the pattern and thus cinematically signal the Virginia Company's intrusion into the Algonquin paradise. Everything has suddenly changed: the light, the framing, the content, the world.

and related (ABABAB). So we expect that pattern to be repeated when shots of the serial killer Buffalo Bill arguing with his intended victim in his basement are intercut with shots of the FBI team preparing to storm a house. We naturally assume that the FBI has targeted the same house in which Buffalo Bill is going about his grisly business. When the sequence eventually reveals that the FBI is, in fact, attacking a different house, the pattern is bro-

ken, thwarting our expectations and setting in motion the suspenseful scene that follows.

Parallel editing is not the only means of creating and exploiting patterns in movies, of course. Some patterns are made to be broken. The six consecutive underwater shots that open Terrence Malick's *The New World* (2005) establish a pattern of peace and affinity. Each shot conveys a harmonious fusion of indigenous people and their natural environment: fish glide past the camera, a smiling Pocahontas runs her hand across the shimmering surface, Algonquin natives swim hand in hand, and Pocahontas glides upward trailing a stream of air bubbles. The cumulative effect of this AAAAAA pattern is quietly powerful—it repeatedly reinforces a feeling of slow-motion tranquility. But the sequence's most expressive moment comes just when this pleasant pattern is broken. The seventh shot rises from the blue waters to cinematically signal the Virginia Company's intrusion into the Algonquin paradise. The underwater A shots were infused with blue; this open-air B shot is dominated by shades of brown. The opening A sequence featured close-framed human subjects; this pattern-breaking B shot is a wide angle of three large European ships. Everything has suddenly changed: the light, the framing, the content, the world.

The preceding examples offer a taste of how important patterns can be to our experience and interpretation of movies. Narrative patterns provide an element of structure, ground us in the familiar, or acquaint us with the unfamiliar; repeating them emphasizes their content. Shot patterns can convey character state of mind, create relationships, and communicate narrative meaning. As we will see in later chapters, nonnarrative patterns such as the repetition of a familiar image or a familiar sound effect (or motif from the movie's musical score) are also important components of film form.

Fundamentals of Film Form

The remaining chapters in this book describe the major formal aspects of film—narrative, mise-en-scène, cinematography, acting, editing, sound—to provide you with a beginning vocabulary for talking about film form more specifically. Before we study these individual formal elements, however, let's briefly discuss three fundamental principles of film form:

❭ Movies depend on light.

❭ Movies provide an illusion of movement.

❭ Movies manipulate space and time in unique ways.

Movies Depend on Light

Light is the essential ingredient in the creation and consumption of motion pictures. Movie images are made when a camera lens focuses light onto either film stock or a digital video sensor. Movie-theater projectors and video monitors all transmit motion pictures as light, which is gathered by the lenses and sensors in our own eyes. Movie production crews—including the cinematographer, the gaffer, the best boy, and many assorted grips and assistants—devote an impressive amount of time and equipment to illumination design and execution. Yet it would be a mistake to think of light as simply a requirement for a decent exposure. Light is more than a source of illumination; it is a key formal element that film artists and technicians carefully manipulate to create mood, reveal character, and convey meaning.

One of the most powerful black-and-white films ever made, John Ford's *The Grapes of Wrath* (1940), tells the story of an Oklahoma farming family forced off their land by the violent dust storms that plagued the region during the Great Depression of the 1930s. The eldest son, Tom Joad, returns home after serving a prison sentence, only to find that his family has left their farm for the supposedly greener pastures of California.

Tom and an itinerant preacher named Jim Casy, whom he has met along the way, enter the Joad house, using a candle to help them see inside the pitch-black interior. Lurking in the dark, but illuminated by the candlelight (masterfully simulated by cinematographer Gregg Toland), is Muley Graves, a farmer who has refused to leave Oklahoma with his family. As Muley tells Tom and Casy what has happened in the area, Tom holds the candle so that he and Casy can see him better [1], and the contrasts between the dark background and Muley's haunted face, illuminated by the flickering candle, reveal their collective state of mind: despair. The unconventional direction of the harsh light distorts the characters' features and casts elongated shadows looming behind and above them [2]. The story is told less through words than through the overtly symbolic light of a single candle.

Muley's flashback account of the loss of his farm reverses the pattern. The harsh light of the sun that, along with the relentless wind, has withered his fields beats down upon Muley, casting a deep, foreshortened shadow of the ruined man across his ruined land [3]. Such sharp contrasts of light and dark occur throughout the film, thus providing a pattern of meaning.

1

2

3

It is useful to distinguish between the luminous energy we call light and the crafted interplay between motion-picture light and shadow known as lighting. Light is responsible for the image we see on the screen, whether photographed (shot) on film or video or created with a computer. Lighting is responsible for significant effects in each shot or scene. It enhances the texture, depth, emotions, and mood of a shot. It accents the rough texture of a cobblestoned street in Carol Reed's *The Third Man* (1949), helps to extend the illusion of depth in Orson Welles's *Citizen Kane* (1941), and emphasizes a character's subjective feelings of apprehension or suspense in such film noirs as Billy Wilder's *Double Indemnity* (1944). In fact, lighting often conveys these things by augmenting, complicating, or even contradicting other cinematic elements within the shot (e.g., dialogue, movement, or composition). Lighting also affects the ways that we see and think about a movie's characters. It can make a character's face appear attractive or unattractive, make the viewer like a character or be afraid of her, and reveal a character's state of mind.

These are just a few of the basic ways that movies depend on light to achieve their effects. We'll continue our discussion of cinema's use of light and manipulation of lighting later (Chapter 5 examines lighting as an element of mis-en-scène; Chapter 6 includes information and analysis of lighting's role in cinematography; Chapter 11 covers how motion-picture technologies capture and use light). For now, it's enough to appreciate that light is essential to movie meaning and to the filmmaking process itself.

Movies Provide an Illusion of Movement

We need light to make, shape, and see movies, but it takes more than light to make motion pictures. As we learned in

Expressive use of light in *The Grapes of Wrath*
Strong contrasts between light and dark (called chiaroscuro) make movies visually interesting and focus our attention on significant details. But that's not all that they accomplish. They can also evoke moods and meanings, and even symbolically complement the other formal elements of a movie, as in these frames from John Ford's *The Grapes of Wrath* (1940).

Lighting and character in *Atonement*

Filmmakers often craft the interplay between illumination and shadow to imply character state of mind. The tragic romance of *Atonement* (2007; director Joe Wright) hinges on the actions of a precocious thirteen-year-old, Briony Tallis. Lives are irrevocably altered when Briony's adolescent jealousy prompts her to accuse the housekeeper's son Robbie of rape. As events unfold, a series of different lighting designs are employed to enhance our perception of Briony's evolving (and often suppressed) emotions as she stumbles upon Cecilia and Robbie making love in the library [1], catches a startled glimpse of her cousin's rape [2], accuses Robbie of the crime [3], guiltily retreats upon Robbie's arrival [4], contemplates the consequences of her actions [5], and observes Robbie's arrest [6].

Chapter 1, movement is what separates cinema from all other two-dimensional pictorial art forms. We call them movies for a reason—cinema's expressive power largely derives from the medium's fundamental ability to move.

Or, rather, it seems to move. As we sit in a movie theater, believing ourselves to be watching a continually lit screen portraying fluid, uninterrupted movement, we are actually watching a quick succession of still photographs called **frames**. There is still some debate among cognitive scientists as to exactly why the brain processes a rapid series of still images as continuous movement. Essentially, when viewing successive images depicting only slight differences from frame to frame at a high enough speed, the brain's visual systems respond using the same motion detectors used to perceive and translate real motion in our everyday lives. For our purposes, what's important is (a) it works, as the marvelously expressive medium we're studying could not exist without this convenient brain glitch, and (b) we recognize the still photographic frame as the basic building block of motion pictures.

In the early days of cinema, when these continuous successions of frames were shot and shown using long strips of celluloid film, filmmakers and exhibitors discovered that the shooting and projection of at least 24 images per second was needed to present smooth, natural looking movement. Projectors were developed that could perform a complex mechanical task 24 times every second: shine light through a frame to project its image, and then move the next frame into place for its moment of projection. A shutter was used to block the light and thus obscure the mechanical movement of each new frame being moved into place, so that the screen was actually momentarily dark at least 24 times every second. Aspects of eye and brain function that blend rapid flashes of light and momentarily retain an image after the eye records it make those moments of darkness undetectable. New rotating multi-blade shutters were soon developed that momentarily interrupted the projection of each frame with a microsecond of black screen, so that audiences were actually seeing two projections of each frame before the projector mechanism replaced it with the next frame. By further increasing the number of projected images flashing across the screen each second, these shutters helped to further smooth the appearance of motion and eliminate any visible flicker on-screen. These days, when most movies are shot on high-definition video using digital cameras, and virtually every movie is viewed digitally—whether in a movie theater using a digital projector or on a digital TV or other device—the brief moments of black are no longer necessary. Most movies are still shot and projected at 24 frames per second, although some recent films (such as Peter Jackson's Hobbit trilogy) have experimented with higher frame rates.

Movies Manipulate Space and Time in Unique Ways

Some of the arts, such as architecture, are concerned mostly with space; others, such as music, are related mainly to time. But movies manipulate space and time equally well, so they are both a spatial and a temporal art form. Movies can move seamlessly from one space to another (say, from a room to a landscape to outer space), or make space move (as when the camera turns around or away from its subject, changing the physical, psychological, or emotional relationship between the viewer and the subject), or fragment time in many different ways. Only movies can record real time in its chronological passing as well as subjective versions of time passing—slow motion, for example, or extreme compression of vast swaths of time.

On the movie screen, space and time are relative to each other, and we can't separate them or perceive one without the other. The movies give time to space and space to time, a phenomenon that art historian and film theorist Erwin Panofsky describes as the *dynamization of space* and the *spatialization of time*.[1] To understand this principle of "co-expressibility," compare your experiences of space when you watch a play and when you watch a movie. As a spectator at a play in the theater, your relationship to the stage, the settings, and the actors is *fixed*. Your perspective on these things is determined by the location of your seat, and everything on the stage remains the same size in relation to the entire stage. Sets may change between scenes, but within scenes the set remains, for the most part, in place. No matter how skillfully constructed and painted the set is, you know (because of the clear boundaries between the set and the rest of the theater) that it is not real and that when actors go through doors in the set's walls, they go backstage or into the wings at the side of the stage, not into a continuation of the world portrayed on the stage.

---

1. Erwin Panofsky, "Style and Medium in the Motion Pictures," in *Film Theory and Criticism: Introductory Readings*, 5th ed., ed. Leo Braudy and Marshall Cohen (New York: Oxford University Press, 1999), pp. 281–283.

By contrast, when you watch a movie, your relationship to the space portrayed on-screen can be flexible. You still sit in a fixed seat, but the screen images move: the spatial relationships on the screen may constantly change, and the film directs your gaze. Suppose, for example, that during a scene in which two characters meet at a bar, the action suddenly flashes forward to their later rendezvous at an apartment, then flashes back to the conversation at the bar, and so on; or a close-up focuses your attention on one character's (or both characters') lips. A live theater performance can attempt versions of such spatial and temporal effects, but a play can't do so as seamlessly, immediately, persuasively, or intensely as a movie can. If one of the two actors in that bar scene were to back away from the other and thus disappear from the screen, you would perceive her as moving to another part of the bar; that is, into a continuation of the space already established in the scene. You can easily imagine this movement due to the fluidity of movie space, more of which is necessarily suggested than is shown.

The motion-picture camera doesn't simply record the space in front of it: it deliberately determines and controls our perception of cinematic space. In the hands of expressive filmmakers, the camera selects what space we see and uses framing, lenses, and movement to determine exactly how we see that space. This process, by which an agent transfers something from one place to another (in this case, the camera transferring aspects of space to the viewer) is known as **mediation**. When we watch a movie, especially under ideal conditions with a large screen in a darkened room, we *identify with the lens*. In other words, viewers exchange the viewpoint of their own eyes for the mediated viewpoint of the camera. The camera captures space differently than do the eyes, which have peripheral vision and can only move through space (and time) along with the rest of the body. The camera's viewpoint is limited only by the edges of the frame. It fragments space into multiple edited images that can jump instantaneously between different angles and positions, looking through variable lenses that present depth and perspective in a number of ways. And yet, because of our natural tendency to use visual information to understand the space around us, the brain is able to automatically accept and process the camera's different way of seeing and use that mediated information to comprehend cinematic space.

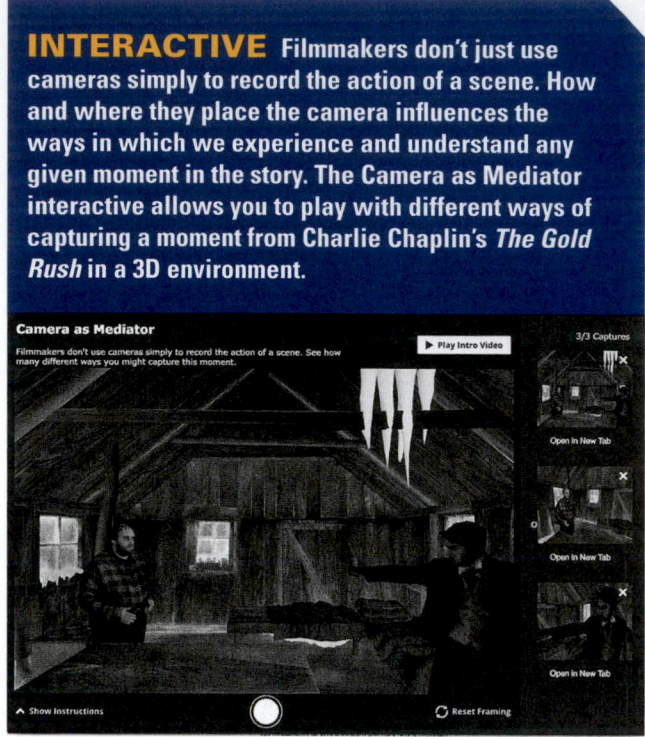

INTERACTIVE Filmmakers don't just use cameras simply to record the action of a scene. How and where they place the camera influences the ways in which we experience and understand any given moment in the story. The Camera as Mediator interactive allows you to play with different ways of capturing a moment from Charlie Chaplin's *The Gold Rush* in a 3D environment.

Cinema's ability to mediate space is illustrated in Charles Chaplin's *The Gold Rush* (1925). This brilliant comedy portrays the adventures of two prospectors: the "Little Fellow" (Chaplin) and his partner, Big Jim McKay (Mack Swain). After many twists and turns of the plot, the two find themselves sharing an isolated cabin. At night, the winds of a fierce storm blow the cabin to the edge of a cliff, leaving it precariously balanced on the brink of an abyss. Waking and walking about, the Little Fellow slides toward the door (and almost certain death). The danger is established by our first seeing the sharp precipice on which the cabin is located and then by seeing the Little Fellow sliding toward the door that opens out over the chasm. Subsequently, we see him and Big Jim engaged in a struggle for survival that requires them to maintain the balance of the cabin on the edge of the cliff.

The suspense exists because individual shots—one made outdoors, the other safely in a studio—have been edited together to create the illusion that they form part of a complete space. As we watch the cabin sway and teeter on the cliff's edge, we imagine the hapless adventurers inside; when the action cuts to the interior of the cabin and we see the floor pitching back and forth,

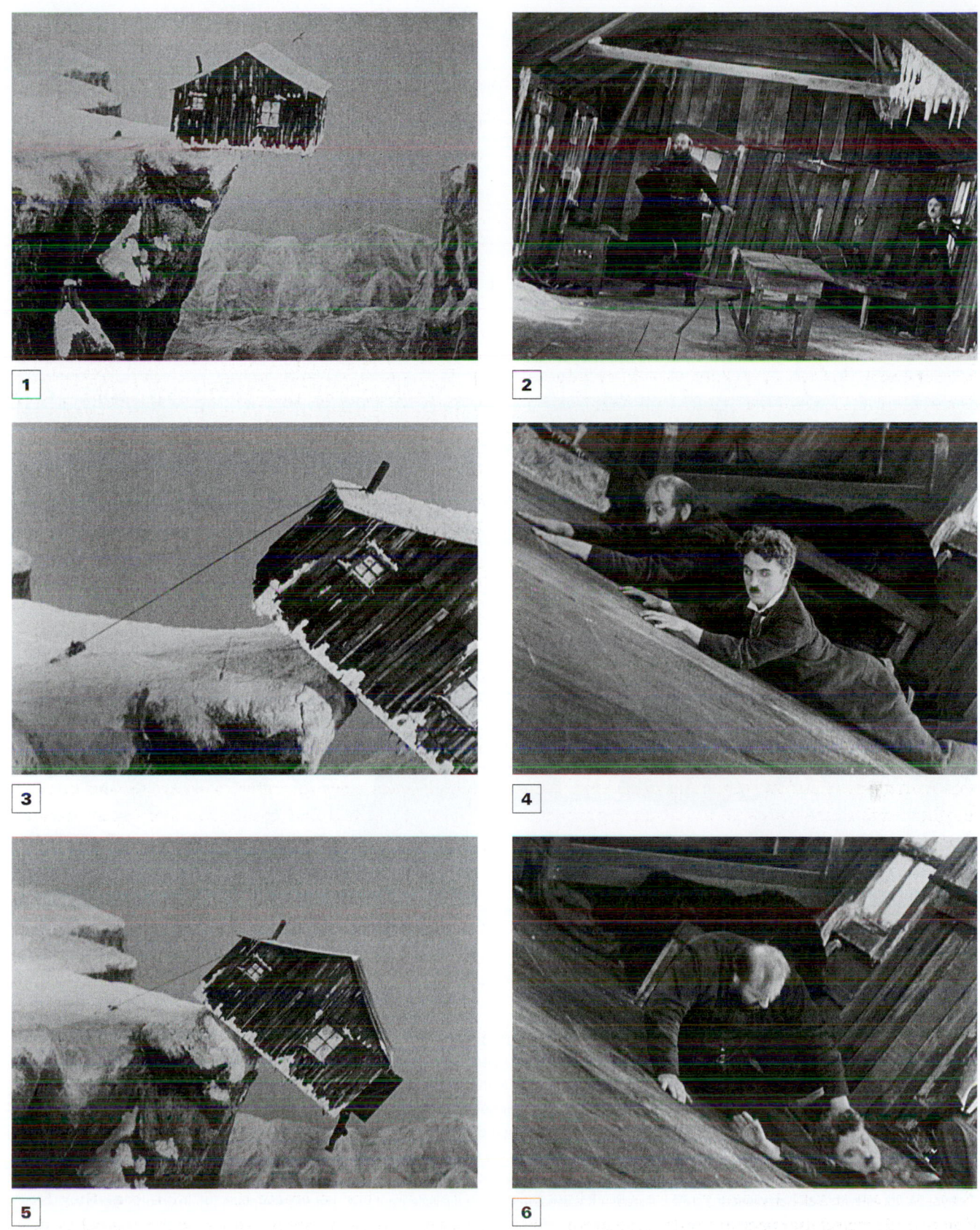

Manipulating space in *The Gold Rush*

Film editing can convince us that we're seeing a complete space and a continuous action, even though individual shots have been filmed in different places and at different times. In Charles Chaplin's *The Gold Rush* (1925), an exterior shot of the cabin [1] establishes the danger that the main characters only slowly become aware of [2]. As the cabin hangs in the balance [3], alternating interior and exterior shots [4–6] accentuate our sense of suspense and amusement.

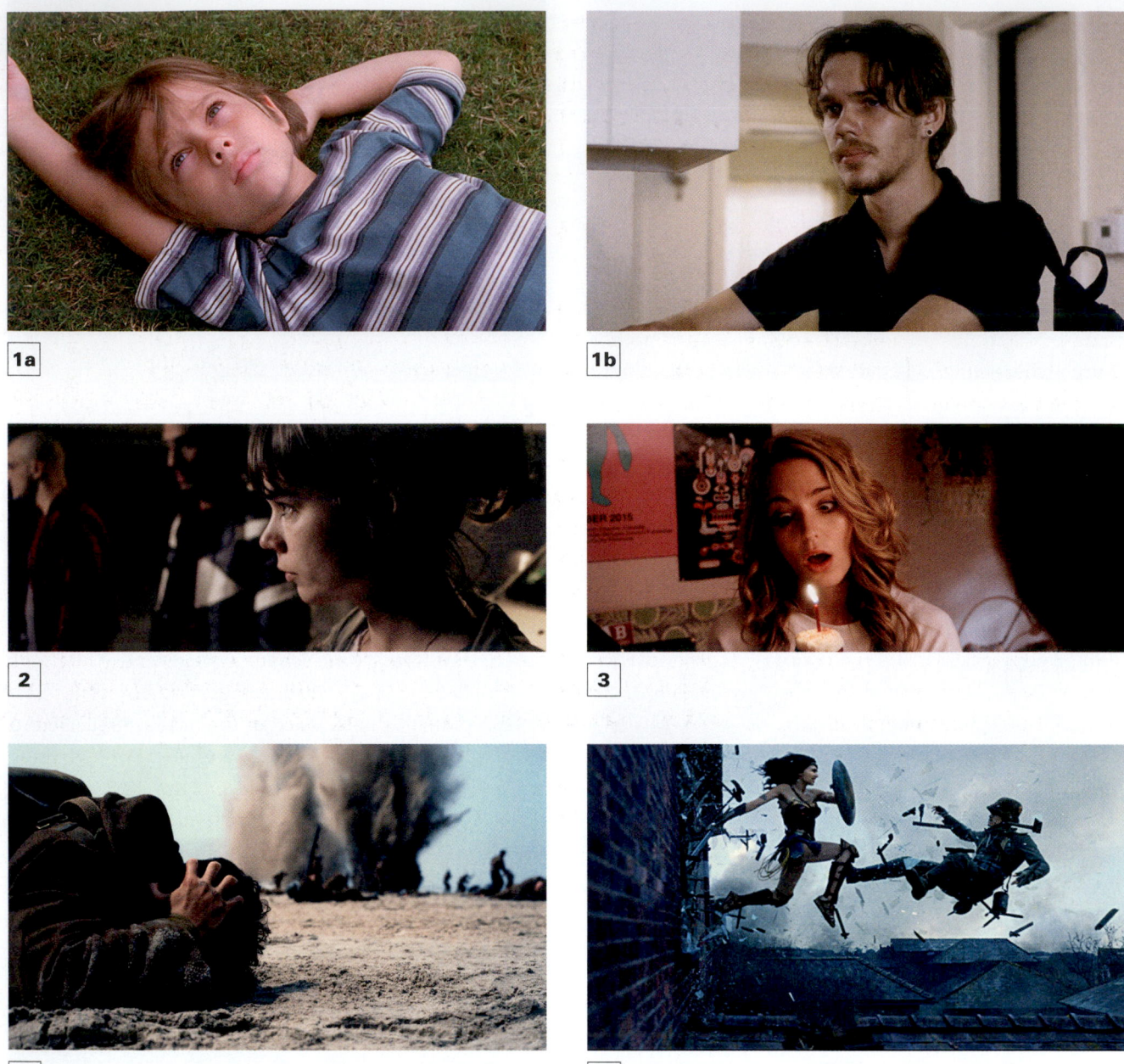

1a

1b

2

3

4

5

Movies manipulate time

A number of recently released films offer ample evidence that rearranging chronology isn't the only way movies manipulate time. Director Richard Linklater shot *Boyhood* (2014) using the same actors over a period of 12 years. The audience literally watches the boy in question grow up on-screen [1]. In contrast, the 140-minute running time of the thriller *Victoria* (2015; director Sebastian Schipper) matches the time it takes the story to elapse. The entire story of a night on the town that goes horribly wrong is conveyed in one unbroken shot [2]. Christopher Landon's horror comedy *Happy Death Day* (2017) takes place all in one day, but that day is repeated multiple times as the protagonist struggles to solve her own recurring murder and break free of the time loop she's stuck inside [3]. Christopher Nolan's World War II epic *Dunkirk* (2017) intertwines three stories with three different timelines: troops stranded on a beach desperately awaiting rescue over the course of 7 days; 24 hours with a civilian pleasure craft enlisted in the evacuation; and a single hour with two fighter pilots [4]. In a fight scene in *Wonder Woman* (2017; director Patty Jenkins), the title character's newfound powers are visualized using ramped speed, a technique in which action speeds up and slows down within a single shot [5].

we imagine the cabin perched precariously on the edge. The experience of these shots as a continuous record of action occurring in a complete (and realistic) space is an illusion that no other art form can convey as effectively as movies can.

The manipulation of time (as well as space), a function of editing, is handled with great irony, cinematic power, and emotional impact in the "baptism and murder" scene in Francis Ford Coppola's *The Godfather* (1972). This 5-minute scene consists of thirty-six shots made at different locations. The primary location is a church where Michael Corleone, the newly named godfather of the Corleone mob, and his wife, Kay, attend their nephew's baptism. Symbolically, Michael is also the child's godfather. Coppola cuts back and forth between the baptism; the preparations for five murders, which Michael has ordered, at five different locations; and the murders themselves.

Each time we return to the baptism, it continues where it left off for one of these cutaways to other actions. We know this from the continuity of the priest's actions, Latin incantations, and the Bach organ music. This continuity tells us not only that these actions are taking place simultaneously but also that Michael is involved in all of them, either directly or indirectly. The simultaneity is further strengthened by the organ music, which underscores every scene in the sequence, not just those that take place in the cathedral. As the priest says to Michael, "Go in peace, and may the Lord be with you," we are left to reconcile this meticulously timed, simultaneous occurrence of sacred and criminal acts.

The parallel action sequences in *The Silence of the Lambs, Way Down East,* and *The Godfather* are evidence of cinema's ability to use crosscutting to represent multiple events occurring at the same instant. Some movies, like *City of God* (2002; directors Fernando Meirelles and Kátia Lund), do parallel action one better, using a split screen to show the concurrent actions simultaneously.

Movies frequently rearrange time by organizing story events in nonchronological order. Orson Welles's *Citizen Kane* (1941) and Todd Haynes's *I'm Not There* (2007) both begin their exploration of a life with that character's death and, for the rest of the film, shuffle the events leading up to that opening conclusion. Movies such as *Love and Mercy* (2014; director Bill Pohlad) inform our perspective on characters and events by alternating between past and present time frames. The science-fiction film *Arrival* (2016; director Denis Villeneuve) re-

Split screen and simultaneous action

Most movies use crosscutting techniques like parallel action to represent more than one event occurring at the same moment. The audience experiences only one event at a time, but the repeated crosscutting implies simultaneity. *City of God* sometimes breaks with convention and splits the screen into multiple frames to present a more immediate depiction of simultaneous action.

orders time in ways that challenge viewer expectations of chronology (and consciousness) when scenes initially assumed to take place in the past are revealed to be glimpses of future events. A number of films, most famously Christopher Nolan's *Memento* (2000) and Gaspar Noé's *Irréversible* (2002), transpose time by presenting their stories in scene-by-scene reverse chronological order. All of these approaches to rearranging time allow filmmakers to create new narrative meaning by juxtaposing events in ways linear chronology does not permit.

John Woo's 1989 action extravaganza *The Killer* maintains conventional chronology but uses many other expressive manipulations of time to tell its story of a kindhearted assassin and the relentless cop determined to capture him. Each of the film's many gun battle scenes features elegant slow-motion shots of either the antihero or one of his unfortunate rivals delivering or absorbing multiple bullets. The slow motion invites the audience to pause and savor an extended moment of stylized violence. The sequences also employ occasional bursts of fast motion that have the opposite effect. These sudden temporal shifts allow Woo and film editor Kung Ming Fan to choreograph cinematic patterns and rhythms that give their fight scenes a dizzying kinetic energy that borders on the outrageous.

Woo expands the audience's experience of time at key points in the story by fragmenting the moment preceding an important action. The film's climactic

Manipulating time in *The Killer*

The world-weary title character in John Woo's *The Killer* (1989) is an expert assassin attempting to cash in and retire after one last hit. Woo conveys the hit man's reluctance to kill again by expanding the moment of his decision to pull the trigger. Film editor Kung Ming Fan fragments the dramatic pause preceding the action into a thirty-four-shot sequence that cuts between multiple images of the intended target [1], the dragon-boat ceremony he is officiating [2, 3], and the pensive killer [4, 5]. The accumulation of all these fragments extends what should be a brief moment into a tension-filled 52 seconds. When the killer finally does draw his weapon, the significance of the decision is made clear by the repetition of this action in three shots from different camera angles [6–8]. The rapid-fire repetition of a single action is one of cinema's most explicit manipulations of time.

gunfight finds the hit man and the cop allied against overwhelming forces. The sequence begins with several shots of an army of trigger-happy gangsters bursting into the isolated church where the unlikely partners are holed up. The film extends the brief instant before the bullets fly with a series of twelve shots, including a panicked bystander covering her ears, a priest crossing himself, and the cop and killer exchanging tenacious glances. The accumulation of these time fragments holds us in the moment far longer than the momentum of the action could realistically allow. The sequence's relative stasis establishes a pattern that is broken by the inevitable explosion of violence. Later, a brief break in the combat is punctuated by a **freeze-frame** (in which a still image is shown on-screen for a period of time), another of Woo's time-shifting trademarks. Bloodied but still breathing, the newfound friends emerge from the bullet-ridden sanctuary. The killer's fond glance at the cop suddenly freezes into a still image, suspending time and motion for a couple of seconds. The cop's smiling response is prolonged in a matching sustained freeze-frame. As you may have guessed, *The Killer* is an odd sort of love story. With that in mind, we can see that these freeze-frames do more than manipulate time; they visually unite the two former foes, thus emphasizing their mutual admiration.

One of the most dazzling manipulations of both space and time the movies have to offer was perfected and popularized by Lana and Lilly Wachowski (as the Wachowski brothers) with their 1999 science-fiction film, *The Matrix*. This effect, known—for reasons that will become obvious—as bullet time, is critical to one of the film's pivotal scenes. In the scene, the hacker-turned-savior-of-humanity Neo transcends real-world physics and bends the Matrix to his purposes for the first time. When one of the deadly digital henchmen known as agents shoots at Neo, the action suddenly reverts to stylized slow motion as Neo literally bends over backward to avoid the projectiles. The slow motion allows us to see "speeding" slugs and lends a balletic grace to Neo's movements. But what makes the moment magical—and conveys our hero's newfound mastery—is the addition of an extra and unexpected time reference: a swooping camera that circumnavigates the slo-mo action at normal real-time speed. To achieve this disorienting and spellbinding combination of multiple speeds, the filmmakers worked with engineers to develop new technology in a process that resembled sequence photography experiments from the earliest days of motion-picture photography (see illustrations on p. 50). Neo's dodging dance was shot not by one motion-picture camera, but by 120 still cameras mounted in a roller-coaster-style arc and snapping single images in a computer-driven, rapid-fire sequence. When all those individual shots are projected in quick succession, the subject appears to move slowly while the viewpoint of the camera capturing that subject maintains its own independent fluidity and speed.

Realism, Antirealism, and Formalism

All the unique features of film form we've just described combine to enable filmmakers to create vivid and believable worlds on the screen. Although not every film strives to be "realistic," nearly all films attempt to immerse us in a world that is depicted convincingly on its own terms. In order to evaluate and appreciate expressive motion pictures, viewers need to understand how cinema engages realism—and its alternatives.

The first movie cameras were primarily intended to record natural images through photography, an approach to content that was reinforced by concurrent artistic movements in painting and literature that were devoted to recording the visible facts of people, places, and social life for working-class and middle-class audiences. In

Movement in *The Matrix*

For Lana and Lilly Wachowski's *The Matrix* (1999), special effects supervisors Steve Courtley and Brian Cox employed a setup much like that used by early pioneers of serial photography (see Chapter 10). They placed 120 still cameras in an arc and coordinated their exposures using computers. The individual frames, shot from various angles but in much quicker succession than is possible with a motion-picture camera, could then be edited together to create the duality of movement (sometimes called bullet time) for which *The Matrix* is famous. The camera moves around a slow-motion subject at a relatively fast pace, apparently independent of the subject's stylized slowness. Despite its contemporary look, this special effects technique is grounded in principles and methods established during the earliest years of motion-picture history.

1895, the pioneering French filmmakers Auguste and Louis Lumière started making some of the first silent movies, and these were devoted to the actual or real (i.e., manifesting a tendency to view or represent things as they really are).

What makes a movie realistic? In the case of the Lumière brothers, it came down to subject matter (content) and style (form). In terms of content, the Lumières documented unrehearsed scenes from everyday life. They did not stylize this "reality" with conspicuous camera angles, compositions, lighting, or edits. In this way, they established some basic approaches to form and content that today's fiction film audiences still associate with cinematic **realism**. These formal components include

Lumière/Méliès

Whether presenting a scene from everyday life, as in Louis Lumière's *Employees Leaving the Lumière Factory* (1895) [1], or showing a fantastical scenario, as in Georges Méliès's *A Trip to the Moon* (1902) [2], motion pictures were recognized from the very beginning for their ability to create a feeling of *being there*, of seeing something that could actually happen. The Lumière brothers favored what they called *actualités*—mini-documentaries of scenes from everyday life—whereas Méliès made movies directly inspired by his interest in magicians' illusions. Yet both the Lumières and Méliès wanted to portray their on-screen worlds convincingly.

naturalistic performances and dialogue; modest, unembellished sets and settings; and wide-angle compositions and other unobtrusive framing. The content tends to concentrate on story lines that portray the everyday lives of "ordinary" people.

In most movie entertainments, every character and situation serves a preordained function in a highly organized plot structure. Because real life is often messy and complicated, the content of movies that strive for realism often takes a more inclusive, less organized approach to the form in which that story is told. These story lines are conveyed without obvious artistic flourishes such as dramatic lighting or dazzling camera moves. But that does not mean realism is devoid of style. On the contrary, fiction movies in this category often adapt formal techniques associated with documentary filmmaking. The down-to-earth authenticity this approach projects makes realism a natural fit for films portraying social issues.

For example, *Fruitvale Station* (2013; director Ryan Coogler) is closely based on the true story of Oscar Grant III, an unemployed San Francisco grocery clerk who was shot and killed on a subway platform by Bay Area Rapid Transit police while on his way home from New Year's festivities in 2009. The script, which recounts the last day of Mr. Grant's life, includes multiple events

and interactions that don't feed directly into the film's plot. Instead, they provide the everyday texture of the protagonist's life and personality. The director cast professional but not widely known actors. He shot the movie at actual locations with a handheld camera using the kind of light-sensitive (and thus grainy) 16mm film stock associated with documentary cinema.

Shortly after the Lumière brothers started making movies based in realism, another groundbreaking French filmmaker began creating movies with different foundations and goals. The work of Georges Méliès displayed an interest in the speculative and fantastic, an approach to content termed **antirealism**. The cinematic antirealism that Méliès practiced considered the viewer's perceptions of reality as a starting point to expand upon or even purposely subvert. His inventive stories featured space travel, monsters, ghosts, and magic. In order to bring this antirealistic content to the screen, Méliès embraced what is now called **formalism**, an approach to style and storytelling that values conspicuously expressive form over the unobtrusive form associated with realism. His films incorporated special effects, elaborate costumes, theatrical performances, and fanciful sets. Contemporary movies that can be considered formalist may use highly stylized and distinctive camera work, editing, and lighting to convey sensational stories set in embellished

Mixing the real and the fantastic

On its surface, *Beasts of the Southern Wild* (2012; director Benh Zeitlin) is very much a realist movie. The story is loosely structured, shot on location with a handheld camera, and everything is gritty: the setting, the characters, and the light-sensitive film stock. Most of the movie looks, sounds, and moves like the real world—until the content and form veer into the fantastic. The protagonist Hushpuppy has recurring visions of icebergs that crumble to reveal—and eventually free—gigantic horned beasts encased inside. Realism comes face to face with both antirealism and formalism when these awesome creatures are confronted by the diminutive Hushpuppy.

1

2

Technology and the appearance of realism

Movies as diverse as the stark drama *Two Days, One Night* (2014; directors Jean-Pierre Dardenne and Luc Dardenne) and the apocalyptic horror film *Cloverfield* (2008; director Matt Reeves) create a sense of realism by employing camera formats and techniques that audiences associate with "reality." *Two Days, One Night* [1] is shot with a relatively smooth handheld technique for a look that resembles that of professional documentary films. *Cloverfield* [2] goes several steps further, shooting in a shaky handheld style and degrading the video image to resemble amateur home movies—the ultimate in unvarnished reality footage.

1

2

Realism versus formalism

These two paintings illustrate the difference between realism and formalism. Thomas Gainsborough's eighteenth-century portrait *The Hon. Frances Duncombe* presents its subject in a form that conforms to our experiences and expectations of how a woman looks [1]. Compare this with *Nude Descending a Staircase, No. 2*, by the twentieth-century French artist Marcel Duchamp [2]. Duchamp has transformed a woman's natural appearance (which we know from life) into a radically altered form of sharp angles and fractured shapes. Both paintings represent women, and each took great technical skill and artistic talent to create; but they differ greatly in their relationship to realism and form.

or imaginary settings. Those settings are often filmed on highly designed sets that purposely reinvent or reject the look of everyday locations.

Wes Anderson's *The Grand Budapest Hotel* (2014) is located at the pinnacle of formalism and antirealism. The fanciful story of an impeccable concierge framed for murder is set in an ornate pink hotel located at the summit of a nearly perpendicular mountain peak above an imaginary town in a fictional country. The filmmakers make no effort to disguise the fact that the exterior set of the titular hotel is a miniature model. The plot is highly structured and includes absurd events like a high-speed sled chase. The larger-than-life characters wear whimsical costumes and makeup, and they are presented by (mostly) famous actors delivering deliberately mannered performances. The cinematography features dramatic lighting, saturated colors, and elaborately staged formal compositions.

Of course, it's important to keep in mind that the two movie examples just discussed—*Fruitvale Station* and

The Grand Budapest Hotel—exist at opposite ends of a realism spectrum. Most films fall somewhere between these two extremes. And the concept of realism should not be confused with a value judgment. Some of the most profound and heartfelt works in cinema could be called antirealist, just as creative innovation can be found in movies classified as realist. Often, our engagement with a movie has less to do with the appearance of realism and more to do with whether we believe it in the moment—which brings us to our next subject.

Verisimilitude

Verisimilitude, the appearance of being true or real, is not the same as realism. A movie doesn't necessarily have to be an accurate portrayal of the world we live in to feel true and real to the viewers watching it. Some of the most popular and successful movies of all time con-

vincingly depict imaginative or supernatural worlds and events that have little or nothing in common with our actual experiences. If the characters and events on-screen feel plausible and consistent within the context of the world of the story—if we are able to believe in what we're seeing while we're seeing it—that film has achieved verisimilitude, regardless of the content presented or the form used to present it. An animated comedy where characters suddenly burst into song may be as verisimilar as a serious drama that is based on actual events.

Oftentimes, verisimilitude is in the eye of the beholder. You can be deeply engaged by the physical verisimilitude of the world being depicted and still be unconvinced by the "unreality" of a character—or by the performance of the actor playing him. And audiences' expectations of believability change over time and across cultures. A film that you found engaging and authentic when you were in kindergarten may seem ridiculous when you revisit it

Verisimilitude and the viewing experience
Cinema's ability to make us temporarily believe in people, places, and events that we know to be imaginary is one of the primary reasons we watch movies. But movies don't have to be realistic to provide verisimilitude. The irrational act of believing in—and caring about—a manufactured reality that is significantly different than our everyday world can provide a special kind of sensation. One of the pleasures of watching Guillermo del Toro's *The Shape of Water* (2017) is the effect of becoming emotionally invested in an interspecies romance between a cleaning woman and a water creature specimen in a government research center.

as an adult. A movie made in Germany in the 1930s may have been considered thoroughly verisimilar by those Germans who viewed it at the time, but it may seem utterly unfamiliar and hence unbelievable to contemporary American viewers. Films that succeed in appearing verisimilar across cultures and generations often enjoy the sort of critical and popular success that prompts people to call them timeless.

What exactly makes a film verisimilar is difficult to quantify. We know it when we see it, or rather, when we *feel* it. Believability seems to be achieved through the right combination of form, content, performance, and intent. But just because it is hard to describe doesn't mean verisimilitude is not important. The movies are an expressive medium perfectly suited for—and devoted to—providing audiences a transcendent and immersive experience. Most of us go to the movies seeking verisimilitude, so most filmmakers employ all of the film form described in this book toward providing it.

Cinematic Language

By cinematic language—a phrase that we have already used a few times in this book—we mean the accepted systems, methods, or conventions by which the movies communicate with the viewer. To fully understand cinema as a language, let's compare it with another, more familiar form of language—the written one you're engaged with this instant. Our written language is based, for the purpose of this explanation, on words. Each of those words has a generally accepted meaning, but when juxtaposed and combined with other words into a sentence and presented in a certain context, each can convey meaning that is potentially far more subtle, precise, or evocative than that implied by its standard "dictionary" definition.

Instead of arranging words into sentences, cinematic language combines and composes a variety of elements—for example, lighting, movement, sound, acting, and a number of camera effects—into single shots. As you work your way through this book, you will learn that most of these individual elements carry conventional, generalized meanings. But when combined with any number of other elements and presented in a particular context, that element's standardized meaning grows more individuated and complex. And the integrated arrangement of all of a shot's combined elements provides even greater expressive potential. So, in cinema, as in the written word, the whole is greater than the sum of its parts. But the analogy doesn't end there. Just as authors arrange sentences into paragraphs and chapters, filmmakers derive still more accumulated meaning by organizing shots into a system of larger components: sequences and scenes. Furthermore, within sequences and scenes a filmmaker can juxtapose shots to create a more complex meaning than is usually achieved in standard prose. As viewers, we analyze cinematic language and its particular resources of expression and meaning. If your instructor refers to the *text* of a movie or asks you to *read* a particular shot, scene, or movie, she is asking you to apply your understanding of cinematic language.

Like any language, cinematic language relies on conventions: a standard and commonly understood way of doing something. The conventions of cinematic language represent a sort of agreement between the filmmaker and the audience about the mediating element between them: the film itself. The filmmaker agrees to use cinematic language in ways that viewers recognize and understand so the audience can comprehend the filmmaker's intended meaning. But without innovations—new and unfamiliar ways of applying cinematic language—those handy conventions would not exist. So, sometimes that agreement must be broken, or at least bent, when an innovative filmmaker seeks new ways to convey meaning and experience. For example, when *Baby Driver* (2017; director Edgar Wright) suddenly cuts from a scene of the adult protagonist and his music collection to a scene depicting a car crash from his childhood, we intuitively understand the movie has momentarily jumped back in time to show us what the character is thinking about, thanks to the filmmaker's use of a conventional *flashback*. But at some point in film history, a filmmaker had to break with convention, and thus challenge viewers' expectations of cinematic language, to innovate this expressive leap in time and space. And even once established, every convention is itself open to further innovation and interpretation. Depending on the way they are created and the context in which they are presented, temporal and spatial leaps can communicate any number of meanings, moods, or ideas.

And you are capable of assimilating each of these ever-evolving permutations, because years of practice watching movies have made you an agile consumer

[2] Design elements such as costumes, props, and set furnishings help communicate the story's early nineteenth-century time period, as well as the upper-class status of Jane's adoptive family.

[4] John Reed is backlit, a lighting direction that renders a figure in silhouette. In this context, the technique differentiates John from our hiding heroine Jane and visually reinforces his cruel and deceptive behavior.

[1] Young Jane is the primary subject of this shot. She is the largest figure in the frame, and she is clearly in focus. She is lit with diffused light that softens her features. Her vulnerable situation—and state of mind—is conveyed via her downcast performance, her comparatively dour dress, and the framing that partially obscures her face.

[3] Jane's literal and figurative detachment is conveyed by the curtains, illumination, shadows, and depth that divides her half of the frame from that occupied by her abusive cousin and aunt.

[5] In contrast to the soft, diffused light that characterizes Jane, Mrs. Reed's portion of the frame is lit with direct, unfiltered light that casts deep shadows and bright highlights. Her distance from Jane, and perhaps even her insensitivity to her niece's situation, is emphasized by the different quality of light, relative size in frame, and indistinct focus.

Cinematic language

Looking at this single image, without even knowing what movie it is from or anything about the various characters pictured in the frame, we can immediately infer layers of meaning and significance. If we think of cinematic language as akin to written language, we can think of this single image from Cary Fukunaga's *Jane Eyre* (2011) as a richly layered "sentence" that communicates by combining and arranging multiple visual elements (or "words" in this analogy) that include lighting, composition, depth, design, cinematography, and performance.

of cinematic language. But, as you may have already discovered, there is much more to this language than the average viewer consciously considers. The following chapters of this book will expand your innate grasp into an informed fluency that empowers you to identify and demonstrate how the movies work to express ideas, tell stories, and engage audiences. Being an active reader of cinematic language is a vital skill in a world increasingly shaped by—and inundated with—motion pictures.

Looking at Film Form: *Donnie Darko*

To better understand how some of these principles of film form function within a single movie, let's examine how they're used in Richard Kelly's *Donnie Darko*. The film was a box office dud in 2001, but it gained critical acclaim and what has proven to be an enduring cult following after its release on VHS and DVD the next year. This popularity—and intense audience interest in the film's sometimes murky meaning—led to the release of an extended director's cut in 2004. For consistency's sake, we will confine our evaluation to the original theatrical release.

Content

What is the content of *Donnie Darko*? That's an interesting question because the search for content is a large part of what makes the movie an absorbing cinematic experience. Throughout the film, events unfold and details emerge that force us as viewers to continually reevaluate our understanding of that content. We are repeatedly provoked to ask if Donnie's mind- and time-bending experiences are real or simply a projection of his diagnosed mental illness. Audiences aren't used to working so hard for their content; the effort *Donnie Darko* demands probably played a part in both the tepid response it received in theaters and its increased popularity on DVD and VHS, formats that allow for repeated viewings. For the purpose of this analysis, let's keep it as simple as possible: the movie is about suburban hypocrisy, high school politics, adolescent alienation—and time travel between parallel universes. The story centers on a troubled and possibly schizo-

phrenic teenager named Donnie Darko who is haunted by a mysterious being that compels him to perform acts of retaliatory destruction.

Expectations

The first scenes of most films prompt basic expectations that shape an audience's engagement with the rest of the movie. These opening moments set the tone and let us know what style of story to expect. Viewers sense if this is reliable or an unpredictable world, determine whether they're watching serious drama or a playful comedy, and form instructive opinions about the characters.

Most movies establish expectations in order to involve and guide the audience. *Donnie Darko* exploits expectations to keep viewers off balance. The film opens with the title character waking from a sound sleep in the middle of a mountain road—a situation that is simultaneously dangerous and ridiculous. So we're still not exactly sure what we're in for as he rides his bike home and we head into the next scenes: a contentious family dinner erupting in political tension and teenage hostility, followed by a confrontation between Donnie and his mother in which we realize he is both in therapy and on medication.

At this stage, past movie experience leads us to presume we've entered a family drama that will chronicle Donnie's struggle with mental illness. That night, a

Who and what is Frank?
The grotesque bunny figure, Frank, plays a central role in the *Donnie Darko* viewing experience. His first appearance complicates expectations about Donnie's mental state, predicts the film's ending, and injects a horror movie mood to what might previously have been assumed to be a conventional troubled teenager story. Frank exists on the border between realism and antirealism. He is a cosmic hallucination dressed in a shaggy homemade costume; he's both a messenger from the future and Donnie's big sister's boyfriend dressed up for Halloween.

strange disembodied voice summons Donnie to sleep-walk out to the front lawn, where he encounters Frank, a tall figure wearing a shaggy homemade costume topped with a grotesque rabbit mask. Based on the previous scenes, we assume that we are experiencing the hallucinations of a disturbed mind. And other, more conflicting expectations are in play as well: the absurdity of a man in a rabbit outfit may lead us to expect something

Pattern in *Donnie Darko*

Donnie Darko uses a simple ABABAB pattern to lull viewers into a sort of cinematic complacency before jolting our senses. The fifteen-shot sequence shifts back and forth seven times between a shot of Eddie Darko [A] and his son Donnie [B] before a new shot of a woman in their path [C] interrupts their conversation. This jarring break in pattern dramatically visualizes the Darkos' sudden realization, allows the audience to experience a shock similar to that of the characters on-screen, and provides a striking introduction to a pivotal figure.

comic, or at least innocuous. Yet there's something scary about the incongruity of the costume that triggers anxious expectations born of horror movie clowns and dolls. Then Frank tells Donnie the world will end in 28 days, 6 hours, 42 minutes, and 12 seconds.

Now, faced with a precise time frame and specific outcome, we instinctively begin to anticipate how this story will conclude, even as we doubt the reliability (and existence) of the source. The next morning, Donnie wakes up on a golf course and stumbles home, only to discover that during his absence a very real jet engine has fallen from the sky and crashed into his bedroom. This sudden intrusion of the undeniably tangible makes us reevaluate our expectations about what kind of movie we're watching, what's at stake, what is real, and what will happen.

Patterns

Like most other movies, *Donnie Darko* uses pattern to convey and compare simultaneous action, fragment dramatic situations for emphasis and juxtaposition, and establish—and then sometimes subvert—expectations. A sequence that occurs early in the film manages to fulfill all of these functions. Donnie's father Eddie is driving him home after school; father and son discuss the mysterious origin of the fallen jet engine. Until its startling conclusion, the scene is presented in a conventional AB shot/reverse-shot pattern: we see Eddie [A] when he speaks, then cut to Donnie [B] for his reaction and response, and so on. On its surface, the pattern presents a practical approach to a two-person conversation filmed in the cramped confines of a moving automobile. But the choice provides opportunities for narrative expression as well. Each shot of Eddie represents the point of view of Donnie, or vice versa. Fragmenting the conversation empowers the filmmakers to select the best dramatic moments to concentrate on either character's dialogue or reaction.

This back-and-forth AB pattern continues for seven repetitions—long enough to lull the viewer into a certain complacency. We're so caught up in the conversation that we may not notice that we haven't been provided a view through the windshield. So when the established pattern is suddenly broken with a shot of the old lady standing in the middle of the street [C], we experience a shock comparable to that of the distracted characters about to run her over. This jarring transition also gives special emphasis to the character it introduces; the lady in the road is Rebecca Sparrow, the one person alive who could have (before she lost her mind) solved the mystery of the fallen jet engine.

Manipulating Space

Pattern is also a component of *Donnie Darko*'s parallel editing sequences. These sequences don't alternate shot by shot like the car scene, but they do exploit a more general back-and-forth pattern between two simultaneous events occurring in distinctly separate spaces. By exploiting the cinema's ability to manipulate space, these

sequences function in much the same way as *The Godfather*'s "baptism and murder" parallel editing sequence described earlier in this chapter. Like that sequence, parallel action in *Donnie Darko* juxtaposes action that appears disturbingly incongruous, even incompatible, until the pattern of repeated juxtaposition compels viewers to perceive meaningful connections in the apparent contrasts. The viewer sees each event in light of the other alternated event and thus vividly experiences the duality of *Donnie Darko*'s universe.

One such sequence intersperses shots of Donnie's therapist telling his dismayed parents about their son's

Parallel action in *Donnie Darko*

The reality of the alternating events in another notable *Donnie Darko* parallel action sequence is not in question, but the juxtaposition—and the simultaneity—is just as significant. While the rest of the town is consumed with raptly watching an inane community talent show, Donnie is burning down the mansion of the charismatic motivational speaker who holds the townsfolk in his sway. The contrast here is less cosmic and more thematic: the sequence compares and contrasts teenage rebellion with slack-jawed conformity.

potentially violent hallucinations with shots of Donnie confronting a very real-seeming Frank using a very large knife. The content of each action undermines the credibility of the alternating other. In comparison to Donnie's experience, the parent/therapist discussion seems obtuse and oblivious; in light of the therapist's diagnosis, Frank's actual existence is in question. In the twisted world of Donnie Darko, these two perspectives don't cancel each other out; they represent an uneasy coexistence between dual realities.

Manipulating Time

It's only logical that a movie about the distortion of time would exploit cinema's ability to distort time. In the film's first high school scene, the filmmakers employ a relentlessly moving camera shifting between "normal," fast, and slow motion to introduce and connect all the characters associated with the setting. The scene starts in slow motion to show Donnie bursting out of the bus and entering the school, then spurts into fast motion to follow the hypervigilant gym teacher, Kitty Farmer. Dreamy slo-mo returns when the camera pivots to Donnie's potential love interest, Gretchen Ross. In this case, the technique serves as a visual representation of character qualities and state of mind, and it also emphasizes the fluid nature of time as posited in the movie's dual universe. Throughout the rest of the movie, shifts in motion speed will return in shots that transition between scenes to remind audiences that, in the *Donnie Darko* countdown to the end of the world, time is possibly malleable, seemingly unpredictable, and certainly unstoppable. Clouds fly across the sky in time-lapse fast motion. Donnie's little sister does slow-motion jumps on her trampoline. Sometimes students scurry out of high school in fast motion, and sometimes the daily ritual is portrayed in graceful slo-mo.

The manipulation of time can also be used to convey a character's thought process and state of mind. Things, temporally and otherwise, get more confused and conflicted for Donnie until it all goes tragically wrong on Halloween night. At his lowest point, Donnie suddenly realizes that he has the power to reset everything. The resulting rapid-fire, thirty-seven-shot sequence that conveys the jumble of memories and revelations flooding his consciousness features thirteen images that visualize time actually reversing itself, an expressive

technique that is as straightforward as playing the shots backward.

Realism, Antirealism, and Verisimilitude

Donnie Darko's normal world is portrayed with relative realism. The locations, sets, costumes, and most of the performances are designed to look and sound like the real world viewers experience every day—or at least an affluent suburban version of it. Even Jake Gyllenhaal's behavior as the disturbed Donnie is what we would expect from a teenager in his situation. The filmmakers have good reason to ground their movie in realism: this is a story about a mundane existence infiltrated by the fantastic. If viewers did not recognize Donnie's world to begin with, it would be difficult to identify with his struggle to navigate the bizarre cosmic quest thrust upon him or to fully appreciate the return to normalcy he ultimately accomplishes.

Yet as we explained earlier in this chapter, cinematic realism is not an absolute value but a broad spectrum. And Donnie Darko intersects this spectrum at multiple points. The film features stylized lighting and editing that falls outside the realm of pure realism, as do at least two broad characters, seemingly included to amplify the film's social commentary: the pompous self-help guru Jim Cunningham and his overzealous disciple Kitty Farmer. And Frank is only one of many examples of antirealism (and formalism) that intrude with increasing frequency as the movie progresses. Long, fluid tendrils emerge from peoples' chests, a black vortex sprouts from the clouds above Donnie's house, and Donnie's ultimate sacrifice resets time to the morning the story began.

But those antirealist elements do nothing to undermine Donnie Darko's ultimate believability. What makes this achievement in verisimilitude so remarkable is that so little of the film's internal logic is ever entirely explained. Even though few viewers can claim to fully comprehend exactly how the story's time loops function, Donnie Darko is a persuasive and engaging movie experience because we believe it when we see it. So much so that fans can now purchase the (fictional) *Philosophy of Time Travel* book that helps Donnie unlock the secrets of the parallel universe, and they can consult an abundance of websites and published articles devoted to the cult movie and its complex concept.

ANALYZING PRINCIPLES OF FILM FORM

At this early stage in your pursuit of actively looking at movies, you may still be wondering what exactly you are supposed to be looking for. For starters, you now recognize that filmmakers deliberately manipulate your experience and understanding of a movie's content with a constant barrage of techniques and systems known as film form and that this form is organized into an integrated cinematic language. Simply acknowledging the difference between form and content, and knowing that a deliberate system is at work, are the first steps toward identifying and interpreting how movies communicate with viewers. The general principles of film form discussed in this chapter can now provide a framework to help you focus your gaze and develop deeper analytical skills. The checklist below will give you some specific elements and applications of form to watch out for the next time you see a film. Using this and the screening checklists in upcoming chapters, you can turn every movie you watch into an exercise in observation and analysis.

SCREENING CHECKLIST: PRINCIPLES OF FILM FORM

✔ A useful initial step in analyzing any movie is to distinguish an individual scene's content from its form. First try to identify a scene's subject matter: What is this scene about? What happens? Once you have established that content, you should consider how that content was expressed. What was the mood of the scene? What do you understand about each character's state of mind? How did you perceive and interpret each moment? Did that understanding shift at any point? Once you know what happened and how you felt about it, search the scene for those formal elements that influenced your interpretation and experience. The combination and interplay of multiple formal elements that you seek is the cinematic language that movies employ to communicate with the viewer.

✔ Do any narrative or visual patterns recur a sufficient number of times to suggest a structural element in themselves? If so, what are these patterns? Do they help you determine the meaning of the film?

✔ Do you notice anything particular about the movie's presentation of cinematic space? What do you see on the screen? Lots of landscapes or close-ups? Moving or static camera?

✔ Does the director manipulate viewers' experience of time? Is this condensing, slowing, speeding, repeating, or reordering of time simply practical (as in removing insignificant events) or is it expressive? If it is expressive, just what does it express?

✔ Does the director's use of lighting help to create meaning? If so, how?

✔ Do you identify with the camera lens? What does the director compel you to see? What is left to your imagination? What does the director leave out altogether? In the end, besides showing you the action, how does the director's use of the camera help to create the movie's meaning?

Questions for Review

1. How and why do we differentiate between form and content in a movie, and why are they relevant to one another?

2. What expectations of film form can filmmakers exploit to shape an audience's experience?

3. What is parallel editing, and how does it use pattern?

4. In what other ways do movies use patterns to convey meaning? How do they create meaning by breaking an established pattern?

5. How do the movies create an illusion of movement?

6. How does a movie manipulate space?

7. How do movies manipulate time?

8. What is the difference between realism and antirealism in a movie, and why is verisimilitude important to them both?

9. What is the relationship between realism and formalism?

10. What is meant by cinematic language? Why is it important to the ways that movies communicate with viewers?

Faces Places (2017). JR and Agnès Varda, directors. Pictured: JR and Agnès Varda.

CHAPTER

TYPES OF MOVIES

3

LEARNING OBJECTIVES

After reading this chapter, you should be able to

- explain how and why movies are classified.
- define narrative, documentary, and experimental movies, and appreciate the ways these types of movies blend and overlap.
- understand the approaches to documenting actual events employed by documentary filmmakers.
- discuss the characteristics that most experimental films share.
- understand what genre is and why it is important.
- explain the most significant (or defining) elements of each of the six major American genres featured in this chapter.
- understand where animation fits into the movie types discussed in the chapter.
- explain the most commonly used animation techniques.

In this chapter, we will discuss the three major types of movies: narrative, documentary, and experimental. Within narrative movies, we will look at the subcategory of genre films, and we will explore six major American film genres in particular. Finally, we will look at a technique—animation—that is often discussed as if it were a type but that is actually used to make movies of all types.

The Idea of Narrative

The word *narrative* is much more than simply a general classification of a type of film. As you will soon see, depending on when and how we use the term, *narrative* might mean several slightly different things. Since we'll be using the term *narrative* in various ways throughout and beyond our exploration of the three essential types of movies, let's discuss some of the ways to approach the term.

When it comes to cinema, nothing is absolute. In the world of movies, a narrative might be a type of movie, the story that a particular film tells, the particular system by which a fictional story is structured, or a concept describing the sequential organization of events presented in almost any kind of movie. Once you become familiar with these different ways of looking at narrative, you will be able to recognize and understand almost any usage that you come across.

A narrative is a story. When people think of any medium or form—whether it's a movie, a joke, a commercial, or a news article—that tells a story, we consider that story a narrative. Journalists will often speak of finding the narrative in a news item, be it coverage of a city council meeting, a national election, or an Olympic swimming competition. By this, they mean that under the facts and details of any given news item is a story. It's the reporter's job to identify that story and organize his reporting in such a way as to elucidate that narrative.

Journalists do this because humans are a storytelling species. We use stories to arrange and understand our world and our lives. So, of course, news articles are not the only place you'll find narrative. Scientists, songwriters, advertisers, politicians, comedians, and teachers all incorporate narrative into the ways they frame and present information. This semester, you will likely hear your professor refer to the narrative of a particular movie. Depending on the context she uses, she might be talking about the story that the film tells, whether that movie is a science-fiction film or a documentary about science.

Narrative is a type of movie. Our most common perception of the word *narrative* is as a categorical term for those particular movies devoted to conveying a story, whether they are works of pure fiction like Alejandro González Iñárritu's *Birdman* (2014) or a fictionalized version of actual events such as *Selma* (2014; director Ava DuVernay). As we have made clear in previous chapters, these narrative films are the focus of this book. We'll discuss the narrative film as a type of movie (along with experimental and documentary films) later in this chapter.

Narrative is a way of structuring fictional or fictionalized stories presented in narrative films. Storytelling is a complicated business, especially when relating a multifaceted story involving multiple characters and conflicts over the course of 2 hours of screen time. Besides being a general term for a story or for a kind of movie, *narrative* is often used to describe the way that movie stories are constructed and presented to engage, involve, and orient an audience. This narrative structure—which includes exposition, rising action, climax, falling action, and denouement—helps filmmakers manipulate the viewer's cinematic experience by selectively conforming to or diverging from audience expectations of storytelling. Chapter 4 is devoted to this aspect of narrative.

Narrative is a broader concept that both includes and goes beyond any of these applications. Narra-

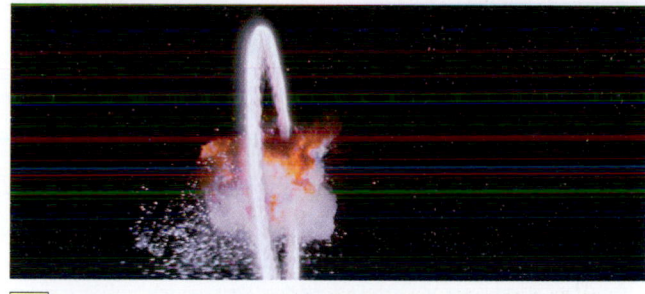

One thing leads to another

The most elemental way of looking at narrative is as a cinematic structure that arranges events in a cause-and-effect sequence. This causality is the basic organizing structure of most movie narratives. Consider the principal events in one of the best-known movies of all time, *Star Wars* (1977; director George Lucas): A starship is boarded by repressive Empire forces. The princess passenger records a plea for help on an android, which escapes to a desert planet. The roving android is captured by scavenging Jawas, who sell it to the farm family of Luke Skywalker, who discovers the message, which sends him in search of Obi-Wan Kenobi, who teaches him the way of the Force and accompanies him on a mission to rescue the princess. One event leads to another and another and another. Decisions are made, which lead to actions, which have consequences, which motivate reactions, which cause subsequent decisions, actions, and consequences. And so it goes. The viewer engages with this logical progression, anticipating probable developments, dreading some and hoping for others.

tive can be defined in a broader conceptual context as any cinematic structure in which content is selected and arranged in a cause-and-effect sequence of events occurring over time. Any time a filmmaker consciously chooses and organizes material so that one event leads to another in a recognizable progression, that filmmaker is employing narrative in its most basic sense. In this case, narrative is not simply the telling of a fictional story, it is a structural quality that nearly every movie possesses, whether it's an avant-garde art film, a documentary account of actual events, or a blockbuster Hollywood fantasy.

Movies do not have to arrange events in conventional order to employ narrative organization. *Sully* (2016; director Clint Eastwood), a fictionalized account of "Sully" Sullenberger (the airline pilot who landed a damaged passenger jet in New York City's Hudson River in 2009), begins with what is soon revealed to be a nightmare—

the plane crashing into a Manhattan building—before launching the story at the start of a National Transportation Safety Board investigation of the incident. Twenty-five minutes later, the movie jumps back to the day of the landing, only to cut back to the "present" just before the plane hits the frigid water. Over the course of the film, the story moves back and forth between the post-incident investigation and the jumble of actions that coincided on the day of the incident itself and also flashes back to past events in Sully's life and to nightmarish visions of what might have happened had he not landed when and

Causal minimalism

A fiction movie need not have a traditional goal-driven plot to be considered narrative. Richard Linklater's *Slacker* (1991) has no central character, no sustained conflict, and tells no single story; yet its structure is very much built on cause-and-effect connections, however tenuous, between the young bohemians who drift in and out of the movie. Beginning with a man getting off a bus (played by Linklater himself), the camera follows one character to another, drifting through a succession of more than a hundred individual participants as they cross paths in Austin, Texas. Each encounter leads to the next, and so forth, in an extended exercise in causal minimalism.

where he did. This approach allows viewers to see what actually happened in direct comparison with the skeptical investigators and even Sully's own self-doubt. The reordered narrative demands that viewers actively engage to recognize the connections presented and reassemble events into a chronology that enables them to fully comprehend the story.

Although nonfiction filmmakers shooting documentary footage obviously can't always control the unstaged events happening before their cameras, contemporary documentary filmmakers often exploit their ability to select and arrange material in a cause-and-effect sequence of events. This very deliberate process may begin even before cameras roll.

Searching for Sugar Man (2012) director Malik Bendjelloul surely recognized the narrative potential of the disappearance and rumored death of Sixto Rodriguez. The American folk singer had never achieved anything approaching notoriety in his own country, but recordings he released in the 1960s made him a superstar in South Africa. Because his music, particularly a song titled "Sugarman," was associated with the country's antiapartheid movement, Rodriguez was still a major cultural figure there, even though he had not toured or recorded—or been heard from at all—in decades. Bendjelloul structured his film as a missing-person investigation filled with tantalizing clues and frustrating dead ends, as well as testimonials to Rodriguez's unique genius that feed the viewer's increasing hunger for a righteous resurrection. *Searching for Sugar Man* reaches its narrative climax with the discovery of Rodriguez, poor and obscure but very much alive, in Detroit, Michigan.

The nonfiction filmmaker's selective role is even more apparent in the Academy Award–winning documentary *Born into Brothels* (2004; directors Zana Briski and Ross Kauffman). The film's events are structured around co-director Briski's explicitly stated intent to use photography to reach and ultimately rescue the children of prostitutes in Calcutta's red-light district. The film's events are arranged in a cause-and-effect structure strikingly similar to that of a conventional fiction movie, where the filmmakers themselves not only select and arrange events, but actively participate in them. Briski engages the children first by photographing them, then by teaching them to take their own photographs. She works to convince the sex workers to allow her greater access to their children. As the children's talents emerge, she leads them on photo-taking expeditions to the beach and the zoo, and even-

tually stages a series of public exhibitions of their work. As the children grow in confidence and ability, the sequence of events builds to a conclusion that engaged and gratified mainstream audiences, as well as the Academy of Motion Picture Arts and Sciences, which awarded the film an Oscar for Best Documentary Feature. Those documentary filmmakers who strive to avoid influencing the events they record still exert a great deal of narrative influence during the editing process.

Most experimental, or avant-garde, movies try to break from the formulas and conventions of more mainstream narrative and documentary films. Even so, they employ narrative according to our most general definition of the concept, despite being more concerned with innovation and experimentation than with accessibility and entertainment.

The complex process of making movies discourages purely random constructions. Filmmakers engaged with planning, capturing, selecting, and arranging footage tend to create sequences that grow logically in some way. The linear nature of motion pictures lends itself to structures that develop according to some form of progression, even if the resultant meaning is mostly impressionistic. Thus nearly every movie, regardless of how it is categorized, employs at least a loose interpretation of narrative.

Types of Movies

Films can be sorted into a variety of systems. The film industry catalogs films according to how they are distributed (theatrical, television, streaming, etc.); how they are financed (by established studios or independent producers); or by their Motion Picture Association of America (MPAA) rating. Film festivals frequently separate entries according to running time. Film-studies curricula often group films by subject matter, the nation of origin, or the era or organized aesthetic movement that produced them.

The whole idea of breaking down an art form as multifaceted as motion pictures into strict classifications can be problematic. Although most movies fall squarely into a single category, many others defy exact classification by any standard. This is because cinematic expression exists along a continuum; no rule book enforcing set criteria exists. Throughout the history of the medium, innovative filmmakers have blurred boundaries and defied classification. Since this textbook is interested primarily in understanding motion-picture *form*, the categories of films that we'll discuss below—narrative, documentary, and experimental—are focused on the filmmaker's intent and the final product's relationship with the viewer.

Narrative Movies

As we learned earlier, the primary relationship of a narrative film to its audience is that of a storyteller. Narrative films are so pervasive, so ingrained in our culture, that before reading this book, you may never have stopped to consider the designation *narrative film*. After all, to most of us, a narrative movie is just a movie. We apply a label only to documentary or experimental films—movies that deviate from that "norm."

What distinguishes narrative films from these other kinds of movies, both of which also tell stories or use other formal aspects of narrative? The answer is that narrative films are directed toward fiction. Even those narrative movies that purport to tell a true story, such as David O. Russell's *American Hustle* (2013), adjust the stories they convey to better serve the principles of narrative structure that filmmakers use to engage and entertain audiences. Events are added or removed or rearranged, and characters are composited—actors (who are usually more attractive than the actual participants they play) add elements of their own persona to the role.

American Hustle acknowledges this necessary manipulation right up front; Russell's movie retelling of con artists caught up in a famous FBI sting operation opens with a title card that replaces the usual "based on a true story" claim with a more candid disclaimer: "Some of this actually happened." Audiences may be attracted to movies marketed as "based on a true story" because of the perception of immediacy or relevance that such a label imparts. But the truth is that very few "true stories" can deliver the narrative clarity and effect that audiences have come to expect from narrative films. In fact, according to the National Transportation Safety Board, *Sully* inaccurately portrayed their investigation as skeptical and confrontational in order to add drama to the fictionalized story.

No matter what the source, typical narrative films are based on screenplays in which nearly every behavior and spoken line are predetermined. The characters are played by actors delivering dialogue and executing action in a manner that not only strives for verisimilitude but also facilitates the technical demands of the motion-picture

Narrative commonality

Even those narrative films bearing an overt ideological message or a dark theme are designed to engage an audience with a story. A twisted formal exercise like David Lynch's Showtime series *Twin Peaks* (2017) [1], a topical crime drama like Taylor Sheridan's *Wind River* (2017) [2], and an animated crowd-pleaser like Wes Anderson's *Isle of Dogs* (2018) [3] all deliver different messages and are designed to appeal to different audiences. But they all employ the same narrative structures and techniques designed to transport viewers into a story, get them invested in the characters, and make them care about the end results, despite knowing up front that none of it is real.

production process. These demands include coordinating their activity with lighting design and camera movement and performing scenes out of logical chronological sequence. This action typically takes place in artificial worlds created on studio soundstages or in locations modified to suit the story and technical demands of production. The primary purpose of most narrative films is entertainment, a stance motivated by commercial intent.

Many narrative films can be broken down still further into categories known as genres. We'll explore that subject later in the chapter.

Documentary Movies

We might say that narrative film and documentary film differ primarily in terms of allegiance. Narrative film begins with a commitment to dramatic storytelling; documentary film is more concerned with recording reality, educating viewers, or presenting political or social analyses. In other words, if we think of a narrative movie as fiction, then the best way to understand documentary film is as nonfiction.

But it would be a mistake to think that simply because documentary filmmakers use actual people, places, and events as source material, their films always reflect objective truth. Whatever their allegiance, all documentary filmmakers employ storytelling and dramatization to some degree in shaping their material. If they didn't, their footage might end up as unwatchably dull as a surveillance video recording everyday comings and goings. As upcoming chapters will repeatedly illustrate, all elements of cinematic language—from the camera angle to the lighting to the sound mix—color our perceptions of the material and so are subjective to some degree. And no documentary subject who knows she is being filmed can ever behave exactly as she would off camera.

So the unavoidable act of making the movie removes the possibility of a purely objective truth. And truth, of course, is in the eye of the beholder. Every documentary filmmaker has a personal perspective on the subject matter, whether she entered the production with a preexisting opinion or developed her point of view over the course of researching, shooting, and editing the movie. The informed documentary viewer should view these mediating factors thoughtfully, always trying to understand how the act of cinematic storytelling and the filmmaker's attitude toward the people and events depicted affect the interpretation of the truth up on the screen.

These complicating factors may have influenced film critic John Grierson, who originally coined the term *documentary* in 1926 to delineate cinema that observed life. Some time after he started making documentaries him-

Nanook of the North

Robert J. Flaherty's *Nanook of the North* (1922), a pioneering nonfiction film, gave general audiences their first visual encounter with Inuit culture. Its subject matter made it significant (and successful), and its use of narrative film techniques was pathbreaking. Flaherty edited together many different kinds of shots and angles, for example, and directed the Inuit through reenactments of life events, some of which—hunting with spears—were no longer part of their lives.

self, Grierson described the approach as the "creative treatment of actuality."

Robert J. Flaherty's pioneering documentary *Nanook of the North* (1922) demonstrates the complex relationship between documentary filmmaking and objective truth. Flaherty's movie included authentic "documentary" footage but also incorporated a great deal of staged reenactments. He reportedly encouraged the Inuit subjects to use older, more "traditional" hunting and fishing techniques for the film instead of their then current practices. However, no one who watches *Nanook* could argue that the film's portrayal of the Inuit and their nomadic northern lifestyle is a complete failure. The challenge for the viewer is to untangle *Nanook*'s nonfiction functions from its dramatic license, to view its anthropology apart from its artifice. We tend to assume that a wide separation exists between fact and fiction, historical reality and crafted story, truth and artifice. The difference, however, is never absolute in any film.

Documentary films can be categorized in a number of ways. If we group these movies according to the intent of the filmmakers regarding content and message, documentaries can be broken into four basic approaches: factual, instructional, persuasive, and propaganda. **Factual**

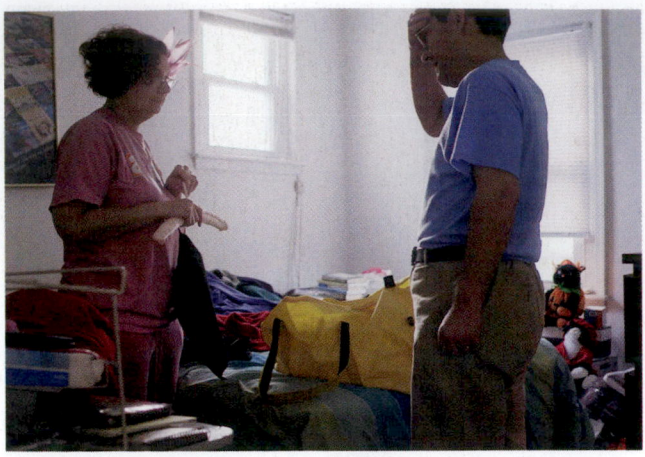

Factual film

The content of factual documentaries need not be "important"; many focus on "ordinary" subjects that offer potential narrative development. These documentaries seek to immerse viewers in an actuality outside their normal experience or observation and to involve audiences with the real-life struggles of a goal-driven protagonist. The factual film *Dina* (2017; directors Antonio Santini and Dan Sickles) chronicles an indomitable woman with autism as she plans her wedding. Her path to marriage is complicated by her fiancé's anxieties and her own painful past.

films, including *Nanook of the North*, usually present people, places, or processes in straightforward ways meant to entertain and instruct without unduly influencing audiences. Early examples include some of the first movies made. In 1896, audiences marveled at the Lumière brothers' short, one-shot films documenting trains arriving, boats leaving, and soldiers marching off to the front. (At that time, the spectacle of moving images impressed viewers as much as, or more than, any particular subject matter.) More recent documentaries that could fall into the factual-documentary classification include *Jane* (2017; director Brett Morgen), a portrait of famed primatologist Jane Goodall's early years studying chimpanzees in the jungles of Tanzania, and *Life, Animated* (2016; director Roger Ross Williams), an account of a boy with autism whose love of Disney characters enables him to communicate with his family and ultimately engage with the outside world.

Instructional films seek to educate viewers about common interests, rather than persuade them to accept particular ideas. Today these movies are most likely to teach the viewer basic skills such as cooking, yoga, or golf swings. They are not generally considered worthy of study or analysis.

Persuasive films were originally called *documentary films* until the term evolved to refer to all nonfiction films. The founding purpose of persuasive documentaries was to address social injustice, but today any documentary concerned with presenting a particular perspective on social issues or with corporate and governmental injustice of any kind could be considered persuasive. Director Gabriela Cowperthwaite's motivation in making *Blackfish* (2013) was not to simply entertain or inform audiences, but to persuade them to oppose the practice of holding orca whales in captivity at animal theme parks. Michael Moore's darkly humorous, self-aggrandizing documentaries take the persuasive documentary a step further. His confrontational and provocative movies address a series of left-of-center political causes, including health care (*Sicko*, 2007), gun control (*Bowling for Columbine*, 2002), and the election of Donald Trump (*Fahrenheit 11/9*, 2018). Dinesh D'Souza is perhaps Moore's best-known conservative counterpart. His persuasive documentaries include *2016: Obama's America* (2012), which argued that the forty-fourth president's upbringing led him to reject American exceptionalism, and the election-year critique *Hillary's America: The Secret History of the Democratic Party* (2016).

Triumph of the Will

The most accomplished (and notorious) propaganda film of all time, Leni Riefenstahl's *Triumph of the Will* (1935) is studied by historians and scholars of film. Much of the blocking of the 1934 Nuremberg Nazi rally was crafted specifically with the camera in mind. Taken from a distant perspective, this shot conveys many concepts that the filmmaker and the Nazis wanted the world to see: order, discipline, and magnitude.

When persuasive documentaries are produced by governments and carry governments' messages, they overlap with **propaganda films**, which systematically disseminate deceptive or distorted information. The most famous propaganda film ever made, Leni Riefenstahl's *Triumph of the Will* (1935), records many events at the 1934 Nuremberg rally of Germany's Nazi party. It thus might mistakenly be considered a "factual" film. After all, no voice-over narration or on-screen commentator preaches a political message to the viewer. But through its carefully crafted cinematography and editing, this documentary presents a highly glorified image of Adolf Hitler and his Nazi followers for the consumption of non-German audiences before World War II.

Regardless of their intent or message, most documentaries draw from the same set of basic elements. Footage that documents subjects (the people the documentary is about) in action and events as they unfold is called **b-roll**. This second-class "b" label is ironic, or at least inaccurate, since these shots almost always offer the most immediate and engaging images and sounds in any documentary.

Interviews with subjects or with experts on the subject matter are traditionally shot with the interviewee speaking to an off-camera interviewer, so that the subject looks off to the right or left side of the frame. The person being interviewed is usually seen from the waist up or sometimes in a close-up of just that individual's head and shoulders, a framing known as a "talking head." The interview is typically edited to remove the questions, and the footage of the interviewed subject is only shown periodically, with much of the interview audio edited separately so that it can be played over other b-roll footage. When the voice of the interviewed subject is heard while we see other images, the interplay between the content of her statements and that of the footage can convey greater perspective and meaning than would be possible with the interview footage alone.

Unlike an interviewed subject, a **narrator** speaks directly to the viewer from outside of the events presented. Typically, the narrator is heard, rather than seen, in the form of **voice-over narration** that explains and comments on the events we see unfolding on-screen.

Archival material is preexisting images and/or sound that is incorporated into the documentary. This material can be almost anything captured previously and by different sources. Types of archival material include radio broadcasts, news footage, historical photographs, official documents, and even home movies. Many

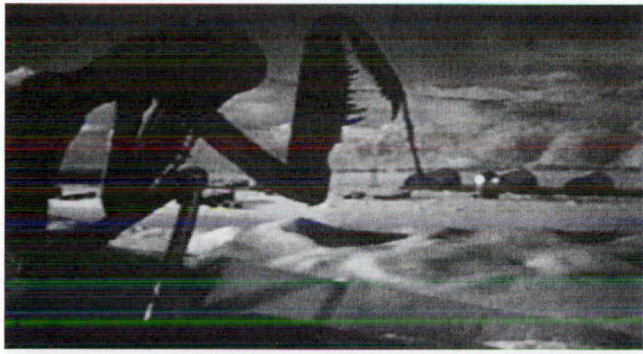

1

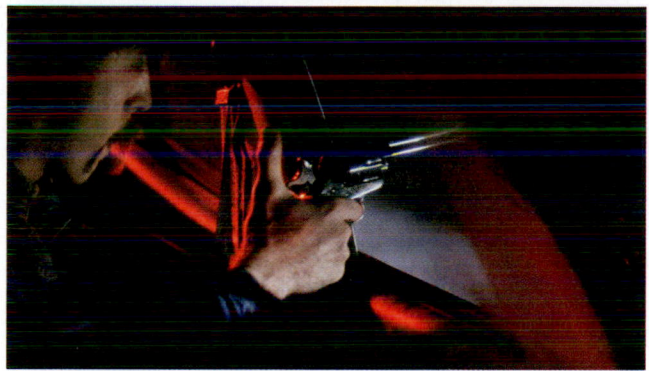

2

3

Evolving documentary elements

The innovative director Errol Morris has put his own stamp on many of the conventional cinematic elements used to make documentaries. The archival material he uses to help visualize the ideas raised by the diverse subjects in *Fast, Cheap, and Out of Control* (1997) [1] includes old low-budget adventure and science-fiction films. In *The Thin Blue Line* (1988) [2], an examination of a murder case, he employs stylized reenactments to illustrate conflicting recollections and accounts of the crime. He expands that practice in another investigation of a suspicious death: the reenactments in *Wormwood* (2017) star well-known actors and have the look of scenes in a classic Hollywood mystery film. In most of his movies, Morris conducts interviews using an Interrotron, a device of his own invention that projects the director's face onto a glass plate placed over the camera lens [3]. The apparatus allows the subject to address responses directly into the lens, which establishes direct eye contact with the viewer.

A persuasive and expository documentary

Categories can help us understand a film's intent, methods, and style, but no single designation can completely define any movie. Ava DuVernay's 2016 documentary *13ᵀᴴ* (named after the constitutional amendment that abolished slavery) uses expert interviews, archival footage and photographs, animation, and graphics to explain the history of the U.S. prison and justice system *and* to make a persuasive argument that laws and policies since the Thirteenth Amendment was ratified have systematically perpetuated a different, but still devastating, form of slavery in the United States.

documentaries incorporate archival media; some documentaries are made up exclusively from this preexisting media. For example, Jason Osder's *Let the Fire Burn* (2013) is constructed entirely from video and film gleaned from newscasts, press conferences, community hearings, and a 1970s documentary. The all-archival documentary looks back at a 1985 police raid on an inner-city Philadelphia compound that led to the deaths of 13 members of the black separatist group MOVE.

Text and graphics are used to convey information in ways that would be impossible or inefficient using filmed images or the spoken word. This information can include statistics, graphs, and maps or even something as simple as text identifying interview subjects, dates, and locations presented on-screen.

Documentary filmmakers, especially those examining events occurring in the past, sometimes must resort to staging re-creations of important actions. These **reenactments** are filmed and presented in ways that make clear their status as fabricated representations of real events. These visual indicators can include stylized lighting, different color values, and animation.

Documentary theorist Bill Nichols considers how the filmmaker uses (or doesn't use) these different cinematic components to help differentiate different modes of documentary filmmaking. He also factors the filmmaker's interaction with the subject, the filmmaker's attitude toward the documentary medium itself, and the viewer's intended experience. Nichols's theories are complex, and it can be difficult to determine where one kind of documentary ends and another begins. But for our purposes, we can think of his six documentary modes in the following relatively simple terms.

Expository documentaries use all of the formal elements listed above to *explain* things to the viewer. These elements are carefully chosen to reinforce the explanation and argument. Typically, an authoritative narrator guides the viewer using narration scripted in advance. If you've ever seen a news magazine show such as *60 Minutes*, you've seen an expository documentary. But expository documentaries need not focus on current events or be bound by conventional application of documentary elements. In documentaries such as *The Civil War* (1990), director Ken Burns seeks to bring history alive by using subtle camera movement to film historical documents, archival photographs, painterly location shots, and posed artifacts. The camera glides and the framing tightens to emphasize details and link them to the narration and historical observations. Burns's use of the effect became so ubiquitous that Apple computers incorporated it into their home-movie-editing software iMovie and openly identified it as the "Ken Burns Effect."

Observational documentaries take a very different approach. These movies seek to immerse the viewer in the middle of the situation or story by relying entirely on b-roll and eliminating as many other signs of mediation as possible. Viewers of an observational documentary won't hear any voice-over narration or see any interviews. They may not even see any text on-screen that identifies locations or subjects. Observational filmmakers typically work with very small crews (as few as one or two people) and use compact portable equipment to shoot large amounts of footage. They seek to become part of the environment so their subjects can eventually disregard their presence and behave as naturally as possible.

Poetic documentaries are expressive nonfiction films that provide a subjective and often impressionistic interpretation of a subject, with an emphasis on conveying mood and generating ideas, rather than providing a realistic observational experience or communicating an information-driven explanation. Godfrey Reggio's Qatsi trilogy demonstrates that documentaries can be poetic while still remaining persuasive. For example, the first film *Koyaanisqatsi* (1982) contains no other sound be-

Observational documentary

The observational approach to documentary was pioneered in the late 1950s and early 1960s by filmmakers participating in a movement known as direct cinema. Their observational films sought to immerse the viewer in an experience as close as is cinematically possible to witnessing events as an invisible observer. Direct cinema films like Albert and David Maysles's *Grey Gardens* (1975; codirectors Ellen Hovde and Muffie Meyer) rely on very small crews and lightweight, handheld equipment to capture the action as unobtrusively as possible. As they filmed *Grey Gardens*, the Maysleses observed that their extroverted subject "Little Edie" Beale [1] was becoming more interested in performing for the filmmakers than in ignoring their presence. Some direct cinema purists may have discouraged or deleted her behavior, but the Maysleses saw Edie's need for recognition, and the delusions that fueled it, as a crucial part of her reality. The filmmakers acknowledged their own participatory role by incorporating their own image (as captured in a mirror) into the movie [2].

sides music. The otherwise silent images are stunningly photographed and almost entirely shown in fast-motion time lapse or graceful slow motion. But the film is not simply visual candy: by juxtaposing beautiful images of the natural world with footage depicting modern life as mechanized, frantic, and ultimately lonely, *Koyaanisqatsi* offers a persuasive argument summed up in the film's subtitle, which is a translation of the Hopi word *koyaanisqatsi*: "life out of balance."

Filmmakers making **participatory** documentaries interact with the subjects and situations they are recording and thus become part of the film. That interaction can be as subtle as the filmmakers letting their voices be heard asking questions offscreen or as conspicuous as the provocateur Michael Moore confronting subjects on camera. Because all documentary filmmakers engage the subjects of their films and make camera and editing choices that influence what we see and hear, some have argued that all documentaries are participatory. **Performative** documentaries are easily confused with participatory documentaries. The participatory filmmaker is a part of the documentary she's directing, and we may even see her on-screen, but the performative filmmaker

takes it a step farther. His interaction with the subject matter is deeply personal and often emotional. His personal experience is central to the way we engage and understand the subject matter.

Reflexive documentaries examine more than their chosen subject; they explore—and sometimes critique—the documentary form itself. The documentary production process becomes part of the experience in ways that may challenge viewer expectations of nonfiction filmmaking conventions. *The Act of Killing* (2012; directors Joshua Oppenheimer, Anonymous, and Christine Cynn) begins as a relatively conventional, expository documentary look-back at the politically motivated massacre of as many as 2.5 million Indonesian citizens in the 1960s and 1970s. What immediately stands out is that Anwar Congo, the former death squad leader being interviewed, makes no attempt to downplay his role in the genocide. On the contrary, he proudly demonstrates his favorite execution methods. The documentary becomes reflexive when the filmmakers harness their subject's brazen narcissism by facilitating (and filming) increasingly elaborate re-creations of torture and murder, all staged by and starring Anwar and his sidekick Herman

1

2

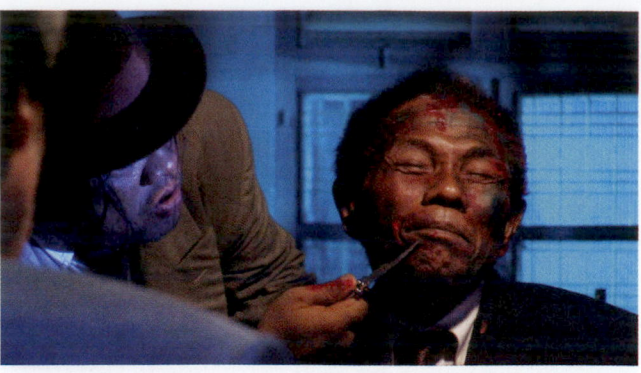

Reflexive documentary

A death squad leader and a paramilitary leader are the subjects of *The Act of Killing*, a documentary that begins as an expository account of the massacre of Indonesian citizens in the 1960s and 1970s. The film turns reflexive when the filmmakers encourage their subjects to stage and star in re-creations of their own crimes. These elaborate, sometimes extravagant, reenactments challenge audience assumptions about nonfiction film and the nature of truth.

Participatory and performative documentaries

When director Morgan Spurlock made himself the subject of the fast-food experiment that is the subject of *Supersize Me* (2004), he was making a participatory documentary. Spurlock is on-screen explaining his plan to eat only McDonald's food for 30 days [1]. We see him purchasing and consuming fast food, and we hear him explaining obesity statistics and questioning doctors, nutritionists, and other experts. When his health begins to seriously deteriorate, his personal soul searching moves the film closer to the performative. Jonathan Caouette's *Tarnation* (2003) is a performative documentary from start to finish. The filmmaker created an emotional portrait of identity, dysfunction, and mental illness from self-shot b-roll, interviews, and reenactments, which is interwoven with home movies, photographs, and answering machine messages from throughout his young life. The resulting performative documentary chronicles his personal struggles and his turbulent relationship with his schizophrenic mother [2].

Koto, a former paramilitary leader and self-described gangster. The resulting spectacle is profoundly disturbing, yet inescapably amusing. Are Anwar and Herman dupes or wily collaborators? Can a movie be a documentary when the filmmakers actively manipulate the peo-

ple and events they document? Does the precise nature of truth matter, so long as the results are entertaining? Parsing these questions is part of the experience of a reflexive documentary like *The Act of Killing*.

More than a century of innovation has blurred the distinctions between these documentary categories and modes. Most documentary movies we consider worthy of study today are nonfiction hybrids that combine qualities of two or more of these foundational approaches to nonfiction filmmaking. This versatility is one reason that documentary continues to enjoy a renaissance unprecedented in the history of cinema. Another reason for documentary's expanding popularity and innovation is that nonfiction filmmakers have new ways to reach viewers, thanks to streaming services like Netflix and Amazon's Prime Video and to video-sharing websites like YouTube.

Experimental Movies

Experimental is the most difficult of all types of movies to define precisely, in part because experimental filmmakers actively seek to defy categorization and convention. For starters, it's helpful to think of experimental cinema as pushing the boundaries of what most people think movies are—or should be. After all, *avant-garde*, the term originally applied to this approach to filmmaking, comes from a French phrase used to describe scouts and pathfinders who explored ahead of an advancing army, implying that avant-garde artists, whether in film or another medium, are innovators who lead, rather than follow, the pack.

The term *experimental* falls along these same lines. It's an attempt to capture the innovative spirit of an approach to moviemaking that plays with the medium, is not bound by established traditions, and is dedicated to exploring possibility. Both *avant-garde* and *experimental* (and other terms) are still used to describe this kind of movie. But since *experimental* is the word most commonly used, is appropriately evocative, and is in English, let's stick with it.

In response to the often-asked question "What is an experimental film?" film scholar Fred Camper offers six criteria that outline the characteristics that most experimental films share. While no criterion can hope to encapsulate an approach to filmmaking as vigorously diverse as experimental cinema, a summary of Camper's list of common qualities is a good place to start:

1. *Experimental films are not commercial.* They are made by single filmmakers (or collaborative teams consisting of, at most, a few artists) for very low budgets and with no expectation of financial gain.

2. *Experimental films are personal.* They reflect the creative vision of a single artist who typically conceives, writes, directs, shoots, and edits the movie with minimal contributions by other filmmakers or technicians. Experimental film credits are short.

3. *Experimental films do not conform to conventional expectations of story and narrative cause and effect.*

4. *Experimental films exploit the possibilities of the cinema* and, by doing so, often reveal (and revel in) tactile and mechanical qualities of motion pictures that conventional movies seek to obscure. Most conventional narrative films are constructed to make audiences forget they are watching a movie, whereas many experimental films repeatedly remind the viewer of the fact. They embrace innovative techniques that call attention to, question, and even challenge their own artifice.

5. *Experimental films critique culture and media.* From their position outside the mainstream, they often comment on (and intentionally frustrate) viewer expectations of what a movie should be.

6. *Experimental films invite individual interpretation.* Like abstract expressionist paintings, they resist the kind of accessible and universal meaning found in conventional narrative and documentary films.[1]

Because most experimental films do not tell a story in the conventional sense, incorporate unorthodox imagery, and are motivated more by innovation and personal expression than by commerce and entertainment, they help us understand in yet another way why movies are a form of art capable of a sort of motion-picture equivalent of poetry. Disregarding the traditional expectations of audiences, experimental films remind us that film—like painting, sculpture, music, or architecture—can be made in as many ways as there are artists.

For example, Michael Snow's *Wavelength* (1967) is a 45-minute film that consists, in what we see, only of an exceedingly slow zoom lens shot through a loft. Although human figures wander in and out of the frame, departing at will from that frame or being excluded from it as the camera moves slowly past them, the film is almost totally devoid of any human significance. Snow's central concern is space: how to conceive it, film it, and encourage viewers to make meaning of it. *Wavelength* is replete with differing qualities of space, light, exposures, focal lengths, and printing techniques, all offering rich possibilities for how we perceive these elements and interpret their meaning. For those who believe that a movie must represent the human condition, *Wavelength* seems empty. But for those who believe, with D. W. Griffith, that a movie is meant, above all, to make us see, the work demonstrates the importance of utterly unconventional filmmaking.

Su Friedrich's experimental films also "make us see," but in different ways. Friedrich's *Sink or Swim* (1990) opens abstractly with what seems to be scientific footage—a microscope's view of sperm cells, splitting cells, a developing fetus—inexplicably narrated by a young girl's voice recounting the mythological relationship between the goddess Athena and her father, Zeus. As the movie's remaining twenty-five segments unfold, the offscreen girl narrator shifts from mythological accounts of paternal

1. Fred Camper, "Naming, and Defining, Avant-Garde or Experimental Film" (n.d.), www.fredcamper.com/Film/AvantGardeDefinition.html (accessed March 19, 2015).

1

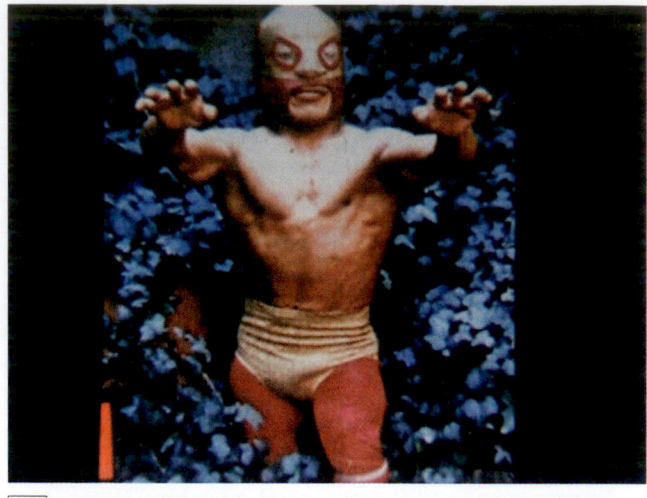

2

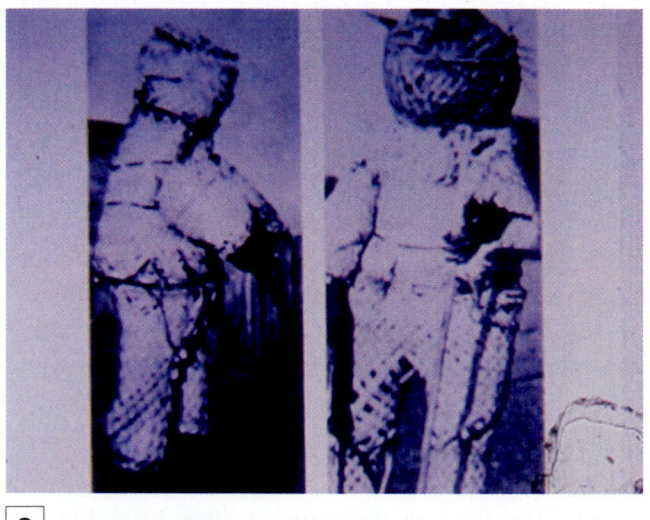

3

4

5

Rearranged footage

A sequence in Craig Baldwin's *Tribulation 99: Alien Anomalies under America* (1992) presents successive images of Mayan carvings [1], Lucha Libre masked wrestlers [2], natives in ceremonial woven suits [3], hooded prisoners [4], and nature footage of snakes [5] to illustrate the narration's breathless claim that displaced aliens hiding below the earth's surface have been forced to mate with reptiles. The power of editing to create meaning through juxtaposition allowed Baldwin to mutate his seemingly random collection of images of wildly disparate origins into a cohesive, if bizarre, story of the malevolent aliens emerging from their subterranean lair to attempt world domination.

relationships to third-person accounts of episodes between a contemporary girl and her father. The episodes are illustrated with candid documentary footage, often featuring men and girls at play, and with what appear to be home movies, edited in a way that obscures their origins. The footage sometimes enforces the narration's mood and content, but just as often conflicts with the girl's story or combines with it so that additional meaning is imparted to both image and spoken word. As the successive layers are revealed, what began as an apparent abstract exercise reveals itself as an autobiographical account of the filmmaker's troubled relationship with her distant and demanding father. Ironically, this experimental approach ultimately delivers a more emotionally complex and involving experience than most conventional narrative or documentary treatments of similar subject matter.

While *Wavelength* explores cinematic space and *Sink or Swim* focuses on personal expression, other experimental films are primarily concerned with the tactile and communicative qualities of the film medium itself. These movies scavenge found footage—originally created by other filmmakers for other purposes—and then manipulate the gleaned images to create new meanings and aesthetics not intended by the artists or technicians who shot the original footage.

To create *Tribulation 99: Alien Anomalies under America* (1992), his feature-length satire of paranoid conspiracy theories, Craig Baldwin collected thousands of still and moving images from a wide variety of mostly vintage sources, including educational films, scientific studies, and low-budget horror movies. By combining, superimposing, and sequencing selected shots, and overlaying the result with ominous text and urgent voice-over narration, Baldwin changes the image context and meaning, thus transforming the way audiences interpret and experience the footage.

Experimental filmmaker Martin Arnold also manipulates preexisting footage to alter the viewer's interpretation and experience with a method that is in many ways the reverse of Baldwin's frenetic collage approach. Arnold's most famous film, *Passage à l'acte* (1993), uses only one sequence from a single source: a short, relatively mundane breakfast-table scene from Robert Mulligan's narrative feature *To Kill a Mockingbird* (1962). Using an optical printer, which allows the operator to duplicate one film frame at a time onto a new strip of film

stock, Arnold stretched the 34-second sequence to over 11 minutes by rhythmically repeating every moment in the scene. The result forces us to see the familiar characters and situation in an entirely new way. What was originally an innocent and largely inconsequential exchange is infused with conflict and tension. Through multiple and rapid-fire repetitions, a simple gesture such as putting down a fork or glancing sideways becomes a hostile or provocative gesture, a mechanical loop, or an abstract dance. Like many experimental films, *Passage à l'acte* deliberately challenges the viewer's ingrained expectations of narrative, coherence, continuity, movement, and forward momentum. The resulting experience is hypnotic, musical, disturbing, fascinating, and infuriating.

It's easy to assume that films that test the audience's expectations of how a movie should behave are a relatively recent phenomenon. But the truth is that filmmakers have been experimenting with film form and reception since the early days of cinema. In the 1920s, the first truly experimental movement was born in France, with its national climate of avant-garde artistic expression. Among the most notable works were films by painters: René Clair's *Entr'acte* (1924), Fernand Léger and Dudley Murphy's *Ballet mécanique* (1924), Marcel Duchamp's *Anémic cinéma* (1926), and Man Ray's *Emak-Bakia* (1926). These films are characterized uniformly by their surreal content, often dependent on dream impressions rather than objective observation; their abstract images, which tend to be shapes and patterns with no meaning other than the forms themselves; their absence of actors performing within a narrative context; and their desire to shock not only our sensibilities but also our morals. The most important of these films, the surrealist dreamscape *An Andalusian Dog* (1929), was made in France by the Spanish filmmaker Luis Buñuel and the Spanish painter Salvador Dalí. Re-creating the sexual nature of dreams, this film's images metamorphose continually, defy continuity, and even attack causality—as in one scene when a pair of breasts dissolves into buttocks.

Although an alternative cinema has existed in the United States since the 1920s—an achievement of substance and style that is all the more remarkable in a country where filmmaking is synonymous with Hollywood—the first experimental filmmakers here were either European-born or influenced by the French, Russians, and Germans. The first major American

Experimental film: style as subject

Among many other random repetitions and animations, Fernand Léger and Dudley Murphy's *Ballet mécanique* (1924) repeatedly loops footage of a woman climbing stairs. This action lacks completion or narrative purpose and instead functions as a rhythmic counterpart to other sections of the film, in which more abstract objects are animated and choreographed in (as the title puts it) a "mechanical ballet."

experimental filmmaker was Maya Deren. Her surreal films—*Meshes of the Afternoon* (1943), codirected with her husband, Alexander Hammid, is the best known—virtually established alternative filmmaking in this country. Deren's work combines her interests in various fields, including film, philosophy, ethnography, and dance, and it remains the touchstone for those studying avant-garde movies.

Concerned with the manipulation of space and time, which after all is the essence of filmmaking, Deren experimented with defying continuity, erasing the line between dream and reality. She used the cinematic equivalent of **stream of consciousness**, a literary style that gained prominence in the 1920s in the hands of such writers as Marcel Proust, Virginia Woolf, James Joyce, and Dorothy Richardson and which attempted to capture the unedited flow of experience through the mind. In *Meshes*, Deren is both the creative mind behind the film and the creative performer on the screen. She takes certain recognizable motifs—a key, a knife, a flower, a telephone receiver, and a shadowy figure walking down a garden path—and repeats them throughout the film, each time transfiguring them into something else. So, for example, the knife evolves into a key and the flower into a knife. These changing motifs are linked visually but also structurally. Deren's ideas and achievements bridge the gap between the surrealism of the French avant-garde films and such dream-related movies as Alain Resnais's *Last Year at Marienbad* (1961), Federico Fellini's *8½* (1963), Ingmar Bergman's *Persona* (1966), and Luis Buñuel's *The Milky Way* (1969).

Deren's work greatly influenced an American underground cinema that emerged in the 1950s. It has since favored four subgenres—the formal, the self-reflexive, the satirical, and the sexual—each of which tends to include aspects of the lyrical approach so typical of Deren. Works of pure form include John Whitney's early experiments with computer imagery in such films as *Matrix I* and *Matrix II* (both 1971); Shirley Clarke's *Skyscraper* (1960), one of several lighthearted, abstract tributes to city life; Peter Kubelka's *Arnulf Rainer* (1960), which created its images through abstract dots; Jordan Belson's *Allures* (1961), using abstract color animation; Robert Breer's *Fist Fight* (1964), which combines animation, images of handwriting, and other material; and Ernie Gehr's *The Astronomer's Dream* (2004), in which he speeds up the images so much that they become vertical purple lines.

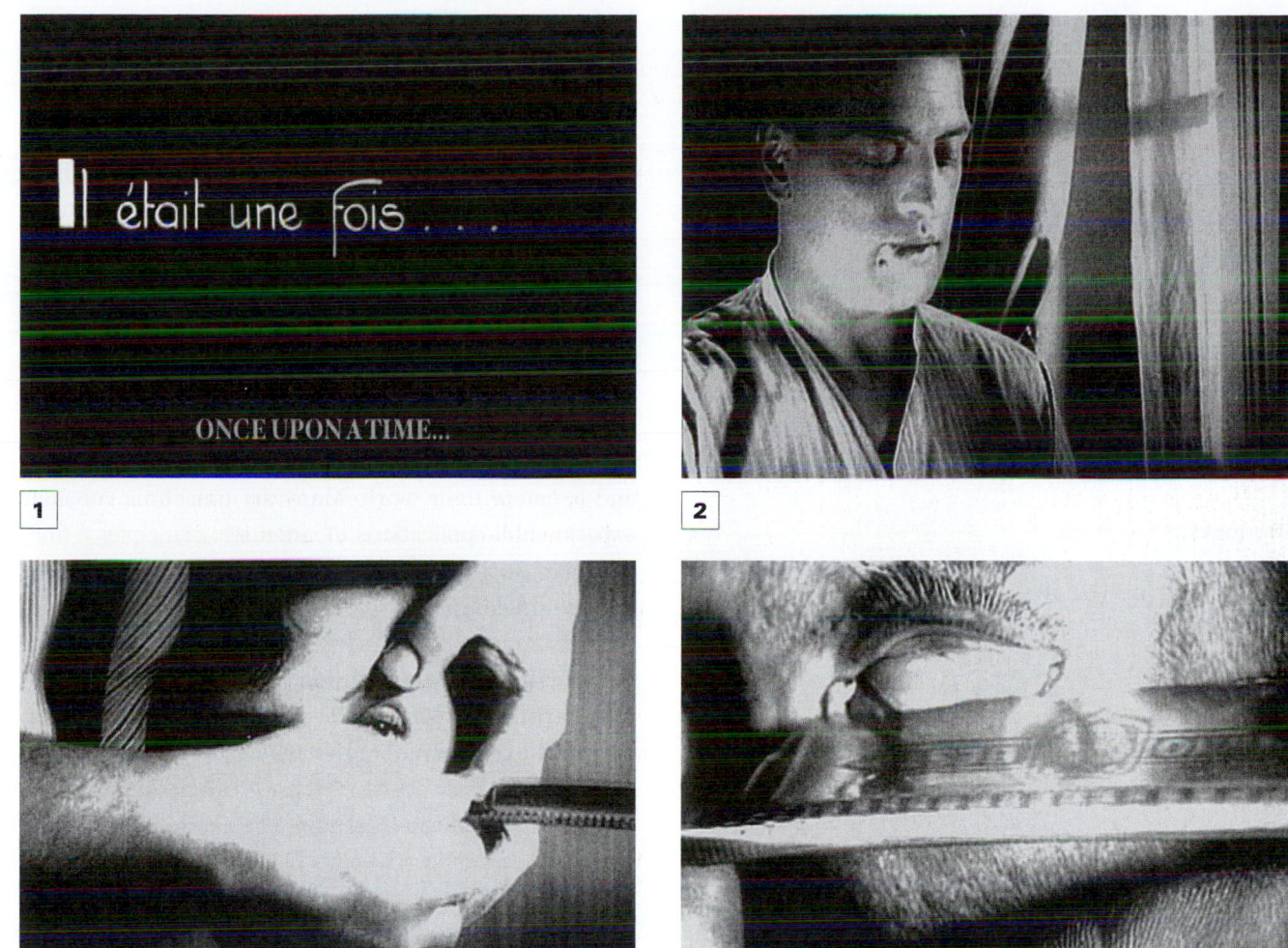

Experimental film: image as shock

Luis Buñuel and Salvador Dalí collaborated to produce *An Andalusian Dog* (1929), one of the most famous experimental films. Through special effects, its notorious opening sequence can be summarized in four shots: [1] the title, "Once upon a time . . . ," which, under the circumstances, is an absurd use of the classic beginning of a nursery story; [2] an image of a man (who has just finished sharpening his straight razor); [3] an image of the hand of a differently dressed man holding a razor near a woman's eyeball with the implication that he will slit it; and [4] an image of a slit eyeball. There is no logic to this sequence, for the woman's eye is not slit; rather the slit eyeball appears to belong to an animal. The sequence is meant to shock the viewer, to surprise us, to make us "see" differently, but not to explain what we are seeing.

Self-reflexive films, meaning those that represent their own conditions of production (movies, in other words, about movies, moviemaking, moviemakers, and so on), include Hans Richter's *Dreams That Money Can Buy* (1947), in the spirit of surrealism; Stan Brakhage's five-part *Dog Star Man* (1962–64), whose lyricism is greatly influenced by Deren's work; Bruce Baillie's *Mass for the Dakota Sioux* (1964), which combines a lyrical vision and social commentary; Hollis Frampton's *Zorn's Lemma* (1970), a complex meditation on cinematic structure, space, and movement; and Michael Snow's *Wavelength* (1967), which we already discussed.

Films that take a satirical view of life include James Broughton's *Mother's Day* (1948), on childhood; Stan van der Beek's *Death Breath* (1964), an apocalyptic vision using cartoons and other imagery; Bruce Conner's *Marilyn Times Five* (1973), which makes its comic points by compiling stock footage from other sources; and Mike

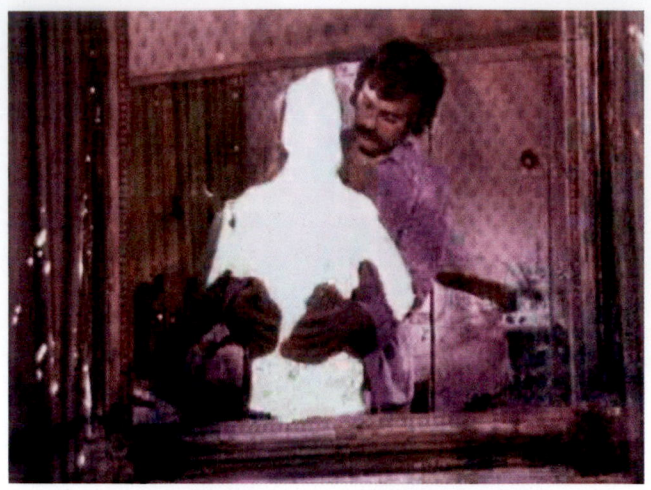

Manipulated footage

Naomi Uman's *Removed* (1999) employs a reductive approach to found-footage filmmaking that made audiences reinterpret and reexamine previously existing footage. She used nail polish and bleach to remove the female character from the emulsion of all 10,000 frames of a 7-minute pornographic movie. The result forces the viewer to experience the objectification of women in a literal—or at least graphic—sense. The film's female character appears as an animated blank space that is physically manipulated by the male actors.

Kuchar's *Sins of the Fleshapoids* (1965), an underground look at the horror genre.

Satirical and sexual films often overlap, particularly in their portrayal of sexual activities that challenge conventional ideas of "normality." Examples of these include Kenneth Anger's *Scorpio Rising* (1964), an explicit homosexual fantasy that is tame by today's standards; Jack Smith's *Flaming Creatures* (1963), a major test case for pornography laws; and many of Andy Warhol's films, including *Lonesome Cowboys* (1968). The directors who made these films tended to be obsessed, as was Deren, with expressing themselves and their subconscious through cinematic forms and images.

These days, movies that seem to be in direct opposition to Camper's experimental film criteria dominate our culture. Popular cinema is largely commercial, universal, and narrative. When most of us think of movies, we picture movies that conceal their artifice, reinforce viewer expectations, and seek a common, accessible interpretation.

While purely experimental cinema rarely penetrates into the mainstream, this highly personal and innovative approach to cinematic expression continues to thrive on the fringes of popular culture. A grassroots "microcinema" subculture has grown out of the affordability and accessibility of digital video formats, personal computer–based editing systems, and video-hosting websites such as YouTube and Vimeo. Most film festivals, from the most influential international competitions to the smallest local showcases, feature experimental programs. Many prestigious film festivals specializing in experimental cinema, such as the Ann Arbor Film Festival, attract hundreds of submissions and thousands of patrons each year. International organizations like Flickr provide experimental filmmakers with an online venue to share and promote their work. Many art museums consider experimental applications of cinematic principles a fine-art form worthy of public display along with painting and sculpture.

Artists such as Bill Viola, Matthew Barney, Pierre Huyghe, and Douglas Gordon have attracted great attention to their avant-garde video installations, which change the traditional ways in which viewers experience and interact with moving images. Christian Marclay handled his experimental film *The Clock* (2010) like a limited edition fine-art print. The movie has never been distributed or broadcast; only seven copies have been sold to museums and collectors. *The Clock* is a precise assembly of thousands of images and lines of dialogue culled from existing movies and television shows, each one indicating a particular chronological moment in a 24-hour cycle.

And, finally, while truly experimental films rarely if ever reach mass audiences, experimental approaches to narrative construction, visual style, and editing techniques do often find their way into movies made by filmmakers sympathetic to the avant-garde's spirit of invention. Many of the Hollywood directors incorporating experimental techniques developed a taste for unconventional innovation in film school or art school or while honing their craft on music videos, commercials, and independent art films. These filmmakers include David Lynch (*Twin Peaks*, 2017), Charlie Kaufman (*Anomalisa*, 2015), Nicholas Winding Refn (*The Neon Demon*, 2016), Daniel Kwan and Daniel Scheinert (*Swiss Army Man*, 2016), Jonathan Glazer (*Under the Skin*, 2013), and Sarah Adina Smith (*Buster's Mal Heart*, 2016). Experimental sensibilities have emerged in a growing number of mainstream productions, from Christian Wagner's wildly kinetic editing

Documentary-narrative fusion

Larry Charles's *Borat: Cultural Learnings of America for Make Benefit Glorious Nation of Kazakhstan* (2006) pushes the documentary-narrative marriage to its extreme by placing the fictional character of Borat (Sacha Baron Cohen) in real-life situations with people who were led to believe that they (and Borat) were the subjects of a documentary about a foreign reporter's exploration of American culture [1]. The result functions as both documentary and narrative: we experience a deliberately structured character pursuing a clearly defined goal, but that pursuit is punctuated with a series of spontaneous explosions of authentic human behavior provoked and manipulated by Borat/Cohen and captured by a documentary film crew. Director Jonathan Glazer took the hybrid a step further in *Under the Skin* (2013), his fiction film about an alien (Scarlett Johansson) who gradually begins to empathize with the humans she was sent to Earth to harvest. Glazer shot most of the movie using hidden cameras, so that many of the people appearing on-screen didn't know they were being filmed. The technique lends a sense of documentary realism to an otherwise fantastic situation. The men attracted to the beautiful extraterrestrial can't help convincingly portraying themselves as unsuspecting victims [2].

in Tony Scott movies such as *Domino* (2005) to the abstracted images in the title sequence that opened each episode of the HBO dramatic series *Vinyl* (2016).

Hybrid Movies

The flexibility of film form has made cross-pollination among experimental, documentary, and narrative approaches an inevitable and desirable aspect of cinematic evolution. The resulting hybrids have blurred what were once distinct borders among the three primary film-type categories. For example, in the short films that accompany this book, Roger Beebe's experimental movie *The Strip Mall Trilogy* (2001) documents a mile-long stretch of strip malls in Florida but so isolates and abstracts the images that he evokes meanings that transcend any architectural or anthropological investigation of commercial suburban development. Ray Tintori's narrative movie *Death to the Tinman* (2007) most certainly tells a

story, but does so with narration, cinematography, performance, and production-design stylings that subvert audience expectations as only an experimental film can.

We've already discussed the importance of narrative to many documentary films. A growing number of narrative feature films that incorporate documentary techniques demonstrate that the borrowing works in both directions. Big-budget blockbusters like Christopher Nolan's *Dunkirk* (2017) shoot sequences in ways that evoke documentary b-roll realism, as do provocative art films such as Darren Aronofsky's *Mother!* (2017). Contemporary directors such as Jean-Pierre and Luc Dardenne (*The Unknown Girl*, 2016), Lance Hammer (*Ballast*, 2008), Benh Zeitlen (*Beasts of the Southern Wild*, 2012), and Ryan Coogler (*Fruitvale Station*, 2013) use small crews, natural lighting, handheld cameras, and nonactors (alongside deglamorized professionals) to lend their gritty narrative films the sense of authentic realism associated with documentary aesthetics and techniques.[2]

2. Many thanks to Dr. James Kruel and University of North Carolina Wilmington professors Shannon Silva, Andre Silva, and Dr. J. Carlos Kase for some of the ideas in this analysis.

1

2

Film-type fusion

Perhaps the film that best exemplifies the fusion of narrative, documentary, and experimental film types is William Greaves's *Symbiopsycho-taxiplasm: Take One* (1968). Greaves employed three camera crews and instructed the first crew to shoot only the series of actors performing the scripted scene, the second crew to film the first crew shooting the scene [1], and the third to shoot the entire multilevel production as well as anything else they judged footage-worthy going on around them. The edited film frequently uses split screen to present several of its multiple layers simultaneously [2]. Greaves intentionally provoked his various crews and casts with vague or contradictory directions, until what amounts to a civil war erupted as some of the film professionals involved began to question the director's intentions and methods. Greaves, who functioned as the director of the actors as well as a sort of actor himself in the dual layers of documentary footage, made sure that every aspect of the ensuing chaos—including private crew meetings criticizing the project—was captured on film and eventually combined into an experimental amalgam that breaks down audience expectations of narrative and documentary, artifice and reality.[3]

Genre

Our brief survey of documentary and experimental cinema demonstrates that both of these primary types of movies can be further divided into defined subcategories. These distinctions are both useful and inevitable. Any art form practiced by ambitious innovators and consumed by a diverse and evolving culture can't help developing in multiple directions. When filmmakers and their audiences recognize and value particular approaches to both form and content, these documentary or experimental subcategories are further differentiated and defined. And the moment such a distinction is accepted, filmmakers and viewers will begin again to refine, revise, and recombine the elements that defined the new categorization in the first place.

Genre refers to the categorization of narrative films by the stories they tell and the ways they tell them. Commonly recognized movie genres include the Western, horror, science fiction, musical, and gangster films. But

this is far from a complete list. The film industry continues to make action movies, biographies (biopics), melodramas, thrillers, romances, romantic comedies, fantasy films, and many others that fall within some genre or subgenre category.

A long list like that may lead you to believe that all films are genre movies. Not so. A quick scan of the movies in theaters during a single week in 2017 reveals many narrative films that tell stories and employ styles that don't fit neatly into any existing genre template. The nongenre titles filling out the top fifteen box office leaders during the last weekend in 2017, for example, included *All the Money in the World* (Ridley Scott), *Coco* (Lee Unkrich; codirector Adrian Molina), *Wonder* (Stephen Chbosky), *Molly's Game* (Aaron Sorkin), and *Ladybird* (Greta Gerwig).

Genre is certainly not the only way that narrative movies are classified. The film industry breaks down films according to studio of origin, budget, target audience, and distribution patterns. Moviegoers often make

3. Amy Taubin, "*Symbiopsychotaxiplasm*: Still No Answers," The Criterion Collection (December 5, 2006), www.criterion.com/current/posts/460.

viewing decisions according to the directors and/or stars of the films available. Film scholars may categorize and analyze a movie based on a wide range of criteria, including its specific aesthetic style, the artists who created it, its country or region of origin, the apparent ideologies expressed by its style or subject matter, or the particular organized cinematic movement it emerged from.

Unlike these film movements (such as French New Wave or Dogme 95), in which a group of like-minded filmmakers consciously conspire to create a particular approach to film style and story, film genres tend to spring up organically, inspired by shifts in history, politics, or society. Genres are often brought about inadvertently—not through any conscious plan, but rather because of a cultural need to explore and express issues and ideas through images and stories. Many classic genres, including Westerns, horror, and science fiction, emerged in literature and evolved into cinematic form during the twentieth century. Others, such as the musical, originated on the Broadway and vaudeville stages before hitting the screen. Some, like the gangster film, were born and bred in the cinema. Cultural conditions inspire artists to tell certain kinds of stories (and audiences to respond to them), the nature of those narratives motivates certain technical and aesthetic approaches, and eventually the accumulation of like-minded movies is detected, labeled, studied, and explicated by cinema scholars.

And, of course, academic scholars are not the only movie lovers who find it useful to categorize films by genre. Genre significantly affects how audiences choose the movies they attend, rent, or purchase. Movie reviewers often critique a film based on how it stacks up against others in its genre. Most movie-rental retailers organize movies according to genre (along with more general catchall classifications like drama and comedy). Online and newspaper theater listings include a movie's genre alongside its rating, running time, and show time.

Of the aforementioned fifteen top-grossing movies for the weekend of December 29, 2017, at least nine could be considered genre films: *Downsizing* (Alexander Payne) is science fiction; *Jumanji: Welcome to the Jungle* (Jake Kasdan) is action-adventure; *Justice League* (Zack Snyder) is a superhero movie; and *Pitch Perfect 3* (Trish Sie) and *The Greatest Showman* (Michael Gracey) are both musicals. *Darkest Hour* (Joe Wright) is a biographical film, a genre that recounts a significant historical period of a notable person's life. *Father Figures* (Lawrence Sher)

1

2

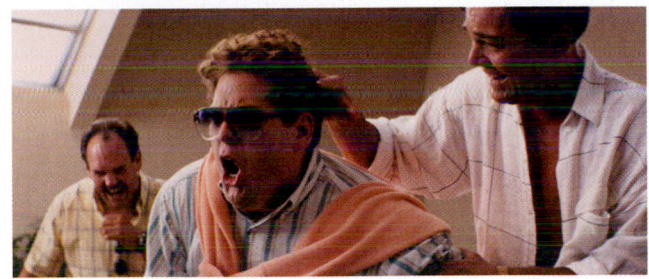

3

Genre study

Scholars find genre films to be especially rich artifacts that can reveal a great deal about the culture that produced and consumed them, as well as about the filmmakers who made them. How does Martin Scorsese, a director associated with gangster films such as *Mean Streets* (1973) [1] and *Goodfellas* (1990) [2], apply the conventions of that genre to the rise and fall of an unscrupulous stockbroker in *The Wolf of Wall Street* (2013) [3]?

is the latest entry in the raunchy arrested-development man-child comedy subgenre. *Star Wars: The Last Jedi* (Rian Johnson) and *The Shape of Water* (Guillermo del Toro) each combine multiple genres, including science fiction and fantasy.

Since genre labels allow us to predict with reasonable certainty what sort of movie to expect, these classifications don't just help audiences make their viewing choices; the people that finance movies often must account for genre when deciding which projects to bankroll.

Genres offer familiar story formulas, conventions, themes, and conflicts, as well as immediately recognizable visual icons. Together, they provide a blueprint for creating and marketing a type of film that has proven successful in the past. Studios and distributors can develop genre-identified stars, select directors on the basis of proven ability in a particular genre; piggyback on the success of a previous genre hit; and even recycle props, sets, costumes, and digital backgrounds. Just as important, the industry counts on genre to predict ticket sales, presell markets, and cash in on recent trends by making films that allow consumers to predict they'll like a particular movie. In other words: give people what they want, and they will buy it. This simple economic principle helps us understand the phenomenal growth of the movie industry from the 1930s on, as well as the mind-numbing mediocrity of so many of the movies the industry produces. The kind of strict adherence to genre convention driven solely by economics often yields derivative and formulaic results.

If genre films are prone to mediocrity, why are so many great filmmakers drawn to making them? Part of the answer can be found, of all places, in a statement by the Nobel Prize–winning poet T. S. Eliot, who wrote: "When forced to work within a strict framework, the imagination is taxed to its utmost—and will produce its richest ideas." Eliot was talking about poetry, but the same concept can be applied to cinema. Creatively ambitious writers and directors often challenge themselves to create art within the strict confines of genre convention.

A genre's so-called rules can provide a foundation upon which the filmmaker can both honor traditions and innovate change. The resulting stories and styles often expertly fulfill some expectations while surprising and subverting others as the filmmaker references, refutes, and revises well-established cultural associations. Genre has intrigued so many of our greatest American and European filmmakers that numerous entries in the canon of important and transformative movies are genre films. *The Godfather* (1972; director Francis Ford Coppola), *Goodfellas* (1990; director Martin Scorsese), and *Bonnie and Clyde* (1967; director Arthur Penn) are all gangster films; Stanley Kubrick's *2001: A Space Odyssey* (1968) is science fiction; Carol Reed's *The Third Man* (1949) and even Jean-Luc Godard's *Breathless* (1960) could be considered film noir; Woody Allen's *Annie Hall* (1977) is a romantic comedy; John Ford's *The Searchers* (1956) is a Western, as is Sergio Leone's *The Good, the Bad and the Ugly* (1966); Stanley Donen and Gene Kelly's *Singin' in the Rain* (1952) is a musical; David Lean's *Lawrence of Arabia* (1962) is a biography and a war movie and an epic.

Still, audiences don't like just the classic films that transcend genre conventions. Genre films have been prevalent since the earliest days of cinema because, contrary to popular perceptions, most movie viewers value predictability over novelty. Elements of certain genres appeal to us, so we seek to repeat an entertaining or engaging cinema experience by viewing a film that promises the same surefire ingredients. We get a certain pleasure from seeing how different filmmakers and performers have rearranged and interpreted familiar elements, just as we are exhilarated by an unexpected deviation from the anticipated path. To put this relationship into gastronomic terms: the most common pizza features a flour-based crust topped with tomato sauce and mozzarella cheese, but it's the potential variety within that familiar foundation that has made pizza one of America's favorite foods.

A less obvious but perhaps more profound explanation for the prevalence of genre lies in the deep roots of genre in our society. Remember that any given genre naturally emerges and crystallizes not because Hollywood thinks it'll sell, but because it gives narrative voice to something essential to our culture. The film industry may ultimately exploit a genre's cultural resonance, but only after cultural conditions motivate enough individual artists and viewers to create the genre in the first place.

For example, no studio executive or directors' club decided to invent horror movies out of thin air. Horror movies exist due to our collective fear of death and the human psyche's need for catharsis. Westerns enact and endorse aspects of American history and the human condition that Americans have needed to believe about themselves. We go to these movies not only to celebrate the familiar, but to enforce fundamental beliefs and passively perform cultural rituals. As our world evolves and audience perspectives change, genre movies adapt to

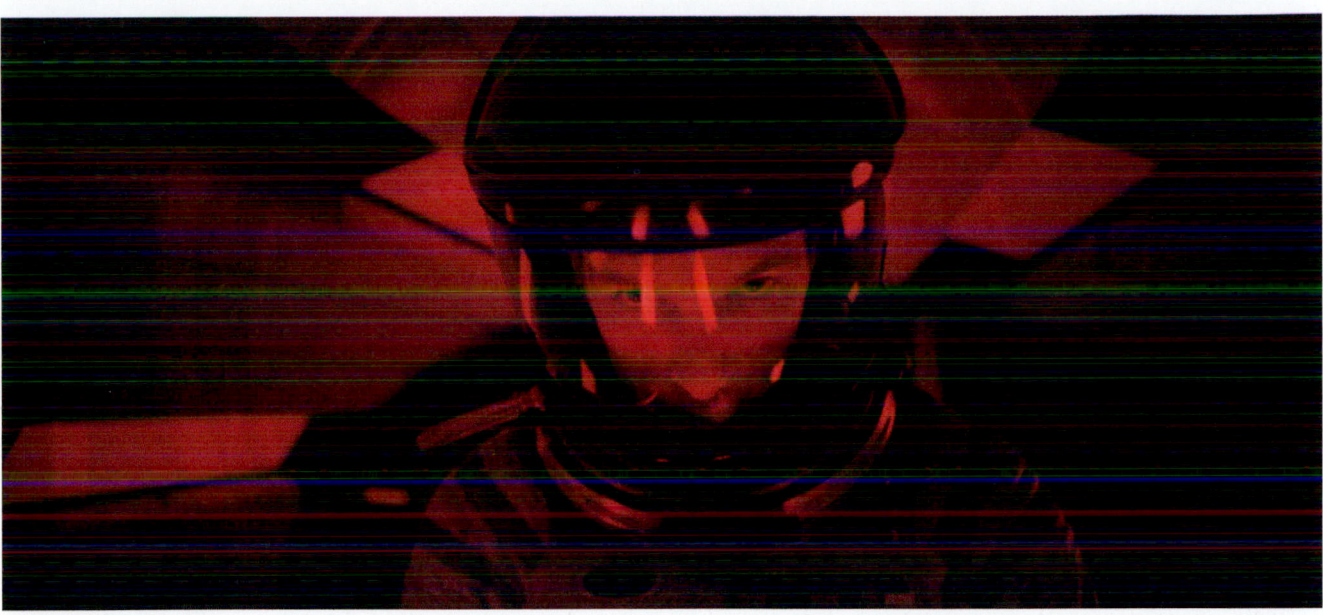

Genre masterpieces
Not all genre movies are disposable formula pictures churned out for the indiscriminate masses. Many of cinema's most revered films are also genre movies. Stanley Kubrick's *2001: A Space Odyssey* (1968) incorporates virtually every standard science-fiction genre element, including speculative setting, special effects, and a decided ambivalence toward the benefits of technology. Yet Kubrick's skills as a storyteller and stylist make *2001* a work of art that transcends conventional attitudes toward genre movies.

reflect these cultural shifts. A Western made during the can-do patriotism of World War II is likely to express its themes differently than one produced at the height of the Vietnam War.

Genre Conventions

Movie genres are defined by sets of conventions—aspects of storytelling such as recurring themes and situations, setting, character types, and story formula, as well as aspects of presentation and visual style such as decor, lighting, and sound. Even the movie stars associated with a particular genre can be considered one of these defining conventions. Keep in mind that these conventions are not enforced; filmmakers don't follow mandated genre checklists. While every movie within any particular genre will incorporate some of these elements, few genre movies attempt to include every possible genre convention.

Story Formulas The way a movie's story is structured—its plot—also helps viewers determine what genre it belongs to. For example, gangster films—from Howard Hawks's *Scarface* (1932) to Ridley Scott's *American Gang-*

ster (2007)—tend to share a plot structure in which an underprivileged and disrespected immigrant joins (or forms) an organized crime syndicate; works his way to the top with a combination of savvy, innovation, and ruthlessness; becomes corrupted by his newfound power and the fruits of his labors; and as a result is betrayed, killed, or captured.

Romantic comedy plots are structured around characters in love as they couple, break up, and reconnect. When they first meet, the two characters (usually a man and a woman) are at odds. They fall in love in spite of, or sometimes because of, this seeming incompatibility. Then they must overcome obstacles to their relationship in the form of misunderstandings, competing partners, social pressures, or friction caused by the aforementioned incompatibility. Eventually the romance will appear doomed, but one half of the couple will realize they are meant for each other and make a grand gesture that reunites the romantic duo.

Theme A movie's *theme* is a unifying idea that the film expresses through its narrative or imagery. Not every genre is united by a single, clear-cut thematic idea, but the Western comes close. Nearly all Westerns share a central conflict between civilization and wilderness: settlers, towns, schoolteachers, cavalry outposts, and lawmen stand for civilization; free-range cattlemen, Indians, prostitutes, outlaws, and the wide-open spaces themselves fill the wilderness role. Many classic Western characters exist on both sides of this thematic conflict. For example, the Wyatt Earp character played by Henry Fonda in John Ford's *My Darling Clementine* (1946) is a former gunfighter turned lawman turned cowboy turned lawman. He befriends an outlaw but falls in love with a schoolteacher from the east. Early Westerns tend to sympathize with the forces of civilization and order, but many of the Westerns from the 1960s and 1970s valorize the freedom-loving outlaw, cowboy, or Native American hero.

Gangster films are shaped by three well-worn, but obviously resonant themes: rags to riches; crime does not pay; absolute power corrupts absolutely. The thematic complexity made possible by the tension between these aspirational and moralistic ideas can give viewers a more meaningful experience than we might expect from a genre dedicated to career criminals.

Character Types While most screenwriters strive to create individuated characters, genre films are often populated by specific character "types." Western protagonists personify the tension between order and chaos in the form of the free-spirited but civilized cowboy or the gunslinger turned lawman. Female characters also personify this tension, but only on one side or the other—as schoolmarm or prostitute, only rarely as a combination of both. Other Western character types include the cunning gambler, the greenhorn, the sidekick, and the settler. John Ford packed nearly every Western character type into a single wagon in his classic Western *Stagecoach* (1939).

The horror or science-fiction film antagonist is almost always some form of "other"—a being utterly different from the movie's protagonist (and audience) in form, attitude, and action. Many of these movie monsters are essentially large, malevolent bugs—the more foreign the villain's appearance and outlook, the better. When the other is actually a human, he often wears a mask designed to accentuate his otherness.

Setting Setting—where a movie's action is located and how that environment is portrayed—is also a common genre convention. Obviously, Westerns are typically set in the American West, but setting goes beyond geography. Most classic Westerns take place in the 1880s and 1890s, an era of western settlement when a booming population of Civil War veterans and other eastern refugees went west in pursuit of land, gold, and cattle trade. The physical location of Monument Valley became the landscape most associated with the genre, not because of any actual history that occurred there, but because the scenic area was the favorite location of the prolific Western director John Ford.

Since science-fiction films are speculative and, therefore, look forward rather than backward, they are usually set in the future: sometimes in space, sometimes in futuristic Earth cities, sometimes in post-apocalyptic desolation, but almost always in an era and place greatly affected by technology. Unlike gangster films, which are almost always urban in setting, horror films seek the sort of isolated locations—farms, abandoned summer camps, small rural villages—that place the genre's besieged protagonists far from potential aid.

Presentation Many genres feature certain elements of cinematic language that communicate tone and atmosphere. For example, horror films take advantage of lighting schemes that accentuate and deepen shadows. The resulting gloom helps to create an eerie mood, but horror films are more than just dark: filmmakers use the hard-edged shadows as a dominant compositional element to convey a sense of oppression, distort our sense of space, and conceal narrative information. Film noir, a genre that also seeks to disorient the viewer and convey a sense of unease (although for very different thematic and narrative reasons), employs many of the same lighting techniques.

Ironically, science-fiction films use the latest high-tech special effects to tell stories that warn against the dehumanizing dangers of advanced technology. In fact, the genre is responsible for many important special effect innovations, from the miniatures and matte paintings that made possible the futuristic city of Fritz Lang's *Metropolis* (1927) to the motion-control cameras and rotoscope animation that launched the spaceships of Stanley Kubrick's *2001: A Space Odyssey* (1968) to the special "virtual camera system" director James Cameron and his *Avatar* (2009) team used to capture actors' expressions and actions as the first step in a revolutionary technical process that transformed the film's cast into aliens inhabiting an all-digital world.

Westerns, a genre clearly associated with setting, feature a great many exterior shots that juxtapose the characters with the environment they inhabit. The human subject tends to dominate the frame in most movie compositions, but many of these Western exterior shots are framed so that the "civilized" characters are dwarfed by the overwhelming expanse of wilderness around them.

Movies in the action genre often shoot combat (and other high-energy action) from many different angles to allow for a fast-paced editing style that presents the action from a constantly shifting perspective. These highly fragmented sequences subject the viewer to a rapid-fire cinematic simulation of the amplified exercise presumably experienced by the characters fighting on-screen.

Stars Even the actors who star in genre movies factor into how the genre is classified, analyzed, and received by audiences. In the 1930s and 1940s, actors worked under restrictive long-term studio contracts. With the studios choosing their roles, actors were more likely to be "typecast" and identified with a particular genre that suited their studio-imposed persona. Thus John Wayne is forever identified with the Western, Edward G. Robinson with gangster films, and Boris Karloff with horror.

These days, most actors avoid limiting themselves to a single genre. When Dwayne Johnson transitioned from professional wrestling to movie stardom, he was initially (and predictably) limited to roles in action films. He still stars in action movies like *The Fate of the Furious* (2017), but he has also headlined comedies like *Central Intelligence* (2016) and voiced (and sang) a lead character in *Moana* (2016), an animated Disney musical. Jennifer Lawrence is just as clearly associated with non-genre dramatic work like *American Hustle* (2013) and *Silver Linings Playbook* (2012) as she is for her starring roles in the superhero X-Men films and the science fiction/fantasy Hunger Games series.

Compiling an authoritative list of narrative genres and their specific conventions is nearly impossible, especially in an introductory textbook. There are simply too many genres, too much cinematic variety and flexibility, and too little academic consensus to nail down every (or any) genre definitively. Nevertheless, the next section offers a closer look at six major American genres to help you begin developing a deeper understanding of how genre functions.

1

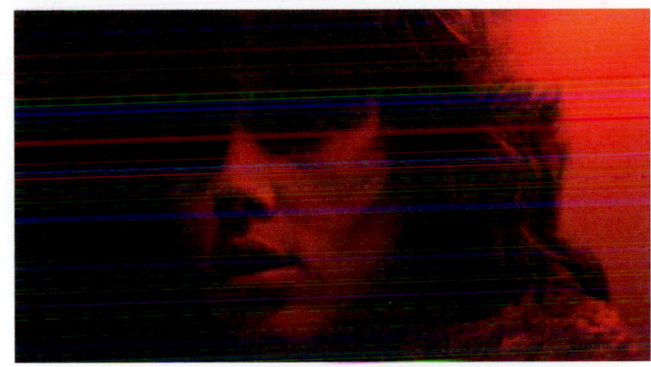

2

3

Multigenre stardom

These days, few actors are associated with a single genre. Scarlett Johansson, since taking on the recurring superhero movie role of the Black Widow in *Iron Man 2* (2010; director Jon Favreau) [1]—a part she has reprised in five subsequent Avengers movies—starred in four very different science-fiction films as well: as a psychokinetic killer in the action-packed *Lucy* (2014), as a lonely alien in the artsy *Under the Skin* (2013) [2], and as the voice of a sentient computer operating system in the cerebral *Her* (2013). During the same period, she also played the elegant movie star Janet Leigh in the biopic *Hitchcock* (2012; director Sacha Gervasi) [3], a cyber-enhanced soldier in the anime-inspired *Ghost in the Shell* (2017), and (as a voice-actor) an animated guitar-playing teenage porcupine in *Sing* (2016).

Six Major American Genres

Gangster

The gangster genre is deeply rooted in the concept of the American dream: anyone, regardless of how humble his origins, can succeed. For much of its history, America's wealth and political power have been wielded primarily by successive generations of a white, Anglo-Saxon, highly educated, and Protestant ruling class. American heroes like Daniel Boone, leaders like Andrew Jackson and Abraham Lincoln, and popular novelists like Horatio Alger Jr. challenged this tradition of power by birthright. Their example gave rise to the notion that anyone with intelligence and spunk can rise to great riches or power through hard work and bold action. The nation's expanding population of working-class American immigrants were eager to embrace this rags-to-riches mythology.

By the turn of the twentieth century, pulp-fiction accounts of the American West had already established the hero as an outsider who lives by his wits and is willing to break the rules to achieve his goals. Two historical events provided the remaining ingredients needed to turn these working-class notions into what we know now as the gangster genre.

First, the Eighteenth Amendment to the Constitution—ratified in 1919—banned the manufacture, sale, and transport of alcohol. This ill-advised law empowered organized crime, which expanded to capitalize on the newfound market for the suddenly forbidden beverages. Many of the criminal entrepreneurs who exploited this opportunity were Irish, Italian, and Jewish immigrants.

What's more, Prohibition legitimized unlawful behavior by making outlaws out of common citizens thirsty for a beer after quitting time. As a result, common

Gangster plot elements

Francis Ford Coppola's The Godfather trilogy (1972–90), perhaps the most famous gangster film series, includes many plot elements common to the genre, including the protagonist's humble origins and his rise to power through a combination of astute management and ruthless violence. But Coppola incorporated genre innovations that differentiated The Godfather movies from more typical gangster films. For example, the protagonist, Michael, is an unwilling crime boss forced into syndicate leadership by circumstances and birthright. The plot elements of a humble origin and the rise to power are presented as flashbacks featuring not Michael, but his father, the man whose death propels Michael into a life of organized crime. Finally, Michael is unusual in that he attains power and prestige but is not destroyed (physically, at least) by corruption and greed.

"crime, wrongdoing, evil or sin." As a result, while early gangster films were among the most violent and sexually explicit movies of their time, the central conflicts and themes they explored were often at odds with one another. For example, the stories were centered around outlaw entrepreneurs who empowered themselves, bucked the establishment, and grabbed their piece of the pie; yet, by the end of the story, this theme of success would give way to a "crime does not pay" message in which the enterprising hero is finally corrupted by his hunger for power and thus defeated by forces of law and order. In many of these films, violent crime was both celebrated and condemned. Movies that had audiences sympathizing with criminals (or at least their goals) at the start would ultimately turn an exhilarating rags-to-riches story of empowerment into a cautionary tale of the consequences of blind ambition. Central characters would achieve their goal, only to be killed either by the law or their own equally ruthless subordinates. Along the way, audiences enjoyed the vicarious thrills of a daring pursuit of power, as well as the righteous satisfaction of seeing order restored.

The antihero

The gangster movie gave the cinema some of its first antiheroes. These unconventional central characters pursue goals, overcome obstacles, take risks, and suffer consequences—everything needed to propel a compelling narrative—but they lack the traditional "heroic" qualities that engage an audience's sympathy. While he may not be courteous, kind, and reverent, he is almost always smart (if uneducated), observant, and brave. More than anything, the gangster-hero is driven by an overwhelming need to prove himself. This need motivates his quest for power, fame, and wealth—and almost always proves to be the tragic flaw that brings about his inevitable downfall. In the final moments of Raoul Walsh's *White Heat* (1949), the psychopathic protagonist Cody Jarrett (James Cagney) declares "top of the world, Ma!" before blowing himself to bits rather than submitting to the policemen who have him surrounded.

While modern gangster narratives have expanded to include a wide range of stories set within the milieu of organized crime, classic gangster plots typically follow this rags-to-riches-to-destruction formula. The protagonist is initially powerless and sometimes suffers some form of public humiliation that both emphasizes his vulnerability and motivates his struggle for recognition. (This humiliation can come at the hands of a governing institution or the ruling gang organization; often, the ensuing conflict pits the gangster hero against both the law and the criminals currently in control.) The hero gains status and eventually grabs power and riches through ingenuity, risk taking, and a capacity for violence.

people—many of them immigrants themselves—began to identify with the bootleggers and racketeers. They were seen as active protagonists who took chances, risked the consequences, and got results—all surefire elements of successful cinema heroes. The stock market crash in 1929 and the resulting economic depression further cemented the public's distrust of authority (i.e., banks and financiers) and the allure of the gangster.

In this specific cultural context, American audiences began to question the authority of discredited institutions such as banks, government, and law enforcement. This viewpoint fed their fascination with the outlaws who bucked those systems that had failed the rest of society. As the Depression deepened, the need for vivid, escapist entertainment increased. Hollywood was the ideal conduit for this emerging zeitgeist; the result was the gangster film.

Just as the gangster film emerged, however, the film industry adopted a production code that forbade movies from explicitly engaging audience sympathy with

Most gangster protagonists are killers, but their initial victims (such as the thugs responsible for the protagonist's initial humiliation) are usually portrayed as deserving of their fate. This pattern shifts as the hero reaches his goal to rule the criminal syndicate. His ambition clouds his vision; he becomes paranoid and power-hungry, and begins to resemble his deposed adversaries. Before he self-destructs, he often destroys—figuratively or literally—characters that represent his last remaining ties to the earnest go-getter who began the story. Frequently, the protagonist expresses last-minute regret for what he has become, but by then it's almost always too late.

More sympathetic secondary characters often serve to humanize the gangster antihero. While the doomed protagonist is nearly always male, the secondary characters who provide a tenuous connection to the Old World values that he must sacrifice on his climb up the ladder usually take the form of a mother or sister. The only other female character typical to the genre is either a fellow criminal or a sort of gangster groupie known as a moll. Whereas the protagonist's mother loves him for his potential humanity, the gangster moll loves him for his potential power and wealth. She is a symbol of his aspirations—an alluring veneer concealing a rotten core.

The protagonist may also have a sidekick—a trusted companion from the old neighborhood—who makes the journey with him. This friend may be responsible for giving the protagonist his first break in the business, only to be eclipsed by the hero later. He is often instrumental in the protagonist's downfall, either as a betrayer or as a victim of the central character's greed and lust for power.

Antagonists come in two forms: law enforcement agents and fellow gangsters. In stark contrast to portrayals in traditional procedurals, the police in gangster movies are portrayed as oppressors who are corrupt, incompetent, or both. They are sometimes in league with the gangster antagonist, the current kingpin who lacks the imagination or courage of our hero. His overthrow is often one of the first major obstacles the protagonist must overcome. Of course, the ultimate antagonist in many gangster movies is the protagonist himself.

Legend has it that when the gangster Willie Sutton was asked why he robbed banks, he replied, "Because that's where the money is." The same sort of logic explains the setting of the vast majority of gangster films. Movies about organized crime are set in urban locations because organized crime flourishes primarily in large cities. The particulars of the setting evolve as the plot progresses. The story usually opens in a slum, develops on the mean streets downtown, and then works its way upward into luxury penthouses.

In contrast to most movie stars, the actors most closely associated with early gangster films were diminutive and relatively unattractive. The authority that actors such as Edward G. Robinson and James Cagney conveyed on-screen was made all the more powerful by their atypical appearance. (In another twist of Hollywood logic, Cagney—whose gangster portrayals were among the most brutal in cinema history—was equally beloved as a star of happy-go-lucky musicals.)

Film Noir

In the early 1940s, the outlook, tone, and style of American genre films grew decidedly darker with the emergence of film noir (from the French for "black film"), a shift clearly denoted by its name. Not that movies hadn't already demonstrated a cynical streak. The gangster movies that surfaced in the previous decade featured antiheroes and less-than-flattering portrayals of our cities and institutions. World War I, Prohibition, and the Great Depression began the trend toward more realistic, and thus bleaker, artistic and narrative representations of the world, as evidenced in the written word of the time. Pulp-fiction writers like Dashiell Hammett had been publishing the hard-boiled stories that formed the foundation of film noir since the early 1930s.

In fact, if not for the efforts of Hollywood and the U.S. government during World War II, film noir might have come along sooner. Instead, gung-ho war movies were designed to build support for the war effort, and lighthearted musicals and comedies were produced to provide needed distractions from overwhelming world events. Yet the same war that helped delay the arrival of film noir also helped give birth to the new genre by exposing ordinary Americans to the horrors of war. Whether in person or through newsreels and newspapers, troops and citizens alike witnessed death camps, battlefield slaughters, the rise of fascism, and countless other atrocities.

Many of the genre's greatest directors, including Otto Preminger, Billy Wilder, and Fritz Lang, were themselves marked by the hardship and persecution they had experienced before leaving war-torn Europe for Hollywood. Others, like Samuel Fuller, fought as American soldiers. The atomic bomb that ended the war also demonstrated that not even a nation as seemingly secure as the United States was safe from its devastating power. The financial boom that the war effort had generated ended abruptly as the soldiers returned home to a changed world of economic uncertainty. Film noir fed off the postwar disillusionment that followed prolonged exposure to this intimidating new perspective.

In part because many of the early noir movies were low-budget "B" movies (so called because they often screened in the second slot of double features), the genre was not initially recognized or respected by most American scholars. Its emphasis on corruption and despair was seen as an unflattering portrayal of the Amer-

Fatalism in film noir

Film noir movies sometimes present information and events in a way that heightens the audience's sense that the hard-luck protagonist is doomed from the moment the story opens. Director and screenwriter Billy Wilder pushed this technique to the extreme in two of his most famous noir movies, both of which reveal the demise of the protagonist. The first moments of *Double Indemnity* (1944) open with antihero Walter Neff (Fred MacMurray) stumbling wounded into his office to confess to the murder he will spend the rest of the story trying to get away with [1]. *Sunset Boulevard* (1950) goes one step further. The entire film is narrated in first-person voice-over by a protagonist (William Holden) presented in the opening scene as a floating corpse [2].

ican character. It was left to French critics, some of whom went on to make genre films of their own, to recognize (and name) the genre.

In fact, the American critic Paul Schrader (himself a filmmaker who has written and directed noir films) feels that film noir is not a genre at all. He claims that "film noir . . . is not defined, as are the Western and gangster genres, by conventions of setting and conflict, but rather by the more subtle qualities of tone and mood."[4] Regardless of how it is classified, film noir has continued to flourish long past the events that provoked its birth, thanks in part to a universal attraction to its visual and narrative style and a lasting affinity for its outlook. Like the eggs they are named for, the hard-boiled characters in film noir have a tough interior beneath brittle shells. The themes are fatalistic, the tone cynical. Film noir may not be defined by setting, but noir films are typically shot in large urban areas (such as Chicago, New York, or Los Angeles). They contain gritty, realistic night exteriors, many of them filmed on location, as opposed to the idealized and homogenized streets built on the studio back lot.

Like his counterpart in the gangster movie, the film-noir protagonist is an antihero. Unlike his gangster equivalent, he rarely pursues or achieves leadership status. On the contrary, the central noir character is an outsider. If he is a criminal, he's usually a lone operator caught up in a doomed attempt at a big score or a wrong-doer trying to elude justice. The private detectives at the center of many noir narratives operate midway between lawful society and the criminal underworld, with associates and enemies on both sides of the law. They may be former police officers who left the force in either disgrace or disgust; or they may be active but isolated police officers ostracized for their refusal to play by the rules. Whatever his profession, the noir protagonist is small-time, world-weary, aging, and not classically handsome. He's self-destructive and thus fallible, often suffering abuse on the way to a story conclusion that may very well deny him his goal and will almost certainly leave him un-redeemed. All this is not to say that the noir protagonist is weak or unattractive. Ironically, the world-weary and wisecracking noir antihero is responsible for some of

4. Paul Schrader, "Notes on *Film Noir*" [1972], in *Film Noir Reader,* ed. Alain Silver and James Ursini (New York: Limelight, 1996), pp. 53–64.

1

2

3

Modern film noir

While many modern noir films, such as Curtis Hanson's *L.A. Confidential* (1997), set their stories in places and times that directly reference the classic noir films of the 1940s, others offer a revised genre experience by relocating noir's thematic, aesthetic, and narrative elements to contemporary times and atypical locations. Rian Johnson's *Brick* (2005) [1] takes place within the convoluted social strata of a suburban high school. Joel Coen's *Fargo* (1996) [2] unfolds on the frozen prairies of rural North Dakota and the snow-packed Minneapolis suburbs. Erik Skjoldbjærg's *Insomnia* (1997) [3] trades ominous shadows for the unrelenting light of the midnight sun in a village above the Arctic Circle.

cinema's most popular and enduring characters. Humphrey Bogart was just a middle-aged character actor before his portrayal of the private detective Sam Spade in John Huston's *The Maltese Falcon* (1941) made him a cultural icon.

World War II expanded opportunities for women on the home front. They took over the factory jobs and other responsibilities from the men who left to fight in Europe and the Pacific. Perhaps as a reflection of men's fear or resentment of these newly empowered women, film noir elevated the female character to antagonist status. Instead of passive supporting players, the femme fatale (French for "deadly woman") role cast women as seductive, autonomous, and deceptive predators who use men for their own means. As a rule, the femme fatale is a far smarter—and thus formidable—opponent for the protagonist than other adversarial characters, most of whom are corrupt and violent though not necessarily a match for the hero's cynical intelligence.

More than virtually any other genre, film noir is distinguished by its visual style. The name *black film* references not just the genre's attitude, but its look as well. Noir movies employ lighting schemes that emphasize

contrast and create deep shadows that can obscure as much information as the illumination reveals. Light sources are often placed low to the ground, resulting in illumination that distorts facial features and casts dramatic shadows. Exterior scenes usually take place at night; those interior scenes set during the day often play out behind drawn shades that cast patterns of light and shadow, splintering the frame. These patterns, in turn, combine with other diagonal visual elements to create a compositional tension that gives the frame—and the world it depicts—a restless, unstable quality.

Film noir plot structure reinforces this feeling of disorientation. The complex (sometimes incomprehensible) narratives are often presented in nonchronological or otherwise convoluted arrangements. Plot twists deprive the viewer of the comfort of a predictable plot. Goals shift, and expectations are reversed; allies are revealed to be enemies (and vice versa); narration, even that delivered by the protagonist, is sometimes unreliable. Moral reference points are skewed: victims are often as corrupt as their persecutors; criminals are working stiffs just doing their job. Paradoxically, this unsettling narrative complexity is often framed by a sort of enforced predictability. Fatalistic voice-over narration telegraphs future events and outcomes, creating a sense of predetermination and hopelessness for the protagonist's already lost cause.

Science Fiction

It seems logical to think of science fiction as being speculative fantasy about the potential wonders of technological advances. But most science-fiction films are not really about science. If we tried to prove the "science" that most sci-fi films present, much of it would be quickly exposed as ridiculous. Instead, the genre's focus is on humanity's relationship with science and the technology it generates.

Science fiction existed as a literary genre long before movies were invented. The genre began in the early nineteenth century as a reaction to the radical societal and economic changes spurred by the industrial revolution. At that time, the introduction of new technologies such as the steam engine dramatically changed the way Americans and Europeans worked and lived. What were once rural agrarian cultures were quickly transformed into mechanized urban societies. Stories are one way that our cultures process radical change, so it didn't take long for the anxiety unleashed by this explosion of technology to manifest itself in the form of Mary Shelley's 1818 novel *Frankenstein; or, The Modern Prometheus.* The subtitle makes evident the novel's theme: in Greek mythology, Prometheus is the Titan who stole fire from Zeu and bestowed this forbidden and dangerous knowledge on mortals not yet ready to deal with its power. Shelley's "monster" represents the consequences of men using science and technology to play God.

Readers familiar with twentieth-century movie versions may think of *Frankenstein* as a horror story. The genres are indeed closely related through their mutual exploitation of audience fears, but the source of the anxiety is different. Horror films speak to our fears of the supernatural and the unknown, whereas science-fiction movies explore our dread of technology and change. Both genres have their roots in folklore that articulates the ongoing battle between human beings and everything that is other than human. In ancient folklore, this "other" was anthropomorphized into monsters (trolls, ogres, etc.) that inhabited (and represented) the wilderness that humans could not control.

1

2

The other in science fiction
Science-fiction films often emphasize a malevolent alien's "otherness" by modeling its appearance on machines or insects. The benevolent visitors in Steven Spielberg's popular science-fiction film *Close Encounters of the Third Kind* (1977) [1] look much more reassuringly humanoid than the hostile invaders his collaborators created for *War of the Worlds* (2005) [2].

Ironically, the same advances in science and technology that allowed cultures to explain away—and thus destroy—all of these old monsters have given voice to the modern folklore of science fiction. For most of us, science is beyond our control. Its rapid advance is a phenomenon that we didn't create, that we don't entirely comprehend, and that moves too fast for us to keep up with. So when it comes to science fiction, the other represents—directly or indirectly—this technological juggernaut that can help us but also has the power to destroy us or at least make us obsolete.

We are not saying that science is an inherently negative force or even that anxiety dominates our relationship with technology. We all love our computers, appreciate modern medicine, and marvel at the wonders of space exploration. But conflict is an essential element of narrative. If everything is perfect, then there's no story. And unspoken, even unconscious, concerns are at the root of a great deal of artistic expression.

Science fiction and special effects

Humanity must escape an Earth ravaged by climate change in Christopher Nolan's science-fiction epic *Interstellar* (2014). To find a habitable planet, a group of scientists must both embrace and overcome human nature to discover and unlock previously inconceivable concepts and technologies. The spaceships they travel in, and the spectacular worlds they encounter, were created using sophisticated digital technology. Ironically, the movie genre founded on audiences' dread of technology also happens to depend heavily on viewers' attraction to high-tech visual effects. The speculative spectacle that audiences expect of science fiction means that most films in the genre feature elaborate sets, costumes, makeup, computer animation, and digital effects.

Science-inspired anxiety is behind the defining thematic conflict that unites most science-fiction movies. This conflict can be expressed in many ways, but for our purposes let's think of it as technology versus humanity or science versus soul.[5] This theme is expressed in stories that envision technology enslaving humanity, invading our minds and bodies, or bringing about the end of civilization as we know it. The antagonist in these conflicts takes the form of computers like the infamous HAL in Stanley Kubrick's *2001: A Space Odyssey* (1968); robots or machines in films like Ridley Scott's *Blade Runner* (1982), the Wachowskis' The Matrix series (1999–2003), and James Cameron's Terminator movies (1984–2003); and mechanized, dehumanized societies in Fritz Lang's *Metropolis* (1927), Jean-Luc Godard's *Alphaville* (1965), and George Lucas's *THX 1138* (1971).

Alien invaders, another common science-fiction antagonistic other, are also an outgrowth of our innate fear of the machine. As soon as humankind was advanced enough to contemplate travel outside the earth's orbit, we began to speculate about the possibility of life on other planets. Our fear of the unknown, combined with our tendency to see Earth as the center of the universe, empowered this imagined other as a threatening force, endowed with superior destructive technology, bent on displacing or enslaving us. The otherness of the most malevolent aliens is emphasized by designing their appearance to resemble machines or insects. In contrast, the science-fiction movies that reverse expectations and portray alien encounters in a positive light typically shape their extraterrestrials more like humans—or at least mammals. You need look no further than *Star Wars'*

---

5. Per Schelde, *Androids, Humanoids, and Other Science Fiction Monsters: Science and Soul in Science Fiction Films* (New York: New York University Press, 1993).

comfortably fuzzy Chewbacca (as opposed to Imperial Stormtroopers and Jabba the Hutt) for evidence of this tradition.

While most science-fiction movies stress the otherness of the antagonist, the opposite is true for the sci-fi protagonist. Science-fiction heroes are often literally and figuratively down-to-earth. They tend to be so compassionate and soulful that their essential humanity seems a liability—until their indomitable human spirit proves the key to defeating the malevolent other.

Because science-fiction narratives often deal with what-ifs, the setting is frequently speculative. If those sci-fi movies are set in the present day, they often heighten the dramatic impact of invasive aliens or time travelers. Most commonly, the genre places its stories in a future profoundly shaped by advances in technology. This setting allows filmmakers to hypothesize future effects of contemporary cultural, political, or scientific trends. These speculative settings may be high-tech megacities or post-apocalyptic ruins. The setting suggests a combination of both in movies such as Ridley Scott's original *Blade Runner* (1982) and the sequel *Blade Runner 2049* (2017) directed by Denis Villeneuve. Of course, outer space is also a popular science-fiction setting for obvious reasons. In many of these examples, the technology-versus-humanity theme is presented in part by dramatizing the consequences of science taking us places we don't necessarily belong—or at least where we are not physically and spiritually equipped to survive. Science-fiction films made before the 1970s tended to feature sterile, well-ordered, almost utopian speculative settings. Movies like Scott's *Alien* (1979), with its grimy industrial space-barge interiors, reversed that trend by presenting a future in which living conditions had degraded rather than evolved.

Horror

Like science fiction, the horror genre was born out of a cultural need to confront and vicariously conquer something frightening that we do not fully comprehend. In the case of horror films, those frightening somethings are aspects of our existence even more intimidating than technology or science: death and insanity. Both represent the ultimate loss of control and a terrifying, inescapable metamorphosis.

To enact any sort of narrative conflict with either of these forces, they must be given a tangible form.

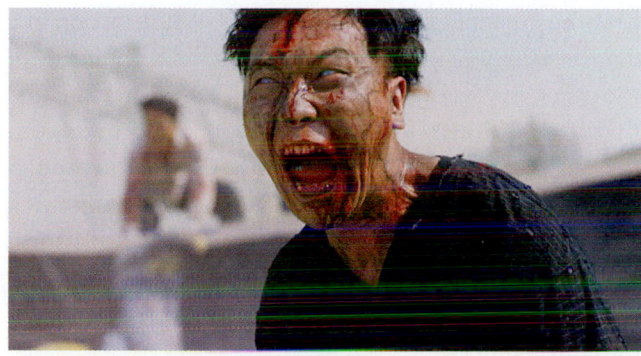

The infectious other

One reason we go to horror movies is to confront our fear of death and insanity, as well as the anxiety that arises out of our ultimate inability to control either condition. As a result, the other that fills the role of antagonist often carries the threat of infection and transformation. The raging zombies in Sang-ho Yeon's *Train to Busan* (2016) [1] are former humans changed into mindless killing machines by a runaway virus. In James Wan's *The Conjuring* (2013) [2], a loving mother is transformed into a demonic witch when she is possessed by a hateful ghost.

And, like horror's sister genre, sci-fi, that form is the "other." Death takes the shape of ghosts, zombies, and vampires—all of which pose a transformative threat to the audience. The only thing scarier than being killed or consumed by the other is actually becoming the other. So it makes sense that the werewolves, demonic possessions, and homicidal maniacs that act as cinematic stand-ins for insanity also carry the threat of infection and conversion.

We could hypothesize that early, primitive religions—even the source of some modern religions—derive from the same essential human need to demystify and defeat these most basic fears. But the difference between movies and religious rituals is the intensity and immediacy that the cinema experience provides. While sitting in a darkened movie theater staring at oversized images of the other, movie viewers are immersed in a shared ritual that exposes them to dread, terror, and ultimately catharsis. We vicariously defeat death (even if the protagonist does not), because we survive the movie and walk back into our relatively safe lives after the credits roll and the lights come up. We experience the exhilaration of confronting the dreaded other without the devastating consequences.

Germany, with its strong tradition of folklore and more developed engagement with the darker aspects of existence (thanks in part to the devastation of World War I), created the first truly disturbing horror movies. Robert Wiene's *The Cabinet of Dr. Caligari* (1920) sees the world through the distorted perspective of a madman; F. W. Murnau's expressionist Dracula adaptation, *Nosferatu, a Symphony of Horror* (1922), associates its other with death and disease. The United States embraced the genre with the release of *Dracula* (1931; director Tod Browning), and thus began Hollywood's on-again, off-again relationship with the horror film. A golden age of Hollywood horror followed, with the monster others at its center taking top billing: *Frankenstein* (1931; director James Whale); *The Mummy* (1932; director Karl Freund); and *The Wolf Man* (1941; director George Waggner).

With the return of prosperity and the end of World War II, the classic "monster"-based horror film faded into mediocrity and relative obscurity until a new generation of audiences with their own fears resurrected the genre. Foreign and independent studios updated and moved beyond the original monster concept with low-budget productions created for the B-movie and drive-in markets. Horror did not return to the mainstream until veteran British directors Alfred Hitchcock and Michael Powell, both of whom were associated with very different motion-picture styles, each unleashed his own disturbing portrait of an outwardly attractive young serial killer. By subverting audiences' expectation of the other, Hitchcock's *Psycho* (1960) and Powell's *Peeping Tom* (1960) shocked audiences and revolutionized the horror genre. Ever since, as our culture's needs and attitudes change, and global awareness of real-life atrocities multiplies, horror has evolved to become one of cinema's most diverse and fluid genres.

A typical horror narrative begins by establishing a normal world that will be threatened by the arrival of the

Horror-movie settings

Most horror stories unfold in settings that isolate potential victims from potential help. Dario Argento's *Suspiria* (1977) goes one step further by placing the young protagonist, Suzy, in an unusually creepy ballet academy in rural Italy. As a newcomer and the only American student, Suzy is not only isolated from the relative security of a populated area, but also must face considerable danger alone, without allies, in unfamiliar surroundings [1]. When Chris Washington, the protagonist of Jordan Peele's allegorical horror movie *Get Out* (2017), agrees to visit his white girlfriend's rich parents, he also finds himself an isolated outsider in a secluded and unfamiliar environment [2]. Instead of evil ballet instructors, he's terrorized by white people who want to possess black men like him in every sense of the word.

other. This monster must be vanquished or destroyed in order to reestablish normalcy. Often, the protagonist is the only person who initially recognizes the threat. Because the other is so far removed from normalcy, the protagonist may reject her own suspicions before she experiences the other more directly and announces the menace to those around her. When her warnings are ignored, the central character is directly targeted by the other. She must either enlist help or face the monster on her own. In the end, the protagonist may destroy the other—or at least appear to. Horror narratives tend to feature resurrections and other false resolutions. Originally, these open endings were meant to give the audience one last scare; now, they are just as likely intended to ensure the possibility of a profitable sequel.

This basic horror plot structure offers a number of typical variants: the protagonist may actually be directly or indirectly responsible for summoning the other, a violation that places even greater responsibility on her to restore the normal world. The protagonist may also have to enlist the help of a mentor or apprentice, or even sacrifice herself, to defeat the antagonistic other. Sometimes the protagonist actually becomes the other. She becomes infected and attempts to deny, and then hide, her encroaching transformation. She may pursue a solution but ultimately faces the decision either to destroy herself or face a complete metamorphosis. Oftentimes, as in similar science-fiction stories, she is somehow saved by the power of her own humanity.

This protagonist is often a loner, someone socially reviled who must save the community that rejects her. We identify with her because she is (initially, at least) unusually fearful, a weakness that allows us the greatest possible identification with her struggle. This characteristic is certainly not limited to horror films. Many movie narratives center on flawed characters because they create high stakes and allow for the kind of character development that satisfies audiences.

While a significant number of horror-film antagonists are one-dimensional killing machines, many of these others are actually more compelling characters than the protagonists charged with destroying them. Vampires fascinate us because they can be as seductive as they are terrifying. Other monsters, such as Frankenstein's monster or his progeny, Edward Scissorhands, may actually display more humanity than the supposedly threatened populace. And, yes, the malevolent father in Stanley Kubrick's *The Shining* (1980) and Freddy Krueger of Wes Craven's *A Nightmare on Elm Street* (1984) may be evil, but they have undeniable personality. Even the masked, robotic killers at the center of the Halloween and Friday the 13th slasher franchises offer more complex histories and motives than their relatively anonymous victims.

Horror-movie settings tend to fall into two categories. The first is the aforementioned "normal world"—a hyperordinary place, usually a small town threatened by invasion of the other. This setting casts the protagonist as the protector of her beloved home turf and violates our own notions of personal safety. Other horror films set their action in remote rural areas that offer potential victims little hope for assistance. A related horror setting places the central character in a foreign, often exotic, environment that lacks the security of the

familiar. The alien customs, language, and landscape disorient the protagonist (and the audience) and diminish any hope for potential support. And, as you may have guessed, regardless of where horror stories are located, they almost invariably stage their action at night.

Besides tapping into our instinctive fears, night scenes lend themselves to the chiaroscuro lighting—the use of deep gradations of light and shadow within an image—that most horror-movie cinematography depends upon. This lighting style emphasizes stark contrasts and shows large areas of deep shadow accented with bright highlights. The light is often direct or undiffused, which creates well-defined shadows and silhouettes, and low-key, meaning the dense shadows are not abated by additional "fill" lights. Horror-genre lighting is sometimes cast from below, an angle of illumination not typical of our everyday experience. The result is the distorted facial features and looming cast shadows known on film sets as "Halloween lighting." Canted camera angles that tilt the on-screen world off balance are used to disorient viewers. Horror-film staging also exploits the use of offscreen action and sound that suggests the presence of peril but denies the audience the relative reassurance of actually keeping an eye on the antagonist.

Halloween lighting in *Bride of Frankenstein*
Like film noir, the horror genre utilizes a style of lighting (referred to as low-key, or chiaroscuro, lighting) that emphasizes stark contrasts between bright illumination and deep shadow. These shadows are used to create unsettling graphic compositions, obscure visual information, and suggest offscreen action. Lighting a subject from below, a technique often referred to as "Halloween lighting," distorts a subject's features by reversing the natural placement of shadows.

The Western

Like most of the major genres, the Western predates the invention of motion pictures. The exploration and settlement of the western United States has fascinated European Americans since the frontier was just a few hundred miles inland from the eastern coast. Set in 1757 and published in 1826, James Fenimore Cooper's *The Last of the Mohicans* is widely considered the first popular novel to explore the tension between the wilderness and encroaching civilization. But the considerably less reputable literature most responsible for spawning the Western movie didn't come along until about 25 years later. Dime novels (so called because of their low cost), short novellas written for young men and semiliterates, delivered sensational adventures of fictional cowboys, outlaws, and adventurers, as well as wildly fictionalized stories starring actual Western figures.

By the 1870s, stage productions and traveling circuslike shows featuring staged reenactments of famous battles and other events were capitalizing on the growing international fascination with the American West. Movies wasted no time getting into the act. Some of the earliest motion pictures were Westerns, including Thomas Edison's 46-second, one-shot vignette *Cripple Creek Bar-Room Scene* (1899) and Edwin S. Porter's groundbreaking *The Great Train Robbery* (1903).

American history inspired the Western, but the genre's enduring popularity has more to do with how Americans see and explain themselves than with any actual event. Westerns are a form of modern mythology that offers narrative representations of Americans as rugged, self-sufficient individuals taming a savage wilderness with common sense and direct action. The concept of the frontier as a sort of societal blank slate is at the heart of this mythology. The Wild West is a land of opportunity—both a dangerous, lawless country in need of taming and an expansive territory where anyone with the right stuff can reinvent himself and start a new life. The mythology label does not mean that these notions cannot be true. It simply acknowledges that certain aspects of the history of the American West have been amplified and modified to serve a collective cultural need.

Earlier in the chapter, we discussed the civilization-versus-wilderness conflict that provides the Western's thematic framework. The tension produced by this conflict is an essential ingredient in virtually every Western narrative. The wilderness can take the form of antago-

Wilderness and civilization

Although many Western narratives favor the forces of order, the outlaw is not always the bad guy. Revisionist Westerns like George Roy Hill's *Butch Cassidy and the Sundance Kid* (1969) mourn the inevitable loss of freedom that accompanies the civilization of the frontier. In that movie, and in many others that reconsidered Western mythology, the protagonists are good-natured outlaws [1]; the righteous avenging posse (presented as a faceless "other" in a technique borrowed from the horror and science-fiction genres) is the dreaded antagonist [2].

nistic forces in direct conflict with the civilizing settlers, such as the Apache Indians in John Ford's *The Searchers* (1956) and *Stagecoach* (1939) or the free-range cattleman of George Stevens's *Shane* (1953). Or it can manifest itself in more metaphorical terms. The wilderness of Ford's *3 Godfathers* (1948), for example, takes the form of the outlaw protagonists' self-interest, which is put in direct opposition with the civilizing effects of social responsibility when the bandits discover an infant orphaned in the desert.

But this sort of duality was nothing new. Many Western characters reverse or combine the thematic elements of order and chaos. Lawmen in movies like Clint Eastwood's *Unforgiven* (1992) are antagonists, and often even a lawman protagonist is a former outlaw or gunfighter. Cowboys—quintessential Western characters—also embody the blurred borders between the West-

1

2

Character duality in the Western

Western protagonists often embody both sides of the genre's thematic conflict between wilderness and civilization. Clint Eastwood's *Unforgiven* (1992) stars Eastwood himself as Bill Munny, a farmer and father enlisted as a hired gun on the basis of his faded (and dubious) reputation as a former gunslinger. Munny resists violent action until the murder of his friend and partner, Ned (Morgan Freeman), reawakens the ruthless desperado within him [1]. Johnny Depp's character in Jim Jarmusch's allegorical Western *Dead Man* (1995) begins his journey west as a hopelessly meek and inept accountant but is gradually transformed into a deadly outlaw by both the figurative and literal wilderness [2].

Whereas gangster icons such as James Cagney are compact and manic, Western stars, from the silent era's William S. Hart through Henry Fonda and John Wayne and on up to Clint Eastwood, are outsized but relatively subdued performers.

All of the tertiary character types found in Westerns have a role to play in this overarching conflict between the wild and settled West. Native Americans are both ruthless savages and noble personifications of dignity and honor. Prostitutes are products of lawlessness but often long for marriage and family. Schoolmarms are educated and cultured, yet are irresistibly drawn to the frontier and the men who roam it. The greenhorn character may be sophisticated back East, but he is an inexperienced bumbler (and, as such, a perfect surrogate for the viewer) when it comes to the ways of the West. His transformation into a skilled cowboy/gunfighter/lawman embodies the Western ideal of renewal.

More than any genre, the American Western is linked to place. But the West is not necessarily a particular place. The genre may be set on the prairie, in the mountains, or in the desert. But whatever the setting, the landscape is a dominant visual and thematic element that represents another Western duality: it's a deadly wilderness of stunning natural beauty. Because setting is of such primary importance, Westerns are dominated by daylight exterior shots and scenes. As a result, Westerns were among the first films to be shot almost exclusively

ern's thematic forces. Cowboys may fight the Indians, but they are also symbols of rootless resisters of encroaching development. Whatever his particular stance and occupation, the Western hero is typically a man of action, not words. He is resistant to—or at least uncomfortable with—the trappings of civilization, even in those common cases where he serves as a civilizing agent. *Shane*'s gunfighter protagonist sacrifices himself to defend the homesteader, but he rides off into oblivion rather than settling down and taking up a plow himself.

The actors associated with the genre reflect the quiet power of the laconic characters they repeatedly play.

LOOKING AT MOVIES
GENRE: THE WESTERN

VIDEO This tutorial explores the form and conventions of the Western.

Civilization and wilderness

This archetypal scene from John Ford's *My Darling Clementine* (1946) demonstrates the tension (and inevitable attraction) between encroaching civilization and the wide open Wild West that lies at the heart of most Western-genre narrative conflicts. Deadly gunfighter turned reluctant lawman Wyatt Earp (Henry Fonda) escorts Clementine (Cathy Downs), a refined and educated woman from the East, to a community dance held in the bare bones of a not-yet-constructed church surrounded by desert and mountains.

on location. (When the Hollywood noir classic *Sunset Boulevard* needs to get a film-industry character out of town, it gets him a job on a Western.) The Western landscape is not limited to background information. The big skies and wide open spaces are used to symbolize both limitless possibility and an untamable environment. For this reason, Westerns favor extreme long shots in which the landscape dwarfs human subjects and the primitive outposts of civilization.

The Musical

The musical tells its story using characters that express themselves with song and/or dance. The actors sing ev-

ery line of dialogue in a few musicals, such as Jacques Demy's *The Umbrellas of Cherbourg* (1964), and those musicals from the 1930s featuring Fred Astaire and Ginger Rogers focus more on dancing than singing. But for the most part, musicals feature a combination of music, singing, dancing, and spoken dialogue.

Unlike many genres, the musical film genre was not born out of any specific political or cultural moment or preexisting literary genre. But musical performance was already a well-established entertainment long before the invention of the movie camera. The long-standing traditions of religious pageants, opera, operetta, and ballet all present narrative within a musical context. Musical comedies similar in structure to movie musicals were popular on British and American stages throughout much of the nineteenth century.

So it was inevitable that the dazzling movement, formal spectacle, and emotional eloquence inherent in musical performance would eventually join forces with the expressive power of cinema. But two hurdles stood in the way of the union. First, the early film industry had to create a workable system for recording and projecting sound—a process more than 25 years in the making. The next obstacle had less to do with mechanical engineering and more with audience perceptions. Because the new medium of motion-picture photography was closely associated with documentation and thus naturalism, the idea of otherwise realistic scenarios suddenly interrupted by characters bursting into song didn't seem to fit with the movies. Therefore, cinema had to establish a context that would allow for musical performance but still lend itself to relatively authentic performances and dramatic situations, as well as spoken dialogue.

The first major movie to incorporate extended synchronized sound sequences provided the solution. Alan Crosland's *The Jazz Singer* (1927) was a backstage musical. This kind of film placed the story in a performance setting (almost always Broadway), so that the characters were singers and dancers whose job it was to rehearse and stage songs anyway. By placing its narrative in this very specific setting, this early musical incarnation established some of the genre's most fixed plot and character elements. Backstage-musical stories typically revolved around a promising young performer searching for her big show-business break, or a talented singer/dancer protagonist pressured by a love interest or family member to leave show business, or a struggling company of singers and dancers determined to mount a big show. Many backstage narratives managed to combine two or more of these standard storylines. These musicals had their own set of character types, including the hard-bitten producer, the gifted ingenue, the insecure (i.e., less talented) star, and the faltering veteran with a heart of gold.

It might be assumed that since the backstage musical's songs were all performed as either rehearsals or productions within the framework of an externalized Broadway show, these songs would be missing the emotional power provided by a direct connection to the characters' lives. But in practice, the lyrics and context were usually presented in such a way as to underscore the performing character's state of mind or personal situation.

1

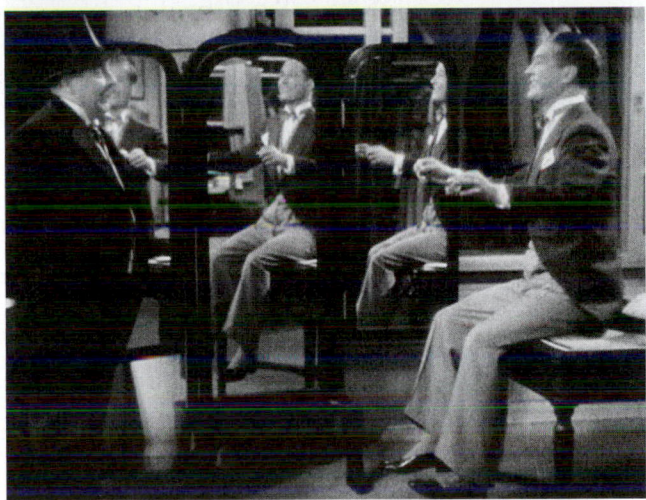

2

Backstage and integrated musicals

Early Hollywood musicals like Harry Beaumont's *The Broadway Melody* (1929) [1] constructed their narratives around the rehearsal and performance of a musical stage show, a setting that provided an intriguing backdrop, narrative conflict, and a context that allowed the characters to sing and dance without testing verisimilitude. Within a few years, integrated musicals like Rouben Mamoulian's *Love Me Tonight* (1932) [2] proved that audiences were already willing to accept characters who burst into song in everyday situations, such as a tailor (Maurice Chevalier) who sings an ode to romantic love as he measures a customer for a suit.

Backstage musicals had been around for only a few years when so-called integrated musicals like Rouben Mamoulian's *Love Me Tonight* (1932) freed the genre from the Broadway setting. (Mamoulian also directed *Applause*, a pioneering 1929 backstage musical.) As the term implies, the integrated musical assimilated singing and dancing with conventional spoken dramatic action;

Contemporary musicals

Like both of its predecessors, *Pitch Perfect 3* (2017; director Trish Sie) is a traditional backstage musical. The principal characters are promising young performers mounting a show in hopes of achieving stardom. Although some songs convey situation and state of mind, they all are delivered in a verisimilar context of rehearsals or performances [1]. Damien Chazelle's *La La Land* (2016) is an integrated musical in which otherwise realistic characters can burst into song at any time to express emotion and enhance a dramatic situation.

characters now could burst into song (or dance) as part of any situation. Of course, most of these musicals reserve musical performance for key dramatic moments, such as when a character declares her love, her goal, or her emotional state. Sometimes these songs are delivered to another character, but they may also be directed inward—a sort of sung soliloquy—or even aimed directly at the viewer.

Part of the pleasure of watching integrated musicals comes from the potentially dramatic shifts in tone and style required to move between dramatic and musical performance. Audiences have learned to appreciate the stylistic prowess required to balance these two seemingly incompatible entertainments, along with the whimsy or poignancy such combinations are capable of generating. Only in a musical can downtrodden factory workers erupt into a celebratory tune, as in Lars von

Trier's *Dancer in the Dark* (2000), or can the drivers stuck in a Los Angeles traffic jam dance out of their cars to sing about moving to Hollywood to pursue show business dreams, as in Damien Chazelle's *La La Land* (2016). The integrated musical, as these examples illustrate, freed the genre from the Broadway backdrop and allowed the musical to apply its unique stylings to a virtually limitless range of stories, characters, and settings.

While traditional musicals still tend to use the romantic comedy for their narrative template, contemporary movies have mixed the musical with a variety of other genres and cinema styles. Director Trey Parker has created credible musicals in the context of an extended *South Park* episode (*South Park: Bigger, Longer & Uncut*, 1999), a Michael Bay–style action movie performed by marionettes (*Team America: World Police*, 2004), and the only prosecuted case of cannibalism in United States history (*Cannibal! The Musical*, 1996). The genre dominated animated features from Walt Disney Studios for almost 60 years. Even television programs have gotten into the act: *The Simpsons*, *Community*, and *The Flash* have all created special musical episodes. The entire *Crazy Ex-Girlfriend* series is an integrated musical; *Glee* was a multi-episode backstage musical.

Evolution and Transformation of Genre

Filmmakers are rarely satisfied to leave things as they are. Thus, as with all things cinematic, genre is in constant transition. Writers and directors, recognizing genre's narrative, thematic, and aesthetic potential, cannot resist blending ingredients gleaned from multiple styles in an attempt to invent exciting new hybrids. The seemingly impossible marriage of the horror and musical genres has resulted in a number of successful horror-musical fusions, including Jim Sharman's *The Rocky Horror Picture Show* (1975), Frank Oz's *Little Shop of Horrors* (1986), and Takashi Miike's *The Happiness of the Katakuris* (2001). Antonia Bird melded horror with another unlikely genre partner, the Western, for her 1999 film *Ravenous*. Sometimes the hybridization takes the form of a pastiche, as in Quentin Tarantino's Kill Bill cycle (*Vol. 1*, 2003; *Vol. 2*, 2004), films that borrow not only from the Japanese *chambara* (sword-fighting) genre but from many Hollywood genres, including the Western, musical, thriller, action, horror, and gangster.

Genres develop inwardly as well. Subgenres occur when areas of narrative or stylistic specialization arise within a single genre. Thus Westerns can be divided into revenge Westerns, spaghetti Westerns, bounty-hunter Westerns, cattle-drive Westerns, gunfighter Westerns, cavalry Westerns, and so on. Zombie movies, slasher flicks, vampire films, the splatter movie, and torture porn are a few of the many manifestations of the horror genre.

To understand how complex a single genre can become, let's consider comedy. Movies are categorized as comedies because they make us laugh, but we quickly realize that each one is unique because it is funny in its own way. Comedies, in fact, prove why movie genres exist. They give us what we expect, they make us laugh and ask for more, and they make money, often in spite of themselves. As a result, the comic genre in the movies has evolved into such a complex system that we rely on defined subgenres to keep track of comedy's development.

The silent-movie comedies of the 1920s featured such legends as Max Linder, Charlie Chaplin, Buster Keaton, Roscoe "Fatty" Arbuckle, Harry Langdon, and Harold Lloyd, many of whom worked for producer Mack Sennett. These films were known as slapstick comedies because aggression or violent behavior, not verbal humor, was the source of the laughs. (The term *slapstick* refers to the two pieces of wood, hinged together, that clowns used to produce a sharp noise that simulated the sound of one person striking another.)

After the arrival of sound, movie comedy continued the sight gags of the slapstick tradition (Laurel and Hardy, the Marx Brothers, W. C. Fields), and it also increasingly relied on verbal wit. Through the 1930s, a wide variety of subgenres developed: comedy of wit (Ernst Lubitsch's *Trouble in Paradise*, 1932); romantic comedy (Rouben Mamoulian's *Love Me Tonight*, 1932), screwball comedy (Frank Capra's *It Happened One Night*, 1934), farce (any Marx Brothers movie), and sentimental comedy, often with a political twist (Frank Capra's *Meet John Doe*, 1941).

By the 1940s, comedy was perhaps the most popular genre in American movies, and it remains that way today, although another group of subgenres has developed, most in response to our changing cultural expectations of what is funny and what is now permissible to laugh at.

These include light sex comedies (Billy Wilder's *Some Like It Hot*, 1959), gross-out sex comedies (Bobby and Peter Farrelly's *There's Something about Mary*, 1998), and neurotic sex comedies (almost any Woody Allen movie), as well as satire laced with black comedy (Stanley Kubrick's *Dr. Strangelove or: How I Learned to Stop Worrying and Love the Bomb*, 1964), outrageous farce (Mel Brooks's *The Producers*, 1968, and Susan Stroman's musical remake, 2005), and a whole subgenre of comedy that is associated with the name of the comedian featured—from Charlie Chaplin in the silent era to Jacques Tati and Jerry Lewis in the 1950s to Whoopie Goldberg and Jim Carrey in the 1990s to more recent headliners such as Will Ferrell, Kevin Hart, and Melissa McCarthy.

The recent wave of what film critic Stephen Holden calls the "boys-will-be-babies-until-they-are-forced-to-grow-up school of arrested-development comedies"[6] seems to have spawned the beginnings of a new comic subgenre. These genre contenders include *The 40-Year-Old Virgin* (2005; director Judd Apatow); *The Hangover* (2009; director Todd Phillips); and *Neighbors* (2014; director Nicholas Stoller). Women characters broke into this formerly all-male subgenre in 2011 with the hit *Bridesmaids* (director Paul Feig). Recent entries include *Girls Trip* (2017; director Malcolm D. Lee) and *Bad Moms* (2016; directors Jon Lucas and Scott Moore).

On one hand, as a form of cinematic language, genres involve filmic realities—however stereotyped—that audiences can easily recognize and understand, and that film distributors can market (e.g., "the scariest thriller ever made"). On the other hand, genres evolve, changing with the times and adapting to audience expectations, which are in turn influenced by a large range of factors—technological, cultural, social, political, economic, and so on. **Generic transformation** is the process by which a particular genre is adapted to meet the expectations of a changing society. Arguably, genres that don't evolve lose the audience's interest quickly and fade away. Horror movies' monsters have evolved from somewhat sympathetic literary figures like *Frankenstein* into increasingly prolific serial killers, then into seductive vampires, and on into apocalyptic zombies.

Westerns began as reverent projections of how the United States saw itself: individualistic, entrepreneurial, and unambiguously righteous. But as perceptions of America grew more complex, so did the genre's depiction

6. Stephen Holden, "Those Darn Kidults! The Menace of Eternal Youth," *New York Times* (November 7, 2008), Sec. C, p. c10.

In 2005, the Western was transformed in a powerful new way in Ang Lee's *Brokeback Mountain* (2005). Set in the 1960s and 1970s, the film features many of the traditional genre elements, including wide open spaces, a taciturn loner incapable of living inside conventional settled society, and ranch hands herding livestock together under difficult conditions. But *Brokeback Mountain* took those elements a significant step further: the cowboys at the center of this story fall in love with one another. At first glance, it might seem that a same-sex romance has no place in a genre rooted in macho action and conservative values. But in fact the more essential components of character duality and the tension between conformity and individuality made the Western a meaningful vehicle for experiencing this passionate but doomed relationship.

And new genres continue to emerge. Superhero movies were first adapted from comic books in the 1930s and 1940s, finally hit the mainstream in 1978 with the big-budget hit *Superman* (director Richard Donner), and their cultural presence has grown ever since. The resulting genre dominates our twenty-first century multiplexes.

The romantic vampire

Ever since Bela Lugosi first portrayed Count Dracula in Tod Browning's 1931 film *Dracula*, forbidden desire has been an essential ingredient of the vampire movie [1]. In recent years, much of the horror has been drained from the subgenre as audiences have fully embraced the vampire as a romantic figure. Films such as *The Twilight Saga: Eclipse* (2010; director David Slade) [2] and television series such as HBO's *True Blood* and CW's *The Vampire Diaries* feature attractive vampires who are ambivalent about their sinister appetites and dark powers—a contradiction that makes them irresistible to their mortal companions.

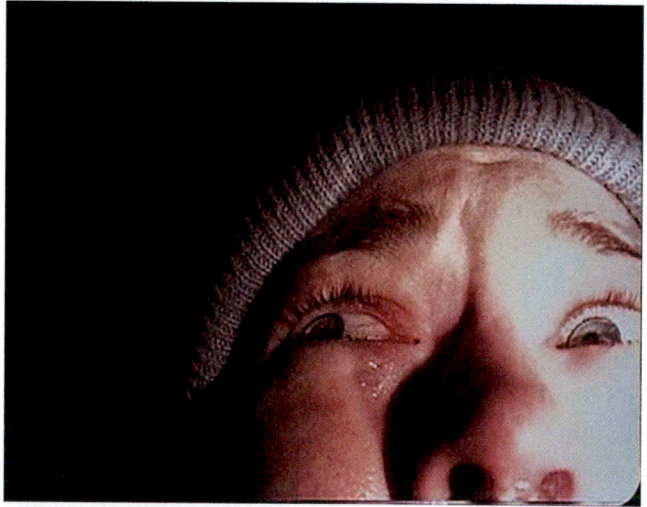

of the American West. For example, the protagonist of Robert Altman's *McCabe and Mrs. Miller* (1971), a Western released at the height of the Vietnam war, is an unscrupulous blowhard named McCabe (Warren Beatty). The civilization he brings to the wilderness is a house of prostitution. The resulting surrounding settlement is ultimately taken over by corrupt real estate speculators who hire hit men to eliminate McCabe. The movie ends with the newly erected church burning down and our bumbling hero forgotten and bleeding to death in a snowbank.

Found footage

In narrative films, the classification *found footage* refers to movies in which everything is presented as if it were preexisting nonfiction footage captured by participants in the events we see on-screen, only to be discovered and revealed later to a public audience. The immediacy and authenticity this "found" footage lends to a fictional story makes this approach especially applicable to horror films. *The Blair Witch Project* (1999) popularized found-footage horror with an Internet campaign that convinced many viewers that the discovered footage was real and the events presented actually happened.

Mixed genre

James Gunn's *Guardians of the Galaxy* (2014) is rife with Western genre archetypes, including righteous renegades, pitiless bounty hunters, a lawless frontier outpost, and a settlement threatened by ruthless savages. The outlaw protagonists risk their freedom (and their lives) to protect a civilization that wants no part of them or their wilderness ways. But this Western takes place in outer space, a speculative setting associated with the science-fiction genre. Showdowns are fought with laser blasters, and everyone rides rocket ships. The mysterious Infinity Stone the characters fight over epitomizes the menace of technology run amok behind the typical science-fiction antagonist.

Superhero movies feature protagonists with special powers that are either acquired via special suits and gadgets or imposed via some combination of freak accident, genetic mutation, immigration to Earth, and/or mad scientist. These protagonists wear costumes, have identity issues, and serve an often skeptical society by fighting super-villains who often have special powers of their own. Story formulas usually involve the origin of the protagonist's powers and/or a high-stakes struggle to defeat a villainous attempt to destroy a city, country, or universe. This mission is compromised by a combination of uncooperative authorities and the hero's love for a vulnerable mortal. The aforementioned identity issues are central to the themes explored by this genre; the same enviable abilities that make the hero super also isolate and burden the secretly flawed man (the superhero is almost always male) behind the mask. Out of necessity and by design, superhero movies offer dazzling special effects, elaborate costumes and makeup, extended action sequences, and stylized performances. This antirealistic visual spectacle feeds a cultural craving for cinematic escapism, yet there is surely more to the genre's popularity. Secret heroes with hidden powers appeal to viewers' inner aspirations. Forward-looking protagonists capable of affecting meaningful change give vicarious satisfaction to audiences that feel powerless to influence a dauntingly complex universe. Any movie that resonates with audiences and inspires imitators that turn a profit could be the beginning of another new movie genre.

What about Animation?

Animation is regularly classified as a distinct type of motion picture. Even the Academy Awards separates the top honor for narrative feature films into "Best Picture" and "Best Animated Feature" categories. Undeniably, **animated films** look different from other movies. But it's important to recognize that, while animation employs different mechanisms to create the multitude of still images that motion pictures require, animation is just a different form of moviemaking, not necessarily a singular type of movie.

In a 2008 interview, director Brad Bird (*Ratatouille, The Incredibles, The Iron Giant*) stresses that process is the only difference between animation and filmmaking that relies on conventional photography. Bird explains: "Storytelling is storytelling no matter what your

1

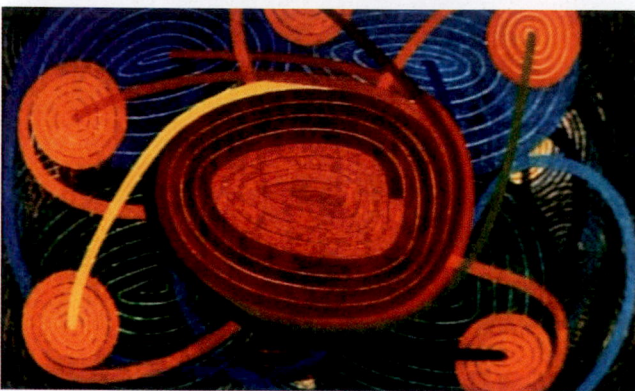

2

3

medium is. And the language of film is also the same. You're still using close ups and medium shots and long shots. You're still trying to introduce the audience to a character and get them to care."[7] In fact, animation techniques have been employed to make every type of movie described in this chapter. We are all familiar with animated narrative feature films; the animation process has been applied to hundreds of stories for adults and children, including examples from every major genre described earlier. In addition, a long tradition of experimental filmmaking consists entirely of abstract and representational animated images. Even documentaries occasionally use animation to represent events, ideas, and information that cannot be fully realized with conventional photography. Brett Morgen re-created undocumented courtroom scenes for portions of his documentary *Chicago 10* (2007); Ari Folman's war memoir *Waltz with Bashir* (2008) claims to be the first fully animated feature-length documentary. Michel Gondry's *Is the Man Who Is Tall Happy?* (2013) is a feature-length "animated conversation" with the linguist and philosopher Noam Chomsky.

Among the countless possible types and combinations of animation, three basic types are used widely today: hand-drawn (also known as traditional or cel animation), stop-motion animation, and computer animation (also known as 3-D animation). To create hand-drawn animation, animators draw or paint images that are then incorporated into a motion picture one drawing at a time. Because 24 frames equal 1 second of film time, the animator must draw 24 separate pictures to achieve 1 second of animation.

In 1914, Winsor McCay's classic animation *Gertie the Dinosaur* required more than 5,000 drawings on separate sheets of paper.[8] The difficulty of achieving fluid movement by perfectly matching and aligning so many characters and backgrounds led, the next year, to the development of cel animation. Animator Earl Hurd used clear celluloid sheets to create single backgrounds that could serve for multiple exposures of his main character. Thus he needed to draw only the part of the image that was in motion, typically the character or a small part of the character. Contemporary "hand-drawn" animation is now produced almost exclusively on computers. The images are still two-dimensional drawings created by animation artists, and they still employ multiple layers (the digital equivalent of cels). But the process of

Alternative animation

Animation isn't just for narrative. *Tower*, Keith Maitland's 2016 documentary about the 1966 shooting spree at the University of Texas at Austin, uses animation to visualize the memories of survivors [1]. The artist Oskar Fischinger began experimenting with abstract animation in 1926 [2]. The fifty avant-garde movies he animated, including *Motion Painting No. 1* (1947), influenced generations of animators and experimental filmmakers. Influential filmmakers like Jan Svankmejer and his stylistic progeny Stephen and Timothy Quay (known as the Brothers Quay) employ stop-motion animation to create dark and surreal movies like the Quays' *The Comb* (1990) [3].

7. Brad Bird, interview with Elvis Mitchell, *The Business*, KCRW Public Radio (May 5, 2008).

8. Charles Solomon and Ron Stark, *The Complete Kodak Animation Book* (Rochester, NY: Eastman Kodak Co., 1983), p. 14.

Persepolis

While digital animation now dominates the animated movie market, hand-drawn films like *Persepolis* (2007) still garner popular and critical attention. Marjane Satrapi's memoir of her childhood and adolescence in Iran and Paris (codirected with Vincent Paronnaud) broke with commercial animation practices by combining its adult subject matter with graphic, mostly black-and-white drawings that emphasized a two-dimensional universe.

drawing, combining, and capturing those images is now accomplished with a series of sophisticated software programs. This traditional method, once the animation standard, has largely been replaced by 3-D computer animation. But beautiful examples still reach theater screens, including Tomm Moore's *Song of the Sea* (2014), Nora Twomey's *The Breadwinner* (2017), and the movies produced by Japan's Studio Ghibli, such as *The Wind Rises* (2013; director Hayao Miyazaki) and *Your Name* (2016; director Makoto Shinkai).

Stop-motion records the movement of objects (toys, puppets, clay figures, or cutouts) with a motion-picture camera; the animator moves the objects slightly for each recorded frame. The objects moved and photographed for stop-motion animation can be full-scale or miniature models, puppets made of cloth or clay, or cutouts of other drawings or pictures. Underneath some figures are armatures, or skeletons, with fine joints and pivots, which hold the figures in place between the animators' careful manipulations.

Among the first American stop-motion films was *The Dinosaur and the Missing Link: A Prehistoric Tragedy* (1915) by Willis H. O'Brien. He went on to animate stop-motion dinosaurs for Harry O. Hoyt's live-action adventure *The Lost World* (1925), then added giant apes to his repertoire with Merian C. Cooper and Ernest B. Schoedsack's *King Kong* (1933) and Schoedsack's *Mighty Joe Young* (1949). Inspired by O'Brien's work on *King Kong*, Ray Harryhausen set out at thirteen to become a stop-motion animator and is now most famous for his work on Don Chaffey's *Jason and the Argonauts* (1963), a Hollywood retelling of the ancient Greek legend. Feature-length animated narrative films that use this technique include Nick Park's *Wallace & Gromit in The Curse of the Were-Rabbit* (2005), Wes Anderson's *Isle of Dogs* (2018), and Tim Burton's *Frankenweenie* (2012). For the stop-motion films *ParaNorman* (2012; directors Chris Butler and Sam Fell) and *Kubo and the Two Strings* (2016; director Travis Knight), the filmmakers at the Laika animation studio adapted digital systems to the stop-motion process. The many interchangeable physical components they used to create different character expressions and poses are designed on computers and fabricated using 3-D printers.

Computer animation uses the virtual world of 3-D computer-modeling software to generate the animation.

This technique is also known as 3-D animation, not because it produces an actual physical three-dimensional object or is necessarily screened using a 3-D projection system, but because the approach digitally constructs virtual characters, objects, and backgrounds in all three dimensions, so that these components can be composed and captured from any perspective or position. John Lasseter's *Toy Story* (1995), produced by Pixar, was the first feature-length computer-animated film. A commercial and critical success, it humanized computer animation and obliterated the fear that computer animation was limited to shiny, abstract objects floating in strange worlds. *Toy Story*'s focus on plastic toys, however, helped disguise the limitations of early digital animation techniques. Six more years of development enabled digitally animated movies such as Pete Docter and David Silverman's *Monsters, Inc.* (2001) to present compelling characters with visually interesting skin, hair, and fur.

The production of digitally animated features begins with less costly traditional techniques that allow filmmakers to test ideas and characters before starting the difficult and expensive computer-animation process. In the early phases, filmmakers use sketches, storyboards, scripts, pantomime, puppets, models, and voice performances to begin developing stories and characters. By creating a digital wire-frame character with virtual joints and anchor points, computer animators use technology to do some of the same work that stop-motion animators do by hand. Typically, a clay model is created and then scanned into the computer with the use of a digital pen or laser scanner. Animal and human actors can be dressed in black suits with small white circles attached to joints and extremities, allowing for "motion capture" of the distinctive actors' movements. The advanced motion-capture technologies developed to animate the Na'vi natives in *Avatar* blur the line between animation and live action.

In digital animation, animators manipulate virtual skeletons or objects frame by frame on computers. To clothe the wire-frame figures with muscle, skin, fur, or hair, the animators use a digital process called texture mapping. Computer animators also "light" characters and scenes with virtual lights, employing traditional concepts used in theater and film. Specialists work on effects such as fire, explosions, and lightning. Compositing is the process of bringing all these elements together into one frame, and rendering is the process by which hundreds of computers combine all the elements at high resolution and in rich detail. Because the backgrounds, surface textures, lighting, and special effects require a tremendous amount of computer-processing power, animators typically work with wire-frame characters and unrendered backgrounds until all elements are finalized. At that point, a few seconds of screen time may take hundreds of computers many hours to render. Although the process is extremely expensive and labor intensive, computer animation's versatility and aesthetic potential have made it the method of choice for studio-produced feature animation. Aardman Animations, the Claymation production company behind the popular Wallace & Gromit movies, designed their project *Flushed Away* (2006; directors David Bowers and Sam Fell) with the stop-motion plasticine look of their popular Wallace & Gromit characters but created every frame of the film on a computer.

With the release of Hironobu Sakaguchi and Moto Sakakibara's *Final Fantasy: The Spirits Within* (2001), audiences were introduced to the most lifelike computer-animated human characters to date. To create these sophisticated representations, the filmmakers used an elaborate process (since dubbed "performance capture"): actors perform scenes in motion-capture ("mocap") suits that record millions of pieces of data that computers use to render the motion of **computer-generated imagery (CGI)** characters on-screen.

This process was so time-consuming and expensive that it contributed to the failure of the film's production company. Nonetheless, *Final Fantasy* gave birth to the first digitally animated human characters. But for many animators and audiences, "realistic" figures are not necessarily the ideal. In 2004, the stylized characters in Pixar's blockbuster *The Incredibles* (director Brad Bird) trumped the motion-capture-guided "lifelike" figures in Robert Zemeckis's *The Polar Express* in both box office and critical response.

Although there are many other potential reasons that audiences and analysts preferred *The Incredibles*, the key issue for many critics was an unsettling feeling that they couldn't shake while watching the characters in *The Polar Express*—a feeling that the whole thing wasn't heartwarming or endearing, but was instead simply creepy. Among fans of computer-generated imagery, there was considerable debate about why, exactly, *The Polar Express* left so many viewers feeling weird and uncomfortable rather than filled with the holiday spirit.

The uncanny valley

If a filmmaker strives for a high level of verisimilitude in computer-generated characters, as Robert Zemeckis did in *The Polar Express* (2004), he may risk taking the humanlike resemblance too far, causing viewers to notice every detail of the characters' appearance or movement that doesn't conform to the way real human beings actually look or move. Our emotional response to these "almost human" characters will, therefore, be unease and discomfort, not pleasure or empathy—a negative reaction known as the "uncanny valley."

Eventually, on blogs and listservs all over the Internet, a consensus was reached: *The Polar Express* had fallen into the "uncanny valley."

The uncanny valley is a theoretical concept first described in 1970 by a Japanese robotics engineer, Masahiro Mori. It states that the closer an object (a robot, an animated character) comes to resembling a human being in its motion and appearance, the more positive our emotional response to that object becomes until suddenly, at some point of very close (but not perfect) resemblance, our emotional response turns from empathy to revulsion. This revulsion or uneasiness, Mori says, is the result of a basic human tendency to look for anomalies in the appearance of other human beings. When an object such as a robot or an animated character is so anthropomorphic that it is nearly indistinguishable from a human being, we monitor the appearance of that object very closely and become extremely sensitive to any small anomalies that might identify the object as not fully human. For whatever reason, these anomalies create in many people a shudder of discomfort similar to the feeling we have when we watch a zombie movie or see an actual corpse. In both cases, what we see is both human and not fully human, and the contradiction produces a very negative reaction. As a result, viewers found it easy to identify and sympathize with the highly stylized characters in *The Incredibles* but responded to the much more realistic figures in *The Polar Express* with unease and discomfort.

Nevertheless, animation and photographed "reality" can and do get along. Animation has been incorporated into live-action movies since the 1920s. Today, many traditionally photographed movies integrate computer-generated animation into characters, backgrounds, and special effects. Computer-animated characters have been convincingly interacting on-screen with flesh-and-blood performers since Gollum in Peter Jackson's Lord of the Rings trilogy (2001–3). Gollum's digital descendants include Caesar in the Planet of the Apes series and the castaway tiger in Ang Lee's *Life of Pi* (2012).

This now commonplace intrusion into conventional motion pictures is only one example of the animation explosion made possible by the recent emergence of new technologies and growing audience demand. As a result, ten animated narrative features were given a major theatrical release in the United States in 2014. Countless more forgo the movie-house release and go straight to DVD. Network and cable television stations, including at least one dedicated entirely to cartoons, broadcast hundreds of animated series, specials, and advertisements. The video-game market exploits animation to create animated characters and situations that allow the viewer an unprecedented level of interaction. Viewers have always been drawn to cinema's ability to immerse them in environments, events, and images impossible in daily life. Animation simply expands that capacity.

Looking at the Types of Movies in *The Lego Movie*

Let's end this chapter by examining one film that borrows from many different types of movies. *The Lego Movie* (2014, directors Phil Lord and Christopher Miller) is the cinematic equivalent of a pastiche, a term applied to a work of art that imitates or appropriates recognizable stylistic elements from a previous work or works.[9] To help understand the concept, think of a pastiche as a collage in which pieces of preexisting drawings and paintings are snipped out and arranged on a new canvas into a cohesive assembly. Even though viewers may be able to identify the source of many of the different pieces, we can still appreciate the new form and draw meaning specific to the resulting self-contained creation. In fact,

9. Roland Green, ed., *Princeton Encyclopedia of Poetry and Poetics*, 4th ed. (Princeton, NJ: Princeton University Press, 2012), p. 1005.

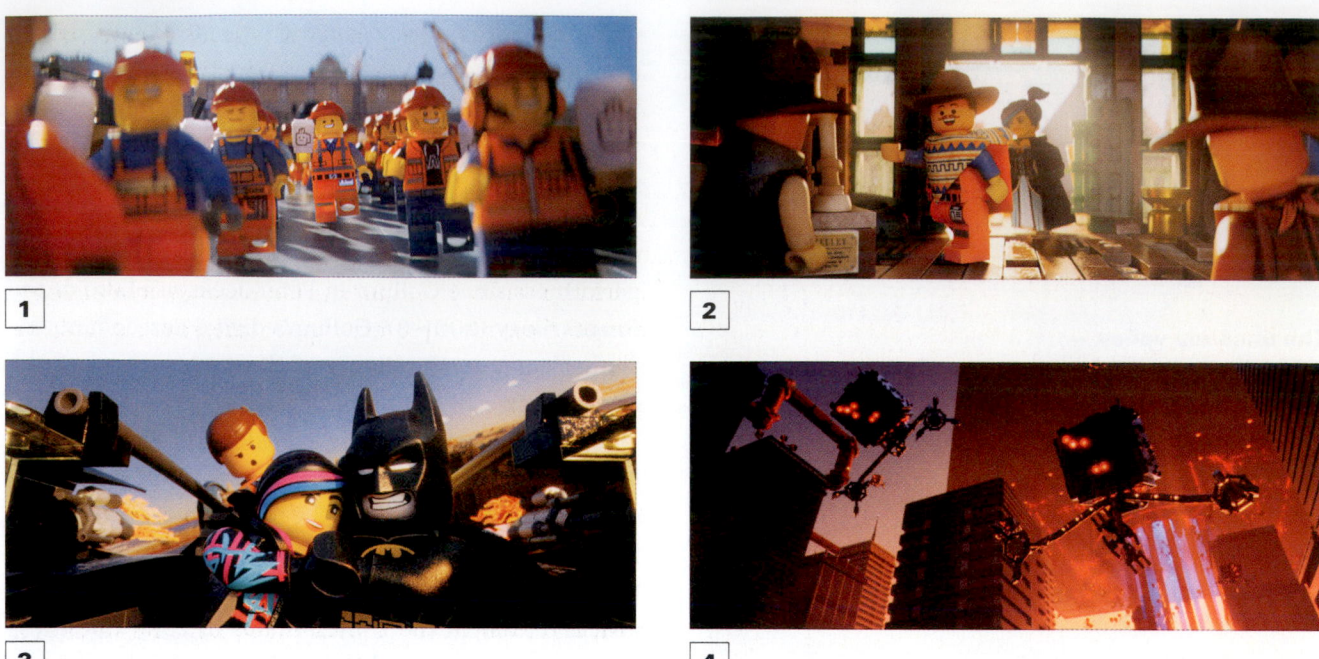

The Lego Movie as genre pastiche

The Lego Movie combines a multitude of genre elements and cultural references to tell a classic quest story. A choreographed musical sequence introduces the primary setting of Bricksburg and establishes the unlikely hero Emmet as a complacent conformist [1]. Later, when he attempts to live up to his "special one" status, Emmet's awkward greenhorn posturing hushes a raucous saloon in a classic Western sequence [2]. Batman is his rival in a romantic comedy love story [3]. Finally, the villain President Business's climactic Kragle attack on Bricksburg unfolds like an epic science-fiction alien invasion [4].

we may get as much pleasure from recognizing the various appropriations as from experiencing the cohesive combination.[10]

The pastiche in *The Lego Movie* begins with the very specific (and unusual) way the film looks and moves. *The Lego Movie* is a big-budget computer-animated extravaganza made by a team of more than 630 professionals, but it owes its distinct style to primitive homemade stop-motion videos. Amateur filmmakers began making short stop-motion animations using Lego bricks in the early 1970s. The interlocking bricks are ideal for building a wide variety of small-scale sets and props, and the Lego figures are easy to pose and position. The technique's unavoidable chunky look and jerky movement gave the movies an endearing common aesthetic. The method gained popularity in the 1990s as affordable consumer-grade digital cameras gave more people access to the

technology necessary to make the movies and the Internet made it possible to share them. The new millennium brought a growing array of Lego products along with increased video streaming bandwidth; soon there were websites, film festivals, and YouTube channels dedicated to what had come to be known as *brickfilms*.

It wasn't long before market forces and creative minds saw the mutual benefit of bringing brickfilms to the big screen. But the producer Dan Lin and the codirectors Phil Lord and Christopher Miller realized that the labor-intensive stop-motion process would be unfeasible for the large scale they envisioned for what would become *The Lego Movie*. So 3-D computer animation was put to work creating an expansive action-packed universe built entirely of plastic bricks. Determined to keep the look and feel of a brickfilm, the animators retained the hand-made method's herky-jerky character movement

1

2

The Lego Movie origins

The computer-animated blockbuster borrowed the distinct style of low-budget stop-motion animations made using Lego bricks, like David Betteridge's 1989 music video for a British group called Ethereal [1]. Although *The Lego Movie* was computer animated, the filmmakers adapted the brickfilms' boxy look and restricted character movements. They even applied realistic-looking chips, scratches, and grime to their digital creations [2].

and even digitally applied fingerprints, scratches, and dirt onto the animated bricks and figures.[11]

But the look wasn't the only element *The Lego Movie* borrowed. The pastiche approach that dominates the film's narrative also is rooted in the brickfilm. Because

Lego sets are often packaged with specific themes, many brickfilms incorporated Lego-version items and figures associated with pirates, police, and space travel or film series such as Star Wars, Lord of the Rings, Harry Potter, and Batman. Brickfilm narratives often referenced or re-created characters, situations, dialogue, and behavior associated with the incorporated components. As the brickfilm evolved, filmmakers increasingly combined elements from multiple, often disparate, sources. A pirate might team up with a spaceman; Harry Potter could duel Darth Vader.

The Lego Movie takes that approach to the extreme. The opening introduces Lord Business (voiced by Will Ferrell) and immediately establishes the film as a pastiche that samples a smorgasbord of cultural and genre sources. With his elaborate costume, diabolical bombast, and homogeneous henchmen, Lord Business is a combination of fantasy film evil wizard and superhero movie super-villain. Lord Business storms a castle for a showdown with Vitruvius (voiced by Morgan Freeman), a character with his own fantasy origins: he is a wise, long-haired, magic-staff-wielding wizard in the mold of The Hobbit's Gandalf and Harry Potter's Professor Dumbledore. Vitruvius declares himself a "master builder," a *Lego Movie* character type with the power to build almost anything from the materials at hand—a disclosure that reveals still more cultural references. Vitruvius was the name of a notable first-century BCE Roman engineer; *The Master Builder* is the title of a famous nineteenth-century play by Henrik Ibsen about a successful but doomed architect. Lord Business defeats Vitruvius, then takes gleeful possession of the mysterious superweapon known as "the Kragle." Vitruvius interrupts the villain's triumphant gloating with a prophecy about a "piece of resistance" that can disarm the Kragle: one day, a "special one"—another master builder—will find a hidden piece of resistance and save the world.

Within two minutes, a familiar story formula has been established. Like Harry Potter, the original Star Wars saga, The Matrix, The Lord of the Rings, and even The Hunger Games series, *The Lego Movie* is structured around an almost impossible quest led by a chosen one to save the world from a seemingly unstoppable evil. This story formula goes deeper than genre; the quest is rooted in what the eminent mythologist Joseph Campbell termed the

11. Meredith Woerner, "The Makers of *The LEGO Movie* Take Apart Their Creation Brick by Brick," https://io9.gizmodo.com/the-makers-of-the-lego-movie-take-apart-their-creation-1516662564 (accessed March 19, 2015).

"monomyth," or "hero's journey." According to Campbell, this basic pattern can be found in the folktales and myths—and movies—of multiple cultures:

> A hero ventures forth from the world of common day into a region of supernatural wonder: fabulous forces are there encountered and a decisive victory is won: the hero comes back from this mysterious adventure with the power to bestow boons on his fellow man.[12]

The cultural prevalence of the hero's journey archetype makes it likely that most viewers of *The Lego Movie* will recall the familiar story pattern the moment it's introduced. So when we meet the construction worker Emmet Brickowoski in the next scene, we instantly recognize him as our hero and anticipate his imminent departure on the aforementioned narrative excursion. He is an oblivious nincompoop, but that does nothing to undermine our assumption. On the contrary, Emmet's incompetence reinforces our expectation. Cinematic history is full of protagonists who initially appear unfit for the challenges to come. So we immediately assume that Emmet will discover the piece of resistance, amass allies, and ultimately prove his unlikely worth to save Bricksburg from President (aka Lord) Business. The predictability does not diminish either our pleasure or investment. When it comes to narrative and genre, much of a viewer's gratification comes not from unexpected revelations, but from experiencing how familiar elements and formulas operate and intersect within a particular scenario—in this case, a multilevel, magical universe constructed entirely out of interlocking plastic bricks and ruled by a meticulous tyrant determined to eliminate innovation by freezing everything in place with the Kragle (i.e., Krazy Glue).

The next few scenes assimilate genre elements and situations to launch Emmet on his quest. First, the kind of elaborately choreographed song-and-dance sequence usually found in an integrated musical establishes Emmet and the rest of Bricksburg's eager ignorance and instruction-following conformity. After stumbling upon the piece of resistance (which is the cap to the Kragle glue), Emmet awakens in the glare of a spotlight to find himself in a spartan interrogation room being questioned by a hostile policeman—a situation found in film noir crime movies and television police procedurals. Emmet himself acknowledges the reference when he asks the Bad Cop: "I watch a lot of cop shows on TV . . . isn't there supposed to be a good cop?" Bad Cop (voiced by Liam Neeson) straps Emmet into the "melting chamber," an elaborate laser-shooting execution apparatus straight out of an early James Bond movie. A master builder named Wyldstyle drops in just in time to rescue Emmet in a scene dominated by action movie presentation elements like fast-paced editing, swooping moving camera, bullet time, and gravity-defying martial arts acrobatics. Emmet and his savior flee a barrage of Bad Cop gunfire and land in an alley, where Wyldstyle immediately constructs a giant motorcycle from the objects at hand.

Wyldstyle's extravagant escape vehicle offers a visual metaphor for how *The Lego Movie* incorporates multiple types of movies into a somewhat cluttered, but ultimately cohesive, whole. None of the many and various components necessarily match, but each fulfills a function in service of a shared purpose. The movie conveys an entertaining cinematic story; the motorcycle propels our protagonists through a chase scene and into a secret portal that leads to a stratified series of discrete worlds and genres. Emmet's journey begins in a Western, adopts a romantic comedy love story, enlists superheroes and cyborg pirates, and culminates with a science-fiction apocalypse.

In the end, the narrative expands into a traditional live-action family drama. *The Lego Movie*'s segregated universe is revealed to be the creation of an adult Lego hobbyist with a strict sense of tradition and a striking resemblance to President Business. It turns out that the narrative's exuberant narrative hodgepodge is the product of his son, a boy too imaginative to be controlled by convention. Emmet's quest is complete when both the father and his Lego counterpart accept the inevitability of innovation. It's only fitting that the humble brickfilm has the last word. *The Lego Movie*'s final credit sequence is a genuine stop-motion animation constructed entirely of actual plastic blocks.

---

12. Joseph Campbell, *The Hero with a Thousand Faces*, 2nd ed. (Princeton, NJ: Princeton University Press, 1949), p. 30.

ANALYZING TYPES OF MOVIES

This chapter's broad survey of the different types of movies should make clear that movies are divided into narrative, documentary, and experimental (and animation) categories, and that each of these has evolved a great variety of ways to express ideas, information, and meaning. What's more, the longer cinema is around, the more ways filmmakers find to borrow, reference, and blend elements from other types to best serve their own vision. Now that you have studied the various ways that movies are differentiated and classified, you should be able to identify what basic type or genre a movie belongs to, recognize how the movie uses the elements of form and content particular to its film type, and appreciate and understand instances when the filmmakers incorporate styles and approaches rooted in other film types.

SCREENING CHECKLIST: TYPES OF MOVIES

✔ If the film is a documentary, is it factual, instructional, persuasive, or propaganda—or a blend of two or more of these documentary approaches? Consider the movie's relationship with the spectator and with relative truth. Does it appear to be attempting to present events and ideas in as objective a manner as is cinematically possible or does it make a specific persuasive argument?

✔ If the film is a documentary, is it expository, observational, poetic, participatory, performative, reflexive, or a hybrid of two or more of these modes? What elements of form and content lead you to this conclusion?

✔ Look for ways in which the documentary employs narrative. Are the events portrayed selected and organized so they tell a story?

✔ Ask yourself how this movie compares to other documentary films you've seen. Think about your formal expectations of nonfiction movies: talking-head interviews, voice-over narration, archival footage, and so on. Does this movie conform to those expectations? If not, how does it convey information and meaning in ways that are different from a typical documentary?

✔ To analyze an experimental movie, try to apply Fred Camper's criteria for experimental cinema. Which of the listed characteristics does the movie seem to fit, and which of them does it diverge from?

✔ Remember that experimental filmmakers often seek to defy expectations and easy characterization. So consider effect and intent. How does the movie make you feel, think, or react? Do you think the filmmaker intended these effects? If so, what elements of form and content contribute to this effect?

✔ When watching an experimental film, be especially aware of your expectations of what a movie should look like and what the movie experience should be. If the movie disappoints or confounds your expectations, do your best to let go of what you've been conditioned to assume, and try to encounter the movie on its own terms. Remember that many experimental movies, unlike documentaries and narrative films, are open to individual interpretation.

✔ Since most of the movies that you study in your introductory film class will be narrative films, you should ask whether a particular film can be linked with a specific genre and, if so, to what extent it does or does not fulfill your expectations of that genre.

✔ Be aware that many movies borrow or blend elements of multiple genres. Look for familiar formal, narrative, and thematic genre elements, and ask yourself how and why this film uses them.

Questions for Review

1. What are the four related ways we can define the term *narrative*?

2. What are the main differences among the three basic types of movies?

3. What are the four basic approaches to content and message documentary cinema? How are these approaches blended and reinterpreted by contemporary documentary filmmakers?

4. What are documentary theorist Bill Nichols's six modes of documentary filmmaking?

5. What are Fred Camper's six characteristics that most experimental films share?

6. What is a hybrid movie? What are some of the ways that documentary, narrative, and experimental movies intersect?

7. What is genre? How does genre affect the way movies are made and received?

8. What are the six sets of conventions used to define and classify film genres?

9. What are the formal and narrative elements common to each of the six movie genres described in the chapter?

10. How does animation differ from the other three basic types of movies?

Three Billboards Outside Ebbing, Missouri (2017). Martin McDonagh, director. Pictured: Frances McDormand.

ELEMENTS OF NARRATIVE

4

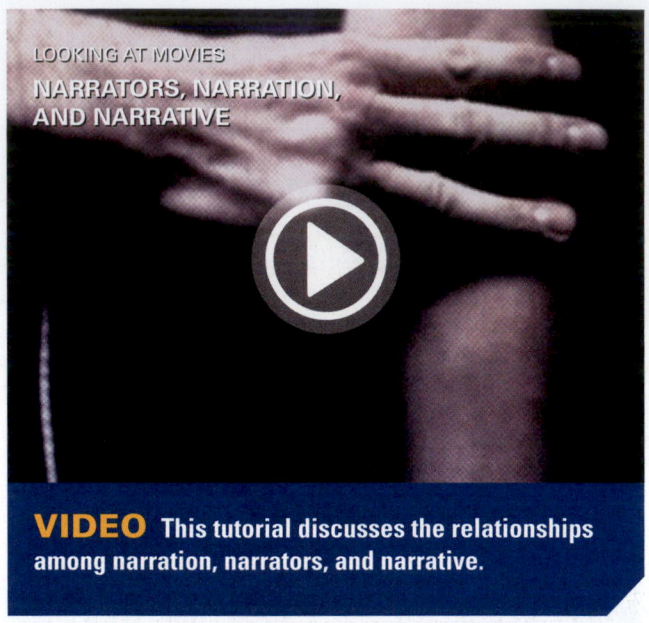

LOOKING AT MOVIES
NARRATORS, NARRATION, AND NARRATIVE

VIDEO This tutorial discusses the relationships among narration, narrators, and narrative.

What Is Narrative?

We've already gotten a good start on exploring the question "What is narrative?" in Chapters 1 and 3. As we begin this chapter dedicated to the subject, we have already learned the following things about narrative:

❯ A narrative is a story.

❯ Narrative movies are fiction films, as opposed to other movie modes, such as documentary or experimental.

❯ At the broadest conceptual level, narrative is a cinematic structure in which the filmmakers have selected and arranged events in a cause-and-effect sequence occurring over time.

❯ When we think of it that way, almost all movies, even documentaries and experimental films, employ some level of narrative.

❯ In fact, narrative permeates more than just the world of movies—it infuses our culture and our lives. Whether we're describing a sporting event, relating

a dream, recalling a memory, or telling a joke, we humans tend to order events so they will convey meaning and engage the recipient.

❯ Because story and storytelling are so ingrained in our everyday lives, including the movies we watch, it's all too easy to take narrative for granted.

To better recognize and understand how it works, we'll first need to break down narrative into the various components that contribute to telling a cinematic story. Let's start with two closely related (and potentially confusing) terms: *narration* and *narrator*.

Narration is the *act of telling* the story. The **narrator** is *who or what tells* the story. In other words, the *narrator* delivers the *narration* that conveys the *narrative*. Filmmakers employ different approaches to the concept of narrator (who or what tells the story) and narration (how that story is told) to shape the viewer's experience of the narrative (the story itself).

In every movie, the camera is the primary narrator. Its narration consists of the many visual elements it captures and arranges in every composition in every shot. A narrative moment in Alfred Hitchcock's *Notorious* (1946) offers an easy example. In the previous scene, we watched the Nazi conspirator Alexander Sebastian discover that his wife, Alicia, is a U.S. government spy. Naturally, he tells his mother, and she begins brainstorming ways to discreetly eliminate his unfaithful spouse. A shot in the next scene begins focused on the betrayed

The camera as narrator

The camera (and everything that implies) is the primary narrator in every film. In this moving camera shot from Alfred Hitchcock's *Notorious*, the camera shows us the Nazi conspirator Alexander urging his wife, Alicia, to drink her coffee [1], moves to fill the screen with a close-up of her cup [2], follows it to her lips [3], and then turns to connect the action to her vengeful mother-in-law [4]. The next shot features Alicia holding her throbbing head [5]. The camera has told us a story: *Alexander and his mother are poisoning Alicia.*

Multiple narrators in *Stranger than Fiction*

In Marc Forster's *Stranger than Fiction* (2006), the third-person narrator doesn't just help *tell* the story—it becomes a player in the narrative itself. Harold Crick hears the voice-over narrating his own story and learns that his character is slated for an imminent demise. His goal of finding the source of the narration and changing his own tragic ending forms the basis of the rest of the story. As the story progresses, we meet the depressed novelist crafting Harold's destiny. Does knowing the character who wrote it make the narration first person or is the novel's text a third-person narrator that exists apart from the novelist character? Or is it narration at all if a character can hear it? Participating in these inconsistencies is part of the fun—and playful strangeness—of *Stranger than Fiction*.

husband as he urges his wife to drink her coffee. The camera drifts down from his smirking face and across the breakfast table until Alicia's coffee cup fills the screen. When she picks it up, the camera follows it to her lips. As Alicia begins to drink, the camera moves over to feature her scheming mother-in-law contentedly stitching her needlepoint. The next shot shows Alicia rubbing her forehead and looking decidedly under the weather. Throughout the sequence, the *camera narrator* tells us that Alicia's coffee is poisoned by selecting what we see and shaping when and how we see it. In other words, the camera tells the story.

And, of course, other cinematic elements contribute to the narration. The lighting, set design, makeup, and performances in each shot, as well as the associations achieved through the juxtaposition of images, all contribute to our engagement with the narrative. Maybe it would be more accurate to state that in every movie, the filmmakers and their creative techniques constitute the primary narrator. Nonetheless, it is a little more streamlined to think of all that as "the camera."

And the camera isn't always a movie's only narrator. Some movies use more than one narrator to deliver the narration. This narration can be in the form of a *character's* particular perspective on the narrative's events.

A **first-person narrator** is a character in the narrative who typically imparts information in the form of **voice-over narration**, which is when we hear a character's voice *over* the picture without actually seeing the character speak the words. This technique of a character speaking to the audience allows us to *hear* one narration—from the first-person character narrator—while simultaneously *watching* the narration provided by our narrator camera.

The combination of these narrator partners may be relatively straightforward, such as in Danny Boyle's *Trainspotting* (1996), when the first-person voice-over primer to heroin addiction delivered by Renton plays over the opening sequences depicting the lives of the addicts that populate the story.

A richer, more complex experience of the narrative is possible when the first-person narration contrasts somehow with what we see on-screen. The first-person narrators of writer/director Terrence Malick's first two films (*Badlands*, 1973, and *Days of Heaven*, 1978) are naive and sometimes deluded young women who attempt to rationalize and even romanticize events and actions we can see for ourselves. The conflict between what the camera is telling us and the perspective provided by the first-person narrator can expand our relationship with the narrative beyond anything a camera alone can deliver.

And some movies push this relationship even further. These films don't limit the first-person narrative to voice-over narration. Instead, the first-person narrator character interrupts the narrative to deliver **direct address narration** directly to the audience, thus breaking the "fourth wall" that traditionally separates the viewer from the two-dimensional fiction on-screen.

Ferris Bueller's Day Off (1986; director John Hughes) features a charismatic slacker who seduces his fellow characters as well as his audience. Ferris frequently pauses the on-screen action to gaze into our eyes and charm us with his own personal take on the story he inhabits. Ferris Bueller follows in the footsteps of other smooth-talking scoundrels who break the fourth wall, most notably Tony Richardson's *Tom Jones* (1963) and Lewis Gilbert's *Alfie* (1966). Other direct address narration is more confrontational. Michel Haneke's *Funny Games* (2007) challenges the viewer to endure a brutal game of cat and mouse played by a pair of psychotic young men. After they take a young family hostage, the attackers goad their victims to wager on their own survival. When their prey try to refuse the bet, one of the attackers turns to confront the audience with a string of questions: "I mean, what do you think? Do you think they stand a chance? You're on their side, aren't you? Who are you betting on, huh?" By breaking the fourth wall in this way, Haneke forces the audience to acknowledge our participation in the violence. The filmmaker implies that, in watching this senseless cruelty, we're complicit in it.

Sometimes the voice-over narrator isn't even someone in the movie. Voice-over narration can also be expressed by a voice imposed from outside of the narrative. Standing at a remove from the action allows this **third-person narrator** to provide information not accessible to a narrator who is also a participant in the story. Like the author of the story, the third-person narrator knows all and can thus provide objective context to any situation.

Wes Anderson's *The Royal Tenenbaums* (2001) opens with a third-person voice-over relating the history of a family of eccentric geniuses delivered in the dispassionate tone of a documentary reporter. But even this seemingly remote narrator provides more than just information. The deadpan delivery layers a sort of literary seriousness over an extended series of comic scenes detailing the family's brilliant successes and staggering failures. Later, the third-person narrator interjects to let us into a character's head at a crucial narrative moment. Royal Tenenbaum, a manipulative con man, has wormed his way back into his estranged family by pretending to be dying of cancer. When he is caught in the lie, his non-apology is predictably slick: "Look, I know I'm going to be the bad guy on this one, but I just want to say that the last six days have been the best six days of probably my whole life." As the words leave his lips, he pauses as if momentarily confused. The third-person narrator speaks up to illuminate the situation: "Immediately after making this statement, Royal realized that it was true." All this goes to show that movies can use a number of possible narrators—even combinations of narrators. Likewise, movies employ more than one approach to *narration*.

Narration can be **omniscient**, meaning it knows all and can tell us whatever it wants us to know. Omniscient narration has *unrestricted* access to all aspects of the narrative. It can provide *any* character's experiences and perceptions, as well as information that *no* character knows. An omniscient camera shows the audience whatever it needs to in order to best tell the story.

An espionage thriller like *Notorious* involves deception, double crosses, and mixed motives. To fully exploit

1

2

3

Narrators

In *The Royal Tenenbaums* (2001), the camera narrator tells us the story by displaying evidence of the children Royal abandoned, as well as the slick con man himself as he delivers what we assume to be the latest in a string of manipulative lies [1]. But the narrative deepens when the third-person voice-over interjects to tell the audience that he's telling the truth this time. In the opening and closing scenes of *The Spectacular Now* (2013; director James Ponsoldt), Sutter Keely helps tell the story in a couple of ways. The camera shows us the character's image and actions on-screen, and his first-person narration (in the form of a surprisingly candid college admissions essay) is delivered in voice-over [2]. The title character in *Deadpool* (2016; director Tim Miller) does more than just break the fourth wall to directly address narration to the audience, but he also repeatedly comments upon the fact that he's a character in a movie.

the intrigue, the camera narrator must show us what is going on with multiple characters and situations. We watch Alicia uncover evidence in the wine cellar proving her husband's Nazi plotting while he hosts a party in oblivious bliss upstairs. We see him plot her death after he learns she's an American spy. We writhe with

Restricted narration in *Black Swan*

Restricted narration makes watching *Black Swan* (2010) both excruciating and ultimately cathartic. The audience must endure every moment of the story locked inside the increasingly unreliable perspective of Nina, a prima ballerina, as the pressures of her role drive her insane. For many viewers, the ultimate experience of sharing Nina's transcendent final performance makes enduring her breakdown worthwhile.

frustration watching her fellow agent (and love interest) blame her disheveled appearance on a hangover, when we know that all she's been drinking is poisoned coffee. A large part of the pleasure in experiencing such a story comes from knowing more than the characters and anticipating what will happen if and when they learn the whole truth.

Another Hitchcock movie, *Rear Window* (1954), tells the story of Jeff Jeffries, a man of action stuck in his apartment in a wheelchair while recovering from a badly broken leg. To amuse himself, Jeff begins spying on his neighbors. The recreational snooping suddenly takes a dark turn when he witnesses what may—or may not—be a murder.

For the viewer, the pleasure of watching Jeff slowly unravel the mystery depends on being restricted to his incomplete understanding of the events unfolding outside his rear window. As a result, Hitchcock chose **restricted narration**, which limits the information it provides the audience to things known only to a single character. This approach encourages the audience to identify with the character's singular perspective on perplexing and frightening events—and invites us to participate in the gradual unlocking of the narrative's secrets.

Steven Soderbergh's *The Limey* (1999) uses a similar approach. For most of the film, the camera narrator restricts the narration. We see and hear only the thoughts, memories, perspectives, and experiences available to the character of Wilson as he doggedly pursues the mystery behind the death of his daughter. In fact, as the narrative progresses, the viewer gradually realizes that the movie's

highly stylized editing is not conveying the story events as they happened, but as they are recalled by Wilson on his way back to England after solving the mystery. It's a sort of visual first-person narration without voice-over.

Of course, nothing in cinema is absolute. Many films shift between restricted and omniscient narration depending on the needs of the story. Movies like *The Limey* enforce restricted narration for most of the story, only to switch to omniscient narration when it serves the narrative to expand our view on the action. For those few times when the narrative demands that the audience witness events outside Wilson's experience, the narration temporarily shifts into omniscient mode.

The deeper you look, the more complex and expressive cinema gets. But the general concepts at the foundation of cinematic storytelling are pretty straightforward. Just remember: the **narrative** is the story; narration is the act of telling the story; the narrator is who or what tells the story. In other words, the *narrator* delivers the *narration* that conveys the *narrative*.

Characters

Whether it's a pregnant teenager trying to find suitable parents to adopt her baby or a hobbit seeking to destroy an all-powerful ring, virtually every film narrative depends on two essential elements: a **character** pursuing a **goal**.

The nature of that pursuit depends on the character's background, position, personality, attitudes, and beliefs. These traits govern how the character reacts to opportunities and problems, makes decisions, acts upon those decisions, and deals with the consequences of those actions. The allies and adversaries (all of whom have traits of their own) that the character attracts are influenced by these traits, as are all interactions between these other various characters. And that pursuit, and all the decisions, actions, consequences, relationships, and interactions that intersect and influence it, is the story.

Imagine how different the story of The Hunger Games series would have been if Katniss Everdeen had been cautious, confident, and privileged instead of the insecure, irreverent, and angry young woman who impulsively volunteers to take her little sister's place at the reaping. Or in the case of the Harry Potter series, what if Ron Weasley, the insecure and unrefined product of a large rambunctious wizard family, had been the boy who lived, instead of the instinctive and strong-willed

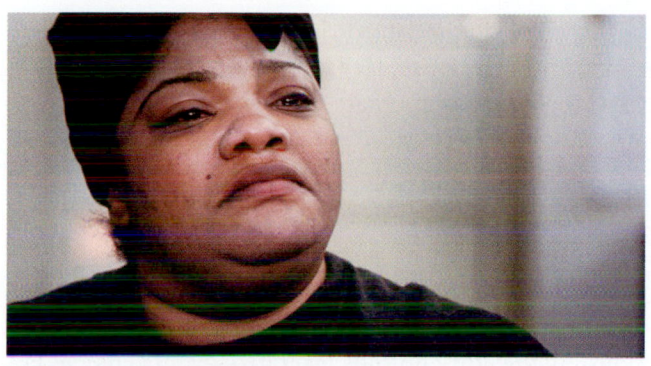

Round and flat characters in *Precious*

Different types of stories, and even different roles within the same story, call for different approaches to character traits, behavior, and development. *Precious: Based on the Novel "Push" by Sapphire* (2009; director Lee Daniels) features two remarkable characters: the illiterate teenager Precious and her abusive mother Mary. Each character is captivating in her own way, and the actresses who played them were both rightfully praised for their powerful performances. But the narrative requires that Mary be a flat character clearly defined by malicious anger and an inability to change [1]. In contrast, Precious must be a round character to drive a narrative built around revelation and transformation. At first glance, Precious appears to be slow-witted and apathetic, but as the story peels away at the layers of her complex personality, we (and Precious herself) learn that she's capable of imagination, ambition, bravery, intelligence, and insight [2].

neglected orphan Harry Potter? Better still, what if the earnest, intelligent, overachieving child-of-muggles Hermione was the *girl* who lived? Even if the goal remained the same in each of these hypothetical narratives, the character's traits would inspire choices and behavior that would lead them to a different path, and thus tell a different story.

The profound effect characters have on narrative comes in handy. After all, there are only so many stories in the world—consider how many movies sound interchangeable when reduced to a short description—but character traits may be assembled in infinite combinations. Each new character makes possible a different take on the same old story. Think of all the love stories or murder mysteries you've watched. The individual personalities falling in love and/or solving (and committing) crimes play a large part in keeping those archetypal narrative approaches fresh. The directors, actors, cinematographers, and designers responsible for putting the characters and their story on-screen build upon the characterizations in the screenplay to develop how exactly each character looks, speaks, and behaves in the movie.

Of course, some characters are more complicated than others. In literature, complex characters are known as **round characters**. They may possess numerous subtle, repressed, or even contradictory traits that can change significantly over the course of the story—sometimes surprisingly so. Because they display the complexity we associate with our own personalities, we tend to see round characters as more lifelike. In contrast, relatively uncomplicated **flat characters** exhibit few distinct traits and do not change significantly as the story progresses.[1] This doesn't mean that one character classification is any more legitimate than the other. Different types of stories call for different approaches to character traits, behavior, and development.

For example, the flamboyant Jack Sparrow is entertaining enough to drive the spectacular success of the Pirates of the Caribbean franchise; no one could call his character boring. But with Jack, what we see is what we get. His character is clearly and simply defined, and at the end of every installment he remains the same lovable scoundrel he was in the opening scene. The Pirates of the Caribbean movies benefit from Jack's flat character.

The coming-of-age drama *An Education* (2009; director Lone Scherfig) calls for a round character. Jenny Mellor is a complicated adolescent—she's smart but naive; she's both ambitious and insecure; she rebels against the same authorities whose approval she craves. Jenny

1. E. M. Forster, *Aspects of the Novel* (New York: Harcourt, Brace, 1927), pp. 103–118.

Character development in *District 9*

Progression is an essential narrative element, and the changes a character undergoes, especially when those changes involve some level of personal growth, are one of the most satisfying progressions movies have to offer. Neill Blomkamp's dystopian science-fiction thriller *District 9* (2009) explores the themes of racism and xenophobia with a story about the forced relocation of unwanted alien squatters. The posturing protagonist Wikus gets what's coming to him when his meddling results in his own inexorable transformation into one of the very aliens he persecuted. But it is the interior changes Wikus experiences that give his story meaning. The more he looks like a monster, the more human he becomes.

falls in love with a charming older man who introduces her to a glamorous new lifestyle of concerts, art auctions, martinis, and sex. She quickly blossoms into a cosmopolitan sophisticate with no use for anything as inane as school. But she does receive an education when David turns out to be a thief and a con man—a married con man at that. Jenny enters the story as a bright girl and leaves it as a wise woman.

Of course, as with most things in the movies, round and flat characters exist not in absolutes, but along a continuum that adjusts according to narrative and cinematic needs. Some characters are rounder than others, and vice versa. And flat characters are no more limited to crowd-pleasing blockbusters than are round characters confined to sophisticated dramas.

No one could call the hyperkinetic and provocative *Black Swan* (2010; director Darren Aronofsky) a simplistic movie. Natalie Portman's powerful performance as Nina, a ballerina driven to madness by her quest to inhabit a demanding role, deserved the critical and popular acclaim it received. Yet in many ways, Nina could be considered a flat character. Her traits are straightforward; she's a fearful, driven perfectionist. Throughout her excruciating journey to the final performance, even as she (apparently) physically transforms, Nina stub-

bornly clings to the same insecurities and flaws that she carried into the story. Her final direct address declaration is evidence of her inability to change.

On the other hand, Peter Quill, the reckless smart aleck at the center of the comic adventure *Guardians of the Galaxy* (2014; director James Gunn), would have to be considered at least somewhat rounded. After all, his seemingly selfish behavior is rooted in a tragic past that complicates any assessment of his actions and intentions. As the story unfolds, narrative events change Peter from an amoral (if amusing) thief to a hero willing to sacrifice himself to save the same civilization that condemned him to prison. Granted, he still steals—but with a strong sense of civic duty.

Whatever the shape of the character, narrative cannot exist if that character does not have a goal. The goal does not just give the character something to do (although that activity is important). It also gives the audience a chance to participate in the story by creating expectations that viewers want to see either fulfilled or surprised. More on that later—for now let's stick to how that goal affects our character.

The primary character who pursues the goal is known as the **protagonist**. The protagonist is sometimes referred to as the hero (or heroine), but this term can be misleading, since engaging narratives do not necessarily depend on worthy goals or brave and sympathetic characters. As Harry Potter or Katniss Everdeen can attest, it's certainly not a liability if the audience happens to like or admire the protagonist. But as long as the protagonist actively pursues the goal in an interesting way, the viewer cannot help becoming invested in that pursuit and, by extension, the story.

Seemingly unsympathetic protagonists chasing less than noble goals are sometimes called **antiheroes**: Walter Neff is a cocky insurance agent whose quest is to murder his lover's husband so he can have her body—and her inheritance—all to himself. Walter's no Boy Scout, but when watching *Double Indemnity* (1944; director Billy Wilder), it's tough not to root for him to get away with murder. Jordan Belfort doesn't kill anyone, but he does manipulate markets, cheat investors, and break innumerable laws to make outrageous profits (which he uses to fuel an aggressively excessive lifestyle). However, while watching *The Wolf of Wall Street* (2013; director Martin Scorsese), we take some pleasure in Belfort's triumphs and can't help pitying him when his empire collapses.

In fact, impeccable characters are rare in modern movies. Narrative craves imperfect characters because those imperfections provide **obstacles**, another essential building block of storytelling. We'll discuss obstacles in the section on narrative structure. For now, simply consider that a romance about a shy, awkward boy in love with the head cheerleader is likely to be much more interesting than a love story between the two most beautiful and popular kids in school. Character imperfections and flaws also give characters room to grow. As the previous discussion of round and flat characters indicated, character development is central to many movie narratives.

In *Precious,* the title character's struggle to escape her violent mother and learn to read transforms her from a numbed victim into an assertive and expressive young woman. Precious's character development makes watching this often-harrowing movie a satisfying and rewarding narrative experience. On the other end of the entertainment spectrum, part of the pleasure of seeing *Big Hero Six* (2014; directors Don Hall and Chris Williams) is the young inventor Hiro's progress from an embittered loner to the dynamic leader of a team of oddball crime-fighters. Even his sidekick Baymax (who is figuratively and literally a round character) experiences character growth. What begins as a benign, inflated health-care robot winds up a sentient superhero.

It's easy to understand what motivates these protagonists to pursue their goals. Precious is abused by her mother and inspired by her new teacher. Hiro discovers that a masked man has stolen his greatest invention. Baymax is programmed to heal. Most narrative relies on this character motivation. If the viewer doesn't believe or understand a character's actions, the story's verisimilitude, and thus the audience's identification with the protagonist's efforts, will be compromised. We believe and connect with the quest Mattie Ross undertakes to track down Tom Chaney in the Coen brothers' *True Grit* (2010; directed by Joel and Ethan Coen) because we know that he killed her father. Sonny Wortzik, the protagonist of Sidney Lumet's *Dog Day Afternoon* (1975), robs a bank (or tries to) because he needs money to pay for his lover's sex-change operation. We might not agree with Sonny's goal or his methods, but understanding the impulse behind his actions allows us to engage in his story.

Some storytellers use expectations of clear character motivation against their audience to create a specific ex-

Goals and needs

The intersection of narrative and character provides for a wide range of narrative structures and outcomes. Not every movie must have a happy ending, and the stories that do provide a happy ending are not always dependent on the protagonist achieving his or her goal. In *Rocky*, the ending is satisfying even though the underdog boxer loses the heavyweight match, because his gutsy performance gives him back the self-respect he was missing at the beginning of the story. Ultimately, the audience identifies with Rocky's psychological need even more than his goal of defeating the mighty Apollo Creed.

perience of the narrative. In David Lynch's *Blue Velvet* (1986), Frank Booth's heinous behavior includes huffing a strange gas, stroking a swatch of velvet, and blurting "mommy" before assaulting his sex slave. Frank's bizarre behavior isn't motivated in a way that we can easily identify, but his outlandish actions only deepen our fascination with this disturbing movie's vivid mystery.

Characters are frequently motivated by basic psychological needs that can profoundly influence the narrative, even when the character is oblivious to the interior motivation directing his or her behavior. This character need often supports the pursuit of the goal. In John G. Avildsen's classic boxing picture *Rocky* (1976), the title character *wants* to win the big fight, but his *need* for self-respect compels him to train hard and endure extraordinary physical punishment on his difficult road to the final bell of the championship bout. The narrative goes to great lengths to establish Rocky's need to regain his self-respect. The movie spends 54 minutes detailing Rocky's pathetic existence and degraded social status before he is offered a goal in the form of a serendipitous shot at a title fight. In the end, Rocky loses the big fight, but the audience still feels rewarded because his gutsy performance proves that he has fulfilled his need.

Sometimes, a story may gain a level of complexity by endowing a character with a need that is, in fact, in direct conflict with his goal. C. C. Baxter, the protagonist of Billy Wilder's *The Apartment* (1960), is a lonely man whose job is crunching numbers at a huge insurance company. C. C. *needs* love, but he *wants* to be a big shot. Sick of being a lowly cog in the company machine, C. C. does everything possible to achieve his goal of being promoted to an executive position, including letting his supervisors use his apartment as a base for their illicit affairs. C. C. is disheartened when he discovers that Fran, the office elevator operator he very much likes, is the mistress his boss Mr. Sheldrake has been entertaining in C. C.'s apartment. But C. C. continues to pursue his goal, even after he discovers the jilted Fran dying of a drug overdose in a suicide attempt. As he nurses Fran back to health, C. C.'s need for love progressively complicates his pursuit of corporate power. Ultimately, Sheldrake rewards C. C.'s discretion with the long-coveted job promotion, and our hero must choose between his goal and his need.

For the purposes of clarity, we've focused our discussion of character on the protagonist. But, of course, most stories require a number of players. And many of these secondary characters, including those who support or share the protagonist's objective as well as those who oppose it, may have their own goals and needs. Typically, the traits and storylines of these characters are not as developed as that of our protagonist. These characters' primary function is to serve the narrative by helping to move the story forward or flesh out the motivations of the protagonist.

Narrative Structure

Movies use a narrative structure that is very similar to the way that events are organized by novelists, short-story writers, playwrights, comedians, and other storytellers. In all these cases, the basic formula that has evolved is calculated to engage and satisfy the receiver of the story.

The use of the word *formula* can be misleading. Most stories may follow the same general progression, but narrative is not a single simple recipe. Like pizza, among the many beauties of narrative structure is its malleability. We all know a pizza when we see it, but very few pies look or taste exactly the same. Once the chef knows the basic formula and the purpose of each individual ingredient, she has a certain amount of creative freedom

when creating her own personal concoction—as long as it still tastes good when it comes out of the oven. Just as good cooks know when and how to bend the rules, so do the most effective cinematic storytellers recognize how to adjust narrative structure to serve their own particular style and story.

In order to organize story events into a recognizable progression, some screenwriters break the narrative into three acts, or sections; others prefer to divide the action into five acts; others—particularly television writers—employ a seven-act structure. Not that it really matters to the audience. Our experience of the story as a continuous sequence of events is not affected by any particular screenwriter's organizational approach to partitioning the narrative development.[2]

For our purposes, we might as well keep it simple. Most narratives can be broken into three basic pieces that essentially function as the beginning, middle, and end of the story. Each section performs a fundamental narrative task. The first act sets up the story; the second (and longest) act develops it; the third act resolves it. Of course, nothing as expressive and engaging as cinematic storytelling can be quite *that* simple. Each of these narrative components involves a few moving parts.

To begin with, the setup in the first act has to tell us what kind of a story we're about to experience by establishing the **normal world**. A movie's first few minutes lay out the rules of the universe that we will inhabit (or at least witness) for the next couple of hours. Once we as viewers know whether we've entered a world of talking dogs or wartime chaos—or whatever the case may be—we'll know how to appraise and approach the events to come. Our expectations of the story also depend on learning the movie's tone. Are we about to watch a grim drama, a whimsical fantasy, or something else altogether? It's up to the events and situations presented in the first act to let us know.

Character, which we already know to be the linchpin of the story, must also be established. The narrative often begins by revealing something about the protagonist's current situation, often by showing him engaged in an action that also reveals some of those essential character traits we discussed earlier in the chapter.

For example, in the Coen brothers' *The Big Lebowski* (1988), we first meet Jeff Lebowski—known to his friends as The Dude—as he shuffles into a supermarket dairy sec-

---

2. David Howard and Edward Mabley, *The Tools of Screenwriting* (New York: St. Martin's Griffin, 1981), p. 24.

Establishing the normal world
The first scene of the Coen brothers' cult movie *The Big Lebowski* tells us what we need to know to understand and evaluate the narrative and its inhabitants. This offbeat comedy features a protagonist who wears a bathrobe in public, samples half and half in the supermarket, and writes checks for 69 cents. We are now armed with an understanding of the character that will help us appreciate The Dude's particular response to the situations the story presents to him.

tion dressed in sunglasses, pajama shorts, flip-flops, and a well-worn bathrobe. The Dude scrutinizes the assortment like a connoisseur in a wine cellar, then cracks open a carton of half and half to sniff the contents. In the next shot, he pays for his selection with a check for 69 cents.

Before we even learn his name, we know that The Dude is a free spirit who plays by his own rules. He's a slob, is not necessarily smart, and is certainly not ambitious—but he does have standards. Thus we already have some of the essential information we'll need to anticipate and appreciate his particular response to the events and situations the narrative is about to present. We have been initiated into the story's comic, absurdist tone and are also becoming acquainted with the movie's normal world: Jeff Lebowski inhabits a decidedly unglamorous Los Angeles sprawl of dilapidated bungalows, strip malls, and bowling alleys.

Now that the character and his world have been established, it's time to get the story started. For this to happen, something must occur to change that normal world. The inciting incident (also known as the **catalyst**) presents the character with the goal that will drive the rest of the narrative.

In The Dude's case, the inciting incident happens the moment he gets home from the supermarket. Two thugs ambush him, shove his head in the toilet, and demand a large amount of missing money. It turns out that it's

a case of mistaken identity—they're looking for a much richer Jeffrey Lebowski. To demonstrate his displeasure with this revelation, one of the attackers urinates on The Dude's beloved rug. The next day, our scruffy little Lebowski goes to see the big Lebowski about getting his rug replaced—and the story has begun.

Most inciting incidents and the resulting character goals are easy to spot. In *Black Swan*, Nina the ballerina is offered a chance at the lead role in *Swan Lake,* so she resolves to dance the part to perfection. When Tom Chaney guns down Mattie Ross's father in Fort Smith, Arkansas, in *True Grit*, the young girl swears vengeance. Dorothy, the protagonist of *The Wizard of Oz* (1939; director Victor Fleming), realizes that there's no place like home after a tornado deposits her among the munchkins.

Not all goals are this straightforward. Some goals shift—Luke Skywalker sets off to rescue a princess but winds up taking on the Death Star. The Dude sets off to replace a rug and winds up a pawn in someone else's mystery. The goal changes every day for William James, the danger-addicted protagonist of Kathryn Bigelow's Iraq war drama *The Hurt Locker* (2008)—but it's always the same goal: defuse the bomb before it explodes. Ultimately, James's toughest battle is with his own inner demons.

Whatever the goal, the nature of the pursuit depends on the individual character. Nina trains, panics, and sprouts black feathers. Mattie gets on the first train to Fort Smith and scours the frontier town for a lawman with true grit. Dorothy follows the Yellow Brick Road. This active pursuit of the goal signals the beginning of the second act.

The moment Dorothy is off to see the Wizard, the audience begins to ask themselves what screenwriters call the central question: Will she ever get back to Kansas? Whether the question whispers within our subconscious mind or we shout it at the screen, it is this expectation, this impulse to learn what happens and how it happens, that keeps us engaged with the narrative. We need to know if Nina will learn to let go and embrace the Black Swan inside her—and hold on to her sanity. We must find out if the spunky teenager Mattie can actually manage to wrangle Rooster Cogburn and track down the elusive Tom Chaney. We want to see if Rocky can beat the odds and defeat Apollo Creed to become heavyweight champ.

Naturally, in most cases, we want the answer to the central question to be yes. The irony, however, is that if the goal is quickly and easily attained, our story is over.

Plot points in *The Grand Budapest Hotel*

Screenwriting specialist Syd Field describes "plot points" as significant events that turn the narrative in a new direction.[3] For example, the development of *The Grand Budapest Hotel* (2014; director Wes Anderson) is profoundly influenced by the death of Madame D. The plot point leads to her convoluted last will and testament being contested by her greedy heirs, her lover Gustave stealing the priceless painting he believes is rightfully his, and a high-stakes search for the butler accused of her murder [1]. Likewise, the moment when Agatha discovers Madame D.'s rightful will hidden in the stolen painting certainly qualifies as a plot point [2]. Gustave inherits her vast fortune, buys the Grand Budapest Hotel, and promotes his faithful protégé Zero to head concierge.

This is where conflict comes in. Narrative depends on obstacles to block, or at least impede, our protagonist's quest for the goal. The person, people, creature, or force responsible for obstructing our protagonist is known as the **antagonist**. Sometimes, the identity and nature of the antagonist are clear-cut. The Wicked Witch is obviously the antagonist of *The Wizard of Oz* because she sets the scarecrow on fire, conjures a field of sleep-inducing poppies, and imprisons Dorothy. But we have to be careful with this term because, while most movies have a single—or at least primary—protagonist, the nature of the antagonist is much more variable. In *The Big Lebowski*, The Dude is beaten and bamboozled by a host of oddballs who each use him for their own obscure purposes. Presumably, the fugitive Tom Chaney is the antagonist of *True Grit*. After all, he gunned down Mattie's beloved father. But he doesn't even appear on-screen until the last third of the movie. Before she discovers (and is taken hostage by) Chaney, Mattie's obstacles are imposed by mostly well-meaning characters concerned for the safety of the plucky young heroine. So, just as not

every protagonist is a hero, not every antagonist is necessarily a villain. The imposing ballet director in *Black Swan* intimidates and manipulates Nina, but he also sincerely wants her to succeed. The restricted narration makes it difficult to determine any actual malice on the part of Nina's gifted understudy. Even the dark forces represented by Nina's apparent hallucinations play a role in pushing her toward greatness. Nina's greatest adversary is herself.

The antagonist need not even be human. Opposition and obstacles are supplied by a persistent shark in Steven Spielberg's *Jaws* (1975); the harsh elements and isolation of the Andes in Frank Marshall's *Alive* (1993); and a very stubborn rock in Danny Boyle's *127 Hours* (2010).

Whatever the source, obstacles are the second act's key ingredient. Let's take a closer look at *127 Hours* to see how obstacles help construct and drive the narrative. We'll start with a quick look at the setup in the first act: In the opening scene, the way the protagonist Aron Ralston packs establishes that he is a loner and an expe-

---

3. This description and elements of Figure 4.1 are based on Syd Field, *Screenplay: The Foundations of Screenwriting*, rev. ed. (New York: Delta, 2005), pp. 19–30.

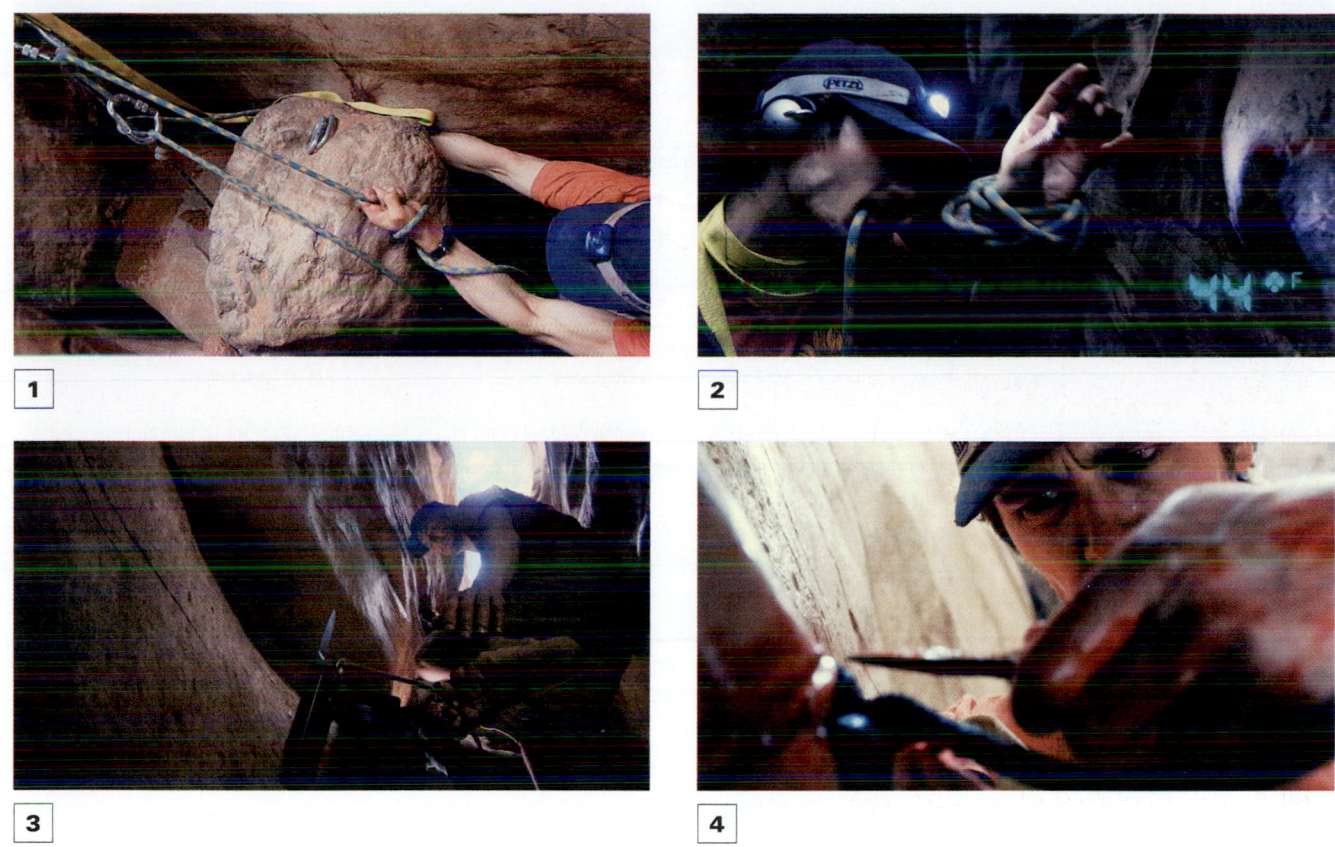

Narrative obstacles in *127 Hours*

Before the Aron Ralston character can finally achieve his narrative goal, he must first engage a series of obstacles. He tries (almost) every possible method of freeing his forearm from the stubborn rock pinning it to a remote canyon wall [1], insulates himself from freezing temperatures with his otherwise useless climbing rope [2], and retrieves his dropped multi-tool with his toes [3]. The crisis comes when Aron must take dramatic action or die [4].

rienced, if overconfident, outdoorsman. As he scrambles around his spartan apartment throwing climbing gear and provisions into a day bag, he doesn't bother to locate his missing Swiss Army knife and ignores a call from his sister. Now that the narration has conveyed some of Aron's flaws, he has some room to grow, and we're prepared to chart and appreciate his development as the adventure unfolds.

Aron ventures into the desert wilds of the remote Canyonlands National Park. Along the way, he reaffirms his character traits by luring two novice hikers to an exhilarating but dangerous plunge into an underground pool before leaving them behind to trek still deeper into the wilderness. In the process of descending a deep slot canyon, Aron dislodges a small boulder. The man and the rock both tumble down the narrow ravine. When they meet again at the bottom, the rock pins Aron's forearm to the canyon wall. This sudden event gives our protago-

nist a goal, supplies the story with conflict and an antagonist, and begins the second act.

The next hour of the movie is devoted to Aron's struggle to free himself. That struggle can be broken down into the series of obstacles he encounters. Aron will overcome some of them, circumvent others, and surrender to still more. Obviously, his tightly wedged forearm is Aron's greatest obstacle. He attempts to yank it loose, he uses his cheap multi-tool to try to chip away at the rock, and he builds a pulley system with his climbing ropes. Nothing works.

Aron must confront other obstacles as well. When he drops his multi-tool, he retrieves it with a long stick gripped between his toes. He defeats the freezing night temperatures by wrapping his climbing ropes around his legs. He rations his water. As time goes on, Aron must also deal with memories, hallucinations, hopelessness, and regret.

Figure 4.1 | NARRATIVE STRUCTURE SCHEMATIC

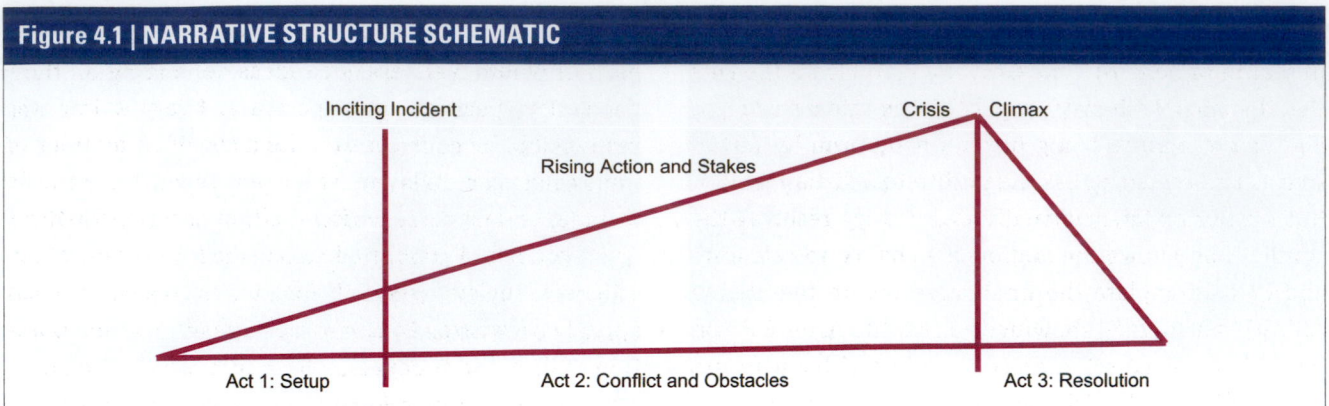

Narrative structure is typically characterized by a three-act format. The first act establishes character, setting, and tone, then introduces a goal with an inciting incident. The second act is structured around the protagonist's pursuit of the goal and the conflict and obstacles that must be confronted before the goal is either gained or lost at the peak of the rising action and stakes. The narrative then falls as the third act resolves the conflict, wraps up ongoing story lines, and gives the viewer a chance to either celebrate or mourn the dramatic result. Diagrams like this are helpful in visualizing a standard structure, but we should keep in mind that the shape any story takes is as flexible as the filmmakers want it to be.

And each time an attempt to dislodge the rock fails or a new obstacle presents itself, the audience asks itself the central question: Will Aron free himself and survive? When his water runs out and he begins to lose his grip on reality, a positive outcome seems increasingly unlikely and the question takes on greater urgency.

This is because the **stakes** are rising. In other words, the deeper we get into the story, the greater the risk to our protagonist. What begins as a possibility of getting lost progresses to the dangers of being trapped, which develops into what appears to be certain death. Of course, the ultimate magnitude of the stakes depends on the movie. By the end of *The Spectacular Now*, a troubled teenager may lose a meaningful friendship. Every life on Earth depends on the mission in *Interstellar* (2014; director Christopher Nolan).

The stakes are rising because the obstacles are becoming increasingly difficult for our protagonist to navigate. Over the course of the second act, narrative typically builds toward a peak, a breaking point of sorts, as the conflict intensifies and the goal remains out of reach. This **rising action** is illustrated in Figure 4.1. The tension it provokes enhances our engagement with the ongoing narrative. As the stakes and action rise in *127 Hours*, Aron undergoes character development. He reevaluates his selfish and solitary lifestyle, appreciates his family, and mourns a squandered relationship. In fact, Aron's encounters with memory provide some of the movie's most meaningful moments.

Eventually, our protagonist must face a seemingly insurmountable obstacle, and our story must reach a turning point and work its way toward resolution and the third and final act. This narrative peak is called the **crisis**. The goal is in its greatest jeopardy, and an affirmative answer to the central question seems all but impossible. In Aron Ralston's case, he's on the verge of death and out of options—almost.

The **climax** comes when the protagonist faces this major obstacle. In the process, usually the protagonist must take a great risk, make a significant sacrifice, or overcome a personal flaw. As the term implies, the climax tends to be the most impressive event in the movie. In *127 Hours*, Aron breaks the bone in his trapped arm, and then saws through what's left with a very dull blade. At the crisis point of *Star Wars: Episode IV—A New Hope* (1977; director George Lucas), Luke Skywalker's fellow fighter pilots have been decimated and the Death Star is within range of the rebel stronghold, so Luke uses the Force to drop two proton torpedoes into the evil Empire's exposed orifice. At the climax of *Black Swan*, Nina realizes she's been stabbed (by herself—it's complicated), but she dances onto the stage and gives the performance of her career.

Once the goal is either gained or lost, it's time for the **resolution**—the third act of falling action, in which the narrative wraps up loose ends and moves toward a conclusion. For some protagonists, the struggle continues well into this final act. After being trapped for 127 hours and amputating his own arm, Aron must still strike out in search of help. In *True Grit*, the recoil from the rifle that dispatches Chaney propels Mattie into a snake pit. She has to endure being bitten on the arm by rattlesnakes and carted across the prairie to a distant doctor. But sooner or later, virtually every story resolves the conflict and allows the audience a chance to celebrate and/or contemplate the final score before the credits roll. We see footage showing the real-life Aron Ralston (yes, it's a true story) as an active hiker with a wife and child. Luke, in blissful ignorance of his family history, enjoys a kiss from the princess. Surrounded by her adoring director and fellow dancers, the black swan declares her perfection. An elderly (and one-armed) Mattie pays homage to the crusty U.S. marshal whose true grit saved her life. Rocky hugs his girlfriend. The Dude abides—and bowls.

The Screenwriter

The screenwriter is responsible for coming up with this story, either from scratch or by adapting another source, such as a novel, play, memoir, or news story. Screenwriters build the narrative structure and devise every character, action, line of dialogue, and setting. And all this must be managed with the fewest words possible. Screenplay format is precisely prescribed—right down to page margins and font style and size—so that each script page represents 1 minute of screen time. The best screenwriters learn to craft concise but vivid descriptions of essential information so as to provide the director, cinematographer, designers, and actors a practical foundation that informs the collaborative creative process necessary to adapt the script to the screen. Many scripts are even described and arranged to take a step beyond written storytelling and suggest specific images, juxtapositions, and sequences. No rules determine how an idea should be developed or an existing literary property should be adapted into a film script, but the process usually consists of several stages and involves many rewrites. Likewise, no rule dictates the number of people who are eventually involved in the process. One person may write all the stages of the screenplay or may collaborate from the beginning with other screenwriters; sometimes the director is the sole screenwriter or co-screenwriter.

Before the breakdown of the Hollywood studio system and the emergence of the independent film, each of the major studios maintained its own staff of writers, each of whom were assigned ideas depending on their particular specialty and experience. Every writer was responsible by contract to write a specified number of films each year. Today, most scripts are written entirely by independent screenwriters (either as write-for-hires or on spec) and submitted as polished revisions. Many other screenplays, especially for movies created for mass appeal, are written by committee, meaning a collaboration of director, producer, editor, and others, including *script doctors* (professional screenwriters who are hired to review a screenplay and improve it). Whether working alone or in collaboration with others, a screenwriter significantly influences the screenplay and the completed movie and, thus, its artistic, critical, and box office success.

Elements of Narrative

Narrative theory (sometimes called *narratology*) has a long history, starting with Aristotle and continuing with great vigor today. Aristotle said that a good story should have three sequential parts: a beginning, a middle, and an end—a concept that has influenced the history of playwriting and screenwriting. French New Wave director Jean-Luc Godard, who helped revolutionize cinematic style in the 1950s, agreed that a story should have a beginning, a middle, and an end—but, he added, "not necessarily in that order." Given the cinema's extraordinary freedom and flexibility in handling time (especially compared to the limited ways the theater can handle time), the directors of some of the most challenging movies ever made—including many contemporary examples—would seem to agree with Godard.

The complexities of narratology are beyond the scope of this book, but we can begin our study by distinguishing between two fundamental elements: story and plot.

Story and Plot

Although in everyday conversation we might use the words *story* and *plot* interchangeably, they mean different things when we write and speak about movies. A movie's **story** consists of (1) all the narrative events that are explicitly presented on-screen plus (2) all the events that are implicit or that we infer to have happened

1

2

Narrative form and the biopic

A biographical movie, or biopic, provides particularly rich opportunities to ask why the filmmakers chose to tell the story the way they did. After all, the facts of the main character's life are objectively verifiable and follow a particular order. But as two recent biopics about the beat poet Allen Ginsberg demonstrate, cinematic storytellers can select and shape that material in many different ways to convey a variety of narrative experiences and interpretations. *Howl* (2010; director Rob Epstein) presents key ideas, sounds, and images from Ginsberg's life and work in a way that rejects the chronological order and cause-and-effect progression we expect from most narrative films. Stylized flashbacks from the poet's earlier life, Ginsberg (James Franco) performing his epic poem "Howl" [1], animation evoking the poem's imagery, and testimony in the obscenity trial incited by the ground-breaking poem are all juxtaposed in a fragmented montage that is just as interested in capturing the spirit of Ginsberg's poetry as it is with presenting a slice of his life. *Kill Your Darlings* (2013; director John Krokidas) is a more conventional coming-of-age narrative that chronicles the young Ginsberg's first year at Columbia University in New York. Young Ginsberg (Daniel Radcliffe) [2] breaks free of his dysfunctional family, is drawn into the orbit of proudly decadent literary rebels, has a sexual awakening, gets his heart broken, and witnesses a crime of passion. Like many biopics, this narrative provides not just a compelling story; it offers viewers a revealing (and often fictionalized) peek at the events and associations that helped form a famous persona.

but are not explicitly presented. The total world of the story—the events, characters, objects, settings, and sounds that form the world in which the story occurs—is called its **diegesis**, and the elements that make up the diegesis are called **diegetic elements**.

LOOKING AT MOVIES
DIEGETIC AND NONDIEGETIC ELEMENTS

VIDEO Learn more about diegetic and nondiegetic elements in this tutorial.

In the first scene of *The Social Network* (2010; director David Fincher), we see actors portraying Mark Zuckerberg and Erica Albright sitting together in a crowded bar. They are having a heated conversation—at least it's heated on one side. Mark is chattering a rapid-fire monologue involving SAT scores in China and rowing crew; Erica is struggling to clarify what exactly he's talking about. Everything we experience in this scene is part of the movie's diegesis, including the other bar patrons and the muffled dissonance of the crowd's chatter mixed with the White Stripes' "Ball and Biscuit" playing on an unseen jukebox. Of course, we pay special attention to what the featured characters say and how they look saying it. From this explicitly presented information, we are able to infer still more story information that we have not witnessed on-screen. They've been here a while—their beers are half empty, and they're in the middle of an ongoing conversation—and they're a couple. Watching their interaction, we can even guess the nature and duration of Mark and Erica's relationship. As the conversation intensifies, we can pick up on still more implicit information. Mark is obsessed with getting into a prestigious student club—his intensity implies that he is

Figure 4.2 | STORY AND PLOT

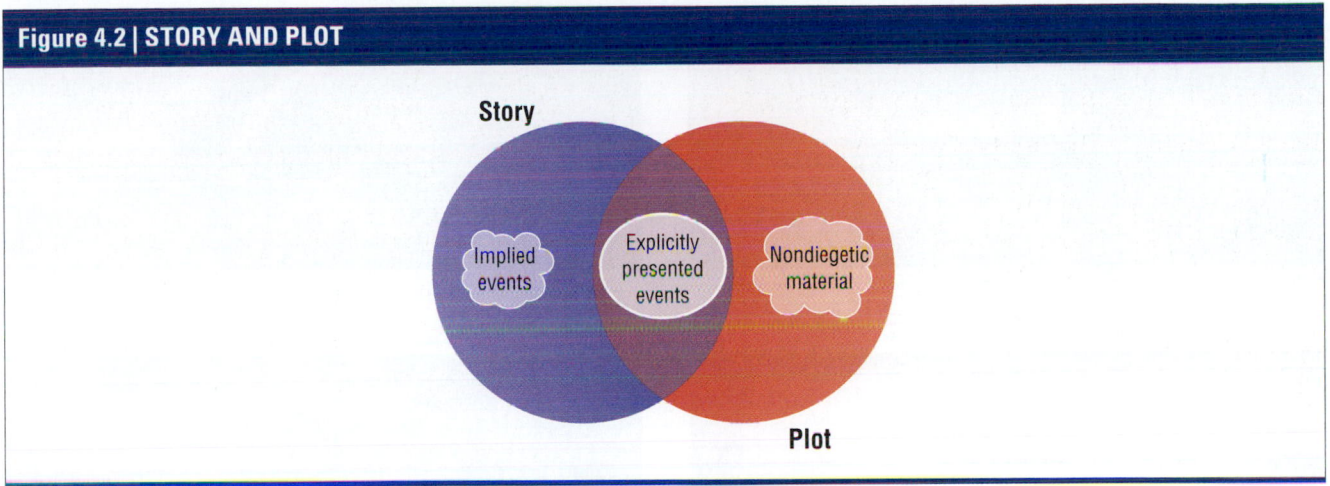

not exactly popular with the elite crowd. We learn Mark is going to Harvard and that he looks down on Erica for merely attending lowly (in his eyes) Boston University. The tone of her angry retort about Mark's Long Island roots lets us imagine a relatively humble upbringing that might be fueling his need for prestige. The story includes everything in the diegesis, every event and action we've seen on-screen, as well as everything we can infer from watching those events.

The **plot** consists of the specific actions and events that the filmmakers select and the order in which they arrange those events to effectively convey the narrative to the viewer. In this scene, what the characters do on-screen is part of the *plot*, including when Erica breaks up with Mark and stalks off, but the other information we infer from their exchange belongs exclusively to the *story*.

The distinction between plot and story is complicated because in every movie, the two concepts overlap and interact with one another. Let's continue exploring the subject by following the jilted Mark as he slinks out of the bar and makes his way back to his dorm. In this sequence, we hear the diegetic sounds of evening traffic, the tread of Mark's sneakers, and the muted chatter of his fellow pedestrians. We watch Mark trudge past the pub, trot across a busy street and down a crowded sidewalk, and jog across campus. As we can see in Figure 4.2, these *explicitly presented events*, and every image and sound they produce, are included in the intersection of story and plot.

But remember that story also incorporates those events *implied* by what we see (and hear) on-screen. In

this particular sequence, implied events might involve the portions of Mark's journey that were not captured in any of the shots used to portray his journey. In addition, everything we infer from these images and sounds, from the supremacy of the great university to the sophistication of the young scholars strolling its campus, is strictly story. The plot concerns only those portions of his journey necessary to effectively convey the Ivy League setting and the narrative idea of Mark's hurrying faster and faster the closer he gets to the sanctuary of his dorm room.

But the plot supplies more than simply this particular arrangement of these specific events. Plot also includes **nondiegetic elements**: those things we see and hear on the screen that come from outside the world of the story, such as score music (music not originating from the world of the story), titles and credits (words superimposed on the images on-screen), and voice-over comments from a third-person voice-over narrator.

For example, back in the bar, moments after Erica storms out, music begins to play over the shot of Mark alone at the table. This music is not the White Stripes song we heard in the background earlier in the scene. Whereas that *diegetic* music came from a jukebox from within the world of the story, this new music is *nondiegetic* score music that the filmmakers have imposed onto the movie to add narrative meaning to the sequence. The music begins as lilting piano notes that help convey the sadness Mark feels after getting unexpectedly dumped. Deeper, darker notes join the score as the music continues over Mark's journey home, allowing us to sense the thoughts of vengeance intruding on Mark's hurt feelings. As he trots up the steps to his dorm, a title

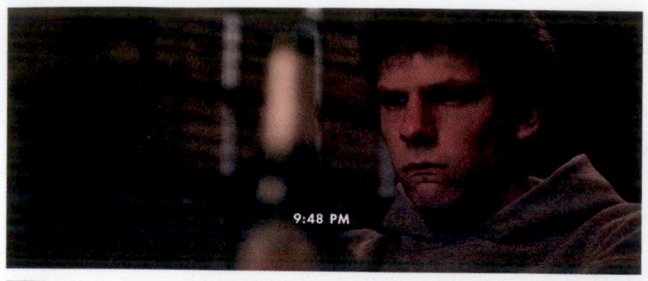

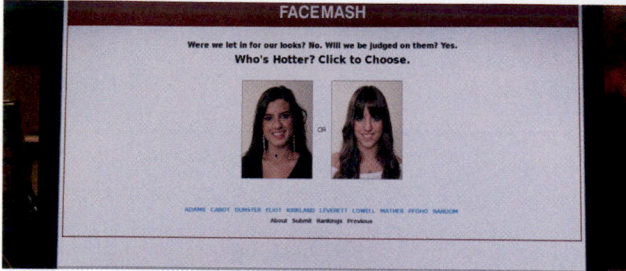

Plot and story in *The Social Network*

The deliberate structure of selected events, as well as nondiegetic elements such as a rhythmic musical score and titles marking the passage of time, compose the *plot* that delivers the *story* of Mark Zuckerberg's social networking epiphany. Causality guides the filmmakers' plot choices: Mark gets a diabolical idea [1], downloads dormitory resident photos [2], uses computer code and an algorithm to create an online game comparing relative female hotness [3], which rapidly escalates into an Internet sensation [4] that crashes the Harvard network—which delights Mark [5]. The specific events and their particular arrangement are plot; the events, along with other actions and meaning they imply but don't show, are the story.

announces the time and place of our story: Harvard University *Fall 2003*. These nondiegetic elements—score music and titles—are not part of the story. But they are an important piece of the plot: the deliberate selection and arrangement of specific events and elements the filmmakers employ to deliver the narrative.

A new sequence begins when Mark arrives home, cracks open a beer, and sits at his laptop. The next 8 minutes of *The Social Network* depict his discovery of the Internet's latent power to enthrall and connect its users.

The *story* conveyed in those 8 minutes includes the following: still stinging from Erica's rejection, Mark blogs a blistering critique of his now ex-girlfriend. Then, an offhand comment from one of his roommates gives Mark an idea. What if he could create a way for other students to compare pairs of female Harvard students and

vote on which woman is hotter? Mark hacks into each of the university's dormitory "Face Book" photo rosters and downloads every possible female resident photo. His friend Eduardo, having read Mark's blog, drops by to console him and winds up getting pressured into creating an algorithm to automatically select and pair photos, then collate and come up with new pairings based on the results. Mark and Eduardo write the necessary code, and "Facemash" goes up on the campus network. Students all across Harvard discover and play and recommend Facemash. The explosion of online participation crashes the university's computer network.

Every event implied by the previous description, including every line of code Mark must write, every gathering happening across campus, every student who plays Facemash, every relative hotness vote they cast, and every roommate cheering them on or reacting with disgust are part of that *story*.

The filmmakers use *plot* to tell us that story. We can't possibly see every line of code, every game of Facemash, every campus activity interrupted and enlivened by the new Internet sensation. So specific events and elements are selected and ordered to present the cause-and-effect chain of events that enables the audience to experience and understand the narrative. Our engagement with the story on-screen is enhanced by the nondiegetic elements the plot layers onto this particular sequence of selected events, including a pulsating musical score and occasional titles announcing the time as the phenomenon spreads.

And, of course, the story and the plot overlap. Every event explicitly presented on-screen, and every diegetic sound generated by those events, qualifies as both story *and* plot.

The relationship between plot and story is important to filmmakers and to the audience. From the filmmaker's perspective, the story exists as a precondition for the plot, and the filmmaker must understand what story is being told before going through the difficult job of selecting events to show on-screen and determining in what order to present them. For us as viewers, the story is an abstraction—a construct—that we piece together as the elements of the plot unfold before us on-screen. Our impressions about the story often shift and adjust throughout the movie as more of the plot is revealed. The plots of some movies—classic murder mysteries, for example—lead us to an unambiguous sense of the story by the time they are done. Other movies' plots reveal very little about the causal relationships among narrative events, thus leaving us to puzzle over those connections, to construct the story ourselves.

As you view movies more critically and analytically, pay attention not only to the story as you have inferred it but also to how it was conveyed through its plot. Understanding this basic distinction will help you to better appreciate and analyze the overall form of the movie.

To picture the relationship between plot and story slightly differently, and to become more aware of the deliberate ways in which filmmakers construct plots from stories, you might watch several different movies that tell a story you are familiar with—such as the classic romantic fairy tale Cinderella, which has been adapted into at least six movies. From the traditional 1950 Walt

Disney animation *Cinderella* to Kenneth Branagh's 2015 live-action version with the same title, and the many updates in between (including Frank Tashlin's 1960 *Cinderfella* and Garry Marshall's 1990 *Pretty Woman*), every version relies on the basic story structure of the well-known fairy tale. This sort of critical comparison will enable you to see more clearly how the plots differ, how the formal decisions made by the filmmakers have shaped those differences, and how the overall form of each movie alters your perception of the underlying story.

When James Cameron planned to make a movie about the sinking of RMS *Titanic*, he had to contend with the fact that there were already three feature films on the subject, as well as numerous television movies and documentaries. Moreover, everyone knew the story. So he created a narrative structure that was based on a **backstory**, a fictional history behind the situation existing at the start of the main story: the story of Rose Calvert's diamond. That device, as well as a powerful romantic story and astonishing special effects, made his *Titanic* (1997) one of the greatest box office hits in history.

Through plot, screenwriters and directors can give structure to stories and guide (if not control) viewers' emotional responses. In fact, a plot may be little more than a sequence of devices for arousing predictable responses of concern and excitement in audiences. We accept such a plot because we know it will lead to the resolution of conflicts, mysteries, and frustrations in the story.

Movies have always looked to literature as a proven source of narrative, style, and cultural resonance—as well as a built-in audience of readers eager to experience a favorite book on the big screen. For example, more than 250 movies—many of them masterpieces in their own right—have been made from Shakespeare's plays, and producers continue to find imaginative ways of bringing other literary classics to the screen. In the past few years alone, cinematic adaptations have been made of the works of distinguished writers such as Charlotte Brontë (*Jane Eyre*, 2011; director Cary Fukunaga), F. Scott Fitzgerald (*The Great Gatsby*, 2014; director Baz Luhrmann), and Thomas Pynchon (*Inherent Vice*, 2014; director Paul Thomas Anderson). *12 Years a Slave* (director Steve McQueen), the 2014 Best Picture Oscar winner, was adapted from a previously obscure but historically significant memoir by the abolitionist Solomon

1

2

Adaptation of literary sources

David Lean's *Great Expectations* (1946) [1] takes place, as Dickens's novel does, in nineteenth-century England. The young protagonist (John Mills, *left*), a student in London named Pip (as in the novel), confronts his previously anonymous benefactor, Magwitch. Fifty-two years later, Alfonso Cuarón's version of the same story (*Great Expectations*, 1998) [2] is set in contemporary America. Finn, a painter in New York City, confronts his previously anonymous benefactor, Arthur Lustig. An analysis of the differences between these two adaptations of the same novel can lead you to a deeper appreciation of the power of filmmakers' decisions regarding plot specifically and film form more generally.

Northup. Popular films such as *Wonder* (2017; director Stephen Chbosky), *Gone Girl* (2014; director David Fincher), and *Fifty Shades of Grey* (2015; director Sam Taylor-Johnson) have been adapted from popular fiction. Some of the most popular films in recent history are adapted from comic books. Marvel Studios, a subsidiary of The Walt Disney Company, was formed to exploit

Marvel Comics's huge accumulated (and copyrighted) library of characters and story lines. The company has released sixteen comic book adaptations since 2008's *Iron Man* and has dozens more adaptations planned for the next 15 years.

Movies are, by their nature, different from the books on which they are based. Peter Jackson's Lord of the Rings trilogy (2001–3) is relatively faithful to the spirit of J. R. R. Tolkien's novels, but Jackson had to eliminate or combine certain characters, details, and events in order to squeeze more than 1,000 pages of source material into three movies. Jackson's subsequent decision to expand Tolkien's whimsical short novel *The Hobbit* into three epic movies had an opposite adaptation effect. Jackson and his fellow screenwriters invented characters, inflated action sequences, and inserted new plot lines—including a tragic love story between an elf and a dwarf, and a revenge-fueled feud between the leader of the dwarves and an Orc chieftain. *The Hobbit: The Battle of the Five Armies* (2014) stretches a relatively modest five-page battle into a bombastic hour-long melee involving ten times the combatants described in the novel.[4]

Order

Bringing order to the plot events is one of the most fundamental decisions that filmmakers make about relaying story information through the plot. Most narrative film plots are structured in chronological order. But, unlike story order, which necessarily flows chronologically (as does life), plot order can be manipulated so that events are presented in nonchronological sequences that emphasize importance or meaning or that establish desired expectations in audiences. *Citizen Kane* (1941; director Orson Welles) presents the biography of Charles Foster Kane, a fictional character inspired by media mogul William Randolph Hearst. Welles and his co-screenwriter, Herman J. Mankiewicz, adopted an approach to plot order so radical for its time that it actually bewildered many viewers. The movie's plot consists of nine sequences, five of which are flashbacks. The film opens with Kane's death, followed by a newsreel that summarizes the major events of Kane's life in more or less chronological order. A third sequence introduces us to Mr. Thompson, a reporter assigned to get additional in-

4. Rachel Nuwer, "The Tolkien Nerd's Guide to 'The Hobbit: The Battle of the Five Armies.'" Smithsonianmag.com (December 19, 2014). https://www.smithsonianmag.com/arts-culture/tolkien-nerds-guide-hobbit-battle-five-armies-180953681/ (accessed February 8, 2015).

Plot order in *Citizen Kane*

To provide a straightforward account of Charles Foster Kane's life and help viewers get their bearings within a highly unconventional plot order, Orson Welles's *Citizen Kane* (1941) begins with a fictionalized mini-documentary. "News on the March" is a satire on the famous weekly newsreel series *The March of Time* (1935–51). The series, shown in movie theaters, mixed location footage with dramatic reenactments. Using this culturally familiar narrative device as an anchor for the rest of the movie, Welles tried to ensure that viewers wouldn't lose their way in the overall plot.

formation about Kane's life—primarily about the meaning of his last word: "Rosebud." Thompson's subsequent investigation is a kind of detective story; each of the five sources he interviews or examines reveals a different perspective on different periods in Kane's life. The order of these sequences is determined not by chronology, but by the order of Thompson's investigation and the memory of his interview subjects. Just as Thompson tries to assemble clues about Kane's life, the audience must assemble the jumbled chronology in which it is presented. The viewer participation required makes watching *Citizen Kane* an engaging, if sometimes disorienting, participatory experience. What's more, once freed from strict chronological order, Welles and Mankiewicz were able to juxtapose events in a way that provided additional context and meaning. For example, having just watched Kane die alone, we comprehend the significance of his leaving home at age eight on a level that would not have been possible if that earlier incident had been presented first. Likewise, our enjoyment of seeing Kane's exuberant idealism when he buys his first newspaper in 1892 is tempered by having previously watched him lose control of his media empire after the 1929 stock market crash.

However challenging it was for its time, the plot structure of *Citizen Kane* has been so influential that it is now considered conventional. One of the many movies that it influenced is Quentin Tarantino's *Pulp Fiction* (1994). The plot of *Pulp Fiction*, which is full of surprises, is constructed in a nonlinear way and fragments the passing of time. We might have to see the movie several times before being able to say, for instance, at what point—in the plot and in the story—the central character Vincent Vega dies.

Christopher Nolan's *Memento* (2000) and Gaspar Noe's *Irreversible* (2002) take manipulation of plot order to the extreme by presenting the events in their respective narratives in reverse chronological order. Each film opens with the story's concluding event, then works its way backward to the occurrence that initiated the cause-and-effect chain. By inverting the sequence in which the audience is accustomed to experiencing events—in life as well as in movies—*Memento* and *Irreversible* essentially challenge viewers to relearn how to align expectation and decipher narrative context. We experience each presented event not in light of the string of actions and reactions that led up to it; our understanding comes only from what happened *after* the action we're currently watching. We start with resolution and work our way toward the inciting incident. In the case of *Memento*, our ignorance of previous events helps us identify with the limited perspective of the movie's protagonist, Leonard—a man incapable of forming new memories.

Plot order in *Memento*

In Christopher Nolan's *Memento* (2000), Leonard Shelby suffers from a disorder that prevents him from forming short-term memories. To remember details of his life, he takes Polaroid snapshots, jots notes on scraps of paper, and even tattoos "The Facts" on his body. The movie's two-stranded plot order, both chronological and reverse chronological, likewise challenges us to recall what we've seen and how the parts fit together.

In Akira Kurosawa's *Rashomon* (1950), we see an innovative variation on the idea of plot order. The same story—the rape of a woman—is told from four different points of view: a bandit, the woman, her husband, and a woodcutter (the only witness of the rape). Kurosawa's purpose is to show us that we all remember and perceive differently, thus challenging our notions of perception and truth.

Events

In any plot, events have a logical order, as we've discussed, as well as a logical hierarchy. Some events are more important than others, and we infer their relative significance through the director's selection and arrangement of details of action, character, or setting. This hierarchy consists of (1) the events that seem crucial to the plot (and thus to the underlying story) and (2) the events that play a less crucial or even subordinate role.

The first category includes those major events or branching points in the plot structure that force characters to choose between or among alternate paths. Damien Chazelle's *Whiplash* (2014) tells the story of Andrew, a talented young drummer who struggles to earn the approval of his demanding and abusive teacher, Terence Fletcher. Andrew's performance in first-year band practice impresses Fletcher, who offers him a coveted spot in his studio band. Later, Fletcher humiliates Andrew for his inability to keep time on a challenging piece, so Andrew practices until his fingers bleed. Each following stage in the plot turns on such events, which force Andrew to take action and make consequential choices.

The second category includes those minor plot events that add texture and complexity to characters and actions but are not essential elements within the narrative. Andrew's relationships with people outside the competitive world of jazz performance create subordinate events. His submissive father, the antithesis of the domineering Fletcher, takes Andrew to old movies. Brimming with newfound confidence after a successful rehearsal, Andrew asks Nicole, the young woman working the concession stand, on a date. Later, Andrew's arrogance embarrasses his father; his ambition compels him to break up with Nicole. These minor or subordinate events enrich and complicate the diegesis (the world of

1

2

Hierarchy of events in *Whiplash*

In Damien Chazelle's *Whiplash* (2014), the student drummer Andrew impresses the school's most demanding teacher, who invites him to join the competitive studio band and thus sets the plot in motion [1]. Andrew's awkward romance with a woman outside the cutthroat culture of his music academy informs the plot through a series of minor events. Her conventional values lend perspective to Andrew's obsessive pursuit of percussion virtuosity [2].

the story) in a narrative film, but no single such event is indispensable to the story.

When filmmakers make decisions about which scenes to cut from a film during the editing phase, they generally look for minor events that, for one reason or another, don't contribute enough to the overall movie. As a critical viewer of movies, you can use this hierarchy of events in diagramming a plot (as a practical way of understanding it) or charting a course of the major and minor events confronting the characters.

Duration

Events, in life and in the movies, take time to occur. **Duration** is this length of time. When talking about narrative movies specifically, we can identify three specific kinds of duration: **story duration** is the amount of time

Screen duration and serialized stories

Serialized dramas presented on cable and streaming services have redefined our relationship with screen duration. The plot duration and the story duration of a conventional feature film each may be of almost any length, but the screen duration is generally limited to somewhere between 90 and 150 minutes. The stories and plots presented in shows like *Game of Thrones* are spread across multiple episodes, which are released in seasons, which can be binge-watched like extremely long movies. With the 2018 release of its eighth season, the screen duration of the *Game of Thrones* "movie" passed 4,000 minutes, or almost 67 hours.

that the implied story takes to occur; **plot duration** is the elapsed time of those events within the story that the film explicitly presents (in other words, the elapsed time of the plot); and **screen duration** is the movie's running time on-screen. In *Citizen Kane*, the plot duration is approximately 1 week (the duration of Thomp-

son's search), the story duration is more than 70 years (the span of Kane's life), and the screen duration is 1 hour 59 minutes, the time it takes us to watch the film from beginning to end without interruption.

These distinctions are relatively simple in *Citizen Kane*, but the three-part relation of story, plot, and screen duration can become quite complex in some movies. Balancing the three elements is especially complex for a filmmaker because the screen duration is necessarily constrained by financial and other considerations. Movies may have become longer on average over the years, but filmmakers still must present their stories within a relatively short span of time. Because moviegoers generally regard films that run more than 3 hours as too long, such movies risk failure at the box office. Figure 4.3 illustrates the relationship between story duration and plot duration in a hypothetical movie. The story duration in this illustration—1 week—is depicted in a plot that covers four discrete but crucial days in that week.

The relationships among the three types of duration can be isolated and analyzed, not only in the context of the entire narrative of the film but also within its constituent parts—in scenes and sequences. In these smaller parts, however, the relationship between plot duration and story duration generally remains stable; in most mainstream Hollywood movies, the duration of a plot event is assumed to be roughly equivalent to the duration of the story event that it implies. At the level of

Figure 4.3 | DURATION: STORY VERSUS PLOT

Imagine a hypothetical movie that follows the lives of two people over the course of 1 week, starting with the moment that they first move into an apartment together as a couple and ending with their parting of ways 7 days later.

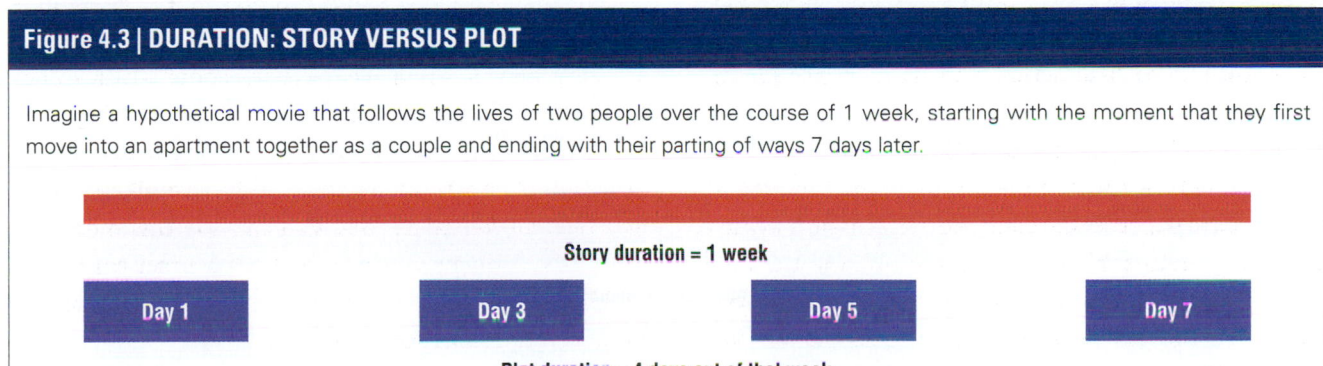

Although the movie's implied story duration is 1 week, the events that are explicitly part of the movie's plot take place during four discrete days within that week (the plot duration). Day 1 in the plot shows the couple moving and settling in. Day 3 shows them already squabbling. Day 5 shows the misguided couple getting ready for and throwing a housewarming party that concludes with a disastrous (but hilarious) argument. Day 7 shows them moving out and then having an amicable dinner over which they agree that the only way they can live with each other is by living apart.

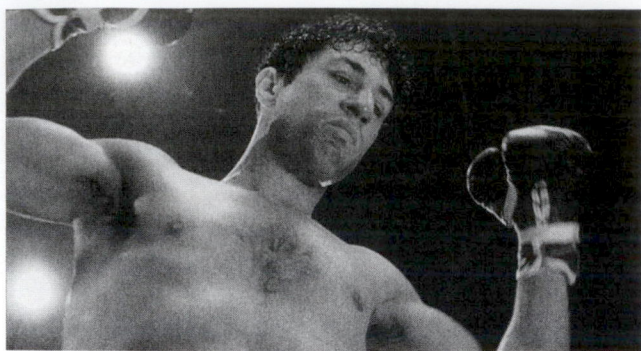 

Summary relationship

A sequence in Martin Scorsese's *Raging Bull* (1980) covers 3 years (story duration) in a few minutes (screen duration). Black-and-white shots of Jake La Motta's (Robert De Niro) most significant boxing matches from 1944 to 1947 are intercut with color shots from home movies that show La Motta and his second wife, Vickie (Cathy Moriarty), during the early years of their marriage.

scenes (a complete unit of plot action), the more interesting relationship is usually between screen duration and plot duration. We can generally characterize that relationship in one of three ways: (1) in a **summary relationship**, screen duration is shorter than plot duration; (2) in **real time**, screen duration corresponds directly to plot duration; and (3) in a **stretch relationship**, screen duration is longer than plot duration.

Both stretch and summary relationships are established primarily through editing techniques (discussed in detail in Chapter 8). The summary relationship is very familiar and occurs much more frequently in main-

stream movies than do the other two. The summary relationship is depicted in Figure 4.4, which illustrates one scene in our hypothetical movie; the screen duration of this scene is 10 minutes, but the implied duration of the plot event is 4 hours.

In *Citizen Kane*, Welles depicts the steady disintegration of Kane's first marriage to Emily Norton through a rapid montage of six shots at the breakfast table that take 2 minutes on the screen but depict 7 years of their life together. Through changes in dress, hairstyle, seating, and their preferences in newspapers, we see the couple's relationship go from amorous passion to sarcastic

---

Figure 4.4 | DURATION: PLOT VERSUS SCREEN

One portion of the plot in this hypothetical movie involves the housewarming party thrown by our ill-fated couple. The implied duration of this event (the plot duration) is 4 hours—from 8 o'clock in the evening to midnight of Day 5.

8:00 PM   Midnight

Day 5

Plot duration = 4 hours

Although the implied duration of the plot event is 4 hours, the actual duration on-screen of the shots that cover this 4-hour event is only 10 minutes (the screen duration). As you can see below, those 10 minutes are divided among 15 discrete shots, each of which features a specific event or discussion at the party.

Screen duration = 15 individual shots = 10 minutes

Real-time relationship in *Timecode*

Mike Figgis's *Timecode* (2000) offers a dramatic and daring version of real time. Split into quarters, the screen displays four distinct but overlapping stories, each shot in one continuous 93-minute take (the length of an ordinary digital videocassette), uninterrupted by editing.

hostility. Summary relationships are essential to telling movie stories, especially long and complicated ones.

Because it is less common than summary, the stretch relationship is often used to highlight a plot event, stressing its importance to the overall narrative. A stretch relationship can be achieved by special effects such as slow motion, particularly when a graceful effect is needed, as in showing a reunited couple running slowly toward one another. It can also be constructed by editing techniques. The "Odessa Steps" sequence in Sergei Eisenstein's *Battleship Potemkin* (1925) uses editing to stretch the plot duration of the massacre: selected single moments are broken up into multiple shots that are overlapped and repeated so that our experience of each event on-screen lasts longer than it would have in reality. Eisenstein does this because he wants us to see the massacre as an important and meaningful event, as well as to increase our anxiety and empathy for the victims.

The real-time relationship is the least common of the three relationships between screen duration and plot duration, but its use has always interested and delighted

Real-time relationship in *Birdman*

An innovative melding of summary and real-time relationships of plot to screen time compels viewers of *Birdman* (2014; director Alejandro González Iñárritu) to experience the same sort of overstimulated exhaustion endured by Riggan, the film's protagonist. In a desperate attempt to restore his reputation, the former superhero franchise movie star is directing and starring in a Broadway play—and it's not going well. Riggan's last-ditch efforts to pull the play (and his life) together are presented in what appears (thanks to hidden edits) to be one very long continuous shot. Watching the movie, our visual senses—and our ingrained cinematic experience—tell us that this unbroken flow of action must represent a real-time relationship between plot and screen duration, but we soon realize that this single shot sneakily slides between and through multiple scenes that take place at different times: an actor injured in rehearsal, the arrival of his hot-shot replacement, a humiliating publicity interview, a disastrous preview performance, and on and on. What looks and feels like a real-time relationship is actually a summary relationship. The constant struggle to process a summary relationship disguised as a real-time relationship lets the viewer experience something comparable to Riggan's manic multitasking.

film buffs. Many directors use real time within films to create uninterrupted "reality" on the screen, but directors rarely use it for entire films. Alfred Hitchcock's *Rope* (1948; screenwriter Arthur Laurents) is famous for presenting a real-time relationship between screen and plot duration. In *Rope*, Hitchcock used the long take (discussed further in Chapter 6)—an unedited, continuous shot—to preserve real time. One roll of motion-picture film can record approximately 11 minutes of action, and thus Hitchcock made an 80-minute film with ten shots that range in length from 4 minutes 40 seconds to 10 minutes.[5] Six of the cuts between these shots are

---

5. Various critics have said that each shot in *Rope* lasts 10 minutes, but the DVD release of the film shows the timings (rounded off) to be as follows: opening credits, 2:09; shot 1, 9:50; shot 2, 8:00; shot 3, 7:50; shot 4, 7:09; shot 5, 10:00; shot 6, 7:40; shot 7, 8:00; shot 8, 10:00; shot 9, 4:40; shot 10, 5:40; closing credits, 00:28.

virtually unnoticeable because Hitchcock has the camera pass behind the backs of people or furniture and then makes the cut on a dark screen; four others are ordinary hard cuts from one person to another. Even these hard cuts do not break time or space, so the result is fluid storytelling in which the plot duration equals the screen duration of 80 minutes.

In most traditional narrative movies, cuts and other editing devices punctuate the flow of the narrative and graphically indicate that the images occur in human-made **cinematic time**, not seamless real time. As viewers, we think that movies pass before us in the present tense, but we also understand that cinematic time can be manipulated through editing, among other means. As we accept these manipulative conventions, we also recognize that classic Hollywood editing generally goes out of its way to avoid calling attention to itself. What's more, it attempts to reflect the natural mental processes by which human consciousness moves back and forth between reality and illusion, shifting between past, present, and future.

LOOKING AT MOVIES
SUSPENSE AND SURPRISE

VIDEO In this tutorial, Dave Monahan discusses the differences between suspense and surprise.

Suspense versus Surprise

It's important to distinguish between suspense, which has been mentioned in the preceding discussions, and surprise. Although they are often confused, suspense and surprise are two fundamentally different elements in the development of many movie plots. Alfred Hitchcock mastered the unique properties of each, taking great care to ensure that they were integral to the internal logic of his plots. In a conversation with French director François Truffaut, Hitchcock explained the terms:

We are now having a very innocent little chat. Let us suppose that there is a bomb underneath this table between us. Nothing happens, and then all of a sudden, "Boom!"

There is an explosion. The public is *surprised*, but prior to this surprise, it has seen an absolutely ordinary scene of no special consequence. Now, let us take a *suspense* situation. The bomb is underneath the table and the public *knows* it, probably because they have seen the anarchist place it there. The public is *aware* that the bomb is going to explode at one o'clock and there is a clock in the decor. The public can see that it is a quarter

to one. In these conditions this same innocuous conversation becomes fascinating because the public is participating in the scene. The audience is longing to warn the characters on the screen: "You shouldn't be talking about such trivial matters. There's a bomb beneath you and it's about to explode!"

In the first scene we have given the public fifteen seconds of *surprise* at the moment of the explosion. In the second we have provided them with fifteen minutes of *suspense*. The conclusion is that whenever possible the public must be informed. Except when the surprise is a twist, that is, when the unexpected ending is, in itself, the highlight of the story.[6]

Because there are no repeat surprises, we can be surprised in the same way only once. As a result, a **surprise**, being taken unawares, can be shocking, and our emotional response to it is generally short-lived. By contrast, **suspense** is a more drawn-out (and, some would say, more enjoyable) experience, one that we may seek out even when we know what happens in a movie. Suspense is the anxiety brought on by a partial uncertainty: the end is certain, but the means is uncertain. Or, even more interestingly, we may know both the result and the means by which it's brought about, but we still feel suspense: we know what's going to happen, so we feel compelled to warn and protect the characters who don't.

6. Alfred Hitchcock, qtd. in François Truffaut, *Hitchcock*, rev. ed. (New York: Simon & Schuster, 1984), p. 73.

Suspense and surprise

We witness a brutal murder committed by what appears to be a woman named Mrs. Bates in Alfred Hitchcock's thriller *Psycho* (1960). So when private detective Milton Arbogast sneaks into Mrs. Bates' house to question someone he thinks is a harmless little old lady, our awareness generates suspense. Every oblivious step he takes as he treads deeper into the creepy house is invested with the tension of the inevitable attack [1]. Hitchcock intensifies the suspense by showing us (but not Arbogast) a shot of Mrs. Bates' bedroom door gliding open. The director saves *Psycho*'s surprise for the end of the movie, when he suddenly reveals shocking new information to the audience *and* the principal characters: Mrs. Bates is long dead, and her timid son is the actual psychotic killer [2].

Repetition

The **repetition**, or number of times, that a story element recurs in a plot is an important aspect of narrative form. If an event occurs once in a plot, we accept it as a functioning part of the narrative's progression. Its appearance more than once, however, suggests a pattern and thus a higher level of importance. Like order and duration, then, repetition serves not only as a means of relaying story information but also as a signal that a particular event has a meaning or significance that should be acknowledged in our interpretation and analysis.

Story events can be repeated in various ways. A character may remember a key event at several times during the movie, indicating the psychological, intellectual, or physical importance of that event.

The **familiar image** is defined by film theorist Stefan Sharff as compositions, graphic elements, sounds, or juxtapositions that a director periodically repeats in a movie (with or without variations) to help inform or stabilize its narrative. By its repetition, the image calls attention to itself as a narrative (as well as visual) element.

Some familiar images are distributed throughout a film as thematic symbols, particularly those where a material object represents something abstract. In *Volver* (2006), director Pedro Almodóvar uses frequent shots of wind turbines in the Spanish landscape as a symbol to help us understand the meaning of the title, a Spanish word that means "turn," "return," or "revolution," as in a circle turning. On the literal level, the story itself turns on the cycle of genetic or behavioral influences that pass from one generation to the next.

The repetition of familiar images can also be used to influence how the audience interprets or experiences the narrative in multiple scenes. The first four shots in the scene depicting Kane's death in the opening minutes of *Citizen Kane* all feature the superimposed image of snow falling across the screen. This visual element is sourced in the snow globe Kane drops after he utters, "Rosebud." The snow image returns 16 minutes later during an event in Kane's childhood that changes his life

LOOKING AT MOVIES
LIGHTING AND FAMILIAR IMAGE IN THE NIGHT OF THE HUNTER

VIDEO This tutorial analyzes the familiar image in Charles Laughton's *The Night of the Hunter* (1955).

forever. That familiar image evokes the audience's initial association with Kane's lonely death and last word, and thus colors the way we experience and interpret young Kane's separation from his mother. The falling snow returns once more in one of the film's final scenes. In a tantrum after his second wife leaves him, Kane tears her bedroom apart—until he stumbles upon the same snow globe we saw him clutching on his deathbed at the beginning of the movie. The snow globe, and the snow inside that swirls when Kane picks it up, reminds us of the two previous scenes featuring the familiar image: one portrayed the influential events that brought Kane to this moment, and the other revealed the eventual consequences of the actions we just witnessed.

Setting

The **setting** of a movie is the time and place in which the story occurs. It establishes the date, city, or country and provides the characters' social, educational, and cultural backgrounds and other identifying factors vital for understanding them—such as what they wear, eat, and drink. Setting sometimes provides an implicit explanation for actions or traits that we might otherwise consider eccentric, because cultural norms vary from place to place and throughout time. Certain genres are associated with specific settings; for example, Westerns with wide open country, film noirs with dark city streets, and horror movies with creepy houses.

Besides giving us essential contextual information that helps us understand story events and character motivation, setting adds texture to the movie's diegesis, enriching our sense of the overall world of the movie. Terrence Malick's *Days of Heaven* (1978) features magnificent landscapes in the American West of the 1920s. At first, the extraordinary visual imagery seems to take precedence over the narrative. However, the settings—the vast wheat fields and the great solitary house against the sky—directly complement the depth and power of the narrative, which is concerned with the cycle of the seasons, the work connected with each season, and how fate, greed, sexual passion, and jealousy can lead to tragedy. Here, setting also helps reveal the characters' states of mind. They are from the Chicago slums, and once they arrive in the pristine wheat fields of the West, they are lonely and alienated from themselves and their values. They cannot adapt and thus end tragically. Here, setting is destiny.

Other films tell stories closely related to their international, national, or regional settings, such as the specific neighborhoods of New York City that form the backdrop of many Woody Allen films. But think of the

Setting in science fiction

Based on Philip K. Dick's science-fiction novel *Do Androids Dream of Electric Sheep?* (1968), Ridley Scott's *Blade Runner* (1982) takes place in 2019 in an imaginary world where cities such as Los Angeles are ruled by technology and saturated with visual information. In most science-fiction films, setting plays an important part in our understanding of the narrative, so sci-fi filmmakers spend considerable time, money, and effort to make the setting come to life.

many different ways in which Manhattan has been photographed, including the many film noirs with their harsh black-and-white contrasts; the sour colors of Martin Scorsese's *Taxi Driver* (1976); or the bright colors of Alfred Hitchcock's *North by Northwest* (1959).

Settings are not always drawn from real-life locales. An opening title card tells us that F. W. Murnau's *Sunrise: A Song of Two Humans* (1927) takes place in "no place and every place"; Stanley Kubrick's *2001: A Space Odyssey* (1968) creates an entirely new space–time continuum; and Tim Burton's *Charlie and the Chocolate Factory* (2005) creates the most fantastic chocolate factory in the world. The attraction of science-fiction films such as George Lucas's *Star Wars* (1977) and Ridley Scott's *Blade Runner* (1982) is often attributed to their almost totally unfamiliar settings. These stories about outer space and future cities have a mythical or symbolic significance beyond that of stories set on Earth. Their settings may be verisimilar and appropriate for the purpose of the story, whether or not we can verify them as "real."

Scope

Related to duration and setting is **scope**—the overall range, in time and place, of the movie's story. Stories can range from the distant past to the narrative present or they can be narrowly focused on a short period, even a matter of moments. They can take us from one galaxy to another or they can remain inside a single room. They can present a rather limited perspective on their world or they can show us several alternative perspectives. Determining the general scope of a movie's story—understanding its relative expansiveness—can help you piece together and understand other aspects of the movie as a whole.

For example, the *biopic*, a biographical film about a person's life—whether historical or fictional—might tell the story in one of two ways: through one significant episode or period in the life of a person or through a series of events covering a longer portion of a person's life, sometimes beginning with birth and ending in old age. For example, Richard Attenborough's *Young Winston* (1972) spans multiple decades and numerous locations to portray the life of the legendary British statesman Winston Churchill. The film begins with his privileged but lonely childhood and then moves through his career as a cavalry officer in India and his subsequent adventures as a war correspondent in South Africa's Sec-

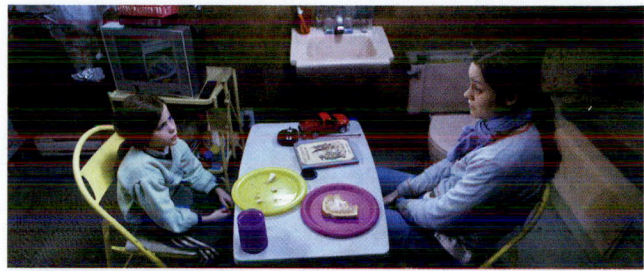

Scope

Scope is integral to the narrative of *Room* (2015; director Lenny Abrahamson). The first 47 minutes of the movie take place entirely inside a small, locked shed; a dirty skylight provides the only view of the outside world. The only characters we see are a captive woman, known only as Ma, her five-year-old son, Jack (who has lived every moment of his life inside the 10- by 10-foot room), and (briefly) Old Nick, the man who holds them prisoner. This narrow scope confines viewers to the mother and child's restricted and intimate existence. When Ma and Jack are finally freed, the sudden overwhelming expansion in scope helps viewers identify with the protagonists' struggles to adjust to life in the wider world.

ond Boer War. The film concludes when Churchill was elected to Parliament at age twenty-six. In contrast, Joe Wright's *Darkest Hour* (2017), the latest Churchill biopic, takes place mostly in interior spaces in London and Kent and covers only his first few eventful weeks as Britain's prime minister. That film ends with his famous "We shall fight on the beaches" speech made to Parliament after the miraculous 1940 evacuation of British forces from Dunkirk. The scope of *Dunkirk*, Christopher Nolan's 2017 war movie covering that same evacuation (and ending with the same speech), is both narrower and broader than *Darkest Hour*. The events in Nolan's film span only 1 week, but the story develops more individual characters, perspectives, and conflicts that take place in relatively far-flung locations, including fighter pilots in the air, desperate evacuees at sea on transport ships, civilians assisting the effort using their personal pleasure craft, and the besieged troops and officers stranded on the broad beaches of Dunkirk itself.

Looking at Narrative in *Stagecoach*

To better understand how the foundations and elements of narrative work together in a single movie, let's consider how they're used in John Ford's *Stagecoach* (1939).

This movie is regarded by many as *the* classic Western, not only for its great entertainment value but also for its mastery of the subjects discussed in this chapter.

Story

The story of *Stagecoach* is based on a familiar convention sometimes called the "ship of fools." Such stories involve a diverse group of people—such as passengers traveling to a common destination or residents of a hotel—who must confront a common danger and, through that experience, confront themselves as individuals and as members of a group. In *Stagecoach*, these people either have been living in or are passing through the isolated frontier town of Tonto. Despite a warning from the U.S. Cavalry that Apache warriors, under the command of the dreaded Geronimo, have cut the telegraph wires and threatened the settlers' safety, this group boards a stagecoach for the 2-day trip to a larger settlement called Lordsburg.

Narration and Narrator

As was typical of John Ford's style throughout his career, the narration in *Stagecoach* is provided by an omniscient camera that has unrestricted access to all aspects of the narrative and, as a result, can convey the experiences and perceptions of any character in ways that enrich the story. For example, the banker Gatewood won't let anyone touch his satchel during the long journey. We understand his attitude and actions because the camera shows us a private moment he uses to steal from his bank's own safe before he barges onto the crowded stagecoach. The camera narrator also reveals information that none of the passengers know, such as when a long-distance view of the lonely stagecoach crossing the vast desert is interrupted when the camera pivots to show us Geronimo and his warriors watching from a hilltop.

Characters

The stagecoach is driven by the good-natured dolt Buck; lawman Marshal Curly Wilcox rides shotgun. The passengers include Dallas, a good-hearted prostitute; Henry Gatewood, the thieving bank president mentioned earlier; Lucy Mallory, the aloof, and (as we later learn) pregnant wife of a cavalry officer; Samuel Peacock, a mousy liquor salesman; Dr. Josiah Boone (aka Doc), a disgraced alcoholic doctor; and Mr. Hatfield, a gambler. The coach picks up a seventh passenger along the way. Ringo is an escaped prisoner. When his horse becomes lame, he stops the stagecoach and is arrested by the marshal before he boards.

Together, Buck, Curly, and their passengers form a sort of composite protagonist in pursuit of a common goal: to reach Lordsburg alive. Many of the characters are after individual goals as well. Curly aims to take Ringo back to prison; Hatfield wishes to protect Lucy (for reasons you'll learn later); Gatewood is trying to get away with his stolen stack of cash; Doc is determined to stay drunk; and Ringo is after the men who murdered his father and brother. Many of these characters are motivated by a psychological need. Both the gambler Hatfield and the drunken Doc need to regain self-respect. Dallas and Ringo—the outcast prostitute and the escaped prisoner—share a mutual need for human kindness and love. Having needs that conflict with their goals, such as the vengeful Ringo's inner need for love, is part of what makes these characters complex and compelling. His repressed desire for civilized normalcy, and the change he undergoes when he surrenders to it (albeit only after killing for revenge), makes Ringo a round character. He's also our primary protagonist, since it is his quest to kill the men who murdered his father and brother, and his not-so-hidden attraction to Dallas, that propel the plot once the common goal of Lordsburg is finally achieved. Ringo is not the only round character: Dallas is a prostitute with a painful past who resists her own desire for love and family. Lucy begins the trip as a judgmental snob; she overcomes deeply rooted prejudices and comes to respect Dallas. Doc is a tangle of contradictions: a disgraced alcoholic capable of pride and purpose. He overcomes his weaknesses to save the day twice, by sobering up to deliver Lucy's baby, and when he stands up to Ringo's enemy, Luke Plummer. Hatfield and Peacock don't necessarily undergo any dramatic changes, but they do possess complex and contradictory traits. Hitchcock is a drifter and a gambler with a reputation for killing rivals, yet he rediscovers a sense of romantic chivalry when he meets Lucy and risks his own life to board the stage to protect her. The normally passive Peacock convincingly asserts authority when he repeatedly shushes his rowdier traveling companions after Lucy gives birth.

The remaining passengers have interesting personalities and are each a vital ingredient in this involving narrative, but since they have no subtle or repressed traits and

The cast of characters in *Stagecoach*

The collective protagonist of *Stagecoach* consists of nine characters: Buck and the lawman Curly [1]; prostitute Dallas and the banker Gatewood [2]; the cavalry officer's wife, Lucy Mallory [3]; the whiskey salesman, Mr. Peacock, and the alcoholic Doc Boone [4]; the gambler Hatfield [5]; and the fugitive Ringo [6].

1

2

The antagonist as other

Ringo's antagonist, Luke Plummer, is not seen on-screen until 80 minutes into the 96-minute story. When we do finally meet him, the portrayal is not sympathetic, but he is at least presented as an individual with his own specific behavior, personality, and motives [1]. In contrast, the insurgent band of Apache warriors that serve as the plot's primary antagonist are presented in ways that exploit audience fears of the unknown other. Although they are described as being led by Geronimo (a well-known Apache leader and the only historical figure in the story), none of the Native American characters seen on-screen are identified by name, speak dialogue, or exhibit individual behaviors [2]. The motivation for their attacks is never discussed. *Stagecoach*'s portrayal of Native Americans as savage others may serve the narrative; it also reveals the prejudices of the filmmakers and their time.

undergo little change over the course of the story, they must be classified as flat characters. Buck is and remains bumbling comic relief, and Curly is a fair and disciplined lawman from start to finish. Gatewood doesn't grow past the selfish coward we meet at the start of the story.

The primary antagonist, for everyone on this journey, is Geronimo, even though he and his warriors appear on the screen only briefly before their climactic attack on the stagecoach. One of the many things that makes *Stagecoach*'s narrative so interesting is that while Geronimo is responsible for many of the narrative obstacles, much of the story's conflict originates in disputes between the characters who share a common goal. For Ringo, Luke Plummer and his brothers are the antagonists. They loom large in the story but do not appear on-screen until just before the final crisis and climax.

Narrative Structure

The narrative structure employed by the screenwriter follows the familiar three-act model established earlier in this chapter. The first act, or setup, establishes the world of Tonto, presented as a rough, prosperous frontier town ruled by a formidable force of social prejudice, the Ladies Law and Order League. The daily stagecoach, a lifeline to the outer world, stops for passengers, mail, news, and other necessities. All its passengers have a reason for going to Lordsburg. The travelers' shared goal of reaching the next town (and surviving the trip) is initiated by a number of inciting incidents: Hatfield recognizes Lucy as the daughter of the officer he served under in the Civil War; Doc and Dallas are exiled by the aforementioned Ladies Law and Order League; Gatewood is on the run with his stolen money; Curly hears that Ringo has escaped from prison. The lawman deduces the fugitive is likely headed for Lordsburg to confront the Plummers and so forces Buck to do his job and drive the stagecoach there. The traveling salesman is compelled to make the trip as well—Doc insists that Peacock comes along once Peacock's case of whiskey samples is discovered. Two inciting incidents occur before the plot opens: the murder of Ringo's brother and father at the hands of the Plummers, and the unspecified event that compels Lucy to try and reach her husband before her baby is born.

In the second act, the protagonists overcome a series of obstacles that stand in the way of their goal, including the loss of cavalry support, the birth of Lucy's baby, the theft of their spare horses, and a destroyed ferry-crossing. Ringo's pursuit of revenge has its own obstacles. Curly arrests him and takes his gun, and his growing love for Dallas threatens to weaken his suicidal resolve to face the three murderous Plummer brothers alone. The stakes rise as we become invested in the endangered characters, especially when we realize two of them are in love and after the arrival of a helpless baby. The shared goal of reaching Lordsburg reaches its crisis when Geronimo's warriors finally attack the stagecoach. Most of the passengers do their part to overcome this final and seemingly insurmountable obstacle in the following climax. Dallas shields Lucy's baby, Doc nurses Peacock's arrow wound and punches the hysterical Gatewood, Hatfield dies nobly, and Ringo scrambles to the lead of the speeding stagecoach horse team after Buck takes a bullet and drops the reins. Thanks to Ringo's heroics, the stagecoach stays racing and out of reach until the cavalry arrives to drive off the attackers. In the third act, when the surviving passengers finally arrive in Lordsburg, most of the conflicts are resolved. Gatewood is arrested, Mrs. Mallory implicitly asks Dallas's forgiveness, and we learn that Mr. Peacock has survived his arrow wound.

But the story isn't over yet, because Ringo's goal has not yet been achieved or lost. When he promises Curly he'll come back and return to prison (if he survives), the kindhearted lawman risks his own goal and lends Ringo his empty rifle. Ringo overcomes this first Lordsburg obstacle when he reveals three bullets (one for each Plummer brother) hidden in his hatband. The stakes keep rising as the plot reminds us of the possibility of a future together for Ringo and Dallas—first when Curly promises to take Dallas to Ringo's "little place" in Mexico, and then when Ringo stops Dallas from entering a bordello to remind her of his marriage proposal before he strides off to face his personal crisis: a three-bullet shootout against a trio of heavily armed men. In the final climax, Ringo dives to the ground with his rifle blazing. A shot of Luke strolling into the saloon makes us fear the worst, but it's a false resolution: the villain drops dead from his wounds before he can drink the glass of whisky that awaits him. The remaining plot lines are then quickly resolved. Curly releases Ringo so he and Dallas can ride off into the desert—presumably en route to wedded bliss on Ringo's ranch across the border.

Plot

The plot of *Stagecoach* covers the 2-day trip from Tonto to Lordsburg and is developed in a strictly chronological way without flashbacks or flash-forwards. The events follow one another coherently and logically, and their relations of cause and effect are easy to discern. Indeed, the eminent French film theorist and critic André Bazin notes that

> *Stagecoach* (1939) is the ideal example of the maturity of a style brought to classic perfection. John Ford struck the ideal balance between social myth, historical reconstruction, psychological truth, and the traditional theme of the Western mise en scène. None of these elements dominated any other. *Stagecoach* is like a wheel, so perfectly made that it remains in equilibrium on its axis in any position.[7]

Order As already noted, Ford maintains strict chronological order in using the journey to structure the story events. The journey provides both chronological and geographic markers for dividing the sequences. Furthermore, it reveals a clear pattern of cause and effect created primarily by each character's desire to go to Lordsburg on this particular day. That pattern proceeds to conflict (created both by internal character interaction and by the external Apache attack, which frustrates the characters' desires), reaches a turning point (the victory over the Apaches), and concludes with a resolution (Ringo's revenge on the Plummers, whose testimony had put him in prison, and his riding off a free man with the woman he loves).

Diegetic and Nondiegetic Elements The diegetic elements are everything in the story except the opening and closing titles and credits and the background music, all of which are, of course, nondiegetic. The filmmakers use our expectations of nondiegetic music to fool (and thrill) viewers during a turning point in the climactic attack on the stagecoach. Nondiegetic score music accompanies the entire 7-minute sequence, so when a bugle call joins the dramatic melody playing over a close-up shot of Lucy mumbling a silent prayer, we assume the notes are part of the background music. But Lucy's eyes widen, and she stops praying to utter aloud "Do you hear it?" For a moment, it seems she's reacting to a desperate delusion, but as the bugle call rises and Lucy confidently declares "They're blowing the charge!" we realize that what we thought was nondiegetic score was in fact the diegetic offscreen sound of the cavalry riding to the rescue.

---

7. André Bazin, "Evolution of the Western," in *What Is Cinema?* trans. Hugh Gray, 2 vols. (Berkeley: University of California Press, 1967–71), II, p. 149.

Diegetic and nondiegetic elements

At the height of the Apache attack, director John Ford uses our expectations against us when he momentarily fools us into thinking the bugles Lucy hears are a hysterical hallucination [1]. The only trumpet notes we hear seem to be part of the dramatic nondiegetic score music. The surprise realization that she's right, and the notes are the diegetic bugle call of the cavalry riding to their rescue [2], makes the miraculous moment especially satisfying.

Events The major events in *Stagecoach*—those branching points in the plot structure that force characters to choose between or among alternate paths—include:

> the passengers' decision to leave Tonto in spite of the cavalry's warning about Geronimo and his troops

> Curly's decision to let Ringo join the party

> the passengers' vote to leave the Dry Fork station for Lordsburg, even though a relief unit of cavalry has not yet arrived

> Dr. Boone's willingness to sober up and deliver the baby

> Dallas's decision at the Apache Wells station to accept Ringo's proposal

> the group's decision to delay departure from Apache Wells until Lucy has rested from childbirth and is ready to travel

> Ringo's attempt to escape at Apache Wells

> the passengers' decision at the burned-out ferry landing to try to reach Lordsburg, even though they realize that an Apache attack may be imminent

> Ringo's willingness to risk his life to bring the coach under control as the Apaches attack

> the arrival of the cavalry soon after the Apache attack has begun

> Curly's decision to reward Ringo's bravery by allowing him 10 minutes of freedom in which to confront the Plummers

> Curly's decision to set Ringo free

The minor plot events that add texture and complexity to characters and events but are not essential elements within the narrative include Gatewood's anxiety about getting to Lordsburg no matter what happens along the route; Peacock's anxiety over Dr. Boone's helping himself to his stock of liquor; Buck's wavering enthusiasm for driving the stagecoach against the odds; Lucy's, Hatfield's, and Gatewood's demonstrations of their self-perceived social superiority; Hatfield's attempt to kill Lucy to spare her from capture at the hands of the Apaches; and Curly's arrest of Gatewood for embezzlement.

Duration The story duration includes what we know and what we infer from the total lives of all the characters (e.g., Lucy's privileged upbringing in Virginia, marriage to a military officer, current pregnancy, and the route of her trip out West up until the moment the movie begins). The plot duration includes the time of those events within the story that the film chooses to tell—here the 2 days of the trip from Tonto to Lordsburg. The screen duration, or running time, is 96 minutes.

1

2

Repetition and familiar image

Although no story events recur in *Stagecoach*, Ford does employ a subtle use of a familiar image at the very end of the movie. Throughout the film, extreme long shots of the stagecoach dwarfed by the vast landscape emphasize the vulnerability of the passengers traveling through Apache country [1]. Having repeatedly experienced the anxiety associated with those images amplifies the satisfaction we feel watching a similar composition that shows Dallas and Ringo riding safely off toward domestic bliss [2].

Suspense

The knowledge that Geronimo is on the warpath before the stagecoach leaves Tonto certainly lends suspense to the events that follow, especially when the original cavalry escort leaves and the promised second escort doesn't materialize. But this is general knowledge that does not clearly indicate a direct threat to our protagonists. Suspense is heightened when more direct evidence of imminent danger is revealed, such as when Ringo spots smoke signals, and when the passengers discover a massacred family at the ravaged ferry crossing and Hatfield spots a line of mounted figures along a distant ridge. The suspense ratchets up considerably when the camera narrator reveals a large gathering of Apache warriors watching the defenseless stagecoach from a hilltop. Our awareness of the imminent attack injects tension into the oblivious passengers' confident conversation as they near the safety of Lordsburg. Even with this forewarning, we can't help but be surprised when their victorious toast is interrupted with the first arrow of the attack.

Setting

The physical setting of *Stagecoach*—the desert and mountains, towns and stagecoach—also represents a moral world, established in its first minutes by the contrast between Geronimo and his Apaches (whom Ford portrays as evil) and the U.S. Cavalry (portrayed as good). It was filmed on settings constructed in Hollywood—the interiors and exteriors of two towns and the stagecoach—and on actual locations in the spectacular Monument Valley of northern Arizona. Beautiful and important as Monument Valley and other exterior shots are to the film, the shots made inside the stagecoach as it speeds through the valley are essential to developing other themes in the movie. As the war with the Apaches signifies the territorial changes taking place outside, another drama is taking place among the passengers. In journeying through changing scenery, they also change through their responses to the dangers they face and their relations with, and reactions to, one another. Understanding the setting helps us to understand many of the other aspects of the movie, especially its meanings. This may be a wilderness, but some settlers have brought from the East and the South their notions of social respectability and status, while others are fleeing such constrictions. For the members of the Ladies Law and Order League, the setting offers them the opportunity to restore the town's moral balance, and Dallas and Dr. Boone are being sacrificed to underscore their efforts.

Scope

The story's overall range in time and place is broad, extending from early events—Ringo's wild past and imprisonment, Dallas's troubled upbringing, Hatfield's Civil War experience, and Lucy's East Coast upbringing—to

1

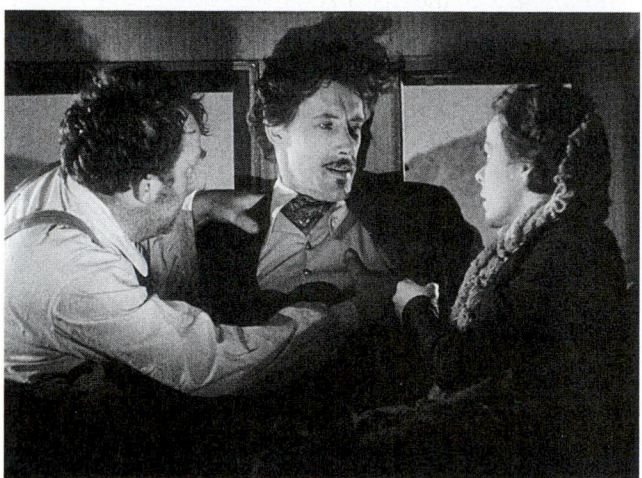

2

Expansive and intimate settings

Stagecoach was the first of the ten Westerns John Ford filmed in Arizona's Monument Valley. The physical landscape of stark desert interspersed with towering mesas and rock formations visually epitomizes his vision of the American West as an ominous but majestic wilderness [1]. But only certain exterior shots were captured in that symbolically (and literally) expansive setting. Much of the narrative occurs in the cramped interior of the stagecoach itself, which was shot inside a Hollywood soundstage. The tight quarters made the ideal setting for developing conflicts between characters representing a diversity of social stations, motivations, and perspectives [2].

those we see on-screen. And although we look essentially at the events on the two days that it takes the stagecoach to go from Tonto to Lordsburg, we are also aware of the larger scope of American history, particularly the westward movement, Ford's favorite subject. Made right before the start of World War II in Europe, *Stagecoach*

presents a historical, social, and mythical vision of American civilization in the 1880s. Ford looked back at the movement west because he saw that period as characterized by clear, simple virtues and values. He viewed the pioneers as establishing the traditions for which Americans would soon be fighting: freedom, democracy, justice, and individualism. Among the social themes of the movie is *manifest destiny*, a term used by conservative nationalists to explain that the territorial expansion of the United States was not only inevitable, but ordained by God. In that effort, embodied in the westward movement, the struggle to expand would be waged against the Native Americans.

One of Ford's persistent beliefs is that civilization occurs as a result of a genuine community built—in the wilderness—through heroism and shared values. In Ford's overall vision, American heroes are always fighting for their rights, whether the fight is against the British, the Native Americans, or the fascists. Precisely because the beauty of Monument Valley means so many different things to different people, it becomes a symbol of the many outcomes that can result from exploration, settlement, and the inevitable territorial disputes that follow. But some later Ford films show that he was troubled by the consequences of expansion, and there seems little doubt that Ford himself is speaking (through Doc) at the end of *Stagecoach*. As Ringo and Dallas ride off to freedom across the border, Doc utters the ironic observation, "Well, they're saved from the blessings of civilization." Dr. Boone's "civilization" includes the hypocritical ladies of Tonto, who force him and Dallas to flee the town; the banker, Gatewood, who pontificates about the importance of banks—"What's good for the banks is good for the country"—while embezzling $50,000 from a payroll meant for miners; and the culture of violence in towns such as Lordsburg. In the 1930s, when *Stagecoach* was made, President Franklin D. Roosevelt singled out the banks as a major cause of the Great Depression and increased the government's regulatory power over them, so we can see that Gatewood (who is not in the original short story that is the source for the *Stagecoach* script) gives the movie contemporary political relevance. In the year after John Ford made *Stagecoach*, in his adaptation of John Steinbeck's *The Grapes of Wrath* (1940)—the story of a dispossessed family journeying through dangerous country to reach a place of safety—the director again put himself fundamentally against the rich and powerful and on the side of the poor and weak.

ANALYZING ELEMENTS OF NARRATIVE

Most of us can hardly avoid analyzing the narrative of a movie after we have seen it. We ask, "Why did the director choose that story?" "Why did he choose to tell it in that way?" "What does it mean?" At the simplest level, our analysis happens unconsciously while we're watching a movie, as we fill in gaps in events, infer character traits from the clues or cues we receive, and interpret the significance of objects. But when we're actively looking at a movie, we should analyze its narrative in more precise, conscious detail. The following checklist provides a few ideas about how you might do this.

SCREENING CHECKLIST: ELEMENTS OF NARRATIVE

✔ Who is the movie's protagonist? What factors and needs motivate or complicate that character's actions?

✔ Consider the movie's major characters. Can you characterize each of them according to complexity (round characters vs. flat)?

✔ What is the narration of the movie? Does it use a narrator of any kind?

✔ What are the differences among omniscient and restricted narration?

✔ Carefully reconstruct the narrative structure of the movie. What is the inciting incident? What goal does the protagonist pursue? How does the protagonist's need influence that pursuit? What obstacles (including the crisis) does the protagonist encounter, and how does she or he engage them?

✔ Keep track of nondiegetic elements that seem essential to the movie's plot (voice-overs, for example). Do they seem natural and appropriate to the film or do they appear to be "tacked on" to make up for a shortcoming in the overall presentation of the movie's narrative?

✔ Are the plot events presented in chronological order? What is the significance of the order of plot events in the movie?

✔ Keep track of the major and minor events in the movie's plot. Are any of the minor events unnecessary to the movie overall? If these events were not included, would the movie be better? Why?

✔ Are there scenes that create a noticeable summary relationship between story duration and screen duration? Do these scenes complement or detract from the overall narrative? Do these scenes give you all the information about the underlying story that you need to understand what has happened in the elapsed story time?

✔ Do any scenes use real time or a stretch relationship between story duration and screen duration? If so, what is the significance of these scenes to the overall narrative?

✔ Is any major plot event presented on-screen more than once? If so, why do you think the filmmaker has chosen to repeat the event?

✔ How do the setting and the scope of the narrative complement the other elements?

Questions for Review

1. What is the difference between narration and narrator?

2. What are the differences between omniscient and restricted narration?

3. What are the differences between (a) the camera narrator and a first-person narrator and (b) a first-person narrator and a third-person narrator?

4. Can a major character be flat? Can a minor character be round? Explain your answer.

5. What is the climax, and how does it relate to the protagonist's pursuit of the goal?

6. How (and why) do we distinguish between the story and the plot of a movie?

7. What is meant by the diegesis of a story? What is the difference between diegetic and nondiegetic elements in the plot?

8. What are major and minor events each supposed to do for the movie's plot?

9. Which of the following is the most common relationship of screen duration to story duration: summary relationship, real time, or stretch relationship? Define each one.

10. What is the difference between suspense and surprise? Which one is more difficult for a filmmaker to create?

Black Panther (2018). Ryan Coogler, director. Pictured: Lupita Nyong'o and Letitia Wright.

MISE-EN-SCÈNE

What Is Mise-en-Scène?

Mise-en-scène is right there on the screen in front of us, but approaching the subject can be daunting because it encompasses so many interconnected components. Even the unfamiliar sound of this hyphenated and accented French term (pronounced "meez-ahn-SEN") is intimidating. But fear not. Like most things cinematic, the more you break it down, the more understandable mise-en-scène reveals itself to be.

Mise-en-scène means literally "staging or putting on an action or scene" and thus is sometimes called *staging*. In fact, the term originated on the theater stage. In a play, a bare stage must be lit up, fitted out with constructed sets, and populated with actors wearing costumes and makeup, all of which is arrayed according to the dramatic needs of each scene.

It is much the same in the movies. A film's mise-en-scène is everything we see in every shot: every object, every person, everything about their surroundings, and how each of these components is arranged, illuminated, and moved around. And very little of this is left to chance—virtually everything on-screen was carefully chosen and placed there by the filmmakers for a reason.

Sometimes those choices are made for reasons of authenticity. If a director wants the viewer to believe the events on-screen are happening in, say, a county courthouse in 1965 in Selma, Alabama, during the civil rights movement (as in Ava DuVernay's *Selma*, 2014), she may stage her shots with objects and elements that reflect that specific situation, place, and era. Other times those choices are driven by the filmmaker's goal of creating mood, conveying character, and telling a story. That same scene in *Selma* uses warm lighting on wood fixtures to evoke a sense of Old South tradition, dresses a man

Mise-en-scène in *Selma*

Director Ava DuVernay uses mise-en-scène in this courthouse scene in *Selma* to evoke an era, manipulate the viewer's narrative expectations, and visualize conflict.

Different directorial approaches to mise-en-scène
Wes Anderson, the director of *Moonrise Kingdom* (2012) [1] and the animated film *Isle of Dogs* (2018), is known for using conspicuous mise-en-scène that favors formal, balanced compositions, stylized settings and costumes, clearly choreographed action, and coordinated color schemes. In movies such as *Children of Men* (2006) [2] and *Gravity* (2013), director Alfonso Cuarón prefers less ostentatious design that emphasizes realism, often in counterpoint to the fantastic events unfolding on screen. In contrast to the more posed look of Anderson's compositions, Cuarón's fluid mise-en-scène unfolds in lengthy, unbroken shots in which actors and the camera are often in seemingly spontaneous motion.

poised to assault Dr. Martin Luther King Jr. in an innocuous cardigan sweater to misguide our expectations, and arranges the actors to emphasize the tense division between the black and the white characters.

As you consider a movie's mise-en-scène, ask yourself whether what you see in a scene is simply appealing decor, a well-dressed actor, and a striking bit of lighting or whether these elements are influencing your understanding of the narrative, characters, and action of the movie. Keep in mind that the director has a purpose for each thing put into a shot or scene, but each of these things does not necessarily have a meaning in and of itself. The *combination* of elements within the frame—

and the context in which they are presented—gives the shot or scene much of its overall meaning.

While decisions about mise-en-scène are driven primarily by the needs of a film's story, mise-en-scène can also be highly personal and can help us distinguish one director's work from another's. Genre formulas can also have a powerful influence on the mise-en-scène of individual films within that genre. You may recall from Chapter 3 the specific kinds of dramatic lighting associated with film noir and the horror genre or the wide open, big-sky settings typical of westerns.

Mise-en-scène is made of four primary components: design, lighting, composition, and movement (also known as kinesis).

Design

Design is the process by which the look of the settings, objects, and actors is determined. Set design, decor, costuming, makeup, and hairstyle design all play a role in shaping the overall design.

Every director counts on a team of professionals to design the look of the movie. The leader of this team is the production designer.

The Production Designer

The director knows the moods and ideas the story must convey in each scene and the character backgrounds, traits, and intentions that must be reflected in costumes and makeup. She is ultimately responsible for guiding and finalizing all decisions that go into determining a film's mise-en-scène. But filmmaking is a collaborative art form, and the director must rely on other experts to advise and execute the design process that serves her vision.

Generally one of the first collaborators that a director hires, the **production designer** is both an artist and an executive and is responsible for the overall design concept (for the *look* of the movie—its individual sets, locations, furnishings, properties, and costumes) and for supervising the heads of the many departments involved in creating that look. These departments include

❯ art (development of the movie's look involves sketch artists, painters, and computer-graphics specialists)

❯ costume design and construction

Even animated films rely on production design

As we can see from this shot in *Trolls* (2016), just because settings, props, costumes, makeup, and lighting are drawn, sculpted, and/or modeled on a computer doesn't mean they aren't designed and composed to create mood, convey character, and tell a story.

> hairstyling

> makeup

> wardrobe (maintaining the costumes and having them ready for each day's shooting)

> location (finding appropriate locations, contracting for their use, and coordinating the transportation of cast and crew between the studio and the locations)

> properties (finding the furniture and objects for a movie, either from a studio's own resources or from specialized outside firms that supply properties)

> carpentry

> set construction and decoration

> greenery (real or artificial greenery, including grass, trees, shrubs, and flowers)

> transportation (supplying the vehicles seen on-screen)

> visual effects (digital postproduction effects)

> special effects (mechanical effects and in-camera optical effects created during production)

The production designer's process begins with the intensive previsualization—imagining, discussing, sketching, planning—that is at the core of all movies. In addition to the director, the film's cinematographer (also known as the director of photography) plays an important role in this visual design process—which makes sense, as he or she will be responsible for lighting and shooting everything the production designer creates and collects. As we will see in the next chapter, the cinematographer helps create the look of the film by selecting film stock or digital format, by overseeing lighting and camera operation, and by manipulating color, saturation, and other visual qualities in a postproduction process called color grading.

Perhaps because the synthesis of mise-en-scène, cinematography, and directing is so crucial, many designers have become directors. Alfred Hitchcock learned about creating visual and special effects, such as expressive lighting, during his early career as an art director (part of the production design team); Ridley Scott worked as a set designer before directing highly designed films like *Alien* (1979) and *Blade Runner* (1982).

Elements of Design

During the process of designing a film, the director and production designer are concerned with several major elements. The most important of these are (1) setting, decor, and properties and (2) costume, makeup, and hairstyle.

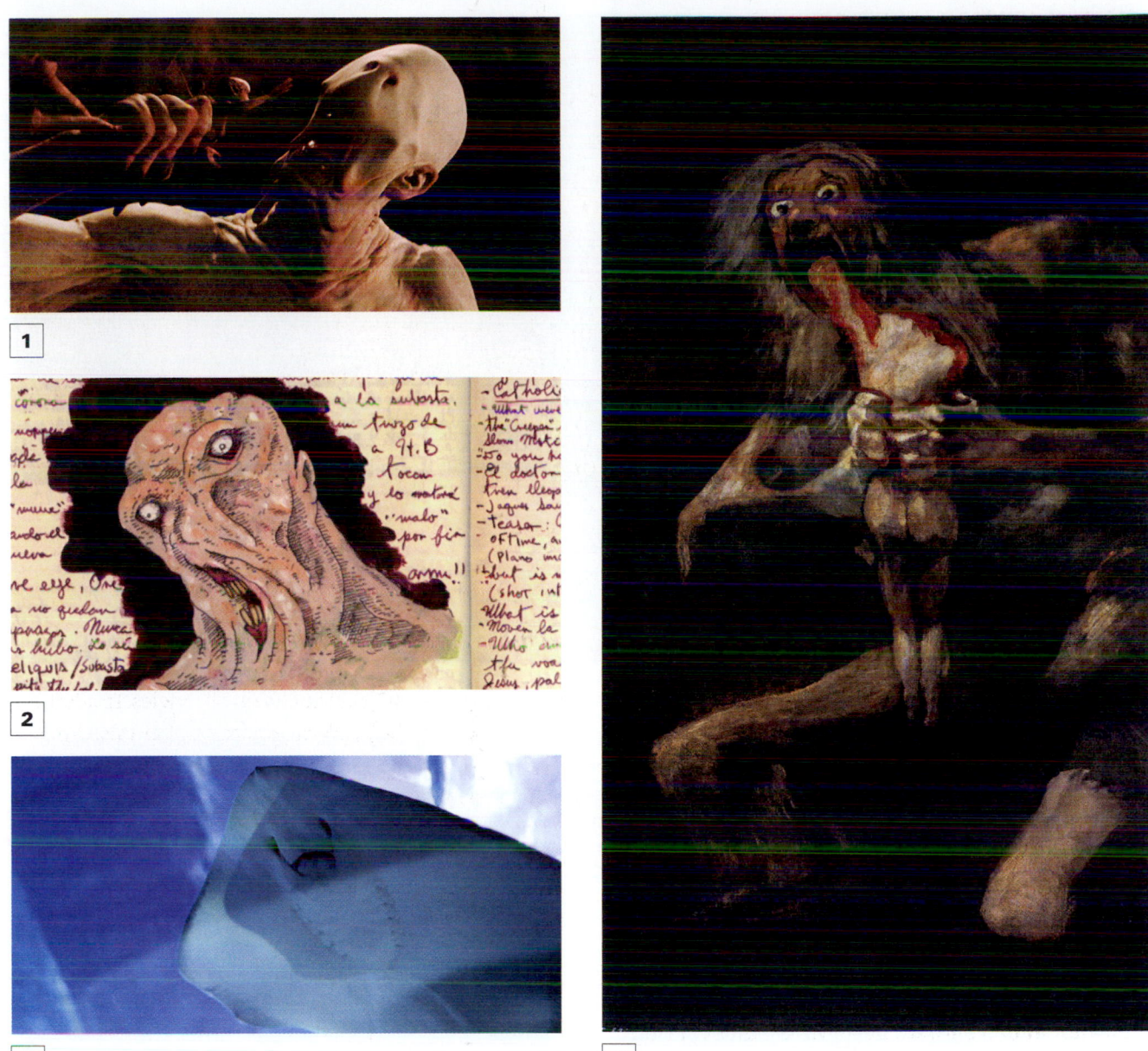

The evolution of a character design
The terrifying Pale Man [1] in Guillermo del Toro's *Pan's Labyrinth* (2006) started as a series of drawings in the director's notebook [2]. As they worked their way through multiple models and sketches, del Toro and his designers were inspired by what he called "the flat faceless effect" of a manta ray [3] and by Francisco Goya's nineteenth-century painting *Saturn Devouring His Son* [4].

Setting, Decor, and Properties The spatial and temporal **setting** of a film is the environment (realistic or imagined) in which the narrative takes place. In addition to its physical significance, the setting creates a mood that has social, psychological, emotional, economic, and cultural significance. The size, layout, and features of the space a character inhabits can tell us a lot about that person's background, circumstances, personality, and even emotional state.

Perhaps the most important decision that a filmmaker must make about setting is to determine when to shoot **on location** and when to shoot on a set. To shoot on location, filmmakers must find existing interior and exterior spaces that suit the needs of their story, then alter the location according to the planned mise-en-scène, a process that may include replacing furnishings, hanging new signage, or repainting walls. Location shooting requires filmmakers to secure access (often for a fee), and

Movie sets are designed for the benefit of the camera

When a movie scene is shot in a studio (rather than at an actual location), the crew making a movie can give us the illusion of a whole room or building when, in fact, they construct only those aspects of a set needed for the benefit of the camera. David Fincher's *The Social Network* (2010) was shot on actual locations as well as in soundstages. This set was designed and constructed to be a life-size representation of the Winklevoss brothers' dormitory rooms at Harvard, but as you can see, the principal room is missing its fourth wall, and lighting equipment is suspended from the ceiling. Through careful framing of each shot, the cinematographer will capture images that make us think this is an actual room. But fake as it is, the designers and decorators were meticulous about details, which one actor said helped him to better understand the characters and situation.

often, to bring in special equipment to power the lights necessary for most motion-picture production.

In the first two decades of moviemaking, the preference was to shoot in exterior locations for authenticity, natural depth, and available light. But location shooting proved expensive and unpredictable, and the evolution of larger studios made it possible to build interior spaces (or sets) that could be more easily configured to meet the needs of the story as well as the film-production process. The first movie sets were little different from theater sets: flat backdrops erected, painted, and photographed in a studio, observed by the camera as if it were a spectator in the theater. Open roofs or skylights provided indoor lighting.

As movie stories and productions grew in scope and sophistication, so did the sets that served them. Movie studios built soundstages—windowless, soundproofed, boxlike buildings that are several stories high and can cover an acre or more of floor space—capable of accom-

modating multiple large sets and virtually unlimited lighting and camera equipment. Some soundstages are large enough to re-create outdoor scenes, complete with

Setting reveals character

In *Ex Machina* (2014), the set design of the home of the reclusive social media billionaire Nathan Bateman conveys not only his vast wealth but also his emotional isolation. The structure is a mostly subterranean labyrinth of sleek and sterile interiors with few direct portals to the outside world.

Spectacular early sets

Giovanni Pastrone's Italian epic *Cabiria* (1914) used massive sets to impress audiences with eye-popping spectacle and convince them that they were witnessing history. The pioneering Italian set designers were later recruited by Hollywood directors, including D. W. Griffith. Then, as now, sets can impart story meaning as well. The design of *Cabiria*'s temple of Moloch conveys tyrannical power and the grotesque evil of a place devoted to human sacrifice.

building exteriors and massive painted backdrops representing distant scenery and sky.

Production studios often also feature back lots: constructed buildings and streets that include classic examples of various types of architecture that can be used again and again, often with new paint or landscaping to help them meet the requirements of a new narrative. A movie set is not reality, but a fragment of reality created as the setting for a particular shot. Only those aspects of the exteriors that are necessary for the benefit of the camera are actually built, whether to scale (life-size) or in miniature. For example, the front of a house may look complete with bushes and flowers, curtains in the windows, and so on, but there may be no rooms behind that facade. Similarly, most interior sets include only the minimum parts of the rooms needed to accommodate the story action and the movement of the camera. Some ambitious filmmakers push past the usual studio practicalities to create immersive sets that lend their settings a more expansive spatial quality. Director Orson Welles and his design team on *Citizen Kane* (1941) created special sets that included ceilings visible in low-angle shots and a complete set of four walls for shots captured from high angles. For Stanley Kubrick's *The Shining* (1980), production designer Roy Walker created what was then

the largest interior set in existence to accommodate the wall-to-wall and floor-to-ceiling moving camera shots that stalk the boy protagonist Danny as he rides his Big Wheel through the Overlook Hotel's seemingly endless series of corridors.

Whether the scene is shot on location or on a set, interior shooting involves the added consideration of **decor** (the color and textures of the interior decoration, furniture, draperies, and curtains) and **properties**, which can be divided into two basic categories: **props** and **set dressing**. Any object handled by actors is considered a prop. The **prop master** works with the production designer to find and select props, then maintains each object and ensures it is ready when the actor needs it for shooting. Set dressing is anything used to create the look of the environment in which the action takes place. Set dressing may include curtains, paint, carpets, and any object visible in the area, such as furniture, books, knickknacks, and other objects or decorations. The **set**

***Arrival* subverts setting expectations**

Everything about the visiting aliens in *Arrival* (2016) is completely outside the understanding of the human scientists tasked with translating their language and deciphering their intent. So, director Denis Villeneuve and his production designer, Patrice Vermette, purposely subverted established movie expectations viewers might have of aerodynamic metal spaceships encrusted with wires, antennae, and other surface details. Each of *Arrival*'s alien egg-shaped craft [1] seems to be made of stone; the interiors are spare, organic, and enormous [2].

Set dressing and props in *Okja*

Decor, set dressing, and props are all capable of expressing meaning that creates mood and aids in our understanding of story and character. Mija, the young protagonist of director Joon-ho Bong's environmental parable *Okja* (2017), lives in a simple but idyllic setting [1]. The rough-hewn objects and decor that make up the *set dressing* communicate a simple lifestyle in harmony with nature that is in stark contrast with the steel and concrete slaughterhouse she infiltrates to rescue her beloved genetically engineered pig Okja [2]. She buys his freedom (and his life) with a *prop*: a solid gold pig that her grandfather purchased with his payment for raising Okja [3]. The prop serves the story and also represents a number of conflicting themes: the grandfather's traditional mind-set, Mija's love for Okja, and the corporate greed personified by the meat industry heiress Nancy Mirando [4].

decorator, a sort of cinematic interior decorator who is in charge of set dressing, supervises a variety of specialists. The late Stephenie McMillan, a set decorator on eight of the Harry Potter films, said that her job was to bring the production designer's vision to life. She believed that the look of a movie should never upstage the actors nor distract from the action.

Costume, Makeup, and Hairstyle   To understand elements of cinematic language, even things as seemingly straightforward as hair, makeup, and costumes, it is often useful to start with how an everyday equivalent functions in our own lives. For most of us, making ourselves presentable to the outside world influences our selection of clothes, cosmetics, and hairstyle. We tend to do our best to appear "attractive."

It is no different in movies. In fact, in most cases, the film industry's impulse to use clothes, makeup, and hairstyling to enhance beauty is even more pronounced, especially in mainstream commercial cinema. Why?

Set design and costumes in *The Leopard*

Luchino Visconti's *The Leopard* (1963) explores the transformation of Sicilian society after the unification of Italy in 1861. In one scene, Angelica, the daughter of a striving bourgeois mayor, wanders an abandoned palace owned by the royal family of her upper-class fiancé. Her bright pink dress stands out in stark contrast against the empty, unadorned walls, visualizing the incongruity between the vibrancy of the ascendant lower classes and the fading of a doomed aristocracy.

Because one of the many reasons we go to the movies is to experience visually pleasing things (gorgeous images, scenic environments, intriguing objects) and beautiful people. So, ever since movies entered the media marketplace, performers have been cast as much (and sometimes more) for their looks as for their acting talent.

During the years of the classical Hollywood studio system, the studios frequently took actors with star potential and gave them major makeovers, dyed and restyled their hair, had their teeth fixed or replaced, and even subjected them to cosmetic surgery, all to create a certain "ideal" masculine or feminine beauty to complement the other decorative aspects of the studio's product. Today, thankfully, actors are not fettered by rigid studio contracts, and our culture's notions of beauty have broadened considerably. But many movies are still in the business of providing beautiful things to look at, so filmmakers often use the styling of actors' hair, makeup, and clothing toward that goal.

Of course, making people pretty is only one way to use costumes, hairstyle, and makeup. Moviemakers are also concerned with verisimilitude. Thanks to centuries of paintings, drawings, prints, and photographs depicting both historical events and everyday life, we are culturally trained to use visual cues—including clothing, hairstyles, and makeup—to identify the period an image represents. Filmmakers tap into this visual vocabulary to tell us where and when a story is taking place and to help us believe the fabricated events we are watching.

That doesn't mean movie characters always look exactly like their real-life counterparts would have appeared in the original era. The hairstyles, clothing design, and makeup practices used in a period film may also be influenced by the fashions in style at the time when the movie was made and marketed. Because designers are products of their times, some of this contemporary influence may be unconscious and unavoidable. But often, designing elements of contemporary style into the mise-en-scène of movies set in the past is done deliberately.

Filmmakers understand that current styles are deeply embedded in audiences' expectations. They want to transport us to a different time and place, but they don't want to distract, confuse, or repulse us with hairstyles, makeup, and garments that don't make sense to our contemporary perspective. How filmmakers conceive and present people, places, and things in a story set in a speculative future or in a wholly imagined fantasy world may also be influenced by contemporary culture.

1

2

Costume and hairstyle convey time and place in *The Get Down* and *Stranger Things*

For Baz Luhrmann's 2016–17 Netflix series *The Get Down* [1], production designer Karen Murphy used details such as afros, sideburns, knit shirts, flared pants, and vintage Pro Keds sneakers to firmly root the story in the Bronx of the late 1970s. *Stranger Things* [2], another Netflix series set just a few years later in small-town Indiana, evoked the era with patterned polos and sweaters, corduroy bell-bottoms, down vests, and feathered hair.

Of course, just as we saw with settings and decor, elements of design may serve multiple functions. In addition to providing visual attractiveness and enhancing verisimilitude, the appearance of characters through costumes, hairstyle, and makeup also provides filmmakers yet another way to convey narrative information and meaning to the viewer.

Costume We choose our clothes for a variety of reasons, including price, fit, and comfort, but we are also—whether unconsciously or deliberately—making selections that communicate an image to those around us. And the image we present often varies with the situation. Most of us don't wear the same kind of clothes to a job interview that we would to class or a party.

Cleopatra values glamour over historical accuracy
The Hollywood studio 20th Century Fox that produced the 1963 epic *Cleopatra* was more concerned with selling their popular star Elizabeth Taylor than with historical accuracy. The costumes Taylor wore in the title role were basically contemporary gowns designed to accentuate the actress's beauty; experts agree that they bear little resemblance to the styles of the late Greco-Roman period.

What we wear in any given situation tells those we encounter something about us. The information conveyed by our clothes is not always accurate; we may be using clothes to imply qualities we don't actually possess (an upstanding orthodontist may buy a motorcycle and put on a bandana and a black leather jacket, but that doesn't make him an outlaw biker). And, of course, our selection is governed or at least influenced by the fashions of the era we live in.

The same goes for film characters. The costumes (the clothing, sometimes known as wardrobe, worn by an actor in a movie) are selected and designed by the filmmakers to provide a sense of authenticity regarding the story's time period and setting and also to help communicate the character's social station, self-image, state of mind, and the public image that the character is trying to project.

Walter Plunkett's clothing designs for the romantic Civil War epic *Gone with the Wind* (1939) were not always historically accurate, but they effectively helped actor Vivien Leigh portray the protagonist Scarlett O'Hara. In the opening scenes, her frilly buttoned-up dress presents Scarlett as a girlish innocent. The next day, when she's on the hunt for a marriage proposal, her new dress, which features a plunging neckline and bare shoulders, reveals her true nature and intent. The outfit doesn't work, and she ends up marrying a different man whom she does not love. He conveniently dies in the war, and soon after, she causes a scandal at a ball when she dances with the notorious scoundrel Rhett Butler while still wearing an all-black mourning gown. As the war reduces her fortunes—and she matures—Scarlett's wardrobe becomes less decorative, more practical, and considerably grimier. Poverty stricken after the war, Scarlett needs money for taxes to save her beloved plantation. Her only chance for a loan is to seduce Rhett, so she orders her former slave to sew a fancy new gown out of old curtains.

Contemporary films employ costumes to convey character progression as well. When Jordan Peele's 2017 horror film *Get Out* introduces us to Rose Armitage, the white girlfriend of African American photographer Chris Washington, the story needs us to believe that she is a progressive and sincerely supportive girlfriend. So, her clothing is cool and casual: a quilted black jacket, denim dress, and ribbed tights. Later, after she has revealed herself to be a racist predator, she changes into a crisp white button-down shirt tucked into fitted khaki slacks.

The title character's costume in Tim Burton's *Edward Scissorhands* (1990) proclaims his status as an absolute outsider. In stark contrast to the bland pastels worn by the conformists who take him in, Edward is clad in an ornate black leather bodysuit that is simultaneously menacing and sexy—and is in direct opposition to his innocent, gentle nature. The suit seems stitched together from multiple spare parts and is held together with straps, buckles, and rivets, a look that implies Edward's assembled origins. (The fact that he has scissors for hands supports this impression.)

Edward Scissorhands takes place in a highly stylized version of contemporary America. But what about costumes in entirely invented settings? When a film involves the future, as in science fiction, the costumes must reflect the social structure and values of an imaginary society. For example, in the dystopian Hunger Games

1

2

3

4

Different characters, different costumes, hairstyles, and makeup

Actor Charlize Theron brings a great range and skill to her performances. Her characterizations are further enhanced by costume, hairstyle, and makeup. To fully inhabit the serial killer Aileen Wuornos in Patty Jenkins's *Monster* (2003), Theron put on weight, partially shaved her eyebrows, thinned and heat-damaged her hair, and wore prosthetic dentures [1]. To play the indomitable Furiosa in *Mad Max: Fury Road* (2015), her skin was soiled, tanned and weathered, her hair was chopped off and darkened, and her left arm was (digitally) amputated [2]. The black makeup across her forehead, a symbol of her allegiance to the tyrant Immortan Joe, gradually wears off as her humanity reemerges. When the emotionally stunted Mavis Gary, her character in *Young Adult* (2011), discovers her high school boyfriend is now a new father, her unwashed hair is pulled back, her eyeliner is smeared, and she wears a baggy T-shirt and sweatpants [3]. She uses clothing, makeup, and wigs to assume an escalating series of more seductive looks in her delusional quest to win him back [4].

series, the regimented workers all wear variations of the same drab conformist uniform, while the clothes worn by the decadent ruling class come in an endless gamut of vibrant colors and flamboyant styles.

Real-world fashion designers constantly borrow from the past to create today's designs, and the same goes for the wardrobe designers inventing costumes for stories set in the future. The characters in the bleak, cynical *Blade Runner* (1982) and *Blade Runner 2049* (2017) films wear clothes that would (mostly) fit right in during the 1940s, when film noir first emerged from Hollywood. The flowing T-shaped garments and the layered armored uniforms worn by characters throughout the continuing Star Wars saga are influenced by traditional Japanese clothing. (It is no coincidence that Japanese samurai films were one of many sources George Lucas drew upon when he invented Star Wars in the first place.)

Makeup and Hairstyle The traditional makeup used to enhance or alter an actor's appearance covers the full range of facial and body cosmetics familiar to consumers (often specially blended to comply with camera and lighting requirements) and **prosthetics**, which are synthetic materials attached to an actor's face or body. Prosthetics can include artificial skin for aging effects; fabricated noses, ears, teeth, and chins to help make an actor look more like a known figure; or the kind of grotesque (or whimsical) appendages and the gory wounds we associate with fantasy and horror films. Actors' bodies may be fitted with prosthetics to increase the illusion of a character's weight, height, or build.

1

2

The appearance of actors' hair is used to create the look appropriate to each character's role in the story. An actor's existing hair may be styled or the actor may be fitted with wigs and other hairpieces. In fact, until the 1960s, actors in almost every film, whether period or contemporary, were required to wear wigs designed for the film for reasons both aesthetic and practical. When shooting out of sequence, which allows continuous scenes to be shot weeks apart, it is particularly difficult to re-create colors, cuts, and styles of hair. In the days before technology made it easy to compare shots captured at different times, an actor's hair might not have matched from shot to shot. Once designed, a wig never changes, eliminating the possibility that an actor's hair could be the source of a continuity error.

The person responsible for all these effects is the **makeup artist**. The makeup artist works closely with the production designer and the cinematographer, as well as with actors themselves, usually accompanying them to the set and performing whatever touch-ups are necessary. In many films, animators and other digital effects artists also alter the appearances of actors to help create characters and lend historical or contextual authenticity. The computer-generated animated layers over live performances using **motion capture** technol-

Historically accurate makeup and hair

During the studio years, film characters' hairstyles were usually based on modified modern looks rather than period authenticity. Two notable exceptions to this practice involve the same actress playing the same character in two different movies shot 16 years apart. The strict historical accuracy that actor Bette Davis brought to her portrayals of Queen Elizabeth I in *The Private Lives of Elizabeth and Essex* (1939) [1] and *The Virgin Queen* (1955) required that she shave her eyebrows and the front half of her head to accommodate a wig in the style worn by the sixteenth-century monarch [2].

Traditional and digital makeup in *Alice in Wonderland*

The hair, costume, and makeup for the Red Queen in Tim Burton's *Alice in Wonderland* (2010) and *Alice Through the Looking Glass* (2016) were influenced by illustrations from Lewis Carroll's original books and by Bette Davis's portrayals of Queen Elizabeth I in two Hollywood studio films. Both traditional and digital techniques were used to create the character we see on-screen. Exaggerated makeup and a massive wig help convey her malicious vanity; her digitally inflated head and impossibly restricted waist complete the effect.

A villain's hairstyle goes against expectations
In the Coen brothers' *No Country for Old Men* (2007), the hair of the character Anton Chigurh is styled in a way not normally associated with portrayals of cold-blooded killers. But somehow, the incongruity of a laughable bowl-cut bob on a ruthless psychopath made actor Javier Bardem's portrayal even more convincing—and terrifying.

ogy have been described as "digital makeup" by the actor Andy Serkis, whose performances have been used to animate characters such as Gollum in the Lord of the Rings and Hobbit films and Caesar in the most recent Planet of the Apes trilogy. Serkis claims that animators follow every expression and movement so closely that the animation counts as makeup. Many animators feel that they contribute more than simply surface embellishment—they create aspects of performance not present in the original motion-capture sessions.

The actor Zoe Saldana is familiar with most approaches to makeup. For her transformation into the compassionate space assassin Gamora in the original *Guardians of the Galaxy* (2014) film and its 2017 sequel, she wore a wig, was covered in multiple layers of green paint, and wore silicone prosthetics over her eyebrows, forehead, and cheekbones. The compassionate space native Neytiri in *Avatar* (2009) began with Saldana's motion-captured performance, which was the basis for the animated character we see on-screen. Her (somewhat) more down-to-earth role as a school psychologist named Mrs. Mollé in *I Kill Giants* (2017) required that she wear minimal traditional makeup and a simple hairstyle. All of Saldana's roles use makeup to convey character and help tell the story. Gamora's look imparts an exotic menace that clashes with an emotional vulnerability she unsuccessfully tries to conceal. Neytiri appears both otherworldly and familiar. Neytiri's people, the Na'vi, are designed to evoke aboriginal peoples and project a sort of feline athleticism that is in stark contrast to the earthling soldiers who discover and exploit

them. Mrs. Mollé's uncomplicated makeup and hair is designed as a counterpoint as well. She is a supportive anchor of normalcy in the protagonist's otherwise unpredictable and often hostile world.

Makeup and hair also contribute to the characterizations in *Get Out* and *Edward Scissorhands* described earlier. As the sincere girlfriend in *Get Out*, Rose Armitage has long flowing hair and stylish bangs. After she betrays her boyfriend Chris, Rose slicks her hair into a tight ponytail. Edward Scissorhands's ghostly pale makeup and lack of eyebrows differentiates (and alienates) him from his more conventionally biological suburban neighbors. The prosthetic scars that cover his face help us sympathize with the hardships of being an abandoned orphan with scissors for hands. Edward's unruly hair tells us something about his self-image and his generous nature. He devotes himself to beautifying the hair of others, but he never turns his talents on himself.

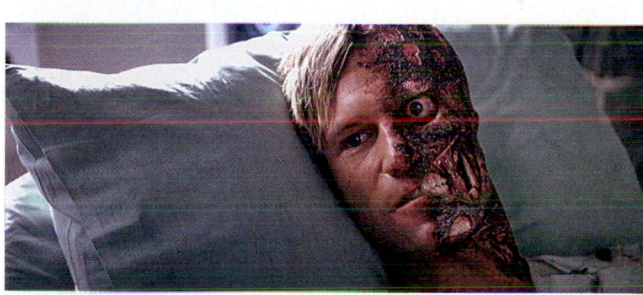

The expressive power of makeup
In Christopher Nolan's *The Dark Knight* (2008), the Joker character's great, gashed red mouth, created through facial painting and prosthetics, is a darkly comic deformation and a visual parallel to the character's dual traits of sadistic humor and true evil [1]. An explosion rigged by the Joker transforms a district attorney into the mutilated villain Two-Face; here, a digital process was used to replace half of the character's face with grisly computer-animated bone, muscle, and scar tissue [2].

Lighting

Illumination and shadow affect the way we see and interpret settings, makeup, and costumes, so during preproduction, most designers include an idea of the lighting in their sketches. Likewise, because lighting can help express mood, tell a story, and convey character, directors often incorporate lighting into the **storyboards** they use to plan the film. When the movie is ready for shooting, these sketches help guide the cinematographer in coordinating the camera and the lighting. During actual production, the cinematographer determines the lighting once the camera setups are chosen. As a key component of composition, lighting creates our sense of cinematic space by illuminating people and things, creating highlights and shadows, and defining shapes and textures. Both on a set and on location, light is controlled and manipulated to achieve expressive effects; except in rare instances, there is no such thing as wholly "natural" lighting in a narrative movie. Documentaries that capture events as they happen often have no choice but to use whatever lighting is available, but events produced for the documentary, such as re-creations and interviews, employ planned, and sometimes even expressive, lighting. Animated movies also use expressive lighting, even when it must be drawn or modeled. We will return to lighting as it relates to cinematography in the next chapter. Here in relation to mise-en-scène, we will concern ourselves with three aspects of the lighting setup: *quality*, *ratios*, and *direction*.

LOOKING AT MOVIES
LIGHTING

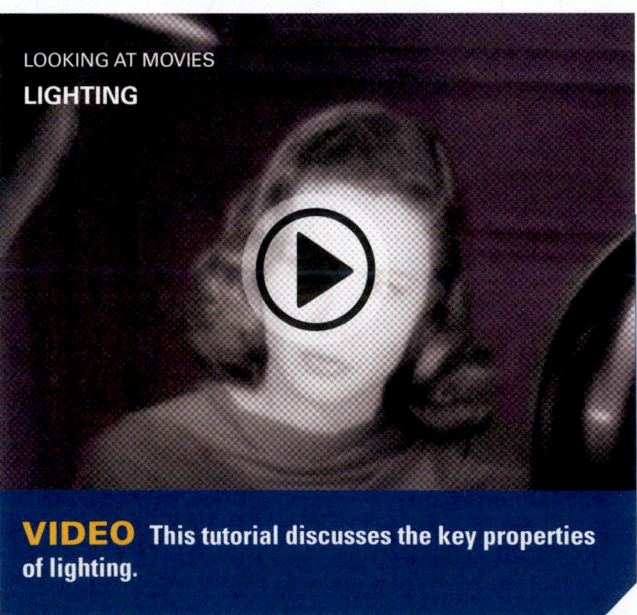

VIDEO This tutorial discusses the key properties of lighting.

1

2

3

Expressive lighting in *City of God*

Lighting plays a powerful role in establishing the setting, character, and tone in *City of God* (2002), a violent story of constantly changing moods that is told with equally rapid changes in lighting style. [1] A rare playful day on the beach is saturated in sunlight. [2] A drug deal in a decaying slum building is depicted with large areas of shadow with the only light filtered through a brick screen. [3] Strobe lights, lens flares, and reflections underscore the rapidly developing chaos at a disco party.

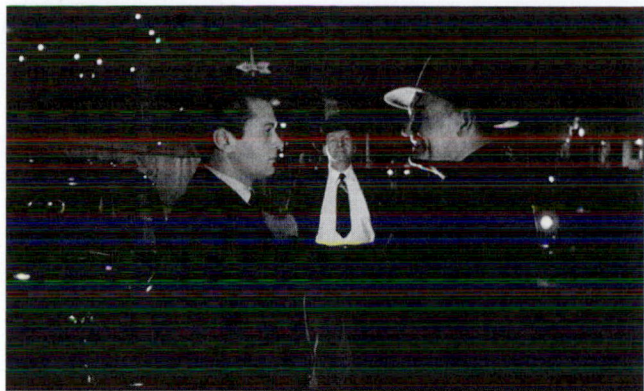

Lighting and setting

A good way to understand how lighting influences our impressions of the setting is to compare the lighting quality of two movies that were filmed in the same setting. Alexander Mackendrick's *Sweet Smell of Success* (1957) paints a cynical portrait of Manhattan as a cutthroat world of schemers and powerbrokers. This scene shot beside the city's Queensboro Bridge uses hard, low-key light to throw sharp pools of light and cast deep shadows [1]. Woody Allen's *Manhattan* (1979) is a romantic and funny appraisal of relationships and the city itself. In its Queensboro Bridge scene, the light is diffused and the edges are soft [2].

Quality

The quality of light used in any situation falls somewhere on a spectrum between hard light and soft light. **Hard light** is direct: the beams of light shine directly from the source to the subject. Hard light creates a clear, sharp border between areas of bright illumination and dark shadows. Hard light is high contrast: details are crisp and defined, which can make hard light less flattering for characters with wrinkles and other facial textures. **Soft light** is diffused: the beams of light are broken up or scattered on their way from the source to the subject. This diffusion can be accomplished by bouncing the light or by passing it through a sort of cloudy paper descriptively

Soft versus hard lighting

In *Citizen Kane* (1941), cinematographer Gregg Toland used lighting ratios and quality to create a clear contrast between characters in the scene in which Charles Foster Kane first meets and woos Susan Alexander. The lighting on the powerful millionaire is harder and relatively low-key, emphasizing his age and worldliness [1]. The inexperienced shopgirl is lit with high-key and soft light that softens her youthful features [2].

dubbed *diffusion*. Soft light is low contrast: where illumination ends and shadow begins is less distinct. Details are also less defined, and so soft light is considered more flattering. One easy way to see the difference between hard and soft light is to compare the interplay between light and shadow in direct sunlight (hard light), as opposed to how light and shadow appear on a cloudy or foggy day (soft light). We can generally (but not always) associate hard lighting with serious or scary situations and soft lighting with romantic or comic stories.

1

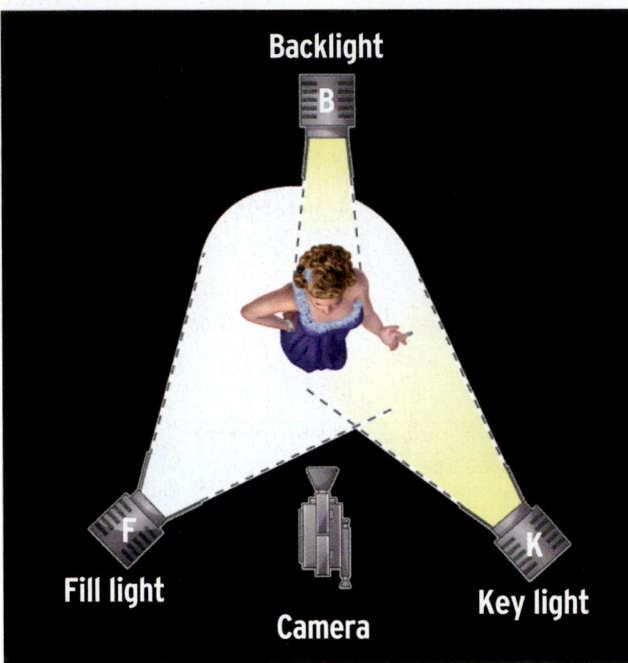

2

Three-point lighting

The Scarlet Empress (1934), a ravishing, high-camp historical drama, is also the director Josef von Sternberg's visual tribute to the allure of Marlene Dietrich. He consistently photographs her with three-point lighting that accentuates her beauty. In this example, the key light casts deep shadows around her eyes and on her right cheek. The fill light softens the depth of the shadows created by the brighter key light. The backlight creates highlights along the edges of her hair and separates her from the background.

Lighting Ratios

The level of illumination on a subject, as compared with the depth of the corresponding shadow, is called its **lighting ratio**. Filmmakers use a number of techniques

to regulate this relationship between light and shadow. The most conventional method is the **three-point system**. Used extensively since the Hollywood studio era (1927–47), the three-point system casts a flattering and natural-looking light on actors. The system uses three sources of light, each aimed from a different direction and position in relation to the subject: key light, fill light, and backlight. The overall character of the image is determined mainly by the relationship between the key and fill lights. The **key light** (also known as the *main,* or *source, light*) is the primary source of illumination and therefore is customarily set first. Positioned to one side of the camera, it creates deep shadows. The **fill light**, which is positioned at the opposite side of the camera from the key light, adjusts the depth of the shadows created by the brighter key light. Fill light may also come from a reflector. The **backlight**, which is also known as a rim light or kicker, provides highlights in the hair and along the edges of the subject. These "rims" of light help make the actor stand out from the background.

When little or no fill light is used, the ratio between bright illumination and deep shadow is very high; the high contrast effect produced is known as **low-key lighting**. Low-key lighting produces the harsh, gloomy atmosphere that we often see in horror films, mysteries, crime stories, and film noirs.

High-key lighting, which produces an image with very little contrast between the darks and the lights, is used extensively in dramas, musicals, comedies, and adventure films. Its relatively even illumination is unobtrusive and does not call particular attention to the lighting style. When the intensity of the fill light equals

Low-key lighting

Vengeance is fulfilled as the title character in *John Wick* (2014) limps away from a bloody and rain-soaked fight with his nemesis. Very hard, extremely low-key lighting helps visualize Wick's grim determination and almost supernatural toughness. Even in his moment of victory, the emotionally (and physically) wounded Wick is portrayed in the darkest possible terms.

1

2

High-key lighting

To create the prison in his dystopian *THX 1138* (1971), George Lucas used the ultimate high-key lighting to suggest a vast and featureless purgatory [1]. Equal ratios of light come from every direction, resulting in a complete lack of shadows. The same technique is used in a different context, and for a different purpose, in Denis Villeneuve's *Arrival.* Extreme high-key lighting gives Dr. Louise Banks's first and only up-close encounter with the aliens an otherworldly eeriness [2].

that of the key light, the result will be the highest of high-key lighting: no shadows at all.

You may have noticed that these terms—*low-key lighting* and *high-key lighting*—are counterintuitive: we *increase* the contrasts to produce low-key lighting and *decrease* them to produce high-key lighting. It would be easier to remember if the terms were low-fill and high-fill instead. After all, cinematographers dim the fill light to achieve low-key lighting and intensify the fill light to get lighting that is high-key. But the terms high-key and low-key are well entrenched after a century of use in the film industry, so we're stuck with them.

Direction

Light can be thrown onto an object or actor from virtually any direction: front, side, back, below, or above. By direction, we also mean the angle of that throw, for the angle helps produce the contrasts and shadows that suggest the source of the illumination and the time of day. As with the other properties of lighting, the direction of

the lighting can also create mood and convey information or meaning regarding the subject being lit.

Backlighting can create dramatic lighting effects, especially when it is the sole light source. When positioned between the light source and the camera, the subject is thrown into silhouette. Eliminating recognizable surface detail by throwing everything we see of the subject into shadow abstracts the character, which can make him or her (or it) more frightening or impressive, depending on the context of the story at that moment.

Lighting from underneath a character (known as **Halloween lighting**, or bottom lighting) reverses the normal placement of illumination and shadows on an actor's face, which distorts the way we see facial features. As you might expect from the name, Halloween lighting is often used in horror films to emphasize that there is

1

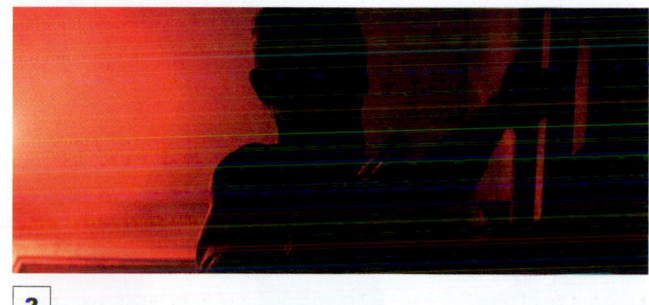

2

Backlighting

In *Citizen Kane*'s pivotal "declaration of principles" scene, Charles Foster Kane hits a high point of righteous sincerity. To emphasize his nobility, backlighting is used to differentiate Kane from his admiring underlings [1]. Silhouetting a character with backlighting has a very different effect in the horror thriller *Don't Breathe* (2016). Backlighting makes the vengeful antagonist all the more imposing [2].

Lighting from below

When a dead body is reanimated in *The Bride of Frankenstein* (1935), the perversity of the act and the deviance of the characters perpetrating it are emphasized with Halloween lighting, the term for aiming the light source up at the subject from below.

Frontal lighting

Detective Mark McPherson falls in love with the title character in *Laura* (1944) when he first meets her. When she becomes his prime suspect, frontal light that flattens her glamorous features visualizes the transformation.

something unnatural about a character or situation. To add to this eerie effect, placing the light source below the subject also throws shadows upward onto walls, where we are not used to seeing them.

Top lighting (light cast on a character from above) usually looks comparatively normal, as the Sun, our most natural light source, is usually in an overhead position. Overhead lighting can be glamorous when it highlights the subject's hair and cheekbones. But if the angle of overhead light is taken to the extreme, the resulting

shadows can obscure an actor's eyes, causing the character to appear threatening or mysterious.

When light is aimed at a subject from the same angle as the camera, no shadows are cast on the actor's face. With no shadows to indicate dimension, the actor's features appear flattened. This literal lack of depth can also convey figurative shallowness: a character lacking insight or courage may be lit with **frontal lighting**.

Lighting from above

In Francis Ford Coppola's *The Godfather* (1972), the enigmatic Don Vito Corleone is often lit with overhead lighting that casts his deep-set eyes into shadow. Partially obscuring the Godfather's eyes enhances his character's mystery and power.

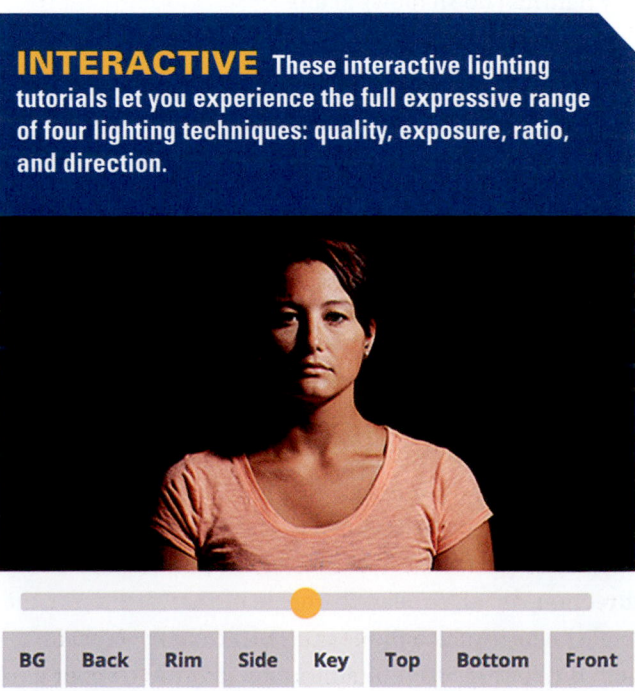

INTERACTIVE These interactive lighting tutorials let you experience the full expressive range of four lighting techniques: quality, exposure, ratio, and direction.

BG · Back · Rim · Side · Key · Top · Bottom · Front

1

2

Lighting imparts character and narrative in
The Night of the Hunter
Cinematographer Stanley Cortez's expressive lighting in *The Night of the Hunter* (1955) sets up the conflict between John, a confused young boy, and Harry, a Bible-quoting serial killer. Both are presented in shadow for the moment of the murderous preacher's arrival outside John's house: John is in silhouette, and Harry is a large, looming shadow cast on his bedroom wall [1]. Throughout the film, Harry's dual nature is underlined with lighting that divides his face between illumination and shadow [2].

Composition

Design and lighting function as elements of mise-en-scène. But what really makes mise-en-scène work is how those visual elements are arranged within each shot. A shot's **composition** is the organization, distribution, balance, and general relationship of objects and figures, as well as of light, shade, line, color, and movement within the frame.

Composition is important for a number of reasons. A consistent approach to composition over the course of

the movie helps ensure that the movie's overall style will have aesthetic unity. How elements are arranged helps guide the viewer's eye through the frame and makes us aware of what elements are most significant at any given moment. Composition can minimize or enhance the appearance of depth in a shot. And, perhaps most important, the way elements are organized on-screen can help viewers understand a character's state of mind and interpret different characters' physical, emotional, and psychological relationships to one another.

Ensuring that each shot's composition serves the movie's narrative, tone, and overall style requires a great deal of planning, so filmmakers use **previsualization** to aid them in visualizing each individual shot and to help them achieve a unified approach to shot compositions. Previsualization can include drawings of planned compositions called storyboards, diagrams of sets that include actor and camera positions called **overheads**, and software that creates three-dimensional models of sets and scenarios.

As a rule, our minds—and by extension our eyes—seek equilibrium and order. On the movie screen, that order

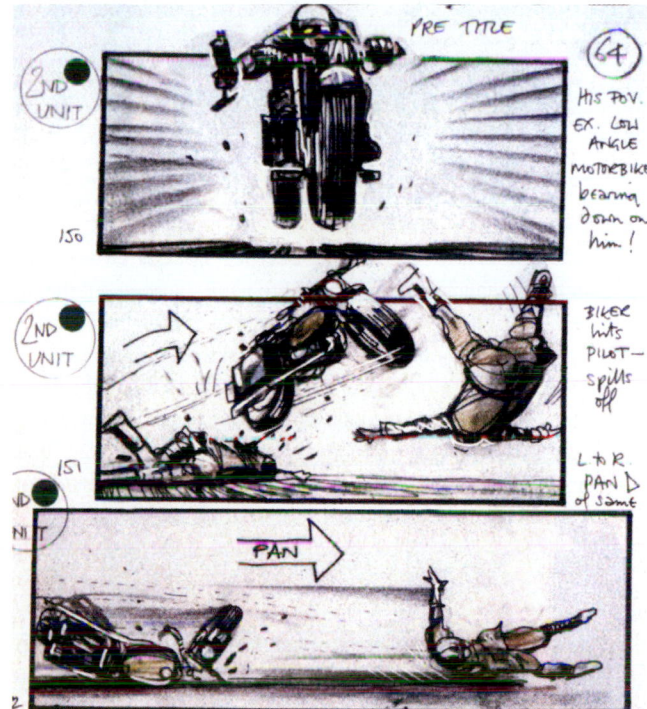

Previsualizing composition with storyboards
Director Martin Campbell worked with storyboard artists to plan compositions and camera moves for the James Bond film *Goldeneye* (1995).

1

2

The **rule of thirds** breaks the frame into three vertical sections and three horizontal sections, resulting in a grid. This grid acts as a guide that filmmakers use to balance visual elements in the frame. It is not an exact science; art is never that simple. The basic idea is that composition is built in basic units of three: top, middle, bottom; left, center, right; foreground, middle ground, and background. Usually, for every visual element placed on one section, there will be a corresponding element in the opposite section to counterbalance the composition. Of course, like all good rules, the rule of thirds allows for a wide variety of applications.

Our gaze is drawn to the area along the top horizontal line of a composition. For this reason, significant information, including the faces of characters, is often placed in this area. Because we humans tend to focus our attention on one another's eyes, close-up compositions often position characters' eyes along this upper line. This alignment has an added benefit. By framing a character's eyes at the level of the upper line, cinematographers can quickly and efficiently establish a practical and aesthetically pleasing amount of space, or **headroom**, above the subject. Sometimes, a story calls for composition that pushes the idea of balance to the next level, resulting in compositions that are so perfectly balanced that one side of the frame virtually mirrors the other. This

Composition and characters

Two shots from William Wyler's *The Best Years of Our Lives* (1946) illustrate how triangular compositions are used to represent the intertwined lives of three veterans. The men meet when they all hitch a ride home from the war in the same decommissioned bomber [1]. Their close physical grouping on that trip reflects the tight emotional bond they have only recently established. Much later, a similar tripoint pattern conveys a much less intimate relationship [2]. Time has changed their lives, and the same old patterns have different meanings within the larger context.

often takes the form of a balanced composition. The inclination toward compositional balance is not limited to narrative movies. Documentary camera operators usually seek balanced visual arrangements when shooting interviews or even while recording impromptu events. Experimental filmmakers that seek to challenge expectations may intentionally exaggerate or subvert balanced composition conventions such as the so-called rule of thirds.

INTERACTIVE In this interactive tutorial on composition, see how many ways you can compose and capture a multitude of interactions and situations presented in a single scenario as you position and scale the camera frame.

1

2

The rule of thirds

Although these two shots from an opening scene in *Hidden Figures* (2016) are composed differently, they each use the rule of thirds. In the closer angle [1], the balanced composition emphasizes the vertical. The overzealous trooper and the defiant Mary are positioned in the grid's left and right sections, with her companions Dorothy and Katherine centered in the background. Each woman occupies a different vertical third in the wider shot [2]; Mary must share hers with the looming officer. The horizontal thirds in the wider shot are divided into highway, car, and sky. Notice how all three of our protagonists' faces fall near the top horizontal line in both compositions. Significant information is often placed in this area of the frame.

symmetry can—depending on the context in which it is used—convey a sense of rigid order, ostentatious ritual, or formal elegance.

By purposely breaking the rule of thirds and denying our expectation of balance, filmmakers can create **com-**

positional stress. This intentional imbalance can communicate many levels of meaning, as always depending on the context in which it is used. A character can be made to appear diminished or disturbed, or a moment can be imbued with a sense of tension or foreboding.

Symmetry

At the beginning of this chapter, we saw an example of the compositional symmetry Wes Anderson used to lend *Moonrise Kingdom* a sort of theatrical whimsy. Stanley Kubrick used symmetry to different effect in *The Shining*. When one of Danny's Big Wheel rides through the Overlook Hotel brings him face to face with the ghosts of murdered twin girls, the scene's sudden uncanny symmetry radiates creepy menace.

Compositional stress

The social marginalization of a guilt-ridden boy is expressed with unbalanced compositions in Lynne Ramsay's *Ratcatcher* (1999).

Sometimes what might appear to be imbalance is actually maintaining a different sort of balance. When a character is looking across the screen, she is typically placed on one end of the frame so that her gaze is balanced with what is called **eye room** (or looking room) on the opposite side of the composition. In our innate visual vocabulary, just the act of looking carries the weight necessary to stabilize a composition. Similarly, a character whose lateral screen movement is tracked by a moving camera is almost invariably given **lead room** on the side of the frame toward which she is moving.

Another application of apparent imbalance is something called **negative space**. We are so accustomed to compositional balance that sometimes when we're presented with a lopsided composition, an expectation is created that something will arrive to restore balance. This technique is often used to generate suspense in narrative contexts featuring someone (or something) whose imminent arrival we anticipate—or fear.

The composition conventions we've just described are primarily concerned with only two dimensions: height and width. After all, a movie screen is two-dimensional. But the world movies depict features a third dimension: *depth*. Since the early days of film, filmmakers have innovated ways to provide audiences the illusion of depth. In the 1930s, as new lenses and lights made it possible to capture depth when photographing images, cinematographers such as Gregg Toland (and

Lead room and eye room

These two different moments in *Run Lola Run* (1998) illustrate the heft a character's gaze or forward momentum can bring to a composition. Most of the many shots depicting Lola dashing across Berlin to save her seemingly doomed boyfriend Manny balance the composition with lead room [1]. In the end, when Lola stares across the screen toward the offscreen (and inexplicably living) Manny, her implied eye room takes up the rest of the composition [2].

Negative space

In a suspenseful scene in *The Lord of the Rings: The Return of the King* (2003), the protagonist Frodo is tricked into becoming lost in a cave. He soon stumbles across a lair filled with massive webs and a sizable collection of silk-wrapped skeletons. When the narrative pauses at this composition, negative space creates the unsettling expectation that the inevitable giant spider will creep from the shadows to fill the empty space.

his directing collaborators John Ford, Orson Welles, and William Wyler) began regularly using depth as a component of composition.

Deep-space composition emphasizes depth by placing significant visual and narrative information on two or more of the three planes of depth—foreground, middle ground, and background—in such a way that not only emphasizes depth but also conveys information, mood, and meaning. This meaning can take many forms, depending on how the levels of depth are presented. Meaning about the situation and relationships presented can be communicated by the relative placement of characters

Deep-space composition and relative size in frame

Alicia, the protagonist of Alfred Hitchcock's *Notorious* (1946), is being slowly poisoned to death by her husband and his Nazi collaborators. In this shot, deep-space composition uses relative size in frame to graphically compare Alicia's vulnerability and weakened condition to the significant threat posed by the poisoned coffee.

LOOKING AT MOVIES
COMPOSING THE FRAME

VIDEO In this tutorial, Dave Monahan discusses the core principles of composition within the frame.

Deep-space composition in *Citizen Kane*

In this deep-space composition from Orson Welles's *Citizen Kane* (1941), cinematographer Gregg Toland exploits all three planes of depth along a line that draws our eye from screen right to screen left. In the foreground telephone booth, the backlit reporter Mr. Thompson calls in his story; in the middle ground, the nightclub headwaiter patiently stands by; and, in a pool of light in the background, the drunk and distraught Susan Alexander Kane, the subject of Thompson's visit, mourns her ex-husband and her misspent life. Each character is photographed in clear focus in a unified setting, yet each occupies a separate physical, psychological, and emotional space.

Deep-space composition, but not deep focus

A scene from *The Little Foxes* (1941) demonstrates that every plane of action need not be in focus to achieve expressive deep-space composition. The invalid Horace has a heart attack shortly after denying his wife Regina the money she wants for a morally dubious investment. He begs her to retrieve his vital medication from an upstairs room, but the vindictive Regina remains motionless. As Horace struggles to reach the stairs in the background, he moves farther and farther out of focus. His increasing fuzziness communicates his rapidly fading grip on life, as well as his wife's efforts to disregard his impending death.

and objects, their relative size in frame, and whether or not a character is in focus.

The way a camera frames the shots in a film can convey meaning in ways that are related to, but go beyond, mise-en-scène and composition. We will discuss some of those ways, including point of view, open and closed framing, and deep-focus photography, in Chapter 6.

Kinesis

One of the most efficient ways to analyze mise-en-scène is to study still images taken from a motion picture. So, it is easy to forget about movement (otherwise known as **kinesis**). Movies don't just move from shot to shot and scene to scene, obviously—people and things move around within the frame, and when the camera moves, the frame itself can move through space. Both of these forms of kinesis are used to "stage or put on an action or scene" and can thus be considered components of mise-en-scène.

Let's start with movement within the frame, or **figure movement**. The word *figure* applies to anything concrete and potentially mobile within the frame. Usually the moving figure is an actor playing a character, but moving figures may also include animals and objects, such as vehicles and props. In movies as well as in theater, figure movement is an essential part of storytell-

Kinesis in action films

Throughout the history of film—from the Hollywood swashbuckler movies, to the many cinematic portrayals of Shakespeare's Hamlet, to martial arts movies—old-fashioned swordplay has always been one of the most exciting forms of movement on-screen. Ang Lee's *Crouching Tiger, Hidden Dragon* (2000), a contemporary update of Hong Kong sword-and-sorcery movies, combined martial arts with elaborate choreography. In playing a nobleman's-daughter-turned-warrior, actor Zhang Ziyi used her training in dance as well as her martial arts skills.

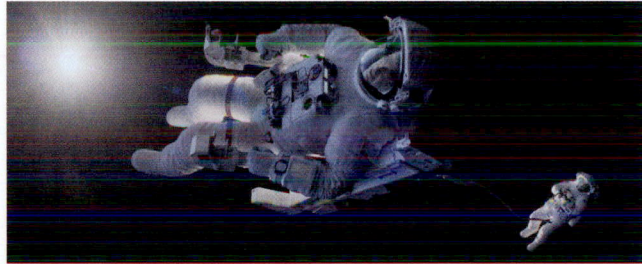

Expressive kinesis

Movies can make anything and anyone move in any way the story calls for. The characters in *Gravity* (2013) float in the vacuum of space, which lends a dissonant dreaminess to their life and death struggle [1]. The character played by dancing legend Fred Astaire in *Royal Wedding* (1951) expresses his love for a woman in a gravity-defying dance up a wall and across the ceiling [2]. A breakthrough moment for the title character in *Forrest Gump* (1994) is conveyed through camera and figure movement when he runs so fast his leg braces fall apart [3].

ing. Both theater and film use **blocking**: predetermined movement of actors that is planned according to the needs of the story. Blocking is usually decided on during a rehearsal process in which the director and actors establish how characters in a given situation might move in relationship to their surroundings and one another. In theater, figure placement and movement is oriented toward an audience sharing a common static viewpoint. Film blocking is oriented toward (and coordinated with) a camera that can be placed anywhere the director wants it to be. A shot's mise-en-scène is determined by what elements are placed within the camera's field of view and by the arrangement (or *composition*) of those elements in relationship to that camera viewpoint. Filmmakers can use figure movement to change the composition during the shot.

Camera movement also affects mise-en-scène. What we see in the frame, and how we see it, changes as the camera moves. The camera may move independently, functioning as a narrator leading us through a setting or situation. And because camera movement is not independent of figure movement, the camera may be used to follow a character or other figure as it moves. We will

explore the many ways the camera can move, and the ways camera movement conveys meaning, in Chapter 6.

In his masterpiece, *Tokyo Story* (1953), Yasujirô Ozu almost never moved the camera within a shot. In fact, even the figure movement is minimal, especially in comparison to modern movies. The relative stillness of *Tokyo Story* helps convey the moods and themes of a story about an elderly couple who are unable to adapt to the modern world inhabited by their self-centered children. Steven Knight's *Locke* (2013), although set almost entirely in a moving car, is also mostly devoid of kinesis. Only one character is seen on-screen, and he is stuck behind the wheel of a car for the entire movie. Movement is limited to reflections gliding across windows and the windshield as Locke's car speeds down a mostly unseen motorway. In this story of a man trapped in a situation he cannot control, the immobility of the camera and the character visually emphasizes his lack of options.

The Mad Max and Fast and Furious franchises fall on the opposite end of the kinesis spectrum. The stories and the mise-en-scène in those movies are built around movement. A large part of the pleasure of watching *Mad Max: Fury Road* (2015) or *The Fate of the Furious* (2017) comes from riding a ridiculously mobile camera as it relentlessly chases souped-up vehicles (and characters) in constant motion at breakneck speeds. Notably, the same actor (Tom Hardy) plays both the immobilized Locke and the latest incarnation of the propulsive Mad Max.

Approaches to Mise-en-Scène

So far, our conversation about mise-en-scène has been focused on its use in particular shots and scenes. But we can also think of mise-en-scène in terms of the overall look and feel of a movie. Other aspects of cinematic language, such as editing and sound, also contribute to a film's comprehensive style, but because design, lighting, kinesis, and composition encompass so much of a viewer's movie experience, the term *mise-en-scène* is often used when discussing the sum of everything the audience sees when watching a certain film.

Mise-en-scène isn't just the specific choices made by individual members of the creative crew, such as lighting and framing by the cinematographer, set designs by the production designer, and costume decisions by the wardrobe department. All of the thousands of choices that go into every film production must be synthesized into a cohesive stylistic strategy. And that's where the director comes in. Her role is to find and execute an approach to mise-en-scène that will best serve the particular story the film is trying to tell. She communicates that approach to the creative team of artists she leads; they

Italian neorealism
Vittorio De Sica's *Bicycle Thieves* (1948) is perhaps the best-loved movie from Italy's neorealist period, in part because its simple story and the naturalistic mise-en-scène focus on the details of ordinary lives. In this scene, a downpour hinders the protagonists' pursuit of an old man who can identify the thief of Antonio's bicycle. The scene was filmed on location with nonactors; when a rainstorm swept through, De Sica incorporated it into the story.

The origins of production design
The silent film pioneer Georges Méliès created the fictional film, using illusions he had learned in his career as a stage magician. In seeking to create magic with the movie medium, he invented a variety of cinematic effects. In so doing, he also invented the film set, and thus we can consider him the first production designer in film history. The image above is from his short film *The Eclipse: Courtship of the Sun and Moon* (1907).

come up with ideas and options; and she makes the final decisions that give the entire film a unified and coherent look and feel.

As a result, we associate some directors with a specific style of mise-en-scène. Recent films directed by Kathryn Bigelow have a restless camera and grittily realistic sets and costumes; the elaborate set pieces in Quentin Tarantino's movies are built around multiple visual references to past genre films; and a movie by Guillermo del Toro combines highly stylized fantasy elements with period-specific details. Many of us can immediately recognize a Wes Anderson movie because of his particular approach to mise-en-scène. It should come as no surprise that many of these directors with distinctive approaches to mise-en-scène often work with the same production designer on successive films: Jeremy Hindle was the production designer for Bigelow's *Zero Dark Thirty* (2012) and *Detroit* (2017); Adam Stockhausen for Anderson's *Moonrise Kingdom* (2012) and *Grand Budapest Hotel* (2014); and David Wasko for Tarantino's *Kill Bill: Volume 1* (2003), *Kill Bill: Volume 2* (2004), and *Inglourious Basterds* (2009).

The director's personal style is not the only factor that can influence a film's mise-en-scène. Over the course of film history, for a variety of cultural and artistic reasons, filmmakers have been inspired to use an enhanced sense of realism to create movies that depict the struggles of ordinary people. Filmmaking developments that aspired to this sort of populist authenticity include the German *Kammerspielfilm* of the silent era, Italian neorealism in the aftermath of World War II, and the Dogme 95 movement launched in 1995 by Danish directors Lars von Trier and Thomas Vinterberg. The films these approaches produced, and the movies made by the many filmmakers they inspired, minimize overtly expressive or otherwise conspicuous mise-en-scène. Instead, costumes, settings, lighting, and composition were selected or designed to depict the places, people, and events on-screen as they would appear in "real" life. Italian neorealist films were shot in actual locations and sometimes cast nonactors. Dogme 95 films adhere to a strict "vow of chastity" that not only requires location shooting but also forbids any lighting or props beyond what is available at the selected setting.

However, just because a movie lacks conspicuous mise-en-scène, we cannot assume the filmmakers did not exercise choice and intent. The existing locations were selected for authenticity—and the qualities and details they brought to the production. The camera positions were determined for both naturalism and effective

| 1 | 2 |
| 3 | 4 |

German expressionism

The highly stylized sets and lighting in *The Cabinet of Dr. Caligari* [1]–[4] emphasized diagonal lines and jagged, pointed graphics to instill a sense of unease and express the subjective state of mind of the story's deranged central character. In some cases, the deep shadows were painted directly on the distorted sets.

1

2

3

4

5

The influence of German expressionism

Expressionistic mise-en-scène has been adopted and adapted by filmmakers since its beginnings in post–World War I Germany. In *The Bride of Frankenstein* (1935), the walls and ceiling beams lean in precarious diagonals at the home of mad scientist Dr. Pretorius [1]. When a small-time author accepts a job offer from a long-lost friend in *The Third Man* (1949), he finds himself drawn into a politically and morally ambivalent post–World War II Vienna, which is represented as shadowy, angular, and mazelike [2]. A deliberately theatrical set in *The Night of the Hunter* conveys the state of mind of Harry, a serial killer about to stab his new wife with a switchblade. Harry sees the murder as the will of God. The pointed roof line and the shafts of light from the gabled window evoke both a church and the murder weapon [3]. In Tim Burton's *Edward Scissorhands* (1990), the shattered roof in the vast empty attic where an Avon lady discovers Edward visually expresses the lonely misfit's emotional anguish [4]. Director David Lynch uses expressionistic visual elements and intentionally mannered or amplified performances in most of his work, including the Showtime series *Twin Peaks: The Return* (2017) [5].

narration. A part may be played by a nonactor wearing her own clothes, but the filmmakers were likely directing that selection.

Movies that depict imaginary worlds (or fanciful versions of our own) usually fall on the opposite end of the mise-en-scène spectrum. Since the beginnings of narrative cinema, filmmakers have used costume, set, and lighting design to express meaning and moods that fall outside the realm of realism. Among the most influential and enduring of these expressive approaches to mise-en-scène originated in Germany after World War I. **German expressionism** was not interested in verisimilitude: design was used instead to give objective expression to subjective (and usually disturbed) human feelings and emotions. Settings and decor were abstracted by twisting the normally horizontal and vertical world of right angles into jagged, pointed diagonals. Lighting was deliberately artificial, emphasizing sharp contrasts, and deep shadows were often cast in the same distorted shapes found in the set design. To ensure complete control and free manipulation of the decor, lighting, and camera work, expressionist films were generally shot in the studio even when the script called for exterior scenes—a practice that was to have an important effect on how movies were later

shot in Hollywood. Even performances were stylized: actors abandoned any attempt at naturalism and instead externalized their emotions to the extreme.

The first great German expressionist film was Robert Wiene's *The Cabinet of Dr. Caligari* (1920). Designed by three prominent artists (Hermann Warm, Walter Reimann, and Walter Röhrig) who used dramatically painted sets to reflect the anxiety, terror, and madness of the film's characters, this movie influenced the design of silent films of the era, as well as horror movies, thrillers, film noirs, and other films to the present day.

Looking at Mise-en-Scène in *Sleepy Hollow*

To conclude this chapter, let's take a close look at *Sleepy Hollow* (1999) to observe how mise-en-scène shapes the overall look and feel of a movie and expresses meaning within individual shots and scenes.

Director Tim Burton credits his understanding of the expressive power of mise-en-scène to his early career as an animator: "In animation, you did everything: draw the backgrounds, draw the characters, you acted it, you cut it, you shot it . . . everything."[1] Burton uses elaborate mise-en-scène in all of his films, whether he's depicting the "real" world in movies such as *Ed Wood* (1994) and *Big Eyes* (2014) or presenting a wholly imagined world such as the simian dystopia of *Planet of the Apes* (2001). A significant number of his movies involve the intersection (or, in some cases, collision) between fantasy and reality. Fanciful creatures cross over into the real world, such as when the kindly suburban Avon lady adopts Edward Scissorhands, or when a hyperactive man-boy abandons his playhouse to search for his stolen bicycle in *Pee-wee's Big Adventure* (1985). More often, the intersection moves in the other direction. Relatively normal characters are transformed by journeys into magical worlds so extraordinary that they are featured in the titles: *Charlie and the Chocolate Factory* (2005), *Alice in Wonderland* (2010), *Miss Peregrine's Home for Peculiar Children* (2016), and *Sleepy Hollow*.

Burton's movie is based somewhat loosely on "The Legend of Sleepy Hollow," a short story by Washington

---

1. Tim Burton, qtd. in Gary Dretzka, "A Head For Horror," *Chicago Tribune* (November 26, 1999), sec. 5.

Irving set in 1790 and first published in 1820. Irving's Sleepy Hollow is an isolated and somewhat backward Dutch settlement with a reputation for spooky folktales, including one about a headless horseman—the ghost of a Hessian soldier decapitated by a cannonball during the American Revolution who rides at night in search of his lost head. The humorous story pokes gentle fun at the unsophisticated characters. Ichabod Crane is a not-very-smart and extremely superstitious schoolteacher who is eager to marry the young Katrina Van Tassel, especially after he realizes how rich her family is. The story's conflict centers on the competition for Katrina's hand between Ichabod and the burly Brom Van Brunt, a late-eighteenth-century equivalent of a jock. The headless horseman appears only once, when he chases Ichabod on a dark night after a party at Katrina's family home. Ichabod disappears, but not necessarily by supernatural means. The story strongly implies that Brom fooled the cowardly schoolteacher into fleeing town by posing as the horseman himself.

In Burton's version, Ichabod Crane (Johnny Depp) is a New York City police constable, whose insistence on progressive police procedures so irritates his superiors that they send him off to the backwoods village of Sleepy Hollow to investigate a series of grisly murders. The enlightened Ichabod assumes (and initially insists) the

murderer is a run-of-the-mill mortal, but he is in for a surprise. The killer is a headless horseman, the murders are bloody beheadings, and our enterprising detective winds up with much more to worry about than marrying Katrina—although he does still manage to fall in love with her.

Sleepy Hollow is a detective story, but it is also a horror movie, so Burton wanted the mise-en-scène to exert a pervasive sense of ominous foreboding and anxiety. He didn't want the movie to have the slick, digital look of many contemporary films filled with computer-generated effects, such as *Star Wars: Episode 1—The Phantom Menace* (1999). Instead, Burton gave *Sleepy Hollow* an old-fashioned, theatrical style modeled on Mario Bava's Italian horror classic *Black Sunday* (1960) and the moody gothic horror movies produced by the British production company Hammer Films in the 1960s and 1970s.

Lighting and Setting

Burton and his cinematographer Emmanuel Lubezki created a visually claustrophobic gloom by permeating nearly every interior and exterior set with smoke generated by fog machines. The thick smoke acts as a sort of super-diffusion, creating a hazy soft light that obscures background details. Burton moved the production to England, in part to take advantage of overcast skies that added to the feeling of perpetually looming dusk. Although we associate soft light with high-key lighting, Lubezki used a low-key ratio so that corners of rooms and other background details fall into shadow. The cinematographer also exposed and processed the film negative in a way that increased contrast and faded color.

We know from the Edward Scissorhands example earlier in the chapter that Tim Burton is no stranger to German expressionism, and with *Sleepy Hollow*, the stylistic approach once again perfectly suited the weird sense of dread he wanted the setting to convey. Production designer Rick Heinrichs incorporated pointed rooftops, diagonal lines, and jagged angles into the design of the village's huddled buildings—a mishmash of architectural styles he dubbed "colonial expressionism."

The village was constructed outdoors in the English countryside, but to give the film the theatrical feel of his classic horror influences, Burton constructed most of the other exterior settings—including an artificial forest of twisted, leafless trees—inside a soundstage. Lighting

Composition
Most of the compositions in *Sleepy Hollow* are tightly framed—the better to convey a feeling of claustrophobia—and conventionally balanced. This moment, shortly after Ichabod's uninvited arrival at a social function, is composed using deep space and the rule of thirds. Ichabod dominates the left third; Katrina gazes upon him from the right vertical. The immediately jealous Brom Van Brunt and his frilly scarf fall in the middle-ground center. Other suspicious bumpkins observe the newcomer from the background. Note how much important narrative information falls on or near the top horizontal line—including a jack-o-lantern, one of the movie's recurring motifs.

1

2

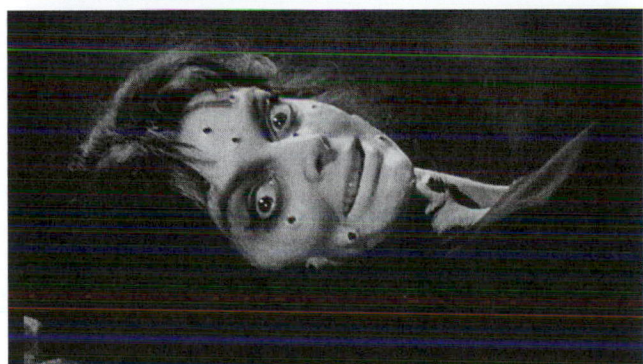

3

Homage to stylistic influences

Tim Burton paid homage to the movies that inspired his mise-en-scène by casting Hammer Films horror star Christopher Lee as the New York City official who sends constable Crane to Sleepy Hollow. In this shot [1], Lee's character is framed against the relief of an American eagle on the wall behind him to evoke the caped Dracula he played in seven Hammer films. The dream sequence featuring the punctured face of Ichabod's murdered mother [2] evokes the image of a resurrected witch from another inspiration, the Italian gothic horror classic *Black Sunday* [3]. Each of the women characters were victims of torture; the puncture wounds in both movies were created with prosthetics.

German expressionism

The "Tree of the Dead" that serves as the horseman's home base is pure German expressionism. The trunk seems to be writhing in agony, with grasping branches jutting out at jagged angles. Artificially generated smoke dilutes the light and almost obscures the surrounding forest. Huge gray backdrops were hung in the soundstage where this scene was shot to provide the illusion of endless fog.

effects, from frail sunlight to flashes of lightning, were achieved using hundreds of lights controlled with dimmer switches and often muted with thick, simulated fog. Painted backdrops were used to represent backgrounds of forest and sky. An illusion of depth was often obtained in these staged exteriors by use of forced perspective, a technique that manipulates relative scale to fool the eye into seeing objects as more distant (or closer) than they actually are. Burton's vintage approach to mise-en-scène extended beyond setting. Although he had to use some digital effects—to create a convincingly headless horseman, for example—he used mechanical in-camera effects as much as possible.

Colonial expressionism

Production designer Rick Heinrichs dubbed his version of expressionist design used to create the village of Sleepy Hollow "colonial expressionism." An overcast sky and the almost total absence of color add to the village's unsettling atmosphere.

Forced perspective

The horseman's fifth execution is set in a field just outside Sleepy Hollow, but the scene was shot in a soundstage. Using small-scale models and exploiting the shroud of artificial fog, the filmmaker fools our eyes into perceiving the trees and windmill in the background to be much farther away than they really are. This *forced perspective* was one of the techniques Tim Burton used to give his movie an old-fashioned theatrical flavor.

Costumes, Makeup, and Hairstyle

Most of us don't know exactly how people in late-eighteenth-century New York dressed, but we know enough to place powdered wigs, breeches, and petticoats somewhere around 1800. So, Tim Burton and his design team use post-colonial fashion to lend this supernatural story a general sense of verisimilitude. But even more important, *Sleepy Hollow*'s costumes, makeup, and hair-

1

2

Costumes and character

The antiquated wigs and waistcoats worn by *Sleepy Hollow*'s leading citizens denote not only their wealth but also their lack of sophistication [1]. The devious Lady Van Tassel is more stylish [2]. The weblike pattern on this gown hints at her evil intentions.

1

2

New York City—before and after

Initially, the metropolis of New York is hardly differentiated from the village of Sleepy Hollow in terms of mood. The city is introduced as a dark mass of soot-stained buildings pouring black smoke into a leaden sky [1]. But upon Ichabod's triumphant return, after he has solved the mystery and the horseman has returned to hell where he belongs, the city is presented as bright and bustling. Fresh snow lightens the street, buildings, and sky as Ichabod and Katrina stroll through a genteel crowd—many of whom wear white costumes [2].

styles help define and differentiate the film's many characters. The village's five most powerful citizens (each doomed to lose his head to the horseman) are conniving scoundrels and/or ignorant cowards and are thus clad in fussy embroidered waistcoats, ornate laced cuffs, and comical wigs or hats. In contrast, our enlightened hero Ichabod Crane wears a plain black coat adorned only with a tastefully understated cravat. His full head of lustrous dark hair is never constrained by a wig or hat. His only accessory is an elaborate set of spectacles that magnify his eccentric intelligence. Katrina Van Tassel functions as Ichabod's temptation as well as savior, so she is dressed in gauzy, lightly colored, and low-cut gowns complemented by a simple star pendant that hints at her secret identity as a practitioner of white witchcraft. Her essential innocence is further emphasized by her pale blonde hair, even paler complexion, and paler still white horse. Lady Van Tassel, Katrina's smiling stepmother, is almost as pale and just as beautiful, but the black

lace and weblike patterns adorning her stylish gowns imply a darker hidden nature. As one might expect from a vengeful fiend summoned from hell, the horseman sports a rotting, black, high-collared cloak. In expository flashbacks and in the scene after he and his own head are reunited, the horseman is played by veteran character actor Christopher Walken, whose already intimidating face is made even more menacing with bright blue contact lenses, a spikey dark wig, and prosthetic sharpened teeth.

Throughout *Sleepy Hollow*, Burton's all-compassing mise-en-scène so effectively envelops the story in relentless dread that when the style finally shifts, viewers experience the same sudden exhilaration as the surviving characters on-screen. Over the course of one forest shot dissolving into the next, the fog lifts, the light brightens, and colored foliage returns to the trees. A few shots later, Ichabod and Katrina are walking hand-in-hand down the sparkling streets of New York City.

ANALYZING MISE-EN-SCÈNE

This chapter has introduced the major elements that together form any movie's mise-en-scène. You should now understand that the term *mise-en-scène* denotes all of those elements taken together to convey meaning, tone, and mood. Using what you have learned in this chapter, you should be able to analyze and discuss mise-en-scène in terms of a shot, a scene, and the overall look of an entire film.

SCREENING CHECKLIST: MISE-EN-SCÈNE

✔ As you watch a film or clip, be alert to the overall mise-en-scène and how it shapes your interpretation and experience.

✔ Identify the elements of the mise-en-scène that seem to be contributing the most to your experience and understanding of story and character in a scene or shot.

✔ Be alert to the composition of individual shots. Where are figures and other significant elements placed? Is the composition balanced or does it use compositional stress? What is the relationship among the figures in the foreground, middle ground, and background?

✔ How is lighting used? Is it simply providing illumination or is it used in a way that contributes to mood or meaning?

✔ How does the shot, scene, or film use kinesis? Is movement minimal or extreme? Is the movement limited to figure movement within the frame, or is the camera moving, or both? How does the movement (or lack thereof) contribute to your experience and understanding of the characters and story?

✔ Does the movie's design have a unified feel? How do the various elements of the design (the sets, props, costumes, makeup, hairstyles, etc.) work together?

✔ Was achieving verisimilitude important to the design of the film? If so, have the filmmakers succeeded in making the overall mise-en-scène feel real, or verisimilar? If the mise-en-scène is stylized, what do you think the filmmakers were attempting to convey with the design?

Questions for Review

1. What is the literal meaning of the phrase *mise-en-scène*? What do we mean by this phrase when we discuss movies?

2. What are the two major components of mise-en-scène?

3. Does a movie's mise-en-scène happen by accident? If not, what or who determines it?

4. Describe the process of developing a movie's mise-en-scène.

5. What are the principal responsibilities of the production designer?

6. Name and briefly discuss the major elements of cinematic design.

7. What is kinesis? What are the two basic forms it takes, and how can each affect composition and our experience of the story?

8. How the lighting for any movie looks is determined, in part, by its quality, ratio, and direction. Explain these terms and the effects they produce.

9. What is composition? Name and briefly discuss how composition uses balance and depth.

10. Describe the different approaches to mise-en-scène and the overall effects they seek to achieve.

CINEMATOGRAPHY

After reading this chapter, you should be able to

- describe the differences among a shot, a setup, and a take.
- understand the role that a director of photography plays in film production.
- describe the basic characteristics of the cinematographic properties of a shot: film stock, lighting, and lenses.
- understand the basic elements of framing, including implied proximity to the camera, depth, camera angle and height, camera movement, open and closed framing, and point of view.
- describe any shot in a movie by identifying
  - its implied proximity to its subject.
  - the angle of the camera.
  - the nature of camera movement, if any, within the shot.
  - the speed and length of the shot.
- describe the relationship between on-screen and offscreen space, and explain why most shots in a film rely on both.
- understand the ways in which special effects are created and the various roles that special effects play in movies.

What Is Cinematography?

Cinematography is the process of capturing moving images on film or a digital storage device. The word comes to us from three Greek roots—*kinesis*, meaning "movement"; *photo*, meaning "light"; and *graphia*, meaning "writing"—but the word was coined only after motion pictures themselves were invented. Cinematography is closely related to still photography, but its methods and technologies clearly distinguish it from its static predecessor. This chapter introduces the major features of this unique art.

Although cinematography might seem to exist solely to please our eyes with beautiful images, it is in fact an intricate language that can (and in the most complex and meaningful films, does) contribute to a movie's overall meaning as much as the story, mise-en-scène, and act-

ing do. The cinematographer (also known as the director of photography, or DP) uses the camera as an expressive instrument. To make an informed analysis of a movie, we need to evaluate precisely how (and how well) the cinematographer, in collaboration with the other creative and technical contributors to the production, has harnessed the many aspects of her craft to express story, mood, and meaning.

The Director of Photography

Every aspect of a movie's preproduction—writing the script, casting the actors, imagining the look of the finished work, designing and creating the sets and costumes, and determining what will be placed in front of the camera and in what arrangement and manner—leads to the most vital step: representing the mise-en-scène on film or video. Although what we see on the screen reflects the vision and design of the filmmakers as a team, the director of photography is the primary person responsible for transforming the other aspects of moviemaking into moving images.

The collaborative relationship between the cinematographer and the director varies from movie to movie, but typically, these two positions form one of the most vital partnerships on the creative crew. The cinematographer's expertise can help shape and advise nearly every aspect of the director's preparation, including set designs, location selection, and especially previsualization storyboards. On set, the DP and director are usually in constant communication as the DP translates the director's vision into specific decisions about how each shot will be photographed. And every choice the DP makes—the lighting, lenses, exposure, focus, camera positions and movements, even the camera model and media format—is largely driven by the needs of the story.

Production Terms and Tasks

The three key terms used in shooting a movie are *shot*, *take*, and *setup*. Because the **shot** is a building block of cinema, *shot* is one of the most common words you'll find in both filmmaking and film study. Yet, because its

Setting up a shot

On an interior setting for *The Social Network* (2010), director David Fincher (*left*) and cinematographer Jeff Cronenweth (*center*)—aided by an unidentified camera operator or technician (*right*)—work with a video-assist camera to set up a shot. Fincher and Cronenweth also worked together on *Fight Club* (1999), *The Girl with the Dragon Tattoo* (2011), and *Gone Girl* (2014). Cronenweth was nominated for an Oscar for Best Cinematography on *The Social Network*.

definition depends on the context in which it is used, the term can cause confusion.

As you learned in Chapter 1, when we're discussing a shot in an edited film, we can define shot as an unbroken span of action captured by an uninterrupted run of the camera. In a completed film, the duration of a shot (as well as its starting point and ending point) is determined by the editor. In that context, a shot is a discrete unit that lasts until it is replaced by another shot by means of a cut or other transition. When you see the term *shot* in every other chapter in this book, it will almost certainly refer to this meaning.

However, during the previsualization and production process, a shot can refer to a specific arrangement of elements to be captured in a particular composition from a predetermined camera position. So, the director may use *shot* when referring to a storyboard or production schedule: "In this shot, let's reposition the juggler behind the zebra." On set, the DP may tell her crew to

"change the lens for the next shot." For various reasons, that planned "shot" may be *taken* a number of times. The director may decide to adjust the blocking, an actor could suggest a different approach, or someone may make a mistake. The term **take** refers to each time that planned shot is captured. That's why, if you are watching a behind-the-scenes program or a fictionalized enactment of a film production, you may hear a crew member call out the next task as something like: "Scene 3, Shot A, Take 6." A **setup** is one camera position and everything associated with it. The crew may shoot a number of different shots (and multiple takes of each of those planned shots) from a single camera position. For example, if a film includes several separate shots of an office-worker character sitting at his desk on different days, all of the shots that can be captured from that particular setup will be shot in succession. The lighting, the actor's hair and wardrobe, and any necessary decor will be adjusted accordingly for each planned shot.

A DP's perceptive eye leads to an unforgettable shot

Although the director of photography must strictly control the cinematographic properties of a movie's shots, the great cinematographers are also alert to unplanned expressive opportunities. In the 1968 movie *In Cold Blood*, a convicted murderer awaiting execution recalls his troubled relationship with his father. During rehearsals, cinematographer Conrad Hall noticed that the production lights shining through the artificial rain running down the set's window projected tear-like images onto actor Robert Blake's face. Before the camera rolled, Hall and director Richard Brooks adjusted the blocking to maximize the effect, resulting in an image that helps reveal the character's hidden emotions.

The cinematographer's responsibilities for each shot and setup, as well as for each take, fall into four broad categories:

1. cinematographic properties of the shot (film stock, lighting, lenses)

2. framing of the shot (proximity to the camera, depth, camera angle and height, scale, camera movement)

3. speed and length of the shot

4. special effects

Although these categories necessarily overlap, we will look at each one separately. In the process, we also examine the tools and equipment involved and discuss what they enable the cinematographer to do.

In carrying out these responsibilities, the DP relies on the assistance of the **camera crew**, which is divided into one group of technicians concerned with the camera and another concerned with electricity and lighting. The camera group consists of the **camera operator**, who controls the camera during the shot, and the **assistant camerapersons (ACs)**. The **first AC** oversees everything having to do with the camera and lenses, including adjusting focus before and during each shot. The **second**

AC prepares the **slate** that is used to identify each shot and take as the camera rolls, notes the lens, exposure, and other information for each shot, and is responsible for moving the camera to each new setup. When film stock is being used, the **loader** feeds that stock into magazines that are then loaded onto the camera. If the production is using digital cameras, the loader's responsibilities are handled by a **digital imaging technician (DIT)**, who archives and manages the digital data being captured. The group concerned with electricity and lighting consists of the **gaffer** (chief electrician), **best boy** (first assistant electrician), other electricians, and **grips** (all-around handypersons who work with both the camera crew and the electrical crew to get the camera and lighting ready for shooting).

Cinematographic Properties of the Shot

The director of photography controls the cinematographic properties of the shot, those basics of motion-picture photography that make the movie image appear the way it does. These properties include the recording medium, lighting, and lenses. By employing variations of each property, the cinematographer modifies the camera's basic neutrality as well as the look of the finished image that the audience sees.

Film and Digital Formats

The cinematographer is responsible for choosing a recording medium for the movie that serves the director's vision. Among the alternatives available are film stocks of various sizes and speeds and a variety of digital media formats. A skilled cinematographer must know the technical properties and cinematic possibilities of each option and must be able to choose the medium that is best suited to the project as a whole.

Movies have been shot on **film stock** since the 1880s. Digital video technology has been accessible to professionals since the 1980s. After George Lucas shot *Star Wars: Episode I—The Phantom Menace* using a high-definition digital camera in 1999, digital cinematography began to slowly take over as the medium of choice for commercial feature films. By 2012, at least half of top-grossing feature films were shot digitally. Today, largely for reasons of cost and convenience, digital formats dominate the feature film and television industries.

Even though most movies are now being shot digitally, a significant number of feature films are still shot on traditional film stock using the same basic materials and techniques filmmakers have employed since cinema's beginnings. It is probably safe to say that most of the films you will watch and study in this course were shot using film. Film stock is available in several standard **formats** (also called *gauges*; widths measured in millimeters): 8mm, Super 8mm, 16mm, Super 16mm, 35mm, 65mm, and 70mm as well as special-use formats such as IMAX, which is 10 times bigger than a 35mm frame. Before the advent of camcorders, 8mm and Super 8mm were popular gauges for amateur home movies. Many documentaries, television programs, and student movies, as well as low-budget narrative feature productions, were once shot on 16mm. Today, most professional narrative productions shooting on film use 35mm.

All of these film-stock gauges are coated with thousands of microscopic silver halide crystals that each react to light to form a tiny piece of the total recorded

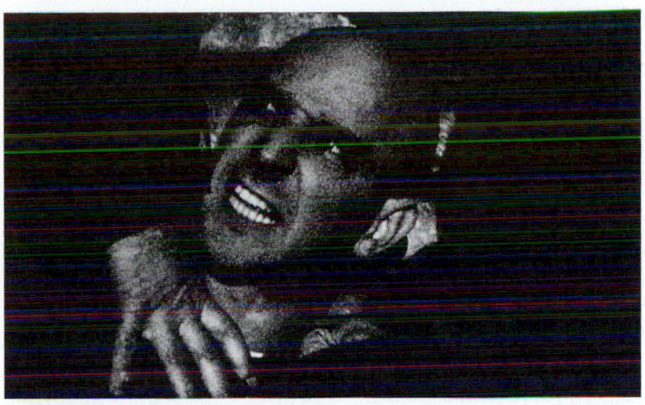

1

2

Practical and expressive use of film stock

The low-budget, independent movie *Pi* (1998; also titled with the symbol π) [1] was the first movie by Darren Aronofsky, a director now known for major releases such as *Black Swan* (2010) and *Mother!* (2017). He and his cinematographer, Matthew Libatique, had financial reasons to use fast 16mm black-and-white film stock. The film format was cheap, and the exposure index allowed them to shoot without large and cumbersome lights. Expressive needs also motivated the choice—the extremely grainy and high-contrast look of this particular film stock perfectly suited the gritty, graphic nature of their story. The visible grain found in 16mm was the primary reason cinematographer Ed Lachman chose the smaller-gauge format to shoot Todd Haynes's *Carol* (2015) [2], a doomed same-sex romance set in 1952. The filmmakers felt that the stock's granular texture captured the look of photographs from the period, and that the swirling grain gave their images "a pulsing of something living underneath the surface."[1]

image on each successive frame. The larger the gauge, the more space there is for crystals. Film formats that capture and hold more fragments of visual information have higher **resolution**: a more detailed, thus sharper,

1. Ed Lachman, qtd. in Paula Bernstein, "Why Ed Lachman Chose to Shoot *Carol* in Super 16mm," *Filmmaker Magazine* (December 7, 2015). https://filmmakermagazine.com/96594-why-ed-lachman-chose-to-shoot-carol-in-16mm/#.WoyeORPwbOY.

image. For optical reasons, too complex to explain here, images recorded on larger formats can also produce a shallower depth of field—the amount of depth in the image that is in focus. The ability to control a reduced slice of focus allows filmmakers a range of expressive and aesthetic options that we'll discuss later in this chapter.

Another variable aspect of film stock is its **speed** (or exposure index)—how sensitive it is to light. "Fast" film stocks have larger crystals that need less light to record an image, whereas "slow" film stocks are fine grained and require more light for a proper exposure. The larger crystals make images shot with fast film stock look grainy, especially compared to the sharper, smoother look of slow film stock. There are uses for both slow and fast film stocks, depending on the shooting environment and the desired visual outcome. Commercial filmmakers seeking the glossy, polished appearance produced by slow stocks are often willing to take on the necessary expense and equipment. A documentary that must shoot without additional lighting would likely use a fast stock, but so might a narrative film that seeks a gritty visual look to convey a particular tone or mood.

Speed and gauge are only two of the characteristics found in the many available film stocks. Other variable qualities include contrast, color temperature, and color saturation. Some movies use multiple stocks in a single film, again for both practical and expressive reasons. For his 1994 movie *Natural Born Killers*, director Oliver Stone constantly switched between eighteen different stocks and formats to give the story a feeling of disorienting instability.

You can touch film stock; you can even hold it up to the light to see each captured image. Footage shot using digital media formats exists only as data stored on a tape, disk, or computer drive. Just like traditional film cameras, digital cameras use lenses, apertures, and shutters. The differences begin when the light hits the recording medium. Instead of film stock, the digital camera uses an electronic sensor that captures fragments of image information not as exposed silver halide crystals but as digital **pixels**. The large amount of resulting data is stored on a hard drive or a solid-state drive (SSD—a memory card similar to a flash drive) in the form of a **codec**: a specialized digital format that compresses all that pixel information into manageably sized files for editing and viewing.

Like their film-stock counterparts, different sensors and codecs captre light, color, contrast, and depth of field

in different ways, so digital cinematographers exercise the same care when selecting digital formats as those shooting film exercise when choosing a film stock. Like the larger film gauges, larger sensors are capable of producing images with a shallower depth of field. Resolution—the detail in the image—is determined by the number of pixels in each frame: 1920 × 1080 pixels, the lowest resolution now available, has 2,073,600 pixels. Professional cameras, and even many consumer cameras, are now capable of capturing 8,294,400 pixels or more for every one of the 24 (or more) images it takes to produce 1 second of a motion picture. But, contrary to popular belief, resolution isn't the determining factor in image quality. The convenient codecs used by our consumer cameras and cell phones greatly reduce the true image resolution. The codecs generated in the cameras used to shoot the movies we see in theaters only slightly compress the data, if at all. Most professional-grade digital movie cameras now feature sensors and other electronics that allow them to shoot uncompressed "raw" footage that supplies the most possible data to the postproduction process, which is where much of the look (in terms of color, contrast, and clarity) of modern films is determined. Beyond these factors, digital cinematographers are primarily concerned with the camera sensor's *dynamic range*: the amount of light a camera's sensor can read from absolute black to absolute white (similar to a film stock's exposure index). A wide dynamic range allows the camera to shoot in a wide range of lighting conditions and capture a spectrum of tonal and color values.

Regardless of which film or digital format they use, virtually all movies are now shot in color, for that is what the public is accustomed to and therefore expects. In 1936, when Hollywood began to use color film stock, 99 percent of the feature releases from major studios were in black and white. By 1968, virtually all feature releases were in color. During the transitional period between 1940 and 1970, the choice between color and black and white needed to be carefully considered, and many films shot in color during that period might have been even stronger if they were shot instead in black and white. John Ford's *The Searchers* (1956), a psychological Western that is concerned less with the traditional Western's struggle between wilderness and civilization than with the lead character's struggle against personal demons, might have been even more powerful shot in black and white instead of color. Doing so might have produced a visual mood, as in film noir, that complemented the darkness at the heart of the movie's narrative. Instead, the choice of color film stock for *The Searchers* seems to have been inspired by industry trends at the time—designed to improve flagging box-office receipts—rather than by strictly artistic criteria.

Black and White Because of its use in documentary films (before the 1960s) and in newspaper and magazine photographs (before the advent of color newspaper and magazine printing), audiences have ironically come to associate black-and-white photography and cinematography with a stronger sense of unidealized realism than that provided by color film stock. But that sheen of authenticity is only one of many connotations intrinsic

to black-and-white cinematography. Depending on the context in which it is used, black-and-white's distinct contrasts and hard edges can look stark, somber, elegant, abstract, or simply different than our regular way of seeing things, which is why it is often used to convey dreams, memories, flashbacks, and historical events. Movies shot in black and white can also have moral or ethical connotations. For good or ill, black and white often carry preconceived interpretations (e.g., black = evil, white = good). As simplistic, misleading, and potentially offensive as these interpretations may be, they reflect widespread cultural traditions that have been in effect for thousands of years. The earliest narrative films, which greatly appealed to immigrant audiences (most of whom could neither read nor speak English), often relied on such rough distinctions to establish the moral frameworks of their stories. Heroes and other morally upright characters wore white, while villains wore black. Later,

Black and white versus color

Stagecoach (1939) [1] was the first film that John Ford shot in Arizona's Monument Valley. The black-and-white cinematography portrayed an Old West that looked and felt different from the depiction using color cinematography in *The Searchers* (1956) [2], one of the last films Ford shot in Monument Valley. Ford might have shot *The Searchers* in black and white, but color was considered more marketable. Almost 60 years later, the same well-entrenched market forces led to *Mad Max: Fury Road* (2015) being released in color [3], although director George Miller originally intended the movie to use bolder, more graphic black-and-white cinematography. In the end, his "Black and Chrome" version [4] was given a limited theatrical and Blu-ray release.

Black and white in *The Seventh Seal*

In *The Seventh Seal* (1957), set during the Black Plague in the Middle Ages, director Ingmar Bergman uses black-and-white cinematography to distinguish faithful innocents (dressed most often in white or gray costumes) from the doubtful and doomed (dressed in black). His monochrome color scheme goes beyond costuming to encompass distinct contrasts in lighting, settings, and props. In a game between Death and the Knight, both characters wear dark costumes, but lighting that illuminates the Knight's blond-white hair, cross-shaped sword, and white chess pieces differentiates the opponents. Spoiler alert: The Knight loses. Nobody beats death, especially not in Swedish art films.

even though both audiences and cinematography became more sophisticated, these distinctions held together the narratives of numerous films in diverse genres, including Westerns, horror films, and film noir.

Tonality, the range of tones from pure white to darkest black, is the distinguishing quality of black-and-white film stock. When making a black-and-white film, set and costume designers closely collaborate with directors of photography to ensure that the colors used in their designs produce the optimal varieties of tones in black and white. Following a process developed during the time of the classical Hollywood studio system, their goal is to ensure a balance of "warm" and "cold" tones to avoid a muddy blending of similar tones. Sometimes the colors chosen for optimal tonality on film are unattractive, even garish, on the set. Audiences are none the wiser, however, because they see only the pleasing tonal contrasts in the final black-and-white movie. Just as different color movies take different approaches to color cinematography (as you will see in the next section), not every black-and-white movie looks the same. Cinema-

tographers use format, design, lighting, and postproduction adjustments to take advantage of tonality and capture the range of whites, blacks, and grays that best suit the story and the director's vision.

Color Although almost all movies today are shot in color, for nearly 60 years of cinema history color was an option that required much more labor, money, and artistic concession than black and white did. Color movies made before 1960 were technically elaborate productions, and in deciding to use color the producers expected the movies to justify the expense with impressive

Black-and-white tonality

Director Ana Lily Amirpour wanted her Iranian vampire western *A Girl Walks Home Alone at Night* (2014) [1] to have a "classic" look but also feel contemporary and gritty. Cinematographer Lyle Vincent selected a particular digital camera codec and coordinated with a postproduction colorist to emphasize deep blacks and high-contrast whites but still retain a middle range of nuanced gray tones. In Pawel Pawlikoski's *Ida* (2014) [2], a novice nun in 1960s Poland discovers a wide range of figurative gray area in her heritage, identity, and faith. The movie's austere digital cinematography uses a wide range of literal grays, with much less emphasis on pure black or white.

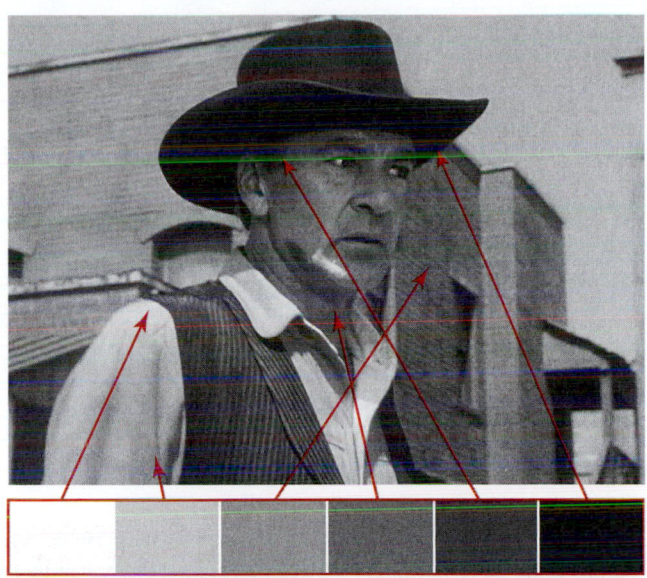

Tonal range

This shot from Fred Zinnemann's *High Noon* (1952) illustrates the tonal range possible in black-and-white cinematography: from absolute white (in the shirt) through a series of grays to absolute black (under the hat's brim). For the purposes of explanation, this illustration includes only six tones out of the complete range. Note that although he is the movie's protagonist, Marshal Will Kane (Gary Cooper) wears a black hat—typically, in less sophisticated morality tales, the symbolic mark of the bad guy.

box-office returns—much like 3-D or IMAX movies today. To gain a better understanding of the period before 1968, when color was not necessarily the default choice, let's take a moment to review the history of color-film technology.

Although full-scale color production began only in the late 1930s, it was possible to create color images soon after the movies were invented, in 1895. The first methods were known as **additive color systems** because they added color to black-and-white film stock. These processes included hand-coloring (drawing color directly onto the processed film), tinting (soaking the film in dye), and toning (a chemical process that replaces the silver halide crystals that make up the dark areas of the image with colored silver salts). Tinting and toning were often used together to extend the color of a single image.

As imaginative as these processes are, they do not begin to accurately reproduce the range of colors that exist in nature. Further experimentation with additive color processing resulted in a crude two-color additive process that used two complementary colors, usually red-orange and blue-green. In 1915, the Technicolor Corporation introduced a two-color additive process, used effectively in aesthetic terms to photograph Albert Parker's impressive epic *The Black Pirate* (1926; cinematographer Henry Sharp).

By the early 1930s, the additive process was replaced by a three-color **subtractive color system** that laid the foundation for the development of modern color cinematography. With this system, color results from the physical action of different light waves on our eyes and optical nervous system, meaning that we perceive these different wavelengths of energy as different colors. Of these colors, three are primary—red, green, and blue. Mixing them can produce all the other colors in the spectrum, and when added together they produce white. The subtractive process takes away unwanted colors from the white light. So when one of the additive primary colors (red, green, blue) has been removed from the spectrum on a single strip of film, what remains are the complementary colors (cyan, magenta, yellow). The first feature-length film made in the three-color subtractive process was Rouben Mamoulian's *Becky Sharp* (1935; cinematographer Ray Rennahan).

In practice, making a Technicolor movie was complicated, cumbersome, and cost almost 30 percent more than comparable black-and-white productions. The Technicolor camera, specially adapted to shoot three strips of film at one time, required a great deal of light. Its size and weight restricted its movements and potential use in exterior locations. Furthermore, the studios were obliged by contract to employ Technicolor's own makeup, which resisted melting under lights hotter than those used for shooting black-and-white films, and to process the film in Technicolor's labs.

For all these reasons, in addition to a decline in film attendance caused by the Great Depression, producers were at first reluctant to shoot in color. By 1937, however, color had entered mainstream Hollywood production; by 1939 it had proved itself much more than a gimmick in movies such as Victor Fleming's *Gone with the Wind* and *The Wizard of Oz*.

In the early 1940s, Technicolor and the Eastman-Kodak Company introduced multilayered color film stocks that essentially replaced the earlier Technicolor system. These stocks, which were less expensive to process, could also be used in conventional cameras with less lighting. Eventually, Kodak's single-strip color film stock improved on these characteristics and became the

The evolution of color

Some silent filmmakers meticulously hand-colored portions of images frame by frame. Because the process was so tedious, only certain shots or scenes were colored, such as this rowdy Western dance scene in Edwin Porter's 1903 *The Great Train Robbery* [1]. Tinting larger quantities of film with dyes let filmmakers use color to differentiate entire scenes or even imply mood or meaning, such as the cold blue used in the climactic blizzard and ice-chase scene in D. W. Griffith's *Way Down East* (1920) [2]. Technicolor's original two-color additive color process, seen here in Albert Parker's 1926 silent epic *The Black Pirate* [3], didn't reproduce true color, but it did represent an important step toward the Technicolor three-color subtractive system that ushered in an era of serious filmmaking in color. The vibrant Technicolor images in *Gone with the Wind* (1939) [4] earned a special commendation at the 1940 Academy Awards ceremony for "outstanding achievement in the use of color for the enhancement of dramatic mood."

standard. But just as Hollywood took several years to convert from silent film to sound, so too the movie industry did not immediately replace black-and-white film with color. During the 1950s, Hollywood used color film strategically, along with the **widescreen aspect ratio**, to lure people away from their television sets and back into theaters.

Now that color cinematography dominates, what we see on the screen looks very much like what we would see in real life. By itself, however, color cinematography doesn't necessarily produce a naturalistic image. Film artists and technicians can manipulate the colors in a film as completely as they can any other formal element. Ultimately, just like its black-and-white counterpart, color cinematography can be used to create realistic or expressionistic images.

Much of Stanley Kubrick's *Barry Lyndon* (1975; cinematographer John Alcott), for example, has a color palette that reflects its temporal setting very well. It's the world of soft pastels and gentle shadows depicted in the eighteenth-century paintings of Thomas Gainsborough and William Hogarth. However, this palette wasn't achieved merely by pointing the camera in a certain direction and accurately recording the colors found there. Instead, the filmmakers used diffused natural lighting, special lenses, and fast film stocks during production, and slightly overexposed the film negative during postproduction processing to render the naturally occurring colors in more subtle and "painterly" shades.

When shooting in color, cinematographers must also consider **color temperature**. Any light source will emit various light wavelengths that register as different colors in a graded spectrum. Sunlight emits light in the blue end of the spectrum, and incandescent lights using traditional tungsten filament bulbs emit light in the orange end of the spectrum. Because the movie camera does not translate this color the way the human eye (and brain) does, a surface that appears white to our eyes may be recorded with a blue or orange hue by the film or sensor. Cinematographers can compensate for this effect by using digital settings or film stocks designed to balance a specific color temperature to something that appears

Pumping up the color in *Tangerine*
To capture the colorful and chaotic life of transgender prostitutes in Los Angeles, director and co-cinematographer Sean Baker shot *Tangerine* (2015) on an iPhone equipped with a lens adaptor and an app that allowed him to control focus and aperture. In postproduction, he intensified and saturated the colors to complement the vibrancy of his characters. The movie's title was inspired by the dominant color to emerge in the color-grading process.

natural to the human eye. Another method is to place a filter (usually a transparent sheet of colored glass or polymer plastic) in front of the lens or light to cut out distinct portions of the color spectrum as the light passes the filter.

Today, when virtually all motion-picture postproduction (and most of the production, too) is done digitally, a great deal of any film's look, including its color, is completed on computers. This work is known as **color grading** (also called color correction), the process of altering and enhancing the color of a motion picture (or video or still image) with specialized software. These

Evocative use of color
Because we experience the world in color, color films may strike us as more realistic than black-and-white films. Many color films, however, use their palettes not just expressively but also evocatively. For Stanley Kubrick's *Barry Lyndon* (1975), cinematographer John Alcott has helped convey both a historical period and a painterly world of soft pastels, gentle shading, and misty textures.

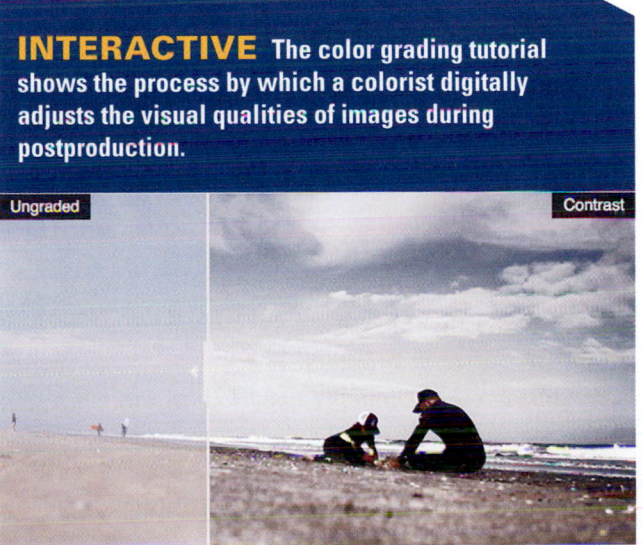

INTERACTIVE The color grading tutorial shows the process by which a colorist digitally adjusts the visual qualities of images during postproduction.

1

2

Expressive color change within a scene

Color isn't just used to give a movie an overall look. Different applications of color hues and vibrancy can be used in different scenes, and even within single scenes, to help convey the mood and meaning appropriate to each moment. For example, in *Fantastic Beasts and Where to Find Them* (2016), notice how the rich browns and golds in the shots of the wizard Newt and his beloved Thunderbird [1] differ from the cool, desaturated blues in the shots of Newt regarding the dreaded Obscurus later in the same scene [2].

Hollywood the center of American movie production in part because of its almost constant sunshine. Even when movies are shot outdoors on clear, sunny days, however, filmmakers often use devices to manipulate that natural light. Daylight can be redirected with *reflectors* and *bounce boards*, diffused with panels of white called *silks*, and shaped with black panels called *flags*. Artificial lights (sometimes called *instruments* to distinguish them from the light they produce) are designed to address a range of cinematic applications and needs. A professional production uses a wide range of lighting instruments, from large 36,000-watt light banks capable of illuminating large areas, to small 25-watt battery-powered LED units designed to simulate the glow a car's instrument panel might cast on a character's face.

To calculate exposure and determine lighting ratios, cinematographers use a handheld light meter to measure how much light is falling on any given surface. Gaffers can adjust the intensity of each instrument in a number of ways: focusing or dispersing the beam, using dimmers, placing heat-resistant screens (called *scrims*) in front of the bulb, or simply moving the instrument closer to or farther from the subject. Lighting instruments are designed to cast direct (hard) light, diffused (soft) light, or both. Hard light cast by some instruments can be softened with the aid of diffusion placed in front of, or even directly onto, the light source. Fresnel lights

days, filmmakers calibrate the way they capture footage to facilitate the technical and creative manipulation that happens largely in postproduction. Those manipulations include exposure, depth of shadows, brightness of highlights, saturation of colors, and color hues. Cinematographers now have to be as knowledgeable about what happens on the computer after shooting as they are about what happens with the camera on the set.

Lighting Sources

In Chapter 5, we discussed how filmmakers use light expressively as part of a movie's mise-en-scène. Now, let's look at some of the tools and techniques cinematographers and gaffers use to achieve lighting quality, direction, and ratios.

There are two fundamental sources of light: natural and artificial. Daylight is the most convenient and economical source, and in fact the movie industry made

Reflector boards

Many scenes of John Ford's *My Darling Clementine* (1946; cinematographer Joe MacDonald) were shot in the sunny desert terrain of Monument Valley in Arizona and Utah. But as this photo shows, a large bank of reflector boards was used when the sunshine was insufficient or when the director wanted to control the lighting.

Fresnel light

A 2000-watt Fresnel light with barn doors and an adjustable lens.

Short-focal-length lens

In Alfonso Gomez-Rejon's *Me and Earl and the Dying Girl* (2015) [1, 2], an antisocial high schooler is ordered by his mother to visit Rachel, a schoolmate he hardly knows, who has been diagnosed with cancer. Cinematographer Chung-hoon Chung used a short-focal-length lens to shoot their awkward exchange. The depth-stretching effect of the wide-angle lens emphasizes the physical and emotional distance between the two embarrassed characters.

feature an adjustable lens that can focus light into a direct, hard beam of maximum intensity or disperse the beam to soften the light and lessen intensity.

Many lighting instruments are equipped with "barn doors": hinged panels used to shape the emitted light and prevent it from falling on areas where it is not needed. As mentioned earlier, black fabric panels called flags are also used to shape and block light.

Lenses

In its most basic form, a camera **lens** is a piece of curved, polished glass or other transparent material. As the "eye" of the camera, its primary function is to bring the light that reflects off the subjects in front of the camera (actors, objects, and settings) into a focused image on the film or sensor inside the camera.

The basic properties shared by all lenses are aperture, focal length, and depth of field. The **aperture** of a lens is an adjustable **iris** (or diaphragm) that controls the amount of light passing through the lens. The greater the size of the aperture, the more light it admits through the lens. The **focal length** of the lens is the distance

(measured in millimeters) from the optical center of the lens to the focal point on the film stock or other sensor when the image is sharp and clear (in focus). Focal length affects how we perceive perspective—the appearance of depth—in a shot, and it also influences our perception of the size, scale, and movement of the subject being shot. The four major types of lenses are designated by their respective focal lengths.

The **short-focal-length lens** (also known as the wide-angle lens, starting as low as 12.5mm) produces wide-angle views and stretches the appearance of depth. It makes the subjects on the screen appear farther and further apart than they actually are. Because this lens exaggerates spatial perspective, subjects moving at normal speeds toward or away from the camera can seem to be moving through space faster than they actually are. Most smartphone cameras have a short-focal-length lens. Fisheye lenses, which are ultra-wide-angle lenses with focal lengths as short as 8mm, push this spatial distortion even further.

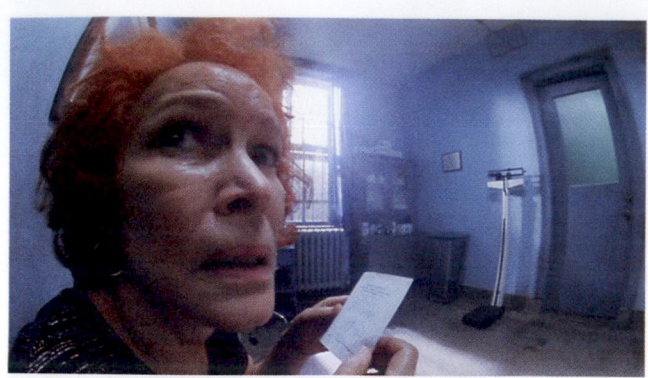

Fisheye lens

The disoriented state of mind of a woman addicted to amphetamines is visualized with the spatial distortion caused by an ultra-wide-angle fisheye lens in Darren Aronofsky's *Requiem for a Dream* (2000).

The **long-focal-length lens** (also known as the telephoto lens; focal lengths ranging from 85mm to as high as 500mm) compresses the appearance of depth, which makes distant subjects look closer and makes objects and subjects on different planes of depth appear to be closer together than they would appear in real life. Because of this spatial flattening effect, subjects moving from the background toward the camera can appear to be making very slow progress through space—almost as if they were walking in place. If you've ever looked through a pair of binoculars, you've experienced a long-focal-length lens.

Although the short and long extremes are used occasionally to achieve certain visual effects, most shots in feature films are made with a **middle-focal-length lens**—from 35mm to 50mm—often called the *normal lens*. Lenses in this range create images that correspond to our day-to-day experience of depth and perspective.

The **zoom lens**, also called the *variable-focal-length lens*, permits the assistant cameraperson to reduce or increase the focal length of the lens between takes or setups without having to change lenses. Changing the focal length in a continuous motion during a shot can make the image "zoom" in or out, thus simulating the effect of movement of the camera toward or away from the subject.

Because zoom lenses contain additional lens elements, they require more light and thus do not produce images as sharp as lenses with fixed focal lengths, which are called **prime lenses**. For this reason, most feature films use prime lenses; zoom lenses are used predominantly for documentary and documentary-style films that require the camera operators to continually adjust focal length to capture ongoing and unpredictable action. In the hands of an accomplished cinematographer, the zoom lens can produce striking effects, but when it is used indiscriminately, as it sometimes is by less skilled filmmakers, it not only feels artificial to an audience but can unintentionally disorient viewers. As with all other aspects of cinematography, the lens used must be appropriate for the story being told.

Long-focal-length lens

This image from Stanley Kubrick's *Barry Lyndon* (1975; cinematographer John Alcott) shows the flattening effect of a long-focal-length lens. The marching soldiers' forward progress seems more gradual as a result.

Middle-focal-length lens

This shot from Billy Wilder's *Sunset Boulevard* (1950) includes the movie's three principal characters. A small orchestra is in the background. The middle-focal-length lens used to make this shot keeps the three principal subjects in normal focus, and the overall image corresponds to our day-to-day experience of depth and perspective.

1

2

Zoom lens

To create documentary visual style for the narrative film *The Hurt Locker* (2008), director Kathryn Bigelow and her cinematographer, Barry Ackroyd, used lightweight, handheld cameras equipped with zoom lenses, which gave them the mobility and flexibility to enter into the action and take viewers with them. A zoom lens allows the camera operator to adjust focal length, so that the camera can provide multiple perspectives on the action within one shot. In this shot, the camera lens begins with an extreme long shot [1] and then immediately shifts to a longer focal length [2] to suddenly thrust us among the coalition soldiers leading the frightened workers to safety. The rapid, fluid movement of the lens between a neutral observation point and a tighter, closer view of the people rushing forward toward the camera not only suggests a documentary immediacy but also increases our involvement with the military forces and workers.

As mentioned earlier in this chapter, the **depth of field** refers to the distance in front of a camera (and its lens) in which the subjects are in apparent sharp focus. Several factors, including light, aperture setting, and gauge or sensor size, can influence the size and placement of that focused area—but to keep things simple,

we'll concentrate here only on how lens focal length affects depth of field. The short-focal-length lens offers a nearly complete depth of field, rendering almost all objects in the frame in focus. The depth of field of the long-focal-length lens is generally a very narrow range, and it leaves the area in front of and behind the in-focus objects dramatically out of focus. The middle-focal-length lens approximates how our human eyes and brains experience space and focus, with a relatively generous field of focus around whatever the camera (or eye) is focused on. Only areas well outside of the specific point of focus will appear less distinct.

In virtually all shooting, cinematographers keep the main subject of each shot in sharp focus to maintain clear spatial and perspectival relations within frames. One option available to cinematographers, however, is a **rack focus**—a change of the point of focus from one subject to another. This technique guides our attention to a new, clearly focused point of interest while blurring the previous subject in the frame.

Framing of the Shot

Framing is the process by which the cinematographer or camera operator uses the boundaries and dimensions

LOOKING AT MOVIES
FOCAL LENGTH

VIDEO This tutorial reviews the effects created by lenses of different focal lengths.

Rack focus

In this shot from Guillermo del Toro's *The Devil's Backbone* (2001), the camera uses depth of field to guide our attention from one subject to another. When the shot begins, the lens is focused on the background where the villainous Jacinto scans the orphanage courtyard for stray witnesses [1]. The lens then shifts focus to the foreground so that Jacinto's elusive prey, the orphan Jamie, snaps into sharp relief [2].

turns the comparatively infinite sight of the human eye into a finite movie image—an unlimited view into a limited view. This process requires decisions about each of the following elements: the implied proximity to the camera of main subjects, the depth of the composition, the camera angle and height space within and outside of the frame, point of view, and the type of camera movement, if any.

At least one decision about framing is out of the cinematographer's hands. Although a painter can choose any size or shape of canvas as the area in which to create a picture—large or small, square or rectangular, oval or round, flat or three-dimensional—cinematographers find that their choices for a "canvas" are limited to a small number of dimensional variations on a rectangle. This rectangle results from the historical development of photographic technology. Nothing absolutely dictates that our experience of moving images must occur within a rectangle; however, thanks to the standardization of equipment and technology within the motion-picture industry, we have come to know this rectangle as the shape of movies.

The relationship between the frame's two dimensions is known as its **aspect ratio** (see Figure 6.1), the ratio of the width of the image to its height. Almost all movies

of the moving image to determine what we see on the screen. Framing involves composition and vice versa, so understanding where one concept ends and the other begins can be difficult. We know from Chapter 5 that composition is the organization, distribution, balance, and general relationship of actors and objects within the space of each shot. Obviously, how the camera frames those elements is a key part of how that arrangement appears on-screen. To understand what distinguishes framing, it helps to consider the term itself: *framing* directly engages the *frame*—the boundaries of the image, including the farthest visible depth and the fourth wall behind the lens—and how what we see and the way in which we see it is shaped by those borders. Framing

Framing and composition

To understand the relationship between framing and composition, it may be helpful to consider the work of a documentary cinematographer such as Kirsten Johnson. Watching her 2016 film *Cameraperson*, which is made up of footage she shot over the course of her long career, we see framing in action. She must continually position and move her camera to compose shots of real people and unrehearsed action. She uses framing to select what we see and composition to make the resulting images visually coherent and engaging.

Figure 6.1 | BASIC ASPECT RATIOS

1.375:1

1.85:1

2.35:1

Although filmmakers seldom use more than one aspect ratio in a movie, in shooting *The Grand Budapest Hotel* (2014), director Wes Anderson differentiated scenes taking place in different time periods by shooting in three different aspect ratios. Scenes set in the 1930s are shot in the Academy 1.375:1 ratio in common use during that decade. Scenes taking place from 1985 to the present are in the 1.85:1 widescreen format, and action set in the 1960s is shot in the 2.35:1 widescreen ratio.

are made to be shown in one aspect ratio from beginning to end. The most common aspect ratios are:

❯ 1.375:1   Academy (35mm flat)

❯ 1.66:1   European widescreen (35mm flat)

❯ 1.85:1   American widescreen (35mm flat)

❯ 2.2:1   Super Panavision and Todd-AO (70mm flat)

❯ 2.35:1   Panavision and CinemaScope (35mm anamorphic)

❯ 2.75:1   Ultra Panavision (70mm anamorphic)

Feature-length widescreen movies were made as early as 1927—the most notable was Abel Gance's spectacular *Napoléon* (1927). In Hollywood, the Fox Grandeur 70mm process very effectively enhanced the epic composition and sweep of Raoul Walsh's *The Big Trail* (1930). Until

Masking in *The Graduate*

Mike Nichols's *The Graduate* (1967) features one of the most famous (and amusing) maskings of the frame in movie history. As the scene ends, Ben Braddock (Dustin Hoffman), framed in the provocative bend of Mrs. Robinson's (Anne Bancroft) knee, asks, "Mrs. Robinson, you're trying to seduce me . . . aren't you?"

the 1950s, when the widescreen image became popular, the standard aspect ratio for a flat film was the Academy ratio of 1.375:1, meaning that the frame is 37 percent wider than it is high—a ratio corresponding to the dimensions of a single frame of 35mm film stock. While this ratio is still often quoted as 1.33:1, the Academy of Motion Picture Arts and Sciences acknowledged in 1932 that the standard of the Academy ratio was widened to 1.375:1 to provide room on the film print for the sound track. Today's more familiar widescreen variations provide wider horizontal and shorter vertical dimensions. Most commercial releases are shown in the 1.85:1 aspect ratio, which is almost twice as wide as it is high. Other widescreen variations include a 2.2:1 or 2.35:1 ratio when projected. In shooting for television broadcast, cinematographers are increasingly using the 1.78:1 aspect ratio. It can be seen on a home TV set with a format of 16:9, which is universal for HDTV.

Occasionally, filmmakers change aspect ratios within a film. Most of Christopher Nolan's *The Dark Knight* (2008) was shot in a widescreen 2.35:1 format, but the top and bottom of the image expanded to the 1.43:1 IMAX frame size during some action scenes. *Hunger Games: Catching Fire* (2013) makes the same aspect ratio switch when the protagonist Katniss enters the Hunger Games

arena. Some Disney films shift aspect ratio when the protagonist experiences a transformation, such as when the princess in *Enchanted* (2007) moves from the animated fantasy world to live-action New York City, and when the Native American protagonist of *Brother Bear* (2003) is changed into a bear. When a filmmaker wants to depict a subject or situation using a frame size and shape other than the one imposed by the chosen aspect ratio, she can also use setting, objects, or even characters to block off, or *mask*, portions of the frame, thus creating a new frame or frames within the standard rectangle. In Mike Nichols's *The Graduate* (1967; cinematographer Robert Surtees), during her initial seduction scene of Ben Braddock (Dustin Hoffman), Mrs. Robinson (Anne Bancroft) sits at the bar in her house and raises one leg onto the stool next to her, forming a triangle through which Ben is framed or, perhaps, trapped.

Implied Proximity to the Camera

Most aspects of cinematic language draw upon the way people instinctively process and react to visual information in their everyday lives. When we're sitting in a dark movie theater, we unconsciously identify with the viewpoint of the camera, which has replaced our own viewpoint. **Implied proximity** refers to the distance between the camera (and thus the viewer) and the subject on-screen. Because a lens with a long enough focal length can allow a camera to film a close-up of a subject standing a hundred feet away, it is important to understand that the distance between the camera and the subject is not always what it seems—thus the term "*implied proximity*." The adjective *implied* also acknowledges that the spatial relationship between the characters on-screen and the viewers in the audience is indicated by cinematic language, rather than any actual measurable distance.

Whether or not that distance is implied or literal, the appearance of a subject's proximity is important to a central aspect of framing and meaning—the whole idea of *significance*. To get a sense of how proximity can connote significance, consider the close-up—a shot in which a character's face fills most of the frame—a framing that filmmakers often use at the moment in a scene that demands the greatest dramatic impact. In our regular, non-movie-watching lives, when someone is right up close to us, and as a result dominates our field of vision, we typically perceive them as especially significant. To understand why, imagine yourself on a crowded dance floor at a club or party. Among all the other distracting things in your field of vision, you see an attractive person looking at you from the opposite end of the room. You may assign that person some significance from that distance, but if that same person strolls right up to you, virtually filling your field of vision, then the person will likely arouse a much more profound physical and emotional reaction. Close-ups often exploit this link between proximity and significance, and it doesn't have to be pleasant. Think of those scenes in horror films in which a monster suddenly dominates the frame, violating and virtually erasing the implied distance between it and you.

Of course, attraction and terror are not the only symptoms of significance, and nearness is not the only degree of proximity that engages our emotions. Each of the possible arrangements of subjects in proximity to each other and to the camera has the potential to convey something meaningful about the subjects on-screen.

Shot Types Implied proximity is the reason behind some of the most common terms for shots used in movies: a close-up implies close proximity, a medium shot is a medium distance, a long shot is a longer distance, and so forth. Depending on the context in which they are used, these shot types can connote significance, convey meaning and a character's state of mind, and elicit emotional responses from the audience. Because the easiest way to remember and recognize the different types of shots is to think about the scale of the human body within the frame, we'll describe them in terms of that scale. But shot types can also be classified by the amount of other kinds of information they provide, including general (or background) information, physical subject information, and psychological subject information.

In the **extreme long shot** (**XLS** or **ELS**), typically photographed at a great distance, the subject is often a wide view of a broad locale surrounding more specific locations where the action takes place. Extreme long shots typically present general background information, rather than a particular featured subject. When used to provide spatial context at the beginning of a scene, the XLS is also an establishing shot. Even when human beings are included in such a shot, the emphasis is not on them as individuals but on their relationship to the surroundings. The XLS may also be used to depict a character dwarfed by his or her environment or for depicting large-scale action, such as a battle scene, in which masses of figures function as a sort of collective subject.

The **long shot** (**LS**) presents background and subject information in equal measure and is as much about setting and situation as any particular character. Long shots are often used as **establishing shots** at the beginning of a scene to indicate where the scene is taking place, who is involved, and what they are doing. The full bodies of characters can be seen, often with enough physical detail to allow us to recognize them, but psychological information (what characters are thinking or feeling) is limited to what can be conveyed through action or gesture.

A **medium long shot** (**MLS**) is neither a medium shot nor a long shot, but one in between. It is used to photograph one or more characters, usually from the knees up. In this shot type, background is reduced, and the subject or subjects begin to predominate. Because the human body is shown in full, or at least nearly so, the MLS is often used for moments of physical action. Because the MLS is widely used in Hollywood movies, the French call this shot the *plan Américain* ("American shot").

1

2

3

4

5

6

7

8

The **medium shot** (**MS**) frames subjects from somewhere around the waist and up, making them large enough in the frame to reduce background to the point of insignificance. The MS is the most frequently used type of shot because it replicates our human experience of proximity without intimacy. We can read increasingly subtle psychological and physical information on the increasingly dominant—and thus significant—subject. Medium shots are often used to convey interaction between multiple subjects: medium shots featuring two subjects are called *two-shots*, a *three-shot* has three subjects, and *group shots* have more than three people.

The **medium close-up** (**MCU**) shows a character from approximately the middle of the chest to the top of the head. The character's face, gestures, and posture can begin to provide the kind of physical and psychological detail and implied proximity we associate with the close-up.

In a **close-up** (**CU**), the subject's face fills the frame, so the camera (and, by extension, the viewer) is up close and personal with the subject. The character's face is close enough to communicate maximum physical and psychological detail—even the subtlest shift in expression can feel monumental. This intimate proximity imparts a heightened sense of significance.

An **extreme close-up** (**XCU** or **ECU**) fills the frame with a part of a subject's face or, oftentimes, with an object revealed in great physical detail. When the XCU enlarges a normally small object to monumental proportions, it may anticipate the use of the object. If an object is isolated and presented with great implied significance, the audience knows, or at least senses, that the object is important and will be used in some significant manner. The resulting expectation can generate suspense or impart to the object a kind of symbolic value.

LOOKING AT MOVIES
SHOT TYPES AND IMPLIED PROXIMITY

VIDEO In this tutorial, Dave Monahan explores the concept of implied proximity and its relationship to various shot types.

Depth

Because the image of the movie screen is two-dimensional and thus appears flat (except for movies shot with 3-D cinematography), one of the most compelling challenges faced by cinematographers has been how to give that image an illusion of depth. From the earliest years of film history, filmmakers have experimented with achieving different illusions of depth. During the 1930s, the traditional method of suggesting cinematic depth was to position significant characters or objects in focus in the foreground or middle ground, with the background in soft focus. The cinematic space is arranged to differentiate the planes of space and draw the viewer's eyes away from the background. With such basic illusions, our eyes automatically give depth to the successive areas of the image as they seem to recede in space.

Shot types

(Facing page) Tom Hooper's *The King's Speech* (2010) uses all of the basic shot types in the opening sequence, in which England's Prince Albert, who suffers from a serious stutter, must give a very public speech in 1934. A huge crowd is gathered to hear him speak, and the speech is also being broadcast across the British Empire. The scene opens with an extreme close-up of a radio microphone [1], a potent symbol of Albert's predicament. Other extreme close-ups opening the scene include the speech text clutched in Albert's hand and Albert's stammering mouth as he attempts to rehearse his delivery [2]. On his way to the podium, the terrified prince receives instructions from an assistant, shown in a medium two-shot [3]. A long shot [4] shows radio technicians operating the huge bank of radio equipment necessary to broadcast the speech around the world. An extreme long shot [5] depicts Albert's view from the podium—the ranks of spectators, officials, and soldiers gathered to hear him speak. The scene builds suspense with a cut back to a medium long shot [6] of a radio engineer anxiously waiting for the prince to begin speaking. A close-up [7] is used for the most significant and agonizing shot in the scene, as Albert struggles to speak. His sympathetic wife watches his futile efforts in a medium close-up [8].

1

2

3

Depth

From the earliest years of film history, filmmakers have experimented with achieving different illusions of depth. In the backstage musical *Gold Diggers of 1933* (1933), Mervyn LeRoy suggested depth by placing the character in the foreground and leaving the rest of the image in a soft-focus background [1]. Rim lighting and top lighting helps separate the foreground subject from the background. During a patriotic musical stage sequence later in the same film, LeRoy and his innovative choreographer, Busby Berkeley, designed shots that fostered the illusion of depth with lines of movement from background to foreground [2]. Legendary cinematographer Gregg Toland helped develop film stocks, lenses, and lighting techniques necessary for deep-space cinematography, which keeps all three planes of depth in sharp focus—as seen in his groundbreaking work on *Citizen Kane* (1941) [3].

Directors of the era such as Rouben Mamoulian and Mervyn LeRoy also experimented with the technique of using camera or figure movement to create lines of movement between the background and foreground to foster the illusion of depth.

Also during the 1930s, however, various cinematographers experimented with creating a deeper illusion of space through cinematographic rather than choreographic means. Of these cinematographers, none was more important than Gregg Toland, who was responsible for bringing the previous developments together, improving them, and using them most impressively in John Ford's *The Long Voyage Home* (1940) and soon after in Orson Welles's *Citizen Kane* (1941). By the time he shot these two films, Toland had already rejected the soft-focus, one-plane depth of the established Hollywood style. He dramatically increased depth of field by

combining the fastest film stock available with greatly increased lighting intensity, which allowed him to close the aperture to the smallest possible setting. All that light required him to work with engineers to design special lenses with coatings that reduced glare.

In *Citizen Kane*, these methods came together to make possible **deep-focus cinematography**, which, using the short-focal-length lens, keeps all three planes of depth in sharp focus. Toland used deep-focus cinematography to create deep-space composition, the compositional approach introduced in Chapter 5 that emphasizes depth by placing significant visual and narrative information on two or more of the three planes of depth. Toland's pioneering work on *Citizen Kane* profoundly influenced the look of subsequent movies. Deep focus (and deep-space mise-en-scène) allowed directors to use blocking to arrange and move actors within the full depth of

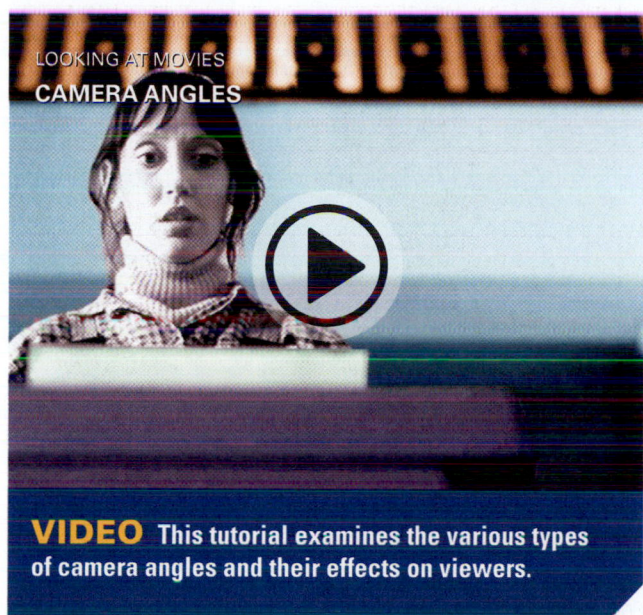

LOOKING AT MOVIES
CAMERA ANGLES

VIDEO This tutorial examines the various types of camera angles and their effects on viewers.

1

2

the setting, which made possible multiple compositions within a single shot. This flexibility made it possible to sustain dramatic action within a single extended shot without cutting, which helped distance Hollywood from the editing-centered theories of the Russian formalist directors like Sergei Eisenstein. French film critic André Bazin emphasizes that deep-focus cinematography "brings the spectator into a relation with the image closer to that which he enjoys with reality" and "implies, consequently, both a more active mental attitude on the part of the spectator and a more positive contribution on his part to the action in progress."[2]

Camera Angle and Height

The **camera angle** is the level and height of the camera in relation to the subject being photographed. Sometimes, the camera's angle on the subject simply reflects spatial relationships between characters and objects seen separately on-screen, as with a shot depicting the point of view of a character looking out of an upstairs window. But oftentimes, camera angles offer filmmakers a range of more expressive possibilities.

Eye Level For most shots in most movies, filmmakers set the camera angle at roughly the same level as the eyes of the characters in the scene. These **eye-level shots**

Eye-level shot

These two shots from the same sequence in Pablo Larraín's *Jackie* (2016) illustrate two uses of the eye-level camera angle. The camera assumes the neutral angle in this medium close-up two-shot [1] of first lady Jackie Kennedy nervously conferring with her social secretary, Nancy Tuckerman, before a White House television interview. During the interview, Jackie glances over to Nancy: this shot [2] represents Jackie's eye-level point of view of Nancy. Notice that the prop television camera is set at Jackie's approximate eye level.

correspond with the way we're most used to seeing our everyday surroundings, including the other people with whom we interact. If the camera is functioning as narrator, the eye-level angle functions as a neutral view of the action on-screen. If the shot represents the point of view of a character, the eye level is a natural angle to represent how and what that character sees. Camera angles take on a wider range of expressive meetings as soon as the filmmakers deviate from this "normal and neutral" viewpoint.

2. André Bazin, "The Evolution of the Language of Cinema," in *What Is Cinema?* trans. Hugh Gray, 2 vols. (Berkeley: University of California Press, 1967–71), I, pp. 35–36.

High-angle shot

In this moment in *Love Me Tonight* (1932), the normally confident Maurice has just been forced to admit that he is only an ordinary tailor, a confession that has cost him the love of his beloved princess. Director Rouben Mamoulian employs a high angle (combined with a framing that diminishes the character's size) to convey Maurice's shame and vulnerability [1]. Sometimes, however, a high-angle shot can be used to play against its traditional interpretation. The sinister villains in this high-angle shot in *North by Northwest* (1959) are the opposite of vulnerable—they're planning a murder. Director Alfred Hitchcock used the spatial implications of the extreme high angle to emphasize their intended victim's predicament: she's oblivious upstairs packing for a flight, and they've just decided to toss her out of the airplane.

High Angle For a **high-angle shot**, the camera is positioned above eye level, so it aims down at the subject. In our everyday conversation, to "look down on someone" indicates that we consider that someone to be inferior. When we literally look down on someone, we are often viewing them from a position of superiority—either we're

Low-angle shot

Two faces, both shot at low angle, convey two different meanings. [1] A low-angle shot of Radio Raheem from Spike Lee's *Do the Right Thing* (1989) portrays him as threatening. The shot conveys the point of view of a pizzeria owner who is intimidated by his boom-box-carrying customer. [2] In *The Shining* (1980), we might expect director Stanley Kubrick to use a high angle for the moment when the helpless Wendy discovers a manuscript that proves her husband Jack is insane. Instead, Kubrick uses a low angle that enlarges the indisputable evidence of his madness in the foreground and denies us the ability to see behind Wendy at a moment when we expect Jack to come sneaking up behind her. The resulting suspense actually intensifies her vulnerability.

physically larger or they are in a comparatively submissive or prone position. In most of its cinematic applications, the high-angle shot draws upon this spatial implication; characters shot with the camera looking down on them are portrayed as vulnerable or weak. However, no cinematic meaning is carved in stone. How we experience and understand any shot depends on the surrounding context.

Low Angle For a **low-angle shot**, the camera is positioned below eye level, so it aims up at the subject. As you

Dutch angle

The off-balance look of the Dutch-angle shot is perfectly suited to the unnatural activities perpetrated by Doctors Frankenstein and Pretorius in *Bride of Frankenstein* (1935). During a 2-minute scene in which the mad scientists equip an assembled corpse with a re-animated heart, director James Whale uses eighteen Dutch-angle shots.

might imagine, the low-angle shot typically conveys the opposite meaning of a high-angle shot. When we say "I look up to her," we're talking about someone we consider our superior. We literally look up at performers on stage, elevated monuments to historical heroes, and physically imposing adversaries. So it makes sense that subjects in low-angle shots generally appear powerful, noble, or threatening. But again, when used in a different context, the low-angle shot can take on very different meanings.

Dutch Angle Our world is built along horizontal and vertical lines; typically, one of the assistant cameraperson's first tasks with each new setup is to level the camera on the tripod so the horizontal and vertical lines align with the framing. For a **Dutch-angle shot** (also called a Dutch tilt or oblique-angle shot), the camera is tilted so that horizontal and vertical lines on set appear as diagonals in the frame. Doing so causes the world on-screen to appear off-balance or misaligned, which is why the Dutch angle is primarily used in scenes depicting unnatural or chaotic events.

Bird's-Eye View A **bird's-eye view shot** (or an *overhead* or *aerial-view shot*) is taken from directly over the subjects, often from an elevated view. Cranes, drones, or aircraft are principally used to capture this extreme

perspective. As most of us don't encounter this viewpoint in our regular lives, the bird's-eye view can be used to impart a sense of disorientation or strangeness to the action on-screen. In a different context, the view from on high can be used to convey omniscience in terms of narration or point of view. In some contexts, the angle can be read figuratively—or even literally—as a God's point of view on the earthly action.

Camera Movement

Any movement of the camera within a shot automatically changes the image we see because the elements of framing that we have discussed thus far—camera angle, level, height, shot types—are all modified when the camera moves within that shot. The moving camera, which can photograph both static and moving subjects, opens up cinematic space, and thus filmmakers use it to achieve many effects. It can search and increase the

Bird's-eye view

Saroo Brierley was a young boy in rural India who became lost in Calcutta, then was sent overseas when he was adopted by an Australian couple. Garth Davis's *Lion* (2016) tells the true story of Brierley's search for his brother and biological mother. Davis juxtaposes two different kinds of bird's-eye view shots to visualize the moment when the adult Saroo finally discovers his lost home using Google Earth: pixilated satellite images on his laptop [1], and vivid bird's-eye shots depicting the forgotten memories they trigger [2].

Camera angles in *M*

In Fritz Lang's *M* (1931), the city of Berlin is gripped in fear during a spree of child murders. In this scene, in which an innocent man becomes the object of a crowd's suspicions, camera angles provide a context for us to distinguish real threats from perceived ones. [1] An accidental meeting between a short man and a little girl is shot as a neutral eye-level long shot. [2] The suspicious man who interrupts the innocent exchange is shown from the short man's perspective, an exaggerated low-angle shot in which the accuser looms threateningly over the camera. [3] A high-angle shot from the perspective of the accuser reinforces the short man's modest stature and relative powerlessness. [4] When we return to an eye-level shot, a crowd—soon to be a mob—fills the tighter framing.

space, introduce us to more details than would be possible with a static image, choose which of these details we should look at or ignore, follow movement through a room or across a landscape, and establish complex relationships between figures in the frame—especially in shots that are longer than average. It allows the viewer to accompany or follow the movements of a character, object, or vehicle and to see the action from a character's point of view. The moving camera leads the viewer's eye or focuses the viewer's attention and, by moving into the scene, helps create the illusion of depth in the flat screen image. Furthermore, it helps convey relationships:

spatial, causal, and psychological. When used in this way, the moving camera adds immeasurably to the director's development of the narrative and our understanding of it.

Within the first decade of movie history, D. W. Griffith began to exploit the power of simple camera movement to create associations within the frame and, in some cases, to establish a cause-and-effect relationship. In *The Birth of a Nation* (1915), within one shot he establishes a view of a Civil War battle, turns the camera toward a woman and small children on a wagon, and then turns back to the battle. From that instinctive, fluid camera movement we understand the relationship between the horror of the battle and the misery that it has created for innocent civilians. Of course, Griffith could have cut between shots of the battle and the bystanders, but breaking up the space and time with editing would not achieve the same subtle effect as a single shot does.

In the 1920s, German filmmakers took this very simple type of camera movement to the next level, perfecting fluid camera movement within and between shots. In fact, F. W. Murnau, who is associated with some of the greatest early work with the moving camera in such films as *The Last Laugh* (1924) and *Sunrise: A Song of Two Humans* (1927), referred to it as the *unchained camera*, thereby suggesting that it has a life of its own, with no limits to its freedom of movement. Since the 1920s, the moving camera has become one of the dominant stylistic trademarks of a diverse group of directors, from Orson Welles and Max Ophüls to Alfonso Cuarón and Alejandro González Iñárritu.

The smoothly moving camera helped change the way movies were made as well as how we see and interpret them. But before the camera was capable of smooth movement, directors and their camera operators had to find ways to create steady moving shots that would imitate the way the human eye/brain sees. When we look around a room or landscape or see movement through space, our eyes dart from subject to subject, from plane to plane, and so we "see" more like a series of rapidly edited movie shots than a smooth flow of visual information. Yet our eyes and brain work together to smooth out the jumps. Camera motion, however, must itself be smooth in order for its audience to make sense of (or even tolerate) the shots resulting from that motion.

There are exceptions, of course: During the 1960s, nonfiction filmmakers began what was soon to become widespread use of the handheld camera. This technique both ushered in entirely new ways of filmmaking, such

LOOKING AT MOVIES
THE MOVING CAMERA

VIDEO In this tutorial, Dave Monahan demonstrates the various types of camera movement.

as *cinéma vérité* and direct cinema, and greatly influenced narrative film style. For the most part, however, cinematographers strive to ensure that the camera does not shake or jump while moving through a shot.

The basic types of shots involving camera movement are the pan, tilt, dolly, and crane shots as well as those made with the Steadicam, the handheld camera, or the zoom lens. Each shot involves a particular kind of movement, depends on a particular kind of equipment, and has its own expressive potential.

Pan and Tilt Shots These most basic moving camera shots use a *head* mounted on a tripod. The tripod is a three-legged, adjustable mechanism that holds the camera steady and can be set at variable heights. The camera attaches to the head, which allows the operator to pivot the camera vertically or horizontally. Your own body provides an easy way to picture the setup: think of your eyes as the lens, your head as the camera, and your neck as the head. Tripods are stationary, so, in this analogy, your body/tripod is standing still. For a **pan shot**, the camera pivots horizontally on a stationary axis; in other words, the camera "looks" from side to side. The pan shot offers us a larger, more panoramic view than a shot taken from a fixed camera; guides our attention to characters or actions that are important; makes us aware of relationships between subjects that are too far apart to be shown together in the frame; allows us to follow people or objects; and attempts to replicate what we

1

2

A tilt shot conveys a psychological relationship in *Citizen Kane*

When his second wife leaves him, Kane tears her room apart in a fit of rage. When his flailing reveals a snow globe on a shelf, his outburst staggers to a stop. The next shot is of Kane's hand gripping the snow globe, which contains a tiny model cabin [1] similar to the one he grew up in. The shot tilts up to his face, where anger has been replaced by wistful sadness [2]. The camera move links the object to the emotion, and we understand that Kane is thinking about his lost childhood.

see when we turn our heads to survey a scene or follow a character.

For a **tilt shot**, the camera pivots vertically; in other words, it "looks" up and down. The tilt shot can do anything a pan does—only vertically. Because our world and our movements are mostly oriented along the horizontal axis, pan shots are the most common of the two. Pan and tilt shots are shot from a stationary tripod, but a camera can also pan or tilt as part of another camera move made from a crane, dolly, or Steadicam.

Dolly Shot A **dolly shot** (also known as a tracking shot) is one taken from a camera mounted on a wheeled platform called a dolly, which can be equipped with either large rubber wheels for smooth soundstage floors or grooved wheels that run on tracks over uneven surfaces. Because it moves smoothly and freely along the ground, the dolly shot is one of the most effective (and consequently most common) uses of the moving camera. Dolly shots can follow characters moving through settings or simulate the point of view of a moving character. A camera narrator shot with a dolly can guide the frame through unfolding situations and convey spatial relationships between one scene element and another. One of the most common dolly shots is the **dolly in**,

which moves the camera toward a stationary subject, causing the subject's size in frame to gradually increase. This visible shift in implied proximity intensifies the significance of a moment, making the technique useful for depicting a character at a moment of realization or decision. You may remember Alicia, the woman married to

A dolly in action

Camera operators follow the action of a street scene using a dolly equipped to roll on tracks over uneven terrain (such as a bumpy city street) during the production of the HBO series *The Sopranos*.

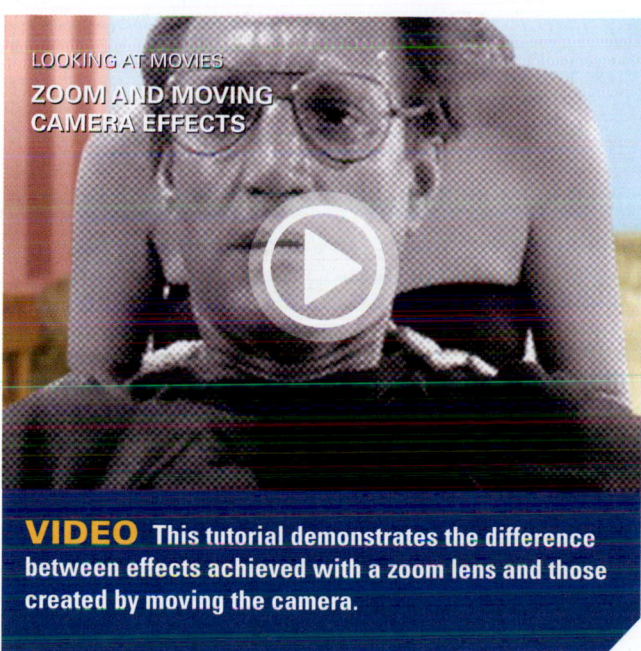

VIDEO This tutorial demonstrates the difference between effects achieved with a zoom lens and those created by moving the camera.

the Nazi conspirator Sebastian in *Notorious* (1946). The moment when she finally figures out her coffee is poisoned is conveyed by a series of dolly-in moves: first of her murderous mother-in-law, then of her devious husband, and finally of Alicia herself. The first two convey a sort of psychological point of view as she realizes who is doing the poisoning, and the third intensifies our experience of her decision to try and make a run for it.

A **dolly-out** movement (moving backwards) can be used for a technique called **slow disclosure** where the camera movement allows new information into the frame that expands or changes the viewer's initial interpretation of the subject or situation. A good example occurs in Stanley Kubrick's 1964 Cold War satire *Dr. Strangelove or: How I Learned to Stop Worrying and Love the Bomb*. When a medium close-up lingers on a bomber pilot staring intently downward, context makes us assume he is a diligent officer monitoring his instrument panel. Then the camera dollies back, widening our viewpoint and revealing that his intent gaze is actually focused on a *Playboy* magazine. Other camera movements can also be used for slow disclosure. In the aforementioned *Notorious*, a high-angle long shot opens on a large formal social function. As the crane shot moves closer and closer to Alicia and Sebastian chatting and greeting guests, the situation appears to be nothing but a cordial gathering, until the camera moves into an extreme close-up of Alicia's hand, which is clutching the

key she stole from Sebastian. What was an elegant party scene is now understood as the backdrop for a dangerous mission into the forbidden wine cellar.

Zoom The zoom is a lens with a variable focal length, which permits the camera operator during shooting to shift from the wide-angle lens (short focus) to the telephoto lens (long focus) or vice versa without changing the focus or aperture settings. It is not a camera movement per se, because only the optics inside the lens are moving in relation to each other and thus shifting the focal length. Still, the zoom can provide the illusion of the camera moving toward or away from the subject. One result of this shift is that the image is magnified when shifting from short to long focal length or demagnified by shifting in the opposite direction.

That magnification is the essential difference between **zoom-in** and dolly-in movements on a subject. When dollying, a camera actually moves through space; in the process, spatial relationships between the camera and the objects in its frame shift, causing relative changes in position between on-screen figures or objects. By contrast, because a zoom lens does not move through space, its depiction of spatial relationships between the camera and its subjects does not change. All a zoom shot does is magnify the image.

Because it depicts movement through space differently than we experience it in our own lives with our own eyes, the movement of a zoom shot can feel artificial. For this reason (and the fact that viewers naturally associate the zoom effect with its use in amateur home videos), zoom shots are rarely used in narrative feature films. However, because the zoom provides documentary filmmakers a fast and practical way to shift perspective when capturing ongoing and unscripted action, the zoom is an accepted technique in nonfiction cinema and in narrative movies presented in a documentary style. You may recall the effective zoom in *The Hurt Locker* described earlier in this chapter.

When combined with the perspective shift of a dolly shot, the magnifying effect of a zoom can create a striking and unsettling distortion of perspective. This so-called "zolly" maintains the size of the subject in frame while the background magnifies or retreats behind them, or vice versa: the background stays the same while the subject enlarges or grows smaller. The unsettling spatial inconsistency is usually used to convey a character realization at a moment of crisis, such as in Steven Spielberg's

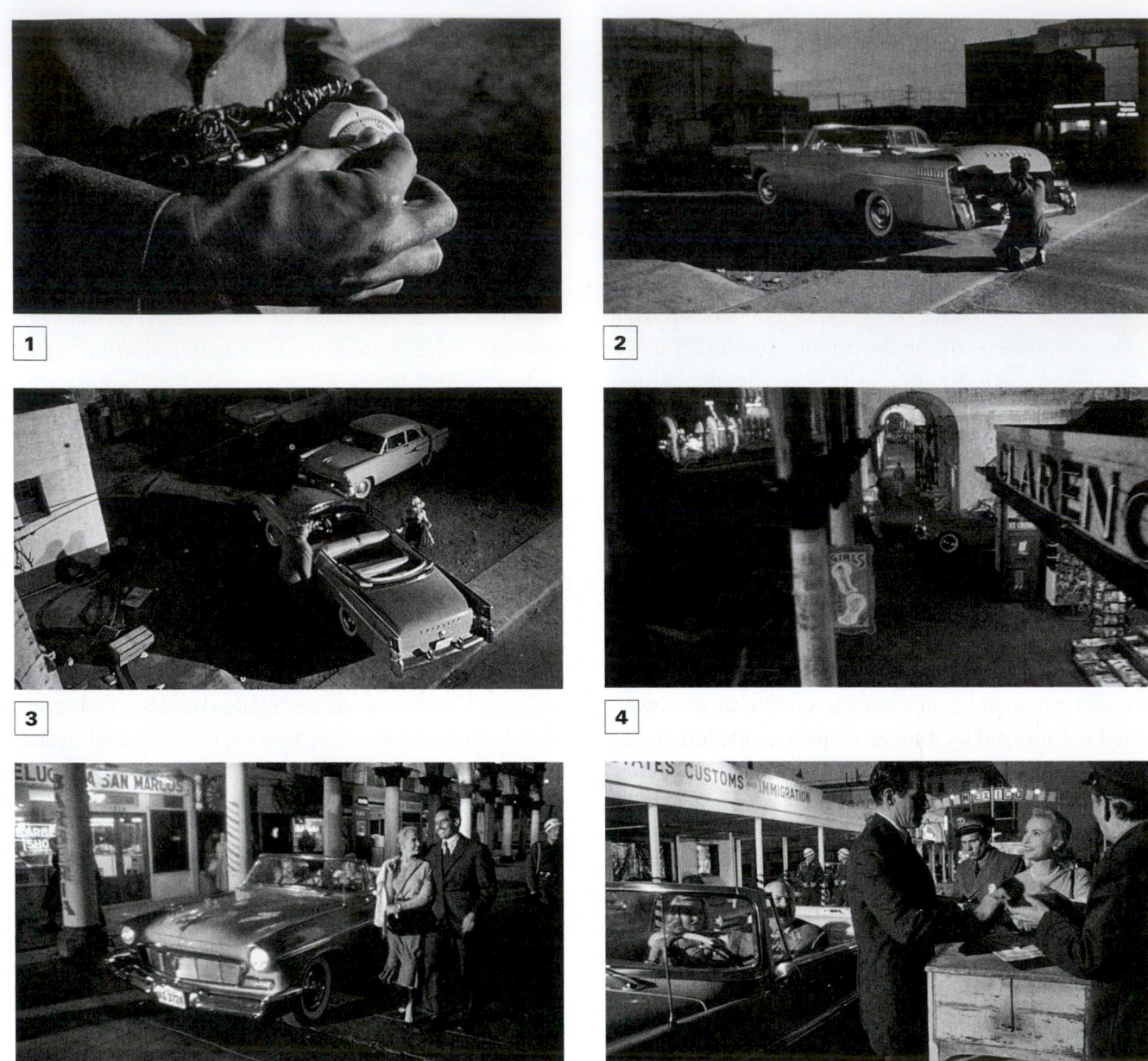

The crane shot in *Touch of Evil*

The virtuoso 3-minute crane shot that opens *Touch of Evil* combines nearly every possible shot type and camera angle into a single fluid movement that sets the scene, introduces characters, and ignites the conflict for the film noir's entire story. The unchained camera starts on an extreme closeup-of a time bomb [1], shows the bomb being slipped into a car trunk [2], lifts to depict the doomed victims in a hig-angle long shot [3], then follows their progress through a seedy border town [4]. Along the way, their path intersects that of the movie's protagonists, Mike and Susan Vargas [5], creating suspense as all the players wait to cross the border [6]—and we anticipate the inevitable explosion.

Jaws (1975) when the sheriff of a tourist town witnesses the signs of a shark attack on a crowded beach.

Crane Shot A **crane shot** is made from a camera mounted on an elevating arm, making it capable of moving freely and smoothly through vertical space. When a camera crane is attached to a dolly or other vehicle, the crane may move freely and smoothly both vertically and horizontally. The crane shot allows filmmakers to combine multiple camera angles and shot types within a single shot, such as the previously described party scene in *Notorious* or the famous opening shot in Orson Welles's *Touch of Evil* (1958). An ascending crane shot is used for slow disclosure in *Gone with the Wind*. The camera begins framed at eye level on Scarlett O'Hara standing beside a few wounded Confederate soldiers, then pulls up and out to a high-angle extreme long shot that reduces her to a tiny, insignificant figure in a vast railroad yard filled with scores of wounded and dead.

Handheld Camera A handheld camera is exactly what it sounds like: the camera operator holds the camera, usually with the help of a mount that allows the bulk of the camera weight to rest on her shoulder. Not even the most skilled operator can completely eliminate the shaking and wobbling associated with a handheld camera. Because news and documentary filmmakers rely on the flexibility of the handheld camera to cover unpredictable ongoing events, its unstable look is often associated with documentary realism. Some narrative films, such as *127 Hours* (2010), *Tangerine*, and *The Hurt Locker* seek a sense of immediacy and authenticity and so are shot mostly, or even entirely, using a handheld camera. The visual instability of the handheld camera can also be used selectively to indicate distressed states of mind or volatile situations. For the opening battle of *Saving Private Ryan* (1998), Steven Spielberg exploited the handheld camera to bring the scene both documentary realism and visual pandemonium. Both documentary realism and visual instability are behind the handheld camera's use in narrative found-footage movies. These fiction films are presented as if the footage was shot by a participant in the action—which is usually chaotic and unpredictable. In found-footage horror movies such as *The Blair Witch Project* (1999), *Rec* (2007), and *Cloverfield* (2008), the rapid pans and jittery framing help to convince viewers that we're experiencing actual documented events and also communicate the terrified state of mind of the camera-operator characters as they cope with, respectively, an unseen witch/ghost, fast zombies, and a gigantic monster.

Steadicam The **Steadicam** is a patented harness device worn by the operator and uses a sophisticated system of counterweights and hydraulics to combine the mobility of the handheld camera with the smoothness of a tracking shot. The camera operator can walk or run up stairs, over uneven surfaces, and through tight spaces where dollies cannot fit.[3] This flexibility has made the Steadicam the method of choice for moving camera shots that extend a

Moving camera conveys a crucial spatial relationship

During *The Shining*'s climactic chase through the hedge maze, the moving camera informs viewers of a key spatial relationship. The shot begins on the young Danny hiding behind a hedge [1], then glides left to reveal his pursuer on just the other side [2]. By uniting Danny's terror with his deranged father, the move also conveys a psychological relationship. The shot was filmed with a Steadicam, but could just as easily have been captured using a dolly.

narrative over time and through space, such as the shot in *The Shining* that follows Danny's long Big Wheel ride through the halls of the Overlook Hotel. This famous early Steadicam shot does more than simply allow the film to keep the rolling Danny in frame. The gliding camera takes on the malevolent spirit of the haunted hotel as it floats along in a kind of relentless lurking pursuit of the oblivious innocent. Later, when his axe-wielding father, Jack, searches for Danny in the hedge maze, the Steadicam pursues the boy from behind in every shot of Danny, while virtually every Steadicam shot of Jack faces the murderous antagonist head on.

---

3. Lighter digital cameras can now be mounted on similar, but smaller, rigs called gimbals that use counterweights and gyroscopes to steady the camera, but the Steadicam still dominates the commercial feature film market.

The longest Steadicam shot

The entire 96-minute running time of Alexander Sukarov's *Russian Ark* (2002) was filmed in a single unbroken shot using a Steadicam moving through intricately choreographed historical reenactments staged throughout the huge Winter Palace of the Russian State Hermitage Museum in St. Petersburg, Russia. Before the advent of digital cinematography, a single shot of this length would have been impossible. The maximum amount of film stock a standard 35mm camera can hold lasts only a little over 11 minutes.

The smoothest-moving camera

The Steadicam is not a camera but rather a steadying mechanism on which any motion-picture camera can be mounted. As seen here, during the filming of Tom Tykwer's *Perfume: The Story of a Murderer* (2006), the operator wears a harness attached to an arm that is connected to a vertical armature, with the camera at the top and a counterweight at the bottom. Unlike the handheld camera, this mechanism isolates the operator's movements from the camera, producing a very smooth shot even when the operator is walking or running quickly over an uneven surface.

Framing: What We See on the Screen

As we learned earlier in this chapter, framing is the process by which the cinematographer uses the borders of the moving image to determine what we see on-screen. Framing is also used to determine what we *don't* see on-screen. The frame of the camera's **viewfinder** (the little window you look into or through when taking a picture) indicates the limited boundaries of the camera's framed perspective on the world. To demonstrate for yourself the difference between the camera's view and your everyday vision, put your hands together to form a rectangular frame, then look through it using one eye. If you move it to the left or the right, move it closer or farther away from your face, or tilt it up or down, you can see instantly how framing (and moving the frame) defines and limits what you see.

Moving that frame makes us aware of the **offscreen space** outside the frame as well as the **on-screen space** inside it. As the film theorist Noël Burch first suggested, the entire visual composition of a shot depends on the existence of on-screen as well as offscreen spaces; both spaces are equally important to the composition and to the viewer's experience of it. Burch divides offscreen space into six segments: the four infinite spaces that lie beyond the four borders of the frame; the spaces beyond the movie settings; and the space behind the camera.

The borders of the frame, and the offscreen spaces beyond them, may be used in a number of ways. Characters may enter or exit the frame from any of the previously listed spaces. Characters on-screen may look offscreen. The image on-screen may represent what a character offscreen is looking at. The filmmaker may use sound, shadow, a character's gaze, or narrative context to hint at the presence of someone (or something) in the space offscreen. Suspecting that something may be hidden outside of the frame can increase our participation in the unfolding narrative as we try to figure out who or what it is: knowing that something is just beyond our view can increase suspense as we predict and anticipate its eventual appearance. Alternatively, the filmmaker can surprise us by moving the frame to suddenly reveal previously hidden information.

Offscreen and on-screen space in *Chinatown*

In his film noir *Chinatown* (1974), Roman Polanski uses offscreen space first to create suspense and then to provide a surprise during a prearranged meeting between the prying detective J. J. Gittes and the menacing tycoon Noah Cross. The scene opens with an LS establishing shot of an empty entryway. Viewers conditioned to having settings populated with characters are made immediately aware of offscreen space, as presumably Gittes and Cross must eventually enter the established setting. And sure enough, we soon see Cross's car through an open door in the background as it passes through the space behind the setting. A moment later, a puff of smoke enters the left side of the frame [1]. Context tells us it's Gittes—we know he's meeting Cross, and we've seen him smoke countless cigarettes in the film's preceding 2 hours of screen time. By placing Gittes offscreen, yet making us aware of his presence, Polanski creates suspense. The viewer wonders if he's hiding or simply waiting—or maybe this is just a transitional moment of vagueness before a powerful confrontation between two antagonists. We are kept in suspense for the 10 long seconds it takes for Cross to enter the frame through the background door, stroll to the foreground, and finally look offscreen and address Gittes. The detective enters the frame to confront Cross with a coroner's report and a pair of shattered eyeglasses that proves Cross committed murder [2]. The framing follows Cross as he ambles into an adjoining garden, leaving Gittes offscreen once again [3]. The persistent Gittes reenters the frame to continue questioning the seemingly imperturbable Cross. After a few moments of conversation, Cross glances offscreen and casually orders an unseen (and unforeseen) enforcer named Claude to confiscate Gittes's evidence [4]. A large hand reaches into the frame [5]. A moment after we see a look of disgusted recognition on Gittes's face, the frame shifts to allow us to share his surprise. Claude is the violent and vengeful security chief that Gittes beat senseless earlier in the story [6].

Table 6.1 | OPEN AND CLOSED FRAMES

	Open	Closed
Visual characteristics	Normal depth, perspective, light, and scale. An overall look that is realistic, or verisimilar.	Exaggerated and stylized depth; out of perspective; distorted or exaggerated light and shadow; distorted scale. An overall look that is not realistic.
Framing the characters	The characters act. They may move freely in and out of the frame. They are free to go to another place in the movie's world and return.	The characters are acted upon. They are controlled by outside forces and do not have the freedom to come and go as they wish. They have no control over the logic that drives the movie's actions.
Relationship of characters to design elements	The characters are more important than the sets, costumes, and other design elements. The design elements support the development of character and story.	Design elements call attention to themselves and may be more important than the characters. Design elements drive the story's development.
The world of the story	The world of the story is based on reality. It changes and evolves, and the framing changes with it. The frame is a window on this world.	The world of the story is self-contained: it doesn't refer to anything outside of itself. It is rigid and hierarchical: everything has its place. The frame is similar to a painting.

Source: Adapted from Leo Braudy, *The World in a Frame: What We See in Films* (1976; repr., Chicago: University of Chicago Press, 1984).

Open and Closed Framing The first and most obvious function of the motion-picture frame is to control our perception of the world by enclosing what we see within a rectangular border. Because it shapes the image in a configuration that does not allow for peripheral vision and thus does not conform to our visual perception, we understand framing as one of the many conventions through which cinema gives form to what we see on the screen. Film theorist Leo Braudy, one of many writers to study the relationship between cinematic arrangement and viewer perception, distinguishes between open and closed films as two ways of designing and representing the visible world through framing it, as well as two ways of perceiving and interpreting it.

Each of these cinematic worlds—open and closed—is created through a system of framing that should remain fairly consistent throughout the film so as not to confuse the viewer. The **open frame** is designed to depict a world where characters move freely within an open, recognizable environment, and the **closed frame** is designed to imply that other forces (such as fate; social, educational, or economic background; or a repressive government) have robbed characters of their ability to move and act freely. The open frame is generally employed in realistic (verisimilar) films, the closed frame in formalist films. In the realistic film, the frame is a "window" on the world—one that provides many views. Because the "reality" being depicted changes continu-

ally, the movie's framing changes with it. In the formalist film, the frame is similar to the frame of a painting or photograph, enclosing or limiting the world by closing it down and providing only one view. Because only that one view exists, everything within the frame has its particular place. As with all such distinctions in film analysis, these differences between open and closed frames are not absolute; they are a matter of degree and emphasis (as shown in Table 6.1).

LOOKING AT MOVIES
POINT OF VIEW

VIDEO This tutorial explores point of view and framing.

The closed frame in *Mother!*

In Darren Aronofsky's closed film, Jennifer Lawrence's character, Mother, is not just confined to the self-contained world of the allegorical story, she is cinematically confined to every frame. Aronofsky used only three types of handheld shots: close framed "singles" on Mother, shots framed over her shoulder, and point-of-view shots showing what she sees. More than half of the movie's running time consists of close-ups of her face.

Directors choose the closed frame when their stories concern characters who are controlled by outside forces and do not have the freedom to come and go as they wish. Design elements frequently drive the story's development. Darren Aronofsky's stylized and allegorical horror film *Mother!* (2017) is by design a closed film. The audience sees only what Jennifer Lawrence's character, identified only as "Mother," perceives and feels—which are feelings of anxiety, abandonment, confusion, anger, and grief. All of these emotions are provoked by outside forces, known as the "visitors," that invade the isolated home she shares with her husband (known as "Him"). Mother (and, by extension, the viewer) never leaves this self-contained setting, with the exception of a scene in which Mother and Him stare at the house as it burns to ashes.

An interesting opportunity to compare open and closed framing presented itself when two different directors from different countries—Jean Renoir (France) and Akira Kurosawa (Japan)—each made their own cinematic adaptation of Russian writer Maxim Gorky's play *The Lower Depths* (1902). Gorky's work gives a pessimistic, dark view of lower-class Russians who share a boarding house, the principal setting of the play. In his 1936 version, Renoir, who generally favors the open frame, sets the story in a Parisian flophouse and allows his characters to move freely in and out of the frame as well as out of the house and into the city beyond. Kurosawa, in his 1957 version, sets the story in seventeenth-century Japan and, like Gorky, keeps the action inside the house. Renoir emphasizes that man's life is left to free will and

chance, while Kurosawa allows his characters little freedom. Renoir's open frame is more relevant to the modern audience, while Kurosawa's relatively closed frame seems claustrophobic by contrast, perhaps reflecting the hierarchical society of the time.

The formulaic nature of these distinctions does not mean that you should automatically categorize movies

Open and closed versions of the same story

Akira Kurosawa's closed version and Jean Renoir's open version of *The Lower Depths* each include a scene where a character recounts a love story she read in a book as if it were her own. Neither Renoir nor Kurosawa stray far from the original play's material in the scene, but the framing differs. Kurosawa's scene takes place in its self-contained setting and uses stylized depth [1]. Renoir uses normal perspective and moves the scene into the city where we can see a world beyond that of the story. Characters freely enter and exit the frame [2].

that you see and analyze as open or closed. Instead, you can recognize the characteristics of each type of film, and you can be aware that certain directors consistently depict open worlds (Jean Renoir, John Ford, Robert Altman) while others are equally consistent in making closed ones (Alfred Hitchcock, Stanley Kubrick, Lars von Trier).

Framing and Point of View

Point of view (or **POV**)—whose viewpoint the image on-screen represents—is implied by the framing of a shot. There are three basic kinds of point of view: (1) omniscient point of view; (2) single-character point of view; and (3) group point of view.

Omniscient point of view shows us what the camera/narrator sees. Typically, we think of omniscient point of view as being fairly neutral, with the camera more or less objectively recording the action of the story. But while omniscient means all-knowing, it does not necessarily mean objective. As we've seen in all of the preceding pages, the camera—as determined by the director and her creative collaborators—uses framing, movement, angles, and all the elements of mise-en-scène

to present characters and situations in specific ways that deliberately shape our perception and interpretation.

Single-character point of view is when framing and editing shows us what a single character is seeing. Typically, a single-character point of view is indicated by a preceding shot showing a character looking offscreen. With the character's gaze established, viewers instinctively understand that the following shot depicts what that character is looking at. The single-character point-of-view shot is almost always followed by a shot of the character reacting to what he or she has just seen. The point-of-view shot itself may be framed to represent the looking character's spatial relationship with the object of his or her gaze or it may be framed in a way that conveys not just what the character is looking at, but how he or she feels about it. Single-character point of view shots should not be confused with over-the-shoulder shots, which also indicate what a character is looking at, but do so by shooting over the character's shoulder, and thus do not directly convey that character's viewpoint. **Group point of view** works much like single-character point of view, but instead of one character seeing something, it is many characters.

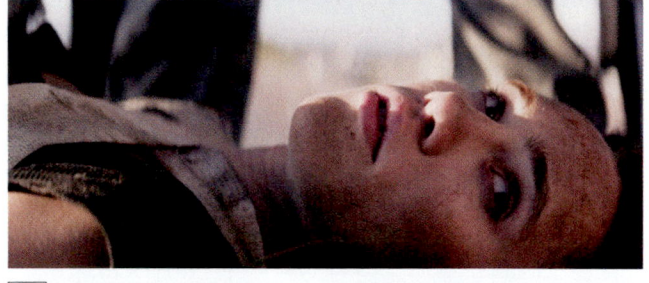

Point of view conveys different perceptions

After Arlen escapes from a band of cannibals in Ana Lily Amirpour's dystopian *The Bad Batch* (2016) [1], her POV of the mysterious man who delivered her from the desert [2] reflects her literal spatial perspective. Later, when she returns a lost child to its father, a former enemy, her POV depicts more than just what she's seeing—the framing suggests the emotional significance of what she is witnessing. Arlen is more than a dozen feet from the reunion [3], but her POV is shown in close-up [4].

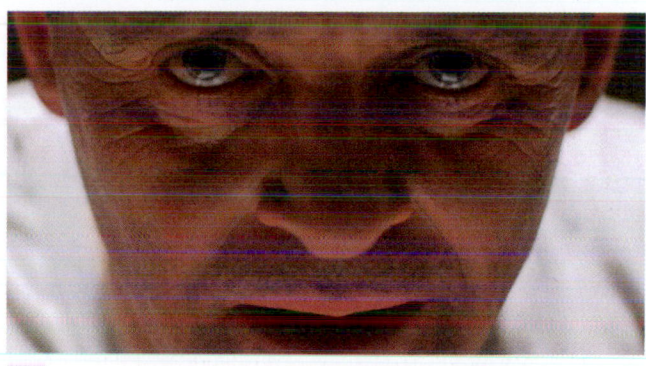

1

2

Separation

Jonathan Demme's 1991 thriller *Silence of the Lambs* contains one of the most extended and powerful separation sequences in movie history. During the main character's final encounter, viewers assume the POV of FBI trainee Clarice Starling to experience the steely gaze of the serial-killer genius Hannibal Lecter [1], then take on the perception of Lecter's POV when he studies the young investigator [2]. The eye-to-eye POV exchange alternates 53 times, with only one brief interruption.

The framing and cinematography may also reflect a physical aspect of how the character sees. The first third of Julian Schnabel's *The Diving Bell and the Butterfly* (2007) is presented almost exclusively in the point of view of the protagonist Jean-Dominique Bauby, who suffered a massive stroke leaving him almost completely paralyzed, having only the use of one eye. The point-of-view shots that put us inside of Bauby's perceptive experience are blurred, flickering, and overexposed. Because this portion of the movie restricts our view to what Bauby himself can see, the point-of-view shots in this portion of *The Diving Bell and the Butterfly* are not motivated by a "character looking" shot or followed by a character reaction shot. A few movies, such as Robert Montgomery's *Lady in the Lake* (1947), Gaspar Noé's *Enter the Void* (2010), and Ilya Naishuller's *Hardcore Henry* (2016) have attempted to tell their entire story in single-character point of view. Confining every shot to this first-person perspective is problematic. Because our eyes and brains experience peripheral vision and movement differently than cameras and lenses, sustained point-of-view shots—especially those that move through space—look artificial to the point of distraction.

Because viewers identify with the lens (the viewpoint of the camera), a single-character point-of-view shot can generate a sort of intensified identification with the character whose viewpoint we have assumed. When we experience a series of shots representing the alternating points of view of two interacting characters, we may experience a sort of participatory cycle that theorist and filmmaker Stefan Sharff called **separation**. It is something of a cinematic role-playing game. On some level, when we're looking at character B through character A's point of view, we assume the perspective of character A. In other words, we literally and figuratively see character B through character A's eyes. When the sequence shifts to character B's point of view of character A, our identification shifts to that of character B. An extended back-and-forth sequence can dramatically intensify our experience of the interaction, which is why filmmakers typically reserve the technique for dramatically significant exchanges.

Speed and Length of the Shot

Thus far, we have emphasized the spatial aspects of how a shot is framed and photographed. But the image we see on the screen also has temporal dimensions: the speed of the movement within the shot and the length (or duration) of the shot itself.

Speed of the Shot

As you have no doubt noticed, most shots in most movies reproduce movement at the speed at which things move in our actual existence. The speed of that movement on-screen depends on frame rate; that is, the number of

still images (frames) the camera captures per second, in combination with the number of still images projected (or played) per second in the movie theater or on your TV or computer. (Projectors use shutters to show each individual image more than once during that second, but the shutter only smooths the appearance of motion—it does not affect the speed of motion.) Action can be shot at any frame rate, but to reproduce the normal speed of the action on-screen, the device that shows us the movie must play it back at the same rate in which it was shot. The number of frames shot and projected per second was standardized at 24 frames per second (fps) in the late 1920s. In recent years, some filmmakers have experimented with higher camera and projector frame rates in an effort to produce sharper images and a more precise reproduction of movement. Peter Jackson's The Hobbit trilogy (2012–14) was shot and projected at 48 fps; Ang Lee boosted the rate to 120 fps for *Billy Lynn's Long Halftime Walk* (2016). These innovators didn't account for a century of cinematic conditioning—we've become accustomed to the way 24 fps reproduces motion and image sharpness. Audiences and critics found the increased frame rates to be too sharp and uncannily precise. So, for the time being at least, most movies are sticking with 24 fps.

Deviations from normal speed are accomplished by altering frame rate during the production phase. This means that directors and cinematographers must decide in advance which shots will appear as fast or slow motion when they are projected to an audience. **Slow motion** is achieved by filming at a higher frame rate. For example, to create a shot where the action happens at half of normal speed, the camera frame rate must be doubled to 48 fps, so that when the shot is played back at 24 fps, it will take up twice the screen time. Slow motion tends to make movement appear more graceful, which makes it useful for a number of applications. It can suggest a character's heightened awareness, impart significance to an

1

2

The slow-motion power walk

Slow motion tends to make movement appear more graceful and elegant, which may explain the ubiquity of the "power-walk" shot featuring a group of characters walking shoulder to shoulder in slow motion toward the camera to express their confidence and cool. Introduced to great effect in films such as Stanley Kubrick's *A Clockwork Orange* (1971) [1] and Philip Kaufman's *The Right Stuff* (1983), and then popularized in Quentin Tarantino's *Reservoir Dogs* (1992), the technique has become a cliché and is regularly parodied in comedies such as Phil Lord and Christopher Miller's *21 Jump Street* (2012) [2].

action that might otherwise be interpreted as mundane, lend an ironic elegance to violence, or suspend viewers in a moment that would normally be fleeting, such as a kiss . . . or an explosion.

Point of view in *The Birds*

Alfred Hitchcock's *The Birds* (1963) takes place in an isolated town suffering increasingly violent bird attacks. This scene, constructed around alternating POV shots, includes a number of different uses of the technique. A shot of the protagonist, Melanie Daniels, and other characters looking out from the cafe where they have taken shelter [1] sets up a group POV of a bird attacking the attendant at a gas station across the street [2]. This group POV accurately depicts the spatial relationship between the group and what they see. But later, when Melanie and other characters look out a different window [3], the group POV shot that follows is framed in a close-up to reflect the significance of what they see: gasoline flowing away from the abandoned pump [4]. Many POV shots later, a series of close-ups of Melanie [5] alternate with POV shots showing her perspective of the flames set by a dropped cigarette as they rush back toward the gas pump. Some POV shots show her emotional perspective and are framed closer to convey significance [6], another reflects her true spatial relationship with the resulting explosion [7]. The final shot in the sequence is a bird's-eye view representing a literal birds' group POV of the havoc they have wrought [8].

Two different uses of the long take

A series of long takes in *The Revenant* [1] thrusts us into the swirling confusion of battle. The long takes hold viewers in real time as the mobile frame weaves together the myriad of events and actions that erupt after Arikara warriors launch a surprise attack on a band of trappers. Godfrey Reggio's experimental documentary *Visitors* (2013) [2] uses the long take to provoke a very different cinematic experience. Viewers accustomed to simply witnessing characters as disconnected spectators are compelled to share a sustained, direct, and mutual gaze with subjects, as in this 2 minute 20 second shot of a gorilla that opens the film. When was the last time you stared into anyone's eyes for that long?

Fast motion is achieved by filming at a lower frame rate. To make action on-screen appear twice as fast as it actually occurred, the cinematographer would shoot it at 12 fps so that when it is projected at 24 fps, that same action will take only half as much screen time as it took in real time. Speeding up the way we humans move can make our actions look ridiculous, and so fast motion is often used for comic effect, as it is in a scene of casual anonymous sex in *A Clockwork Orange*. But in the right hands and in the right context, fast motion can be as expressive as slow motion. As we saw in the *Donnie Darko* case study in Chapter 2, fast motion can be used to present time as malleable, even volatile. In Luc Besson's *Lucy* (2014), fast-motion time lapses visualize the title char-

acter's sudden drug-induced ability to process almost limitless information. Time lapses of passing clouds are often used to signal a passage of time, as in Francis Ford Coppola's *Rumble fish* (1983). In the final shots of Jean-Pierre Jeunet's *Amélie* (2001), fast-motion footage of a couple riding a scooter expresses the exuberance of new-found love.

Length of the Shot

The length, or duration, of a shot is determined by a combination of factors: the kind of story being told, the dramatic demands of particular scenes within that story, and the approach to cinematic language the director and his creative collaborators (filmmakers) bring to that story. Ultimately, of course, the duration of most shots as we see them on-screen is determined by the editor, but it is important to know that directors design their shots with editing in mind. Shot length is another expressive tool that must be considered before production begins. Movies directed by Billy Wilder and Woody Allen, both of whom place more emphasis on writing and performance, have average shot lengths of around 17 seconds, whereas shot lengths in movies by directors who design their films to exploit editing, such as Baz Luhrmann or Edgar Wright, might have average shot lengths of less than 2 seconds. The average shot length in the last four films directed by Béla Tarr, a filmmaker known for his use of the long take, is a whopping 178 seconds.

We'll talk more about shot duration when we explore editing in Chapter 8. While we're still on the subject of cinematography, let's focus on the **long take**, which is a shot that lasts significantly longer than a conventional shot. There are two basic approaches to the long take: (1) those that exploit the mobile frame, and (2) those that hold the viewer in a state of relative stasis. **Mobile framing** uses a moving camera and blocking to present multiple viewpoints, compositions, and actions within a single unified shot. Ordinarily, we refer to a *sequence* as a series of edited shots characterized by inherent unity of theme and purpose. This kind of long take is sometimes referred to as a **sequence shot** because it enables filmmakers to present a unified pattern of events— usually with a structured dramatic trajectory—within a single period of time in one shot. Although they eliminate the need for editing, sequence shots are by no means easy. These long takes require filmmakers to coordinate moving actors and objects with a moving camera, which requires focus shifts, complex lighting setups, rehearsals, and multiple takes. Uniting all these events in one unbroken visual, dramatic, temporal, and spatial experience holds viewers viscerally present in a way that makes these virtuosic sequence shots among the most compelling experiences cinema has to offer. The entire running time of *Russian Ark* and the 200-second opening crane shot in *Touch of Evil* (illustrated earlier in the chapter) are each sequence shots. The latter film's director, Orson Welles, is known for his masterful use of the technique, beginning with *Citizen Kane*. Alfonso Cuarón is another director associated with this kind of long take. His film *Children of Men* (2006), which contains sixty-two shots that could be considered long takes, brought extensive use of sequence shots into mainstream commercial cinema, a trend that has continued with Alejandro González Iñárritu's *Birdman* (2014) and *The Revenant* (2015) and Cuarón's own *Gravity* (2013). Notably, all four of these recent movies were shot by the cinematographer Emmanuel Lubezki, all were nominated for the Academy Award for Best Cinematography, and all but *Children of Men* won. The most impressive long take in the Oscar-less *Children of Men* occurs during a raging battle between revolting militants and government soldiers as the protagonist, Theo, attempts to escort the new mother, Kee, and her miraculous infant (the only baby in the world—it's a long story) to safety. Over the course of the sequence shot's 6 minute 17 second duration, Theo scrambles through street battles, is captured by vengeful radicals who take Kee and her child, narrowly avoids execution, dodges tank and machine gun fire to access a decimated building, searches the rapidly crumbling structure, finds Kee, and confronts his nemesis.

Which brings us to another approach to the long take—one that intensifies the viewer experience not with movement or visual dexterity, but by holding the viewer in a moment or encounter until we are forced to realign and deepen the way we engage the subject on-screen. The aforementioned Béla Tarr uses this approach in many of his films, including and especially in his most recent movie, *The Turin Horse* (2011). Tarr describes the 2 hour 35 minute movie, which is made up entirely of long takes, as being about the daily repetition of life and the heaviness of human existence. The 4½-minute opening shot contains multiple viewpoints, but all of the same subject and action: a horse pulling a cart and

A long take in close-up

In Jonathan Glazer's *Birth* (2004), Nicole Kidman plays Anna, a young widow who gradually becomes obsessed with a ten-year-old boy who claims to be the reincarnation of her deceased husband. A 2-minute-long close-up on her face while she sits at a public concert allows Kidman to subtly express the conflicting emotions and disturbing thoughts running through her mind and holds viewers long enough and close enough to fully experience the depth of her suppressed anxiety.

driver down a desolate rural road. Locked in this relatively unchanging shot, the viewer experiences the journey, and the time it takes, in a way that approaches the experience of the subjects themselves. Deprived of the constant shifts in perspective and unfolding action most films provide, we are compelled to observe details and contemplate the situation in a way that would be impossible with a typical edited sequence.

Special Effects

Special effects is a general term reserved for technology used to create images that would be too dangerous, too expensive, or simply impossible to achieve with traditional cinematographic approaches. For audiences, a major attraction of movies has always been their ability to create illusion. Indeed, the first special effect appeared in Alfred Clark's *The Execution of Mary Stuart* in 1895, the year the movies were born. To depict the queen's execution, Clark photographed the actor in position, stopped filming, and replaced the actor with a dummy, then started the camera and beheaded the dummy.

Mechanical effects in *Swiss Army Man*

For their farcical but strangely moving buddy movie *Swiss Army Man* (2016), directors Daniel Kwan and Daniel Scheinert (known collectively as "the Daniels") innovated a series of relatively low-tech mechanical effects that made Manny, the soulful and supernaturally resourceful corpse played by Daniel Radcliffe, to appear to spray gallons of water and shoot rocks from his mouth, chop logs with his arm, and set himself on fire. Multiple life-size dummies were made from molds of Radcliffe for different purposes: dropping and throwing, carrying, and—for the film's infamous first scene—using simulated flatulence for the corpse to appear to propel itself through the water. For the shot above, which lasts only seconds, the real Radcliffe was towed behind a boat and ridden by his costar, Paul Dano.

As is often the case with movie terminology, the names used to categorize special effects are somewhat convoluted. In this case, we can blame the vagaries on the evolution from film to digital capabilities. During the celluloid era, **mechanical effects** were those created and photographed on set; **optical effects** were created by manipulating the image and/or film negative "in-camera" during production and/or during the film-stock processing after the negative had been exposed. These days, when the postproduction process (even for those few films shot on film stock) is completed on computers, the term **visual effects** refers to those effects created and integrated using computers in postproduction. The current specific use of *special effects* is synonymous with mechanical effects: any effect generated on set that can be photographed by the camera. These effects may also be referred to as *practical effects*.

Now that we have that straight, let's quickly consider some of the many effects filmmakers use to create movie magic. Filmmakers employ a very broad range of special (or mechanical) effects. These can be purposely noticeable: makeup using prosthetics, imaginary creatures using animatronics (essentially a mechanical puppet, like the shark in *Jaws*), pyrotechnics (controlled explosions), gunshots and the wounds they produce, cables that allow characters to float or fly, and atmospheric effects such as

rain and wind produced using suspended perforated water pipes and industrial fans. Integrated special effects may be less ostentatious: carefully crafted miniature models (known as miniatures) stand in for large structures, landforms, or objects; forced perspective and painted backdrops simulate distant objects and landscapes. A special effect called the process shot placed actors in front of a screen that had images projected onto it from the opposite side. You may notice this so-called "rear projection" in driving scenes from older movies.

To create his speculative science-fiction/noir Los Angeles, *Blade Runner* (1982) director Ridley Scott relied primarily on production design and practical mechanical effects such as atmospheric rain, smoke, and steam. The iconic aerial tracking shot over the city that opens the movie was achieved using forced perspective and miniatures equipped with thousands of tiny lightbulbs. Part of this approach was practical—visual effects were new and limited in 1982—but Scott also wanted the film to have a classic "lived-in" look that computers couldn't then deliver.

Optical effects in the celluloid era could be as simple as the "stop trick" used to depict the aforementioned queen's execution or as complicated as the Schüfftan process (named for its inventor, Eugen Schüfftan), which integrated actors onto shots of sets built in miniature by using etched mirrors to expose the two very different elements precisely onto the same image. Other optical effects include the similar but simpler matte shot, which exposed an image onto one portion of the negative but kept another portion unexposed so it could be filled with an exposure of another element later. *The Great Train Robbery* (1903) featured an early example of this technique to show the passing countryside through the window of a baggage car that was stationary when the scene was filmed. In *Blade Runner*, Scott used a much more advanced version of this technique, in which mechanically calibrated camera moves enabled settings to be photographed multiple times to create layers of visual information within a single shot.

In the digital age, computer-generated imagery (CGI) has largely eclipsed optical effects, replacing them with visual effects that can create settings and backgrounds with more accuracy and less cost. CGI backgrounds are often used for spectacular imaginary worlds in fantasy and science-fiction films, but are also used to enhance backgrounds to allow scenes set in contemporary (and even relatively mundane) locales to be shot on a sound-

The virtual and the "real"

Director Denis Villeneuve had a huge budget and state-of-the-art visual effects at his disposal for the sequel *Blade Runner 2049* (2017), but he still avoided CGI and the green screen whenever possible because it denies actors the opportunity to interact organically with their surroundings. His point is ironically illustrated in the shot above, in which an actor on a physical set faces a superimposed video projection. Both *Blade Runner* films examine the distinctions between what is artificial and what is real, a theme visualized in the way color, relative size, and a sort of variegated video-texture is applied to the simulated woman addressing the protagonist—who is himself a simulated human.

stage or at a more convenient location. Actors can be placed within digitally generated settings by filming the actors against a uniformly colored backdrop (usually bright green, hence the term *green screen*) and then applying chroma keying, a process that digitally removes that color so it can be replaced with computer-generated images.

Motion capture (also known as motion tracking or mocap) is a specific visual effect in which a live-action subject wears a bodysuit fitted with reflective markers that enables a computer to record each movement as digital images; they are then translated, with as much manipulation as desired, into models on which the screen figures are based. When the images include facial contours and expressions, the process is called *performance capture*. As spectacular as some special effects can be, however, the goal of virtually all of the effects previously described is almost always to create verisimilitude—an illusion of reality or a believable alternative reality—within the imaginative world of even the most fanciful movie. Well over 100 visual effects shots (of vehicles, landscapes, cityscapes, bullet strikes, and bodies) enhanced the stark realism of the drug war along the U.S.–Mexico border in Denis Villeneuve's *Sicario* (2015).

Subdued but substantial visual effects also made possible the verisimilitude of his science-fiction follow-up *Arrival* (2016), in which our perceptions of time and space

Early special effects

For Fritz Lang's *Metropolis* (1927) a pioneering science-fiction film, the city of the future was a model created by designer Otto Hunte. Special effects photography turned this miniature into a massive place on-screen, filled with awe-inspiring objects and vistas.

1

2

Creating a convincing cybercharacter

Benedict Cumberbatch didn't simply provide the voice for Smaug, the colossal psychotic dragon in *The Hobbit: The Desolation of Smaug* (2013). Director Peter Jackson and his second unit director, Andy Serkis (the actor who created Gollum, considered cinema's first truly convincing cybercharacter), enlisted Cumberbatch to use motion-capture and performance-capture technology to inform the 3-D computer animators as to the dragon's movements and expressions.

are ultimately invalidated by visiting aliens that bear no resemblance to traditional depictions. That same year, Scott Derrickson's *Dr. Strange* (2016) also upended conventional notions of time and space, but applied its avalanche of visual effects toward an entirely different cinematic experience: overwhelming psychedelic spectacle. And yet, that film's seamless visual effects are also carefully crafted to help viewers believe in the visually dazzling events and images unfolding on-screen—at least while they're watching them.

The capabilities of visual effects will certainly continue to expand as the capacity and speed of computer software and hardware evolves. These ever more sophisticated and spectacular visual effects are already playing major roles in the expansion of other motion-picture media such as gaming and virtual reality. It won't be long before the effects in *Dr. Strange* look as quaint as the

rear-projection highway traffic flickering behind actors pretending to drive in movies of the 1950s. Of course, capacity doesn't always equal utility, and bigger is not always better. The ever-present danger is that the visual effects spectacle will crowd out cinematic stories that seek instead to increase our understanding of human life and the world we live in.

Looking at Cinematography in *Moonlight*

Moonlight, a 2016 film directed by Barry Jenkins, is about a gay black man struggling to attain acceptance and selfhood in a hypermasculine culture. His story is divided into three chapters, each titled after the name he is given (or gives himself) at a different stage in his life. In "Little," the first chapter, the protagonist is a fragile child in Miami trying to reconcile the differences between himself and other boys. With no friends and scarce support from his troubled mother, the emotionally withdrawn Little finds an unlikely father figure in a crack dealer named Juan. Besides Juan and his girlfriend, Teresa, a sympathetic neighborhood boy named Kevin is the closest thing to a friend Little has to hold onto. "Chiron," the second chapter, chronicles a difficult period of the protagonist's adolescence. His mother is addicted to crack, Juan is dead, and Chiron is tormented by a bully named Terrel. Chiron has his first sexual experience with Kevin, but before their relationship has any chance of evolving further, Kevin is pressured by Terrel into beating up Chiron in front of a crowd of other high school students. Heartbroken and humiliated, Chiron attacks and seriously injures Terrel and is subsequently arrested. The final chapter is titled "Black," which was Kevin's nickname for Chiron and is now the name the grown man has adopted after reinventing himself as a muscular and street-hardened crack dealer in Atlanta. After an unexpected call from Kevin, Black impulsively drives to Miami to see his first and only love, the person whose betrayal changed the course of his life.

Technical decisions made by *Moonlight*'s director of photography, James Laxton, were motivated primarily by aesthetic and expressive considerations. Laxton shot on the Arri Alexa XT, a digital camera that has a sensor capable of delivering the dynamic range needed to shoot in a variety of lighting situations with a minimum of arti-

Cinematography in *Moonlight*

This shot of Juan driving the streets of the Liberty City neighborhood of Miami demonstrates the low-key lighting and saturated colors used in *Moonlight*, as well as the shallow depth of field and impressionistic bokeh achieved through the use of anamorphic lenses.

ficial lighting (primarily lightweight LED instruments). The sensor also provided exceptional color reproduction, especially in terms of skin tones. Laxton and Jenkins wanted a look that diverged from the documentary realism typically expected of independent films dealing with social issues. To achieve an incongruous dreamlike quality that placed viewers in the protagonist's solitary perspective, they shot virtually every scene using only a single key light with no fill, maximizing deep shadows to sculpt the characters' faces. Footage was exposed at levels that gave the postproduction colorist the ability to provide rich, saturated colors, deep shadows, and bright highlights. The camera was equipped with anamorphic lenses, which squeeze the maximum possible visual information onto the camera sensor. More important, these specialized lenses dramatically narrow the depth of field in every shot. This thin slice of focus allowed the filmmakers to visually isolate Chiron and other characters and subjects within the depth of the image. Anamorphic lenses are oval (as opposed to standard spherical lenses), which means that out-of-focus reflections and lights in the image background (known as *bokeh*) are rendered in the same unusual oval shape, which adds another subtle layer of unorthodoxy to the film's style.

Although the Alexa camera is capable of shooting raw footage, Jenkins and Laxton elected to shoot in a codec

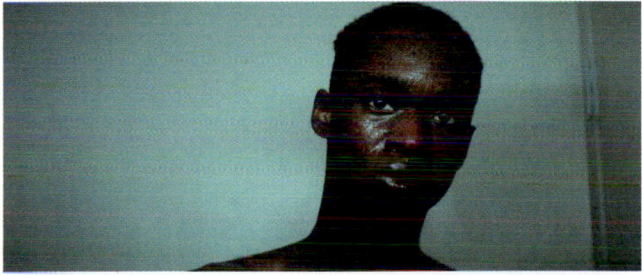

Expressive use of color and light

In *Moonlight*'s second chapter, a flickering fluorescent bathroom light and a sickly green tone imbues the character Chiron with an awkward ugliness in the moment the normally gentle young man decides to seek revenge on his tormentor [1]. In a matching bathroom mirror sequence in the third chapter, the light is similar, but the color has shifted to blue to emphasize the cold and hardened nature the character has since adopted [2].

Moving camera diminishes the subject

Perhaps the most poignant moving camera shot in *Moonlight* uses depth and relative size in frame. After Terrel has threatened to beat up Chiron after school, the camera pulls back as Chiron himself retreats against the wall behind him, reducing his size in comparison to the indifferent students strolling past him.

that compressed the data because they felt that any loss in visual information would be more than offset by the ability to shoot longer without filling the camera's data storage card. Letting the camera roll continually helps actors immerse themselves in a dramatic situation without the distraction of cutting and slating new takes.

Most of *Moonlight* was shot using a handheld camera and a Steadicam in a fluid style that reduces the reliance on editing to assemble sequences and scenes. The flowing camera work allowed Laxton to follow action and capture performances as they unfolded, such as in a sequence in the third chapter where the adult Kevin prepares a meal for Black. Pans and tilts convey literal and figurative connections throughout this story of a boy desperate to connect with others. During Little's first dinner with Juan and Teresa, the camera glides back and forth between the loving partners. Point-of-view shots are often connected to the looking character with a pan instead of the traditional edit. The accumulated and intimidating male gaze that the protagonist endures while interacting with other boys is conveyed with pans along rows of distrustful faces. Unlike our usual experience of the handheld camera, most of this footage is relatively smooth, with the exception of the shot that gives us our first look at Little. When we first meet the character, an erratic handheld camera chases Little as he flees from a group of hostile boys. The instability of the camera effectively conveys the child's helpless panic. A particular application of the moving camera, in which the frame rapidly circles characters, was used once in each chapter to present a sort of dangerous, assertive masculinity. The dizzying effect of background information flying

rapidly past a relatively static subject is both destabilizing and exhilarating, and thus effectively visualizes the menace and allure of male power. We experience it first as an introduction to Juan as he meets with one of his street dealers, and again when Terrel intimidates Kevin into punching Chiron, and finally when we see the reinvented Black cruising his drug territory in a shot that equates his new persona with both his nemesis and his mentor.

Some of the most striking cinematic moments in *Moonlight* are accomplished with point of view. In a number of sequences, character interaction is portrayed using separation, with each subject staring directly into the camera lens. This eyeline exploits our tendency to identify with the lens, causing an intensified identification with the character offscreen whose point of view we have assumed as we stare directly back into the opposing character's eyes. These sequences are used in key moments of the story, including when Chiron repeatedly refuses to stay down after Kevin hits him. In every case

Separation and point of view

This separation sequence in *Moonlight* compels the audience to assume alternating points of view between the withdrawn Little [1] and his raging mother, Paula [2], at a point in which her life is spiraling out of control. The juxtaposed viewpoints are connected to the viewer and to each other through each character's direct gaze. Color and light differentiate the opposing characters.

but one, the technique employs juxtaposed close-ups. But in what may be the film's most dramatic example, the interacting characters are shown in medium shots and medium long shots. Consumed with fear and guilt after being confronted by Juan, Little's mother, Paula, glares and screams at her offscreen son. Little, unable to comprehend or return her rage, offers no emotion in response. The opposing characters are differentiated with color, light, and design. Paula's angry world is dark and discordant, with lurid clashing colors. In contrast, Little's contained defiance is presented in whites and blues—colors associated with his relationship with Juan and Teresa. The sequence shifts between the mother and son five times before each walks off the screen in turn.

Framing is used to place viewers inside the world of the story at a turning point in Little's struggle for acceptance and affection. For the scene in which Juan teaches Little to swim, James Laxton brought the camera into the ocean so that the water washed in and out of the frame and across our intimate viewpoint. The filmmakers had scheduled 6 hours to shoot this crucial scene but were forced to capture the action in a mere 90 minutes when an unexpected storm blew in. It turned out to be one of filmmaking's many happy accidents. The rushed takes lend the scene a dynamic spontaneity, and the rapidly

Learning to swim in _Moonlight_
When the Atlantic Ocean leaks into frame, it implies a larger world outside of the screen's limited perspective. By washing over our viewpoint, it makes us feel as if we're in the water with the characters.

darkening skies convey a progressive passage of time. But _Moonlight_'s innovative and effective cinematography was no accident. The movie's economical but expressive cinematic techniques demonstrate what digital cinematography can do when in the hands of skilled artists and craftspeople. Cinematographer James Laxton and director Barry Jenkins earned Oscar nominations in their respective categories, and _Moonlight_ became the lowest-budget film in the history of the Academy Awards to be named Best Picture.

ANALYZING CINEMATOGRAPHY

This chapter has provided an overview of the major components of cinematography—the process by which a movie's mise-en-scène is recorded onto a film or digital medium. More than just a process, however, cinematography is very much a language used by directors and their collaborators (most notably, directors of photography) to convey meaning, transmit narrative information, and influence the emotional responses of viewers. Now that you know something about the basic cinematographic tools available to filmmakers, you can pay greater attention to the particulars of this language while looking at movies.

SCREENING CHECKLIST: CINEMATOGRAPHY

✔ Determine whether the cinematographic aspects of the film—the qualities of the film stock or digital codec, lighting, lenses, framing, angles, camera movement, and use of long takes—add up to an overall look. If so, try to describe its qualities.

✔ Take note of moments in the film when the images are conveying information that is not reflected in characters' action and dialogue. These moments are often crucial to the development of a movie's themes, narrative, and meaning.

✔ Are special effects used in the film? To what extent? Are they appropriate to, and effective in, telling the story? Are they effective in making something look real when it isn't?

✔ Also keep track of camera angles other than eye-level shots. If there are high- or low-angle shots, determine whether they are POV shots. That is, is the high or low angle meant to represent another character's point of view? If so, what does the angle convey about that character's state of mind or perspective? If not, what does it convey about the person or thing in the frame?

✔ Be alert to the framing of individual shots, and make note of how the boundaries of the image are used to tell the story. Is the frame mobile? Do characters interact with offscreen space? Is the story world outside of the frame indicated, and if so, how and why? Do characters engage you as a viewer with their direct gaze?

✔ Can you determine whether the colors of a shot or scene have been artificially manipulated through the use of color filters, different film stocks, or chemical or digital manipulation to convey meaning, create a mood, or indicate a state of mind?

✔ Pay attention to camera movement in the film. Sometimes camera movement is used to produce visual excitement or to demonstrate the filmmaker's technological virtuosity. At other times it is playing an important functional role in the film's narrative. Be alert to these differences, and take note of meaningful uses of camera movement.

✔ Note when the cinematography calls attention to itself. Is this a mistake or misjudgment by the filmmaker or is it intentional? If intentional, what purpose is served by making the cinematography so noticeable?

Questions for Review

1. What are the differences among a setup, a shot, and a take?

2. A cinematographer depends on two crews of workers. What is each crew responsible for?

3. How the lighting for any movie looks is determined, in part, by its source and direction. Explain these terms and the effect each has on the overall lighting.

4. What are the four major lenses used on movie cameras? What is the principal characteristic of the image that each lens creates?

5. Based on proximity to the camera, what are the three most commonly used shots in a movie? What principle is used to distinguish them?

6. Describe the differences and relationship between framing and composition.

7. The movie camera can shoot from various angles. What are they? What meaning does each imply? Do these implications always hold true?

8. What are the basic types of camera movement?

9. What is a long take? What can it achieve that a short take cannot? What is the difference between a long take and a long shot?

10. Special effects create images that might not be possible with traditional cinematography. What are the basic ways to create special effects?

Phantom Thread (2017). Paul Thomas Anderson, director. Pictured: Daniel Day Lewis and Vicky Krieps.

>>>>>>

CHAPTER

ACTING | 7

What Is Acting?

It's easy to define narrative, mise-en-scène, or cinematography because those formal aspects of filmmaking depend in part on techniques and conventions that are widely accepted by filmmakers. Acting, by comparison, presents a different challenge because there is no one way to do it; every actor is a master of his or her own technique in creating characters. Yet Joaquin Phoenix, one of today's most impressive actors, does not even try to define his work, and it's not a cliché to say that it speaks for itself. In *Her* (2013; director Spike Jonze), Phoenix plays Theodore Twombly, a lonely introvert who falls in love with Samantha, the female voice of his computer's operating system, voiced by Scarlett Johansson, whom we hear but never see. Their relationship falls apart when Samantha dumps him (she has thousands of cyberlovers just like him). It's both funny and sad when Theodore is devastated by something that is as impossible as it is peculiar. Throughout, Phoenix's portrayal of this character sustains the film's development. He is almost always on the screen, something that only a very few actors in film history have ever accomplished, and he amazes us with his control as an actor. Although he worked closely with the director, costar,

and supporting actors, Joaquin Phoenix delivers the movie.

Screen acting of this kind is an art in which an actor uses imagination, intelligence, psychology, memory, vocal technique, facial expressions, body language, and an overall knowledge of the filmmaking process to realize, under the director's guidance, the character created by the screenwriter. The performance and effect of that art can seem mysterious and magical when we're enjoying a movie, and acting turns out to be even more complex than we might at first assume.

Our initial interest in a movie is almost always sparked by the actors featured in it. As the critic Pauline Kael said, "I think so much of what we respond to in fictional movies is acting. That's one of the elements that's often left out when people talk theoretically about the movies. They forget it's the human material we go to see."[1] The power of some actors—Jennifer Lawrence or Tom Hanks, for example—to draw an audience is frequently more important to a movie's financial success than any other factor. For this reason, some observers regard screen actors as mere commodities, cogs in a machine of promotion and hype designed only to generate revenue. Although even the most accomplished screen actors can be used as fodder for promotional campaigns, such a

The camera and the actor
English film actor Michael Caine has compared the movie camera to an impossibly attentive lover who "hangs on your every word, your every look; she can't take her eyes off you. She is listening to and recording everything you do, however minutely you do it."[2] That appears to be exactly what the camera is doing in this expressive close-up of Caine as Thomas Fowler in Phillip Noyce's *The Quiet American* (2002). The business and art of Hollywood moviemaking intersect when "bankable" stars such as Michael Caine take on challenging, unglamorous roles that transcend their physical attractiveness.

view overlooks the many complex and important ways that skillful acting can influence the narrative, style, and meanings of a film. Actor Cate Blanchett believes that "when acting works, when performance works, when theater's great, when films connect—whether it's a piece of profound satire or a work of great drama—it expands what it means to be human."[3] Writer-director-producer-actor Orson Welles, who questioned nearly every other aspect of filmmaking dogma, firmly believed in the importance of acting: "I don't understand how movies exist independently of the actor—I truly don't."[4]

Despite its central importance, acting is also the aspect of filmmaking over which directors have the least precise control. Directors may describe literally what they want from their principal collaborators—for example, screenwriters or costume designers—but they can only suggest to actors what they want. That becomes quite different when a director-screenwriter like Paul Thomas Anderson writes parts specifically for the actors he casts. This approach has led to many memorable performances—for example, by Daniel Day-Lewis in *Phantom Thread* (2017) and *There Will Be Blood* (2007) or Amy Adams and Philip Seymour Hoffman in *The Master* (2010)—in which the director, screenwriter, and actor enjoy an unusually close collaboration. However, screen actors, or at least experienced screen actors, know that the essential relationship is between them and the camera—not between them and the director or even the audience. Actors interpret the director's guidance in the area between them and the lens—an intimate and narrowly defined space that necessarily concentrates much of the actors' energy on their faces. Through composition, close-ups, camera angles and movements, and other cinematic techniques, movie actors always come closer to the audience and appear larger than actors on the stage do.

The camera makes possible an attention to detail that was impossible before the invention of cinema, mainly because stage acting forced actors to project their voices and their gestures to the back of the theater. Screen acting, as an experience, can be as tight and intimate as examining a painting at arm's length. As American screen actor Joan Crawford put it, "A movie actor paints with the tiniest brush."[5]

Movie Actors

The challenges facing movie actors in interpreting and pretending to be their characters, and the responsibilities involved in performing those characters on the screen, are very different from the challenges and responsibilities facing stage actors. Stage actors convey their interpretations of the characters they play directly to the audience through voice, gesture, and movement. By contrast, movie actors, using gesture and movement—and voice since the coming of sound—convey their characters directly to the camera. In turn, that camera is what makes the movie actor's performance so different from the stage actor's. Stage actors play to a large audience and must project their voices so they can be heard throughout the theater. They must avoid the soft speech, subtle facial expressions, or small gestures that are fundamental tools of the movie actor.

Stage actors, who must memorize their lines, have the advantage of speaking them in the order in which they were written. This in turn makes it much easier to maintain psychological, emotional, and physical continuity in a performance as the play proceeds. By contrast, movie actors are subject to the shooting schedule. For budgetary and logistical reasons, most shots are not made in the sequence indicated in the screenplay, so movie actors learn only those lines that they need for the moment. Therefore, movie actors bear the additional burden, particularly on their memory, of creating continuity between related shots, even though the shots may have been made days, weeks, or even months apart.

Judith Anderson had an illustrious stage career before achieving fame as a movie actor as Mrs. Danvers in Alfred Hitchcock's *Rebecca* (1940). She emphasizes how each form affects an actor's movements. On the stage she is free (to move where she wants, scratch her ear if she wants, add a bit of business if she wants), but on the screen she is constrained by the physical space before the camera, the lighting and other technical aspects, and

3. Qtd. in Melena Ryzik, "Desperate Times Call for Her," *New York Times* (February 13, 2014): p. C1, www.nytimes.com/2014/02/13/movies/awardsseason/cate-blanchett-has-front-runner-oscar-status.html (accessed February 6, 2015).

4. Orson Welles and Peter Bogdanovich, *This Is Orson Welles*, ed. Jonathan Rosenbaum (New York: HarperCollins, 1992), p. 262.

5. Joan Crawford, qtd. in Lillian Ross and Helen Ross, *The Player: A Profile of an Art* (New York: Simon & Schuster, 1962), p. 66.

LOOKING AT MOVIES
PERSONA AND PERFORMANCE

VIDEO This short tutorial discusses the importance of persona to our experience of acting performances.

the much greater size of the image on the screen as opposed to the natural appearance of an actor on the stage.[6]

To achieve the goal of maintaining continuity (as we will discuss in Chapter 8), editing is a major factor in putting shots together and creating the performance. During a play, the stage actor performs each scene only once; in the shooting of a movie, the actor may be asked to do many takes before the director is satisfied with the performance. Before a shot is made, the movie actor must be prepared to wait, sometimes for long periods, while camera, lighting, or sound equipment is moved or readjusted; the stage actor faces no such delays or interruptions.

Although the theater and the movies are both collaborative arts, once the curtain goes up, stage actors need not think much about the backstage crew, for the crew will perform scenery or lighting changes according to a fixed schedule. Movie actors, however, must play directly to the camera while dozens of people are standing around just outside the camera's range. These people are doing their jobs, but also watching and listening to everything the actors do. Some people are there because they have to be (e.g., the director, script supervisor, cinematographer, sound recordist, makeup artist, hairstylist); others are there waiting to make the necessary changes in scenery, properties, or lighting required for

the next shot. Over the years, some temperamental actors have succeeded in closing the set to all but the most essential personnel, but that is an exceptional practice. Traditionally, however, movie sets have been closed to visitors, particularly the media.

Although there are probably as many types of actors as there are actors themselves, for the purposes of this discussion, we can identify four key types:

1. actors who take their personae from role to role (personality actors)

2. actors who deliberately play against our expectations of their personae

3. actors who seem to be different in every role (chameleon actors)

4. actors who are often nonprofessionals or people who are cast to bring verisimilitude to a part

In our everyday lives, each of us creates a persona, the image of character and personality that we want to show the outside world. For movie actors, those personae are their appearance and mannerisms of moving and delivering dialogue—unique creations that are relatively consistent from role to role and from performance to performance. Actors' personae are usually (but not always) rooted in their natural behavior, personality, and physicality. Current actors defined by their personae include Tom Cruise, Amy Schumer, and Will Smith. Even more versatile actors, not just those who are popular action or comedy stars, rely on persona. Among them are Susan Sarandon, Morgan Freeman, and Benicio Del Toro.

For many movie actors, the persona is the key to their careers as well as an important part of film marketing and why we choose particular movies over others. One reason audiences go to movies is to see a certain kind of story. That's a big part of what the concept of genre is all about. You go to a romantic comedy, an action movie, a horror film, or a comic-book adaptation because you know what to expect, and you want what you expect. Having made your choice on the basis of story, you should get familiar and appealing narrative structures, cinematic conventions, character types, dramatic situations, and payoffs.

The same thing goes for persona-identified actors such as Tom Cruise. He's not only good-looking, but he proj-

6. See interview with Anderson on Disc 2 of the Criterion Collection DVD release of *Rebecca* (2001).

Cate Blanchett's complete transformation as Bob Dylan

In *I'm Not There* (2007; director Todd Haynes), Cate Blanchett transforms her glamorous self into Jude, a skinny, ragged, androgynous folksinger at the beginning of his career: Bob Dylan. In this image, Jude is responding to an obnoxious British journalist who questions his motives in switching from acoustic to electric guitar in 1965. To understand how accomplished Blanchett's portrayal is, compare her Dylan with the real Dylan as he appears in D. A. Pennebaker's *Dont Look Back* (1967) or Martin Scorsese's *No Direction Home: Bob Dylan* (2005).

ects an interesting balance of arrogance and vulnerability that appeals to many viewers. When you go to a Tom Cruise movie (the kind where the star's name is the most important factor in your choice), you have an expectation of the kind of performance he's going to give you, based on his persona. And you expect to see that performance, that persona, in the context of a certain kind of story. Part of the fun comes from seeing that persona in different kinds of movies, enjoying its interaction with a particular role or genre. So part of the reason you might go to see Cruise in Michael Mann's *Collateral* (2004) is to see how a personality we associate with heroic roles is applied to a hit man or, in *Rock of Ages* (2012; director Adam Shankman), an aging sex-and-drugs fueled rock star. Having enjoyed him as a macho master spy in the Mission Impossible movies, you may be curious to see how the playful arrogance he brought to Ethan Hunt manifests itself in the role of a desk-bound military hack forced to fight alien invaders in Doug Liman's *Live Die Repeat: Edge of Tomorrow* (2014) or as a reckless, double-dealing spy/smuggler in Liman's *American Made* (2017).

Sometimes an actor with a familiar, popular persona takes on a role that goes against what we expect; for example, Jack Nicholson as Warren Schmidt in Alexander Payne's *About Schmidt* (2002) or Cate Blanchett as Jude in Todd Haynes's *I'm Not There* (2007). A major factor affecting our enjoyment of actors in such roles is not just the role, but the strange sensation of seeing an actor whose persona we have come to know well play a totally different sort of role. In Nicholson's case, the normally crafty, strong, menacing man portrays a powerless, mundane, befuddled, and cuckolded insurance salesman. In Blanchett's career, we are astonished to see an actor known for her regal beauty in such roles as Queen Elizabeth I in Shekhar Kapur's *Elizabeth* (1998) or Lady Galadriel in Peter Jackson's The Lord of the Rings trilogy (2001–3) when she undergoes a complete physical transformation as Jude, one of six different interpretations, by six different actors, of Bob Dylan in Todd Haynes's *I'm Not There* (2007). Blanchett is famous for her ability to change her distinctly Australian accent to meet the needs of any role. She can speak the Queen's English as Elizabeth and Galadriel or, with a pitch-perfect accent redolent of New York's upper East Side, she can become Jasmine Francis, a woman on the verge of a nervous breakdown, in Woody Allen's *Blue Jasmine* (2013). In *I'm Not There*, she hits the mark squarely with her interpretation of Dylan's twangy Midwestern

The versatile Tilda Swinton

Male actors like Johnny Depp and Jeff Bridges aren't the only chameleons capable of delivering diverse performances as very different characters. Tilda Swinton's many roles in the past decade include the tormented mother of a mass murderer [1] in Lynne Ramsay's *We Need to Talk About Kevin* (2011), a centuries-old nonconformist vampire [2] in Jim Jarmusch's *Only Lovers Left Alive* (2013), a powerful master of the mystic arts [3] in *Doctor Strange* (2016; director Scott Derrickson), and two pairs of feuding twin sisters in two different films: rival gossip columnists Thora and Thessaly Thacker in the Coen brothers' 2016 comedy *Hail Caesar!*, and the estranged siblings Lucy and Nancy Mirando [4] fighting for control of their father's meat-empire in Bong Joon-ho's topical satire *Okja* (2017).

speech. In creating her gender-bending portrait of a diffident, slightly androgynous singer, she uses every technique in the actor's stock besides her voice: movements and gestures, wig, makeup, eyeglasses, costumes, and props.

On the other side of the acting scale is the chameleon actor, named for the lizard that can make quick, frequent changes in its appearance in response to the environment. Chameleon actors adapt their look, mannerisms, and delivery to suit the role. They surprise us as persona actors when they are cast, as Jack Nicholson or Charlize Theron often are, in a role we do not expect—one that extends their range. For example, Jeff Bridges often looks (and acts) so different in roles that he's unrecognizable at first. You may not realize that the shaggy Dude (aka Jeff Lebowski) in the Coen brothers' *The Big Lebowski* (1998) is played by the same actor that played the bald industrialist villain Obadiah Stane in *Iron Man* (2008; director Jon Favreau), the grizzled U.S. Marshal

Rooster Cogburn in the Coens' *True Grit* (2010), and the laconic but persistent Texas Ranger Marcus Hamilton in *Hell or High Water* (2016; director David Mackenzie). Indeed, along with such multitalented colleagues as Leonardo DiCaprio, Tilda Swinton, Brad Pitt, and Christian Bale, Bridges is a marvel of flexibility.

Johnny Depp, an actor who makes quick and frequent changes in the roles he plays, has reached star status without any fixed persona. Although he's earned the reputation as the ideal *nonnaturalistic* actor for such Tim Burton movies as *Edward Scissorhands* (1990), *Charlie and the Chocolate Factory* (2005), *Sweeney Todd: The Demon Barber of Fleet Street* (2007), and *Alice in Wonderland* (2010), he's also played an astonishing range of very different roles, such as Raoul Duke/Hunter S. Thompson in Terry Gilliam's *Fear and Loathing in Las Vegas* (1998); the cocaine king George Jung in Ted Demme's *Blow* (2001); Sir James Matthew Barrie, the author of

Peter Pan, in Marc Forster's *Finding Neverland* (2004); and Lord Rochester, the seventeenth-century English poet, in Laurence Dunmore's *The Libertine* (2004). In the current phase of his career, among other roles, he's played the charming scoundrel Captain Jack Sparrow in five Pirates of the Caribbean movies; the gangster James "Whitey" Bulger in Scott Cooper's *Black Mass* (2015); the titular dark wizard in David Yates's *Fantastic Beasts: The Crimes of Grindelwald* (2018); and even Donald Trump in Jeremy Konner's satire *Donald Trump's The Art of the Deal: The Movie* (2016).

Finally, there are the nonprofessional actors, real-life people who take roles in feature films (not documentaries) to play characters whose lives are much like their own. The earliest movies were cast with only nonprofessionals, and the tradition has remained in movies that call for such casting. Memorable examples include almost all the movies in the Italian neorealist tradition, including an entire community re-creating their daily lives in Ermanno Olmi's *The Tree of Wooden Clogs* (1978). Michel Gondry recruited a group of Bronx high school students to act as Bronx high school students in *The We and the I* (2012). Similarly, Laurent Cantet recruited François Bégaudeau, as the teacher, and a group of mixed-race students, many of them immigrants, for *The Class* (2008), his film about the challenges of teaching in a French school. In *The Best Years of Our Lives* (1946), William Wyler's powerful movie about three veterans of World War II, a nonprofessional almost steals the movie away from the professionals when Harold Russell, who lost both arms in the conflict, portrays the challenges facing such a handicapped man. In *Beasts of the Southern Wild* (2012; director Benh Zeitlin), the two leading characters are played by nonprofessionals Quvenzhané Wallis and Dwight Henry. And in Lynne Ramsay's *Ratcatcher* (1999), a haunting film about a Scottish slum kid, fledgling actor Tommy Flanagan plays the lead.

Although previous generations of stage actors knew that their duty was to convey emotion through recognized conventions of speech and gesture (mannerisms), screen actors have enjoyed a certain freedom to adopt individual styles that communicate emotional meaning through subtle and highly personal gestures, expressions, and varieties of intonation. American screen actor Barbara Stanwyck credited director Frank Capra with teaching her that "if you can think it, you can make the audience know it. . . . On the stage, it's mannerisms. On the screen, your range is shown in your eyes."[7] In addition, many different types of inspiration fuel screen acting; many factors guide actors toward their performances in front of the camera.

Consider the work of Meryl Streep, who has been nominated eighteen times for an Oscar. That's more nominations than any actor in the history of the Academy Awards (15 for Best Actress, 2 wins; 3 for Best Supporting Actress, 1 win). Despite her success in more than fifty feature films, Streep, like many seasoned actors, finds it difficult to describe her talent. She says it is

> an art that I find in its deepest essence to be completely mysterious. . . . I have been smug and willfully ignorant. I've cultivated a deliberate reluctance to investigate my own method of working because I'm afraid of killing the goose. I'm afraid if I parse it I won't be able to do it anymore.[8]

Streep has played an astonishing variety of fictional and actual people on the screen. Fictional characters include Anna in Karel Reisz's *The French Lieutenant's Woman* (1981), a particularly interesting movie because Anna, a film actor, is creating the character of Sarah, a romantic of the Victorian era; Sophie Zawistowksi, a woman haunted by her Nazi-era past, in Alan J. Pakula's *Sophie's Choice* (1982); or Miranda Priestly in David Frankel's *The Devil Wears Prada* (2006), where the character, though fictional, is thought to have been influenced by Anna Wintour, the longtime editor of *Vogue*. By contrast, you might also study Streep's portrayals, often controversial with audiences, of such real people as Karen Blixen, the Danish novelist writing under the name of Isak Dinesen, in *Out of Africa* (1985; director Sydney Pollack); Julia Child, America's irresistible master of French cooking, in *Julie & Julia* (2009; director Nora Ephron); Margaret Thatcher, the British prime minister, in *The Iron Lady* (2011; director Phyllida Lloyd), or *Washington Post* newspaper publisher Kay Graham in Steven Spielberg's *The Post* (2017). Given

7. Barbara Stanwyck, qtd. in *Actors on Acting for the Screen: Roles and Collaborations*, ed. Doug Tomlinson (New York: Garland, 1994), p. 524.

8. Jennifer Greenstein Altmann, "Meryl Streep Talks about the 'Mysterious' Art of Acting" (December 1, 2006), www.princeton.edu/main/news/archive/S16/49/92S82 (accessed February 5, 2014).

this variety that requires her to be different in every role, Streep says: "Acting is not about being someone different. It's finding the similarity in what is apparently different, then finding myself in there."[9]

A director's individual style plays a significant role in how actors develop their characters. The many approaches include encouraging actors to identify with characters (e.g., Elia Kazan), promoting a style loosely referred to as method acting (Terrence Malick); favoring spontaneity, unpredictability, and sometimes improvisation (Richard Linklater); and encouraging actors to see their performances from a cinematographic point of view and explicitly imagine how their gestures and expressions will look on-screen (Alfred Hitchcock). This latter approach encourages actors to think more than to feel, to perform their roles almost as if they are highly skilled technicians whose main task is to control one aspect of the mise-en-scène (performance), much as set designers control the look and feel of sets, sound mixers control sound, directors of photography control camera work, and so on.

No matter what type a movie actor is—how definite or changeable the persona is, how varied the roles are, how successful the career is—we tend to blur the distinction between the actor on-screen and the person offscreen. The heroes of today's world are performers—athletes, musicians, actors—and a vast media industry exists to keep them in the public eye and encourage us to believe that they are every bit as fascinating in real life as they are on the screen. Inevitably, some movie actors become rich and famous without having much art or craft in what they do. Essentially, they walk through their movies, seldom playing any character other than themselves. Fortunately, for every one of these actors there are many more talented actors who take their work seriously; try, whenever possible, to extend the range of roles they play; and learn to adapt to the constantly shifting trends of moviemaking and public taste.

One definition of great acting is that it should look effortless, but that takes talent, training, discipline, experience, and hard work. It also takes the skills necessary for dealing with pressures that range from getting older (and thus becoming more apt to be replaced by a younger, better-looking actor) to fulfilling a producer's expectation that you will succeed in carrying a multimillion-dollar production and making it a profitable success.

As we continue this discussion of acting, remember that it is not actors' personal lives that count, but their ability to interpret and portray certain characters. In today's world, where the media report actors' every off-screen activity, especially indiscretions, maintaining the focus required for good acting poses a challenge. Although the media have always done this, the behavior of some of today's actors not only is more reckless but also is seldom covered up by a studio's public-relations department like it was in Hollywood's golden age.

The Evolution of Screen Acting

Early Screen-Acting Styles

The people on the screen in the very first movies were not actors but ordinary people playing themselves. The early films caught natural, everyday actions—feeding a baby, leaving work, yawning, walking up and down stairs, swinging a baseball bat, sneezing—in a simple, realistic manner. "Acting" was simply a matter of trying to ignore the presence of the camera as it recorded the action. In the early 1900s, filmmakers started to tell stories with their films and thus needed professional actors. Most stage actors at the time scorned film acting, however, and refused to take work in the fledgling industry.

Therefore, the first screen actors were usually rejects from the stage or fresh-faced amateurs eager to break into the emerging film industry. Lack of experience (or talent) wasn't the only hurdle they faced. Because no standard language of cinematic expression or any accepted tradition of film direction existed at the time, these first actors had little choice but to adopt the acting style favored in the nineteenth-century theater and try to adapt it to their screen roles. The resulting quaint, unintentionally comical style consists of exaggerated gestures, overly emphatic facial expressions, and bombastic mouthing of words (which could not yet be recorded on film) that characterized the stage melodramas popular at the turn of the twentieth century.

In 1908, the Société Film d'Art (Art Film Society), a French film company, was founded with the purpose

9. www.goodreads.com/quotes/140679-acting-is-not-about-being-someone-different (accessed February 5, 2014). See also Karina Longworth, *Meryl Streep: Anatomy of an Actor* (London: Phaidon Press, 2014).

of creating a serious artistic cinema that would attract equally serious people who ordinarily preferred the theater. Commercially, this was a risky step not only because cinema was in its infancy but also because, since the sixteenth century, the French had seen theater as a temple of expression. Its glory was (and remains) the Comédie-Française, the French national theater. To begin its work at the highest possible level, the Société Film d'Art joined creative forces with this revered organization, which agreed to lend its actors to the society's films. In addition, the society commissioned leading theater playwrights, directors, and designers, as well as prominent composers, to create its film productions.

Sarah Bernhardt (1844–1923), adored by her public as *la divine Sarah*, was the first great theatrical actor to appear in a movie, Clément Maurice's *Le Duel d'Hamlet* (*Hamlet*, 1900, 2 min.), a short account of Hamlet's duel with Laertes. She appeared in at least seven features, the most important of which is *Les Amours d'Elisabeth, Reine d'Angleterre* (*Queen Elizabeth*, 1912, 44 min.), directed by Henri Desfontaines and Louis Mercanton and produced by the Société Film d'Art.

As interesting as it is to see one of the early twentieth century's greatest actors as Elizabeth I, it is even more interesting to observe how closely this "canned theater" resembled an actual stage production. The space we see is that of the theater, which is limited to having actors enter and exit from stage left or right. It is unlike the cinema, where characters are not confined to the physical boundaries imposed by theater architecture. For all her reputed skill, Bernhardt's acting could only echo what she did on the stage. Thus we see the exaggerated facial expressions, strained gestures, and clenched fists of late-nineteenth-century melodrama. Although such artificiality was conventional and thus accepted by the audience, it was all wrong for the comparative intimacy between the spectator and the screen that existed even in the earliest movie theaters.

Despite its heavy-handed technique, *Queen Elizabeth* succeeded in attracting an audience interested in serious drama on the screen, made the cinema socially and intellectually respectable, and therefore encouraged further respect for the industry and its development. What remained to be done was not to teach Sarah Bernhardt how to act for the camera, but to develop cinematic techniques uniquely suitable for the emerging narrative cinema as well as a style of acting that could help actors realize their potential in this new medium.

D. W. Griffith and Lillian Gish

American film pioneer D. W. Griffith needed actors who could be trained to work in front of the camera, and by 1913 he had recruited a group that included some of the most important actors of the time: Mary Pickford, Lillian and Dorothy Gish, Mae Marsh, Blanche Sweet, Lionel Barrymore, Harry Carey, Henry B. Walthall, and Donald Crisp. Some had stage experience, some did not. All of them earned much more from acting in the movies than they would have on the stage, and they all enjoyed long, fruitful careers (many lasting well into the era of sound films).

Because the cinema was silent during this period, Griffith worked out more naturalistic movements and gestures for his actors rather than training their voices. The longer stories of such feature-length films as *The Birth of a Nation* (1915), *Intolerance* (1916), *Hearts of the World* (1918), and *Broken Blossoms* (1919) gave the actors more screen time and therefore more screen space in which to develop their characters. Close-ups required them to be more aware of the effect that their facial expressions would have on the audience, and actors' faces increasingly became more important than their bodies (although, in the silent comedies of the 1920s, the full presence of the human body was virtually essential for conveying humor).

Under Griffith's guidance, Lillian Gish invented the art of screen acting. Griffith encouraged her to study the movements of ordinary people on the street or in restaurants, to develop her physical skills with regular exercise, and to tell stories through her face and body. He urged her to watch the reactions of movie audiences, saying, "If they're held by what you're doing, you've succeeded as an actress."[10] Gish's performance in *Broken Blossoms* (1919) was the first great film performance by an actor. Set in the Limehouse (or Chinatown) section of London, the movie presents a stylized fable about the love of an older Chinese merchant, Cheng Huan (Richard Barthelmess), for an English adolescent, Lucy Burrows (Gish). Lucy's racist father, the boxer Battling Burrows (Donald Crisp),

10. Lillian Gish with Ann Pinchot, *Lillian Gish: The Movies, Mr. Griffith, and Me* (Englewood Cliffs, NJ: Prentice-Hall, 1969), pp. 97–101, quotation on p. 101. See also Jeanine Basinger, *Silent Stars* (New York: Knopf, 1999).

Lillian Gish in *Broken Blossoms*
Lillian Gish was twenty-three when she played the young girl Lucy Burrows in D. W. Griffith's *Broken Blossoms* (1919). It was, incredibly, her sixty-fourth movie, and she gave one of her long career's most emotionally wrenching performances.

beats her for the slightest transgression. Enraged by her friendship with the merchant, Burrows drags her home, and when Lucy hides in a tiny closet, he breaks down the door and beats her so savagely that she dies soon after.

The interaction of narrative, acting, extremely confined cinematic space, and exploitation of the audience's fears gives this scene its beauty, power, and repulsiveness. Seen from various angles within the closet, which fills the screen, Lucy clearly cannot escape. Hysterical with fear, she finally curls up as her father breaks through the door. At the end, she dies in her bed, forcing the smile that has characterized her throughout the film. Terror and pity produce the cathartic realization within the viewer that Lucy's death, under these wretched circumstances, is truly a release.

In creating this scene, Gish invoked a span of emotions that no movie audience had seen before and few have seen since. Her performance illustrates the qualities of great screen acting: appropriateness, expressive coherence, inherent thoughtfulness/emotionality, wholeness, and unity. Amazingly, the performance resulted from Gish's own instincts—her sense of what was right for the

climactic moment of the story and the mise-en-scène in which it took place—rather than from Griffith's direction:

> The scene of the terrified child alone in the closet could probably not be filmed today. To watch Lucy's hysteria was excruciating enough in a silent picture; a sound track would have made it unbearable. When we filmed it I played the scene with complete lack of restraint, turning around and around like a tortured animal. When I finished, there was a hush in the studio. Mr. Griffith finally whispered: "My God, why didn't you warn me that you were going to do that?"[11]

Gish gives a similarly powerful performance—her character shoots the man who raped her—in Victor Sjöström's *The Wind* (1928), and her work in confined spaces influenced such later climactic scenes as Marion Crane's (Janet Leigh) murder in the shower in Alfred Hitchcock's *Psycho* (1960) and Jack Torrance's (Jack Nicholson) attempt to get out of a bathroom where he is trapped in Stanley Kubrick's *The Shining* (1980).

With the discovery and implementation of the principles of screen acting, Gish (and her mentor, Griffith) also influenced excellent performances by her contemporaries: Emil Jannings in F. W. Murnau's *The Last Laugh* (1924) and Janet Gaynor and George O'Brien in Murnau's *Sunrise: A Song of Two Humans* (1927), Gibson Gowland in Erich von Stroheim's *Greed* (1924), and Louise Brooks in G. W. Pabst's *Pandora's Box* (1929).

The Influence of Sound

Not long after Griffith and Gish established a viable and successful style of screen acting, movie actors faced the greatest challenge yet: the conversion from silent to sound production. Instead of instantly revolutionizing film style, the coming of sound in 1927 began a period of several years in which the industry gradually converted to this new form of production (see Chapter 9). Filmmakers made dialogue more comprehensible by developing better microphones; finding the best placements for the camera, microphones, and other sound equipment; and encouraging changes in actors' vocal performances. At first they encased the camera, whose overall

---

11. Gish, *Lillian Gish,* p. 200. For another version of how this scene was prepared and shot, see Charles Affron, *Lillian Gish: Her Legend, Her Life* (New York: Scribner, 2001), pp. 125–131.

size has changed relatively little since the 1920s, in either a bulky soundproof booth or the later development known as a **blimp**—a soundproofed enclosure, somewhat larger than a camera, in which the camera may be mounted so that its sounds do not reach the microphone.

Such measures prevented the sounds of the camera from being recorded, but they also restricted how freely the camera—and the actors—could move. Actors accustomed to moving around the set without worrying about speaking now had to limit their movements to the circumscribed sphere where recording took place. Eventually, technicians were able to free the camera for all kinds of movement and find ways of recording sound that allowed the equipment and actors alike more mobility.

As monumental as the conversion to sound was in economic, technological, stylistic, and human terms, Hollywood found humor in it. It's the subject of one of the most enjoyable of all movie musicals: Stanley Donen and Gene Kelly's *Singin' in the Rain* (1952). This movie vividly and satirically portrays the technical difficulties of using the voice of one actor to replace the voice of another who hasn't been trained to speak, trying to move a camera weighted down with soundproof housing, and forcing actors to speak into microphones concealed in flowerpots. As film scholar Donald Crafton writes:

> Many of the clichés of the early sound cinema (including those in *Singin' in the Rain*) apply to films made during this period: long static takes, badly written dialogue, voices not quite in control, poor-quality recording, and a speaking style with slow cadence and emphasis on "enunciated" tones, which the microphone was supposed to favor.[12]

How did the "talkies" influence actors and acting? Although sound enabled screen actors to use all their powers of human expression, it also created a need for screenplays with dialogue, dialogue coaches to help the actors "find" their voices, and other coaches to help them master foreign accents. The more actors and the more speaking a film included, the more complex the narrative could become. Directors had to make changes, too. Before sound, a director could call out instructions to the actors during filming; once the microphone could

Early sound-film acting

Sound technicians on the earliest sound films were challenged with recording the actors' voices with stationary microphones, which restricted their movements. This problem was solved later with microphones suspended on **booms** outside the camera's range and capable of moving to follow a character's movements. In looking backward, the classic movie musical *Singin' in the Rain* (1952; Stanley Donen and Gene Kelly, directors) found nothing but humor in the process of converting movie production to sound. In the background of this image, we see a reluctant and uncooperative actor, Lina Lamont (Jean Hagen, *right*), next to Don Lockwood (Gene Kelly, *left*). A microphone concealed in the bodice of her gown is connected by wire to the loudspeaker in the glass booth in the foreground, where the exasperated director and sound recordist discover that it has recorded only Miss Lamont's heartbeat. Obviously, they'll have to find a different microphone placement if they want to hear her voice. And if you've seen the movie, you know that her voice is so bad that she had little chance of making the transition to sound movies.

pick up every word uttered on the set, directors were forced to rehearse more extensively with their actors, thus adopting a technique from the stage to deal with screen technology. Though many actors and directors could not make the transition from silent to sound films, others emerged from silent films ready to see the addition of sound less as an obstacle than as the means to a more complete screen verisimilitude.

An innovative production from this period is Rouben Mamoulian's *Applause* (1929; sound-recording technician Ernest Zatorsky). After several years of directing

12. Donald Crafton, *The Talkies: American Cinema's Transition to Sound, 1926–1931* (New York: Scribner, 1997), p. 14.

theater productions in London and New York, Mamoulian made his screen-directing debut with *Applause*, which is photographed in a style that mixes naturalism with expressionism. From the opening scene, a montage of activity that plunges us into the lively world of burlesque, the film reveals Mamoulian's mastery of camera movement. But when the camera does not move, as in the many two-shots full of dialogue, we can almost feel the limited-range microphone boom hovering over the actors, one step beyond the use of flowerpots. In contrast to the vibrant shots with the moving camera, these static shots are lifeless and made even more confusing by the loud expressionist sounds that overwhelm ordinary as well as intimate conversations.

Obviously, such limitations influence how we perceive the acting, which is *Applause*'s weak point throughout. Most likely because Mamoulian knew that symphonies of city sounds and noises would be the main impression of many scenes, the actors have little to say or do. However, the movie remains interesting thanks to a new technique in sound recording that Mamoulian introduced and that soon became common practice. Earlier, all sound in a particular shot had been recorded and manipulated on a single sound track. Mamoulian persuaded the sound technicians to record overlapping dialogue in a single shot using two separate microphones and then mix them together on the sound track. When April Darling (Joan Peers), her head on a pillow, whispers a prayer while her mother, Kitty (Helen Morgan), sits next to her and sings a lullaby, the actors almost seem to be singing a duet—naturally, intimately, and convincingly.[13]

The conversion to sound, a pivotal moment in film history that simultaneously ruined many acting careers while creating others, has long fascinated movie fans. And it has been treated with pathos as well as humor in movies other than those discussed here, including Billy Wilder's *Sunset Boulevard* (1950) and Michel Hazanavicius's *The Artist* (2011).

Acting in the Classical Studio Era

From the early years of moviemaking, writes film scholar Robert Allen, "the movie star has been one of the defining characteristics of the American cinema."[14] Most simply, a movie star is two people: the actor and the character(s) he or she plays. In addition, the star embodies an image created by the studio to coincide with the kinds of roles associated with the actor. That the star also reflects the social and cultural history of the period when that image was created helps explain the often rapid rise and fall of stars' careers. But this description reveals at its heart a set of paradoxes, as Allen points out:

> The star is powerless, yet powerful; different from "ordinary" people, yet at one time was "just like us." Stars make huge salaries, yet the work for which they are handsomely paid does not appear to be work on the screen. Talent would seem to be a requisite for stardom, yet there has been no absolute correlation between acting ability and stardom. The star's private life has little if anything to do with his or her "job" of acting in movies, yet a large portion of a star's image is constructed on the basis of "private" matters: romance, marriage, tastes in fashion, and home life.[15]

The golden age of Hollywood, roughly from the 1930s until the 1950s, was the age of the movie star. Acting in American movies then generally meant "star acting." During this period, the major studios gave basic lessons in acting, speaking, and movement, but because screen appearance was of paramount importance, they were more concerned with enhancing actors' screen images than with improving their acting.

During the golden age, the studio system and the star system went hand in hand, and the studios had almost complete control of their actors. Every 6 months, the studio reviewed an actor's standard 7-year **option contract**: if the actor had made progress in being assigned roles and demonstrating box-office appeal, the studio

---

13. In his next films, Mamoulian made other innovations in sound, including the sound flashback in *City Streets* (1931) and the lavish use of contrapuntal sound in the opening of *Love Me Tonight* (1932).

14. For a study of stars in Hollywood from which this section liberally draws, see Robert C. Allen and Douglas Gomery, *Film History: Theory and Practice* (New York: Knopf, 1985), pp. 172–189, quotation on p. 174 (reprinted as Robert C. Allen, "The Role of the Star in Film History [Joan Crawford]," in *Film Theory and Criticism: Introductory Readings*, 5th ed., ed. Leo Braudy and Marshall Cohen [New York: Oxford University Press, 1999], pp. 547–561).

15. Allen and Gomery, *Film History*, p. 174.

picked up the option to employ that actor for the next 6 months and gave him or her a raise; if not, the studio dropped the option, and the actor was out of work. The decision was the studio's, not the actor's. Furthermore, the contract did not allow the actor to move to another studio, stop work, or renegotiate for a higher salary. In addition to those unbreakable terms, the contract had restrictive clauses that gave the studio total control over the star's image and services; it required an actor "to act, sing, pose, speak or perform in such roles as the producer may designate"; it gave the studio the right to change the name of the actor at its own discretion and to control the performer's image and likeness in advertising and publicity; and it required the actor to comply with rules covering interviews and public appearances.[16]

These contracts turned the actors into the studios' chattel. To the public, perhaps the most fascinating thing about making actors into stars was the process of changing their names. Marion Morrison became John Wayne, Issur Danielovitch Demsky became Kirk Douglas, Julia Jean Mildred Frances Turner became Lana Turner, and Archibald Leach became Cary Grant. Name and image came first, and acting ability often was considered secondary to an actor's screen presence or aura, physical or facial beauty, athletic ability or performance skills, or character "type." Although many stars were also convincing actors capable of playing a variety of parts (e.g., Bette Davis, Henry Fonda, Barbara Stanwyck, Jimmy Stewart), surprisingly little serious attention was paid to screen acting. As Charles Affron observes:

> An almost total absence of analytical approaches to screen acting reflects the belief that screen acting is nothing more than the beautiful projection of a filmic self, an arrangement of features and body, the disposition of superficial elements. Garbo is Garbo is Garbo is Garbo. We mortals are left clutching our wonder, and

victims of that very wonder, overwhelmed by our enthusiasm and blinded by the light of the star's emanation.[17]

In her comprehensive study *The Star Machine*, Jeanine Basinger offers a list of observations of what a movie star is:

> A star has exceptional looks. Outstanding talent. A distinctive voice that can easily be recognized and imitated. A set of mannerisms. Palpable sexual appeal. Energy that comes down off the screen. Glamour. Androgyny. Glowing health and radiance. Panache. A single tiny flaw that mars their perfection, endearing them to ordinary people. Charm. The good luck to be in the right place at the right time (also known as just plain good luck). An emblematic quality that audiences believe is who they really are. The ability to make viewers "know" what they are thinking whenever the camera comes up close. An established type (by which is meant that they could believably play the same role over and over again). A level of comfort in front of the camera. And, of course, "she has something," the bottom line of which is "it's something you can't define."[18]

Today, film acting has become the subject of new interest among theorists and critics in semiology, psychology, and cultural studies who wish to study acting as an index of cultural history and an aspect of ideology.[19] This approach stresses that stars were a commodity created by the studio system through promotion, publicity, movies, criticism, and commentary. As Richard Dyer notes, "Stars are involved in making themselves into commodities; they are both labour and the thing that labour produces. They do not produce themselves alone."[20] Such analyses tend to emphasize the ways in which culture makes meaning rather than the art and expressive value of acting, the ways in which actors make meaning.

16. Tino Balio, *Grand Design: Hollywood as a Modern Business Enterprise, 1930–1939* (New York: Scribner, 1999), p. 145.

17. Charles Affron, *Star Acting: Gish, Garbo, Davis* (New York: Dutton, 1977), p. 3. See also Roland Barthes, "The Face of Garbo," in *Film Theory and Criticism*, ed. Braudy and Cohen, pp. 536–538; Alexander Walker, *Stardom: The Hollywood Phenomenon* (New York: Stein and Day, 1970); and Leo Braudy, "Film Acting: Some Critical Problems and Proposals," *Quarterly Review of Film Studies* (February 1976): 1–18.

18. Jeanine Basinger, *The Star Machine* (New York: Knopf, 2007), pp. 3–4.

19. See Richard Dyer, *Stars*, new ed. (London: British Film Institute, 1998); and his *Heavenly Bodies: Film Stars and Society* (New York: St. Martin's Press, 1986). See also Richard deCordova, "The Emergence of the Star System in America," *Wide Angle* 6, no. 4 (1985): 4–13; Carole Zucker, ed., *Making Visible the Invisible: An Anthology of Original Essays on Film Acting* (Metuchen, NJ: Scarecrow Press, 1990); and Christine Gledhill, *Stardom: Industry of Desire* (New York: Routledge, 1991).

20. Dyer, *Heavenly Bodies*, p. 5.

What makes a movie star?

Jeanine Basinger's list of observations on what makes a movie star could have been written about Cary Grant, for her criteria fit him perfectly. Regarded by the public, as well as critics and colleagues, as the finest romantic comedian actor of his time, the handsome actor was often cast as a glamorous, high-society figure in a series of 1930s screwball comedies, including George Cukor's *The Philadelphia Story* (1940). In this image, Grant's wide-open, handsome face and laid-back manner mask the charming wiles of a man who succeeds in remarrying a former wife, played by Katharine Hepburn. He played against some of Hollywood's most glamorous stars, including Mae West, Marlene Dietrich, Audrey Hepburn, Ingrid Bergman, Doris Day, and Grace Kelly. Long before the birth of the independent production system, Grant was unique among Hollywood actors by not signing a studio contract but rather controlling every aspect of his career himself, including the directors and actors he wanted to work with and the roles he wanted to play. Perhaps the high point of his career was working with Alfred Hitchcock on *Suspicion* (1941), *Notorious* (1946), *To Catch a Thief* (1955), and *North by Northwest* (1959), films in which he still plays a lighthearted rogue. His assets—sleek good looks, ease, lack of self-consciousness, physical grace, and natural comic sense—make him one of the great movie actors of all time; some say the greatest.

Materialistic as it was, the star system dominated the movie industry until the studio system collapsed. It was replaced by a similar industrial enterprise powered essentially by the same motivation of making profits for its investors. However, because every studio had its own system, creating different goals and images for different stars, there was no typical star. For example, when Lucille Fay LeSueur (also known early in her theater career as Billie Cassin) went to Hollywood in 1925, MGM

decided that her name must be changed and altered her image to be that of an ideal American "girl." Through a national campaign conducted by a fan magazine, the public was invited to submit names. The first choice, "Joan Arden," was already being used by another actress, so Lucille LeSueur became Joan Crawford, a name that she objected to for several years. However, her new name became synonymous with the public's idea of a movie star—indeed, one proclaimed by MGM to be a "star of the first magnitude."[21]

Crawford's career soon took off, reaching a high level of achievement in the mid-1930s when she became identified with the "woman's film." Subsequently, in a long series of films, she played women who, whether by family background or social circumstances, triumphed over adversity and usually paid a price for independence. No matter what happened to them, her characters remained stylish and distinctive in their looks—chic, self-generated survivors. Like many other stars, Crawford became indelibly associated with the roles she played. Yet she received little serious acclaim for her acting until the mid-1940s, when she left MGM for Warner Bros. For Michael Curtiz's *Mildred Pierce* (1945), her first film there, Crawford won the Academy Award for Best Actress—her only Oscar, although she received two more nominations. After her success at Warner Bros., Crawford worked for various major studios and independents, shedding her image as the stalwart, contemporary American woman. Sometimes her performances were excellent, as in Curtis Bernhardt's *Possessed* (1947), David Miller's *Sudden Fear* (1952), and, costarring with Bette Davis, Robert Aldrich's *What Ever Happened to Baby Jane?* (1962).

Davis was a star of another sort, leading a principled and spirited fight against the studio and star systems' invasion into virtually every aspect of actors' personal and professional lives. In fact, Davis's career (from 1931 to 1989) comes as close to any as demonstrating these systems at their best and worst. In the mid-1930s, when she walked out of Warner Bros. demanding better roles, the studio successfully sued her for breach of contract. She returned to work rewarded by increased respect, a new contract, and better roles. But her career sagged after World War II, for she had reached her early forties, an age at which female actors are seldom offered

1

2

The movie star

Elizabeth Taylor epitomizes what we mean by the term *movie star*: talent, beauty, sex appeal, and a glamour that dazzled the world. As a child star, the product of the studio system, she appeared in such movies as *Lassie Come Home* (1943) and *National Velvet* (1944). As a teenager, she came to prominence as Angela Vickers [1] in George Stevens's *A Place in the Sun* (1951), a romantic but tragic melodrama. During her most fruitful period—the 1950s and 1960s—she starred in such movies as George Stevens's *Giant* (1956), Richard Brooks's *Cat on a Hot Tin Roof* (1958), Joseph L. Mankiewicz's *Suddenly, Last Summer* (1959), and Daniel Mann's *BUtterfield 8* (1960). Her career took a brief downward spin with Mankiewicz's *Cleopatra* (1963), one of the most lavish, expensive, and unsuccessful films of all time. A survivor, she recovered in two impressive roles: Martha [2] in Mike Nichols's *Who's Afraid of Virginia Woolf?* (1966) and Katharina in Franco Zeffirelli's *The Taming of the Shrew* (1967). In all, Elizabeth Taylor appeared in more than fifty films and was awarded three Oscars as Best Actress. Long after she quit her acting career, she remained a star, lending her name and reputation to raising hundreds of millions of dollars for AIDS research and other humanitarian causes.

good parts. Ironically, playing just such a character—an older stage actress in danger of losing roles because of her age—she triumphed in Joseph L. Mankiewicz's *All about Eve* (1950), generally regarded as her greatest performance. During her long career, Davis was nominated eleven times for the Academy Award for Best Actress, winning for Alfred E. Green's *Dangerous* (1935) and William Wyler's *Jezebel* (1938). Nominations for an Oscar as Best Actor or Best Actress involve a peer-review process in which only actors vote. Davis's record of nominations is exceeded only by Meryl Streep's (seventeen nominations), Katharine Hepburn's (twelve), and Jack Nicholson's (eight).

Method Acting

During the studio years, movie acting and the star system were virtually synonymous. Although acting styles were varied, the emphasis was on the star's persona and its effect at the box office—on the product, not the process, of acting. And as production processes were regularized, so too was acting. Even so, screen acting in the 1930s and 1940s was not formulaic or unimagina-

tive; quite the contrary. On Broadway, however, stage actors were becoming acquainted with a Russian theory that became known as method acting. Method acting did not make a major impact on Hollywood until the 1950s, but it marks a significant point in the evolution of screen acting from the studio system's reliance on "star acting" in the 1930s and 1940s to a new style.

What Americans call method acting was based on the theory and practice of Konstantin Stanislavsky, who co-founded the Moscow Art Theater in 1897 and spent his entire career there. In developing what became known as the **Stanislavsky system** of acting, he trained students to start by conducting an exhaustive inquiry into their characters' background and psychology. With an understanding of those aspects, they could then work from the inside out. In other words, they had to *be* the character before successfully *playing* the character. Whether that works on the stage or screen is another issue.

Stanislavsky's ideas influenced the Soviet silent film directors of the 1920s—Sergei Eisenstein, Aleksandr Dovzhenko, Lev Kuleshov, and Vsevolod I. Pudovkin—all of whom had learned much from D. W. Griffith's work. But they often disagreed about acting, especially about how it was influenced by actors' appearances and by editing, which could work so expressively both for and against actors' interpretations.

Among this group, Pudovkin, whose *Film Acting* (1935) was one of the first serious books on the subject, has the most relevance to mainstream movie acting today. Although he advocates an explicitly Stanislavskian technique based on his observations of the Moscow Art Theater, he writes from the standpoint of film directors and actors working together. Because film consists of individual shots, he reasons, both directors and actors work at the mercy of the shot and must strive to make acting (out of sequence) seem natural, smooth, and flowing while maintaining expressive coherence across the shots. He recommends close collaboration between actors and directors as well as long periods devoted to preparation and rehearsal. He also advises film actors to ignore voice training because the microphone makes it unnecessary, notes that the close-up can communicate more to the audience than overt gestures can, and finds that the handling of "expressive objects" (e.g., Charlie Chaplin's cane) can convey emotions and ideas even more effectively than close-ups can.

Through his teaching and books, especially *An Actor Prepares* (1936), Stanislavsky had a lasting impact on Broadway and Hollywood acting. Actor Stella Adler taught principles of method acting to members of the experimental Group Theatre, including Elia Kazan. In 1947, Kazan, now a director, helped found the Actors Studio in New York City. In 1951, Kazan was replaced by Lee Strasberg, who alienated many theater people including Kazan, Adler, Arthur Miller, and Marlon Brando. Today the studio is guided by three alumni: Ellen Burstyn, Harvey Keitel, and Al Pacino. In 1949, Adler went her own way and founded the Stella Adler Studio of Acting, where Marlon Brando was her most famous and successful student.

These teachers loosely adapted Stanislavky's ideas. They used his principle that actors should draw on their own emotional experiences to create characters as well as his emphasis on the importance of creating an ensemble and expressing the subtext, the nuances lying beneath the lines of the script. The naturalistic style that they popularized (and called **method acting**, more pop-

ularly known as the *Method*) encourages actors to speak, move, and gesture not in a traditional stage manner but just as they would in their own lives. Thus it is an ideal technique for representing convincing human behavior on the stage and on the screen. The Method has led to a new level of realism and subtlety, influencing such actors, in addition to those already mentioned, as James Dean, Montgomery Clift, Marilyn Monroe, Morgan Freeman, Robert De Niro, Jack Nicholson, Jane Fonda, Sidney Poitier, Dustin Hoffman, Daniel Day-Lewis, and Shelley Winters, among many others.[22]

To understand method acting, you have to see it. Fortunately, there are some wonderful examples, including James Dean's three movie roles—Cal Trask in Elia Kazan's *East of Eden* (1955), Jim Stark in Nicholas Ray's *Rebel without a Cause* (1955), and Jett Rink in George Stevens's *Giant* (1956). Marlon Brando gave equally legendary performances as Stanley Kowalski in Elia Kazan's *A Streetcar Named Desire* (1951), reprising the stage role that made him famous, and as Terry Malloy in Kazan's *On the Waterfront* (1954). Other notable performances, out of many, include those by Paul Newman as Eddie Felson in Robert Rossen's *The Hustler* (1961), Shelley Winters as Charlotte Haze Humbert in Stanley Kubrick's *Lolita* (1962), and Faye Dunaway as Evelyn Cross Mulwray in Roman Polanski's *Chinatown* (1974). Each of these performances exhibits the major characteristics of method acting: intense concentration and internalization (sometimes mistaken for discomfort) on the actor's part; low-key, almost laid-back delivery of lines (sometimes described as mumbling); and an edginess (sometimes highly neurotic) that suggests dissatisfaction, unhappiness, and alienation. In directing *The Misfits* (1961), with a script by playwright Arthur Miller, John Huston (not a method director) must have been bewildered by the range of acting talent in front of his camera: Clark Gable, a traditional Hollywood star in any sense of the word, who always could be counted on to deliver a reliable performance; Thelma Ritter, an equally seasoned supporting player who invariably played the role of a wisecracking sidekick; and several method actors (Eli Wallach, Montgomery Clift, and Marilyn Monroe), whose performances, by contrast with the rest of the cast, seem out of touch and clumsy. Absent here is

---

22. See Carole Zucker, "An Interview with Lindsay Crouse," *Post Script: Essays in Film and the Humanities* 12, no. 2 (Winter 1993): 5–28. See also Foster Hirsch, *A Method to Their Madness: The History of the Actors Studio* (New York: Norton, 1984); and Steven Vineberg, *Method Actors: Three Generations of an American Acting Style* (New York: Schirmer, 1991).

1

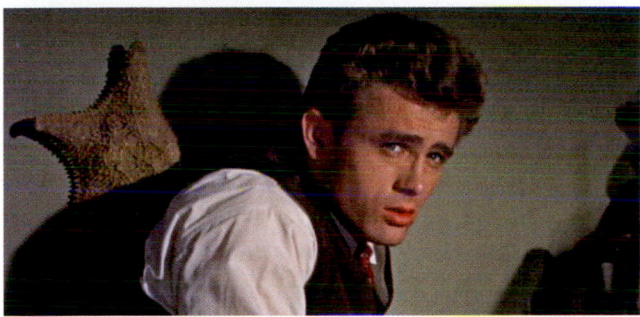

2

Elia Kazan and method acting

Elia Kazan is notable, among many other things, for directing two of the iconic method-acting achievements: Marlon Brando as Terry Malloy in *On the Waterfront* (1954)—here [1] we see Kazan (*center*) and Brando (*right*) on location during the filming—and James Dean [2] as Cal Trask, a troubled teenager, in *East of Eden* (1955).

the ensemble method acting obvious in Elia Kazan's movies.

No matter what school or style of acting is involved, it is clear that memorable acting results from hard work, skill, imagination, and discipline.

Screen Acting Today

From the earliest years, the development of movie acting has relied on synthesizing various approaches, including those already discussed. Contemporary actors employ a range of physically or psychologically based approaches. Some action stars, like Vin Diesel, rely primarily on physical effect; others, like Bruce Willis, rely both on physical

prowess and a distinct persona that has evolved from the early wise-guy days to a more world-weary one. Directors also take different approaches toward actors. Robert Altman, for example, who was particularly good at capturing the mood of an ensemble of actors within a narrative, encouraged improvisation and the exploration of individual styles. Joel Coen, in contrast, tends to regard acting as a critical component of the highly stylized mise-en-scène within the often cartoonlike movies that he creates with his brother, Ethan.

In Altman's *The Player* (1992), Tim Robbins plays Griffin Mill, a Hollywood producer, at once emotively and satirically. He uses his big, open face and charming manner to draw us into Mill's professional and existential crises, then turns edgy enough to distance us as Mill becomes a murderer and ruthless careerist. In Altman's *Kansas City* (1996), Jennifer Jason Leigh delivers an emotional hurricane of a performance as the cheap, brassy, tough Blondie O'Hara, a Jean Harlow wannabe. Her scowl, furrowed brow, rotten teeth under big red lips, and screeching-cat voice leave no room for the kind of gently ironic distance that Robbins creates in *The Player*.

In the Coens' *The Hudsucker Proxy* (1994), however, both Robbins and Leigh tailor their performances to fit the madcap mood and mannered decor of an Art Deco screwball comedy. Indeed, part of the movie's appeal lies in watching an ensemble of actors working in this style. Channeling Cary Grant and Rosalind Russell in Howard Hawks's *His Girl Friday* (1940) and Spencer Tracy and Katharine Hepburn in Walter Lang's *Desk Set* (1957), Robbins plays Norville Barnes, a goofy mailroom clerk who becomes company president, and Leigh plays Amy Archer, a hard-boiled, wisecracking newspaper reporter. Robbins and Leigh's zany comic interaction fits perfectly in the Coens' jigsaw puzzle, which lovingly pays tribute to an era when movie style often transcended substance.

Today, actors struggle to get parts and to create convincing performances, and, like their earlier counterparts, they seldom have the chance to prove themselves across a range of roles. Once **typecast**—chosen for particular kinds of roles because of their looks or "type" rather than for their acting talent or experience—they continue to be awarded such parts as long they bring in good box-office receipts. No star system exists to sustain careers and images, but now, as in earlier periods of movie history, some individuals use films to promote themselves. Think of the music stars, sports stars,

Contemporary star power

Unlike some actors who become movie stars almost overnight, Robert Downey Jr. began appearing in avant-garde movies directed by his father at the age of five. Working in the independent era, he was able to choose a range of roles that revealed his extraordinary talent. Downey's breakthrough as a major performer came with Richard Attenborough's *Chaplin* (1992), for which he received an Oscar nomination as Best Actor. He continued to demonstrate his remarkable versatility in serious roles in Robert Altman's *Short Cuts* (1993), Oliver Stone's *Natural Born Killers* (1994), Richard Loncraine's *Richard III* (1995), and Michael Hoffman's *Restoration* (1995). Between 1996 and 2001, his acting career faltered because of his drug abuse. Except for his role in Curtis Hanson's *Wonder Boys* (2000), he was cast in relatively unimportant projects. He returned to serious roles, deserving serious attention, in such movies as George Clooney's *Good Night, and Good Luck* (2005) and David Fincher's *Zodiac* (2007). These days, virtually all of his screen time is devoted to lead roles in two successful, ongoing franchises: Tony Stark in Marvel's Iron Man and Avengers movies, and Sherlock Holmes in the film series of that name. In this image, we see Downey as the brilliant, arrogant, and intense Tony Stark, aka Iron Man.

or other celebrities who sometimes appear in a movie or two but leave no mark on the history of film acting.

The transition from studio production to independent production has markedly affected the livelihood of actors and the art of acting. The shape of the average career has fundamentally changed. Fewer major movies appear each year, so actors supplement film work with appearances on television shows, in advertisements, and in theater. (Salaries and contractual benefits, such as residual payments for television reruns, provide excellent financial security.) Moreover, actors are finding fewer quality roles because today's average movies are comedies that target the under-thirty audience (and such comedies rely on physical and often scatological humor rather than verbal wit).

Some extremely versatile actors—Jennifer Lawrence, Johnny Depp, Leonardo DiCaprio, Samuel L. Jackson,

Nicole Kidman, Julianne Moore, and Oscar Isaac, to name a few—have, after two or three successful films, become stars quickly. The greater their drawing power at the box office, the greater the urgency to promote them to top rank and cast them in more films. As independent agents, however, they can contract for one film at a time and thus hold out for good roles rather than having to make a specific number of films for a given studio. In addition, these newcomers can negotiate a new salary for each film, and they routinely make more money from a single picture than some of the greatest stars of classical Hollywood made in their entire careers. Furthermore, they usually work under their own names. But because they maintain their status by audience reaction and not a studio's publicity office, such actors often face highly unpredictable futures.

Let's look more closely at the careers and earnings of two of the most important and popular movie stars in history: Bette Davis, who was at the top during the studio era, and Nicole Kidman, who is at the top today. Although they are both well regarded for their professional approach to performances in a range of film genres—melodrama, comedy, historical and period films, and romantic dramas—their careers exhibit significant differences that result from the different production systems in which each star worked (see Chapter 11).

Bette Davis (1908–1989), who began her movie career on Broadway, went to Hollywood at the age of twenty-two. Over a career that spanned fifty-two years, she appeared in eighty-nine movies, fifty-nine of them under contract to Warner Bros. Her breakthrough role was in John Cromwell's *Of Human Bondage* (1934); she won her first Oscar as Best Actress in 1936 and again in 1939, when she reached the peak of her career in William Wyler's *Jezebel* (1938). She sued Warner Bros. in an attempt to get better roles in better pictures (she was forced, by contract, to make a lot of mediocre films) but lost her case. (In essence, Davis had to fight for what actors of Kidman's generation take for granted: the right to pick the roles they want to play.) However, Davis did get better roles (and unwisely rejected some juicy ones, including *Mildred Pierce* [1945] and *The African Queen* [1951]). She was so well paid in the 1940s that she was known around Hollywood as the fourth Warner brother. The years between 1939 and 1945 were marked by major successes—Edmund Goulding's *Dark Victory* (1939), Michael Curtiz's *The Private Lives of Elizabeth and Essex*

Stardom: then and now

Bette Davis, an actress who became a legend for playing strong-willed and often neurotic female characters, was in top form as Leslie Crosbie in *The Letter* (1940). In the movie's electric opening scene, she pumps five bullets into her lover [1], then pleads self-defense in court. Nicole Kidman, like Davis, is famous for her professionalism and versatility. Unlike Davis, however, she has almost totally controlled her career. Thus she has been far more adventurous in the roles she chooses to play, and the result is a filmography of considerable depth and range. She is well known for her willingness to take risks in highly individual movies, such as *Birth* (2003; director Jonathan Glazer), in which she plays a woman who becomes convinced that her husband has been reborn as a young boy, and the Civil War drama *The Beguiled* (2017; director Sophia Coppola), in which she plays the emotionally mysterious headmistress of an isolated girls school [2] who takes in, nurses, and eventually poisons a wounded Union soldier.

(1939), William Wyler's *The Letter* (1940) and *The Little Foxes* (1941), Irving Rapper's *Now, Voyager* (1942) and *The Corn Is Green* (1945)—but by 1950, her studio career was over. As one of the first freelancers in the independent system, she revived her career with her greatest performance in Joseph L. Mankiewicz's *All about Eve* (1950). However, she was then forty-one, the "barrier" year that usually relegates women actors to character parts. She had her share of them, including Robert Aldrich's *What Ever Happened to Baby Jane?* (1962). Her career went downhill, although there were still a few good movies and loyal fans; her penultimate role was a moving performance in Lindsay Anderson's *The Whales of August* (1987). A demanding perfectionist to the end, she walked off the set of her final film just before she died. Bette Davis, a name synonymous with Hollywood stardom, ranked second (after Katharine Hepburn) on the American Film Institute's poll of the greatest female actors.

Bette Davis is an icon of movies past, and Nicole Kidman is a screen legend for today. Unconstrained by a studio contract, she is free to choose her roles. She has worked with a variety of directors, including Gus Van Sant, Jane Campion, Stanley Kubrick, Baz Luhrmann, and Yorgos Lanthimos. Where Davis had some say over her directors (all of whom were studio employees), Kidman has worked with outsiders, insiders, kings of the megaplexes, and avant-garde experimenters. Kidman (b. 1967) began her movie career in Australia at the age of fifteen and has since made sixty films (as of 2018), all independently produced. Her breakthrough movie was Tony Scott's *Days of Thunder* (1990), after which her career took off in such films as Gus Van Sant's *To Die For* and Joel Schumacher's *Batman Forever* (1995), Jane Campion's *The Portrait of a Lady* (1996), Stanley Kubrick's *Eyes Wide Shut* (1999), Baz Luhrmann's *Moulin Rouge!* (2001), and Stephen Daldry's *The Hours* (2002), for which she won the Oscar for Best Actress for her portrayal of Virginia Woolf. Another turning point came in 2003, when she made three different movies with three very different directors: Lars von Trier's *Dogville*, Robert Benton's *The Human Stain*, and Anthony Minghella's *Cold Mountain*. Kidman is willing to tackle serious melodrama (Sydney Pollack's *The*

Interpreter, 2005), light comedy (Nora Ephron's *Bewitched*, 2005), edgy, experimental concepts (Steven Shainberg's *Fur: An Imaginary Portrait of Diane Arbus*, 2006), and comic drama (Noah Baumbach's *Margot at the Wedding*, 2007) as well as a serious domestic drama (*Rabbit Hole*, 2007; director John Cameron Mitchell), a psychological thriller (*The Beguiled*, 2017; director Sophia Coppola), and a romantic biopic (*Grace of Monaco*, 2014; director Olivier Dahan). When Bette Davis turned forty-one, her career (despite her success that year with *All about Eve*) began its downward spiral. Ironically, Kidman, now fifty-one, remains at the peak of her career and continues to get roles worthy of her experience and talent.

Let's consider their earning power. In her career, we estimate that Bette Davis earned around $6 million, which in today's money is about $10 million.[23] Until 1949, her salary was set by contract; her highest studio earnings were $208,000 for the years 1941–43. Her highest poststudio earnings came with her last movie, for which she was paid $250,000. Kidman made $100,000 on her first movie and today receives up to $17 million per picture. During the first 25 years of her ongoing movie career, Kidman has earned $230 million. That's twenty-three times what Davis earned over an entire 52-year career! Davis worked under a Warner Bros. contract, and the studio kept the lion's share of profits from her films. Kidman is free to negotiate the terms of her salary and her share of the profits for her movies, terms that are determined by a far more complicated equation than a studio contract. These estimates do not include fees for television acting, advertising work, DVD sales, and so on. Stars of Davis's era made far less money from advertisements than, say, Kidman, who is the face in Chanel's print and television campaigns, for which she earns millions each year. The most revealing indicator separating the "old" from the "new" Hollywood, as far as actors are concerned, is clearly the freedom to choose roles and negotiate earnings.

Earnings are influenced by an actor's popularity with audiences. There are two basic ways of measuring this popularity: box-office receipts and popularity polls. Among the popularity polls, the Harris Poll, conducted by a leading market-research company, is probably as reliable as any poll of America's favorite movie stars. The 2016 Harris Poll results are as follows:

1. Tom Hanks
2. Johnny Depp
3. Denzel Washington
4. John Wayne
5. Harrison Ford
6. Sandra Bullock
7. Jennifer Lawrence
8. Clint Eastwood
9. Brad Pitt
10. Julia Roberts

Looking over this list, two questions are immediately obvious. First, if women constitute the bulk of the movie audience, why is this list dominated by men? And how did John Wayne make the list at all, much less at number 4? He died in 1979!

Indeed, John Wayne has been on Harris's top-ten list every year since he died. An actor of many parts, he is as durable a Hollywood legend as has ever existed. Wayne is a far better actor than many people give him credit for. He was indelibly linked to the Western and, in private life, to right-wing politics. On-screen, he represented a kind of American male virtue that many people admire. Wayne is an acting icon who has a solid place in American cultural ideology. The people who were polled here neglected to vote for many fine and popular actors, but the results represent the unpredictability of Hollywood fame. When an actor who made his last movie—Don Siegel's excellent *The Shootist*—in 1976 gets fourth place today, that's stardom!

In another poll, the Vulture entertainment blog released its 2015 ranking of "the most valuable" stars, those most likely to positively affect a movie's gross. Here are the top ten stars on its 2015 list:

---

23. The figures cited here are based, in part, on information provided by newspaper and magazine articles and by the online database pro.imdb.com and do not include fees for television acting, advertising work, DVD sales, and so forth.

An icon of the new Hollywood

Working wholly within today's independent system of movie production, an actor like Jeff Bridges does not have the security of a studio contract or the opportunity of developing and perpetuating a legendary character, such as John Wayne did. Nonetheless, Bridges has earned universal respect as one of Hollywood's most talented and resilient actors. His characters have become legendary: Ernie in John Huston's *Fat City* (1972), Nick Kegan in William Richert's *Winter Kills* (1979), Starman/Scott Hayden in John Carpenter's *Starman* (1984) [1], Jeffrey "The Dude" Lebowski in Joel Coen's *The Big Lebowski* (1998), and Marcus Hamilton in David Mackenzie's *Hell or High Water* (2016). In Joel and Ethan Coen's *True Grit* (2010) [2], he played a character first developed by John Wayne in the 1969 film of the same name. To date, Bridges has made seventy-three films, earned six Oscar nominations (three for best supporting actor and three for best actor), and won the Best Actor Oscar for his role as Bad Blake in Scott Cooper's *Crazy Heart* (2009).

A durable Hollywood legend

In a career spanning 46 years and 180 movies, John Wayne starred in war movies, romantic comedies, and historical epics, but he is best known for his roles as the hero in great Westerns, particularly those directed by John Ford and Howard Hawks. His first starring role, at age twenty-three, was as a winsome young scout in Raoul Walsh's *The Big Trail* (1930) [1], a spectacular epic of a wagon train going west. Wayne's last film, at sixty-seven, was Don Siegel's *The Shootist* (1976). In it he plays an aging gunslinger ("shootist"), dying of cancer, out to settle some old scores [2]. Wayne himself died of cancer three years after completing the film.

1. Jennifer Lawrence
2. Robert Downey Jr.
3. Leonardo DiCaprio
4. Bradley Cooper
5. Dwayne Johnson
6. Tom Cruise
7. Hugh Jackman
8. Sandra Bullock
9. Channing Tatum
10. Scarlett Johansson

An interesting list, to be sure, and you'll find these names on other lists, if not in the same order. You'll notice that many of the most popular stars, including the three oldest (Clint Eastwood, Tom Hanks, and Denzel Washington) are not necessarily the most bankable. In fact, only two of the actors that people seem to like the best are also considered among Hollywood's most bankable stars, and they're both women: Jennifer Lawrence and Sandra Bullock.

Technology and Acting

As discussed in Chapter 6, "Cinematography," for every advance in the world of special effects, the narrative and the acting that propels it lose some of their importance. Movies such as Stanley Kubrick's *2001: A Space Odyssey* (1968) and Steven Spielberg's *E.T. the Extra–Terrestrial* (1982) made us familiar, even comfortable, with nonhuman creatures that had human voices and characteristics; John Lasseter, Ash Brannon, and Lee Unkrich's *Toy Story 2* (1999), with its shiny, computer-generated graphics, took this process another step forward.

Although digital technology is now affecting all aspects of filmmaking, we don't have to worry about it replacing actors entirely. Audiences say they choose movies that include their favorite actors. But alongside real actors, computer-generated imagery (CGI) can create convincing characters such as the avatars digitally created to interact with the Na'vi, the blue-skinned humanoids in James Cameron's *Avatar* (2009) and its sequels. Its mix of real and computer-generated actors did not stop *Avatar* from becoming the highest-grossing movie of all time. Human viewers respond to humanity on-screen; audience polls confirm that many viewers choose movies to see their favorite actors perform. So,

although digital technology is now dominating all aspects of filmmaking, we don't have to worry about it replacing actors entirely. But digital animation technology has advanced to the point that real actors, supplemented by motion capture and CGI, can create compelling animated characters capable of convincingly interacting with live-action performers. The actor Andy Serkis describes the digital effects used to animate his motion-capture performances as "digital makeup." His performance as Gollum in The Lord of the Rings films *The Two Towers* and *The Return of the King* (2002 and 2003; director Peter Jackson) ushered in a new era of digitally enhanced performance that continues to evolve, largely thanks to Serkis's continuing contributions to the craft in roles such as the chimpanzee protagonist Caesar in the Planet of the Apes reboot series and Snoke, the evil Supreme Leader of the First Order in *Star Wars: The Last Jedi* (2017; director Rian Johnson).

Let's also note the distinction between whole characters created entirely by digital technology and real actors transformed by digital makeup (see "Costume, Makeup, and Hairstyle" in Chapter 5). Director David Fincher used both procedures when faced with the challenge of casting actors to play the real-life, identical Winkelvoss twins in *The Social Network* (2010). Since Aaron Sorkin's screenplay is a fictional account of a true incident,

Movie technology produces identical twins
It's not a tabloid headline but a fact. With the help of an ingenious use of technology, two different actors appear on-screen as identical twins in *The Social Network*.

it would have been acceptable to alter the story and cast actors as fraternal rather than identical twins. Instead, Fincher cast Armie Hammer and Josh Pence, respectively, in the roles of the identical Winklevoss twins, Cameron and Tyler. Throughout their scenes, Hammer acted alongside Pence, and through the postproduction use of motion-capture technology and digital grafting of Hammer's face onto Pence's, they appear on the screen as identical twins, as you can see in the image on the previous page (*left to right*: Hammer as Cameron, Pence as Tyler). Using two different actors in these roles allows the actors to develop characters with different personalities; using digital grafting ensures the facial similarity necessary for depicting identical twins. While the result is totally convincing in this specific situation, there aren't many movies about identical twins.

Computer-generated characters might have the same fate as some of the other innovations that Hollywood has periodically employed to keep the world on edge, such as the short-lived Sensurround, which relied on a sound track to trigger waves of high-decibel sound in the movie theater that made viewers feel "tremors" during Mark Robson's *Earthquake* (1974); or the even shorter-lived Odorama process, involving scratch-and-sniff cards, for John Waters's *Polyester* (1981). Indeed, the use of computer technology to replace actors is one side effect of our current fascination with virtual reality. Although the evolving film technology may enable filmmakers to realize their most fantastic visions, we should remember, as film theorist André Bazin has so persuasively argued, that such developments may extend and enrich the illusions that the movies create at the expense of the film artists themselves, including directors, designers, cinematographers, editors, *and* actors.[24]

Casting Actors

Casting is the process of choosing and hiring actors for both leading and supporting roles. In the studio system of Hollywood's golden years, casting was done in several ways, but the overall process was supervised by a central casting office. Often a director, producer, writer, or studio head already had his or her own idea of an actor for a particular role. That choice could be solely based on the actor's looks, screen presence, or overall charisma. Actors were under contract (typically required to appear in seven films over 5 years), and studio heads, mindful of this, often based casting decisions on availability rather than suitability for the role. The "bad" movies of those years are full of such mechanical casting decisions. Studios also announced the availability of a role with an "open call" that could produce crowds of applicants, many of whom were dismissed after cursory consideration. Between 1930 and 1950, hundreds of movies were produced each year, so thousands of would-be actors were living in Hollywood, hoping for the big break that would make them a movie star. Unknown actors were often given **screen tests** (filmed auditions) to see how they looked under studio lighting and how they sounded in recordings. Predatory and unscrupulous studio heads, producers, and directors also used the "casting couch" to determine which actors (both male and female) were willing to trade sex for work.

Today, casting has moved into the front office and become more professional. Independent casting directors (CDs) work under contract to independent producers or directors on a film-by-film basis. For example, Juliet Taylor, who has worked with a long list of major directors, has cast more than thirty of Woody Allen's films. The CD typically scouts talent wherever actors are working, whether it's movies, theater, or commercials, and maintains regular contact with a variety of actors. Casting directors are represented by their own professional association, the Casting Society of America (CSA), and will soon be eligible for Oscar nominations and awards.

Actors learn about casting through direct contact by CDs, producers, directors, or screenwriters, as well as through online audition listings posted by casting services and industry publications such as *Backstage*. After initial interviews, they may be asked to read for parts, either alone or with other actors, or to take screen tests. If they are chosen for the part, negotiations in most cases are handled by their agents. But if they belong to one of the actors' unions—the Screen Actors Guild (SAG) or the American Federation of Television and Radio Artists (AFTRA)—the conditions of their participation are governed by union contract.

---

24. André Bazin, "The Myth of Total Cinema," in *What Is Cinema?* trans. Hugh Gray, 2 vols. (Berkeley: University of California Press, 1967–71), I, pp. 17–22.

Factors Involved in Casting

Although casting takes many factors into account, in theory the most important is how the prospective actors' strengths and weaknesses relate to the roles they are being considered for. In reality, casting—like every other aspect of movie production—depends heavily on the movie's budget and expected revenues. An actor's popularity in one film often leads to casting in other films. As we've seen, the polls that rate actors are based on very different criteria. Still, the key factor in casting is who brings in the most money, which after all other considerations is what the movie business is all about. Just as Hollywood traditionally has repeatedly made movies in popular genres (such as action films or romantic comedies), so too has the industry repeatedly cast the same popular actors in order to sell tickets. A director may think that Denzel Washington is the right person for the lead in her new film, but if the producer does not have the $20 million that Washington currently makes per film, some further thinking is needed. Yet valuable actors like Washington frequently have waived all or part of their salaries because they believe in a particular film project. In such cases, an actor might agree to accept a percentage of the profits should the movie be successful. Other general factors considered in casting include an actor's reputation and popularity; prior experience on the screen or stage; chemistry with other actors, particularly if ensemble acting scenes are part of the script; results of a screen test or reading, often required for newcomers or those about whom the director and others are uncertain; and, equally important, the actor's reputation for professionalism, reliability, ability to withstand the physical challenges of filming certain productions, and personal behavior on the set.

A good CD must have a strong artistic sense of which actors are right for the roles in question, a comprehensive knowledge of all the acting talent available at a particular time for a particular movie, a memory capable of remembering an actor's achievements on-screen, and the ability to avoid playing favorites and keep the process as professional as possible. He or she must be able to coordinate a liaison between directors, producers, writers, and actors in reaching casting decisions while working with everyone from nervous newcomers to the egomaniacs among acting royalty. Although the CD can make or break an actor's career, the final decision rests with the director and/or producer. Once that decision has been made, the CD must handle the deals that determine the terms of the contract. The role and the actor's suitability are generally the determining factors in casting choices, although other considerations, such as cost and marketability, also influence many decisions. Happily, Hollywood has continued to shed casting practices that contradicted social reality. These days, most roles are filled by actors who correspond with the race or ethnicity of a character as written. Increasingly, filmmakers are casting ethnic minority actors in roles for which no specific race or ethnicity is specified or required, a practice labeled "color-blind" or "nontraditional" casting. As a result, contemporary audiences have been exposed to an expanding number of brilliant performances delivered by African American, Native American, Latino, and Asian actors.

Aspects of Performance

Types of Roles

Actors may play major roles, minor roles, character roles, cameo roles, and walk-ons. In addition, roles may be written specifically for bit players, extras, stuntpersons, and even animal performers. Actors who play

Character actors

Although Franklin Pangborn was never a household name, his face was instantly recognizable in the more than 200 movies he made over a career that spanned four decades. With his intimidating voice and fastidious manners, he was best known for playing suspicious hotel clerks, imperious department-store floorwalkers, and sourpuss restaurant managers. Here he's the threatening bank examiner J. Pinkerton Snoopington in the W. C. Fields classic *The Bank Dick* (1940; director Edward F. Cline).

major roles (also called *main, featured,* or *leading roles*) become principal agents in helping to move the plot forward. Whether stars or newcomers, they appear in many scenes and ordinarily, but not always, receive screen credit above the title.

In the Hollywood studio system, major roles were traditionally played by stars such as John Wayne, whose studios counted on them to draw audiences regardless of the parts they played. Their steadfastness was often more important than their versatility as actors, although Wayne surprises us more often than we may admit. One strength of the studio system was its grooming of professionals in all its creative departments, including actors who ranged from leads such as Henry Fonda and Katharine Hepburn to character actors such as Andy Devine and Thelma Ritter. Ritter is unforgettable as the wisecracking commentator on Jeff's (James Stewart) actions in Alfred Hitchcock's *Rear Window* (1954) and Devine is best remembered as the Ringo Kid's (John Wayne) loyal friend in John Ford's *Stagecoach* (1939). Indeed, one of the joys of looking at movies from this period comes from those character actors whose faces, if not names, we always recognize.

Stars may be so valuable to productions that they have **stand-ins**, actors who look reasonably like them in height, weight, coloring, and so on and who substitute for them during the tedious process of preparing setups or taking light readings. Because actors in major roles are ordinarily not hired for their physical or athletic prowess, **stuntpersons** double for them in scenes requiring special skills or involving hazardous actions, such as crashing cars, jumping from high places, swimming, and riding (or falling off) horses. Through special effects, however, filmmakers may now augment actors' physical exertions so that they appear to do their own stunts. In effect, the computer becomes the stunt double. Nonetheless, ten stunt boxers were cast for Clint Eastwood's *Million Dollar Baby* (2004), indicating, at least, that some activities cannot be faked on the screen, particularly activities that could damage an actor's looks or cause other serious injuries.

Actors who play **minor roles** (or *supporting roles*) rank second in the hierarchy. They also help move the plot forward (and thus may be as important as actors in major roles), but they generally do not appear in as many scenes as the featured players. **Bit players** hold small speaking parts, and **extras** usually appear in nonspeaking or crowd roles and receive no screen credit. **Cameos**

The importance of minor roles

In John Huston's *The Maltese Falcon* (1941), Humphrey Bogart stars as the hard-boiled private eye Sam Spade. Gladys George has a small part as Iva Archer, Spade's former lover and the widow of his business partner, Miles Archer (Jerome Cowan). In this scene, George delivers a strongly emotional performance, against which Bogart displays a relative lack of feeling that fills us in on relations between the characters. Stars' performances often depend on the solid and even exceptional work of their fellow actors. The unusually fine supporting cast in this movie includes Hollywood greats Mary Astor, Peter Lorre, and Sydney Greenstreet, who received an Oscar nomination for Best Supporting Actor.

are small but significant roles often taken by famous actors, as in Robert Altman's Hollywood satire *The Player* (1992), which features appearances by sixty-five well-known actors and personalities. **Walk-ons** are even smaller roles, reserved for highly recognizable actors or personalities. As a favor to his friend Orson Welles, with whom he'd worked several times before, Joseph Cotten played such a role in Welles's *Touch of Evil* (1958), where he had a few words of dialogue and literally walked on and off the set.

Animal actors, too, play major, minor, cameo, and walk-on roles. For many years, Hollywood made pictures built on the appeal of such animals as the dogs Lassie, Rin Tin Tin, Asta, and Benji; the cat Rhubarb; the parakeets Bill and Coo; the chimp Cheeta; the mule Francis; the lion Elsa; the dolphin Flipper; and the killer whale Willy. Most of these animals were specially trained to work in front of the camera, and many were sufficiently valuable that they, like other stars, had stand-ins for setups and stunt doubles for hazardous work. Working with animal performers often proves more complicated than working with human actors. For example, six Jack Russell terriers, including three puppies, played the title character in Jay Russell's *My Dog Skip* (2000), a tribute to that indomitable breed.

Preparing for Roles

In creating characters, screen actors begin by synthesizing basic sources, including the script, their own experiences and observations, and the influences of other actors. They also shape their understanding of a role by working closely with their director. This collaboration can be mutually agreeable and highly productive or it can involve constant, even tempestuous arguments that may or may not produce what either artist wants. Ideally, both director and actor should understand each other's concept of the role and, where differences exist, try to agree on an approach that is acceptable to both. Director Sidney Lumet, known for his keen understanding of how actors work, recognizes that acting is a very personal thing. He writes:

> The *talent* of acting is one in which the actor's thoughts and feelings are instantly communicated to the audience. In other words, the "instrument" that the actor is using is himself. It is *his* feelings, *his* physiognomy, *his* sexuality, *his* tears, *his* laughter, *his* anger, *his* romanticism, *his* tenderness, *his* viciousness, that are up there on the screen for all to see.[25]

He emphasizes that the difference between the actor who merely duplicates a life that he or she has observed and the actor who *creates* something unique on the screen depends on how much the actor is able to reveal of himself.

Different roles have different demands, and all actors have their own approaches, whether they get inside their characters, get inside themselves, or do further research. Bette Davis, whose roles were often assigned to her by studios, said, "It depends entirely on what the assignment happens to be. . . . [But] I have never played a part which I did not feel was a person very different from myself."[26] Jack Lemmon, a method actor who generally chose his own roles, explained, "It's like laying bricks. You start at the bottom and work up; actually I guess you start in the middle and work to the outside."[27]

Building a character "brick by brick" is an approach also used by Harvey Keitel and John Malkovich, who might have varied this approach slightly when he played himself in Spike Jonze's *Being John Malkovich* (1999). Liv Ullmann and Jack Nicholson believe that the actor draws on the subconscious mind. Ullmann says, "Emotionally, I don't prepare. I think about what I would like to show, but I don't prepare, because I feel that most of the emotions I have to show I know about. By drawing on real experience, I can show them."[28] In describing his work with director Roman Polanski on *Chinatown* (1974), Nicholson says that the director "pushes us farther than we are conscious of being able to go; he forces us down into the subconscious—in order to see if there's something better there."[29] Jodie Foster works from instinct, doing what she feels is right for the character.[30] To create The Tramp, Charlie Chaplin started with the character's costume: "I had no idea of the character. But the moment I was dressed, the clothes and the make-up made me feel the person he was."[31] Alec Guinness said that he was never happy with his preparation until he knew how the character walked; Laurence Olivier believed that he would not be any good as a character unless he "loved" him;[32] and Morgan Freeman says that some of his preparation depends on the clothes he is to wear.[33]

If you are familiar with Alec Guinness only through his role as Obi-Wan Kenobi in the first three Star Wars

25. Sidney Lumet, *Making Movies* (New York: Knopf, 1995), pp. 59–60.

26. Bette Davis, "The Actress Plays Her Part," in *Playing to the Camera: Film Actors Discuss Their Craft*, ed. Bert Cardullo, Harry Geduld, Ronald Gottesman, and Leigh Woods (New Haven, CT: Yale University Press, 1998), pp. 177–185, quotation on p. 179.

27. Jack Lemmon, "Conversation with the Actor," ibid., pp. 267–275, quotation on p. 267.

28. Liv Ullmann, "Conversation with the Actress," ibid., pp. 157–165, quotation on p. 160.

29. See the entry on Jack Nicholson in Tomlinson, ed., *Actors on Acting for the Screen*, pp. 404–407, quotation on p. 405.

30. See the entry on Jodie Foster, ibid., pp. 196–197.

31. Charles Chaplin, *My Autobiography* (New York: Simon & Schuster, 1964), p. 260.

32. See the entry on Alec Guinness in Tomlinson, ed., *Actors on Acting for the Screen*, pp. 232–233; and Laurence Olivier, *Confessions of an Actor: An Autobiography* (1982; repr., New York: Penguin, 1984), pp. 136–137.

33. From an interview with James Lipton, *James Lipton Takes on Three* on Disc 2 of "Special Features" in the widescreen DVD release of *Million Dollar Baby* (2004).

1

2

films, looking at a range of his movies will provide you with a master class in the art and craft of acting. A short list would include *Kind Hearts and Coronets* (1949), *The Bridge on the River Kwai* (1957), *Our Man in Havana* (1959), *Tunes of Glory* (1960), *Lawrence of Arabia* (1962; perhaps his finest performance), and *Hitler: The Last Ten Days* (1973). You might also study his performance as George Smiley in the TV series *Tinker Tailor Soldier Spy* and then compare and contrast it with Gary Oldman's in the movie version (2011). Guinness never defined acting per se; he didn't need to, for his acting says it all.

Olivier, one of the greatest stage and screen actors of the twentieth century, defined acting in various ways, including as "convincing lying."[34] Although Olivier stands out for the extraordinary range of the roles he undertook on both stage and screen and for his meticulous preparation in creating them, this remark suggests that he had little patience with theories of acting. Indeed, when asked how he created his film performance as the king in *Henry V* (1944; directed by Olivier), he replied simply, "I

Actors with many faces

Alec Guinness seems to have no predictable persona, playing characters as diverse as Obi-Wan Kenobi and Adolf Hitler. He is also famous for playing characters who first appear to be meek and indecisive, but surprisingly turn out to have inner strength. As George Smiley in *Tinker Tailor Soldier Spy* (1979) [1], a British master spy who has all the answers, Guinness is calm and professorial with horn-rimmed glasses and a scarf to protect against a chill. He fools his smug colleagues into believing he doesn't have a clue, but in the end, he proves that appearances can indeed be misleading. Gary Oldman is another British actor noted for the wide range of different characters he plays, including assassin Lee Harvey Oswald; Count Dracula; Ludwig von Beethoven; Harry Potter's guardian, Sirius Black; Winston Churchill; and George Smiley, in the recent movie version of *Tinker Tailor Soldier Spy* (2011) [2], where he's as cool and cerebral as Guinness, but with a characterization all his own.

Laurence Olivier's *Henry V*

Laurence Olivier in the first screen adaptation of *Henry V* (1944); this very popular film, produced during a troubled time (World War II), was uniformly praised for the quality of its acting. The many previous screen adaptations of Shakespeare's plays had been mainly faithful records of stage productions, but Olivier's film, his first as a director, benefited from his understanding of cinema's potential as a narrative art, his extensive acting experience, his deep knowledge of Shakespeare's language, and his sharp instincts about the national moods in Great Britain and the United States. *Henry V* received an Oscar nomination for Best Picture, and Olivier received a nomination for Best Actor as well as an Oscar for his outstanding achievement as actor, producer, and director in bringing *Henry V* to the screen.

34. Olivier, *Confessions of an Actor*, p. 20.

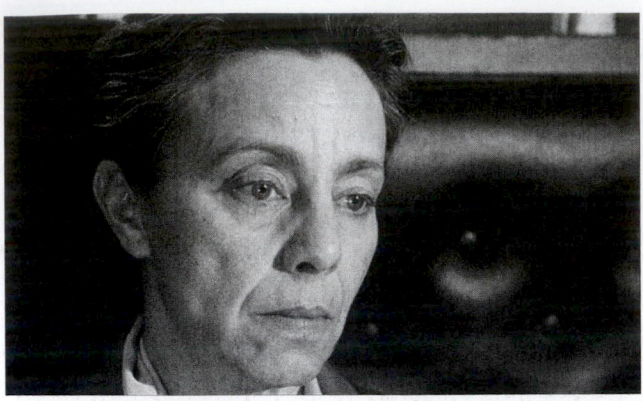

How to read a face

In directing *The Man from London*, Béla Tarr uses many of the film noir traits: black-and-white imagery, slow-motion cinematography, long takes, and haunting close-ups. This image marks the film's ending, where Tarr holds the expression of Mrs. Brown (Ági Szirtes)—a woman who just learned of her husband's murder—for a mesmerizing length of time. What is she feeling? Despair, grief, disbelief are all possibilities. But her face holds many secrets, and we bring our own experiences watching the entire film to bear on our interpretations.

transform it into what we hope or want to see: sadness, courage, inspiration, whatever we choose. Mamoulian's influence can be seen in *The Man from London* (2007; codirectors Béla Tarr and Ágnes Hranitzky), where the long final close-up, in high-contrast black-and-white, is of a grieving widow's expressionless face. As in the shot of Garbo, this is a face that says everything and nothing. It brings the full force of a single shot to make us think and interpret what we see.

Naturalistic and Nonnaturalistic Styles

We have all seen at least one movie in which a character, perhaps a whole cast of characters, is like no one we have ever met or ever *could* meet. Either because the world they inhabit functions according to rules that don't apply in our world or because their behaviors are extreme, such characters aren't realistic in any colloquial sense of the word. But if the actors perform skillfully, we are likely to accept the characters as believable within the context of the story.

Actors who strive for appropriate, expressive, coherent, and unified characterizations can render their performances naturalistically as well as nonnaturalistically. Screen acting appears naturalistic when actors re-create recognizable or plausible human behavior for the camera. The actors not only look like the characters should (in their costume, makeup, and hairstyle) but also think, speak, and move the way people would offscreen. By contrast, nonnaturalistic performances seem excessive, exaggerated, even overacted; they may employ strange or outlandish costumes, makeup, or hairstyles; they might aim for effects beyond the normal range of human experience; and they often intend to distance or estrange audiences from characters. Frequently, they are found in horror, fantasy, and action films.

What Konstantin Stanislavsky was to naturalistic acting, German playwright Bertolt Brecht was to nonnaturalistic performance. Brecht allied his theatrical ideas with Marxist political principles to create a nonnaturalistic theater. Whereas Stanislavsky strove for realism, Brecht believed that audience members should not think they're watching something actually happening before them. Instead, he wanted every aspect of a the-

don't know—I'm England, that's all."[35] Olivier had made this film to bolster British morale during the last days of World War II, and thus he wanted *Henry V* to embody traditional British values.

The great silent-era director F. W. Murnau emphasized intellect and counseled actors to restrain their feelings, to *think* rather than *act*. He believed actors to be capable of conveying the intensity of their thoughts so that audiences would understand. Director Rouben Mamoulian gave Greta Garbo much the same advice when she played the leading role in his *Queen Christina* (1933). The film ends with the powerful and passionate Swedish queen sailing to Spain with the body of her lover, a Spanish nobleman killed in a duel. In preparing for the final close-up, in which the queen stares out to sea, Garbo asked Mamoulian, "What should I be thinking of? What should I be doing?" His reply: "Have you heard of *tabula rasa*? I want your face to be a blank sheet of paper. I want the writing to be done by every member of the audience. I'd like it if you could avoid even blinking your eyes, so that you're nothing but a beautiful mask."[36] Is she remembering the past? Imagining the future? With the camera serving as an apparently neutral mediator between actress and audience, Garbo's blank face asks us to

35. Laurence Olivier, qtd. in Donald Spoto, *Laurence Olivier: A Biography* (New York: HarperCollins, 1992), pp. 111–112.

36. Rouben Mamoulian, qtd. in Tom Milne, *Rouben Mamoulian* (Bloomington: Indiana University Press, 1969), p. 74.

atrical production to limit the audience's identification with characters and events, thereby creating a psychological distance (called the **alienation effect** or **distancing effect**) between them and the stage. The intent of this approach is to remind the audience of the artificiality of the theatrical performance.

Overall, this theory has had little influence on mainstream filmmaking. After all, unlike theater, cinema can change—as often as it wants—the relationship between spectators and the screen, alternately alienating them from or plunging them into the action. However, we do see this approach when actors step out of character, face the camera, and directly address the audience (a maneuver, more common in theater than cinema, known as *breaking the fourth wall*—the imaginary, invisible wall that separates the audience from the stage). Although the distancing effect can destroy a movie if used inappropriately, breaking the fourth wall works effectively when audience members are experiencing things like the character does *and* the character has the self-confidence to exploit that empathy.

In the late 1920s in Berlin, Brecht discovered Peter Lorre, who later became one of the most distinctively stylized actors on the American screen. They worked closely together on several stage productions at the same time that Lorre was preparing the lead role of Hans Beckert, a child murderer, in Fritz Lang's *M* (1931). Lorre's magnificent performance—particularly in the final scene, which is one of the most emotional in movie history—reflects the influence of Brecht's theories and directing. Lorre creates a duality—Beckert and the actor detached from the character who comments on his actions—and while it is not pure direct address (he is addressing a "jury" in a kangaroo court), we are absolutely riveted by the power and strangeness of Lorre's conception of the role.

Tom Edison (Paul Bettany) frequently addresses his idealistic views directly to the viewer in Lars von Trier's *Dogville* (2003), which in overall style owes much to Bertolt Brecht's influence. In Max Ophüls's *Lola Montès* (1955), the Circus Master (Peter Ustinov) addresses the circus audience, of which, we understand, we are members. For comic effect, *Deadpool* (Ryan Reynolds) breaks the fourth wall in Tim Miller's 2016 film of the same name. Various characters speak directly to the viewer in Spike Lee's *Do the Right Thing* (1989). There is a much more solid tradition of direct address in the European theatrical cinema of such directors as Jean-Luc Godard,

1

2

Naturalistic versus nonnaturalistic performances

Naturalistic and nonnaturalistic performances sometimes overlap, but these categories help us relate actors' contributions to a filmmaker's overall vision. In *Knocked Up* (2007), Seth Rogen's naturalistic performance as a reformed slacker becomes part of director Judd Apatow's clear-eyed depiction of the consequences of unprotected sex. Here [1], Rogen tells his pregnant girlfriend, who has decided to keep their baby, that he's ready to do whatever it takes to support her. He then congratulates himself by saying "awesome" in recognition of his newfound maturity. Johnny Depp's nonnaturalistic performance as the title character in *Edward Scissorhands* (1990) [2] enables director Tim Burton to draw us into the exaggerated, downright weird world of this story. Burton's film is about fantasy, the way things might be in that world. Rogen's and Depp's performances differ widely, but they suit their respective movies. Imagine how out of place either character would be in the other's world!

Chantal Akerman, Eric Rohmer, Ingmar Bergman, and Michael Haneke, among others.

In Buddy Giovinazzo's *No Way Home* (1996), Tim Roth gives a naturalistic performance as Joey, a slow but principled young man who is just out of prison. He has taken the rap for an assault he did not commit and returns to Staten Island to find that the people who framed him and circumstances in the community are just as rotten as they were when he left. Determined not to associate with his low-life brother and former friends or return to a life of crime, he boards a bus and heads for undiscovered country. In Boaz Yakin's *Fresh* (1994), Sean Nelson naturalistically plays the title character—a young, black Brooklynite working as a courier for a dope dealer between going to school and looking out for his older sister. In Tim Burton's *Edward Scissorhands* (1990), Johnny Depp gives a nonnaturalistic performance as the title character, a kind of Frankenstein's monster—scary, but benevolent—created by a mad inventor who died before his work was finished. Edward lives in a deteriorating Gothic castle on a mountaintop that overlooks a nightmarishly pastel suburb, to which he eventually moves. The decor and costumes identify him immediately as a metaphor for the ultimate outsider. But the challenge to Depp as an actor is not only to acknowledge just how different he appears to others ("hands," scars, makeup, hairstyle), which he does in a very self-conscious and often comic manner (e.g., using his hands to shred cabbage for cole slaw). He also has to humanize this character so that he can be accepted as a member of the community.

Improvisational Acting

Improvisation can mean extemporizing—delivering lines based only loosely on the written script or without the preparation that comes with studying a script before rehearsing it. It can also mean playing through a moment, making up lines to keep scenes going when actors forget their written lines, stumble on lines, or have some other mishap. Of these two senses, the former is most important in movie acting, particularly in the poststudio world; the latter is an example of professional grace under pressure.

Improvisation can be seen as an extension of Stanislavsky's emphasis that the actor striving for a naturalistic performance should avoid any mannerisms that call attention to technique. Occupying a place somewhere between his call for actors to bring their own experiences to roles and Brecht's call for actors to distance themselves from roles, improvisation often involves collaboration between actors and directors in creating stories, characters, and dialogue, which may then be incorporated into scripts. According to film scholar Virginia Wright Wexman, what improvisers

> seem to be striving for is the sense of discovery that comes from the unexpected and unpredictable in human behavior. If we think of art as a means of giving form to life, improvisation can be looked at as one way of adding to our sense of the liveliness of art, a means of avoiding the sterility that results from rote recitations of abstract conventional forms.[37]

For years, improvisation has played a major part in actors' training. But it was anathema in the studio system, where practically everything was preprogrammed, and it remains comparatively rare in narrative moviemaking. Actors commonly confer with directors about altering or omitting written lines, but this form of improvisation is so limited in scope that we can better understand it as the sort of fertile suggestion making that is intrinsic to collaboration. Although certain directors encourage actors not only to discover the characters within themselves but also to imagine what those characters might say (and how they might act) in any given situation, James Naremore, an authority on film acting, explains that even great actors, when they improvise, "tend to lapse into monologue, playing from relatively static, frontal positions with a second actor nearby who nods or makes short interjections."[38]

Among the director-actor collaborations that have made improvisation work effectively are Bernardo Bertolucci and Marlon Brando (*Last Tango in Paris*, 1972); Robert Altman and a large company of actors (*Nashville*, 1975; *Short Cuts*, 1993; *Gosford Park*, 2001); Mike Leigh and various actors (*Another Year*, 2010); and John Cassavetes and Gena Rowlands (*Faces*, 1968; *A Woman under the Influence*, 1974; *Gloria*, 1980).

The Cassavetes-Rowlands collaboration is particularly important and impressive, not only for what it accomplished but also for the respect it received as an experimental approach within the largely conventional film industry. "John's theory," Rowlands explains,

---

37. Virginia Wright Wexman, "The Rhetoric of Cinematic Improvisation," *Cinema Journal* 20, no. 1 (Fall 1980): 29. See also Maurice Yacowar, "An Aesthetic Defense of the Star System in Films," *Quarterly Review of Film Studies* 4, no. 1 (Winter 1979): 48–50.

38. James Naremore, *Acting in the Cinema* (Berkeley: University of California Press, 1988), p. 45.

Improvisation

"You talkin' to me?...You talkin' to me?" Screenwriter Paul Schrader wrote no dialogue for the scene in Martin Scorsese's *Taxi Driver* (1976) in which Travis Bickle (Robert De Niro) rehearses his dreams of vigilantism before a mirror. Before filming, De Niro improvised the lines that now accompany this well-known moment in film history, a disturbing, darkly comic portrait of an unhinged mind talking to itself.

is that if there's something wrong, it's wrong in the writing. If you take actors who can act in other things and they get to a scene they've honestly tried to do, and if they still can't get it, then there's something wrong with the writing. Then you stop, you improvise, you talk about it. Then he'll go and rewrite it—it's not just straight improvisation. I'm asked a lot about this, and it's true, when I look at the films and I *see* that they look improvised in a lot of different places where I know they weren't.[39]

Improvised acting requires directors to play even more active roles than if they were working with prepared scripts, because they must elicit actors' ideas for characters and dialogue as well as orchestrate those contributions within overall cinematic visions. Ultimately, directors help form all contributions, including those of actors. Nearly all directors who employ improvisation have the actors work it out in rehearsal and then lock it down for filming, perhaps radically changing their plans for how such scenes will be shot. This is how, for example, Martin Scorsese and Robert De Niro worked out the

originally silent "You talkin' to me?" scene in *Taxi Driver* (1976).

Unless directors and actors have talked publicly about their work, we seldom know when and to what extent improvisation has been used in a film. Because we know that Cassavetes prepared his actors with precise scripts that they refined with extensive improvisational exercises, by studying the original script we can prepare to look for the improvisation, to judge its usefulness, and to determine whether improvised performances seem convincing or, ironically, less convincing than scripted ones.

Directors and Actors

Directors and actors have collaborated closely since the days when D. W. Griffith established the art of screen acting with Lillian Gish. Inevitably, such relationships depend on the individuals: what each brings to his or her work, what each can do alone, and what each needs from a collaborator. Such different approaches taken by different directors in working with actors are as necessary, common, and useful as the different approaches taken by different actors as they prepare for roles.

Some veterans of the studio system, such as William Wyler and George Cukor, are known as "actors' directors," meaning that the directors inspire such confidence they can actively shape actors' performances. Although Wyler may have enjoyed the trust of Bette Davis, Fredric March, Myrna Loy, Barbra Streisand, and other notable actors, the atmosphere on the set was considerably tenser when Laurence Olivier arrived in Hollywood for his first screen role, as Heathcliff in Wyler's *Wuthering Heights* (1939). Olivier had already earned a considerable reputation on the London stage and was frankly contemptuous of screen acting, which he thought serious actors did only for the money. Wyler, on the other hand, was one of Hollywood's great stylists, a perfectionist who drove actors crazy with his keen sense of acting and love of multiple takes. Everyone on the set perceived the tension between them. Wyler encouraged Olivier to be patient in responding to the challenges involved in acting for the camera, and eventually Olivier overcame his attitude of condescension to give one of his greatest film performances.

39. Gena Rowlands in Tomlinson, ed., *Actors on Acting for the Screen*, p. 482.

In developing his relationships with actors, director John Ford encouraged them to create their characters to serve the narrative. He preferred to work with the same actors over and over, and his working method never changed. John Wayne, who acted in many of Ford's films and has been described as the director's alter ego, said Ford gave direction "with his entire personality—his facial expressions, bending his eye. He didn't verbalize. He wasn't articulate, he couldn't really finish a sentence. . . . He'd give you a clue, just an opening. If you didn't produce what he wanted, he would pick you apart."[40] Newcomers faced a challenge in getting it right the first time. Similarly, Otto Preminger, the director of *Laura* (1944), was so predictably cruel to his actors that he was known as Otto the Ogre.

However rigid Ford's approach may at first seem, we find it in similarly fruitful collaborations between Rouben Mamoulian and Greta Garbo, Josef von Sternberg and Marlene Dietrich, John Huston and Humphrey Bogart, William Wyler and Bette Davis, François Truffaut and Jean-Pierre Léaud, Akira Kurosawa and Toshirô Mifune, Satyajit Ray and Soumitra Chatterjee, Martin Scorsese and Robert De Niro, Spike Lee and Denzel Washington, and Tim Burton and Johnny Depp. These directors know what they want, explain it clearly, select actors with whom they work well, and then collaborate with them to create movies that are characterized in part by the seamless line between directing and acting. Alexander Mackendrick, director of the classic *Sweet Smell of Success* (1957), was once asked how to get an actor to do what he needed him to do. "You don't," he said. "What you do is try to get him to *want* what you need" [emphasis added].

By contrast, the line that *can* exist between directing and acting is evident in the work of director Alfred Hitchcock, who tends to place mise-en-scène above narrative, and both mise-en-scène and narrative above acting. Hitchcock's movies were so carefully planned and rehearsed in advance that actors were expected to follow his direction closely, so that even those with limited talent (e.g., Tippi Hedren in *The Birds*, 1963; and Kim Novak in *Vertigo*, 1958) gave performances that satisfied the director.

On the other hand, Stanley Kubrick, who controlled his films as rigidly as Hitchcock, was more flexible. When directing *Barry Lyndon* (1975), a film in which fate drove the plot, Kubrick gave his principal actors, Ryan O'Neal and Marisa Berenson, almost nothing to say and then moved them about his sumptuous mise-en-scène like pawns on a chessboard. When working with a more open story, however, he encouraged actors to improvise in rehearsal or on the set. The results included such memorable moments as Peter Sellers's final monologue as Dr. Strangelove (and the film's last line, *"Mein Führer, I can walk!"*) and Jack Nicholson's manic "Heeeere's Johnny!" before the climax of *The Shining* (1980). Malcolm McDowell in *A Clockwork Orange* (1971) and Tom Cruise and Nicole Kidman in *Eyes Wide Shut* (1999) are also said to have worked out their performances in improvisations with the director. Perhaps the most extreme example is director Werner Herzog, who, in directing *Heart of Glass* (1976), hypnotized the entire cast each day on the set to create what he called "an atmosphere of hallucination, prophecy, visionary and collective madness."

How Filmmaking Affects Acting

Actors must understand how a film is made, because every aspect of the filmmaking process can affect performances and the actors' contributions to the creation of meaning. At the same time, audiences should understand what a movie actor goes through to deliver a performance that, to their eyes, seems effortless and spontaneous. Here are some of the challenges an actor faces.

With some exceptions, most production budgets and schedules do not have the funds or the time to give movie actors much in the way of rehearsal. Thus actors almost always perform a character's progression entirely out of sequence, and this out-of-continuity shooting can also force those who are being filmed in isolation to perform their parts as though they were interacting with other people. When these shots are edited together, the illusion of togetherness is there, but the actors must make it convincing. Actors must time their movements and precisely hit predetermined marks on the floor so that a moving

40. John Wayne, qtd. in Joseph McBride, *Searching for John Ford: A Life* (New York: St. Martin's Press, 2001), p. 299.

camera and a focus puller know where they will be at every moment; they must often direct their gaze and position their body and/or face in unnatural-feeling poses to allow for lighting, camera position, and composition. These postures usually appear natural on-screen but don't feel natural to the actors performing them on the set.

Movie actors must repeat the same action/line/emotion more than once, not just for multiple takes from a single setup but also for multiple setups. This means that they may perform the close-up of a particular scene an hour after they performed the same moment for a different camera position. Everything about their performance is fragmented, and thus they must struggle to stay in character. Finally, actors are sometimes required to work with acting and dialogue coaches, physical trainers, and stunt personnel. For all the reasons listed here, delivering a convincing screen performance is very challenging.

In the following chapters we will examine editing and sound and the ways they relate to acting and meaning. Here we'll look briefly at how acting is affected by framing, composition, lighting, and the types and lengths of shots.

Framing, Composition, Lighting, and the Long Take

Framing and composition can bring actors together in a shot or keep them apart. Such inclusion and exclusion create relationships between characters, and these in turn create meaning. The physical relation of the actors to each other and to the overall frame (height, width, and depth) can significantly affect how we see and interpret a shot.

The inciting moment of the plot of Orson Welles's *Citizen Kane* (1941) and one of the principal keys to understanding the movie—for many viewers, its most unforgettable moment—occurs when Charles Foster Kane's (Welles) mother, Mary Kane (Agnes Moorehead), signs the contract that determines her son's future. It consists of only six shots, two of which are long takes. Relying on design, lighting, cinematography, and acting, Welles creates a scene of almost perfect ambiguity.

In designing the scene, Welles puts the four principal characters involved in the incident in the same frame for the two long takes but, significantly, divides the space within this frame into exterior and interior spaces: a young Charles (Buddy Swan) is outside playing with the Rosebud sled in the snow [1], oblivious to how his life is being changed forever; meanwhile, Mary, her hus-

1

band Jim (Harry Shannon), and Walter Parks Thatcher (George Coulouris) are in Mrs. Kane's boardinghouse [2] for shots 1 through 3 (images [1] to [5]) and outside for shot 4 [6]. In shot 3 (images [3] to [5]), this division of the overall space into two separate physical and emotional components is dramatically emphasized after Mary signs the contract [4] and Jim walks to the background of the frame and shuts the window, symbolically shutting Charles out of his life and also cutting us off from the sound of his voice. Mary immediately walks to the same window and opens it [5], asserting her control over the boy by sharply calling "Charles!" before going out to explain the situation to him.

The two long takes carry the weight of the scene and thus require the adult actors to work closely together in

2

3

4

5

parts of shot 3 [4] and with the boy in parts of shot 4 [6]. They begin inside the house as a tightly framed ensemble confronting one another across a small table—their bodies composed and their faces lighted to draw attention to the gravity of the decision they are making—and continue outdoors, where these tensions break into the open as young Charles learns of his fate.

The lighting also helps create the meaning. Lamps remain unlit inside the house, where the atmosphere is as emotionally cold as the snowy landscape is physically cold. Outside, the light is flat and bright; inside, this same bright light, reflected from the snow, produces deep shadows. This effect appears most clearly after the opening of shot 3, when Mary Kane turns from the window [3] and walks from the background to the foreground. As she does, lighting divides her face, the dark and light halves emphasizing how torn she feels as a mother in sending Charles away.

To prepare for the long take, Welles drilled his actors to the point of perfection in rehearsals, giving them amazing things to do (such as requiring Moorehead to pace up and down the narrow room) and then letting this preparation pay off in moments of great theatrical vitality. Look closely, for example, at the performance of Agnes Moorehead, with whom Welles had worked in radio productions.[41] Moorehead knew exactly how to use the tempo, pitch, and rhythm of her voice to give unexpected depth to the familiar melodramatic type she plays here. In the carefully designed and controlled setting—the long room, dividing window, and snowy exterior—Mrs. Kane, whose makeup, hairstyle, and costume are those of a seemingly simple pioneer woman, reveals herself to be something quite different. She is both unforgettably humane as she opens the window and calls her son sharply to the destiny she has decreed and, given that her only business experience has been in running a boardinghouse, surprisingly shrewd in obviously having retained Thatcher to prepare the contract that seals this moment. In fact, this is one of the few scenes in the movie in which a female character totally dominates the action—not surprising, for it is a scene of maternal rejection.

As Mary Kane throws open the window, she cries out, "Charles!" in a strained, even shrill, voice that reveals

41. Welles reportedly called Agnes Moorehead "the best actor I've ever known"; qtd. in Simon Callow, *Orson Welles: The Road to Xanadu* (New York: Viking, 1995), p. 512.

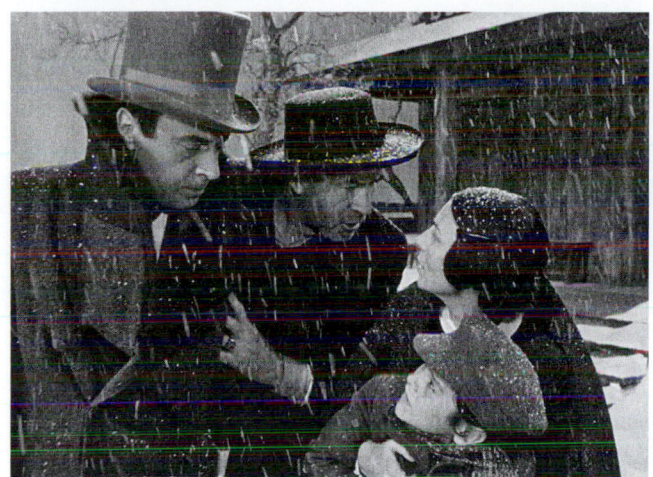

6

7

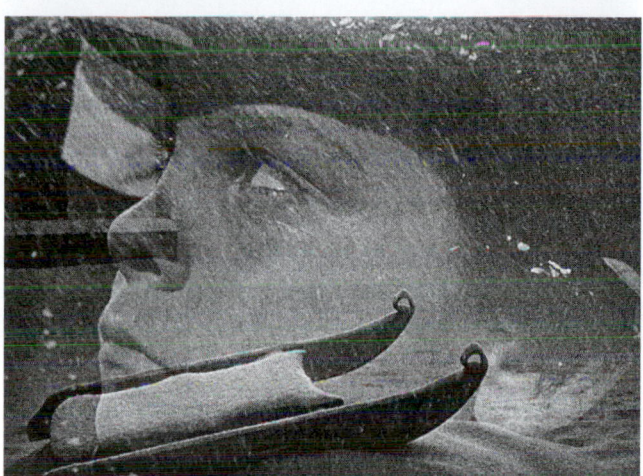

8

her anxiety about what she is doing; yet a moment later, sounding both tender and guilty, she tells Thatcher that she has had Charles's trunk packed for a week. Should we read the cold mask of her face [7] as the implacable look of a woman resigned to her decision or as a cover for maternal feelings? Does it reflect the doubt, indecision, and dread any person would feel in such a situation? Is it the face of sacrifice? Is it all of these possibilities and more? And how should we read Charles, who, in the span of a moment, goes from playful to wary to angry to antagonistic [8]?

Although the downtrodden Jim Kane protests his wife's actions, when Thatcher coolly informs him that he and his wife will receive $50,000 per year, he feebly gives in, saying, "Well, let's hope it's all for the best"— a remark that invariably, as it should, provokes laughter from viewers. And Thatcher, wearing a top hat and dressed in the formal clothes of a big-city banker, sends contradictory signals. He's precise in overseeing Mrs. Kane's signature, dismissive of Mr. Kane, fawning as he meets Charles, and angry when Charles knocks him to the ground. In encouraging this kind of richly nuanced acting and its resulting ambiguity, Welles shifts the challenge of interpretation to us.

As this scene shows, the long take, used in conjunction with deep-focus cinematography, gives directors and actors the opportunity to create scenes of unusual length as a well as a broader and deeper field of composition. In addition, the long take encourages ensemble acting that calls attention to acting, not editing between shots. Although we tend to think of actors and their performances as acts of individual creativity, we should keep in mind that one actor's performance often very much depends on another's. Indeed, it may rely on an ensemble, or group, of actors.[42]

Ensemble acting—which emphasizes the collaborative interaction of a group of actors, not the work of an

42. Further study of the long take should consider the work of the great Japanese director Kenji Mizoguchi and notably the Lake Biwa episode in *Ugetsu* (1953). Other notable uses of the technique can be seen in Jean-Pierre Melville's *Le Doulos* (1962), which includes a virtuoso 8-minute single shot; Werner Herzog's *Woyzeck* (1979); Lisandro Alonso's *Los Muertos* (2004), where most of the movie is divided into very long takes; and Pedro Costa's *Colossal Youth* (2006), where real time and very long takes are the norm. *Avalanche* (1937), a work by Japanese director Mikio Naruse, includes a sequence of very brief shots that are edited together so seamlessly that they provide the visual equivalent of a single long take.

***Boyhood*'s ensemble of actors celebrates a milestone**

Here, we see members of the cast celebrate the principal character's (Mason Evans Jr.) high school graduation. *Left to right*: Mason Evans Sr. (Ethan Hawke), Mason Evans Jr. (Ellar Coltrane), his mother Olivia (Patricia Arquette), Olivia's mother (Libby Villari), and his sister Samantha (Lorelei Linklater). It's a milestone for them all, young and old, near the conclusion of 12 years of intermittent filming during which they all grew up together and developed as characters.

individual actor—evolved as a further step in creating a verisimilar mise-en-scène for both the stage and the screen. Typically experienced in the theater, ensemble acting is used less in the movies because it requires the provision of rehearsal time that is usually denied to screen actors. However, when a movie director such as Richard Linklater (*Boyhood*, 2014) chooses to use long takes and has the time to rehearse the actors, the result is a group of actors working together continually in a single shot. Depending on the story and plot situation, this technique can intensify the emotional impact of a specific plot situation by having all of the involved characters on the screen at the same time.

As with so many other innovations, Orson Welles pioneered ensemble acting in *Citizen Kane* (1941) and *The Magnificent Ambersons* (1942), and its influence was quickly seen in the work of other directors, notably William Wyler in *The Little Foxes* (1941) and *The Best Years of Our Lives* (1946). A particularly challenging assignment for a group of actors was Richard Linklater's *Boyhood* (2014). The film focuses on newcomer Ellar

Coltrane, who's six when the movie begins and eighteen when it ends. Filmed in 4-day sections over that 12-year span, it shows what movies usually manipulate through editing: the passage of time. Coltrane's passage from a boy to a teenager is played out on the movie screen. It requires the actors, including Ethan Hawke and Patricia Arquette, to stay in character over that period and to be comfortable with showing their natural aging, unaltered by makeup or digital effects. It's a unique achievement in moviemaking, in a minor way comparable to Michael Apted's 7 Up series of documentaries (1964–2012), which followed the lives of a group of real British seven-year-olds and recorded their progress every seven years until they reached age fifty-six.

The Camera and the Close-Up

The camera creates a greater naturalism and intimacy between actors and audience than would ever be possible on the stage, and thus it serves as screen actors' most important collaborator. Nowhere is the camera's effect

Acting and the close-up

Carl Theodor Dreyer's *The Passion of Joan of Arc* (1928) vividly and unforgettably illustrates the power of the close-up. Most of this silent movie's running time is taken up with contrasting close-ups of Joan (played by Maria Falconetti, a French stage actress who never again appeared on film) and of her many interrogators during the course of her trial. As Joan is questioned, mocked, tortured, and finally burned at the stake, we witness an entire, deeply moving story in her face. Thus we respond to a single character's expressions as they are shaped by the drama and the camera.

on the actor's role more evident than in a close-up. The true close-up isolates an actor, concentrating on the face; it can be active (commenting on something just said or done, reminding us who is the focus of a scene) or passive (revealing an actor's beauty). Thus actors' most basic skill is understanding how to reveal themselves to the camera during the close-up.

All great movie actors understand, instinctively or from experience, what to do and not do with their faces when the camera moves in. They must temporarily forget their bodies' expressive possibilities, stand as close to the camera as they would to a person in real life, smoothly balance their voices because the microphone is so close, and focus on the communicative power of even the slightest facial gesture.

Close-ups can shift interpretation to the viewer, as in the 2-minute-long close-up of Anna (Nicole Kidman) in Jonathan Glazer's *Birth* (2004; see Chapter 6, p. 227), or they can leave little room for independent interpretation, as in Marlene Dietrich's opening scene as Amy Jolly in Josef von Sternberg's *Morocco* (1930; cin-

ematographer Lee Garmes). On the deck of a ship bound for Morocco, the mysterious and beautiful Amy drops her handbag. A sophisticated, older Frenchman— Monsieur La Bessiere (Adolphe Menjou)—kneels at her feet to retrieve her things and then offers to assist her in any way he can when she arrives at her destination. In a relatively quick close-up, Amy looks off into space and tells him she will not need any help. Design elements further distance us from the actress and the character: Dietrich wears a hat with a veil, and thus the shot is "veiled by the 'Rembrandt' light, by the fog, by the lens, and by the diaphanous fabric."[43] Although we do not yet know who Amy is, what she does, or why she's going to Morocco, we certainly understand La Bessiere's interest.

Close-ups can also reveal both the process of thinking and the thoughts at its end. In a close-up during the

Artistic collaboration and the close-up

In *Morocco* (1930), Marlene Dietrich's beautiful face is made to appear even more haunting and enigmatic by director Josef von Sternberg's mise-en-scène and Lee Garmes's black-and-white cinematography. Dietrich, too, instinctively understood the kind of lighting and camera placement that was right for her role and the narrative as well as for the glamorous image she cultivated in all her movies. In this medium close-up, she stands on the deck of a ship at night and appears distant, almost otherworldly, as she is bathed in soft, misty "Rembrandt lighting." One half of her face is bright, part of the other half is in shadow. Her face is further framed and softened by her hat and veil and by shooting her against a background that is out of focus. In all likelihood, Garmes also placed thin gauze fabric over the lens to further soften the image. This is the first appearance of Dietrich's character in the movie, so we know little about her but can already discern that she is not only alluring but mysterious. But one thing we know for sure: the Dietrich face, as it appeared on the screen, was the conscious creation of the actress, director, and cinematographer.

43. Naremore, *Acting in the Cinema*, p. 141.

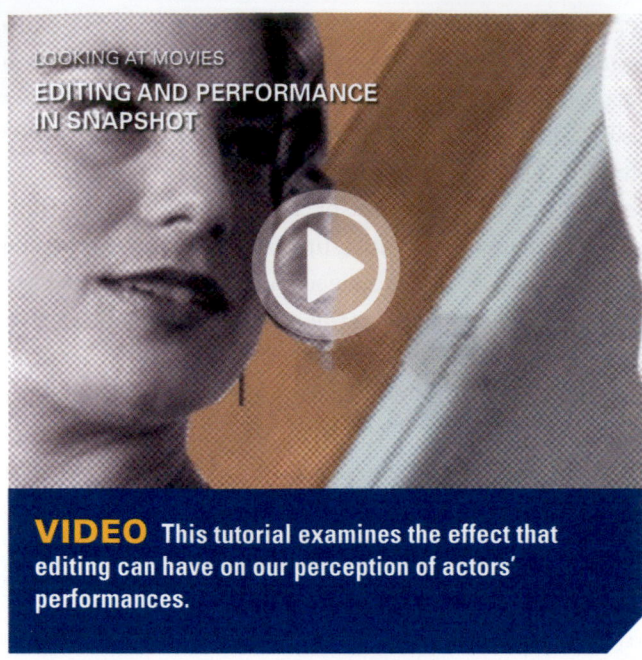

LOOKING AT MOVIES
EDITING AND PERFORMANCE
IN SNAPSHOT

VIDEO This tutorial examines the effect that editing can have on our perception of actors' performances.

climactic moment of John Ford's *The Searchers* (1956), Ethan Edwards (John Wayne) transforms from a hateful to a loving man as he halts his premeditated attempt to murder his niece, Debbie (Natalie Wood), and instead lifts her to the safety of his arms. The shot gives us no time to analyze why he has changed his mind—we see only the results of that change.

In a bar scene in Elia Kazan's *On the Waterfront* (1954), Terry Malloy (Marlon Brando), playing the tough guy, tells Edie Doyle (Eva Marie Saint) his philosophy: "Do it to him before he does it to you." Up to this point, he has remained aloof after witnessing the mob's murder of Edie's brother, an attitude he continues to display until Edie, who is trying to do something about the corruption on the waterfront, asks for his help. Stopped in his tracks, Terry sits down, and a series of close-ups reveals the shakiness of his unfeeling posture. In a soft, caring, but slightly nervous voice (in this bar setting, surrounded by other tough guys, he's a little self-conscious of being tender with a woman), he tells her, "I'd like ta help" and so reveals to her, the camera, and the audience a more sensitive man under the macho mannerisms.

Acting and Editing

Because a screen actor's performance is fragmented, the editor has considerable power in shaping it. We've already emphasized that the actor is responsible for maintaining the emotional continuity of a performance, but even the most consistent actor delivers slightly different performances on each take. Editors can patch up mistakes by selecting, arranging, or juxtaposing shots to cover these differences. They control the duration of an actor's appearance on the screen and how that time is used. When aspects of an actor's performance that originally were deemed acceptable appear in the editing stage to interrupt the flow of the narrative, the development of the character, or the tone of the movie, the editor, in consultation with the director, can dispense with it completely by leaving that footage on the cutting-room floor. In short, the editor has the power to mold a performance with more control than most directors or even the actors themselves.

Looking at Acting

Given all the elements and aspects in our discussion of an actor's performance, how do we focus our attention on analyzing acting? Before looking at some recognized criteria, let's discuss how we can bring our own experiences to the task. An actor's performance on the screen goes beyond what we see and hear; it also includes many intangibles and subtleties. That alone makes the analysis of acting much more challenging. Breaking down and cataloging other elements of cinematic language—whether narrative, mise-en-scène, production design, or cinematography—and using that information to analyze their usefulness and effectiveness is much easier than analyzing acting. Yet acting (perhaps second only to narrative) is the component most people use to assess movies. We feel an effective, natural, moving performance in a more direct way than we respond to other cinematic aspects of most films, and we feel both qualified and compelled to judge films by their performances.

What accounts for this sense of entitlement? Why are we so fixated on actors? Why do we so frequently judge the quality of the movie by the (often intangible) quality of the actors' performances? There are several reasons. First, although cinematic language has a considerable effect on the way we look at a movie, we also identify with characters and, of course, with the actors who inhabit those characters. Second, we identify with characters who pursue a goal. We get involved with this pursuit, which is driven by and embodied by the actors who inhabit the characters, because a movie narrative is

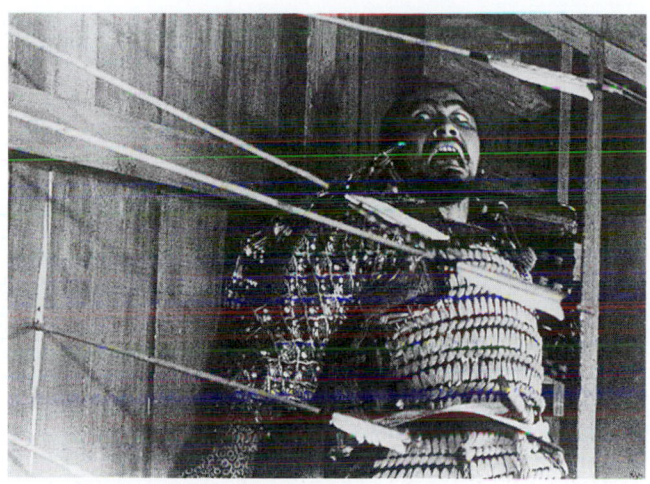

Assessing acting performances

[1] Toshirô Mifune in the death scene of Lord Washizu in Akira Kurosawa's *Throne of Blood* (1957) and [2] Holly Hunter in Jane Campion's *The Piano* (1993), a performance for which she won the Oscar for Best Actress. To analyze an actor's performance, we need to consider its context—the particular movie in which it appears. Kurosawa's film draws on a specific genre—the *jidai-geki*, or historical drama—that is traditionally full of action; Campion's film draws on history but focuses more on psychology than on action. Thus Mifune uses ritualized, nonnaturalistic facial expressions and body language; and Hunter, who speaks only in voice-over, appears more naturalistic, inner directed, subdued.

constructed to exploit what most involves us. We don't even have to like the characters as long as we believe them. Third, we identify with characters because of our own behavior as people. Although cinematic language draws from our instinctive responses to everyday visual and audio information, we don't consciously notice and process it as much as we do human behavior. We are people watchers by nature, necessity, and desire. We are constantly analyzing behavior. When you say hello to a friend or ask a professor a question or order a cup of coffee from a waiter, you are noticing and processing and reacting to human behavior. Is the friend happy? Does the professor think you're stupid? Is the waiter paying attention?

Finally, our identification with characters and the actors who play them has something to do with our own personality. We too behave in a way that is consistent with our general character or state of mind, and beyond that, we are also engaged in role-playing. You present yourself differently, depending on where you are, what's going on, and who you're with. You behave differently with a police officer than you do with your mother or your professor, differently with a new friend than with an old one.

Now that we've looked at some of the reasons for our reactions to actors and acting, how do we analyze their performances? What are the criteria of a good performance? In their everyday moviegoing, people tend to appreciate acting subjectively. They like an actor's performance when he or she looks, speaks, and moves in ways that confirm their expectations for the character (or type of character). Conversely, they dislike a performance that baffles those expectations.

This approach, though understandable, can also be limiting. How many of us have sufficient life experiences to fully comprehend the range of characters that appear on the screen? What background do we bring to an analysis of a performance such as that of Humphrey Bogart as a cold-blooded private eye in John Huston's *The Maltese Falcon*, or Taraji P. Henson as an overlooked African American mathematician in *Hidden Figures* (2016; director Theodore Melfi), or Daniel Day-Lewis as a possessive 1950s fashion designer in Paul Thomas Anderson's *Phantom Thread* (2017)?

Movie acting may be, as legendary actor Laurence Olivier once said, the "art of persuasion."[44] Yet it is also a formal cinematic element, one as complex as design or cinematography. To get a sense of how movie acting works on its own and ultimately in relation to the other formal elements, we need to establish a set of criteria more substantial than our subjective feelings and reactions.

44. Olivier, *Confessions of an Actor*, p. 51.

Evil, pure evil

In *12 Years a Slave*, Michael Fassbender plays Edwin Epps, as evil a character that ever appeared on-screen. He's a racist, a liar, an alcoholic, and a sadist, traits that manifest themselves in his actions rather than in his appearance. He may not "look" evil, but his treatment of his slaves is almost unbearable to watch. Movies like these should convince us not to confuse the actor with the part.

Because every actor, character, and performance in a movie is different, it is impossible to devise standards that would apply equally well to all of them. Furthermore, different actors, working with different directors, often take very different approaches to the same material, as you can judge for yourself by comparing the many remakes in movie history. Within the world of a particular story, your goal should be to determine the quality of the actor's achievement in creating the character and how that performance helps tell the story. Thus you should discuss an actor's specific performance in a specific film, for example, by discussing how Michael Fassbender's acting in Steve McQueen's *12 Years a Slave* (2013) serves to create the character of Edwin Epps, the alcoholic, sadist plantation owner. In your analysis, tell the story of that film without being influenced by expectations possibly raised by your having seen Fassbender in other movies, including those directed by McQueen: *Hunger* (2008) and *Shame* (2011).

In analyzing any actor's performance, you might consider the following criteria:

❯ *Appropriateness.* Does the actor look and act naturally like the character he or she portrays, as expressed in physical appearance, facial expression, speech, movement, and gesture? If the performance is nonnaturalistic, does the actor look, walk, and talk the way that character might or should?

Paradoxically, we expect an actor to behave as if he or she were *not* acting but were simply living the illusion of a character we can accept within the context of the movie's narrative. Such appropriateness in acting is also called *transparency*, meaning that the character is so clearly recognizable—in speech, movement, and gesture—for what he or she is supposed to be that the actor becomes, in a sense, invisible. Most actors agree that the more successfully they create characters, the more we will see those characters and not them.

❯ *Inherent thoughtfulness or emotionality.* Does the actor convey the character's thought process or feelings behind the character's actions or reactions? In addition to a credible appearance, does the character have a credible inner life?

An actor can find the motivations behind a character's actions and reactions at any time before or during a movie's production. They may come to light in the script (as well as in any source on which it is based, such as a novel or play), in discussions with the director or with other cast members, and in spontaneous elements of inspiration and improvisation that the actor discovers while the camera is rolling. No matter which of these aspects or combinations of them reveal the character's motivation, we expect to see the actor reflect them within the character's consciousness or as part of the illusion-making process by which the character appears. To put it another way, the characters must seem vulnerable to forces in the narrative. They must be able to think about them and, if necessary, change their mind or feelings about them.

❯ *Expressive coherence.* Has the actor used these first two qualities (appropriateness and inherent thoughtfulness/emotionality) to create a characterization that holds together?

Whatever behavior an actor uses to convey character, it must be intrinsic, not extraneous to the character, "maintaining not only a coherence of manner, but also a fit between setting, costume, and behavior."[45] When an actor achieves such a fit, he or she is playing in character. Maintaining expressive

45. Naremore, *Acting in the Cinema*, p. 69.

My Week with Marilyn is a week to remember

Eddie Redmayne plays Colin Clark, a young film school graduate who lands a job as an assistant to Marilyn Monroe (Michelle Williams), who is making a movie in London. Williams gives an outstanding performance as the screen goddess, in all her fragility and craziness, as well as vulnerability in falling for Eddie, a naive, lovesick puppy. The week they spend together, much of it alone, may be something many men dream about, but it's based on a true story. When Monroe's movie work is finished, she returns to Hollywood and her new husband, Arthur Miller. Although she leaves Colin with a broken heart, Michelle Williams's versatile portrayal of Monroe provides some level of understanding.

coherence enables the actor to create a complex characterization and performance, to express thoughts and reveal emotions of a recognizable individual without veering off into mere quirks or distracting details.

❯ *Wholeness and unity.* Despite the challenges inherent in most film productions, has the actor maintained the illusion of a seamless character, even if that character is purposely riddled with contradictions?

Whereas expressive coherence relies on the logic inherent in an actor's performance, wholeness and unity are achieved through the actor's ability to achieve aesthetic consistency while working with the director, crew, and other cast members; enduring multiple takes; and projecting to the camera rather than to an audience. However, wholeness and unity need not mean uniformity. The point is this: as audience members we want to feel we're in good hands; when we're confused or asked to make sense of seemingly incoherent elements, we want to know that the apparent incoherence happened intentionally, for an aesthetic reason, as part of the filmmakers' overall

vision. For example, if a given character suddenly breaks down or reveals himself to be pretending to be somebody he isn't, the actor must sufficiently prepare for this change in the preceding scenes, however he chooses, so that we can accept it.

Michelle Williams

To begin applying these criteria, we'll take a look at the work of Michelle Williams in Derek Cianfrance's *Blue Valentine* (2010) for which she earned an Oscar nomination for Best Actress. She is part of a long tradition of actors who play strong female characters in a man's world. A short list would include Joan Crawford, Bette Davis, Faye Dunaway, Jane Fonda, Jodie Foster, Lillian Gish, Diane Keaton, Frances McDormand, Ellen Page, Julia Roberts, Barbara Stanwyck, and Uma Thurman. Many of them—including Crawford, Davis, and Stanwyck—worked primarily in the studio system. As discussed earlier in this chapter, these actors worked under contractual obligations that severely limited their opportunities.

Michelle Williams is one of a younger generation of actors—including Carey Mulligan, Jennifer Lawrence,

1

Cindy and Dean are married

Cindy and Dean's wedding takes place in the office of a justice of the peace. She wears a white lace dress and cries tears of joy as she looks up at Dean and repeats the vows. The couple has taken a great risk in getting married, but they are happy as they begin their life together. The director chose to shoot all scenes of the couple's past on film stock, and the bright light flooding the office fades the colors of her face and Dean's jacket (*right*), making the image look old, as was intended.

2

The marriage falls apart

Two incidents, among others, indicate that Cindy and Dean's marriage is falling apart. In [1], Cindy, upset when their pet dog is killed by a passing car, watches stoically as Dean buries the body in their yard. It's an omen of what's to come, just as Dean's attempt to rekindle their marriage in the "Future Room" of a motel backfires. Soon, looking haggard [2], Cindy has one last fight with Dean. She's determined not to give in to his pleas for another chance and, within minutes, he walks out of her life. The use of digital cinematography for these scenes gives them the real-life look of a documentary film.

Lupita Nyong'o, and Jessica Chastain—who are enriching the art of acting. They work in today's independent production system and are almost completely free to choose their movies, roles, and sometimes even their directors, costars, and other collaborators. They work as often as they want, taking time off to meet the challenges of acting on the stage, to enjoy lucrative promotional opportunities, usually for luxury goods and services, and to enjoy private life.

Williams was born in Montana and raised in California, where, after completing the ninth grade, she quit school to pursue an acting career. With her gamine-like features, she began her movie career with comedies—Andrew Fleming's *Dick* and Jamie Babbit's *But I'm a Cheerleader*, both 1999—before moving on to serious drama with Erik Skjoldbjærg's *Prozac Nation* (2001). Between 1999 and 2014, she'd completed more than thirty movies. She is best known for her portrayals of intelligent, determined women, including Emily in Thomas McCarthy's *The Station Agent* (2003); Alma in Ang Lee's *Brokeback Mountain* (2005), for which she earned an Oscar nomination for Best Supporting Actress; Wendy in Kelly Reichardt's *Wendy and Lucy* (2008); and Emily in Reichardt's *Meek's Cutoff* (2010). Her other movies include *Deception* (2008; director Marcel Langenegger),

Synecdoche, New York (2008; director Charlie Kaufman), and *Shutter Island* (2010; director Martin Scorsese). After *Brokeback Mountain*, another turning point in Williams's career was her portrayal of Marilyn Monroe in Simon Curtis's *My Week with Marilyn* (2011), for which she garnered an Oscar nomination for Best Actress. More recently, she received her fourth Oscar nomination (for Best Supporting Actress) for her performance in Kenneth Lonergan's *Manchester by the Sea* (2016).

Blue Valentine is a story about a marriage that was off course from the beginning, a union of Cindy (Michelle

Williams), a talented, promising young woman, and Dean (Ryan Gosling), a romantic who is contented with only being her husband, not striving for more. His love for her is genuine, hers isn't, and it's clear from almost the beginning that she is not committed. It is basically a two-person story that requires two superb actors to handle the characters' development from needy teenagers to disillusioned parents. She's a pre-med student living at home and looking after her aging grandmother; he works for a moving company. He may be a high school dropout, but he doesn't lack intelligence, sensitivity, or a desire to be a good husband and father. But it doesn't help their situation that she's running away from her unhappy parents, that he hasn't seen his parents in some time, that their child was fathered by Cindy's high school boyfriend, or that she attempted to abort it before agreeing to start a family with Dean.

They move to rural Pennsylvania, where Cindy works as an aide in a doctor's office and Dean as a house painter, a job that he jokingly says allows him to starting drinking at eight in the morning. She soon becomes disillusioned with him and their life together. From the marriage to the ultimate breakup, their situation changes dramatically, and the movie charts those changes through frequent flashbacks that show her falling for his boyish charm and promise of a life together to the nasty fight that ends it all. Their happy memories of the time before they were married are contrasted to a climactic weekend spent in the "Future Room" of a theme motel, an arrangement that Dean hopes will rekindle their love. When it doesn't, he provokes an ugly argument at the doctor's office where she works; consequently, she is fired, and he walks off into the distance, with their young daughter begging him to come back, as the movie ends.

Such a story—so unlike *Stella Dallas* (1937) and so recognizable in our time—requires two actors who can truthfully convince us of the characters' range of intellect and emotions as they watch their marriage crumble. Williams and Gosling were so committed to bringing the story to the screen that they served as the film's executive producers. Thus they helped to formulate the process by which the movie would be shot. Indeed, this is an excellent example of how filmmaking affects acting, especially in a low-budget, independent movie such as *Blue Valentine*. The actors and director agreed that the film would be made in three stages. As we've already noted, the movie relies heavily on continual flashbacks that contrast the first part of this couple's relationship, which was happy, with the last part, which was not. So the first stage was to shoot those happy scenes, all together, with seldom more than one take for each. There were no rehearsals. And the director, Derek Cianfrance, chose to shoot on traditional film stock because it lends a romantic quality to the footage. The second and third stages were shot using digital cameras calibrated for a bright and clinical look, contrasting markedly from the film footage. The second stage began when the two principal actors—joined by Faith Wladyka, who plays Frankie, their daughter—spent a month "living" their parts in the house used for the actual shooting. (They simulated this marriage here only during the day, returning to their real-life homes at night.) In this unusual mode of working, they ripped apart the happy years, determining what Cindy and Dean would have been like in the subsequent years, and then improvised much of the dialogue for the next stage of shooting. The third stage was to shoot the marriage as it dissolves. Here, the director shot many takes. Intercutting both kinds of footage gives the movie a discernible texture that helps the viewer separate past from present. Also, to emphasize the status of the marriage, you'll notice that in the first part of the film, the cinematographer almost always uses two-shots with the couple together in the frame, and in the second part, he shoots them in separate frames.

Blue Valentine is the director's second feature film—Cianfrance's previous experience was mostly with television documentaries—and while he uses a unique method of creating the film, he also intuitively understands how to let Williams and Gosling work together to create their characters. They built on mutual trust and spent 8 hours a day living together in a fully functional house where Gosling and Williams, like Dean and Cindy, did nothing but bicker with each other. After a month, they were all ready to shoot "the present" and were so fully prepared in their parts that they didn't have to act. (Cianfrance also directed Gosling in *The Place Beyond the Pines* [2013], an ambitious, complex story about fathers and sons.)

In her role as Cindy in *Blue Valentine*, Williams uses her intelligence and insight to create a character who is determined to make the best of her life, but whose stoic acceptance of reality prevails until she can stand it no longer. The director takes this strong story, of which he is a co-screenwriter, and lets it run an emotional course that is clearly established by the spontaneous interaction of the two principal actors. Its measured pace builds slowly to the ultimate blowup. Of the two characters, many viewers will find Gosling to be the more sympathetic. He emphasizes Dean's loyalty, sense of humor, kind heart, and genuine but failed efforts to understand his wife's unhappiness. He makes it clear that Dean is incapable of evolving or changing. Like the cigarette that is perpetually dangling from his lower lip, he's predictable. But while Cindy is the more determined of the two to reverse her discontent, she does it at the cost of destroying Dean. It's a grim story, hard to watch in the rawness of its emotions and in its ambiguous ending. Shattered, Dean walks off; Cindy is now a single mother with no job and an uncertain future. But she has not been defeated.

Using those characteristics that we have just defined as the key to analyzing an actor's performance, we can see that Williams looks and acts naturally, as we would expect of the character that she defines. Cindy keeps a messy house and takes little notice of her appearance, but she is engaged in something more important: balancing her tender empathy for Dean with her strong resolve to change her life. At first, their sexual life together seems satisfactory, but she soon regards it mechanically and then with resentment. They're both caring parents, but Dean works harder at it than she does. She's initially and passively resentful of Dean's lack of ambition, and then, in despair, challenges him to be more than he is (or could be). Williams conveys the thought process and feelings behind Cindy's actions and reactions primarily through gesture and physical movement: you can feel her physical resentment for her husband when he tries to make love to her. And the dialogue, which was improvised, has the honest rawness to be convincing. The frequent flashbacks to happier times require the actors to break the unity of their performances to accommodate the changes that have occurred between them then and now. Because Dean doesn't change, Cindy most clearly registers these changes. We see them in her appearance, voice, and mannerisms. In high school she's a sweet, passive kid, foolishly in love with the wrong man. Williams finds great joy in Cindy's singing and dancing in the street with Dean and dressing up for their wedding. But in later life, there is little joy, and she makes Cindy into a hard, resentful, unforgiving woman. Shooting as they did, Williams (and Gosling) faced difficult challenges in maintaining expressive coherence. Ultimately, she creates a characterization that has the wholeness of its contradictory parts.

Finally, there's a truthfulness that comes with her seemingly effortless performance, a naturalness that only a born actor can create. Williams not only looks and acts like such a character in physical appearance, facial expression, speech, movement, and gesture but also understands—and can make us understand—all kinds of feelings, ranging from vulnerability to strength.

ANALYZING ACTING

Our responses to actors' performances on-screen are perhaps our most automatic and intuitive responses to any formal aspect of film. Thus it is easy to forget that acting is as much a formal component of movies—something made—as mise-en-scène, cinematography, and editing are. And yet, acting is clearly something that must be planned and shaped in some manner; the very fact that films are shot out of continuity demands that actors approach their performances with a rigor and consciousness that mirrors the director's work on the film as a whole. This chapter has presented several different things to think about as you watch film acting in other movies. Using the criteria described in the previous section, remaining sensitive to the context of the performances, and keeping the following checklist in mind as you watch, you should be able to incorporate an intelligent analysis of acting into your discussion and writing about the movies you screen for class.

SCREENING CHECKLIST: ACTING

✔ Why was this actor, and not another, cast for the role?

✔ Does the actor's performance create a coherent, unified character? If so, how?

✔ Does the actor look the part? Is it necessary for the actor to look the part?

✔ Does the actor's performance convey the actions, thoughts, and internal complexities that we associate with natural or recognizable characters? Or does it exhibit the excessive approach we associate with nonnaturalistic characters?

✔ What elements are most distinctive in how the actor conveys the character's actions, thoughts, and internal complexities: body language, gestures, facial expressions, language?

✔ What special talents of imagination or intelligence has the actor brought to the role?

✔ How important is the filmmaking process in creating the character? Is the actor's performance overshadowed by the filmmaking process?

✔ Does the actor work well with fellow actors in this film? Do any of the other actors detract from the lead actor's performance?

✔ How, if at all, is the actor's conception of the character based on logic? How does the performance demonstrate expressive coherence?

✔ Does the actor's performance have the expressive power to make us forget that he or she is acting? If it does, how do you think the actor achieved this effect?

Questions for Review

1. How does movie acting today differ from movie acting in the 1930s through the 1960s?

2. Why is the relationship between the actor and the camera so important in making and looking at movies?

3. How did the coming of sound influence movie acting and actors?

4. What's the difference between movie stars and movie actors? Why do some critics emphasize that movie stars are a commodity created by the movie industry?

5. What factors influence the casting of actors in a movie?

6. How are naturalistic and nonnaturalistic movie acting different?

7. What is improvisational acting?

8. How do framing, composition, lighting, and the long take affect the acting in a movie?

9. Given the range of techniques available to movie actors, why do we say that their most basic skill is understanding how to reveal themselves to the camera during the close-up?

10. What do you regard as the most important criteria in analyzing acting?

>>>>>

CHAPTER

EDITING

8

LOOKING AT MOVIES
EDITING TECHNIQUES IN SNAPSHOT

VIDEO This tutorial provides an overview of the nature and importance of film editing, using a scene from Andrew Lund's short film *Snapshot* as an example.

What Is Editing?

Editing is the selection and arrangement of shots and sounds. Film editors determine what you see, how long you see it, and the order in which you see it. Because most editing is designed to go unnoticed, and because the sequential arrangement of shots can so effectively represent unfolding action as to seem effortless and inevitable, people often mistakenly think of editing as simply a selection and assembly process—removing the mistakes and stringing together the best takes. In fact, although directors and cinematographers design shots with editing in mind, very few movies predetermine the order and duration of every shot. Filmmakers recognize the expressive power of creative editing, and the form of most movies is meant to evolve throughout post-production. Directors count on editors to use concepts and techniques unique to their craft to mold moments, establish pace, shape performances, and structure—sometimes even reimagine—scenes and stories.

The basic building block of film editing is the shot, and its most fundamental tool is the **cut**. The cut can be thought of in several ways. The first is as part of the editor's process. When an editor selects a shot for use in a sequence or scene, she determines an *in-point* (the frame at which the shot will appear on-screen) and an *out-point* (the final frame we will see before that shot is replaced with another shot). Each time the editor executes an in-point or out-point, she is making a *cut*. The term dates back to the days when editors literally cut processed film stock with a device called a splicer (virtually all movies are now edited digitally on computers). The second way we can think of a cut pertains to watching a film. In that context, a cut is an instantaneous transition from one shot to another shot. The third common use of the term *cut* refers to any edited version of a sequence, scene, or movie. For example, a director may tell her editor: "Let's take a look at your latest cut of this scene."

To further understand the role of editing, let's examine the relationship between film production and post-production. The best directors and cinematographers plan and capture action in ways that facilitate the creative editing process. Many scenes are recorded using **coverage**—multiple angles and shot types covering the same action—in order to provide the editor the freedom to select the best possible viewpoint for each dramatic moment. Camera positions, framing, and blocking of different shots for a single scene are planned and executed

Documentary editing

Director Amanda Lipitz and editor Penelope Falk used a complex combination of different kinds of documentary footage to construct *Step*, an inspiring portrait of the members of a high school girls' step team as they strive to win a competition and improve their lives. Falk conveys the story and its themes of injustice and resilience by intercutting shots gleaned from more than 400 hours of footage, which included interviews with team members and their coach; b-roll chronicling rehearsals, performances, and the girls' struggles in school and at home in inner-city Baltimore; and archival footage depicting the racial tensions in their city after the death of a young man at the hands of the police.

in ways that ensure the editor will be able to preserve spatial and temporal continuity when constructing the scene. Multiple takes of the same shot may be captured to provide editors a variety of different approaches to performance or camera movement.

All of this raw material adds up. A commercial narrative feature film's shooting ratio (the proportion of footage shot to footage used in the completed movie) is commonly as high as 20:1, meaning that for every 1 minute you see on the screen, 20 minutes of footage has been discarded. Francis Ford Coppola's *Apocalypse Now* (1979), an epic film whose story was greatly shaped in postproduction, had a then almost unheard-of shooting ratio of 95:1. For contemporary stunt-heavy movies that require multiple cameras to capture complex action on an even greater scale, the ratio can be significantly higher, especially now that digital cinematography makes capturing numerous takes relatively cost-effective. The action extravaganza *Mad Max: Fury Road* (2015) used 480 hours of raw footage to construct its 120-minute

running time—a shooting ratio of 240:1. Documentary films can have similarly lopsided shooting ratios, but for different reasons. Unlike narrative films that are scripted and storyboarded in advance, many documentary films chronicle actual events and real-life subjects engaged in unrehearsed activity. A documentary filmmaker may enter a project with no clear idea of what story will ultimately emerge from her accumulated footage. For these films, the story is largely discovered during postproduction. Thus, every action, statement, and image that could possibly serve that story must be captured for potential use in the editing process.

The Film Editor

Like other primary members of the collaborative filmmaking team, the editor on a movie works closely with the director. During the preproduction phase, they may discuss storyboards and other previsualization materials.

1

2

Director and editor

Director John Ford [1] said that he edited the movie in the camera; in other words, he carefully visualized beforehand how the movie would look and then shot footage that could only be edited according to his plan. He minimized choices to retain creative control and prevent the studio bosses from meddling with his edit. But editors such as Dorothy Spencer [2] certainly helped to craft Ford's films in postproduction. She edited seventy-five Hollywood films, including two of Ford's masterpieces: *Stagecoach* (1939) and *My Darling Clementine* (1946). Her work on *Stagecoach* earned Spencer the first of her four Academy Award nominations for Best Film Editing.

For some scenes, the editor may even edit storyboards into an *animatic* (a video produced by sequencing storyboard images and adding sound), which is used to help envision how planned shots will work in the edit. During production, an editor may cut together rough versions of completed scenes to assist the director in determining if additional footage is needed.

Of course, most of the editor's contributions happen after shooting is completed. During postproduction, the director-editor relationship can take many forms. A select group of classical Hollywood directors, including John Ford and Alfred Hitchcock, so precisely planned each shot, juxtaposition, and sequence prior to shooting that they claimed their movies were essentially edited before the cameras even rolled. Contemporary director Steven Soderbergh does those old masters one better: he shoots and edits most of his own films under the pseudonyms of Peter Andrews and Mary Ann Bernard. At the other end of the spectrum, some directors rely on editors to craft their raw footage into a completed film with little to no oversight.

Of course, the typical director-editor relationship falls somewhere in between those two extremes. Before the edit begins, the director and editor discuss each scene's story, tone, and narrative function. After reviewing the footage provided, the editor communicates observations regarding performance, emphasis, important dramatic moments, event structure and order, and other potential expressive opportunities. The editor shares each draft version of every scene with the director so they can discuss what works and what doesn't. The editor takes notes and continues working on progressive versions, getting and applying feedback until the project is completed. Although the director has the final say on all decisions, editors are known to feel very strongly about particular cuts. Kevin Tent, the editor of *Election* (1999), reportedly believed so fervently in the unconventional rapid-fire sequence of thirty-seven consecutive close-ups he used in a key scene, he offered his skeptical director, Alexander Payne, the contents of his wallet to accept the idea. Convinced, Payne relented—and took the $75. It's a funny story, but it also demonstrates the serious role

An editor reshapes a movie

When director Woody Allen shot what would eventually become *Annie Hall* (1977), he intended the movie to be a self-deprecating satire of his alter-ego character, Alvy Singer. But, after exhaustively reviewing the film's extensive raw footage, editor Ralph Rosenblum discovered that the story of Alvy's relationship with the character of Annie Hall was far more compelling. As he explains in his memoir *When The Shooting Stops . . . The Cutting Begins*, Rosenblum sacrificed countless comically brilliant scenes (much to Allen's initial chagrin) and restructured many others to ultimately reveal the endearing romantic comedy that won Oscars for Best Picture, Best Director, and Best Actress.

the editor plays as an invested storyteller. Editors have the power to create moments and ideas not present in the original script. They often eliminate material that was planned and performed but reveals itself to be unnecessary. When captured footage proves inadequate (and reshoots are not an option), editors must innovate ways to convey necessary information using added sound, offscreen dialogue, and sometimes even by repurposed footage from other scenes.

In addition to the director, the editor works closely with a number of other collaborators during postproduction. Assistant editors function as media managers: importing, labeling, organizing, and archiving terabytes of digital video and sound files. Coeditors help draft scenes and sequences. The postproduction supervisor shepherds the project through picture editing, and the concurrent and subsequent steps required before the final digital export: scoring, sound design, sound mixing, visual effects, and color grading and correction. The many stages the edit goes through on its way to completion are collectively termed *workflow*.

Once the footage is prepared by the assistant editors, the editor begins work on a first-draft edit known as the *rough cut*. As part of this process, she may create multi-

ple versions of the same scene or sequence for purposes of comparison. Today's digital editing allows for this level of experimentation as opposed to the old physical process of splicing processed film stock, which restricted editors to only one edited assembly at a time. The creative freedom made possible by digital editing may account for the fact that contemporary movies run longer and contain more individual shots than do earlier films. A typical Hollywood movie made in the 1940s and 1950s runs approximately 110 minutes and is composed of about 1000 shots; today's movies typically run between 120 and 140 minutes and consist of 2000 to 3000 shots.

Over the course of postproduction, the edit moves through successive versions working toward the *fine cut*. Throughout this process, the editor edits the footage (or *picture*), as well as the dialogue, which is typically the only sound recorded on set during production. She makes notes regarding potential sounds or score to be added later and may even insert temporary "scratch" sound to help inform editing decisions that rely on or influence the use of sound. The rest of the sound is handled by the sound editor and the sound designer, who will coordinate with the editor and director as the cut progresses to determine, design, and record sounds and music for each scene. Ultimately, the editor submits the *picture lock* version, the final edit of the film footage. The picture and dialogue must be finalized before the rest of the creative team can add sounds, music, and visual effects, then color grade the images, and finally mix together the many separate tracks of accumulated sound.

Functions of Editing

Film editing has five primary functions:

1. Organize fragmented action and events.
2. Create meaning through juxtaposition.
3. Create spatial relationships between shots.
4. Create temporal relationships between shots.
5. Establish and control shot duration, pace, and rhythm.

None of these functions work autonomously. Like all things cinematic, fragmentation, juxtaposition, spatial and temporal connections, and pace and rhythm are all interconnected and interdependent.

Fragmentation

Editing relies on **fragmentation**, the breaking up of stories, scenes, events, and actions into multiple shots that provide a diversity of compositions and combinations with which to convey meaning. This aspect of film form draws upon a sort of cinematic gestalt: the idea that our minds can intuitively organize a continuous stream of incomplete pieces into a coherent whole.

Many scenes are shot using coverage, or **master scene technique**, meaning that the action is photographed multiple times with a variety of different shot types and angles so that the editor will be able to construct the scene using the particular viewpoint that is best suited for each dramatic moment—a practice known as **classical cutting**. Often, directors begin shooting a single scene with a long shot that covers the characters, setting, and action in one continuous take. With this **master shot** as a gen-

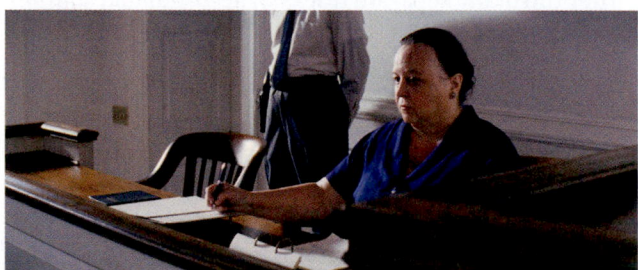

Master scene technique

For this courtroom scene in *Loving* (2016), director Jeff Nichols covered the action using medium close-ups of Richard Loving [1], Mildred Loving [2], and the judge [3]; medium shots of the judge [4], the court secretary [5], and the Lovings and their lawyer [6]; and a master shot [7]. Editor Julie Monroe cut between these seven shots, using most of them multiple times, to tell the scene's story: the Lovings being charged with illegal interracial marriage and ordered to leave the state of Virginia.

eral foundation, the scene's action is captured repeatedly using more specific framing, so that a single character's dialogue and blocking may be captured multiple times using a variety of shot types. In the editing room, the editor can begin the scene with the master shot, then cut closer as the story dictates: full shots during physical action, medium two-shots for interactions, close-ups for reactions, extreme close-ups for details, and so forth. The master shot can be integrated whenever setting or spatial relationships need to be reestablished. This conventional outside-in structure is not the editor's only option. For example, she may find it more effective to open the scene with a close-up detail and gradually (or suddenly) open up the framing to reveal the setting and situation. Conversations between characters are often captured and edited using the **shot/reverse shot** method. The entire interaction is filmed with the camera first framed on one character (the camera usually positioned just behind the second character's shoulder), then the camera is moved to a reverse position facing the second character from a corresponding position just behind the first character's shoulder. Even coverage as simple as a shot/reverse shot gives the editor a great deal of creative freedom. She can control the pace of the conversation and which character's face we're seeing at any particular moment in the exchange. We often need to see the character speaking, but sometimes it may be more compelling to see a character reacting to dialogue delivered by an offscreen character.

Scenes can also be broken up and integrated with other scenes using **parallel editing** (or **crosscutting**), a technique that cuts back and forth between two or more actions happening simultaneously in separate locations. You may recall the parallel editing sequences discussed as part of our examination of patterns in Chapter 2. *Way Down East* (1920) crosscuts between a suicidal woman stumbling through a snowstorm and the desperate search by the man who secretly loves her. The parallel editing sequence in *The Silence of the Lambs* (1991) takes advantage of our expectation of a direct relationship between the different crosscut actions to fool us into thinking the FBI agents swarming a house in one action are closing in on the serial killer we see in the other action. That trick works because viewers assume spatial, causal, or narrative relationships between the intertwined actions, since that is almost invariably the case. One of the things that makes parallel editing so compelling is the participation the technique requires of the viewer. As soon as we recognize that the movie is shifting between simultaneous

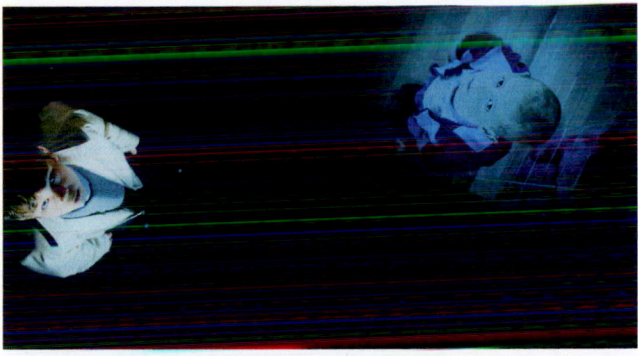

Intercutting

Danny Boyle's *T2: Trainspotting* (2017) picks up the story of a group of friends 20 years after the events depicted in its predecessor *Trainspotting* (1996). In the second film, the characters are middle aged, dissolute, and depressed. Editor Jon Harris repeatedly intercuts scenes with brief shots of the men as children, when their lives still carried the potential for happiness. The intercutting lends a melancholy perspective to the contemporary conflict.

events, we start trying to figure out how the events are related and how those relationships affect the narrative. Often, parallel editing sequences resolve by uniting the separate actions. Joel and Ethan Coen's comedy *Raising Arizona* (1987) crosscuts between five simultaneous actions after the habitual criminal H. I. "Hi" McDunnough decides to steal diapers at gunpoint from a convenience store. His outraged wife, Ed, abandons him, driving away with their supposedly adopted (actually stolen) son in the family station wagon, forcing Hi to abandon his loot and flee on foot. He is pursued by a pistol-packing convenience store clerk, the police, and a pack of dogs. Ed soon decides to rescue Hi and joins the pursuit. What makes the sequence fun is wondering where each participant is in relation to our flawed protagonist, when and how all these various paths will cross, and what will happen when they do. Ultimately, Ed decides to rescue her hapless husband. Their parallel actions intersect when she picks him up (and punches him). Thus reunited, the happy family snags the dropped diapers and resumes the getaway.

Crosscutting should not be confused with **intercutting**, the insertion of shots into a scene in a way that interrupts the narrative. Examples of intercutting include **flashbacks**, flash-forwards, shots depicting a character's thoughts, shots depicting events from earlier or later in the plot, and associative editing that inserts shots to create symbolic or thematic meaning through juxtaposition.

Comparative split screen

Split screen can do more than show different physical viewpoints of the same or simultaneous action. Marc Webb's romantic comedy *500 Days of Summer* (2009) uses split screen to convey state of mind. When Summer throws a party and invites her ex-boyfriend Tom (who is still in love with her), cold reality plays out side by side with Tom's heartbreakingly unrealistic expectations [1]. Thirty-two years earlier, Woody Allen's romantic comedy *Annie Hall* used split-screen sequences to compare and contrast the perspectives of the couple concerned. One sequence places Annie and Alvy's respective psychotherapy sessions side by side as they relate diverging interpretations of the same events [2].

Admittedly, that's a long list. Think of it this way: If the cutting *crosses* back and forth between two or more *simultaneous* actions, you're watching *crosscutting*. *Intercutting* applies to any other edits that *insert* shots into a scene from outside the action of that scene.

Editors are not limited to cutting shots together; editing can also break the screen into multiple frames and images, a technique known as **split screen**. Like parallel editing, split screen typically depicts one or more simultaneous actions, but since those actions are uninterrupted and adjacent (rather than crosscut), the comparisons they evoke and the relationships they imply are even more conspicuous. *The Rules of Attraction* (2002), Roger Avary's sardonic story of tangled relationships at a private university, uses split screen to trace the converging physical paths of two characters in a way that makes a possible emotional connection seem inevitable. When their paths finally cross, the split screens merge back into a unified whole. A split-screen sequence in Tom Tykwer's *Run Lola Run* (1998) creates suspense by showing Lola's desperate sprint to reach her father on one side of the frame while showing her father's leisurely departure from work on the other side. The actions shown in split-screen sequences don't have to occur in separate locations. Sometimes split screen can be used to fragment action happening in the same place at the same time for expressive reasons not as well suited to parallel editing. When young Napoleon picks a fight with his entire dormitory, Abel Gance's silent epic *Napoleon* (1927) captures the chaos of the ensuing pillow fight (it's more serious than it sounds) by breaking the screen into nine equal sections, all of which show different angles on the same melee. Darren Aronofsky uses split screen in *Requiem for a Dream* (2000) to combine close-ups of characters' faces with extreme close-ups of their actions or points of view in a way that would otherwise be impossible in the frame. For example, a love scene places one image of a character's loving gaze alongside another image of her finger stroking her partner's lips. In another sort of love scene, a close-up of a woman's face on the top of the frame gazes down on extreme close-ups of the "diet pills" to which she will soon be addicted. The

LOOKING AT MOVIES

THE EVOLUTION OF EDITING:
CONTINUITY AND CLASSICAL CUTTING

VIDEO This tutorial explores the history of the major innovations in continuity (or classical) editing in early cinema.

relative size of the drugs in the split frame conveys their power over their user.

Even relatively brief moments are routinely fragmented in ways that allow editors to individually accentuate specific components of a single action. For example, during the *Raising Arizona* parallel editing chase scene described earlier, a 7-second action of a chained dog attacking (and just missing) Hi is conveyed in a sequence of nine shots. The first four shots alternate between Hi's point of view of the dog racing toward him and the dog's moving-camera point of view of his intended victim. The final five shots, all less than a half-second long, are each devoted to highly specific canine-related subjects: the dog's final lunge, its teeth snapping inches from Hi's nose, its chain snapping taught, its collar jerking back, and finally its hard landing. This kind of fragmentation does more than emphasize each discrete component of the attack: the rapid-fire barrage of images infuses a feeling of energy into the action. For this reason, fight scenes in action movies are often fragmented in a similar fashion. Darren Aronofsky used the term *hip-hop montage* for his use of a similar technique that fragments a single action in a way that also condenses time. In *Requiem for a Dream,* a jarring cause-and-effect series of extreme close-ups (that are each extremely short and extremely specific) captures the process, as well as the exhilaration, of taking drugs. Repeating the technique five times over the course of the movie's first 30 minutes helps convey the ritual (and habitual) aspect of the characters' substance abuse. Shortening and speeding up the sequence each time it occurs suggests their accelerating addiction.

Juxtaposition and Meaning

Juxtaposition refers to placing two shots together in sequence. The creation and communication of meaning through juxtaposition, a concept known as **montage editing**, is an essential aspect of editing that affects nearly every cut in every film. Montage editing can be as simple as showing the exterior of a building, then cutting to a shot of people in a room. Neither shot by itself conveys that the room is inside the building, yet when we watch the shots put together (or juxtaposed), that is exactly what we assume. Likewise, when we see a shot of someone looking, followed by a shot of a tree, we intuitively understand that the person is looking at the tree. One shot tells us "that person is looking"; the other shot tells us "here is a tree." Only the juxtaposition of those

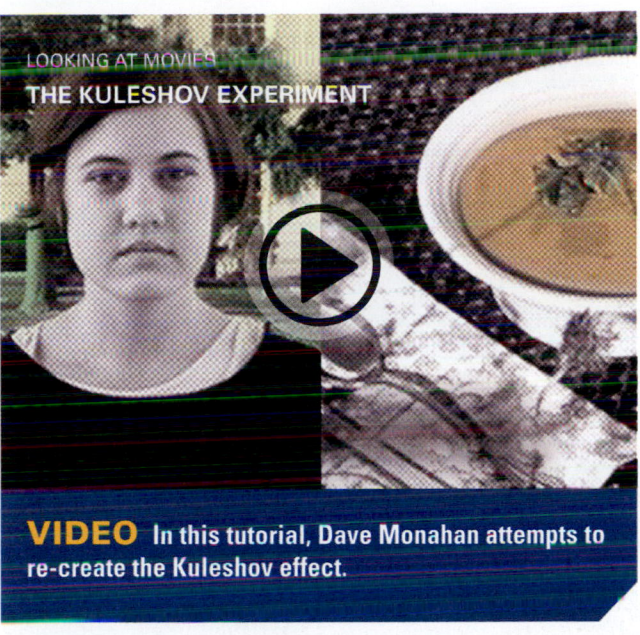

LOOKING AT MOVIES
THE KULESHOV EXPERIMENT

VIDEO In this tutorial, Dave Monahan attempts to re-create the Kuleshov effect.

shots provides a third and new meaning: "that person is looking at a tree."

The early Russian film theorists and filmmakers placed meaning through juxtaposition at the center of their approach to filmmaking. These pioneers, including Sergei Eisenstein, Vsevolod Pudovkin, and Lev Kuleshov, were the first filmmakers to systematically explore the expressive capacity of editing. In the 1920s, Kuleshov conducted an experiment in which he juxtaposed a shot of an actor wearing a neutral expression with a number of other shots and then screened them in sequence for a test audience. When viewers saw the man paired with a shot of a bowl of soup, they not only assumed he was looking at the soup but also interpreted his expression as one of hunger. When shown the same shot of the expressionless actor, but juxtaposed instead with the image of a girl in a coffin, viewers assumed a relationship between the character and the corpse and felt the actor was expressing grief or remorse. Another juxtaposition, this time with an attractive woman reclined on a couch, caused viewers to read his expression as lustful. With this simple experiment, Kuleshov demonstrated a creative capacity of film editing that editors still use: the juxtaposition of images to create new meaning not present in any single shot by itself.

Pudovkin expanded upon the idea with an experiment showing that shot order can influence meaning. He started with three different close-up shots: A, a pistol

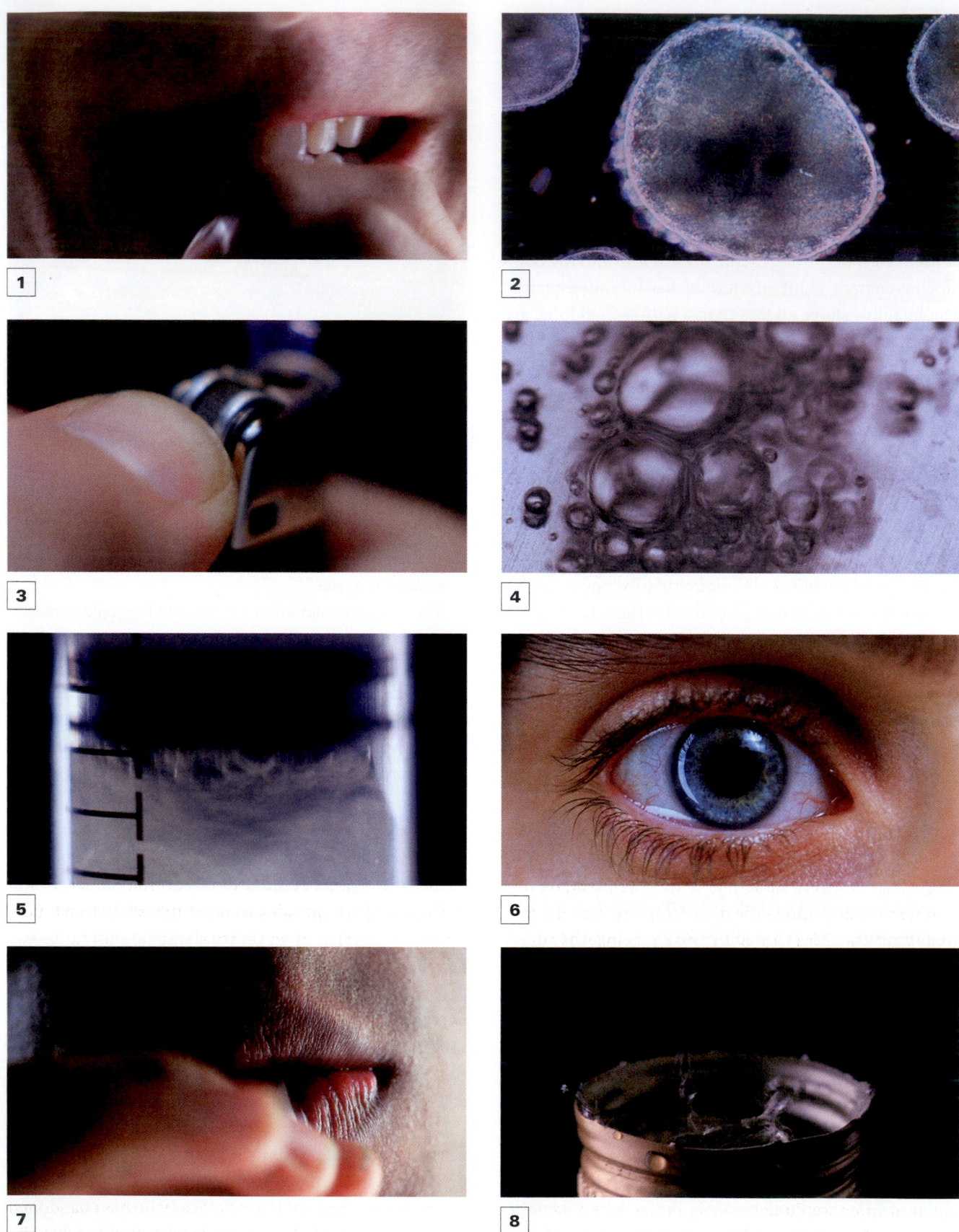

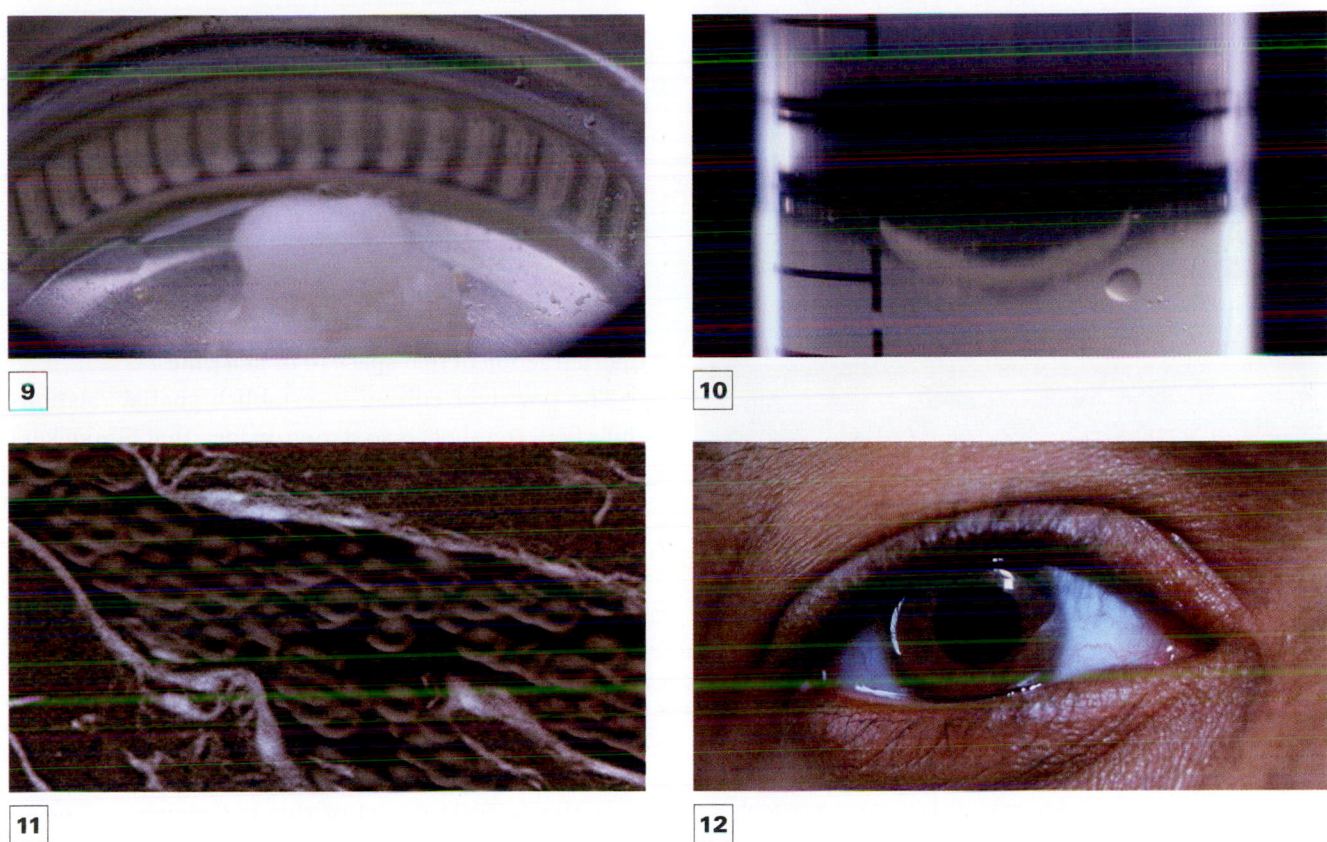

9　10

11　12

Hip-hop editing in *Requiem for a Dream*

In *Requiem for a Dream*, a fast 5-second sequence fragments the experience of two characters shooting heroin into twelve extreme close-ups. The technique condenses time and shows each cause-and-effect step of the process—right down to the cellular level. In narrative terms, the sequence cinematically simulates the intoxicating rush that draws the protagonists into an ultimately devastating addiction. Director Darren Aronofsky likens the expressive rapid-fire string of images and juxtaposition to the musical sampling of early hip-hop, an observation that led him to dub his technique *hip-hop montage*.

being pointed; B, a man looking frightened; and C, the same man smiling. When the shots were shown in the BAC order, viewers understood the BA juxtaposition (frightened man/gun) as the man being frightened by the gun. When the third shot of the man smiling was added, viewers assumed that the man had overcome his fear and was demonstrating courage. But when a different audience was shown the same shots in a new CAB sequence (smiling man/gun/frightened man), they interpreted the man as reacting with cowardice. Pudovkin's experiment was significant in asserting the flexibility of the viewers' psychology.

The montage editing previously described functions on a relatively intuitive level. We apprehend the meaning even when we do not overtly notice how it is being conveyed. **Associative editing**, also known as *intellectual editing*, uses juxtaposition to impart meaning in a way that we usually can't help but notice. This approach

pairs contrasting or incongruent images in a manner that implies a thematic relationship. Sergei Eisenstein's *October* (1928), an account of the Bolshevik Revolution of October 1917, includes some of the earliest and most famous examples of associative editing. In one scene, shots of a mechanical peacock are intercut with shots of a provisional governor to suggest the man is vain and corrupted by power.

The climactic sequence of Francis Ford Coppola's epic Vietnam War film *Apocalypse Now* (1979) uses parallel editing to incorporate associative juxtapositions that lend symbolic meaning to the movie's final act(s) of violence. Special Operations Officer Benjamin Willard has been sent on a mission to assassinate Colonel Walter Kurtz, a rogue Special Forces officer who has abandoned his command and led his troops into the jungle, where he has established himself as a ruthless philosopher king. When Willard ultimately kills Kurtz with a machete, the

Associative editing

In the opening scene of Luc Besson's science fiction-thriller *Lucy* (2014), a recent acquaintance pleads with Lucy to deliver a briefcase to a mysterious Mr. Jang [1]. When editor Julien Rey inserts a shot of a mouse approaching a baited trap [2], associative editing tells us the true nature of this dangerous situation. After Lucy takes the bait and enters a hotel to make the delivery, the editor intercuts shots of predatory cheetahs and their gazelle prey as the protagonist's situation goes from bad to worse.

scene unfolds in parallel with a native sacrifice happening outside. Juxtaposing shots of Willard slashing Kurtz with shots of tribespeople slaughtering a passive water buffalo portrays Kurtz as a complicit participant and depicts his execution as a ritual sacrifice performed in an attempt to purge his assassin's—and America's—sins. Coppola does something similar with parallel and associative editing in a sequence from *The Godfather* (1972) discussed in Chapter 2. In that case, juxtaposing shots that depict a succession of mob murders with shots of a baptism ceremony equates the killings with a sacred rite of passage and points out the hypocrisy of the new crime boss who ordered the murders as he vows to renounce Satan.

Spatial Relationships between Shots

One of the most powerful effects of film editing is to create a sense of space in the mind of the viewer. When we are watching any single shot from a film, our sense of the overall space of the scene is necessarily limited by the height, width, and depth of the film frame during that shot. But as other shots are placed in close proximity to that original shot, our sense of the overall space in which the characters are moving shifts and expands. The juxtaposition of shots within a scene can cause us to have a fairly complex sense of that overall space (something like a mental map) even if no single shot discloses more than a fraction of that space to us at a time.

The power of editing to establish spatial relationships between shots is so strong, in fact, that filmmakers have almost no need to ensure that a real space exists whose dimensions correspond to the one implied by editing. Countless films, especially historical dramas and science-fiction films, rely heavily on the power of editing to fool us into perceiving their worlds as vast and complete even as we are shown only tiny fractions of the implied space. Because our brains effortlessly make spatial generalizations from limited visual information, George Lucas was not required, for example, to build an entire to-scale model of the *Millennium Falcon* to convince us that the characters in *Star Wars* are flying (and moving around within) a vast spaceship. Instead, a series of cleverly composed shots filmed on carefully designed (and relatively small) sets could, when edited together, create the illusion of a massive, fully functioning spacecraft.

In addition to painting a mental picture of the space of a scene, editing manipulates our sense of spatial relationships among characters, objects, and their surroundings. For example, the placement of one shot of a

INTERACTIVE The editing interactive allows you to rearrange the same three shots to change the way we interpret and engage a single narrative scenario.

Spatial relations in a space chase

In 1977, George Lucas used a series of small sets to create the illusion of the massive *Millennium Falcon* in the original *Star Wars*. Six films later, in J. J. Abrams's *Star Wars: The Force Awakens* (2015), editing helps represent the interior space of a freighter huge enough to swallow the *Millennium Falcon* whole. Combining footage shot on two relatively modest sets—the intersection of two long corridors and a small crawl space—editors Maryann Brandon and Mary Jo Markey use fragmentation, juxtaposition, crosscutting, and screen direction to create the impression of a large labyrinth of passageways during a chaotic chase scene involving the ragtag protagonists, a couple of ruthless death gangs, and a trio of ravenous space monsters.

person's reaction (perhaps a look of concerned shock) after a shot of an action by another person (falling down a flight of stairs) immediately creates in our minds the thought that the two people are occupying the same space, that the person in the first shot is visible to the person in the second shot, and that the emotional response of the person in the second shot is a reaction to what has happened to the person in the first shot. To communicate all of these spatial relationships, editors rely on the juxtaposition of shots to convey meaning not contained in any single shot by itself—further evidence that the tendency of viewers to interpret shots in relation to surrounding shots is the most fundamental assumption behind all film editing.

Temporal Relationships between Shots

Nearly every cut an editor makes provides an opportunity to expand or condense time. For the most part, this temporal manipulation is more practical than expressive. The pace of an exchange between characters in separation can be sped up or slowed down by either trimming or maximizing the actor's pauses between lines. Time nearly always elapses between the last shot of one scene and the first shot of the next. And unnecessary action—and the time it consumes—is routinely removed from within scenes in a way that we've become conditioned to accept and understand without even noticing the missing time. For example, in Paul Greengrass's *The Bourne Supremacy* (2004), narrative suspense requires that we watch every step of a secret operative's casual arrival home; context tells us the fugitive Jason Bourne will be waiting for him—and that the operative may even be expecting Bourne. To go through the necessary buildup without wasting precious screen time, the film's editors used seven shots totaling 42 seconds: a car driving down the street, the operative climbing out of the parked car, the operative walking toward his door holding his key, the operative starting to walk through the now-unlocked door, the operative's hand entering a code into a security system console, the operative beginning to remove his overcoat, and the (now coatless) operative entering his kitchen. The audience gets the full agonizing benefit of expecting Bourne to pop up at any second, but the movie doesn't have to spend the several minutes the full arrival home would have actually consumed.

1

2

An ellipsis launches *Lawrence of Arabia*

In David Lean's *Lawrence of Arabia* (1962), set during World War I, British Lieutenant T. E. Lawrence is a mischievous misfit who puts matches out with his fingers to impress his fellow junior officers. When an intelligence official orders him to track down and enlist rebellious Bedouin tribesmen to fight their mutual enemies, Lawrence lights the official's cigarette and considers the flame. Instead of putting it out with his fingers, Lawrence says the dangerous mission "is going to be fun," then blows out the match [1]. An ellipsis cuts to the Arabian Desert [2], instantly propelling Lawrence (and the viewer) from the relative comforts of British headquarters to an unforgiving landscape where our protagonist's courage will be tested by more than matchsticks. The juxtaposed moments are separated by many days and miles, but the thematic connection is immediate in every sense of the word.

Oftentimes, editing is used to jump from one moment to another in ways that are more evident—and more expressive. This temporal leap between shots is called an **ellipsis**. These cuts often interrupt the action of a scene unexpectedly, usually in the middle of a continuing action, and involve significant leaps of time. The direct connection of images and actions that would normally be temporally and spatially distant empowers the filmmaker to create meaning with juxtaposition that otherwise would have been impossible. The ellipsis also makes viewers fill in the gap in the story for themselves, a participatory experience that can be more rewarding than

1

2

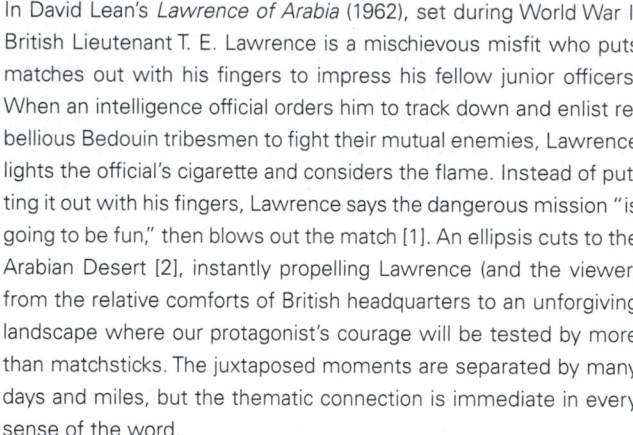

3

Ellipses for comic effect

Edgar Wright's zombie apocalypse comedy *Shaun of the Dead* (2004) repeatedly uses sudden jumps in time and space to generate jarring juxtapositions for comic effect. Two such ellipses happen in rapid order as the protagonists finally begin to realize their slacker existence is under siege. A shot of Shaun and Ed frantically clubbing undead invaders in their backyard [1] cuts to the roommates in their usual sofa spots drinking tea and eating ice cream [2] while a TV newscaster reports that those bitten by zombies turn into zombies themselves. Another ellipsis then jumps to Shaun and Ed timidly calling upstairs to their recently bitten roommate [3].

watching those missing events unfold on-screen. For example, in Gus Van Sant's *Drugstore Cowboy* (1989), a policeman offers an ultimatum to Bob, a drug addict and thief. Bob can tell him where the stolen drugs are hidden or the police will tear his house apart looking for them. Before Bob can answer, an ellipsis shows us the scattered debris of an exhaustive and destructive search. The function of this ellipsis is not simply to save screen time. Skipping past the cause (Bob's refusal to cooperate) to jump straight to the effect (his destroyed house) invites us to imagine the defiance and vicious consequences in a way that is ultimately more compelling—and amusing.

A **montage sequence** is an integrated series of shots that rapidly depicts multiple related events occurring over time. Music or other sound often accompanies the sequence to further unify the presented events. Although all aspects of editing are related, the *montage sequence* should not be confused with *montage editing. Montage*—from the French verb *monter,* "to assemble or put to-gether"—is French for "editing." Because French schol-ars and filmmakers were the among the first to take cinema seriously as an art form, their broad term wound up applied to more than one specific editing approach. *Montage sequences* are usually used to condense time when an accumulation of actions is necessary to the narrative, but developing each individual action would consume too much of the movie's duration. Common multi-event narrative progressions (such as a charac-ter falling in love, undergoing a makeover or similar transformation or training for some sort of occasion or competition) are so often represented using a montage sequence that the technique is sometimes the object of parody. But the montage sequence can be both useful and effective, and its application is not limited to these time-condensing tropes.

Wes Anderson's quirky coming-of-age comedy *Rush-more* (1998) employs four distinct montage sequences, each for a different narrative reason, and each set to an infectious 1960s British rock song. The first sequence conveys important character information and helps ex-plain why the irrepressible protagonist Max Fisher is one of the worst students at the Rushmore Academy. Nineteen artfully staged compositions, each portraying Max's role in a different extracurricular activity, quickly demonstrate Max's ridiculously ambitious participation in every possible school club. The second montage se-quence condenses and combines multiple story develop-ments: Max's continuing crush on the Rushmore teacher Rosemary Cross, his developing friendship with industri-alist Herman Blume, his adjustment to public high school after being expelled from Rushmore, fellow student Margaret Yang's interest in Max, and the spark of attrac-tion between Rosemary and Herman. After Max discov-ers Herman and Rosemary's romance, a third montage

1

2

Citizen Kane **montage sequence**

While many montage sequences have been used to portray char-acters falling in love, one of cinema's most eloquently expressive examples of the technique chronicles the opposite process. This *Citizen Kane* (1941) montage sequence, set entirely in the same dining room, opens with a two-shot that dollies in on the newlyweds Charles and Emily flirting in close proximity [1], then cuts back and forth between single medium shots of each as they talk together over breakfast. As the sequence progresses, the characters grow older and the dialogue grows colder until a slow-disclosure dolly-out reveals the former lovers now sit silently at opposite ends of a long table [2].

sequence efficiently chronicles the escalating feud be-tween Max and his former friend. Finally, after Rose-mary rejects both Max and Herman, a training montage sequence pokes gentle fun at the cliché as it shows the heartbroken friends reunited and working together in a misguided attempt to win Rosemary back.

Sometimes the temporal relationship between shots doesn't condense or propel time. Editors can juxtapose shots in sequence in a way that *extends* an action across time. The same Soviet innovators who brought us associative editing and the Kuleshov effect innovated editing techniques that manipulate time in this way. The famous "Odessa Steps" sequence in Sergei Eisenstein's *Battleship Potemkin* (1925) begins with **overlapping action**, the repetition of parts or all of an action using multiple shots. This repetition holds viewers momentarily in a single instant of time, which assigns emphasis and significance to the extended action. In this case, a young woman gaping in shock is shown three times in rapid succession. This overlapping action is followed by a succession of shots showing people fleeing down the steps before the cause—advancing Cossack soldiers—is revealed. Overlapping action is used throughout the sequence, most notably when a young mother collapses after being shot by the Cossacks. Forty-two years later, in Arthur Penn's *Bonnie and Clyde*, overlap editing was again used to depict someone falling after being shot, only this time the victim was a notorious bank robber. Editor Dede Allen sets up the film's climactic scene with a series of shots (including a last meaningful glance between the outlaw couple) that extend the moments before the protagonists are gunned down by police in a hail of machine-gun fire. The sequence is heavily fragmented; twenty-five shots in 23 seconds are used to depict the attack that kills Bonnie and Clyde. But this brief burst of action itself is extended with slow-motion cinematography and five overlapping action cuts of Clyde falling to the ground.

Editing can even suspend the viewer in a single instant. The **freeze-frame** suddenly stops a shot to hold on a single "frozen" image of the arrested action. The editor accomplishes this by simply repeating the same frame for whatever length of time is required for the desired effect. Martin Scorsese frequently uses the freeze-frame in his gangster film *Goodfellas* (1990) to hold our gaze on a specific image while the first-person voice-over narration from protagonist Henry Hill relates his memories and observations. The juxtaposition of the arrested action and the voice-over can convey meaning that neither the image nor the audio could do on its own. In one montage sequence chronicling young Henry's induction to gangster life, his father savagely beats him for skipping school to do odd jobs for the neighborhood mobsters.

During an unusually long 15-second freeze-frame that suspends the beating, Henry matter-of-factly continues his narration—suggesting his blithe acceptance that violence is now part of his life. Francois Truffaut's film *The 400 Blows* (1959) ends with one of the most famous freeze-frames in cinema history. This character study of a troubled and misunderstood adolescent concludes with the protagonist Antoine escaping a youth detention center. He runs away to the beach, a place he's always wanted to visit, where a long take follows him as he trots to the water. But when he gets there, he doesn't seem to know what to do. When Antoine turns to the camera, the image freezes and an optical zoom brings us in close to the ambiguous expression on his face. This unexpected

1

2

Freeze-frames and final shots

The famous freeze-frame at the end of *The 400 Blows* [1] was the inspiration for the freeze frame that concludes George Roy Hill's 1969 western *Butch Cassidy and the Sundance Kid* [2]. The two movies use the same technique in the same place, but the context and the meanings are different. Antoine in *The 400 Blows* doesn't know what will happen next, and neither do we, but context and sound make it clear that Butch and Sundance most certainly die in a blaze of gunfire. Hill's movie is about the end of the old West and the beginning of the era that would mythologize it. Instead of showing the humbled heroes' bloody defeat, the final frozen image transforms the flawed characters into legendary Western archetypes.

(at the time audacious) ending denies resolution, which is appropriate, since Antoine doesn't know what's going to happen to him next, either. The freeze-frame makes us spend time contemplating the uncertainty of both the boy's state of mind and his future.

Duration, Pace, and Rhythm

There is no such thing as fast or slow cutting. Every cut in every film happens instantaneously; there is no variation in the time it takes a cut to move from one shot to another. The characteristic that determines the speed with which we experience edited sequences is not the cut between shots, but the **duration** of each of the assembled shots, as measured in frames (usually 24 per second), seconds, and (occasionally) minutes. Our perception of the duration of any shot is affected by the content that shot presents. A shot with relatively straightforward content, such as a close-up of a coffee cup, can be on-screen for a relatively short amount of time because the viewer only needs a moment to understand and absorb that content before she is instinctively ready for the next image. Holding on that simple coffee cup for anything longer than a few seconds, past the point where the audience has absorbed all of its available information, may even make the viewer uneasy. In contrast, a shot containing a great deal of information, such as an establishing shot with background detail and multiple interacting characters, typically takes longer for the viewer to process and thus may be held on-screen for significantly more time before the audience is ready to move on to another viewpoint. This interplay between duration and information is known as the **content curve** because it can be visualized as a bell curve, with the peak representing that point of optimum duration where a cut will typically occur. Editors often use the concept when deciding—or sometimes just sensing—how long to make each individual shot.

Editors can also deviate from standard practice for expressive purposes. If the editor cuts before the peak—that is, before the viewer has had time to fully comprehend the content and prepare for the next shot—the technique can disorient the audience or create a sense of excitement as viewers attempt to keep up with the accelerated pace. A series of shots cut at this point amplifies the effect. Music videos, commercials, and action movies take full advantage of the phenomenon, but often run

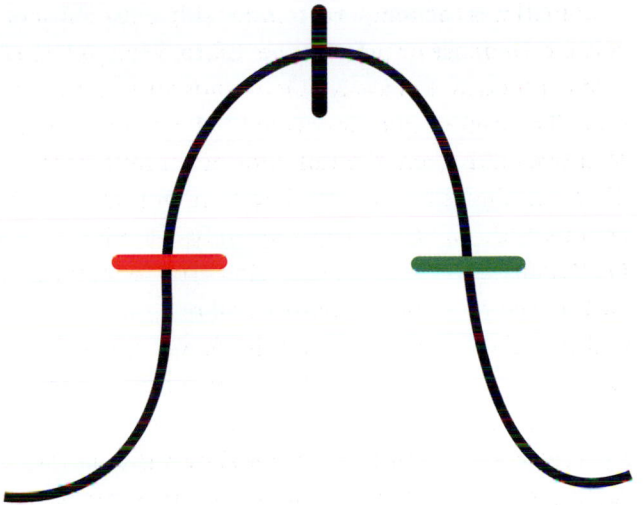

The content curve
The black line at the peak of this bell curve represents the conventional point in any shot where the audience has absorbed all immediately available information and is instinctively ready to see another shot. Cutting before that peak (represented by a red line) or after that peak (represented by a green line) changes the way the viewer interprets and experiences the shot.

the risk of visually exhausting their audiences and thus diminishing the intended experience. Very short shots that cut before the peak of the content curve are also used to simulate flashes of lost or suppressed memories. Sydney Lumet's *The Pawnbroker* (1964) is about an alienated Holocaust survivor who has repressed his painful past and rejected meaningful human contact. As events in his present life force him out of his self-imposed isolation, fragmented memories begin to force their way back into his consciousness, which editor Ralph Rosenblum presents as very short intercut shots that are initially over before we can fully comprehend their content. As the story progresses, the shots get longer until they are no longer cut off before the peak of the content curve, and we finally understand the events responsible for his damaged psyche.

Holding a shot until after the peak of the content curve, past the point where the viewer has processed all of the immediately available information, can make the viewer feel trapped. Béla Tarr didn't intend his film *The Turin Horse* (2011) as entertainment; he wanted viewers to experience the heaviness of human existence. The extremely long takes in the film force us to endure

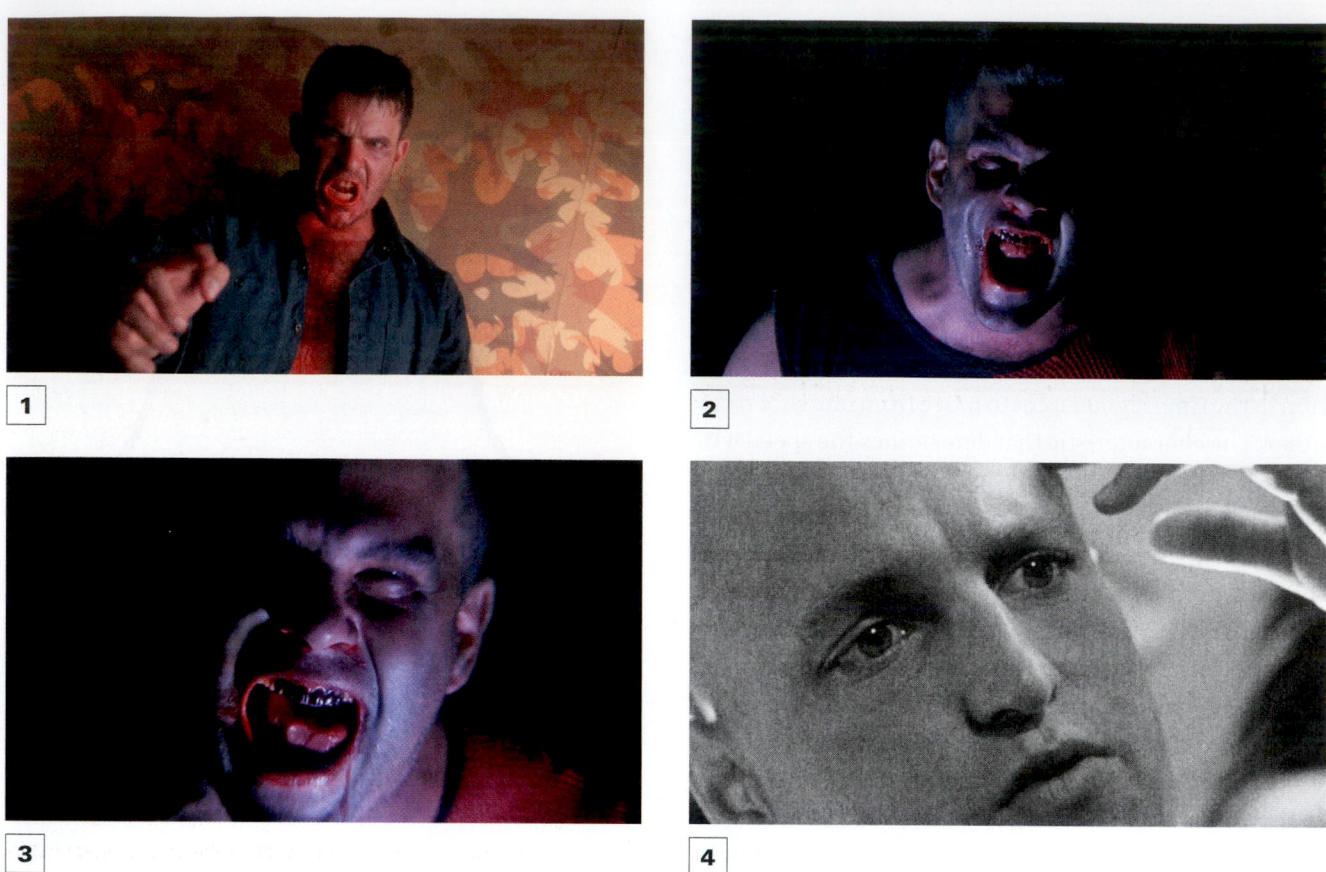

Cutting before the peak of the content curve

The content curve is used to convey repressed memories in Oliver Stone's *Natural Born Killers* (1994). When a TV reporter asks the imprisoned Mickey Knox about his father, the normally cool mass murderer is momentarily shaken. Editing shows us why. Three very short images of a snarling man (8 frames long [1], 1 frame long [2], and 1 frame long [3]) flash across the screen so quickly the viewer can only register a sense of violent rage before the sequence cuts back to Mickey [4] for 20 frames—long enough for us to read his unsettled expression. Duration and juxtaposition give us a glimpse of Mickey's suppressed past that he does not share with the reporter.

the mundane tasks that fill the characters' bleak lives in real time. But being stuck in a shot beyond when we would normally be ready to move along does not have to be unpleasant. In some contexts, extended duration causes viewers to look deeper into an image in search of meaning not readily apparent at first glance. Consider the close-up of the gorilla in *Visitors* (2013) from the discussion of the long take in Chapter 6. If the shot had cut after a few seconds, viewers may have only registered: "There's a gorilla." But when compelled to stare into the primate's eyes for more than 2 minutes, we can't help but contemplate her existence and perspective.

When the editor employs patterns of duration over time, she is using pace and rhythm. Those two terms are often used interchangeably, but there are important differences. **Pace** is the speed at which a shot sequence

flows. The pace of a scene or sequence is accomplished by using shots of the same general duration. An action sequence using a series of short-duration shots could be described as *fast paced*. A *slow-paced* sequence made up of shots of a similarly long duration might be found in a serious dialogue-driven drama. **Rhythm** in editing applies to the practice of changing the pace, either gradually or suddenly, during a scene or sequence.

The German thriller *Run Lola Run* (1998) makes use of pace and rhythmic shifts to create a sense of urgency, punctuate key moments, and convey state of mind in an opening sequence in which Lola gets a call from her boyfriend, Manny. We learn that she was supposed to give Manny a ride earlier that morning but didn't show up because her scooter was stolen. Manny, a low-level criminal, needed the lift to deliver a bag of cash to his boss.

Cutting after the peak of the content curve

In Stanley Kubrick's Cold War satire *Dr. Strangelove or: How I Learned to Stop Worrying and Love the Bomb* (1964), a deranged general explains a bizarre conspiracy theory to an officer he has taken prisoner. The ridiculous situation is made all the more awkward when it is presented in a single extended shot lasting more than 2 minutes that makes the viewer feel as trapped as the general's hostage. The longer duration also allows us to notice details we may have missed in a shorter shot, such as the decorative pistols on the wall, which are framed so that they appear to be pointed at the anxious victim of the general's paranoia.

1

2

The duration, the pace, and the rhythm

The climactic three-way standoff in Sergio Leone's Western *The Good, the Bad, and the Ugly* (1966) starts with an extreme long shot [1] lasting 36 seconds that establishes the spatial relationship between the three gunslingers described in the film's title. The next seventy-three shots cut back and forth between shots of the characters as they size each other up and wait for their moment to draw and fire. The tension increases as shots get closer and shorter and the pace gradually increases over the course of three rhythmic shifts. By the time the bullets fly, the final three extreme close-ups each last only a fraction of a second. The shot of Angel Eyes ("the Bad") going for his gun lasts 5 frames (less than one-quarter of a second) [2].

When Lola didn't show up, he was forced to take the subway. While on the train, Manny assisted a homeless man who had stumbled, leaving the bag momentarily unattended. At that moment, Manny noticed police on board, so he reflexively ducked out of the train. This first section of the sequence is covered in fifty-three shots that crosscut between images of Lola in her bedroom, Manny in a phone booth, and shots depicting the events Manny is recounting. The average shot length is about 2½ seconds, setting a brisk pace appropriate to the building tension, which is reinforced by the subtle but steady beat of the underlying score music.

The sequence's first major rhythmic shift covers the next series of shots, which depict Manny's recollection of what happened after he exited. A 4-second shot of Manny walking onto the subway platform is followed by a shot that is only 4 frames (or one-sixth of a second) long: the bag of cash left behind on the seat. The image comes and goes so quickly, we barely have time to register the content before it is replaced by a half-second shot of Manny. This pattern (4 frames of the bag, followed by a half-second of Manny) is repeated twice more, with the short shots functioning as flashes of memory juxtaposed

with the slightly longer shots of Manny's face registering realization.

The rhythm shifts again as Lola and Manny each repeatedly voice that terrible realization—*the bag*—in a rhythmic sequence of ten shots (all less than a second long), that bounces back and forth between Lola and Manny three times before settling on images showing Lola repeating the words four times from different angles.

After two relatively long shots (4 seconds and 3 seconds) that show Manny trying (but not succeeding) to get back on the train, a series of five 1½-second shots cuts back and forth between Manny and the departing bag—another sudden rhythmic shift that ratchets up the tension before resolving with a 4-second shot of the train departing the station. That relatively long shot begins a series of eight shots of similar duration showing the homeless man picking up the bag, seeing the bundles of cash inside, and stepping off the train with it as we hear Manny and Lola frantically speculate about what happened to the lost money.

That temporary lull in pace sets us up for the final climactic shifts in rhythm that convey Manny's escalating anxiety. A series of twelve shots, all 16 frames (two-thirds of a second) or less long, cuts between the homeless man exiting the subway and the various countries (in Manny's imagination) the new owner may have taken the money. Suddenly, the rhythm shifts again for a 2-second panic-attack barrage of fifty shots, each only 1 frame long. The first half pummels the viewer with exotic locations one might use a found fortune to visit. The final burst intersperses a repeated image of the ruthless crime boss, Ronnie, staring directly into the camera.

Major Approaches to Editing: Continuity and Discontinuity

The world we live in today is inundated with motion pictures. From our modern perspective, it may be difficult to imagine how astounding, and potentially confounding, movies were to their first audiences. No one at the beginning of the twentieth century had any experience with photographic images that moved, much less moving pictures that jumped instantaneously between different viewpoints and points in time. In most of the world, the first filmmakers to employ editing were in the business of entertainment. To attract and satisfy audiences, they had to develop methods that exploited the expressive power of cinema without confusing their fledgling viewers. They also recognized the movies' unprecedented capacity to transport viewers into a different world and so took care to avoid reminding audiences they were watching a manufactured illusion. The **continuity editing** that evolved out of these concerns seeks to keep viewers oriented in space and time, to ensure a smooth and subtle (preferably invisible) flow between shots, and to maintain a logical connection between adjacent shots and scenes. Because commerce and coherence are still vital elements of mainstream movies, continuity editing

remains predominant in most of the movies and television produced today.

But movies are a malleable medium. Even in cinema's infancy, some filmmakers were more concerned with ideas and expression than with orientation and invisibility. They embraced **discontinuity editing**, which emphasizes dynamic, often discontinuous relationships between shots, including contrasts in movement, camera angle, and shot type. This approach deliberately incorporates abrupt spatial and temporal shifts between shots, especially if doing so conveys meaning or provokes reaction. Instead of seeking to make viewers forget they are watching a movie, discontinuity editing calls attention to itself as an element of cinematic form. Discontinuity editing was pioneered by the same Soviet filmmakers whose experiments and innovations with juxtaposition and order we discussed earlier in this chapter. Eisenstein, Kuleshov, Pudovkin, and others influenced the maverick directors of the French New Wave of the 1950s and 1960s, who in turn inspired a generation of Hollywood and independent filmmakers looking for expressive alternatives to conventional continuity. The resulting discontinuous editing techniques include associative editing, the freeze-frame, split screen, the jump cut, and the ellipsis.

Like realism and antirealism, continuity and discontinuity are not absolute values but are instead tenden-

LOOKING AT MOVIES
THE EVOLUTION OF EDITING: MONTAGE

VIDEO This tutorial explores montage and discontinuity editing in Sergei Eisenstein's film *Battleship Potemkin.*

Continuity editing in the classic *Casablanca*

This scene that introduces the protagonist of the Hollywood classic *Casablanca* (1942) flows smoothly from shot to shot, each of which has a meaning that is directly related to those that precede and follow it. The moving camera and the editing always let us know us exactly where we are in space and in the story.

cies along a continuum. An average Hollywood movie may exhibit continuity in some parts and discontinuity in others, even if the movie's overall tendency is toward conventional continuity. Similarly, an experimental film that is mostly discontinuous may include scenes that employ continuity editing. Many of today's creative film-makers use whichever approach best suits the expressive needs of the story at any given moment. We've already encountered plenty of evidence of this practice earlier in this chapter. For example, *Butch Cassidy and the Sundance Kid* employs conventional continuity right up until its very last shot, when a discontinuous freeze-frame best provides the narrative the thematic resolution it requires. *Lucy* inserts associative images, such as incautious mice and hunted gazelles, into sequences that otherwise adhere to standard continuity.

Conventions of Continuity Editing

Continuity editing seeks to achieve logic, smoothness, sequential flow, and the temporal and spatial orientation of viewers to what they see on the screen. As with so

1

2

3

4

Discontinuity in the groundbreaking *Breathless*

The scene that opens Jean-Luc Godard's seminal French New Wave film *Breathless* (1960) makes little or no attempt to orient viewers in time and space. There are no clear spatial cues to tell us if the woman in shot [2] is looking at the smoking man in shot [1] or the car in shot [3]. When the scene cuts to the man stealing the car [4], nothing in the coverage or the edit makes it clear where he is in relationship to his accomplice or even if it is the same car we saw before. Godard's use of discontinuity compels the viewer to figure out spatial, temporal, and even narrative relationships using the images provided.

many conventions of film production, the conventions of continuity editing remain open to variation, but in general, continuity editing ensures that

❯ what happens on the screen makes as much narrative sense as possible.

❯ screen direction is consistent from shot to shot.

❯ graphic, spatial, and temporal relations are maintained from shot to shot.

Maintaining a coherent sense of space in a medium that comprises constantly shifting viewpoints is one of continuity editing's primary functions. Filmmakers have developed a number of different techniques to help viewers maintain their bearings from shot to shot.

Shot Types and Master Scene Technique As we learned earlier in this chapter, the master scene technique provides the editor with a variety of different shot types covering the same action so that the scene may be

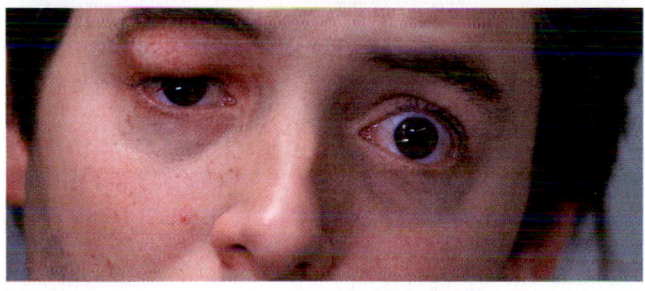

The three-shot salvo

Intentional discontinuity in the form of a jarring sequence of increasingly closer shots all captured from the same camera angle is sometimes used to punctuate particularly shocking moments, in this case a high school teacher's sudden realization he's been caught falsifying the student body president election results in Alexander Payne's *Election* (1999).

constructed using the framing that best serves each dramatic moment. The master shot is a long shot covering most or all of the scene's action. The editor uses the master shot to provide the viewer with a kind of reference map: whenever the location, background detail, and spatial relationship of the characters need to be established (or reestablished), she can simply cut to the master shot before proceeding with the rest of the scene. Typically, coverage is captured in spatial increments (long shot, medium long shot, medium shot, medium close-up, close-up, etc.) so that the editor can move gradually

between different implied proximities and thus avoid jarring leaps in spatial perspective. Cinematographers also vary the angle of their camera position in relation to the subject when shooting coverage so that when the editor does cut from, say, a medium shot to a close-up of the same character, there is enough variation in framing to avoid a jarring effect that makes the subject appear to "jump" forward or backward. This so-called **30-degree rule** states that the camera should shift at least 30 degrees between different shot types of the same subject. Filmmakers sometimes intentionally break this rule to intentionally "jump" in at (or away from) a character or object multiple times in quick succession, an effect called the **three-shot salvo**.

The 180-Degree Rule and Screen Direction Screen direction applies to both the movement of subjects in the frame and to the direction each subject faces in relation to other characters. If either is inconsistent from shot to shot, the scene risks losing its spatial coherence. For example, if we are watching two different characters interact across different shots, as long as character A is facing left and character B is facing right, we intuitively understand that characters A and B are facing each other, even if we don't see them together in the same frame. But if character A is suddenly facing right in her shots, just like character B, it now appears as if they are both looking in the same direction, rather than speaking face to face. To

LOOKING AT MOVIES
THE 180-DEGREE RULE

VIDEO This tutorial illustrates the 180-degree system by analyzing its use in a scene from Alfred Hitchcock's *Vertigo*.

Figure 8.1 | THE 180-DEGREE SYSTEM

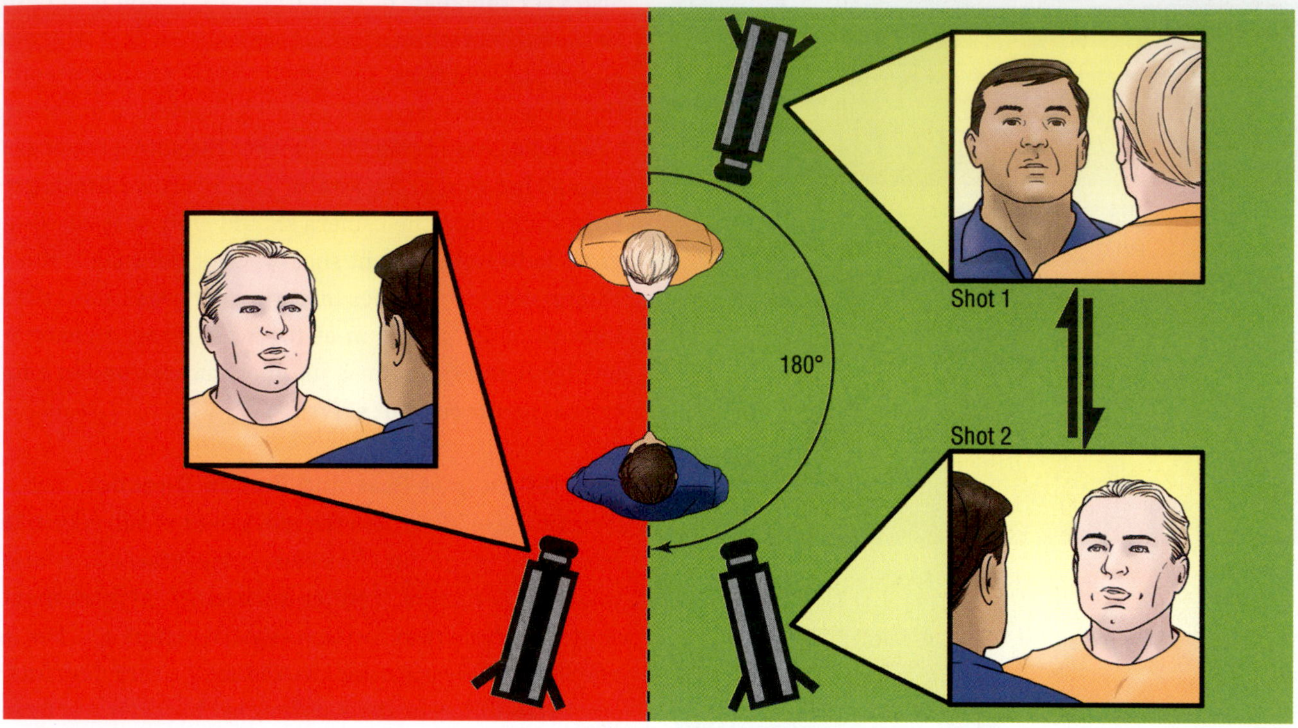

Shots 1 and 2 are taken from positions within the same 180-degree space (green background). When viewers see the resulting shots on-screen, they can make sense of the actors' positions relative to each other. If a camera is placed in the opposite 180-degree space (red background), the resulting shot reverses the actors' spatial orientation and thus cannot be used in conjunction with either shot 1 or shot 2 without confusing the viewer.

help editors avoid this spatial disjunction, cinematographers devised the **180-degree rule**. This system uses an imaginary line (called "the line," or the **axis of action**) drawn between the interacting characters being photographed (Figure 8.1). Once the line is determined, the camera remains on the same side of the line as it moves from position to position to capture different shots. As long as the camera stays within the 180-degree half-circle defined by that line, the characters on-screen will remain in the same relative spatial orientation regardless of which shots the editor chooses to use when cutting the scene.

Editing Techniques That Maintain Continuity

In addition to the fundamental building blocks—master shot coverage and maintaining screen direction with the 180-degree system—various editing techniques are used to ensure that graphic, spatial, and temporal relations are maintained from shot to shot.

Match Cuts Editors use a match cut to carry an element from one shot into the next shot using action, graphic content, or eye contact. These **match cuts** help create a sense of continuity between contiguous shots in the same scene or between shots that connect different scenes.

Match-on-Action Cut Cutting during a physical action helps hide the instantaneous and potentially jarring shift from one camera viewpoint to another. When connecting one shot to the next, a film editor often ends the first shot in the middle of a continuing action and starts the connecting shot at the same point in the same action. As a result, the action flows so continuously over the cut between different moving images that most viewers fail to register the switch. For example, suppose a class-

Crossing the line for dramatic effect

Cinematographers and directors are careful to follow the 180-degree rule on set, so that editors can maintain spatial continuity when constructing sequences involving multiple shots with multiple characters. Keeping the camera in the half-circle defined by the imaginary line (the axis of action) drawn between the characters ensures that each subject will remain on the same side of the frame in every shot. But sometimes, the filmmakers intentionally "jump the line" and shoot from the opposite side of the axis of action to provide the editor an opportunity to punctuate a key moment. When the war hero Billy first meets NFL cheerleader Faison in Ang Lee's *Billy Lynn's Long Halftime Walk* (2016), the shots depicting their awkward small talk (a medium two-shot [1], and a series of shot/reverse shots like [2] and [3]) are all framed from one side of the axis of action so that Billy is screen right and Faison is screen left. But the moment their encounter turns serious—when Faison asks Billy about his religious faith—the coverage "jumps the line" so that the characters switch positions on screen [4]. This sudden discontinuity grabs our attention and signals that this meet-cute is heading in a new direction.

room scene included the action of a student standing to ask a question. The coverage may include a medium long shot of the assembled students, as well as a medium close-up of the student who asks the question. If the editor wanted to cut from the general shot of the students to the medium close-up focused on the student asking the question, she could end the medium long shot in the middle of the student's action of standing and begin the subsequent medium close-up at approximately the same point in that action. The continuous act of standing would carry the viewer's eye over the switch between spatial viewpoints.

Eyeline Match Cut When looking at others, we humans are naturally drawn to the eyes. Filmmakers use this tendency to create spatial continuity between sequenced shots depicting interacting characters. On set, camera positions are calculated so that if one actor's gaze is aimed in a particular direction offscreen in one shot, the direction of the other actor's eyes is mirrored in the corresponding shot. The direction in which an actor looks is known as his or her *eyeline*. When the editor cuts between two such corresponding shots, the resulting **eyeline match cut** creates a logical and spatial connection between the juxtaposed images.

Match-on-action and eyeline cuts in *Stagecoach*

Near the conclusion of John Ford's *Stagecoach* (1939), Doc Boone fearlessly confronts Luke Plummer, the outlaw that murdered his friend's father and brother. In response to Doc's casual request, Luke slings a bottle of whisky down the bar. Doc catches the bottle with practiced ease, then holds eye contact with Luke as he takes a drink—a display of confidence that unnerves the outlaw. A match-on-action edit uses the movement of the bottle to cut from the medium long shot of the gathered patrons [1] to a medium shot of Doc [2]. An eyeline match cut then uses Doc's assured gaze [3] to make a spatial, logical, and meaningful connection to Luke's corresponding reaction [4].

Graphic Match Cut By repeating a similar shape, color, or other compositional element from one shot to the next, the graphic match cut implies a direct link between the events and content presented in the two different shots. For this reason, graphic match cuts are often used to bridge scenes taking place in the present to sequences depicting past events or memories. For example, when the diabolical hypnotherapist Missy Armitage hypnotizes the protagonist Chris Washington in Jordan Peele's *Get Out* (2017), a graphic match cut between two com-positionally similar extreme close-ups of fingers nervously scratching on the armrests of chairs links Chris's current situation with a hypnotically imposed childhood memory. The fluid nature of time in Denis Villeneuve's *Arrival* (2016) is conveyed when an embrace between protagonist Louise Banks and her daughter cuts to a similarly composed shot of her hugging fellow scientist Ian Donnelly. When that cut happens, we assume the graphic match is signaling the connection between a memory and a present event. Only later do we come to

1

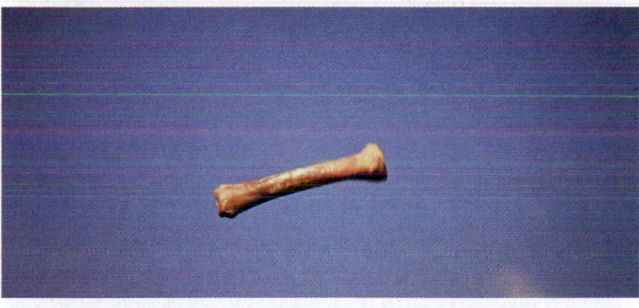

2

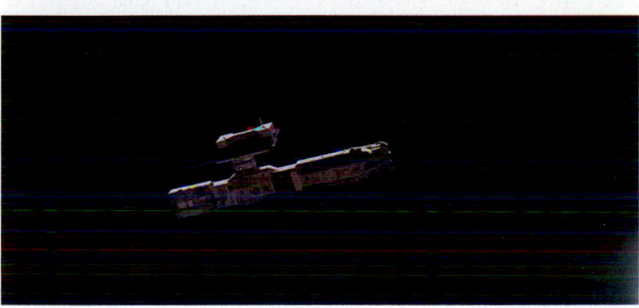

3

Graphic match cut in *2001: A Space Odyssey*

An instantaneous graphic match cut conveys an evolutionary leap spanning millions of years in Stanley Kubrick's *2001: A Space Odyssey* (1968). After a prehistoric tribe of hominids discovers the first tool—a bone used as a weapon against an enemy band—one of the proto-humans celebrates the invention by tossing it in the air [1]. A shot tracking the bone's trajectory [2] cuts to a spacecraft of the same general shape and position in the frame [3]. Eons of incremental advances driven by the desire of the human race to harness knowledge are suggested in this graphic match cut, which itself harnesses other editing techniques. The cut is perhaps the most dramatic ellipsis in cinematic history, and it uses associative editing to equate the first primitive tool with advanced space-age technology.

understand that the causal and temporal relationship actually moves in the opposite direction: the mother-daughter embrace happens in the future; Ian will eventually marry Louise and father the girl. But not all graphic matches connect events happening at different times.

For example, at the end of the infamous shower murder sequence in *Psycho* (1960), director Alfred Hitchcock matches two circular shapes: bloody water washing down a round shower drain, and the lifeless eye of victim Marion Crane. Here the graphic match cut implies a metaphorical visualization of Marion's life ebbing away.

Point-of-View Editing Point-of-view editing also uses a character's eyeline to create connections between subjects in separate shots, but instead of simply imparting a spatial relationship between interacting characters, the point-of-view edit seeks to convey the viewpoint and perspective of a character's offscreen gaze. Most frequently, a point-of-view edit juxtaposes an objective shot of a character looking offscreen with a shot of an object, person, or action. The juxtaposition causes the viewer to interpret the second shot as the object of the looking character's gaze. This framing of this point-of-view shot often reflects a spatial relationship between the looking character and the looked-at object. However, if the filmmakers wish to communicate how the looking character feels about the object of her gaze, the second shot can be framed in a way that conveys significance, rather than distance.

Other Transitions between Shots

Jump Cut The term *jump cut* is often generally (and incorrectly) applied to any noticeably discontinuous edit, but this particular editing technique defies our expectations of continuity in a very specific way. A **jump cut** is created when two shots of the same subject taken from the same camera position are edited together so that the action on-screen seems to jump forward in time. This jump usually amounts to a matter of moments; the effect is often created using a single shot of an ongoing action. The editor simply removes a portion of the shot and then relinks the remaining footage. *Breathless,* the influential French New Wave film cited earlier in this chapter, was among the first to intentionally (and repeatedly) violate conventional continuity with jump cuts that call attention to the movie's construction. For example, during a scene of the young lovers Michel and Patricia primping and flirting in the bathroom of Patricia's apartment, editor Cécile Decugis cuts five pieces out of one continuous shot, creating five obvious jump cuts. Decugis may have

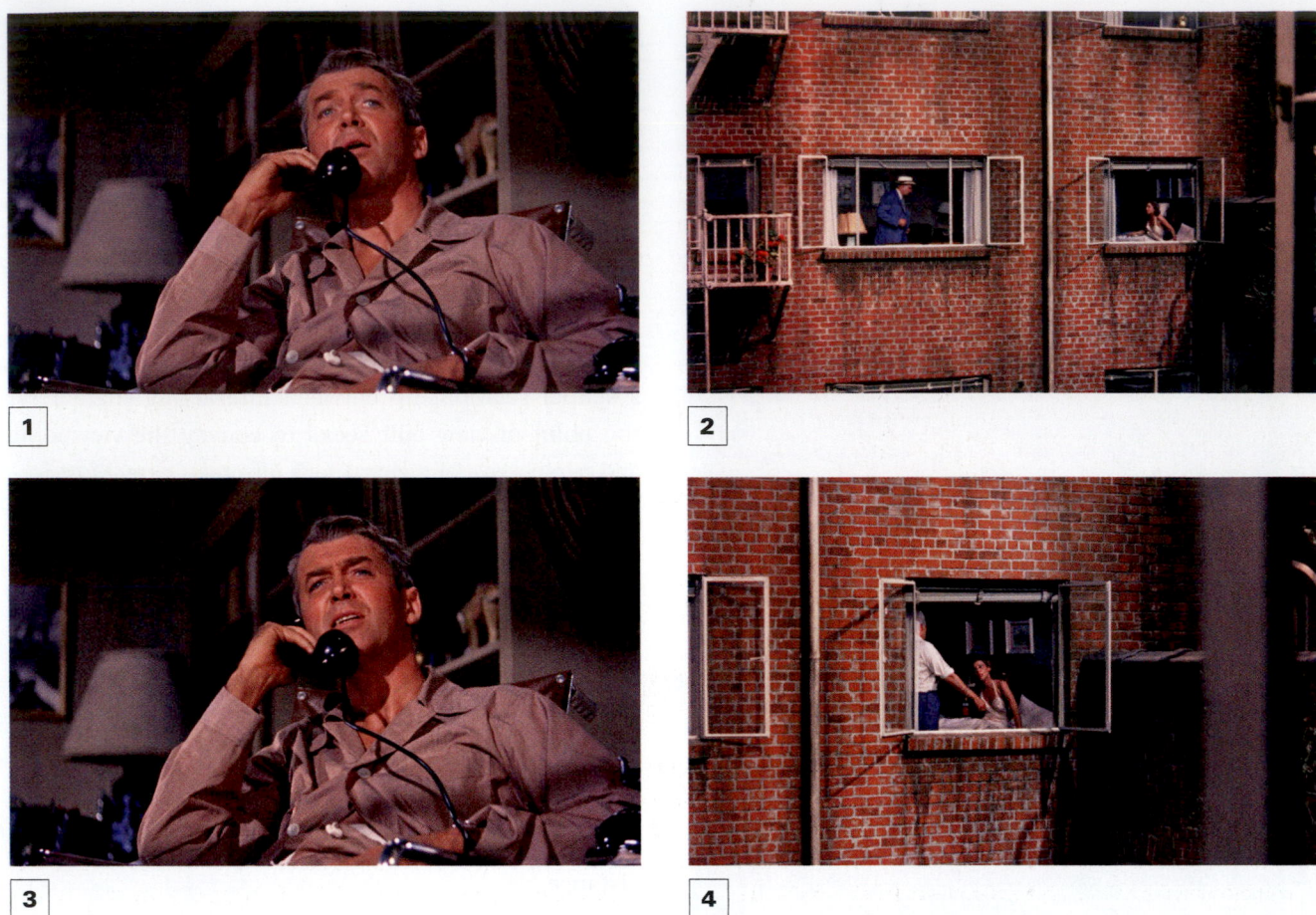

Point-of-view editing

Alfred Hitchcock's *Rear Window* (1954) tells the story of L. B. Jefferies, an adventurous globe-trotting photographer stuck in his New York City apartment with a broken leg. To alleviate his boredom, Jefferies observes his neighbors. This point-of-view editing sequence conveys his initial curiosity about a seemingly unhappy couple in the apartment across the courtyard—an interest that will eventually draw him into a murder mystery. An initial shot of Jefferies looking offscreen [1] is followed by a second shot that depicts his point of view with a wide framing that reflects the physical distance between Jefferies and the neighbors [2]. The sequence cuts back to Jefferies [3] as his expression indicates growing interest. The cut to the next point-of-view shot [4] confirms that impression. The tighter framing conveys a psychological relationship, not a spatial one. Jefferies hasn't moved, yet the quarreling couple he's looking at is larger in the frame, and thus reads as more significant to his state of mind. As this brief setup suggests, *Rear Window* exploits the expressive power of point-of-view editing to explore themes of perception and voyeurism.

made the jump cuts to add a sense of spontaneity to the encounter or she may have simply edited out unnecessary material without regard for traditional continuity. The sequence accomplishes both. In contemporary films, intentional jump cuts are often used to express a lack or loss of control in scenes featuring disturbed or distressed characters. When the protagonist of Vincent Gallo's *Buffalo 66* (1998) strides through a bus station in search of a restroom, a series of jump cuts helps viewers feel his distracted desperation.

Fade Unlike the cut, which moves from shot to shot instantaneously, the **fade** transitions between shots over multiple frames. The first shot *fades out* (gets progressively darker) until the screen is entirely black. After a moment, the succeeding shot *fades in* (becomes increasingly exposed). The editor can control the duration of every step of the process; the fade-out, the moment of pure black, and the fade-in can each be as long or as short as the edit requires. Fades are traditionally used as transitions from one scene to another. Because the darker/

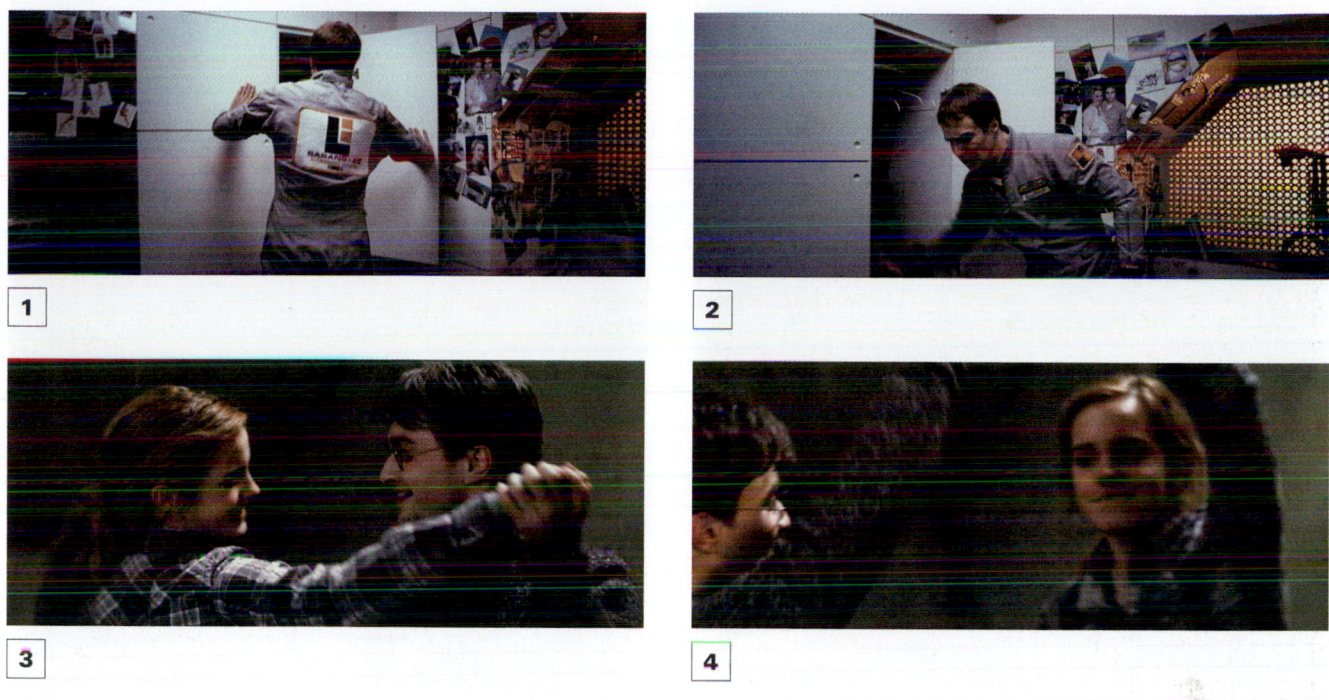

Jump cuts

In Duncan Jones's dystopic science-fiction film *Moon* (2009), the lonely caretaker of an automated lunar mining station becomes convinced that clones of himself are hidden somewhere in the sealed complex he inhabits. His desperate search of the facility is presented in an escalating series of jump cuts that lurch through his ongoing action [1, 2]. But jump cuts aren't limited to conveying distress. When Harry and Hermione share a dance in David Yates's *Harry Potter and the Deathly Hallows, Part 1* (2010), their mood is somber and their movements are cut using continuity editing. But when the friends relax and begin to have fun, the editing signals the shift from careworn to carefree with a playful series of jump cuts [3, 4].

black/lighter progression mimics the setting and rising of the Sun, a visual indicator of passing time in our everyday lives, the fade is often used to emphasize the passage of time between scenes. It should be noted that almost every transition from one scene to the next involves the passage of time, including those accomplished with an instantaneous cut. Fades and other transitions simply add additional weight to the temporal shift. A slow fade at the end of a scene can also lend a solemn sense of finality to the end of a dramatic scene, such as after the gunslinger-turned-lawman Wyatt Earp vows to avenge his young brother's death at the boy's makeshift grave in John Ford's classic Western *My Darling Clementine* (1946). Fades can also be used within a scene, as in John Boorman's *The General* (1998), the story of the notoriously brazen thief Martin Cahill. A night scene in which he breaks into the home of a wealthy family is presented in eleven brief segments, each separated by a fade. Cahill's stealth and self-confidence are under-

scored by the buoyant rhythm of the fades, which convey both the passage of time and the character's calm state of mind.

Fading into and out of colors other than black defies expectations and adds new potential meanings. Perhaps the most common such deviation is the fade to white. Because this approach to the fade involves the image being overwhelmed with light, the fade to white is often used to communicate a feeling of transcendence or oblivion, as in the transition between the final shot and the end credits of Lynne Ramsay's *We Need to Talk About Kevin* (2011). After 17 years attempting to raise and love her emotionally detached and violent child, a mother visits the boy as he is being prepared to serve a prison sentence for a massacre that claimed, among others, his father and sister. As she walks away from the son that destroyed everything she loved, including himself, the mother experiences a devastating ambivalence that combines overwhelming loss and euphoric release, which is

Fade and dissolve in *My Darling Clementine*

When a shot of Wyatt Earp at his brother's grave [1] fades [2] to a shot of Tombstone's main street [3], the transition imbues a sense of solemnity and emphasizes an important passage of time. In the grave scene, Earp has just taken on the position as town marshal. In the scene following the fade, he's been at the job for a while. Later in the story, when a shot of Earp cavorting at a church dance [4] dissolves [5] into a shot of a communal Sunday dinner [6], the dissolve's combined images help stress Earp's (and Tombstone's) increasing civilization.

visually expressed when her point of view of the prison hallway is gradually consumed in white. In *Cries and Whispers* (1972), Ingmar Bergman builds the emotional intensity of his story by cutting back and forth between scenes of the past and the present and ending most of those scenes with a fade-out to a blood-red screen. Bergman has said that he thinks of red as the color of the human soul; his film's sets also often feature the color. The set designs and these edit transitions function in a symbolic system that suggests the cycles of life, love, and death.

Dissolve A dissolve is similar to the fade in a number of ways. Both the fade and the dissolve are commonly used to transition between scenes but are sometimes used within scenes or sequences: both are gradual rather than instantaneous, and the editor controls the duration of each. The differences lie in appearance and usage. With a **dissolve**, the first shot is gradually replaced with the second shot, with no intervening period of a solid color. Instead, the first shot appears to dissolve into the second, so that both images exist simultaneously for a moment before the first shot is completely replaced with the new image. (It sounds more complicated than it looks; usually, this entire process lasts only a matter of a second or two.) Dissolves are also used to emphasize a passage of time between scenes, but because the dissolve combines the two shots so that they momentarily share the screen, the technique is also often used to imply a relationship between the people, objects, or events depicted in the scenes connected by the transition. A good example can be found in *My Darling Clementine*, when a scene depicting the normally rough and tumble Marshal Earp participating in a church dance dissolves to a shot of him carving meat at a communal Sunday dinner. A cut or a fade might have sufficed to get from the last shot of the dance scene to the first shot of the dinner scene, but the dissolve more effectively conveys the relationship between the events: both depict the former gunfighter's evolving role as a civilizing force in the community.

Wipe Like the dissolve and the fade, the **wipe** is a transitional device—often indicating a change of time, place, or location—in which shot B wipes across shot A vertically, horizontally, or diagonally to replace it. A line between the two shots suggests something like a windshield wiper. A soft-edge wipe is indicated by a blurry line; a hard-edge wipe by a sharp line. A jagged line sug-

gests a more violent transition. Unlike the subtler cut, fade, and dissolve transitions, the ostentatious and old-fashioned wipe is rarely used in contemporary films. On those rare occasions when filmmakers do employ the wipe, they usually do so to evoke a previous era. The wipes in *Star Wars* (1977) recall the look of the old 1930s *Flash Gordon* adventure movies that in part inspired director George Lucas. The overt flamboyance of the wipe is also sometimes used to add a level of graphic energy to montage sequences, such as the one that introduces the various scoundrels who populate Guy Ritchie's raucous 2001 crime caper *Snatch*.

Iris-in and iris-out

Volker Schlöndorff's *The Tin Drum* (1979) contains an iris transition that denotes the passage of time, as well as the fall of a woman's fortunes. In a full-screen image, we see the young prosperous Anna selling freshly killed geese. This image irises out [1] until the compressed circular image around the young Anna transitions to another image [2] with a subsequent iris-in revealing Anna as a middle-aged woman with only turnips to sell. This iris transition dramatically and economically portrays the social shift in Germany caused by World War I.

Iris Shot An **iris shot** appears on the screen in two ways. The **iris-out** begins with the image shown as a large circle, which shrinks and closes in around the subject, leaving the rest of the surrounding screen in black. The **iris-in** works in the opposite direction. The image begins as just a small circle in a field of black, and then expands. These terms can be confusing, since the circle of an iris-*in* is actually expanding *out*ward. In this case, the "in" refers to the shot image, which is expanding *in*to the frame and *in*to the edit. Likewise, the shot in an iris-out is being moved *out* of the sequence to be replaced by another image. Like the wipe, the iris-in and iris-out are associated with early cinema and thus are rarely used in modern films. But these transitions still carry expressive potential in the right context. For example, in Gus Van Sant's *To Die For* (1995), an iris-out conveys the state of mind of Suzanne Stone Maretto, a small-town woman obsessed with becoming a TV celebrity. When her unambitious husband proposes that she abandon her pipe dreams and help him work at the family restaurant, an iris-out takes over Suzanne's point of view to squeeze his oblivious face into a tiny circle, which then closes to black, thus visualizing her contempt.

Looking at Editing: *City of God*

As a viewer, you can get a sense of the overall effects of an editor's decisions by studying a film as a creative whole. But you can effectively analyze an editor's contributions to a film only by closely examining specific scenes and sequences. For this reason, we will limit this case study to the intertwined scenes that make up *City of God*'s opening credit sequence. To understand the editing in any scene, we need to determine the scene's intent. To do that, we must first ask ourselves a series of questions.

> What is the story of the scene, and how does that story contribute to the movie's overall narrative?

> What mood or tone does the scene impart? How does it make you feel?

> What meaning and information do you comprehend while watching and after watching the scene?

Once you are able to identify what the scene is trying to do, you can be prepared to evaluate how editing is applied toward those goals.

City of God is a 2002 film set in the 1970s in the *favela* ("shanty town") of Cidade de Deus (aka City of God) outside Rio de Janeiro, Brazil. The movie relates the rise of organized crime in the slum through a number of interconnected characters, principally Li'l Zé, the sociopathic leader of a criminal gang, and Rocket, a young photographer struggling to escape the favela's poverty and violence. Editor Daniel Rezende packs a lot of story into the 155 shots that make up the film's first 3½ minutes. A boisterous outdoor party is underway in the crowded favela: musicians play, drinks are mixed, and food is prepared. A chicken about to be slaughtered for stew meat slips out of the string that binds his foot and bolts an escape down the slum's narrow winding alleyways. Li'l Zé spots the runaway bird and orders his motley gang of young men to catch it. A chaotic chase ensues. Nearby, Rocket and a friend walk and talk about Rocket's plan to take a risky photo as a way to get a job at a newspaper. Meanwhile the chase continues. When a man carrying a load of pots and pans momentarily hampers the pursuit, Li'l Zé pushes him down, draws a pistol, and threatens the man. The chicken flies into a street, where it is almost run over by a passing police truck. Rocket and his friend, who are now walking down the same street, find themselves facing both the chicken and the armed thugs pursuing her. Li'l Zé orders Rocket to catch the chicken, but his attempt to comply is interrupted when policemen pile out of the truck, the gang members draw their guns, and our protagonist finds himself caught between the heavily armed adversaries.

This opening credit sequence serves a number of functions. It introduces and differentiates the two principal characters: Li'l Zé and Rocket. It also establishes the setting as crowded and dirty, but also vibrant, colorful, and full of life. Rocket's impossible position is clearly visualized and dramatized in the sequence's final standoff. Perhaps most important, the central conflict of Rocket's struggle to escape the favela is presented metaphorically in the form of a desperate chicken. The sequence's tone is one of exhilaration and volatility, a mood that places the viewer squarely inside life in the favela. The scene that follows this sequence jumps back in time to begin the story in the 1960s when the characters are children. Knowing how Li'l Zé and Rocket end up changes the way we understand and interpret the story of their begin-

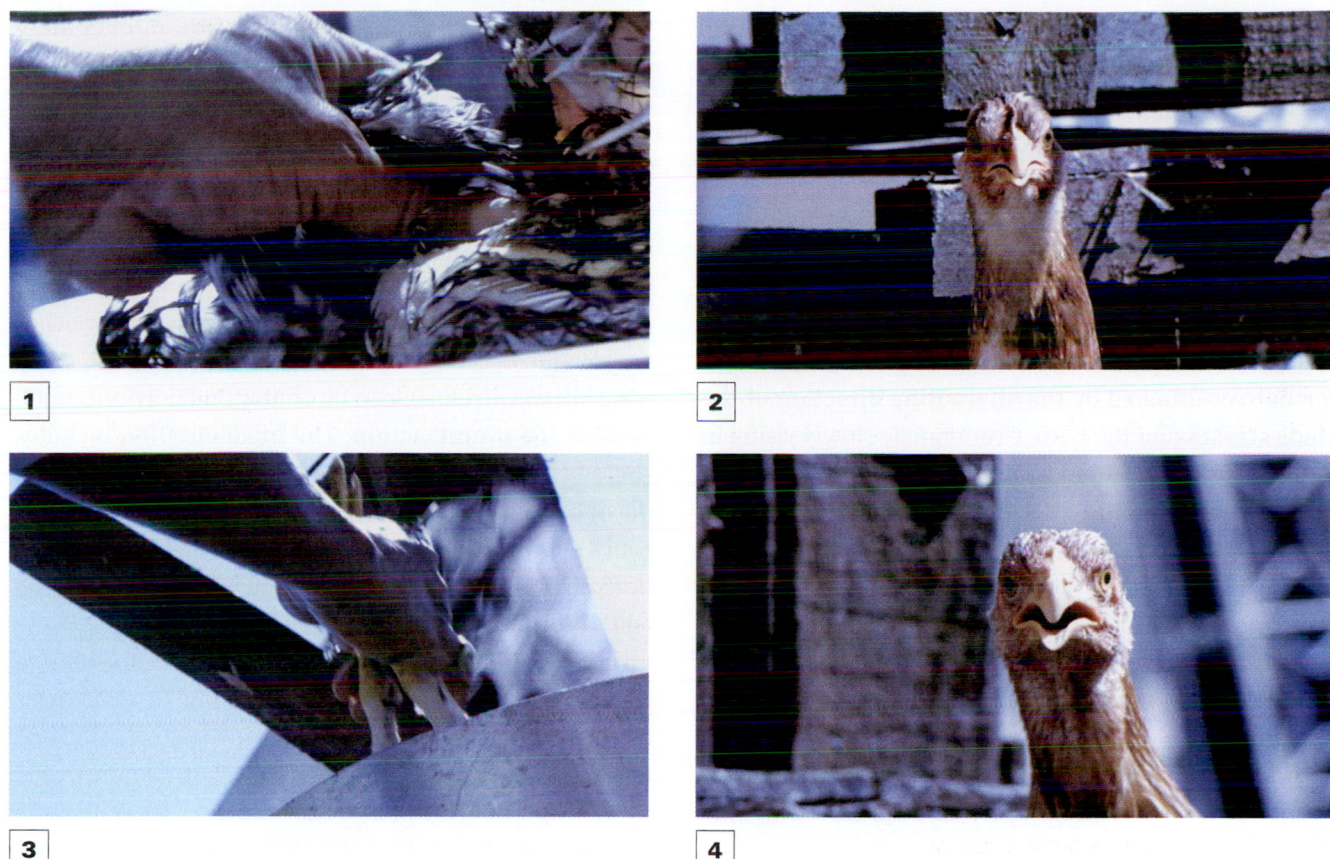

Montage editing creates a fowl performance

The opening sequence in *City of God* demonstrates the montage editing principle Lev Kuleshov tested with his famous experiment: the juxtaposition of images can create new meaning not present in any single shot by itself. When we see shot [1] and shot [2] juxtaposed in sequence, we assume the chicken is watching another chicken being plucked and interpret its expression as one of trepidation. Later in the same sequence, the juxtaposition of a chicken carcass lowered into a pot [3] with a close-up of our star chicken [4] makes us believe that witnessing its fellow hen's fate is increasing its anxiety.

nings. In addition, the chicken-chase scene and its aftermath is repeated and extended at the end of the movie. When we ultimately see the scenes again, we know that the photo Rocket seeks is an image documenting Li'l Zé's criminal activities. Seeing the action once more in the context of previous events alters our experience the second time around. The stakes are higher, since we have now come to care about Rocket and his goals—and have learned to fear Li'l Zé.

Because editors must work with the footage provided, how a scene is shot has a profound influence on the way that scene is cut. For this reason, considering the way in which a scene was photographed is another useful step in any editing analysis. Director Fernando Meirelles wanted to give the film a sense of realism, so he cast mostly nonactors (many of whom were residents of the

favela where the story is set) and enlisted the documentary filmmaker Kátia Lund as his codirector. Much of the movie—and this scene in particular—was shot documentary style, with mobile handheld cameras capturing action as it unfolded. This approach imbues the footage with a dynamic energy that serves the story's tone, but it also limits the editor's ability to employ conventional continuity. Most of the cuts in this sequence use discontinuity and fragmentation, which reinforce the anarchic vitality of the setting, characters, and story.

The Opening Sequence

Sharpening the knife The scene begins with a black, silent screen. The film's first shot, a sudden extreme close-up of a knife blade stroked quickly across a stone, is on-screen less than a half-second before it is replaced by a cut to black that lasts just over 1 second. This black-blade-black pattern repeats three more times, with each knife shot lasting less than 11 frames, thus pushing the limits of the content curve—we have just enough time to recognize the content before the image is over. Interspersing longer durations of black makes these short knife shots feel even more abrupt, and the back and forth pattern initiates a propulsive visual rhythm that is further accentuated by the alternating direction of the blade strokes and the Latin drum music slowly rising in the background. These images of implied violence, and the way they are presented and repeated, create an instant and exhilarating expectation. We know that any blade shown repeatedly and up close is bound to be used. The pattern is broken by an 11-frame extreme close-up of a guitarist's hand gripping a fretboard. The Sun flares in the frame, and this burst of light is used to create a graphic match cut to a camera flash in the next shot: an intercut image of Rocket taking a photograph. This camera pulls back, and the film's title appears—but only

for 44 frames (less than 2 seconds) before another knife stroke takes its place. Even the movie's title card doesn't merit much screen time in this frenetic sequence.

The chicken gets the gist The next 43-second section maintains the rapid-fire pace with sixty-six shots with an average shot length of 16 frames. No master shot is employed, so we are never exactly sure where we are or where each element is in relation to the many other people and objects that populate the scene. In fact, every image is an extreme close-up containing only one small piece of the overall action. The fragmentation includes shots of vegetables being chopped, instruments being played, people dancing, butchered chickens, and—of course—the knife being sharpened. Many of these actions are overlapped and repeated in ways that add to the edit's percussive nature. Interspersed throughout these myriad fragments are seven different close-up shots of a particular chicken in the act of looking. Rezende uses montage editing to convey the chicken's state of mind and tell a story. The same principles Kuleshov demonstrated in his experiment impel us to interpret the chicken's

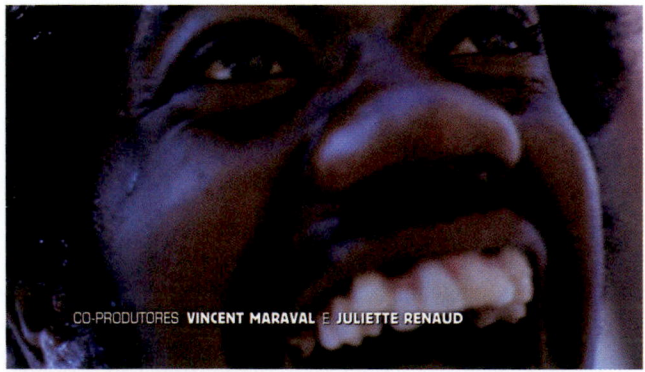

CO-PRODUTORES **VINCENT MARAVAL** E **JULIETTE RENAUD**

1

PRODUÇÃO EXECUTIVA **ELISA TOLOMELLI**

2

3

Editing differentiates characters

During *City of God*'s opening scene, Li'l Zé himself is portrayed in an overlapping action jump cut linking two extreme close-ups of his laughing face [1, 2]. His distorted features combine with the discontinuity to imply instability and menace. The protagonist Rocket is introduced in a way that clearly differentiates the young photographer from his volatile nemesis. The sustained and smooth shot [3] is in stark contrast to the fast-paced handheld fragmentation that dominates the rest of the sequence.

expression as increasingly fearful each time the bird's staring face is juxtaposed with another extreme close-up. Editing makes it seem as if she is ogling the knife being sharpened, a carrot being chopped, and another, less fortunate chicken having its throat cut, getting plucked, being lowered into boiling water, and finally gutted.

The chicken escapes The next fourteen shots present a rhythmic and narrative shift. The average shot duration almost doubles, and only three images of the party are included. The action is still highly fragmented, but the focus is now clearly on the chicken. Three sequential shots show different discontinuous angles of the chicken tugging on, pecking at, and slipping free of its string leash. In a conventional continuity–style sequence, these actions would seem disjointed, but by this stage in the sequence, viewers have been conditioned to a different way of seeing. A single 19-frame shot of a hand striking a tambourine separates the leash sequence from another fragmented action: five shots depict the chicken jumping off the party platform and flapping to the alleyway below. The final downward tilt shot of this leap to freedom leads to a kind of comparative match cut that extends the downward movement of the chicken's landing over the cut to another downward tilt shot to reveal the blood and feathers of less rebellious poultry. A rhythmic shift concludes the sequence with a 4½-second shot (more than twice as long as any other shot in the scene thus far) of the chicken peering around a corner and treading cautiously into a walkway. At least the chicken *seems* to be peering and treading, thanks to the previous juxtapositions that have invested the runaway fowl with a goal-driven personality. This sustained shot provides a reprieve from the nonstop action and editing, as well as a sort of false resolution. For a brief moment, it seems the chicken is safe at last.

The Chase, Part 1 That expectation is quickly shattered when Li'l Zé notices the loose chicken and gleefully orders his gang to capture the bird. The young crew leaps into action, and so does the determined chicken. The average shot duration lengthens to two full seconds in this fifteen-shot sequence. But the pace doesn't necessarily diminish, since the wider-framed shots contain setting details, multiple subjects, and physical action. This more complex subject matter takes longer to process, which means that it takes the viewer more time to feel in-

Violating the 180-degree rule to convey character
The camera viewpoint jumps back and forth across the axis of action [1–3] to repeatedly reverse spatial orientation during a recurring action in a way that conveys the violent instability of the character Li'l Zé.

stinctively ready for the next shot. The chase through the winding alleyways is disorderly, but not necessarily discontinuous. Although the action is captured with a handheld camera from constantly shifting perspectives, the unbroken action of the running men unifies the

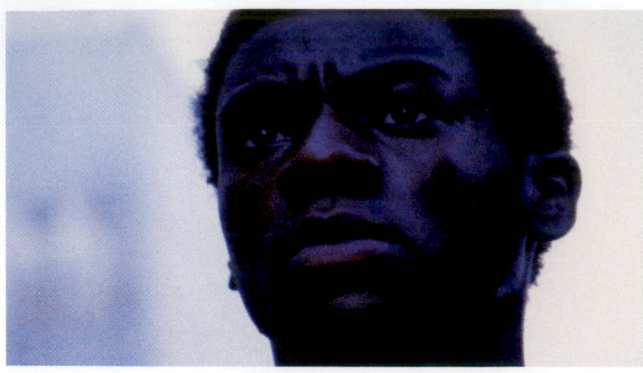

1

2

Point-of-view editing

The final moments of *City of God*'s opening sequence uses point-of-view juxtapositions like this one [1, 2] to structure the scene around the protagonist Rocket.

multiple angles and allows for cuts that match on the action of their movements.

Parallel Editing One minute forty-three seconds into the film, an extended and stable shot suddenly interrupts the pandemonium of the chicken chase. At 13½ seconds, the shot of Rocket and a friend discussing a photograph is almost three times longer than any other shot in the film's opening sequence. This sudden rhythmic and stylistic shift clearly differentiates the protagonist from the chaos that precedes his appearance. As Rocket walks off the screen, a cut to Li'l Zé leading his minions drops us back into the action.

The Chase, Part 2 This sequence of twenty-four shots picks up the pace of the chase by shortening the average shot length to 1¼ seconds. When the gang's pursuit intersects the path of a man carrying a load of tin cookware, discontinuity is again employed to characterize Li'l Zé as dangerously unstable. The gang leader shoves the man to the ground in one shot. For the next shot, the camera violates the 180-degree rule by crossing the line to show a reversed composition of the characters performing the same overlapped action. The camera then once again jumps the line back to its original position to repeat the same action in the opposite spatial orientation we just witnessed. A measure of continuity returns when a match-on-action is used to link the two to a shot depicting Li'l Zé drawing his gun to threaten his victim. But it doesn't last—Li'l Zé's action of yelling after his scrambling underlings is conveyed with a jump cut. The pursuit continues with alternating shots of the sprinting gang and the fleeing chicken until the chase sequence finally concludes with five shots that fragment the action of the chicken taking a flying and flapping leap into a city street.

The Standoff in the Street The parallel actions of Rocket and Li'l Zé (and the chicken) converge in the opening's final sequence of twenty-two shots. A change in pace momentarily reduces the manic energy; the 2¼-second average shot length is the longest we've experienced so far. But the tension doesn't fully dissipate; it simply refocuses. The moment the chicken runs into Rocket, the young photographer takes over as the target of the gang and the center of the scene. This pivotal position is reflected in the editing that uses point of view to structure the remaining shots around Rocket. He is either the looking character whose point of view the next shot depicts or the subject of a point-of-view shot that follows a looking shot of Li'l Zé and his gang. The scene's final shot uses the act of looking to launch a graphic match cut that propels the story back in time. As Rocket crouches defensively and looks back and forth between the police and the gang, the camera rapidly circles the trapped protagonist until the shot dissolves into an image of the character as a child hunkered in defense of a soccer goal.

1

2

A moving graphic match transition

A revolving shot of Rocket [1] dissolves into a shot that matches the camera movement as well as the subject's crouching posture [2]. This graphic match transitions to a Rocket as a child in a scene set in the previous decade.

ANALYZING EDITING

Studying a film as a whole can provide you with a sense of the editing styles and techniques the movie employs. But to effectively analyze how editing shapes your experience, you must closely examine specific scenes and sequences, paying attention to the ways in which individual shots have been selected, linked, and ordered. Don't let editing's intentional invisibility make you miss cuts and other transitions. Resist the tendency to consider editing an inevitable assembly of predetermined shots. Remember that fragmentation, juxtaposition, and duration can impart meaning, mood, and state of mind.

SCREENING CHECKLIST: EDITING

✔ Determining the intent of a scene will help you understand how and why editing is used. Ask yourself what is the story of the scene, and how does that story contribute to the movie's overall narrative? What mood does the scene make you experience? What meaning and information do you derive from watching the scene?

✔ Are actions and events presented in a single unbroken shot or are they fragmented into multiple shots? If fragmentation is used, how does it affect your understanding and experience?

✔ Remember that juxtaposing two images can create new meaning not present in either shot by itself. What kind of juxtapositions in the scene or sequence impart a third and new meaning?

✔ Look for different types of match cuts in the film. What sort of visual or narrative information is each match cut conveying?

✔ Is editing used to convey spatial relationships between characters, objects, and actions? If so, how?

✔ Does the scene use point-of-view editing? If so, does the point-of-view shot convey a spatial or psychological relationship?

✔ How does time function in the sequence? Is time condensed between shots? Are transitions used to indicate or emphasize a movement through time?

✔ Do any shots seem to be cut before or after the peak of the content curve? How does deviating from a standard approach to duration change the way you experience and interpret the shot?

✔ As each shot cuts to the next shot in the scene or sequence, tap your finger to get a feeling for the pace of the editing. How would you describe that pace? Does it stay constant or does it speed up or slow down? How do rhythmic shifts and patterns affect mood and meaning?

✔ Are there any moments in the scene in which the traditional conventions of continuity editing are violated in some way? Describe how these moments appear on-screen. What do you think is the significance of these discontinuous edits? What information, meaning, or mood do they impart?

✔ Keep track of the types of transitions from shot to shot and scene to scene. Are the transitions smooth and subtle or intentionally jarring? What information and meaning, if any, is conveyed by the transition?

Questions for Review

1. What is the basic building block of film editing?
2. What are the five primary functions of editing?
3. What are some of the differences between editing of narrative movies and documentaries?
4. How does editing influence and inform the way movies are shot?
5. What is continuity editing? What does it contribute to a movie?
6. What is the purpose of the 180-degree system? How does it work?
7. Name and describe the various types of match cuts.
8. What is the difference between crosscutting and intercutting?
9. How is the content curve used to determine the duration of a shot?
10. What is discontinuity editing? Given the dominance of continuity editing in mainstream filmmaking, what role does discontinuity editing usually play?

Dunkirk (2017). Christopher Nolan, director. Pictured (*looking up*): Fionn Whitehead.

SOUND

LEARNING OBJECTIVES

After reading this chapter, you should be able to

- explain the assumptions influencing contemporary sound design.
- differentiate among sound recording, sound editing, and sound mixing.
- understand the perceptual characteristics of sound: pitch, loudness, and quality.
- name and define the principal sources of film sound.
- describe the difference between diegetic and nondiegetic sound.
- distinguish between the four major types of film sound.
- explain the functions of film sound.
- describe how sound can call attention to both the spatial and temporal dimensions of a scene.
- explain how sound helps to create meaning in a movie.

What Is Sound?

The movies engage two senses: vision and hearing. Although some viewers and even filmmakers assume that the cinematographic image is paramount, what we hear from the screen can be at least as significant as what we see on it, and sometimes what we hear is more significant. Director Steven Spielberg says, "The eye sees better when the sound is great." Sound—talking, laughing, singing, music, and the aural effects of objects and settings—can be as expressive as any of the other narrative and stylistic elements of cinematic form. What we hear in a movie is often technologically more complicated to produce than what we see. In fact, because of the constant advances in digital technology, sound may be the most intensively creative part of contemporary moviemaking. Spielberg, for one, has also said that, since the 1970s, breakthroughs in sound have been the movie industry's most important technical and creative innovations. He does not mean "using the technology to show off" by producing gimmicky sounds that distract you from the story being told, but rather sound used as an integral storytelling element.[1]

Christopher Nolan's *Inception* (2010) is a case in point. As seems appropriate for a science-fiction action movie

about the creative powers of the human mind—how our thoughts and dreams create imaginary worlds—the story is complex and intellectually challenging. And the sound design, which shifts seamlessly between imagination and reality, and our perceptions of them, is equally caught up in its own intricacies. Richard King is responsible for the memorable sound editing of *Inception* and many other distinguished movies, including *War of the Worlds* (2005; discussed later in this chapter). His style produces sound that is multilayered and deeply textured, incorporating a bold and aggressive mix of sounds and music that complement the vivid visual and special effects. Virtually all of the sounds were produced in the studio, including the incredible sounds of the weapons, vehicles, explosions, and scenes of destruction.

Stanley Kubrick's *The Shining* (1980) opens with a series of helicopter point-of-view shots that, without the accompanying sound, might be mistaken for a TV commercial. In these shots, we see a magnificent landscape, a river, and then a yellow Volkswagen driving upward into the mountains on a winding highway. Whereas we might expect to hear a purring car engine, car wheels rolling over asphalt, or the passengers' conversation, instead we hear music: an electronic synthesis by composers Wendy Carlos and Rachel Elkind of the *Dies Irae*, one of the most famous Gregorian chants, which became the fundamental music of the Roman Catholic Church. The *Dies Irae* (literally, "the day of wrath") is based on Zephaniah 1:14–16, a reflection on the Last Judgment. It is one section of the Requiem Mass, or Mass for the Dead. Experiencing the shots together with the sound track, we wonder about the location, the driver, and the destination. What we hear gives life to what we see and offers some clues to its meaning. The symbolic import and emotional impact of this music transforms the footage into a movie pulsating with portentous energy and dramatic potential. Once we identify this music, we suspect it is warning us that something ominous is going to happen before the movie ends. Thus forewarned, we are neither misled nor dissatisfied.

The sound in the scenes just described (or in any movie scene) operates on both physical and psychological levels. For most narrative films, sound provides cues that help us form expectations about meaning; in some cases, sound actually shapes our analyses and interpretations. Sound calls attention not only to itself but also to

---

1. Rick Lyman, "A Director's Journey into a Darkness of the Heart," *New York Times* (June 24, 2001), sec. 2, p. 24.

Sound as meaning

Inception is about an illegal espionage project that enters the subconscious minds of its targets to gain valuable information. Dominic Cobb, the leader of the team, has hired Ariadne, a gifted young architecture student, to design labyrinthine dreamscapes for this work, but she (like the viewer) is still in the learning stage. In this image, they sit in a Parisian café that is part of a larger street scene exploding all around them. Ariadne (like the viewer) is astonished to see that they sit unhurt while the perceivable world is destroyed around them, but then Ariadne awakens in the design studio to realize that she has been dreaming this episode. The action is crafted with such visual and aural detail that everything we see—flower pots, people, wine glasses, tables, chairs, automobiles—explodes in its own unique way and with its own unique sound. Every sight and sound image has been created and implanted in Ariadne's dream to show her (and the viewer) the power of the "dreams within dreams" project in which she is now a key player.

silence, to the various roles that each plays in our world and in the world of a film. The option of using silence is one crucial difference between silent and sound films; a sound film can emphasize silence, but a silent film has no option. As light and dark create the image, so sound and silence create the sound track. Each property—light, dark, sound, silence—appeals to our senses differently.

In film history, the transition to sound began in 1927. It brought major aesthetic and technological changes in the way movies were written, acted, directed, and screened to the public (see Chapters 10 and 11). After the first few sound movies, where sound was more of a novelty than a formal element in the telling of the story, a period of creative innovation helped integrate sound—vocal sounds, environmental sounds, music, and silence—into the movies. The results of this innovation can be seen and heard in some of the great movies of the 1930s, including Rouben Mamoulian's *Applause* (1929), Fritz Lang's *M* (1931), and Ernst Lubitsch's *Trouble in Paradise* (1932). Comparing one or more of these movies to several silent classics will help you to understand how profoundly sound changed the movies.

Like every other component of film form, film sound is the product of specific decisions by the filmmakers. The group responsible for the sound in movies, the **sound crew**, generates and controls the sound physically, manipulating its properties to produce the effects that the director desires. Let's look more closely at the various aspects of sound production controlled by the sound crew.

Sound Production

Sound production consists of four phases: design, recording, editing, and mixing. Although we might suppose that most of the sounds in a movie are the result of recording during filming (such sounds are called *production sounds*), the reality is that most film sounds are constructed during the postproduction phase (and thus are called *postproduction sounds*). But before any sounds are recorded or constructed, the overall plan for a movie's sound must be made. That planning process is called *sound design*.

Design

Sound design is the art of creating the sound for a film. As motion-picture sound has become increasingly innovative and complex, the result of comprehensive sound design, the sound designer's role has become more well known. Given its name by film editor Walter Murch—the sound designer for such movies as Francis Ford Coppola's *The Conversation* (1974) and *Apocalypse Now* (1979) and Anthony Minghella's *The English Patient* (1996) and *Cold Mountain* (2003)—sound design combines the crafts of editing and mixing and, like them, involves matters both theoretical and practical.[2]

Although many filmmakers continue to understand and manipulate sound in conventional ways, sound design has produced major advances in how movies are conceived, made, viewed, and interpreted. Until the 1970s, the vast majority of producers and directors thought about sound only after the picture was shot. They did not design films with sound in mind and frequently did not fully recognize that decisions about art direction, composition, lighting, cinematography, and acting would ultimately influence how sound tracks would be created and mixed. They considered sound satisfactory if it could distract from or cover up mistakes in shooting and create the illusion that the audience was hearing what it was seeing.

By contrast, the contemporary concept of sound design rests on the following basic assumptions:

❭ Sound should be integral to all three phases of film production (preproduction, production, and postproduction), not an afterthought to be added in postproduction only.

❭ A film's sound is potentially as expressive as its images.

❭ Image and sound can create different worlds.

❭ Image and sound are co-expressible.

A sound designer treats the sound track of a film the way a painter treats a canvas. For each shot, the designer first identifies all the sounds necessary to the story and plot. The next step is laying in all the background tones (different tones equal different colors) to create the support necessary for adding the specific sounds that help the scene to function. According to Tomlinson Holman (the creator of Lucasfilm's THX sound technology), "Sound design is the art of getting the right sound in the right place at the right time."[3] Today, many directors—Joel Coen and David Lynch, among others—are notable for their comprehensive knowledge and expressive use of sound.

Before sound design was widely accepted, the responsibilities for sound were divided among recording, rerecording, editing, mixing, and sound-effects crews; these crews sometimes overlapped but often did not. In the industry's attempt to integrate all aspects of sound in a movie, from planning to postproduction, the sound designer began to supervise all these responsibilities—a development initially resented by many traditional sound specialists, who felt their autonomy was being compromised. It is now conventional for sound designers (or supervising sound editors) to oversee the creation and control of the sounds (and silences) we hear in movies. They are, in a sense, advocates for sound.

During preproduction, sound designers encourage directors and other collaborators to understand that what characters hear is potentially as significant as what they see. This is especially true for point-of-view shots, which focus characters' (and audiences') attention on specific sights or sounds. Sound designers encourage screenwriters to consider all kinds of sound; working with directors, they indicate in shooting scripts what voices, sounds, or music may be appropriate at particular points. They also urge their collaborators to plan the settings, lighting, cinematography, and acting (particularly the movement of actors within the settings) with an awareness of how their decisions might affect sound. During production, sound designers supervise the implementation of the sound design. During postproduction, after the production sound track has been cut along with the images, they aid the editing team. But although their results may far exceed the audience's expectations of clarity and fidelity, sound designers keep their eyes and ears on the story being told. They want audiences not only to regard sound tracks as seriously as they do visual images but also to interpret sounds as integral to understanding those images.

---

2. Randy Thom, "Designing a Movie for Sound" (1998), www.filmsound.org/articles/designing_for_soundelder.htm (accessed February 4, 2006).

3. Tomlinson Holman, *Sound for Film and Television* (Boston: Focal Press, 1997), p. 172.

Recording

The process of recording sound is very similar to the process of hearing. Just as the human ear converts sounds into nerve impulses that the brain identifies, so the microphone converts sound waves into electrical signals that are then recorded and stored. The history of recording movie sound has evolved from optical and magnetic systems to the digital systems used in today's professional productions. Of the various types of film sound (which will be described later in the chapter), dialogue is the only type typically recorded during production. Everything else is added in the editing and mixing stages of postproduction.

The recording of production sound is the responsibility of the production sound mixer and a team of assistants, which includes, on the set, a sound recordist, a sound mixer, a microphone **boom** operator, and wranglers (in charge of the power supply, electrical connections, and cables). This team must place and/or move the microphones so that the sound corresponds to the space between actors and camera and the dialogue will be as free from background noise as possible.

On set, the motion-picture camera is responsible only for recording the image; the dialogue sound is recorded using a separate sound recorder, an approach known as **double-system recording**. Before any dialogue shot is captured on set, an assistant "claps" the hinged pieces of a simple device called the slate (also known as a clapboard or sticks) to create a simultaneous image and sound "mark" that are used to line up (or synchronize) the separate image and sound recordings in postproduction, a process referred to as synching. Newer digital slates place matching electronic mark on the corresponding elements instead of relying on actual visual and sound cues. This system allows both for maximum quality control and for the manifold manipulation of sound during postproduction editing, mixing, and synchronization. Once the sound has been recorded and stored, the process of editing it begins.

Editing

The editor is responsible for the overall process of editing and for the sound crew, which consists of a supervising sound editor, sound editors (who usually concentrate on their specialties: dialogue, music, or sound effects), sound mixers, rerecording mixers, sound-effects person-

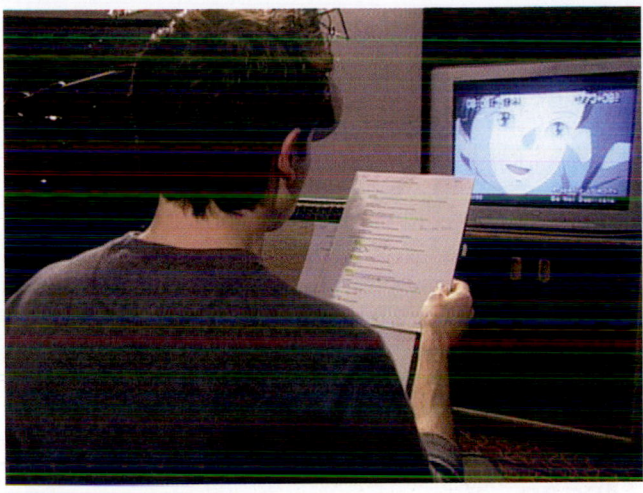

ADR in action

For the American version of Hayao Miyazaki's animated movie *Spirited Away* (2001), it was necessary to rerecord the characters' voices using English-speaking actors and the ADR (automatic dialogue replacement) system. Here, Jason Marsden (the voice of Haku), standing in front of a microphone and holding his script, lip-synchs his lines to coordinate with the action on the monitor in the background.

nel, and Foley artists. The editor also works closely with the musical composer or those responsible for selecting music from other sources. In the editing room, the editor is in charge; but the director and the sound designer may also take part in the process.

The process of editing, of both pictures and sounds, usually lasts longer than the shooting itself. Sound editing takes up a great deal of that time, because a significant portion of the dialogue and all of the sound effects and music are created and/or added during postproduction. Included in this process is the addition of Foley sounds (discussed later in the chapter) for verisimilitude and emphasis and the creation and layering of ambience using traffic, crowd voices, and other background sounds.

Filmmakers first screen the **dailies** (or rushes), which are synchronized picture/sound work prints of a day's shooting. From these they select the usable individual shots from among the multiple takes, sort out the **outtakes** (any footage that will not be used), log the usable footage so it is easy to follow through the rest of the process, and decide which dialogue needs rerecording and which sound effects are necessary. If ambient or other noises have marred the quality of the dialogue recorded during photography, the actors are asked to come back, view the faulty scene, and perform the dialogue again while watching a looped (repeating) recording of the moment in question, a process known as **automatic dialogue replacement (ADR)**, or looping. It's very much like selective lip-synching; when an acceptable rerecording that matches the take has been made, an ADR editor inserts it into the movie. Finally, the sound-editing team synchronizes the sound and visual tracks. Because the entire editing and mixing process is now done digitally, a certain amount of overlap can occur between the sound editing and mixing stages.

Mixing

Mixing is the process of combining all of the different individual edited tracks of dialogue, sound effects, music, and so forth, into one composite sound track to play in synchronization with the edited picture.

The number of sound tracks used in a movie depends on the kind and amount of sound needed to tell each part of the story; thus, filmmakers have an unlimited resource at their disposal. No matter how many tracks are used, they are usually combined and compressed during the final mixing. Working with their crew, sound mixers adjust the relative loudness and various aspects of sound quality; filter out unwanted sounds; and create, according to the needs of the screenplay, the right balance of dialogue, music, and sound effects. The result is a sort of "audio mise-en-scène" that emphasizes significant sound elements in the mix, just as a visual composition uses placement and size in frame to feature significant subject matter in a shot. Sound elements that are mixed with lower loudness may not be emphasized, but they may still contribute to a scene's mood or meaning, much like background or other less prevalent visual elements affect the way we interpret composed images.

This resembles the typical recording process for popular music, in which drums, bass, guitars, vocals, and so on are recorded separately and then mixed and adjusted to achieve the desired acoustic quality and loudness. The ideal result of sound mixing is clear and clean, so whatever the desired effect is, the audience will hear it clearly and cleanly. Even if what the filmmakers want is distorted or cluttered sound, the audience will hear that distortion or clutter perfectly.

With this background on the four basic stages of sound production—what goes on during sound design, recording, editing, and mixing—we're ready now to look more closely at the actual characteristics that make up the sounds we hear in real life as well as in the movies.

Describing Film Sound

When talking or writing about a movie's sound, you should be able to describe a sound in terms of its perceptual characteristics (determined by its pitch, loudness, quality, and fidelity), its source (where it comes from), and its type (vocal or musical, for example). To that end, let's begin by taking a closer look at the perceptual characteristics of sound.

Pitch, Loudness, Quality

The **pitch** (or level) of a sound can be high (like the screech of tires on pavement), low (like the rumble of a boulder barreling downhill), or somewhere between these extremes. Pitch is defined by the **frequency** (or speed) with which it is produced (the number of sound waves produced per second). Most sounds fall somewhere in the middle of the scale. But the extremes of high and low, as well as the distinctions between high pitch and low pitch, are often exploited by filmmakers to influence our experience and interpretation of a movie.

In Victor Fleming's *The Wizard of Oz* (1939; sound by Douglas Shearer), the voice of the "wizard" has two pitches—the high pitch of the harmless man behind the curtain and the deep, booming pitch of the magnificent "wizard." Each helps us to judge the trustworthiness of the character's statements. Pitch is used to convey a character's state of mind in Stanley Kubrick's *The Shining* (1980). Wendy is already afraid of her increasingly agitated husband, Jack, when she enters the vast room where he's been diligently working on his novel. The low, ominous notes dominating the abstract score music underline her dread as she treads closer to his now-unoccupied typewriter. When Wendy sees that all of his hours of writing have been devoted to writing the same ten words over and over again, the pitch of the musical tones rise to signal that dread has turned to alarm. By the time Jack creeps up behind her, Wendy is consumed with panic, and the notes of the score are shrieking at the highest possible pitch.

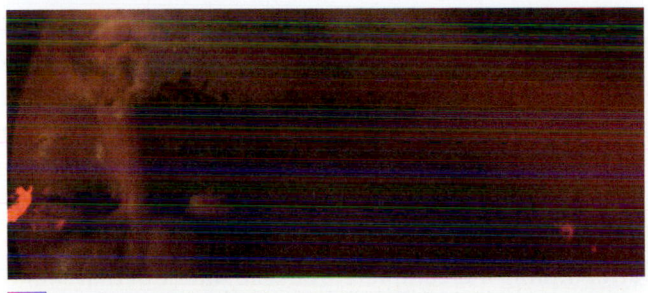

Sound and state of mind

The sound design of the first scene in Francis Ford Coppola's Vietnam war epic *Apocalypse Now* (1979) helps us experience the state of mind of the troubled protagonist, Captain Benjamin L. Willard. In the opening images, firebombs explode across a jungle but produce no sound; all we hear is a haunting Doors song. These incongruous elements are revealed to be Willard's dreamlike musings when the picture dissolves to his inverted face [1]. As military helicopters cross the images superimposed over Willard [2], the reverberations of their rotating blades morph into the sound of the ceiling fan, back in the real world, in the sweltering Saigon hotel room where he is stuck awaiting orders [3]. Later, as Willard explains (in voice-over) his consuming need to return to the jungle, the ambient noises of the city surrounding him are gradually replaced with the sounds of wild birds and insects.

Sound moves through the air in a wave that is acted upon by factors in the physical environment. Think of this as analogous to the wave that ripples outward when you throw a rock into a pond—a wave that is acted upon by the depth and width of the pond. The **loudness** (or volume or intensity) of a sound depends on its **amplitude**, the degree of motion of the air (or other medium) within the sound wave. The greater the amplitude of the sound wave, the harder it strikes the eardrum and thus the louder the sound. Again, although movies typically maintain a consistent level of moderate loudness throughout, filmmakers sometimes use the extremes (near silence or shocking loudness) to signal something important or to complement the overall mood and tone of a scene. In *The Shining*, during the scene in which Wendy and Jack argue and she strikes him with a baseball bat, Kubrick slowly increases the loudness of all the sounds to call attention to the growing tension.

The **quality** (also known as timbre, texture, or color) of a sound includes those characteristics that enable us to distinguish sounds that have the same pitch and loudness. In music, the same note played at the same volume on three different instruments (say, a piano, violin, and oboe) will produce tones that are identical in frequency and amplitude but very different in quality. The sound produced by each of these instruments has its own **harmonic content**, which can be measured as wavelengths. In talking about movie sounds, however, we do not need scientific apparatus to measure the harmonic content, because most often we see what we hear.

In the opening sequence of Francis Ford Coppola's *Apocalypse Now* (1979; sound designer Walter Murch), the sound comes from many sources—including helicopters, the fan in a hotel room, explosions, jungle noises, a smashed mirror, the Doors' recording of "The End," voice-over narration, and dialogue—each contributing its own qualities to an overall rich texture. Although many of these sounds are distorted or slowed down to characterize both the dreamlike, otherworldly quality of the setting and Captain Benjamin L. Willard's (Martin Sheen) state of mind, they have been recorded and played back with such accuracy that we can easily distinguish among them.

Fidelity

Fidelity is a sound's faithfulness or unfaithfulness to its source. Ang Lee's *The Ice Storm* (1997; sound-effects designer Eugene Gearty) faithfully exploits the sounds of a violent ice storm to underscore the tragic lives of two dysfunctional Connecticut families, the Hoods and the

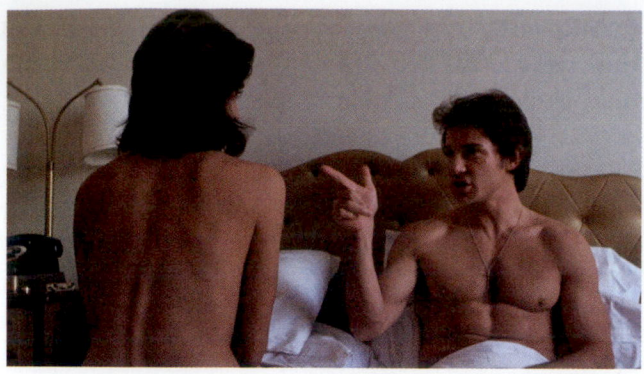

Nonfaithful sound

In *Mean Streets* (1973), Martin Scorsese uses nonfaithful sound when Charlie, after making love to Teresa, playfully points his fingers at her as if they were a gun and pulls the "trigger." We hear a gunshot, but there is no danger, for this is just a lovers' quarrel.

Carvers. At the climax of the movie, in the midst of the storm, Lee meticulously observes the phenomena and records the sounds of icy rain as it falls on the ground or strikes the windows of houses and cars, icy branches that crackle in the wind and crash to the ground, and the crunch of a commuter train's wheels on the icy rails. As the marriage of Ben and Elena Hood (Kevin Kline and Joan Allen), which is already on the rocks, completely falls apart, the ice storm has a powerful, even mystical effect on the lives of these characters, and its harsh breaking sounds serve as a metaphor for their frail lives while providing an audibly faithful reminder of the power of nature.

An excellent early example of a sound effect that is not faithful to its source occurs in Rouben Mamoulian's *Love Me Tonight* (1932). During the farcical scene in which "Baron" Courtelin tells Princess Jeanette, whom he is wooing, that he is not royalty but just an ordinary tailor, pandemonium breaks out in the royal residence. As family and guests flutter about the palace singing of this deception, one of the princess's old aunts accidentally knocks a vase off a table. As it hits the floor and shatters, we hear the incongruous sound of a bomb exploding, as if to suggest that the aristocratic social order is under attack.

Sources of Film Sound

By *source*, we mean "the location from which a sound originates." Obviously, as mentioned already, most of the sounds heard in a movie literally originate from post-production processes. But when we talk about source, we're speaking of the implied origin of that sound, whether it's a production sound or a postproduction sound. For example, the sound of footsteps that accompany a shot of a character walking along a sidewalk may have been constructed by Foley artists in a sound studio after filming was completed, but the source of that sound is implied to be on-screen—created by the character while walking.

The terms used to describe the source of a movie sound are *diegetic* or *nondiegetic*, *on-screen* or *offscreen*, and *internal* or *external*. Let's look at how these sounds are used in movies.

Diegetic versus Nondiegetic

As you know from the "Story and Plot" section in Chapter 4, the word *diegesis* refers to the total world of a film's story, consisting perceptually of figures, motion, color, and sound. **Diegetic sounds** come from a source within a film's world; they are the sounds heard by both the movie's audience and characters. **Nondiegetic sounds**, which come from a source outside that world, are heard only by the audience. Most diegetic sound gives us an awareness of both the spatial and the temporal dimensions of the shot from which the sound emanates; most

Diegetic sound in action

In John Schlesinger's *Midnight Cowboy* (1969), right after stepping in front of an oncoming car (which screeches to a halt and honks its horn), "Ratso" Rizzo (*right*) interrupts his conversation with Joe Buck (*left*) to shout one of the most famous movie lines of all time: "I'm walkin' here!" Even surrounded by everyday Manhattan pedestrian and traffic noise, Rizzo's nasal voice and heavy "Noo Yawk" accent help characterize him as the extremely eccentric and comic foil to Buck, a new and unseasoned arrival in the big city.

Diegetic and nondiegetic sounds share a scene

The Lobster (2015; director Yorgos Lanthimos) is a dystopian satire depicting a world in which unpaired adults are forced to stay at a remote resort. Those who cannot find a suitable (and willing) partner within 45 days are forcibly transformed into animals. The sappy romantic music we hear in a scene in which the mostly doomed single residents attend a dance lends a sense of irony to their absurd and sad situation. This music is clearly sourced in the scene [1] and is thus diegetic. But when the protagonist, David, crosses the dance floor in search of a potential partner, the band's diegetic song is temporarily replaced by dramatic—and nondiegetic—orchestral score music that emphasizes his anxiety in this high-stakes situation [2].

nondiegetic sound has no relevant spatial or temporal dimensions. For example, the electronic music that plays during the opening sequence of Stanley Kubrick's *The Shining* (1980) is completely nondiegetic: we're not supposed to assume that the music is coming from the sky, or playing on the car radio, or coming from any location in the scene on-screen.

Diegetic sound can be either internal or external, on-screen or offscreen, and recorded during production or constructed during postproduction. The most familiar kind of movie sound is diegetic, on-screen sound that occurs simultaneously with the image. All of the sounds that accompany everyday actions and speech depicted on-screen—footsteps on pavement, a knock on a door, the ring of a telephone, the report from a fired gun, ordinary dialogue—are diegetic.

Nondiegetic sound is offscreen and recorded during postproduction, and it is assumed to be inaudible to the characters on-screen. The most familiar forms of nondiegetic sound are musical scores and narration spoken by a voice that does not originate from the same place and time as the characters on the screen. When Redmond Barry attracts the attention of the countess of Lyndon in Stanley Kubrick's *Barry Lyndon* (1975) during a visually magnificent scene accompanied by the equally memorable music from the second movement of Franz Schubert's Trio no. 2 in E-flat Major (D. 929, op. 100) for piano, violin, and cello, the instrumentalists are nowhere to be seen; furthermore, we do not expect to see them. We accept, as a familiar convention, that this kind of music reflects the historical period being depicted but does not emanate from the world of the story.

The standard conventions of diegetic and nondiegetic sound may be modified for other effects. In Bobby and Peter Farrelly's *There's Something about Mary* (1998), for example, the "chorus" troubadour, Jonathan exists outside the story, which makes him and his songs nondiegetic even though we can see him. The Farrellys play with this concept by having Jonathan get shot accidentally in the climactic scene and thus become part of the story.

On-Screen versus Offscreen

On-screen sound emanates from a source that we can see. **Offscreen sound**, which can be either diegetic or nondiegetic, derives from a source that we do not see. When offscreen sound is diegetic, it consists of sound effects, music, or vocals that emanate from the world of the story. When nondiegetic, it takes the form of a musical score or narration by someone who is not a character in the story. Note that on-screen and offscreen sound are also referred to, respectively, as simultaneous and nonsimultaneous sound. **Simultaneous sound** is diegetic and on-screen; **nonsimultaneous sound** occurs familiarly when a character has a mental flashback to an earlier voice that recalls a conversation or an earlier sound that identifies a place. We recognize the sound too because its identity has previously been established in the movie.

Somewhere between on-screen and offscreen sound is **asynchronous sound**. We are aware of it when we sense a discrepancy between the things heard and the things seen on the screen. It is either a sound that is closely related to the action but not precisely synchronized with it or a sound that either anticipates or follows the action to which it belongs. Because we cannot see its source, asynchronous sound seems mysterious and raises our curiosity and expectations. Thus it offers creative opportunities for building tension and surprise in a scene.

Asynchronous sound was used expressively in some of the first sound movies by such innovators as King Vidor, Rouben Mamoulian, and René Clair. For example, in his classic *Le Million* (1931), director René Clair uses asynchronous sound for humorous effect when we see characters scrambling to find a valuable lottery ticket and hear the sounds of a football game. Another classic example (with a variation) occurs in Alfred Hitchcock's *The 39 Steps* (1935). A landlady enters a room, discovers a dead body, turns to face the camera, and opens her mouth as if to scream. At least, that's what we expect to hear. Instead, as she opens her mouth, we hear the high-pitched sound of a train whistle, and then Hitchcock cuts to a shot of a train speeding out of a tunnel. The sound seems to come from the landlady's mouth, but this is in fact an asynchronous sound bridge linking two simultaneous actions occurring in different places.

Most movies provide a blend of offscreen and on-screen sounds that seems very natural and verisimilar, leading us to almost overlook the distinction between them. Some uses of sound, however, call attention to themselves; for example, when a scene favors offscreen sounds or excludes on-screen sounds altogether, we usually take notice. The total absence of diegetic, on-screen sound where we expect it most can be disturbing, as it is in the concluding, silent shots of a nuclear explosion in Sidney Lumet's *Fail-Safe* (1964). It also can be comic, as in the conclusion of Stanley Kubrick's *Dr. Strangelove or: How I Learned to Stop Worrying and Love the Bomb* (1964) when the otherwise silent nuclear explosion is accompanied by nondiegetic music (Vera Lynn singing "We'll Meet Again").

In Robert Bresson's *A Man Escaped* (1956), a member of the French Resistance named Lieutenant Fontaine is being held in a Nazi prison during World War II. Once he has entered the prison, he never sees outside the walls, although he remains very aware, through offscreen sound, of the world outside. In fact, sounds of daily life—church bells, trains, trolleys—represent freedom to Fontaine.

Internal versus External

An **internal sound** occurs whenever we hear what we assume are the thoughts of a character within a scene. The character might be expressing random thoughts or a sustained monologue. In the theater, when Shakespeare wants us to hear a character's thoughts, he uses a solilo-

Internal sound in *Hamlet*

To be, or not to be; that is the question:
Whether 'tis nobler in the mind to suffer
The slings and arrows of outrageous fortune,
Or to take arms against a sea of troubles,
And, by opposing, end them.[4]

Few lines cut deeper into a character's psyche or look more unflinchingly into the nature of human existence, and yet it's not hard to imagine how ineffective these well-known lines might be if simply recited at a camera. In his *Hamlet* (1948), actor-director Laurence Olivier fuses character and psyche, human nature and behavior, by both speaking his lines and rendering them, in voice-over, as the Danish prince's thoughts while simultaneously combining, in the background, music and the natural sounds of the sea. Olivier's version of *Hamlet* was the first to apply the full resources of the cinema to Shakespeare's text, and his innovativeness is especially apparent in the sound.

4. William Shakespeare, *The Tragedy of Hamlet, Prince of Denmark*, act 3, scene 1.

quy to convey them, but this device lacks verisimilitude. Laurence Olivier's many challenges in adapting *Hamlet* for the screen included making the title character's soliloquies acceptable to a movie audience that might not be familiar with theatrical conventions. Olivier wanted to show Hamlet as both a thinker whose psychology motivated his actions and a man who could not make up his mind. Thus in his *Hamlet* (1948), Olivier (as Hamlet) delivered the greatest of all Shakespearean soliloquies—"To be, or not to be"—in a combination of both spoken lines and **interior monologue**. This innovation influenced the use of internal sound in countless other movies, including subsequent cinematic adaptations of Shakespeare's plays.

External sound comes from a place within the world of the story, and we assume that it is heard by the characters in that world. The source of an external sound can be either on-screen or offscreen. In John Ford's *My Darling Clementine* (1946), Indian Charlie is drunk and shooting up the town of Tombstone. The townspeople are afraid of Charlie, and the sheriff resigns rather than confront him, so Wyatt Earp—who is both on-screen and offscreen during the scene—is appointed sheriff and takes it upon himself to stop the chaos that Charlie has created.

The scene effectively combines both on-screen and offscreen sounds. The characters (and the viewer) hear the offscreen sounds of Charlie shooting his gun inside the saloon followed by the offscreen sounds of women screaming; then the women appear on-screen as they run from the saloon with Charlie right behind them, still shooting his gun. When Earp, on-screen, starts to enter the building through an upstairs window, we hear the offscreen screams of the prostitutes who are in the room as he says, "Sorry, ladies." Offscreen, Earp confronts Charlie and conks him on the head, for we hear the thud of Charlie falling to the saloon floor. This is followed by an on-screen shot of Earp dragging Charlie out of the saloon to the waiting crowd. This use of sound demonstrates Earp's courage and skill while treating his serious encounter with Charlie with a comic touch.

Types of Film Sound

The types of sound that filmmakers can include in their sound tracks fall into four general categories: (1) vocal sounds (dialogue and narration), (2) environmental sounds (ambient sound, sound effects, and Foley sounds), (3) music, and (4) silence. As viewers, we are largely familiar with vocal, environmental, and musical sounds. Vocal sounds tend to dominate most films because they carry much of the narrative weight, environmental sounds usually provide information about a film's setting and action, and music often directs our emotional reactions. However, any of these types of sound may dominate or be subordinate to the visual image, depending on the relationship that the filmmaker desires between sound and visual image.

Vocal Sounds

Dialogue, recorded during production or rerecorded during postproduction, is the speech of characters who are either visible on-screen or speaking offscreen—say, from an unseen part of the room or from an adjacent room. Dialogue is a function of plot because it develops out of situations, conflict, and character development. Further, it depends on actors' voices, facial expressions, and gestures and is thus also a product of acting. By expressing the feelings and motivations of characters, dialogue is one of the principal means of telling a story. In most movies, dialogue represents what we consider ordinary speech, but dialogue can also be highly artificial.

During the 1930s, screwball comedies invented a fast, witty, and often risqué style of dialogue that was frankly theatrical in calling attention to itself. Among the most exemplary of these films are Ernst Lubitsch's *Trouble in Paradise* (1932), Howard Hawks's *Bringing Up Baby* (1938), and Preston Sturges's *The Lady Eve* (1941). Each of these movies must be seen in its lunatic entirety to be fully appreciated, but they nonetheless provide countless rich individual exchanges.

Movie speech can take forms other than dialogue. For example, French director Alain Resnais specializes in spoken language that reveals a character's stream of consciousness, mixing reality, memory, dream, and imagination. In Resnais's *Providence* (1977), Clive Langham, an elderly novelist, drinks heavily as he drifts in and out of sleep. Through the intertwining strands of his interior monologue, we learn of his projected novel—about four characters who inhabit a doomed city—and of his relationships with members of his family, on whom his fictional characters are evidently based. Langham's monologue and dialogues link the fantasy to the reality of what we see and hear; in this way, sound objectifies what is ordinarily neither seen nor heard in a movie.

Narration, the commentary spoken by either off-screen or on-screen voices, is frequently used in narrative films, where it may emanate from a third-person narrator (thus not one of the characters) or from a character in the movie. In the opening scene of Stanley Kubrick's *The Killing* (1956), when Marvin Unger enters the betting room of a racetrack, a third-person narrator describes him for us. This offscreen narrator knows details of Unger's personal life and cues us to the suspense of the film's narrative.

In Terrence Malick's *Badlands* (1973), the character of Holly narrates the story in first-person voice-over, helping us understand her loneliness, her obsession with her older boyfriend, Kit, her participation in a series of brutal murders, and her inability to stop. This technique enhances our appreciation of her character because rather than simply reinforcing what we are seeing, Holly's understanding and interpretation of events differ significantly from ours. She thinks of her life with Kit as a romance novel rather than a pathetic crime spree.

In *The Magnificent Ambersons* (1942), Orson Welles uses both offscreen and on-screen narrators. Welles himself is the offscreen, omniscient third-person narrator who sets a mood of romantic nostalgia for the American past while an on-screen "chorus"—a device that derives from Greek drama—of townspeople gossip about what is happening, directly offering their own interpretations. Thus the townspeople are both characters and narrators.

Multiple voice-over narrators are also used effectively in two movies where such narration underscores the solitude and stress of characters living in small towns: Paolo and Vittorio Taviani's *Padre Padrone* (1977), a documentary-like account of the lives of sheepherders in the Sardinian countryside, and Atom Egoyan's *The Sweet Hereafter* (1997). Egoyan's eloquent, disturbing movie concerns the fatal crash of a school bus and its aftereffects on the townspeople who have lost children. Two principal characters voice the narration—the bus driver, Dolores Discolt, and Nicole Burnell, a teenager who survived the crash. In scenes where these two are giving sworn testimony, Egoyan brilliantly employs the contrasts between the women in age, experience, and perspective. Since we have seen the crash in flashback, we know that Dolores gives an accurate account of the last moments before the crash; however, Nicole deliberately lies as she accuses the bus driver of speeding and causing the crash.

[1]

[2]

On-screen and offscreen narration

Billy Wilder's *Double Indemnity* (1944) uses on-screen narration in a unique way. Walter Neff, a corrupt insurance investigator, is pictured here recording his confession of murder on an office Dictaphone [1]. His story leads to flashbacks that fill us in on events leading to that confession. We see Elliot, the protagonist of the cable TV show *Mr. Robot*, on-screen [2] when he delivers his narration, but he doesn't say it out loud. Instead, the sound design allows us to hear this narrator speaking directly to us from outside of his regular thoughts and actions. Elliot's unreliable narration illuminates some events and misrepresents or misinterprets others.

Nicole's narration is made all the more haunting because she reads (both on-screen to two children and offscreen to underscore the narrative) from the Robert Browning translation of *The Pied Piper of Hamelin* (1888), the legendary German folktale about a piper, masquerading as a rat catcher, who lures a town's children to their death in a river. Although there are parallels between this story and the movie narrative, Nicole's voice-over at the movie's conclusion shows that she has mixed fiction and fact, truth and lies. Angry about what life has handed her—an abusive father and an accident that has crippled her for life—she reads the fictional account of a "strange and new . . . sweet hereafter" and lies to prevent her abusive father from gaining damages from a lawsuit. The sound of her innocent, pure voice reading the grim folktale masks a tragedy as powerful as the bus crash itself.

Environmental Sounds

Ambient sound, which emanates from the ambience (or background) of the setting or environment being filmed, is either recorded during production or added during postproduction. Although it may incorporate other types of film sound—dialogue, narration, sound effects, Foley sounds, and music—ambient sound should not include any unintentionally recorded noise made during production, such as the sounds of cameras, static from sound-recording equipment, car horns, sirens, footsteps, or voices from outside the production. Filmmakers regard these sounds as an inevitable nuisance and generally remove them electronically during postproduction. Ambient sound helps set the mood and atmosphere of scenes, and it may also contribute to the meaning of a scene.

Consider the ambient sound of the wind in John Ford's *The Grapes of Wrath* (1940). Tom Joad, who has just been released from prison, returns to his family's Oklahoma house to find it empty, dark, and deserted. The low sound of the wind underscores Tom's loneliness and isolation and reminds us that the wind of Dust Bowl storms reduced the fertile plains to unproductive waste and drove the Joads and other farmers off their land. In Satyajit Ray's "Apu" trilogy—*Pather Panchali* (1955), *The Unvanquished* (1956), and *The World of Apu* (1959)—recurrent sounds of trains establish actual places, times, and moods, but they poetically express characters' anticipations and memories as well. These wind and train sounds, respectively, are true to the physical ambience of Ford's and Ray's stories, but filmmakers also use symbolic sounds as a kind of shorthand to create illusions of reality. In countless Westerns, for example, tinkling pianos introduce us to frontier towns; in urban films, honking automobile horns suggest the busyness (and business) of cities.

Sound effects include all sounds artificially created for the sound track that have a definite function in telling the story. All sound effects, except those made on electronic equipment to deliberately create electronic sounds, come from "wild" recordings of real things, and it is the responsibility of the sound designer and the sound crew to pick and combine these sounds to create the hyperreality of the film's sound track. (*Wild recording* is any recording of sound not made during synchronous shooting of the picture.) In Ray's *Pather Panchali*, two children, Apu and Durga, find their family's eighty-year-old aunt, Indir Thakrun, squatting near a sacred pond and think she is sleeping. As Durga shakes her, the old woman falls over, her head hitting the ground with a hollow sound—a diegetic, on-screen sound effect—that evokes death.

In the 1930s, Jack Foley, a sound technician at Universal Studios, invented a special category of sound effects: **Foley sounds**. There are two significant differences between Foleys and the sound effects just described. The first is that traditional sound effects are created or recorded "wild" and then edited into the film, whereas Foleys are created and recorded in sync with the picture. To do this, the technicians known as Foley artists have a studio equipped with recording equipment and a screen for viewing the movie as they create sounds in sync with it. The second difference is that traditional sound effects can be taken directly from a library of prerecorded effects (e.g., church bells, traffic noises, jungle sounds) or created specifically for the movie. By contrast, Foley sounds are unique. As an example of the latter, the sound technicians working on Peter Jackson's *The Lord of the Rings: The Fellowship of the Ring* (2001) needed the sounds of arrows shooting through the air, so they set up stationary microphones in a quiet graveyard and shot arrows past the mikes to record those sounds.

Foley artists use a variety of props and other equipment to simulate everyday sounds—such as footsteps in the mud, jingling car keys, the rustling of clothing, or cutlery hitting a plate—that must exactly match the movement on the screen. Such sounds fill in the soundscape of the movie and enhance verisimilitude, but they also convey important narrative and character information. Although these sounds match the action we see on the screen, they can also exaggerate reality—both loud and soft sounds—and thus may call attention to their own artificiality. Generally, however, we do not consciously notice them, so when they are truly effective, we cannot distinguish Foley sounds from real sounds.

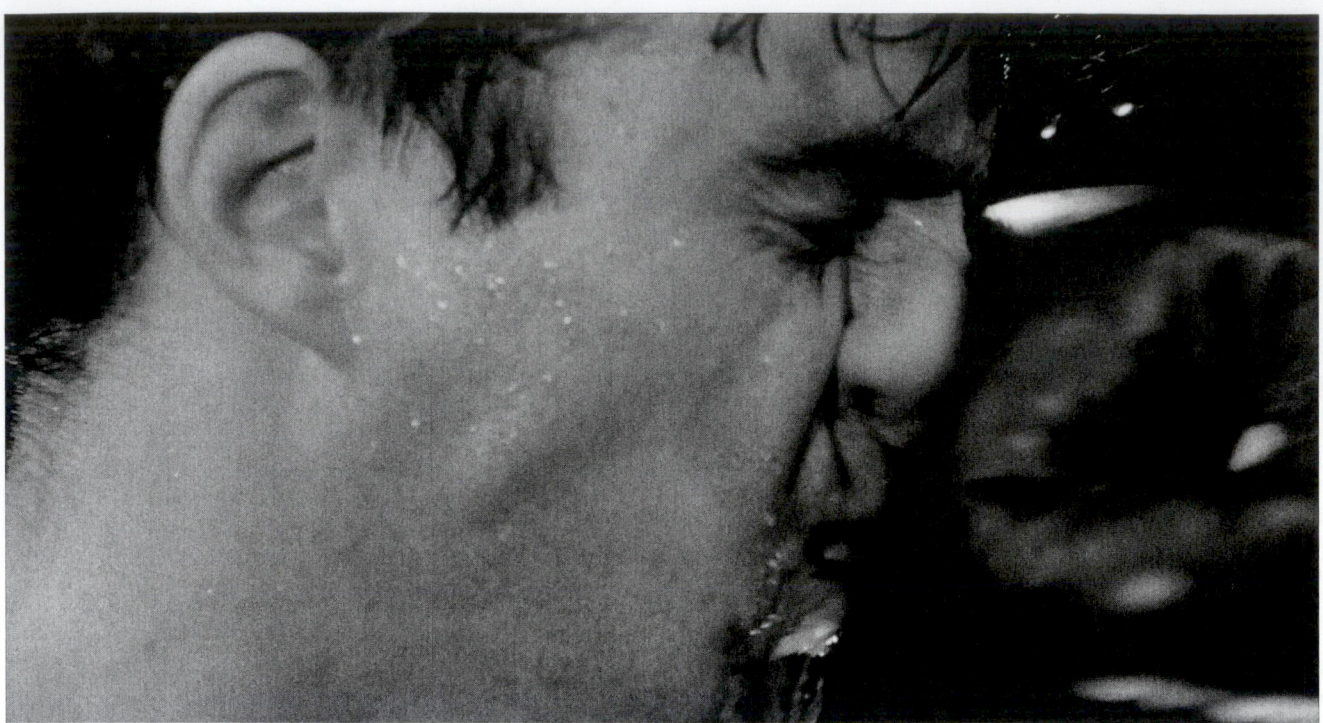

Sound effects in *Raging Bull*

The boxing film against which all others are measured is Martin Scorsese's *Raging Bull* (1980). Based on former middleweight champion Jake La Motta's memoir of the same title, this movie fully employs every aspect of filmmaking technology as it re-creates the experience of being in the ring. Close-ups don't get much more vivid than this one, which depicts La Motta's glove slamming into and breaking fighter Tony Janiro's nose; blood spurts and sweat flies. The image moves from powerful to unbearable, however, when accompanied by the Foley sounds of impact, collapse, and explosion.

In Martin Scorsese's *Raging Bull* (1980; sound by Frank Warner), brutal tape-recorded sounds from boxing matches are mixed with sounds created in the Foley studio. Many different tracks—including a fist hitting a side of beef, a knife cutting into the beef, water (to simulate the sound of blood spurting), animal noises, and the whooshes of jet airplanes and arrows—all work together to provide the dramatic illusion of what, in a real boxing match, would be the comparatively simpler sound of one boxer's gloves hitting another boxer's flesh.

The artistry involved in using all the various sources and types of sound has permanently established the role of the sound designer and exponentially increased the number of sound-related job titles, and therefore new employment, in the field of movie sound. All of these jobs are reflected in the large number of sound artists and technicians receiving screen credit. Furthermore, these roles have made necessary the invention and development of new equipment for sound recording, editing, and mixing and have brought change to many theaters, which have had to install expensive new equipment to process the superb sound made possible by the digital revolution.

Music

Music is used in many distinct ways in the movies, but in this discussion we are concerned principally with the kind of music that Royal S. Brown, an expert on the subject, describes as "dramatically motivated . . . music composed more often than not by practitioners specializing in the art to interact specifically with the diverse facets of the filmic medium, particularly the narrative."[5]

5. Royal S. Brown, *Overtones and Undertones: Reading Film Music* (Berkeley: University of California Press, 1994), p. 13.

Music, sound, and rhythm in *Baby Driver*

Edgar Wright's *Baby Driver* (2017) uses music and other sounds—and even the lack of sound—to place its audience inside the perspective of its protagonist. The getaway driver prodigy who calls himself Baby suffers from tinnitus, a constant high-pitched ringing in his ears. Baby wears earbuds and listens to music on an iPod to drown out the ringing, and we hear what he hears. His playlist becomes the score for many of the movie's scenes, including breakneck chase scenes [1] and romantic interludes [2]. Because the earbuds produce clear sound, and overwhelm most other sounds, Baby's song selections have the same acoustic quality as score music. The driving rhythms of the songs propel the fast-paced rhythmic editing in many of the film's action scenes; their celebratory tone alters the way we feel about otherwise violent events. When things go (very) bad after a bank robbery, and Baby loses his iPod in the ensuing chase, the usual festive music is replaced by the high-pitched whine of his tinnitus [3], a sound that adds to our experience of his anxiety.

Such music can be classical or popular in style, written specifically for the film or taken from music previously composed for another purpose, written by composers known for other kinds of music (e.g., Leonard Bernstein, Aaron Copland, Philip Glass, and Igor Stravinsky) or by those who specialize in movie scores (e.g., Elmer Bernstein, Carter Burwell, Bernard Herrmann, Ennio Morricone, Rachel Portman, Tôru Takemitsu, John Williams, and Hans Zimmer, among many others). It also can be music played by characters in the film or by offscreen musicians (i.e., diegetic or nondiegetic). Some of Hollywood's most prolific contemporary composers were formerly rock musicians: Oingo Boingo's Danny Elfman has scored more than ninety films, including sixteen Tim Burton movies; Devo's Mark Mothersbaugh, another prolific composer, has scored more than seventy-five films, including Wes Anderson's first four movies. Songwriter and singer Randy Newman's twenty-seven composer credits include eight animated features produced by Pixar. Jonny Greenwood, the lead guitarist of the English alternative rock group Radiohead, is also the composer of the lush orchestral score for Paul Thomas Anderson's *Phantom Thread* (2017), as well as the scores for Anderson's previous three films: *There Will Be Blood* (2007), *The Master* (2012), and *Inherent Vice* (2014).

Like other types of sound, music can be intrinsic, helping to tell the story, whether it pertains to plot, action, character, or mood; indeed, music plays an indispensable role in many movies. Perhaps the most familiar form of movie music is the large symphonic score used to set a mood or manipulate our emotions.[6] Few old-Hollywood films were without a big score by masters of the genre such as Max Steiner (who scored Victor Fleming's *Gone with the Wind*, 1939). Although recent movies have relied mainly on less ambitious scores, big scores are still used when large stories call for them. These movies include Peter Jackson's The Lord of the Rings trilogy (2001–3; composer Howard Shore), James Cameron's *Avatar* (2009; composer James Horner), Wes Anderson's *The Grand Budapest Hotel* (2014; composer Alexandre Desplat), and the Star Wars (1977–2019) movies, all of which (with the exception of the "Star Wars Story" anthology series) were scored by John Williams.

Movie music can be equally effective when it creates or supports ideas in a film, as in Orson Welles's *The*

6. See Larry M. Timm, *The Soul of Cinema: An Appreciation of Film Music* (New York: Simon & Schuster, 1998), ch. 1.

Audio assault and deception in *Dunkirk*

For *Dunkirk* (2017), director Christopher Nolan and his sound team used every audio element at their disposal to immerse audiences in the overwhelming chaos of the 1940 Battle of Dunkirk. The thundering sounds of military aircraft and bomb strikes were mixed at maximum volume—so much so that much of the film's dialogue is lost in the cacophony. Composer Hans Zimmer's score employed an audio illusion caused by the Shepard tone, which is achieved by layering three separate tones, each of which is separated by an octave. Each of the three tones repeats an ascending scale in a continual loop. Because the three scales fade in and out in turn, audiences always hear at least two at a time but don't notice when the successive scales fade and begin again. This system tricks our brains into interpreting the sound as continually rising in pitch, an effect that subtly but ceaselessly intensifies tension in *Dunkirk*'s battle scenes.

Tragedy of Othello: The Moor of Venice (1952). Welles takes a deterministic view of Othello's fate, but he depicts the two central characters, Othello and Desdemona, as being larger than life, even as they are each destined for an early death.

Accompanying their funeral processions is a musical score that leaves no question that these tragic circumstances are the result of fate. In fact, in their cumulative power the sights and sounds express the inexorable rhythm of all great tragedies. The complex musical score covers several periods and styles, but to most ears it resembles medieval liturgical music. Deep, hard, dirgelike piano chords combine with the chanting of monks and others in the processions, spelling out (even drawing us into) the title character's inevitable deterioration and self-destruction.

For John Curran's *We Don't Live Here Anymore* (2004), a dark melodrama about marital infidelities, composer

Michael Convertino has written a score that builds with the suspense and establishes the mood of anxiety that hangs over everyone involved. By contrast, Don Davis's score for the Wachowskis' *The Matrix* (1999) uses the sounds of brass and percussion instruments and songs by the Propellerheads and Rage Against the Machine to match the world of the story's synthetic technological environment. Davis also scored the music for the two sequels (*The Matrix Reloaded* and *The Matrix Revolutions*, both 2003).

Irony often results from the juxtaposition of music and image because the associations we bring when we hear a piece of music greatly affect our interpretation of a scene. Take, for example, composer Ennio Morricone's juxtaposition of "Ave Maria" with shots of Brazilian natives and missionary priests being slaughtered by Portuguese slave traders in Roland Joffé's *The Mission* (1986); Quentin Tarantino's use of Stealers Wheel's carefree,

Songs inspire a movie

Miraculous things happen, and people and events connect in unexpected ways, throughout Paul Thomas Anderson's *Magnolia* (1999). Part of what inspired Anderson in writing his screenplay was hearing then-unreleased recordings by American pop-rocker Aimee Mann. In some cases, connections between the songs and the narrative are explicit, as when the lyrics to "Deathly" (Now that I've met you / Would you object to / Never seeing each other again) become a line of dialogue: "Now that I've met you, would you object to never seeing me again?" At the film's emotional climax, [1] Claudia Wilson Gator, [2] Jim Kurring, [3] Jimmy Gator, [4] Quiz Kid Donnie Smith, [5] "Big Earl" Partridge and his nurse, Phil Parma, and [6] Stanley Spector—all in different places and different situations—sing along with Mann's "Wise Up."

groovy "Stuck in the Middle with You" to choreograph the violent cop-torture scene in *Reservoir Dogs* (1992); or Pier Paolo Pasolini's *Accatone* (1961), where the director contrasts urban gang violence with themes from the *St. Matthew Passion* by Johann Sebastian Bach. Another memorable juxtaposition of violent imagery with music (Bach's Passacaglia and Fugue in C Minor [BWV 582] for organ) is used in *The Godfather* (see Chapter 2, p. 47). Perhaps the boldest experiment in juxtaposing music and image occurs in Sergei Eisenstein's *Alexander Nevsky* (1938), which depicts the thirteenth-century conflict be-

tween Crusader knights and the Russian people. Here, using a complex graph, the director integrated Sergei Prokofiev's original musical score, note by note, with the visual composition, shot by shot. This mathematical and theoretically rigorous experiment results, at its best, in a sublime marriage of aural and visual imagery, which has been influential, particularly in such epic movies as Stanley Kubrick's *Spartacus* (1960) and Irvin Kershner's *The Empire Strikes Back* (1980).

Neil Jordan makes a more sustained use of such juxtaposition in *The Crying Game* (1992), a political

1

2

Great music, bad boy

A principal theme of Stanley Kubrick's *A Clockwork Orange* (1971), the loss of moral choice through psychological conditioning, is developed by a focus on Alex [1], a worthless, violent character, here staring at a poster of the German classical/Romantic composer Ludwig van Beethoven [2]. Alex's only good trait is his love for Beethoven's Ninth Symphony—especially the setting of Friedrich von Schiller's "Ode to Joy," music that represents all that is most noble in the human spirit, in its finale. Here, however, this music is used ironically to underscore Alex's desire to preserve his freedom to do what he wants (which consists mostly of violent acts), even though society tries to socialize him away from these acts (using a fascistic treatment that attempts to turn him into a "clockwork orange"). In the somewhat muddled world of this controversial film, we're supposed to be glad that Alex is still sufficiently human to embrace Beethoven *and* resist brainwashing.

and psychological thriller that is also a frank, revealing movie about loneliness, desire, and love. Its music helps underscore the developments in its story. A man named Fergus falls in love with a woman named Dil, but rejects her when he discovers she is transgender. Over the course of the story, Fergus's love for Dil overcomes his prejudice, so much so that he takes a prison rap for her. At the end of the movie, Dil is visiting Fergus in prison, and as the camera pulls back to the final fade-out and closing credits, we hear Tammy Wynette and Billy Sherrill's country-western classic "Stand by Your Man," sung by Lyle Lovett. The song emphasizes Dil's dedication, but also pokes fun at the traditional notions of gender identification that initially threatened Dil's relationship with Fergus. The opening credits of *The Crying Game* use a popular old song in a similar way. Percy Sledge singing the R&B classic "When a Man Loves a Woman" (by Cameron Lewis and Andrew Wright) provides the perfect introduction, although we do not know it at the time, to what will evolve into a love story that transcends contemporary gender expectations.

Among directors, Tom Tykwer is notable for his use of music to enhance the pace, or tempo, of *Run Lola Run* (1998), in which the relentless rhythm of the techno-music matches the sped-up, almost surreal pace of the action. Significantly, this music does not change with developments in the action, so it takes on a life of its own. Indeed, any action movie with many exciting chase sequences, such as Paul Greengrass's *The Bourne Supremacy* (2004), could become routine if the music did not change significantly to suit the participants, location, and outcome of each chase. In *The Bourne Supremacy*'s spectacular chase through Moscow traffic, Jason Bourne, whose own musical theme is played by a bassoon, successfully eludes the Russian police—but not before many vehicles are destroyed. The sound in this scene is an expressive mix of ambient sounds, Foley sounds, sound effects, and John Powell's score. Indeed, it's impossible to disentangle these elements. The loud sounds of sirens, screeching tires, shattered glass, gunshots, and revving car engines accentuate the violent action. Meanwhile the music, which is softer in volume, is a full orchestral score mixed with Russian folk themes and electronic sounds, including techno-music. The chase ends with a final smashup and silence.

Many directors use music to provide overall structural unity or coherence to a story. In Wes Anderson's *Moonrise Kingdom* (2012), *Noye's Fludde* (Noah's Flood), a children's opera by British composer Benjamin Britten, is at the heart of the story. As a boy, Anderson was in a production of the opera, which made a very strong impression, and he says, "It is the colour of the movie in a way."[7] This music is used when a local church is putting on the opera with a cast of children. Audiences hear it again when a hurricane threatens the island and towns-people gather in the church, where a recording of the opera is being played. Then, amid songs by Hank Williams and Françoise Hardy, Alexandre Desplat interpolates another familiar Britten work, *The Young Person's Guide to the Orchestra*, with his own take on that work, into the final credits sequence. This passage is so fresh and imaginative that it's almost worth the price of admission. Furthermore, if you tend to walk out during the final credits, it should cure you of that bad habit forever.

A movie such as Stephen Daldry's *The Hours* (2002), which tells a story spanning some 80 years in three different settings with three different women, presents a unique challenge to a musical composer to find some way to unify all these elements. The movie's narrative concerns the different ways these three women are affected by Virginia Woolf's 1925 novel *Mrs. Dalloway*, including the novelist herself in the 1920s; an American housewife, Laura Brown, in the 1940s; and a New York professional woman, Clarissa Vaughan, in the present. Therefore, viewers might expect a three-part musical score with one distinct sound for each historical period and location, and perhaps even a distinct theme for each principal character. However, composer Philip Glass takes a very different course.

A New Age classical composer with minimalist tendencies, Glass links the three stories with recurring musical motifs played by a chamber orchestra of a pianist and five string players. To create further unity among the lives of the three women, Glass emphasizes the bond that Woolf's novel has created among them by avoiding music from the periods in which they lived. The tensions in the score pull between the emotional and cerebral, underscoring the tensions that the characters experience in this psychological melodrama.

Finally, film music may emanate from sources within the story—a television, a radio or stereo set, a person singing or playing a guitar, an orchestra playing at a dance. For example, Ridley Scott's *Black Hawk Down* (2001) depicts a complex and failed attempt by a group of U.S. Army Rangers to depose a Somalian warlord—a conflict between Americans and African Muslims. For this film, composer Hans Zimmer decided against writ-

Diegetic music

Debra Granik's *Winter's Bone* (2010) is a horrific narrative film that shows how methamphetamine abuse destroys the lives of people in the rural Ozarks. Actor Jennifer Lawrence gives a brilliant performance as Ree Dolly, a teenager who takes charge and tries to keep her family together under the worst of circumstances. Her efforts are hampered by local traditions of patriarchy, secrecy, and resistance to authority, but in this image, when she listens to local bluegrass musicians, including Marideth Sisco singing "High on a Mountain," she momentarily forgets the strife. Here, a traditional folk song offers her and the others a moment of peace and reveals a creative side of their culture.

ing the sort of score we hear in other classic war movies, such as Coppola's *Apocalypse Now* (1979) or Oliver Stone's *Platoon* (1986).

Instead of using familiar classical themes for theatrical effect, Zimmer relies heavily on diegetic music that emanates from soldiers' radios, street musicians, or mosques. Thus the score juxtaposes Western and African music, Irish tunes, and songs by Elvis Presley and popular groups such as Alice in Chains, Stone Temple Pilots, and Faith No More on the one hand, and traditional Muslim prayer music and chants, mournful piano and strings, African pop music, and tribal drums on the other. At times, such as the beginning of the attack on the marketplace, Zimmer fuses elements of both. His "score" goes beyond music to include many sound effects that function as rhythmic elements (the constant hum of military and civilian vehicles, the beating of helicopter rotor blades, the voices of American soldiers and African crowds). In this expanded sense of a musical score, Zimmer and Jon Title, the sound designer, worked together to create an original, seamless entity

7. Qtd. in www.brittenpears.org/page.php?pageid=771 (accessed September 8, 2014).

that makes few distinctions between music and other sounds. Of course, in *Black Hawk Down* sometimes music is just music and sound effects are just sound effects. But the major achievement here is the fusion of sounds.

With this score, Zimmer does not make conflict appear to be the work of godlike warriors (such as the helicopter gunships in *Apocalypse Now*) but rather conveys the hell of war, reinforces the bond among the soldiers, and helps us understand the agony they suffer on each other's behalf. Near the end, we hear his "Leave No Man Behind," a beautiful tapestry of piano and strings that includes familiar patriotic musical motifs, and his soft, martial arrangement of the heartbreaking Irish ballad "Minstrel Boy," sung by Joe Strummer & The Mescaleros. This score, derived from many sources—both diegetic and nondiegetic—is not background music but central to portraying the movie's almost unbearable tension.

Although a movie's characters and its viewers hear diegetic music, which can be as simple as sound drifting in through an open window, only viewers hear nondiegetic music, which usually consists of an original score composed for the movie, selections chosen from music libraries, or both. John Carney's *Once* (2006) is a contemporary love story about a "Guy" and a "Girl." Its song lyrics virtually replace the meager dialogue. The story is simple enough: boy meets girl, boy sings to girl, girl helps boy to perfect his songs, boy gets music contract and leaves girl to make his first recording. Its goofy charm depends almost completely on this diegetic music.

Nondiegetic music is recorded at the very end of the editing process, so that it can be matched accurately to the images. In recording an original score, the conductor and musicians work on a specially equipped recording stage that enables them to screen the film and tailor every aspect of the music's tempo and quality to each scene that has music (similar to the way that Foley sounds are created). Further adjustments of the sounds of individual musicians, groups of musicians, or an entire orchestra are frequently made by sound technicians after these recording sessions and before the final release prints. Similar efforts are made to fit selections taken from music libraries with the images they will accompany.

Silence

As viewers, we are familiar with all the types of film sound that have been described in this chapter, but we may be unfamiliar with the idea that silence can be a sound. Paradoxically, silence has that function when the filmmaker deliberately suppresses the vocal, environmental, or musical sounds that we expect in a movie. When so used, silence frustrates our normal perceptions. It can make a scene seem profound or even prophetic. Furthermore, with careful interplay between sound and silence, a filmmaker can produce a new rhythm for the film—one that calls attention to the characters' perceptions. *The Silence before Bach* (2007), a film by the legendary Spanish surrealist director Pere Portabella, does just that. It's a feast for the ears and eyes, providing an avant-garde filmmaker's look at how the music of Bach and the contemporary world might interact.

A similar achievement distinguishes Carlos Reygadas's *Silent Light* (2007), a film that is as visually beautiful as it is aurally spare. It records a year in the lives of Flemish Mennonite farmers living in Mexico, God-fearing people who are as silent as the extraordinary sunlight in which they work. It is not a documentary, but a celebration of the life cycle, reminiscent of Ermanno Olmi's *The Tree of Wooden Clogs* (1978) and Terrence Malick's *The Tree of Life* (2011). Another most unusual movie, Pat Collins's *Silence* (2012), follows a sound recordist who wanders the fields of Ireland in search of pure sound—natural, not man-made. This hybrid feature/documentary takes place amid magnificent scenery. And, based on the theories of American composer John Cage, the sound design results in a film that has a quiet intensity. The sound design of Malgorzata Szumowska's *In the Name Of* (2013) is uncredited, perhaps because it is mainly a silent movie composed of such powerful images that little sound is required. The story—about a priest who cannot reconcile his calling with his sexual attraction to young men—is also about a man who cannot, because of his vows, talk freely about his feelings. The perfection of the mise-en-scène, acting, and use of natural sounds help the director to tell this difficult story.

Classic directors such as Ingmar Bergman (e.g., *Wild Strawberries*, 1957) and Michelangelo Antonioni (e.g., *The Red Desert*, 1964) control their own sound designs, imaginatively using silence to evoke the psychological alienation of their characters. Akira Kurosawa's *Dreams* (1990) consists of eight extremely formal episodes, each based on one of the director's dreams. The third episode, "The Blizzard," tells of four mountain climbers trapped in a fierce storm. We hear what they hear when they are

Yummy.

The sound of silence

In *Uncle Boonmee Who Can Recall His Past Lives* (director Apichatpong Weerasethakul), there is silence everywhere in the Thai settings. In this tranquil image, Boonmee and his sister-in-law Jen are sampling honey harvested at Boonmee's farm. Except for a few words, the only sound we hear is the soft hum of the bees and some distant ambient sound, perhaps a gentle wind or small river. This aesthetic pervades the entire movie, especially in the scenes where ghosts from Boonmee's family appear. Of course, we cannot call this a "silent film," but it powerfully demonstrates how to tell a story primarily with visual images.

conscious, but when they are exhausted and near death, they (and we) hear almost nothing.

As the episode begins, we hear the climbers' boots crunching the snow, their labored breathing, and the raging wind. They are exhausted, but the leader warns them that they will die if they go to sleep. Nonetheless, they all lie down in the snow. The previous loud sounds diminish until all we hear is the low sound of the wind. Then, out of this, we hear the sweet, clear, high sounds of a woman singing offscreen. The leader awakens to see a beautiful woman on-screen—the specter of Death—who says, "The snow is warm. . . . The ice is hot." As she covers the leader with shimmering fabrics, he drifts in and out of sleep, trying to fight her seductive powers—all in silence.

Ultimately, Death fails to convince the leader to give up. When it's clear that he has regained his consciousness and strength, he is able to hear the loud storm again. Death disappears, accompanied by wind and thunder. Perhaps her beauty has given the leader the courage to resist death and thus save the group. The other men awaken; they, of course, have not seen or heard any of this. We then hear muted trumpets, horns, and alpine music—all nondiegetic sounds signifying the climbers' victory over the weather and death. Ironically, when they awaken in the bright sunshine, the climbers recognize

that they have slept in the snow only a few yards away from the safety of their base camp. What is the meaning of this dream? Perhaps that life equals consciousness and, in this instance, awareness of sound.

While movies such as *Dreams*, Jean-Pierre Melville's *Le Cercle Rouge* (1970), or Patrice Chéreau's *Gabrielle* (2005) are important for calling our attention to the imaginative use of silence, no other contemporary movie has done this better than Joel and Ethan Coen's *No Country for Old Men* (2007). Although Carter Burwell is credited for the score, the sound track of this tense, bloody thriller has only 16 minutes of music. Likewise, there is very little dialogue. In this absence, the sound effects are particularly striking and memorable: gunshots, the prairie winds, car doors slamming and engines roaring, the scrape of a chair or footsteps in a creepy hotel, and the beeping tracking device that facilitates the movie's violent ending. When long sections of a movie are as conspicuously silent as this one, audiences automatically are obliged, perhaps ironically, to listen more carefully. However, unlike the approach in many thrillers, where sound creates suspense and even helps the audience to anticipate what might happen, we don't have that to guide us here. Indeed, many of the movie's characters also have to strain to hear and identify sounds.

In *Uncle Boonmee Who Can Recall His Past Lives* (2010), the acclaimed Thai director Apichatpong Weerasethakul has made a film about reincarnation that may also seek to transform cinema itself by emphasizing silence rather than sound. Significantly, it won the Palme d'Or for the best feature film at the 2010 Cannes Film Festival, and it is like nothing you have ever seen or heard on the screen. The story, based on the Buddhist belief in reincarnation, is about Boonmee, who is dying of kidney disease and believes that he can see ghosts from his past. His belief is powerful enough to call forth apparitions of his late wife, with whom he discusses the afterlife. It's all treated very matter-of-factly with superimposed images of the dead appearing on the screen. Thus we (and some other characters) see the wife too, just as she was in life. One ghost returns reincarnated as a monkey, another as a catfish. The director's radical vision involves a careful observation of ordinary life in scenes shot in long takes and real time and using very austere sound design. He does not reject sound, for we hear the standard types of film sound, all of them diegetic, including vocal sounds (some dialogue, a short offscreen interior monologue, monks' prayers), music (from a TV melodrama, a stringed instrument), and environmental sounds of all kinds, including jungle noises, insects, water, and rainfall. Indeed, the combination of long takes in which there is little action and the soft, low tones of these sounds is hypnotic. Perhaps ironically, the overwhelming and calming silence of this place defines it. The silence of the perceivable world and the afterworld is Weerasethakul's most powerful sound.

Types of Sound in Steven Spielberg's *War of the Worlds*

Let's take a close look at how important sound is to one movie in particular: Steven Spielberg's *War of the Worlds* (2005; sound designer Richard King; musical score John Williams). To do this, we'll catalog the types of sounds we hear in the movie. Because the sound design of this movie is so complex, it would be impossible to identify every sound that we hear, but the following discussion offers a sense of the many types of sound incorporated into the overall sound design.

The movie begins with shots of protoplasm as seen through a microscope, accompanied by the deep, soothing voice of the narrator speaking the opening lines of H. G. Wells's 1898 novel *The War of the Worlds*, on which the screenplay was loosely based:

> No one would have believed in the last years of the nineteenth century that this world was being watched keenly and closely by intelligences greater than man's and yet as mortal as his own; that as men busied themselves about their various concerns they were scrutinised and studied, perhaps almost as narrowly as a man with a microscope might scrutinise the transient creatures that swarm and multiply in a drop of water.

The ominous nature of this text, along with the grave voice of the narrator (Morgan Freeman), lets us know that we're in for a thrilling story. Furthermore, these few lines establish the basis of the sound design. Those "intelligences greater than man's" inhabit the colossal tripods, which make thunderous noises. By contrast, humankind is a puny thing, prone to making incredulous assumptions about what is happening and then whimpering or crying about it. Big/little, loud/soft: that's the pattern underscoring this conflict.

As the action begins with Ray Ferrier working at a New Jersey container port, we hear the ambient sounds

Sounds introduce conflict

At the beginning of Steven Spielberg's *War of the Worlds* (2005; sound designer Richard King), we hear loud, high-pitched sounds (accompanying eerie atmospheric effects) and realize that something terrible is going to happen. Here, Ray Ferrier (Tom Cruise) and his daughter, Rachel (Dakota Fanning), brave the roaring winds to watch the darkening skies.

The tripods' warning

For the first time, Ferrier sees and hears the foghorn-like warning "voice" of the tripods. He and his neighbors, who do not yet understand what's happening, seem stunned by the tripods—as much by their massive size as by their ominous sounds.

of this industrial operation; traffic in and around the area; the television in Ray's apartment (bringing an ominous news report of violent lightning strikes in Ukraine); and dialogue between Ray, his ex-wife, Mary Ann, and their children, Rachel and Robbie, who are spending the weekend with their father. From this point on, however—when the movie rapidly enters the surreal world of the story—most of the sounds we hear are the work of sound engineers and technicians: the violent lightning storm that incites the action, sudden winds that make the laundry flap wildly on the line, shattering glass as a baseball breaks a window, the earthquake that splits the

Flight from terror

Ferrier, driving a van that he has stolen, and his two children (who are hiding from danger on the floor of the car) flee their New Jersey town as it is destroyed by the tripods. Notable here are the sound effects of crumbling steel bridges, vaporizing concrete highways, and debris falling everywhere.

Panic

The tripods cause a whirlpool that capsizes a ferry overcrowded with people trying to escape. Sounds here include the hornlike "voices" of the tripods, the screams of the crowd (those still on deck and those already in the river), the buckling steel of the ferryboat, underwater sounds, and John Williams's musical score.

streets and enables the giant tripods to emerge, electrical flashes that emanate from the tripods, and the sounds of explosions, falling debris, shattered glass, and people being vaporized as the tripods wreak havoc. There are also implied sounds, such as what Robbie is listening to on his iPod, that we cannot hear.

As the crisis in this New Jersey town worsens, we are overwhelmed by the sounds of fires, explosions, bridges and highways collapsing, and the screeching tires of the car as Ray drives frantically out of town. When Ray and his children reach the temporary safety of his ex-wife's new house, there are more lightning storms, heavy winds, and the sounds of a jet aircraft crashing on the front lawn. Many of these sounds were produced in the Foley lab.

During a lull before the tripods appear again, we hear more ambient sounds: Rachel's shrill screams, a radio report on the status of the emergency broadcast system, a passing convoy of army tanks and trucks, and car horns in the heavy traffic as the Ferriers approach a ferry on the Hudson River. At the ferry landing we hear the deafening roar of a freight train as it passes in the night, the jangling of the warning bells at the train's crossing, a female ferry employee shouting instructions through a megaphone, and the ferry's deep-sounding horns. The crowd there is furious at Ray for having a car in which to escape and begins to attack it; we hear loud crowd noises, individual voices, gunshots, and the sounds of the car's windows being smashed. Amid all this pandemonium, Rachel looks up to the sky and hears geese

honking as they fly by—a classic omen of the horror to come. There is very little music in this part of the film (the rising action of the plot), but we hear from a radio somewhere the sound of Tony Bennett singing "If I Ruled the World." Since viewers know that a new demonic force now rules the world, it's a particularly ironic use of music.

The Ferriers manage to get on the ferryboat, but their escape is thwarted when the boat is caught in a whirlpool and capsizes, throwing cars and passengers overboard. The sounds of this action are faithful and vivid. We also see and hear people thrashing underwater as they seek safety. By now, the tripods are on the scene, their huge tentacles (with their own peculiar noises) grabbing people out of the Hudson and gobbling them up into their nasty "mouths." Of course, the three members of the Ferrier family escape all of this.

On the riverbank, we see an Armageddon-like scene—what might be the final conflict between the tripods and humanity—and hear the sounds of the massive tripods crashing through the landscape, army tanks firing missiles at them, and helicopters and fighter jets above also firing missiles and dropping bombs. The scene is complete chaos, and we hear ambient noises of the crowds rushing back and forth. While all this is happening, Robbie Ferrier pleads with his father for independence and escapes into the fray.

As the crowds disperse, and a semblance of quiet and order returns, Ray and Rachel are welcomed into the basement of a nearby farmhouse by Harlan Ogilvy. Soon

Armageddon

As the tripods attack the fleeing crowds and devastate the landscape, military jets and missiles fail in their attempts to subdue them. We hear the sounds of the tripods and the chaos they create. Aircraft, music, and various electronic sounds add to the doomsday atmosphere.

the sounds of his sharpening a large blade provide another omen that the battle is not yet over and that this man may also become an evil force for Ray to reckon with. We even suspect that Ogilvy is a murderer and that Ray and Rachel are in harm's way, but in fact he just wants to annihilate the tripods.

The basement is full of sounds that further establish the imminent evil: scurrying rats; the soft, whirring sound of a tripod's tentacle as it searches the labyrinth of rooms; rippling water that is pooling there; and the sounds of the stealthy grasshopper-like creatures that have emerged from inside the tripods. Meanwhile, as Rachel continues to scream, her father attempts to calm her

by singing; she sings also. But Harlan has now decided to take on the tripods himself—an act that Ray knows will prove fatal for him and his daughter—so Ray kills Harlan (offscreen), apparently beating him to death with a shovel, as indicated by the accompanying heavy drumlike sound.

When Ray and his daughter emerge from the basement, they are confronted with a desolate landscape and an entire arsenal of eerie sounds associated with the tripods and other creatures. For an instant all is quiet (a rare moment in this very noisy movie), and then the tripods strike again with all the familiar sounds we have come to expect. Ray attempts to hide in a car, which is smashed by the tripods; Rachel and Ray scream as they are grabbed separately by the tentacles that are swirling everywhere like giant snakes.

It is already clear, though, that the Ferriers can withstand anything. Fulfilling that expectation, they once again escape—to Boston, where the tripods self-destruct in violent explosions and fireworks. We hear the last sputtering bursts of flame, the gushing red fluid, and the last gasps of the creatures. At the conclusion, as leaves blow across a Boston street (reminding us of the winds in New Jersey at the beginning of this adventure), Rachel and Robbie reunite with their mother, who has been visiting her own mother for the weekend. We hear somber piano music and soft, muted horns as the camera surveys the dead landscape.

The musical score for *War of the Worlds* was written by John Williams, the most famous composer of film music alive today. But the movie's sound effects, more than its music, produce the fright that is the heart of

Farmhouse refuge

Rachel and her father take shelter in the house of Harlan Ogilvy. Their initial meeting is a moment of comparative quiet that's rare for this movie; all we hear is Harlan's soft voice and the offscreen sounds of distant battles being fought outside.

Rachel captured

As her father screams, "No! No!" a tentacle of one of the tripods swoops down and captures Rachel. Other sounds include Rachel's screams and the ominous, insistent musical score that suggests the inevitability of this incident.

Home, devastated home

At the conclusion of Spielberg's *War of the Worlds*, Ray, his daughter, Rachel, and his son, Robbie, are reunited with the children's mother. The soft, muted horns suggest a happy ending, but as Ray and his family tearfully celebrate their reunion, the camera reveals the full extent of the havoc wrought by the alien invaders. Whatever future the Ferriers may have is uncertain.

the story. Contrary to viewers' expectations (if we are familiar with Williams's other work), Williams does not create a musical theme for each of the major characters—although there is a recurring, low-key motif for the tripods. Nor does he leave us with one of his memorable "wall of sound" experiences. We are frightened when we see the unfamiliar tripods, and Williams underscores that fear with atonal music, but he also understands that what we see in this movie demands a level of sound effects that necessarily assigns music a secondary role.

It's interesting to compare Steven Spielberg's movie adaptation of *War of the Worlds* with Orson Welles's classic radio adaptation. Spielberg spent some $135 million to make the movie and employed hundreds of artists and technicians in the fields of sound and special effects. Welles's budget (estimated at $2,000) paid for his eleven-person radio cast, small crew, and studio orchestra. We cannot easily compare a blockbuster movie released in 2005 with a radio show broadcast in 1938, not only because of the differences in the two media but also because the radio audience then was less media-savvy than movie audiences of today. But for anyone who has turned off the lights and listened to Welles's production—the most famous of all radio broadcasts—it's clear how he was able to convince millions of people in the audience that aliens had actually landed and that humankind was in mortal danger. At some level Spielberg instinctively understood this because, like Welles, ultimately he created fright through sound.

Functions of Film Sound

Primarily, sound helps the filmmaker tell a movie's story by reproducing and intensifying the world that has been partially created by the film's visual elements. A good sound track can make the audience aware of the spatial and temporal dimensions of the screen, raise expectations, create rhythm, and develop characters. Either directly or indirectly, these functions give the viewer clues to interpretation and meaning. Sounds that work directly include dialogue, narration, and sound effects (often Foley sounds) that call attention (the characters' or ours) to on-screen or offscreen events.

In John Ford's *My Darling Clementine* (1946), "Doc" Holliday tosses his keys noisily on the hotel desk to underscore his desire to leave town if Clementine won't keep her promise to leave before him. In Charles Laughton's *The Night of the Hunter* (1955), Harry Powell covets the large sum of money that he knows is hidden somewhere around the farm. His stepchildren, John and Pearl, have kept the money hidden inside Pearl's doll, but Pearl is too young to understand what's going on and has cut two of the bills into figures that she calls "Pearl" and "John." When Harry comes out of the house to tell the children that it's bedtime, they quickly restuff the crackling bills into the doll. Although we hear this sound, Harry doesn't; but a moment later, in a small but easily missed visual moment in the wide frame, we see

INTERACTIVE In this interactive tutorial, see how sound plays a major role in how movies convey meaning, mood, and narrative. Experience a single silent scene in several very different ways, thanks to three distinct soundscapes created by a professional sound designer.

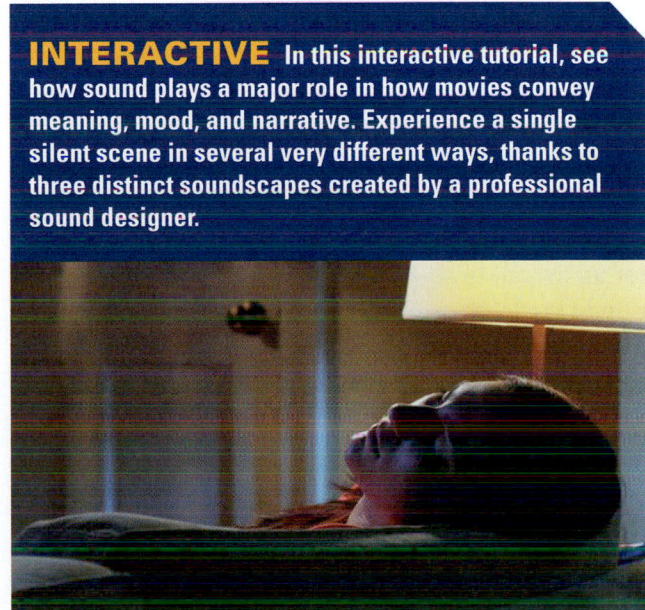

and hear the two "Pearl" and "John" bills blowing across the path toward Harry. This ominous coincidence adds tension to the scene because we fear that Harry will surely hear it too, look down, and discover the children's secret. Happily, at least for the moment, he doesn't. The sound effects in both of these films were created by Foley artists.

Sounds that function indirectly help create mood and thus may help the audience interpret scenes subconsciously. Tomlinson Holman, a sound expert, points out that viewers differentiate visual elements in a movie far more easily and analytically than they do sound elements. The reason is that they tend to hear sound as a whole, not as individual elements. Filmmakers can take advantage of viewers' inability to separate sounds into constituent parts and use sound to manipulate emotions, often via the musical score. In *Bride of Frankenstein* (1935), director James Whale uses low-pitched music to accentuate the terror of the scene in which a lynch mob pursues the Monster through the woods. In Steven Spielberg's *Jaws* (1975), composer John Williams uses four low notes as the motif for the shark—the sound of fear being generated in an otherwise placid environment.

Whether direct or indirect, sound functions according to conventions, means of conveying information that are easy to perceive and understand. In this section, we look at some of these conventions.

Audience Awareness

Sound can define sections of the screen, guide our attention to or between them, and influence our interpretation. *Once upon a Time in the West* (1968), Sergio Leone's masterfully ironic reworking of the Western genre, begins with a scene at the Cattle Corner railroad stop somewhere in the Arizona desert. This scene is notable for an overall mise-en-scène that emphasizes the isolation of the location and the menacing behavior of three desperadoes waiting for a man called Harmonica to arrive on the Flagstone train. Within that setting, the director and his sound engineers have created a memorable audio mise-en-scène for the opening scene. Running approximately 14 minutes, this sequence uses various diegetic sounds that we perceive as emanating from very specific points on and off the screen.

Sound that defines cinematic space

The tapestry of sounds that underscores the opening of Sergio Leone's *Once upon a Time in the West* (1968) is based on recurring sounds (squeaking windmill) [1], sounds heard only once (whimpering dog), sounds that advance the narrative (an approaching train), sounds that emphasize the tension of the situation in which three desperadoes wait for a train (buzzing fly, dripping water), and sounds that remind us of the outside world (the clackety-clack of the telegraph—until it is disabled by one of the desperadoes) [2].

This scene is worth studying both for its montage of sounds and for its convincing way of pinpointing their sources. This sound tapestry is composed almost entirely of sound effects: a creaking door inside the crude station, the scratch of chalk as the station agent writes on a blackboard, a squeaking windmill, the clackety-clack of a telegraph machine, water slowly dripping from the ceiling, a man cracking his knuckles, various animals and insects (a softly whimpering dog, loudly buzzing fly, and chirping bird in a cage), the distant sound of a train approaching and the closer sounds of its chugging steam engine, the music from Harmonica's harmonica, and the sounds of the shootout in which Harmonica swiftly kills the three waiting desperadoes.

We see and hear clearly the source of each of these sounds. Because we are in the desert, there is no background sound per se (except the sound of the train approaching); at two brief moments we hear voices and, at the end, only a hint of Ennio Morricone's musical score. This sound design helps us distinguish the individual sounds and also helps us understand how they are arranged in relation to one another. Furthermore, it creates a brooding suspense and raises fundamental questions about the narrative and characters: Who are these desperadoes? Who are they waiting for? Why do they seem to betray Harmonica the moment he arrives? Why does he kill them?

In addition to directing our attention to both the spatial and temporal dimensions of a scene, as in *Once upon a Time in the West*, sound creates emphasis by how it is selected, arranged, and (if necessary) enhanced. In Robert Altman's *The Player* (1992), sound helps us eavesdrop on the gossip at one table in a restaurant and then, even more deliberately, takes us past that table to another in the distance where the protagonist is heading and where the gossip will be confirmed. Because the scene takes place on the terrace of an exclusive restaurant in Beverly Hills—the guests all seem to be in the motion-picture business—the sound makes us feel as if we're among them, able to see the rich and famous come and go and, more relevant here, able to hear what they're saying, even if they think they aren't being overheard.

Audience Expectations

Sounds create expectations. For example, in a scene between a man and a woman in which you hear quiet music, the sounds of their movements, and a subtle sound of moving clothes, you might expect intimacy between the characters. However, in a similar scene in which the characters are not moving and you cannot hear their clothes—and instead you hear the harsh sound of traffic outside or a fan in the room—you might expect something other than intimacy. Sound also requires precise timing and coordination with the image. For example, when a simple scene of meeting in a doorway is accompanied by a musical chord, we know that the incident is significant, even if we do not know how it will evolve. But in a scene where a small boy is taken away by a bad guy at a carnival, and we hear only the carnival music and loud crowd sounds and then see the look of terror on the parents' faces when they realize their child is gone, dramatic music is probably not needed.

When a particular sound signals an action and that sound is used repeatedly, it plays on our expectations.

Sound that thwarts audience expectations

A classic example of sound thwarting audience expectations occurs in Alfred Hitchcock's *The 39 Steps* (1935). A landlady enters a room, discovers a dead body, turns to face the camera, and opens her mouth as if to scream [1]. At least, that's what we expect to hear. Instead, as she opens her mouth we hear a sound that resembles a scream but is slightly different—a sound that, because it is out of context, we may not instantly recognize. Immediately, though, Hitchcock cuts to a shot of a train speeding out of a tunnel [2], and the mystery is solved: instead of a scream, we have heard the train whistle blaring a fraction of a second before we see the train.

In Ridley Scott's *Alien* (1979), sound (along with visual effects) plays an impressive role in helping to create and sustain the suspenseful narrative. This science-fiction/horror movie tells the story of the crew of a commercial spacecraft that takes aboard an alien form of "organic life" that ultimately kills all but one of them, Lieutenant Ellen Ripley.

One device used to sustain this suspense is the juxtaposition of the familiar "meow" sounds made by Ripley's pet cat, Jonesy, against the unfamiliar sounds made by the alien. After the alien disappears into the labyrinthine ship, three crew members—Ripley, Parker, and Brett—attempt to locate it with a motion detector. This device leads them to a locked panel that, when opened, reveals the cat, which hisses and runs away from them. Because losing the cat is Brett's fault, he is charged with finding it by himself. We hear his footsteps as he proceeds warily through the craft, calling "Here, kitty, kitty . . . Jonesy, Jonesy," and we are relieved when Brett finds the cat and calls it to him. Before the cat reaches Brett, however, it sees the alien behind him, stops, and hisses. Alerted, Brett turns around, but he is swiftly killed by the creature. This sound motif is repeated near the end of the film, when Ripley prepares to escape on the craft's emergency shuttle but is distracted by the cat's meow.

Expression of Point of View

By juxtaposing visual and aural images, a director can express a point of view. In countless movies, for example, the sounds of big-city traffic—horns honking, people yelling at one another, taxis screeching to a halt to pick up passengers—express the idea that these places are frenetic and unlivable. Similarly, when a movie is set in other distinct environments—seashore, desert, mountain valley—the natural sounds associated with these places (the placid, turbulent, and stormy rhythms of the sea; the howling winds of the desert sands; the cry of a lone wolf in an otherwise peaceful valley) reflect the director's point of view of landscape and often the thoughts or emotional mood of the characters.

Alfred Hitchcock is a master of expressing his point of view through sound. In *The Birds* (1963), for example, one of the few of his movies that does not have background music, Hitchcock uses a design of electronic bird sounds to express his point of view about the human chaos that breaks out in an unsuspecting town that has been attacked by birds. Bernard Herrmann, who composed the scores for many Hitchcock movies including *Psycho* (1960), was the uncredited sound designer on this one. Its highly stylized sound track consists of a jux-

taposition of natural sounds and computer-generated bird noises. Elisabeth Weis, an authority on film sound, writes:

> [In] *The Birds*, screeches are even more important than visual techniques for terrorizing the audience during attacks. Indeed, bird sounds sometimes replace visuals altogether. . . . Hitchcock carefully manipulates the sound track so that the birds can convey terror even when they are silent or just making an occasional caw or flutter. . . . Instead of orchestrated instruments there are orchestrated sound effects. If in *Psycho* music sounds like birds, in *The Birds* bird sounds function like music. Hitchcock even eliminates music under the opening titles in favor of bird sounds.[8]

Directors of visionary movies—those that show the past, present, or future world in a distinctive, stylized manner—rely extensively on sounds of all kinds, including music, to create those worlds. In *2001: A Space Odyssey* (1968), where the world created comes almost totally from his imagination, Stanley Kubrick uses sounds (and the absence of them) to help us experience what it might be like to travel through outer space. The barks and howling of the apes in the prologue reflect Kubrick's point of view that aggression and violence have always been a part of the world—indeed, that such behavior removes the distinction between such concepts as *primitive* and *civilized*. The sounds of switches, latches, and doorways on the space shuttles have a peculiar hollow sound all their own. The electronic sounds emanating from the monolith reflect its imposing dignity but also mirror the awe and fear of the astronauts who approach it.

Although Werner Herzog usually shoots his visionary movies with direct sound (meaning that it is recorded on-site), he frequently augments that sound with haunting musical scores by the German group Popol Vuh. These sounds, as well as Herzog's very deliberate use of silence, are part of what elevates such films as *Aguirre: The Wrath of God* (1972), *Nosferatu the Vampyre* (1979), and *The Enigma of Kasper Hauser* (1974) beyond being mere poetic movies to being philosophical statements about human life. *Aguirre* recounts the failed attempt of Don Lope de Aguirre, a sixteenth-century Spanish explorer, to conquer Peru and find the fabled city of El Do-

---

8. Elisabeth Weis, *The Silent Scream: Alfred Hitchcock's Sound Track* (Rutherford, NJ: Fairleigh Dickinson University Press, 1982), pp. 138–139.

rado. From the opening to the closing moments of this extraordinary movie, it is clear that Aguirre is mad. Indeed, Kinski's performance as Aguirre leaves no doubt that he is possessed by ruthless ambition and greed.

Herzog's style is frequently called hallucinatory (as well as visionary) because it produces a feeling in the viewer of being somewhere between fantasy and reality, which is exactly where Aguirre is. In the opening scene, in which Aguirre and his forces slowly descend a steep mountainside toward a river, most of the action is shot in real time, helping us to understand just how arduous and dangerous the expedition will be. The primary sounds are people's low voices, footsteps on the path, and Popol Vuh's minimalist score, which mixes electronic and acoustic sources with choral monotones. This music makes clear Herzog's view of the futility of Aguirre's quest. Thus at the end, when Aguirre is alone on a drifting raft spinning slowly out of control on the river (photographed impressively from a helicopter, which, of course, we do not hear), we are not surprised to hear this musical score again—except that now Aguirre too seems to understand the futility of his quest. This reuse of music reinforces the prophetic nature of the director's point of view.

Rhythm

Sound can add rhythm to a scene, whether it's accompanying or juxtaposed against movement on the screen. In *Citizen Kane* (1941; sound by Bailey Fesler and James G. Stewart), in the comic scene in which Kane moves into the *Inquirer* office, Orson Welles uses the rhythms within overlapping dialogue to create a musical composition—one voice playing off another in its pitch, loudness, and quality [see "Looking at (and Listening to) Sound in Orson Welles's *Citizen Kane*" later in this chapter]. In Atom Egoyan's *The Sweet Hereafter* (1997), two conversations overlap, joined in time but separated in on-screen space: Wendell and Risa Walker talk with each other while Mitchell Stevens speaks with his daughter, Zoe, on a cell phone.

A **montage** of sounds is a mix that ideally includes multiple sources of diverse quality, levels, and placement and usually moves as rapidly as a montage of images. Such a montage can also be orchestrated to create rhythm, as in the famous opening scene of Rouben Mamoulian's *Love Me Tonight* (1932)—one of the first films

to use sound creatively—in which the different qualities of sounds made by ordinary activities establish the "symphony" that accompanies the start of the day in an ordinary Parisian neighborhood.

Jean-Pierre Jeunet and Marc Caro pay homage to Mamoulian's sound montage in *Delicatessen* (1991). One comic scene in the film functions like a piece of music, with a classic verse-chorus-verse-chorus-verse-chorus pattern. When a butcher, Monsieur Clapet, makes love to his mistress, Mademoiselle Plusse, the mattress and frame of the bed squeak noisily and in an increasing rhythm that matches their increasing ardor. As the tempo increases, we expect the scene to end climactically. Playing on our expectations, though, Jeunet and Caro cut

Sound and characterization

The opening montage in Francis Ford Coppola's *Apocalypse Now* (1979) sets a high visual and sonic standard. But Coppola and his collaborators meet and perhaps exceed that standard during the "helicopter attack" scene, in which the lunatic Lieutenant Colonel Kilgore leads a largely aerial raid on a Vietnamese village. Accompanying horribly magnificent images of destruction and death are the sounds of wind, footsteps, gunfire, explosions, airplanes, helicopters, crowd noise, shouting, dialogue, and Richard Wagner's "Ride of the Valkyries." Although the grand operatic music gives unity, even a kind of dignity, to the fast-moving, violent, and disparate images, its main effect is to underscore Kilgore's megalomania.

back and forth between the lovers and other inhabitants of the building, who hear the squeaking bed and subconsciously change the rhythm of their daily chores to keep time with the sounds' escalating pace. The sequence derives its humor from the way it satisfies our formal expectations for closure (the sexual partners reach orgasm) but frustrates the tenants, who just become exhausted in their labors.

Characterization

All types of sound—dialogue, sound effects, music—can function as part of characterization. In Mel Brooks's *Young Frankenstein* (1974), when Frau Blücher's name is mentioned, horses rear on their hind legs and whinny. It becomes clear in context that she is so ugly and intimidating that even horses can't stand to hear her name, so for the rest of the movie, every time her name is mentioned, we hear the same sounds.

In *Jaws* (1975), Steven Spielberg uses a sound effect to introduce Quint, the old shark hunter. When Quint enters a community meeting called in response to the first killing of a swimmer by the shark, he draws his fingernails across a chalkboard to show his power and bravery: he is affected neither by a sound that makes most people cringe nor, by extension, by the townspeople or sharks. We might also observe that this sound is as abrasive as Quint is.

Musical themes are frequently associated with a character's thoughts, as in Lasse Hallström's *My Life as a Dog* (1985), where Björn Isfält's score reflects the melancholic state of mind of a boy yearning for his dead mother, or in Joseph L. Mankiewicz's *The Ghost and Mrs. Muir* (1947), where Bernard Herrmann's score reflects a widow's loneliness in an isolated house on a cliff overlooking the sea. Musical themes can also help us to understand the setting in which characters live. Miranda July's *Me and You and Everyone We Know* (2006) is an offbeat indie feature that tells the overlapping stories of a diverse group of people living in Los Angeles and looking for love, affection, or whatever they can find. These people—young, old, married, single, black, Hispanic, and white—are poignant in their somewhat goofy yearnings, and Michael Andrews's whimsical musical score (including solo guitar, solo piano, solo organ, pop songs, and a hymn) reflects their casual lifestyles and provides the perfect comment on their activities. Animals can also be identified by a significant musical

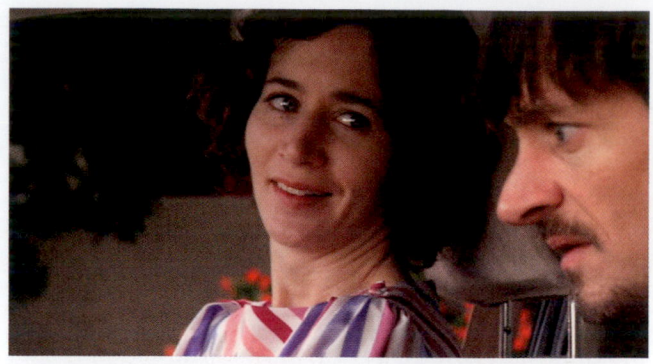

Music supporting characterization
Richard and Christine are just two of the endearing characters looking for love in *Me and You and Everyone We Know*. When they meet initially, nothing clicks, at least not for Richard. But later they discover that they live in the wacky world of L.A. and view it in the same detached way. The musical score does not create a theme for them; instead, it echoes their casual way of living and loving.

theme, as with John Williams's memorable one for Hedwig, Harry's owl in the Harry Potter series.

Musical themes often identify characters, occurring and recurring on the sound track as the characters make their entrances and exits on the screen. But music can also underscore characters' insights. In Sam Mendes's *American Beauty* (1999), for example, Lester Burnham is having a midlife crisis. Although a wide variety of diegetic popular music helps identify the musical tastes of the Burnham family, it is an original theme that helps identify and sustain Lester's longing for a different life, literally a "bed of roses"—and roses are the symbol of Lester's lust for his daughter's friend Angela. Lying on his bed, Lester has this fantasy—shots of rose petals floating on him are intercut with shots of Angela naked among the rose petals on the ceiling above him—and we hear a peaceful theme played by a Javanese gamelan orchestra. The repetitiveness and quality of this music emphasize Lester's mood of wanting to escape to another world.

Continuity

Sound can link one shot to the next, indicating that the scene has not changed in either time or space. **Overlapping sound** carries the sound from a first shot over to the next before the sound of the second shot be-

LOOKING AT MOVIES
SOUND IN SNAPSHOT

VIDEO This short tutorial shows how sound functions in a short scene from Andrew Lund's *Snapshot*.

gins. Charles Laughton's *The Night of the Hunter* (1955) contains an effective sound bridge: Harry Powell, a con man posing as an itinerant preacher, has murdered his wife, Willa, placed her in an automobile, and driven it into the river. An old man, Birdie Steptoe, out fishing on the river, looks down and discovers the crime.

Through shot A, an underwater shot of great poetic quality in which we see Willa in the car, her floating hair mingling with the reeds, we hear Harry singing one of his hymns; that music bridges the cut to shot B, where Harry, continuing to sing, is standing in front of their house looking for his stepchildren. Hearing Harry's hymn singing over Willa's submerged body affects the meaning of this scene in two ways: it both adds to the shot's eerie feeling of heavenly peace (with her gently undulating hair, diffused light, etc.) associated with what should be a grisly image and connects Harry directly to the murder. In addition, his calm, satisfied, even righteous attitude reinforces the interpretation that he sees his killings as acts of God. When the picture catches up with the sound to reveal Harry calmly stalking the murdered woman's children, the dramatic tension is increased because of the association between Harry and Willa's body that the sound bridge has reinforced.

Joel Coen's *The Man Who Wasn't There* (2001) is a dark, twisted neo-noir film. It contains a smoothly edited sequence of fifteen shots, thirteen of which are linked by overlapping, nondiegetic bits of a Beethoven piano sonata and two of which show Ed Crane listening to Rachael Abundas playing the sonata (diegetic music). In a life filled with conflict and tragedy, Ed has found "peace" listening to Rachael play this particular sonata, and this sequence is made all the more peaceful by its lyrical theme. But Carter Burwell, the movie's composer, must have chosen this sonata—no. 8 in C Minor, op. 13—for its subtitle, *Pathétique*, as a pointedly ironic reminder that Crane sees himself as a loser and so does everyone else.

Emphasis

A sound can create emphasis in any scene: it can function as a punctuation mark when it accentuates and strengthens the visual image. Although some movies treat emphasis as if it were a sledgehammer, others handle it more subtly. In Peter Weir's *The Truman Show* (1998), Truman Burbank unknowingly has lived his entire life in an ideal world that is in fact a fantastic television set contained within a huge dome. When after 30 years he realizes the truth of his existence, he overcomes his fear of water and attempts to sail away. To deter him, the television producer orders an artificial storm, which temporarily disables Truman. But the Sun comes out, he wakes up, and he continues his journey, thinking he is free. Suddenly the boom of one of his sails pierces the inside of the great dome with a sound that is unfamiliar to him—indeed, one of the most memorable sounds ever heard in a movie. His first reactions are shock, anguish, and disbelief. How could there be an "end" to the horizon?

Distinct as this sound is, it has nothing of the sledgehammer effect. Rather, it underscores Truman's quiet, slow epiphany of who and where he is. His next reaction is the awareness that something is very wrong with his world. Cautiously touching the dome's metal wall, he says, "Aah," indicating a further insight into his situation. He walks along the edge of the "horizon," mounts a surreal staircase, pauses for a moment to talk with the show's producer, and finally walks through an exit door to the first free day of his life. The unique sound of the boom piercing the metal dome, underscored by the chord progressions of Burkhard Dallwitz's score, is nothing like the ordinary sound of a boat bumping against a dock. And although it is a real sound, it is not a natural one. This is a symbolic sound that both emphasizes

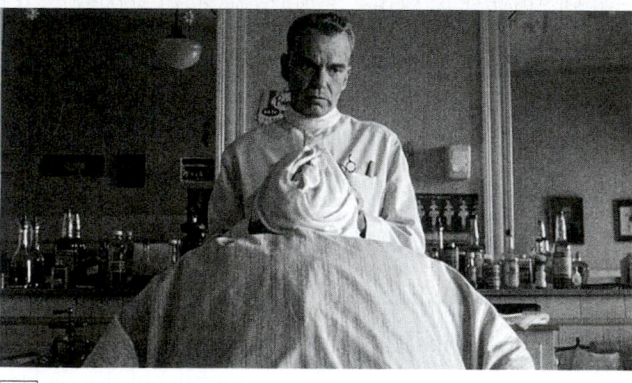

Overlapping music

A fifteen-shot sequence in Joel Coen's *The Man Who Wasn't There* (2001) documents a futile attempt by Ed Crane to find a man who has swindled him out of $10,000. The sequence is one of many in the movie that show the decent but ineffectual Crane coming to grips with his life as an ordinary barber while his wife and everyone else around him set higher goals. The sequence is underscored with the nondiegetic and diegetic sounds of Beethoven's *Pathétique* piano sonata. Here are five shots from the middle of the sequence: Crane [1] tries to locate Creighton Tolliver, the swindler, by phone; [2] checks the man's business card; and [3] listens to Rachael "Birdy" Abundas, a teenage neighbor, playing a Beethoven piano sonata. [4] Rachael's father, Walter, also listens. [5] Crane is back at his job in the barber shop. When he asks, "How could I have been so stupid?" we understand the appropriateness of the filmmakers' choice of this Beethoven sonata to underscore his self-insight.

Truman's captivity and heralds his liberation from a world of illusion.

In Adrian Lyne's version of *Lolita* (1997), the sexual ambiguity of a confrontation between Humbert Humbert and his nemesis, Clare Quilty, is punctuated by the insistent sound of an electric bug zapper. In action movies, such as *Sin City* (2005; directors Frank Miller and Robert Rodriguez), the sounds of violent action are greatly emphasized so that fists hit with a bone-crunching "thunk" and cars crash with a deafening noise. The same exaggerated emphasis applies to many animated movies, in which the violence is loud but usually harmless.

Looking at (and Listening to) Sound in Orson Welles's *Citizen Kane*

During the 1930s, the first decade of sound in film, many directors used sound as an integral part of their movies. Their innovations were all the more significant because most of them had little or no prior background in sound.

Between 1933 and 1938, Orson Welles established himself as one of the most creative innovators in American radio broadcasting. Before Welles, radio broadcasting had been a wasteland lacking in creativity, but Welles approached the medium the way he approached the theater and, later, the movies: experimenting and making things different.

As always, Welles was a one-man show: writer, director, producer, actor. As writer, he specialized in making modern adaptations of classic literary works; as producer, he cast famous stage and movie actors, generally saving the most important part for himself; and as director, he orchestrated voices, sound effects, narration, and music in a complex mix that had never been tried before, at least on the scale that he created. There was no commercial television broadcasting at the time, and Welles understood the power of pure sounds, without images, to entertain, educate, and engage listeners. He also understood the power of radio to shock people, as his notorious 1938 production of H. G. Wells's *The War of the Worlds* proved. Indeed, the awesome imagination behind that one radio broadcast made Orson Welles world famous overnight and was instrumental in his recruitment by Hollywood.

Welles's complex sound design for *Citizen Kane* (1941; sound by Bailey Fesler and James G. Stewart) is a kind of deep-focus sound that functions much like deep-focus cinematography. Indeed, we can confidently call Welles the first sound designer in American film history for his comprehensive use of sound to establish, develop, and call our attention to the meanings of what we see. In this discussion, we will look more closely at the impressive uses of sound in the party scene that celebrates Kane's acquisition of the *Chronicle* staff for the *Inquirer*. In addition to the combined staff of reporters, musicians, waiters, and dancers, the principal characters are Charles Foster Kane, Mr. Bernstein, and Jed Leland. The setting for the party is the *Inquirer*'s offices, which have been decorated for the occasion. The room is both deep and wide, designed to accommodate the deep-focus cinematography. Welles made his complicated sound design possible by covering the ceilings with muslin, which concealed the many microphones necessary to record the multiple sounds as the scene was shot.

We hear these multiple sounds simultaneously, distinctly, and at the proper sound levels in relation to the camera's placement, so that the farther we are from the sound, the softer and less distinct the sound becomes.

Sound mise-en-scène

The mise-en-scène of this party scene from Orson Welles's *Citizen Kane* (1941) clearly reflects what's going on both visually and aurally. Leland and Bernstein are talking, and even though there are competing sounds around them, their voices are distinct because they have been placed close to a microphone in a medium shot. Note that Kane (Welles), both visually and aurally, dominates this scene through his presence in the middle background of each shot.

When Bernstein and Leland are talking, for example, they appear in medium shots, and their dialogue is naturally the loudest on the sound track. However, they literally have to shout to be heard because of the pitch, loudness, and quality of the competing sounds: the music, the dancing, the crowd noise.

We can say that the sound has its own mise-en-scène here. Although these diegetic, on-screen sounds were recorded directly on the set, some additions were made during the rerecording process. Reversing the ordinary convention of composing the music after making the rough cut of a film, Bernard Herrmann wrote the music first, and Robert Wise edited the footage to fit the music's rhythm.

Sources and Types

The sound in this scene is diegetic, external on-screen. It was recorded during both production and postproduction and is diverse in quality, level, and placement. The types of sound include overlapping voices, ordinary dialogue, and singing; music from an on-screen band; sound effects; and ambient noise. Welles's handling of sound dominates this scene: he makes us constantly aware of the sources, the types, and the mix and (unsurprisingly) doesn't use much silence. However, two signs mounted on walls read "SILENCE" and thus, as relics of an earlier period, remind us how quiet these same offices were before Kane took over from the previous editor. Through this visual pun, Welles employs a touch of silence during the loudest sequence in *Citizen Kane*.

Functions

Given what was possible in sound design and recording in 1941, the sound montage in this party scene is an ex-

Complex mix of sound
In addition to the distinct voices of the three main characters and those of the guests, there is a brass marching band—all of this constituted a sound design and mix that was very advanced for its time.

traordinary achievement. It creates the spatial, temporal, emotional, and dramatic setting of the action, and also heightens our expectations and fears about Kane's future in journalism and politics. This complexity set it far ahead of its time and deeply influenced the development of movie sound. The sound montage in this party scene functions in many ways. Here are some notable ones:

> Guides our attention to all parts of the room, making us aware of characters' relative positions (e.g., the contrast between Kane and the others)

> Helps define the spatial and temporal dimensions of the setting and the characters' placement within the mise-en-scène (e.g., the sound is loud when the source is closer to the camera)

> Conveys the mood and the characters' states of mind (e.g., the sound is frantic and loud and gains momentum until it almost runs out of control, underscoring the idea that these men, Kane and reporters alike, are being blinded and intoxicated by their own success)

> Helps represent time (e.g., the sound here is synchronous with the action)

> Fulfills our expectations (e.g., of how a party of this kind might sound and of the fact that Kane

Sound creates mood
At this party, where spirits are high, almost everyone joins in the act, including Kane, the performers, and Kane's staff of reporters, here pretending as if they were members of the band.

is continuing on his rapid rise to journalistic and political power)

> Creates rhythm beyond that provided by the music (within the changing dramatic arc that starts with a celebration involving all the men and ends with one man's colossal display of ego)

> Reveals, through the dialogue, aspects of each main character (e.g., establishes a conflict between Kane and Leland over personal and journalistic ethics, one in which Bernstein predictably takes Kane's side)

> Underscores one principal theme of the entire movie (e.g., the song "There Is a Man" not only puts "good old Charlie Kane" in the spotlight—he sings and dances throughout it—but also serves as the campaign theme song when he runs for governor and becomes a dirge after his defeat; at the same time, while the lyric attempts to answer the question "Who is this man?" it has no more success than the rest of the movie)

> Arouses our expectations about what's going to happen as the film evolves (e.g., the marching band signals both that the *Inquirer* won over the *Chronicle* and that the *Inquirer* "declares" war on Spain—a war the United States will win)

> Enhances continuity with sound bridges (the smooth transitions from shot to shot and scene to scene within the sequence)

> Provides emphasis (e.g., the sound of the flashlamp when the staff's picture is taken punctuates Kane's bragging about having gotten his candy; after Kane says, "And now, gentlemen, *your complete attention, if you please,*" he puts his fingers in his mouth and whistles; the trumpets' blare)

> Enhances the overall dramatic effect of the sequence

This overwhelming sound mix almost tells the story by itself.

Characterization

All the functions named in the previous section are important to this particular sequence and the overall film. In this section, we will look more closely only at how the sound helps illuminate the characters of Charles Foster Kane, Mr. Bernstein, and Jed Leland. Even though their dialogue is primarily a function of the narrative, its vocal delivery brings it to life. Long after you have seen the movie, you remember the characters, what they said, and the voices of those who portrayed them. As one legacy of his radio experience, Welles planned it that way.

Who is this man?
"Who is this man?" a line in Kane's campaign song "There Is a Man," might function as a subtitle for the movie itself and allows Kane—singing, dancing, and mugging his way through the act—to show a lighter side of his many-faceted personality.

Sound effects
Welles rarely missed an opportunity to use sound effects expressively, as here, where the bright light of the old-fashioned flash unit illuminates the scene and punctuates his bragging about acquiring the *Chronicle* staff: "I felt like a kid in a candy store!"

Sound aids characterization in *Citizen Kane*

[1] Standing at opposite ends of the banquet table, Bernstein (*background*) and Kane (*foreground*) banter back and forth as if they were a comedy duo. [2] Welles dominates the scene with sound. Putting his fingers between his lips, Kane gets the attention of his guests and loudly calls for their "complete attention." [3] Bernstein (*left*) and Leland (*right*) join in the singing of "There Is a Man," but Leland, now disillusioned with Kane, sings only to be polite.

Each of the actors playing these characters has a distinctive speaking voice that is a major part of their characterization. Indeed, their voices are part of the key to our understanding of their characters. The depth and resonance of Welles's voice, coupled with its many colors (or qualities) and capabilities for both nuance and emphasis, enhance his ambiguous portrayal of the character. In several distinct areas, the sound of his voice deepens our understanding of this contradictory figure. It helps Kane flaunt his wealth and his power as the *Inquirer*'s publisher: when he brags to the new reporters about feeling like a "kid in a candy store" and having gotten his candy, his remarks are punctuated by the sound of the photographer's flashlamp. However, this sound may also be interpreted as Welles's way of mocking Kane's bragging.

Kane dominates the table of guests with the announcement that he is going to Europe for his health—"forgive my rudeness in taking leave of you"—but there is in fact nothing physically wrong with him, as we learn when he calls attention to his mania for collection (and wealth) by sarcastically saying, "They've been making statues for two thousand years and I've only been buying for five." This conversation between Kane and Bernstein is directed and acted as if it were a comedy routine on a radio show or in a vaudeville theater between the "top banana" (Kane) and the "straight man" (Bernstein). The implied nature of this exchange is something that 1940s audiences would have instinctively understood.

The sound in this scene helps Kane build on his power, not only as the boss and host of the party—"And now, gentlemen, *your complete attention*, if you please"— but also as the flamboyant and influential publisher: "Well, gentlemen, are we going to declare war on Spain, or are we not?" He's in charge because he's the boss, and the boss's voice also dominates his employees. As he asks this question, the band enters, playing "Hot Time in the Old Town Tonight," and is followed by women dancers carrying toy rifles. When Leland answers, "The *Inquirer* already has," Kane humiliates him by calling him "a long-faced, overdressed anarchist." Even though he says this humorously, he uses the tone of his voice, as well as his words, to humiliate his subordinate.

The song about "good old Charlie Kane"—here the excuse for more of Welles's vocal theatrics—later becomes his political campaign theme, so the sound in this scene connects us with later scenes in which we hear this musical theme again. By participating in the singing and dancing, Kane continues to call "complete attention" (his words) to himself. Through both visual and aural imagery, Kane remains in the center of the frame for most of the scene, either directly on-screen himself or indirectly reflected in the windows. His voice dominates all the other sounds in this scene because it always seems to be the loudest.

Leland and Bernstein are different from one another in family background, education, level of sophistication, and relationship to Kane, and their conversation about journalistic ethics establishes another major difference: these characters' voices are also quite different from Kane's voice. Leland has the soft patrician voice of a Virginia gentleman, while Bernstein's voice reflects his New York immigrant-class upbringing. Leland gently questions Kane's motives in hiring the *Chronicle*'s staff and wonders why they can change their loyalties so easily, but the pragmatic Bernstein bluntly answers, "Sure, they're just like anybody else. . . . They got work to do, they do it. Only they happen to be the best in the business." Their reading of these lines embodies one of the movie's major themes: journalistic ethics. Even their singing sets them apart. Bernstein sings as if he's having a good time, but Leland seems to sing only to show his good manners. Their differences, including the differences in their voices, ultimately determine their future relationship with Kane.

Themes

Sound serves many functions in this scene, including the development of several major themes and concerns:

> *Kane's youthful longings fulfilled.* A major strand of the narrative conveys Kane's lifelong bullying of others, mania for buying things, and egomania as a reaction to being abandoned by his parents at an early age. Here he begins the scene by addressing the new reporters and likening his acquisition of the *Chronicle* staff to a kid who has just gotten all the candy he wants. This statement is punctuated by the sound of a flashbulb.

> *Kane's ruthless ambition.* The mix of burlesque dancing, loud music, and serious conversation about ethics only underscores Kane's determination to do whatever is necessary to attain his goals.

> *Kane's disregard for ethics and principles and his relation with his two closest associates.* Kane's domination of the scene is made personal by his humiliation of Leland (throwing his coat at Leland, as if Leland were a lackey) and teasing of Bernstein ("You don't expect me to keep any of those promises, do you?"), a further reference to the "Declaration of Principles" that Kane flamboyantly writes and prints on the first page of the *Inquirer*. The dialogue in this scene (and those scenes that precede and follow it) further clarifies the relationships among Kane, Bernstein, and Leland.

The care and attention that Welles and his colleagues enthusiastically gave to the sound design of this scene was virtually unprecedented in 1941 and was seldom equaled until the 1970s. In giving this rowdy party the appearance of a real event, not something staged for the cameras, the sound—along with the visual design, mise-en-scène, acting, and direction, of course—plays a major role in depicting a crucial turning point in the narrative.

ANALYZING SOUND

By this point in our study of the movies, we know that like everything else in a movie, sound is manufactured creatively for the purposes of telling a story. As you attempt to make more informed critical judgments about the sound in any movie, remember that what you hear in a film results from choices made by directors and their collaborators during and after production, just as what you see does. This chapter has provided a foundation for understanding the basic characteristics of film sound and a vocabulary for talking and writing about it analytically. As you screen movies in and out of class, you'll now be able to thoughtfully appreciate and describe how the sound in any movie either complements or detracts from the visual elements portrayed on-screen.

SCREENING CHECKLIST: SOUND

✔ As you analyze a shot or scene, carefully note the specific sources of sound in that shot or scene.

✔ Also keep notes on the types of sound that are used in the shot or scene.

✔ Note carefully those moments when the sound creates emphasis by accentuating and strengthening the visual image.

✔ Does the sound in the shot, scene, or movie as a whole help develop characterization? If so, how does it do so?

✔ In the movie overall, how is music used? In a complementary way? Ironically? Does the use of music in this movie seem appropriate to the story?

✔ Do image and sound complement one another in this movie or does one dominate the other?

✔ Does this film use silence expressively?

✔ In this movie, do you hear evidence of a comprehensive approach to sound—one, specifically, in which the film's sound is as expressive as its images? If so, explain why you think so.

Questions for Review

1. What is sound design? What are the responsibilities of the sound designer?
2. Distinguish among recording, rerecording, editing, and mixing.
3. What is the difference between diegetic and nondiegetic sources of sound?
4. What are the differences between sounds that are internal and external; on-screen and offscreen?
5. Is a movie limited to a certain number of sound tracks?
6. How do ambient sounds differ from sound effects? How are Foley sounds different from sound effects?
7. Can the music in a movie be both diegetic and nondiegetic? Explain.
8. How does sound call our attention to both the spatial and temporal dimensions of a scene?
9. Cite an example of sound that is faithful to its source and an example that is not.
10. What is a sound bridge? What are its functions?

as radical and provocative as Godard's. Also you might browse through a comprehensive history of film, such as the ten-volume *History of American Cinema* series (University of California Press). Such comprehensive histories are written over many years, and often by many people. Because of this, most film historians don't undertake such massive projects. Most people who practice film history instead focus their energies on studying specific moments, movements, and phenomena. Jeanine Basinger's *I Do and I Don't: A History of Marriage in the Movies* (New York: Knopf, 2012) provides a masterful account of its subject. C. S. Tashiro's *Pretty Pictures: Production Design and the History Film* (Austin: University of Texas Press, 1998) focuses on just one aspect of film production—production design—even as it ranges widely over the full chronology of film history. In both broad and specific studies, the film historian is interested equally in change—those developments that have altered the course of film history—and stability, meaning those aspects that have defied change. Film

What Is Film History?

In just over a hundred years, the cinema, like the classical art forms before it—architecture, fiction, poetry, drama, dance, painting, and music—has developed its own aesthetics, conventions, influence, and, of course, history. Broadly defined, film history traces the development of moving images from early experiments with image reproduction and photography through the invention of the movies in the early 1890s and subsequent stylistic, financial, technological, and social developments in cinema that have occurred up to now.

To get some idea of the scope and depth of that record, you should start looking at as many of the movies as possible that made history. Because that could take years, a good way to start is by seeing one or both of the following compilation films. The first is *Histoire(s) du cinéma* (1998) by Jean-Luc Godard, one of the world's great film directors. Consistent with Godard's argumentative reputation, this highly original account, whose title correctly suggests that there is more than one way to look at this subject, is full of clips that will challenge your thinking. The second is Mark Cousins's *The Story of Film: An Odyssey* (2011), a 15-hour series made for British television. Cousins, an Irish filmmaker and critic, has gathered a highly personal list of movies

A major turning point in film history

Billy Wilder's *Sunset Boulevard* (1950) is a haunting film noir about film history. Norma Desmond (Gloria Swanson), an aging silent-movie star who (in the 1950s) still represents the glamour and allure of the silent era, hopes to revive her career in the sound era with the help of Joe Gillis (William Holden), an aspiring screenwriter. Her fantasies are apparent in one of her most famous (and unintentionally funny) lines: "I am big. It's the movies that got small." Unfortunately, she isn't big anymore, and the movies just kept getting bigger and better after the conversion to sound, one of the major turning points in film history. All Desmond has left is her dreams, and *Sunset Boulevard* is all the more poignant because Gloria Swanson herself was actually one of the greatest stars of the silent era.

history is not, to quote film historians Robert C. Allen and Douglas Gomery, "a list of film titles or an academically respectable trivia contest. It has the much more important and complex task of explaining the historical development of a phenomenon on which billions of dollars and countless hours have been spent."[1]

Like other historians, film historians use artifacts to study the past. These artifacts include the various machines and other technology—cameras, projectors, sound recording devices, and so on—without which there would be no movies. Artifacts might include notes from story conferences, screenplays, production logs, drawings, outtakes, and other objects relevant to the production of a particular movie. Of course, they might also include first-person accounts by people involved with the movie, newspaper and magazine articles, and books about the production and the people involved in it. Obviously, the most important artifacts to the film historian are the movies themselves.

Film history includes the history of technologies, the people and industrial organizations that produce the movies, the national cinemas that distinguish one country's movies from another's, the attempts to suppress and censor the movies, and the meanings and pleasure that we derive from them. Gaining knowledge about these and other aspects of film history is pleasurable and interesting in itself. But as you graduate from merely watching movies to looking at movies in a critically aware way, your knowledge of film history will also give you the perspective and context to understand and evaluate the unique attributes of movies from the past as well as the more complex phenomena of today's movies.

Basic Approaches to Studying Film History

There are many approaches to studying film history, including studies of production, regulation, and reception. But the beginner should know the four traditional approaches: the aesthetic, technological, economic, and social. In what follows, we describe each and cite one or two studies that exemplify each approach.[2]

The Aesthetic Approach

Sometimes called the *masterpiece approach* or *great man approach*, the aesthetic approach seeks to evaluate individual movies and/or directors using criteria that assess their artistic significance and influence. Ordinarily, historians who take this approach will first define their criteria of artistic excellence and then ask the following questions: What are the significant works of the cinematic art? Who are the significant directors? Why are these movies and these directors important?

Historians who take the aesthetic perspective do not necessarily ignore the economic, technological, and cultural aspects of film history—indeed, it would be impossible to discuss many great movies without considering these factors—but they are primarily interested in movies that are not only works of art but also widely acknowledged masterpieces.

The most comprehensive, one-volume international history that takes an aesthetic approach is David A. Cook's *A History of Narrative Film*, 5th ed. (New York: Norton, 2016). Other aesthetic studies are on the auteur theory, which holds that great movies are the work of a single creative mind; one outstanding study in this field is James Naremore's *On Kubrick* (London: BFI, 2007).[3]

The Technological Approach

All art forms have a technological history that records the advancements in materials and techniques that have affected the nature of the medium. Of all the arts, though, cinema seems to rely most heavily on technology. Historians who chart the history of cinema technology examine the circumstances surrounding the

1. Robert C. Allen and Douglas Gomery, *Film History: Theory and Practice* (New York: Knopf, 1985), p. 21.

2. These four traditional categories are covered in Allen and Gomery, *Film History*, chs. 4–7. Jon Lewis and Eric Smoodin, eds., *Looking Past the Screen: Case Studies in American Film History and Method* (Durham, NC: Duke University Press, 2007), pp. 4–5, identify four other categories: industrial systems, regulatory systems, reception, and representation.

3. Film critic Andrew Sarris defines the auteur theory in his *The American Cinema: Directors and Directions, 1929–1968* (New York: Dutton, 1968), pp. 19–37. See also Pauline Kael's famous rebuttal, "Circles and Squares," in *Film Theory and Criticism: Introductory Readings*, ed. Gerald Mast and Marshall Cohen, 2nd ed. (New York: Oxford University Press, 1979), pp. 666–691. Sarris's essay is also included in this anthology (pp. 650–665), but it should be read in the context of his pioneering 1968 study, cited here.

development of each technological advance as well as subsequent improvements. They pose questions such as: When was each invention made? Under what circumstances, including aesthetic, economic, and social, was it made? Was it a totally new idea or one linked to the existing state of technology? What were the consequences for directors, studios, distributors, exhibitors, and audiences?

By studying how the major developments (including the introduction of sound, the moving camera, deep-focus cinematography, color film stock, and digital cinematography, processing, and projection) occurred, historians show us how the production of movies has changed and can also evaluate whether that change was significant (like widescreen processes) or transitory (like Smell-O-Vision). This approach cuts across artists, studios, movements, and genres to focus on the interaction of technology with aesthetics, modes of production, and economic factors.

An excellent example of such a study is by David Bordwell, Janet Staiger, and Kristin Thompson, *The Classical Hollywood Cinema: Film Style and Mode of Production to 1960* (New York: Columbia University Press, 1985). For a study of a specific technological subject, see John Belton's *Widescreen Cinema* (Cambridge, MA: Harvard University Press, 1992).

The Economic Approach

The motion-picture industry is a major part of the global economy. Every movie released has an economic history of its own as well as a place in the economic history of its studio (policies of production, distribution, and exhibition) and the historical period and country in which it was produced.

Historians interested in this subject help us to understand how and why the studio system was founded, how it adapted to changing conditions (economic, technological, social, historical), and how and why different studios took different approaches to producing different movies, how these movies have been distributed and exhibited, and what effect this had on film history. They study how and why the independent system of production superseded the studio system and what effect this has had on production, distribution, and exhibition. They are also concerned with such related issues as manage-

ment and organization, accounting and marketing practices, and censorship and the rating system. Finally, they try to place significant movies within the nation's economy as well as within the output of the industry in general and the producing studio in particular.

Excellent studies include Douglas Gomery's *The Hollywood Studio System: A History* (London: BFI, 2005), Joel W. Finler's *The Hollywood Story*, 3rd ed. (London: Wallflower, 2003), and Tino Balio's *Grand Design: Hollywood as a Modern Business Enterprise, 1930–1939*, History of the American Cinema series, vol. 5 (Berkeley: University of California Press, 1995).

The Social History Approach

Because society and culture influence the movies, and vice versa, the movies serve as primary sources for studying society. Writing about movies as social history continues to be a major preoccupation of journalists, scholars, and students alike. Philosopher Ian Jarvie suggests that, in undertaking these studies, we ask the following basic questions: Who made the movies, and why? Who saw the films, how, and why? What was seen, how, and why? How were the movies evaluated, by whom, and why?[4]

In addition, those interested in social history consider such factors as religion, politics, and cultural trends and taboos. They ask to what extent, if any, a particular movie was produced to sway public opinion or effect social change. They are also interested in audience composition, marketing, and critical writing and reviewing in the media, from gossip magazines to scholarly books. Overall, they study the complex interaction between the movies—as a social institution—and other social institutions, including government, religion, and labor.

Landmark studies include Robert Sklar's *Movie-Made America: A Cultural History of American Movies*, rev. and updated ed. (New York: Vintage, 1994), and Richard Abel's *Americanizing the Movies and "Movie-Mad" Audiences, 1910–1914* (Berkeley: University of California Press, 2006).

Although some areas in the study of film history may require experience and analytic skills beyond those possessed by most introductory students, you can use your familiarity with film history in writing even the most basic analysis for a class assignment.

---

4. This paraphrase of Ian Jarvie comes from Allen and Gomery, *Film History*, p. 154.

Figure 10.1 | CAMERA OBSCURA

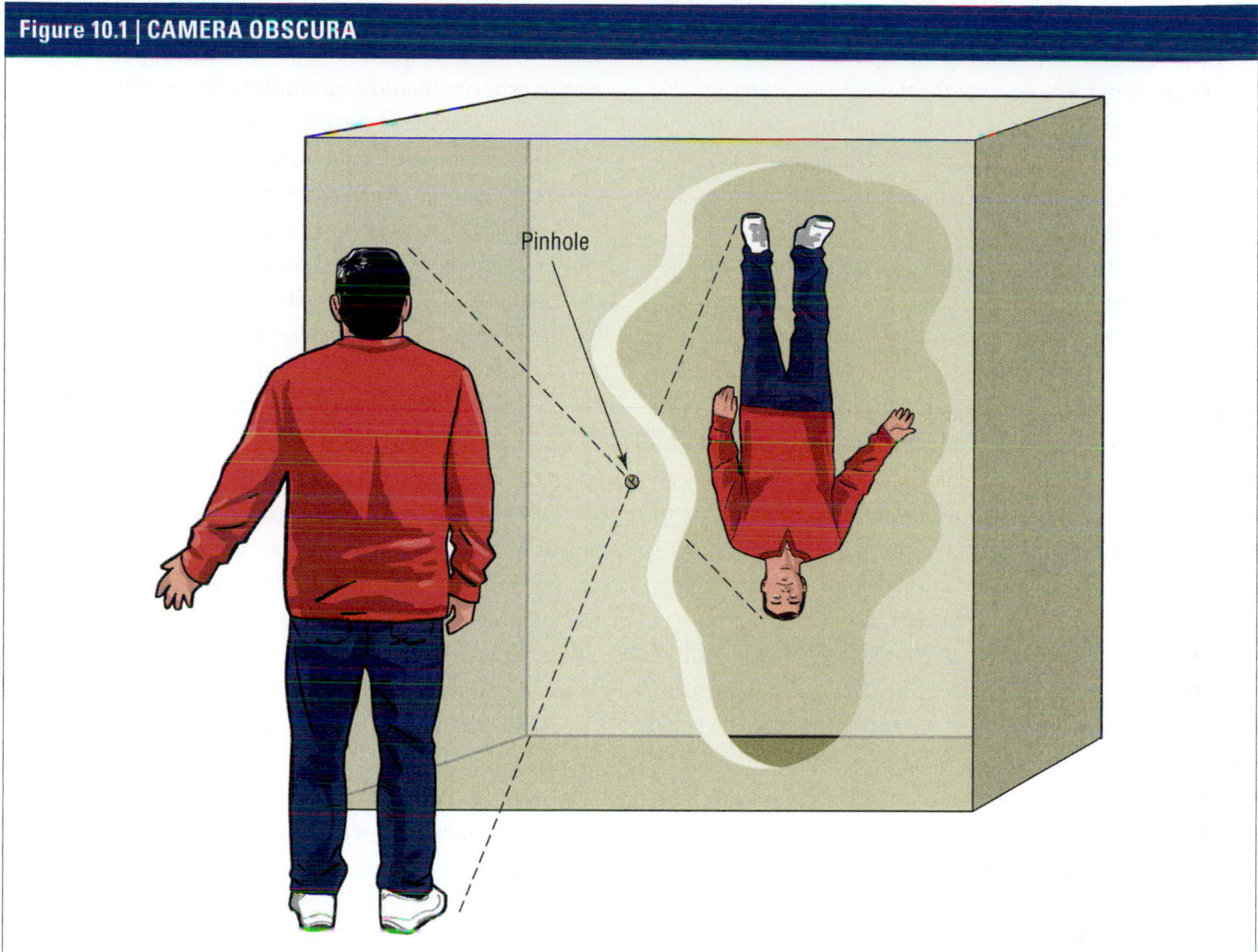

Pinhole

Before the advent of photosensitive film, the camera obscura was used to facilitate lifelike drawing. In this simple schematic, for example, the interior "wall" upon which the upside-down image is projected was usually whitened; an artist could place a piece of drawing paper on the wall and trace the image onto it.

Which approach—aesthetic, technological, economic, or social—will we take in this chapter? Where they are relevant, we will consider them all.

A Short Overview of Film History

Precinema

Before we discuss the major milestones of film history, let's look at some of the key technological innova-

tions that made movies possible.[5] First among these is photography.

Photography In one sense, movies are simply a natural progression in the history of photography. The word **photography** means, literally, "writing with light" and technically, "the static representation or reproduction of light." The concept has its beginnings in ancient Greece. In the fourth century BCE, the Greek philosopher Aristotle theorized about a device that later would be known as the **camera obscura** (Latin for "dark chamber"; Figure 10.1). In the late fifteenth century, Leonardo da

5. This discussion of early film technologies is necessarily brief. For more on key filmmaking technologies, see Chapter 11, "How the Movies Are Made."

Vinci's drawings gave tangible form to the idea. Both simple and ingenious, the camera obscura may be a box or it may be a room large enough for a viewer to stand inside. Light entering through a tiny hole (later a lens) on one side of the box or room projects an image from the outside onto the opposite side or wall. An artist might then trace the image onto a piece of paper.

Photography was developed during the first four decades of the nineteenth century by Thomas Wedgwood, William Henry Fox Talbot, and Sir John Herschel in England; Joseph-Nicéphore Niépce and Louis-Jacques-Mandé Daguerre in France; and George Eastman in the United States. In 1802, Wedgwood made the first recorded attempt to produce photographs. However, these were not camera images as we know them, but basically silhouettes of objects placed on paper or leather sensitized with chemicals and exposed to light. These images faded quickly, for Wedgwood did not know how to fix (stabilize) them. Unaware of Wedgwood's work, Talbot devised a chemical method for recording the images he observed in his camera obscura. More important was the significant progress he made toward fixing the image, and he invented the **negative**, or negative photographic image on transparent material, that makes possible the reproduction of the image.

Niépce experimented with sunlight and the camera obscura to make photographic copies of engravings as well as actual photographs from nature. The results of this heliographic ("Sun-drawn") process—crude paper prints—were not particularly successful. But Niépce's discoveries influenced Daguerre, who by 1837 was able to create, on a copper plate treated with chemicals, an image remarkable for its fidelity and detail. In 1839, Herschel perfected hypo (short for hyposulfite thiosulfate, or sodium thiosulfate), a compound that fixed the image on paper and thus arrested the effect of light on it. Herschel first used the word *photography* in 1839 in a lecture at the Royal Society of London for the Promotion of Natural Knowledge. What followed were primarily technological improvements on Herschel's discovery.

In 1851, glass-plate negatives replaced the paper plates. More durable but heavy, glass was replaced by gelatin-covered paper in 1881. The new gelatin process reduced, from 15 minutes to 0.001 second, the time necessary to make a photographic exposure. This advance made it possible to record action spontaneously and simultaneously as it occurred. In 1887, George Eastman began the mass production of a paper "film" coated with gelatin emulsion; in 1889, he improved the process by substituting clear plastic (film) for the paper base. Although other technological improvements followed, this is the photographic film we know today.

This experimentation with optical principles and still photography in the nineteenth century made it possible to take and reproduce photographic images that could simulate action in the image. But simulation was not enough for the scientists, artists, and members of the general public who wanted to see images of life in motion. The missing step between still photography and cinematography was discovered with the development of series photography.

Series Photography **Series photography** records the phases of an action. In a series of still photographs, we see, for example, a man or a horse in changing positions that suggest movement, though the images themselves are static. Within a few years, three men—Pierre-Jules-César Janssen, Eadweard Muybridge, and Étienne-Jules Marey—contributed to its development.

In 1874, Janssen, a French astronomer, developed the **revolver photographique** (or chronophotographic gun), a cylinder-shaped camera that creates exposures automatically, at short intervals, on different segments of a revolving plate. In 1877, Muybridge, an English photographer working in California, used a group of electrically operated cameras (first twelve, then twenty-four) to produce the first series of photographs of continuous motion. On May 4, 1880, using an early projector known as the **magic lantern** and his **zoopraxiscope** (a version of the magic lantern, with a revolving disk that had his photographs arranged around the center), Muybridge gave the first public demonstration of photographic images in motion—a cumbersome process, but a breakthrough.

In 1882, Marey, a French physiologist, made the first series of photographs of continuous motion using the **fusil photographique** (another form of the chronophotographic gun), a single, portable camera capable of taking twelve continuous images. Muybridge and Marey later collaborated in Paris, but each was more interested in using the process for his own scientific studies than for making or projecting motion pictures as such. Marey's invention solved the problems created by Muybridge's use of a battery of cameras, but the series was limited to forty images—a total of 3 or 4 seconds.

The experiments that Janssen, Muybridge, and Marey conducted with various kinds of moving pictures were

1 **2**

Series photography

Eadweard Muybridge's famous series of photographs documenting a horse in motion were made possible by a number of cameras placed side by side in the structure pictured here [1]. The cameras were tied to individual trip wires. As the horse broke each wire, a camera's shutter would be set off. The result of this experiment—a series of sixteen exposures [2]—proved that a trotting horse momentarily has all four feet off the ground at once (see the third frame). Series photography has been revived as a strategy for creating special effects in contemporary movies.

limited in almost every way, but the technologies needed to make moving pictures on film were in place and awaited only a synthesis.

1891–1903: The First Movies

Who invented the movies?[6] Historic milestones such as this are seldom the result of a few persons working together on a single idea but rather the collaborative product of many dreams, experiments, and inventions. It did not occur in one moment, but rather took place in four major industrialized countries—the United States, France, England, and Germany—in the years just before 1895. Furthermore, in attempting to answer the question, we must distinguish between moving pictures that were projected onto a surface for an audience and those that were not.

In 1891, William Kennedy Laurie Dickson, working with associates in Thomas Edison's research laboratory, invented the **Kinetograph** (the first motion-picture camera) and the **Kinetoscope** (a peephole viewer). The first motion picture made with the Kinetograph, and the earliest complete film on record at the Library of Congress, was Dickson's *Edison Kinetoscopic Record of a Sneeze* (1894), popularly known as *Fred Ott's Sneeze*, which represents, on Edison and Dickson's part, a brilliant choice of a single, self-contained action for a single, self-contained film of very limited length. Edison's staff made their movies, including *Fred Ott's Sneeze*, inside a crude, hot, and cramped shack known as the **Black Maria**. The Black Maria was really the first movie studio, for it contained the camera, technicians, and actors. The camera, fixed on a trolley, was limited in its motion, able only to move closer to or away from the subject. Light was provided by the Sun, which entered through an aperture in the roof, and the entire "studio" could be rotated to catch the light. Edison demonstrated the Kinetoscope to various audiences, public and private. And in April 1894, the first Kinetoscope parlor opened in New York City, thus inaugurating the history of commercial movies.

Although the visual image seen in the Kinetoscope peephole viewer was moving, it could be enjoyed by only

6. An invaluable history of the invention of the movies, and one on which this section draws, is Charles Musser's *The Emergence of Cinema: The American Screen to 1907*, History of the American Cinema, vol. 1 (New York: Scribner, 1990; repr., Berkeley: University of California Press, 1994).

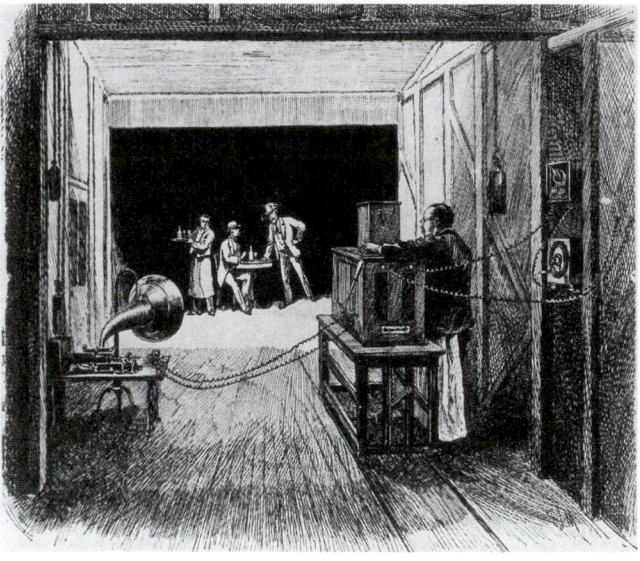

Edison's Kinetograph and the Black Maria

These images show Thomas Edison's Black Maria, the first motion-picture "studio," pictured from the outside [1] and the inside [2]. The interior view shows how awkward and static the Kinetograph was thanks to its bulk and its need to be tethered to a power source. In addition, the performers had very little room to move, and the environment was hot and airless. The makeshift quality of the studio, as well as its relatively modest size, is evident from the external view.

one person at a time. In the same month, the Lathams—Woodville and his two sons, Grey and Otway, former Edison employees—used their movie projector, the Ei-doloscope, to show a movie to the press. Although Edison put down the significance of this demonstration, it was

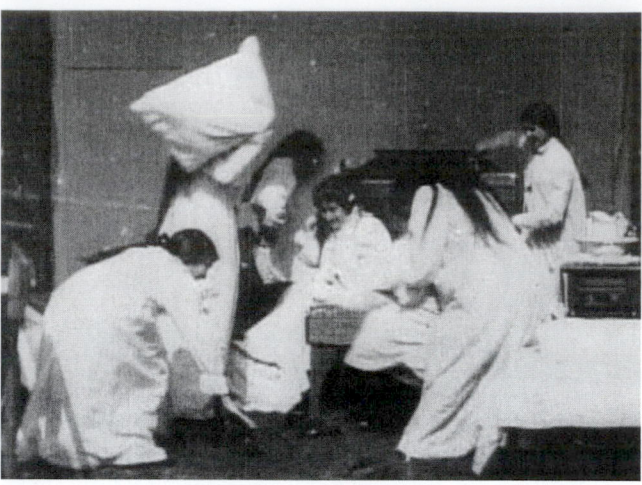

Short records of real life

Before narrative or editing, Thomas Edison's first movies (about 30 seconds in length) were simple records of ordinary people and events: a man and woman kissing, a young woman dancing, a man getting a shave and haircut in a barber shop, and a woman and child feeding doves in a barnyard. In *Seminary Girls* (1897), we see young girls having a rare moment of fun in a harmless pillow fight until the school's matron interrupts them. The scene, obviously staged for the stationary camera, was photographed in Edison's first studio, the Black Maria.

the first time an invited audience had seen projected motion pictures in the United States. Meanwhile, in November in Germany, another pair of brothers, Max and Emil Skladanowsky, projected short films in Berlin. Co-incidentally, in France, two brothers (teams of brothers figure significantly in this story) named Auguste and Louis Lumière invented the Cinématographe, a far more sophisticated device than either the Kinetoscope or the Eidoloscope. In December 1895, they used it to project a movie on a screen set up in a small room inside a public café that was converted into a theater. (They had already projected it throughout Europe for small, invited audiences.) Although that movie, *Employees Leaving the Lumière Factory* (1895), which the Lumières called an *actualité* (a documentary view of the moment), was only 1 minute in length, it captivated the audience with its depiction of a spontaneous event. The Cinématographe—a hand-cranked device that served as camera, projector, and film printer—was equally amazing. In 1896, Edison unveiled his own projector, the Vitascope, in a New York City theater.

The projection of moving pictures to a paying audience ended the prehistory of cinema and freed it to

Real life as seen through the artists' lens

At first glance, Auguste and Louis Lumière's *Children Digging for Clams* (1896) may seem similar to Edison's *Seminary Girls* as a simple record of an ordinary activity. But the differences between them show that the Lumières were artists with a natural sense of style. Not only was it longer (44 seconds) and shot outdoors (with a stationary camera), but it also employs a deep composition. Across the foreground, in a diagonal line, we see the clam-digging children; in the middle ground, we see adults, probably their parents, keeping an eye on them; and in the background, we see other people, the shoreline, and the horizon. As far as composition goes, nothing could be simpler; but by shooting it outdoors in a natural landscape, the Lumières provide an aesthetically pleasing interpretation of an actual event rather than just a documentary record.

Méliès the magician

Georges Méliès, who was by trade a magician, took naturally to motion pictures, which are primarily an illusion. He quickly understood that he could make the camera stop and start (what we now call stop-motion photography) and, with this technique, make things vanish and reappear (sometimes in a new form). Like all magicians, he reveled in fooling the public. In *Long Distance Wireless Photography* (1908), Méliès plays the inventor of a process for transmitting photographs from one place to another and dupes his clients. When a man and woman ask for a demonstration, he photographs them and, behind them, projects unflattering images of them. Annoyed at this deception, they try to destroy the studio, but are chased away in a scene of slapstick comedy. Here, Méliès shows a prophetic but comic insight into two events that were decades away: the electronic transmission of photographs and television. The action is staged for the camera as if it were happening on a theater stage, and the movie, which is nearly 6 minutes in length, tells a complete story.

become the art form of the twentieth century. Aesthetically, the work of the first filmmakers cannot compare in any way with today's movies, yet they managed, in a few years' time, to establish the basic types of movies: short narratives, documentary depictions of real life, and experimental movies with special effects that foreshadow today's animation. In addition, they recognized that the movies—like the contemporary steam engine, electricity, and the railroad—would attract paying customers and make them a great deal of money. What they probably did not envision was the power of the movies to shape attitudes and values.

After a few years of experimenting with very short movies, a minute or two in length and hardly more than a novelty, Edison, the Lumière brothers, and other new filmmakers realized that the cinema needed new forms and conventions. It was clear that the movies needed to

be less a curiosity that the public would soon tire of and more a durable and successful commercial entertainment. They had to compete with and draw from other popular art forms, such as literature and theater.

Paramount among the early innovators of film form was a Frenchman, Georges Méliès. In the late 1890s he began to make short narrative movies based on the theatrical model of short, sequential scenes shot from a fixed point of view. The only editing within these self-contained scenes was for cuts or in-camera dissolves. Rudimentary as these movies were, according to film historian David A. Cook, Méliès was "the cinema's first narrative artist,"[7] famous for innovating many technical and narrative devices. He is best known for his use

7. David A. Cook, *A History of Narrative Film*, 5th ed. (New York: Norton, 2016), p. 14.

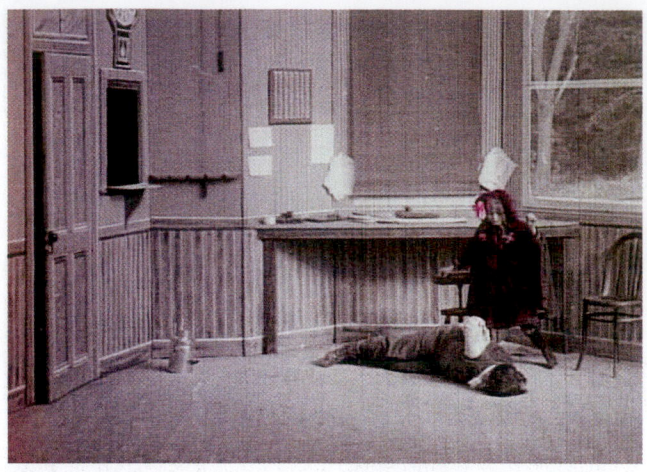

The beginnings of cinematic narrative

Realizing that they needed to tell stories, the early filmmakers began to develop conventions of cinematic narrative. Among these artists were Georges Méliès in France, G. A. Smith in England, and Edwin S. Porter in the United States. In *Life of an American Fireman* (1903) and *The Great Train Robbery* (1903), Porter broke away from the prevailing step-by-step, one-shot–one-scene editing of Méliès and invented an early form of continuity editing in which he built a scene made up of shots that seemed chronologically continuous from one shot to the next. We make sense of this, as well as create meaning, by mentally connecting the shots into a logical narrative. Porter also cuts back and forth in time, showing simultaneous events taking place in different locations. For example, in *The Great Train Robbery*, the robbers begin their heist by shooting and tying up a telegraph operator at a train station; then they board the next train, rob the passengers, uncouple the engine, and head off. As they reach what they think is safety, Porter cuts back to the telegraph office, where (as shown here) a little girl, presumably the operator's daughter, discovers her father and revives him. Porter then cuts directly to a barn dance, where the operator and the little girl report what has happened. Porter then jumps ahead to the outlaws and the final shoot-out, continuing to use ellipsis when necessary to keep the action moving to the conclusion.

of special effects—still captivating today—in such landmark films as *A Trip to the Moon* (1902) and *The Impossible Voyage* (1904).

Another early pioneer, Edwin S. Porter, was a director working with Edison and by 1903 had established a relatively sophisticated approach to narrative filmmaking in such pioneering films as *The Great Train Robbery* (1903; 12 min.), which used multiple camera positions, interior and exterior settings, and crosscutting (inter-

cutting) that made it possible to depict parallel actions occurring simultaneously. He also established the concept that the shot was the basic structural unit of a movie and pioneered the idea of continuity editing. *The Great Train Robbery* was the first major milestone in the development of the American narrative film as well as the first "Western."

1908–1927: Origins of the Classical Hollywood Style—The Silent Period

The "silent era" of film history is distinguished by Edwin S. Porter's and D. W. Griffith's developments in narrative form, the crystallization of the classical Hollywood style, the ascendance of Hollywood as the center of the world's motion-picture industry, the development of movie genres, and early experiments with color and animation.

The "classical Hollywood cinema"[8] refers here to the traditional studio-based style of making motion pictures in both the silent and sound periods. Although the rudiments of the classical style can be seen in the work of Edwin S. Porter, it began its ascendancy with the release of D. W. Griffith's *The Birth of a Nation* (1915) and continues, with various modifications, to identify the cinematic conventions used by most filmmakers today.

The classical Hollywood style is built on the principle of "invisibility" that we discussed in Chapter 1. This principle generally includes two parts. The first is that the movie's form (narrative, cinematography, editing, sound, acting, and so forth) should not call attention to itself. That is, the narrative should be as economical and seamless as possible, and the presentation of the narrative should occur in a cinematic language with which the audience is familiar. The second part is the studio system itself, a mode of production that standardized the way movies were produced. Management was vertically organized, meaning that a strong executive office controlled production, distribution, and exhibition; hired all employees, including directors and actors; and assigned work to them according to the terms of their contracts, thus ensuring a certain uniform style for each studio. While we know that such principles were sometimes ignored in practice, they nonetheless serve a pur-

8. A concept popularized by film scholars David Bordwell, Janet Staiger, and Kristin Thompson, in *The Classical Hollywood Cinema: Film Style and Mode of Production to 1960* (New York: Columbia University Press, 1985).

pose in helping us chart the course of stylistic history. Thus, for example, we can understand and appreciate just how radical Orson Welles's approach was in *Citizen Kane* (1941) when he deliberately called attention to technique and, in so doing, challenged the perceived limitations of the classical Hollywood style and the studio system itself.

By 1907, a small film effort had started in and around Hollywood, its founders lured by the favorable climate and variety of natural scenery. While they were nearly all uneducated immigrants, their business practices were consistent with the ruthless tactics of other Gilded Age entrepreneurs. D. W. Griffith made his first movie there in 1910; in 1911, the first studio was built; and by 1912, some fifteen film studios were operating. By 1914, the American film industry was clearly identified with Hollywood. As a forward-looking sign of this growth, the industry invested heavily in movie theaters, some of which were dubbed "palaces" for their imposing architecture, lavish interiors, and seating for hundreds and sometimes thousands of people. It also established other "firsts," including trade journals, movie fan magazines, movie reviews in general-circulation newspapers, the star system, and a film censorship law.

During this period, filmmakers began to replace short films (generally one reel in length) with feature-length movies (four or more reels). The term *feature* came to mean major works that stood out on a program that might include shorter films as well. In these early days, the length of one reel was 10–16 minutes, depending on the speed of projection. The longer format permitted filmmakers to tackle more complicated narratives and also emphasized the quality of the production, including mise-en-scène, cinematography, acting, and editing. The growing middle-class audience liked longer narratives and more polished productions and was willing to pay more to see such movies. Accordingly, producers could book them for extended runs and, of course, make more money. The transformation of the nickelodeon into the movie palace, which exceeded in splendor any legitimate theater and thus had an attraction all its own, further established the cinema as a serious artistic endeavor. Thus, with changes in a film's length, content, quality, and exhibition came the first major restructuring of the movie industry. The second was to come with the advent of sound, and the third with the development of the independent system of production. The movies took on the modern production system and

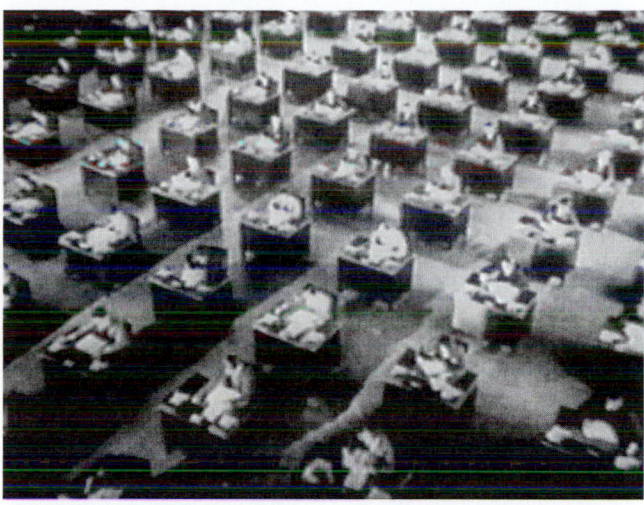

A great silent movie challenges the American dream
King Vidor was one of several important directors working in the early 1920s who learned his art from D. W. Griffith. In *The Crowd* (1928), Vidor dared—in the Roaring Twenties, a period of relative prosperity before the stock-market crash of 1929—to make a social critique of the American dream of opportunity and getting ahead. It tells the tragic story of a man who refuses to conform in the New York business world, suggested by the office environment pictured here, which reduces him and other employees to nonentities. The story seems to end with the promise of future happiness for the man and his wife, but it's really ambiguous, leaving us to use our own values and experiences to come to grips with the characters' fate. In the silent-movie period, exhibitors were sometimes offered the choice of alternate endings, particularly for movies with a controversial conclusion. Vidor shot seven different endings for *The Crowd* and offered two of them to the theater owners. (Here we refer to what the director called the "realistic" ending.)

the cinematic conventions that, however much they have changed, we know today.

The first multiple-reel movies included J. Stuart Blackton's *The Life of Moses* (1909, five reels), D. W. Griffith's *Enoch Arden* (1911; 34 min.), *The Loves of Queen Elizabeth* (1912; directors Henri Desfontaines and Louis Mercanton, 44 min.), a film from France, and such Italian epics as *Dante's Inferno* (1911, 5 reels; director unknown), Enrico Guazzoni's *Quo Vadis?* (1913; 120 min.), and Giovanni Pastrone's *Cabiria* (1914; 181 min.). In 1914, clearly the turning point, Edwin S. Porter released *Tess of the Storm Country* (1914; 80 min.) and directed an astonishing twenty features before retiring from film directing the next year. Cecil B. DeMille, another industry founder, began his feature film career with *The Squaw Man* (1914; 74 min.) and made fourteen features

The first female director

Among early filmmakers, Alice Guy Blaché stands out as the first female director in film history. Born in France, where she worked with the Gaumont Film Company, she came to the United States shortly after 1907, founded her own studio, and made dozens of narrative films, most of which are lost. *Making an American Citizen* (1912; 16 min.) is unremarkable in its theatrical staging and acting but is well photographed and edited. What's most important is its outspoken feminist message. It tells the story of Ivan and his wife, new Russian emigrants. Ivan believes in the Old World custom of wife abuse. In this shot, a well-dressed New Yorker threatens Ivan when he catches him beating his wife (note the Statue of Liberty in the background). This and other encounters with liberated American males (including a judge who sentences him to prison) convince him to love and respect his wife. With the happy ending, he is, as the title card proclaims, "Completely Americanized." Guy Blaché was not only ahead of her time as a film director but also highly optimistic in her views about American male-female relationships.

in 1915 alone. Griffith's *Judith of Bethulia* (61 min.) was released in 1914 and *The Birth of a Nation* (187 min.) in 1915.

Every 10 years since 1952, the influential British publication *Sight & Sound* asks a large panel of international film critics to choose the ten greatest movies. In polls between 1952 and 2002, the list always included at least one silent film (there were five in 1952). The latest poll (2012) listed three silent films: no. 5, *Sunrise* (1927; director F. W. Murnau); no. 8, *Man with the Movie Camera* (1929; director Dziga Vertov); no. 9, *The Passion of Joan of Arc* (1928; director Carl Theodor Dreyer). All were

released at the high point of the silent era, between 1926 and 1930, when sound was slowly transforming the movie industry. Many other outstanding silent films from that period also deserve mention: *The Crowd* (1926; director King Vidor), *Berlin: Symphony of a Metropolis* (1927; also called *Symphony of a Great City*; director Walter Ruttmann); *An Italian Straw Hat* (1927; director René Clair), *The Circus* (1928; director Charles Chaplin); *The Wind* (1928; director Victor Seastrom); *Un chien Andalou* (1928; directors Luis Buñuel and Salvador Dalí); *Pandora's Box* (1929; director G. W. Pabst); *A Cottage on Dartmoor* (1929; director Anthony Asquith); and *Earth* (1930; director Alexandr Dovzhenko).[9]

The social impact of the silent movies during this period established trends that continue today. They appealed to all socioeconomic levels and stimulated the popular imagination through their establishment and codification of narrative genres and character stereotypes, particularly those that reinforced prejudices against Native Americans, African Americans, and foreigners in general. Their depiction of certain types of behavior considered immoral provoked calls for censorship, which would become an even bigger problem in the next decade and on into today and raised issues of movie content and violence. Although most jobs in the film industry remained male-dominated for the next 50 years, at least acting jobs for women were plentiful from the beginning. Two female directors were at work—Lois Weber and Alice Guy Blaché—and the African American actor Bert Williams starred in his first movie in 1915.

The movie director was central to developing the art of the motion picture in these early years. D. W. Griffith would soon emerge as the most important of these figures, and *The Birth of a Nation* would become known as one of the most important and controversial movies ever made. While its racist content is repugnant, its form is technically brilliant. Griffith, who borrowed freely from other early filmmakers, was an intuitive and innovative artist. In this legendary movie we see him perfecting and regularizing (if not inventing) a style that included a dazzling set of technical achievements: the 180-degree system; cutting between familiar types of shots (close-up, medium shot, long shot, extreme long shot, and soft-focus shot); multiple camera setups, accelerated montage, and panning and tilting; and the exploitation of camera angles, in-camera dissolves and fades, the flash-back, the iris shot, the mask, and the split screen. He also highly valued using a full symphonic score and, more important, developing screen acting by training actors for the special demands of the silent cinema. At that time the longest (3 hours) and most expensive ($2.7 million) American movie yet made, *The Birth of a Nation* attracted enormous audiences, garnered the critics' praise, and earned, within 5 years of its opening, approximately $178 million (both are 2014 figures adjusted for inflation). However, the social and political stance of this film's story had another impact.

Born in Kentucky, Griffith was in sympathy with the antebellum South. He tells his story by distorting history and reaffirming the racist stereotypes of his time and background. The movie provoked controversy and riots and was banned in many Northern states. Yet this profoundly American epic, a work of vicious propaganda, is also a cinematic masterpiece that garnered international prestige for American silent movies. Unfortunately for the future history of the movies, it demonstrated how a manipulative movie could appeal to the public's worst prejudices and make a fortune as a result. Griffith made other films, including such silent masterpieces as *Intolerance* (1916), *Broken Blossoms* (1919), *Way Down East* (1920), *Orphans of the Storm* (1921), and *Dream Street* (1921), a very early but unsuccessful attempt to add recorded voices to a movie. Nonetheless, his career was virtually finished by 1931.

The most successful American silent feature movies were epics (Erich von Stroheim's *Greed*, 1924), melodramas (King Vidor's *The Big Parade*, 1925), and comedies. Comedy in particular was a major factor in Hollywood's early success. These films starred gifted comic actors (Buster Keaton, Charles Chaplin, Roscoe "Fatty" Arbuckle, Harold Lloyd, Stan Laurel, and Oliver Hardy) and had innovative directors (Mack Sennett and Hal Roach). They included such enduring silent movies (shorts, series, and features) as Chaplin's *The Gold Rush* (1925) and Keaton's *The General* (1926).

According to a 2013 study by the Library of Congress, almost 70 percent of the silent feature films made in the United States are lost due to various reasons, including neglect, poor cataloging, or the natural deterioration of film negatives. Efforts are continually being made to find

The Birth of a Nation

The turning point in D. W. Griffith's great epic (1915) comes in the middle of the movie, as the title card says: "And then, when the terrible days were over and a healing time of peace was at hand . . . came the fated night of April 14, 1865." The scene is Ford's Theatre in Washington, D.C., where a gala performance is being held to celebrate General Robert E. Lee's surrender. In this shot, President and Mrs. Abraham Lincoln enter and greet the enthusiastic audience. Moments later, he is assassinated, ending Part I, "War," and opening Part II, "Reconstruction," a saga of Southern white racism that is the most controversial part of the movie.

copies of these films in foreign countries, but it is a sad ending to one of America's great artistic achievements.[10]

Other notable films produced in this period include Robert J. Flaherty's *Nanook of the North* (1922), regarded as the first significant documentary film. The art of animation progressed in the hands of such artists as Otto Messmer (the Felix the Cat series), Walt Disney, who made his first cartoons in 1922, and Max and Dave Fleischer, who experimented with color and sound in the early 1920s and whose most endearing character was Betty Boop. Benefiting from Griffith's enormous influence, other filmmakers made improvements in design, lighting, cameras and lenses, the use of color, special effects, and editing equipment. Nothing, of course, would be more important than the experiments with sound that led to the complete transformation of the movie industry after 1927. In the meantime, however, international developments were influencing film history.

10. See http://carpetbagger.blogs.nytimes.com/2013/12/04/majority-of-silent-films-are-lost-study-finds/ (accessed December 18, 2013).

1919–1931: German Expressionism

During part of the period just discussed, Eastern and Western Europe were engulfed in chaos. World War I (1914–18), in which many millions of people died, pitted the United Kingdom, Russia, Italy, and the United States against Germany, Austria-Hungary, the Ottoman Empire, and Bulgaria. (The United States, isolationist and opposed to the war, did not enter the conflict until 1917.) In March 1917, the Russian Revolution overthrew Czar Nicholas II. These events changed the world order.

By the end of the war, Germany had suffered a humiliating defeat. But a new democratic government emerged, known unofficially as the Weimar Republic. Seeking to revitalize the film industry and create a new image for the country, the government subsidized the film conglomerate known as UFA (Universum-Film AG). Its magnificent studios, the largest and best equipped in Europe, enabled the German film industry to compete with those of other countries as well as attract filmmakers from around the world. This organization led to Germany's golden age of cinema, which lasted from 1919 to Adolf Hitler's rise to power in 1933. Its most important artistic component was the German Expressionist film, which flourished from 1919 to 1931.

German film artists entered the postwar period determined to reject the cinematic past and enthusiastically embrace the avant-garde. Expressionism had flourished in Germany since the early twentieth century in painting, sculpture, architecture, music, literature, and theater. After the war, it reflected the general atmosphere in postwar Germany of cynicism, alienation, and disillusionment. German Expressionist film presents the physical world on the screen as a projection, or expression, of the subjective world, usually that of the film's protagonist. Its chief characteristics are distorted and exaggerated settings; compositions of unnatural spaces; the use of oblique angles and nonparallel lines; a moving and subjective camera; unnatural costumes, hairstyles, and makeup; and highly stylized acting. The classic examples are Robert Wiene's *The Cabinet of Dr. Caligari* (1920), Paul Wegener and Carl Boese's version of *The Golem* (1920), F. W. Murnau's *Nosferatu, a Symphony of Horror* (1922)—the first vampire film—and *The Last Laugh* (1924), Fritz Lang's *Metropolis* (1927) and *M* (1931), G. W. Pabst's *Pandora's Box* (1929), and Josef von Sternberg's *The Blue Angel* (1930).

The most famous expressionist film, and the one traditionally cited as the epitome of the style, is Wiene's *The Cabinet of Dr. Caligari*. What we remember most about

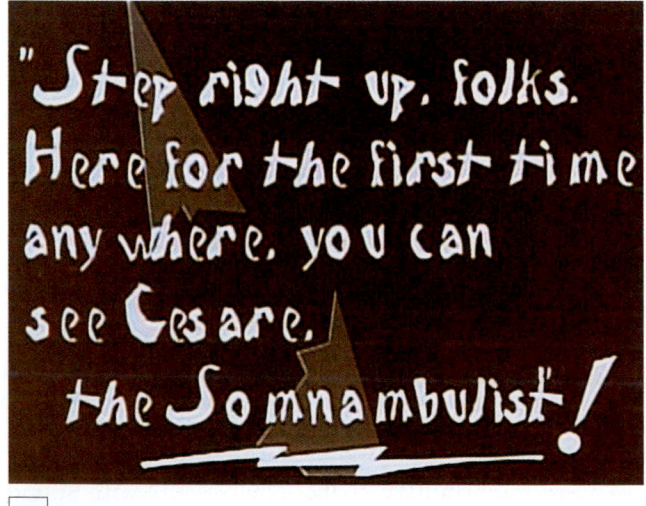

1

2

Inside *The Cabinet of Dr. Caligari*

In Robert Wiene's eerie, foreboding movie (1920), Dr. Caligari (Werner Krauss) operates a carnival attraction featuring a somnambulist (sleepwalker) named Cesare (Conrad Veidt); the "cabinet" in the title refers to the type of early freak show called a "cabinet of curiosities" as well as to the coffin-like box in which Cesare "sleeps" until Caligari awakens him and orders him to commit murders. The title card [1], written in exaggerated letters, speaks in a folksy tone while echoing the graphics of the movie's painted settings. The power of these settings is evident when we see [2] Dr. Caligari (*left*) attempting to rouse Cesare (*right*), who is presumably "asleep" while standing upright in Caligari's cabinet.

1

2

The Cabinet of Dr. Caligari's influence

Robert Wiene's *The Cabinet of Dr. Caligari* (1920) is traditionally cited as the best example of German Expressionist film. But expressionist elements also figure strongly in F. W. Murnau's *Nosferatu, a Symphony of Horror* (1922), the first of many film adaptations of the Dracula story, and *The Last Laugh* (1924), a charming fable about social justice. Their narratives could not be more different, yet these films are linked by their reliance on expressionist design. In contrast to *Dr. Caligari*, where the expressionism relies mostly on graphic effects, those in *Nosferatu* rely primarily on cinematic effects: low camera angles, makeup and costume design, lighting, and editing create an eerie mise-en-scène [1]. And even though the vampire figure is truly scary (Nosferatu is played by the memorable Max Schreck, who, pictured here with Gustav von Wangenheim as the real-estate agent, looks like a rat), the movie also manages to make him a sympathetic human being. [2] Far more sympathetic—and far more realistic—is the principal character of *The Last Laugh*, an unnamed hotel porter played equally memorably by Emil Jannings. Here, expressionism can be seen in the mise-en-scène and actor's movements as well as in the composition, play of light and shadow, and exaggerated costume, all of which are subtler than what we see in either *Dr. Caligari* or *Nosferatu*. *The Last Laugh* is also important for its impressive use of the moving camera and the camera's subjective point of view.

this disturbing, complicated story of fantasy and horror told by a madman is its design. The floors, walls, and ceilings of the interior sets are sharply angled; windows admit no natural light, though shafts of illusionistic light and shadow are painted on the walls and floors of the sets; dim staircases seem to lead nowhere; the calligraphy of the titles is bizarre, as is the color tinting—blue, sepia, rose, and green (in the 1996 restored DVD edition). All this differentiates night from day and underscores the different moods. The exterior sets are equally artificial; buildings, piled on top of one another, jut upward at strange angles.

German Expressionist film was a short-lived but unforgettable phenomenon that disappeared within 12 years after it began. There are aesthetic, political, economic, and social reasons for this. Even though these films gave birth to the horror-film genre, German audiences did not crave a steady diet of them. As far as politics goes, because expressionism emphasized the inner rather than the outer world, Hitler (now rising to power) saw it as a revolt against the traditional values that he sought to preserve. With their lavish studio settings, expressionist films were expensive to make. Furthermore, foreign films were taking an increasing share of the German market, prompting the German film industry to copy them in order to hold its market share. When the government tightened control of UFA, it became clear that Hitler would curtail freedom of expression when he came to power in 1933. Thus many great German filmmakers were lured to the United States, stimulating the aesthetics of Hollywood production for decades to come. Soon, certain tendencies of the expressionist look became evident in Hollywood's psychological dramas, horror movies, and, most notably, the film noir. To quote film historians Gerald Mast and Bruce F. Kawin, "It is difficult to imagine the history of American cinema without this infusion of both visual imagery and thematic commentary from Weimar Germany."[11]

11. Gerald Mast and Bruce F. Kawin, *A Short History of the Movies*, 11th ed. (New York: Pearson/Longman, 2010), p. 193.

1918–1930: French Avant-Garde Filmmaking

In the 1920s, Paris was the world's center of avant-garde experimentation in painting, literature, drama, music, and film. It was a time when the philosophical approaches of surrealism, cubism, dadaism, and expressionism led to an explosion of artistic styles and movements. The French Avant-Garde film movement included both intellectuals and artists who took their inspiration not only from Karl Marx and Sigmund Freud but also from the experimental French filmmakers who preceded them in the earliest years of the movies: Georges Méliès, Ferdinand Zecca, Max Linder, Émile Cohl, Jean Durand, and Louis Feuillade, pioneering artists who influenced the course of avant-garde and experimental filmmaking around the world.

The French movies that we will discuss tend to fit into one of three different types: (1) short dadaist and surrealist films of an anticonventional, absurdist nature; (2) short naturalistic psychological studies; or (3) feature-length films that also emphasize pure visual form.

Dada and surrealism were two European movements in the arts that sought, provocatively and irreverently, to shock the viewer with surprises and unexpected juxtapositions. Specifically, they attempted to re-create the free play of the mind in its perceptions, dreams, or hallucinations. Dadaist and surrealist cinema attacks normal narrative conventions by eliminating causality, emphasizing chance and unexpected occurrences, and creating strange and shocking relationships among images. The result is a visual world that appears to be neurotic, unnatural, and illogical, resisting analysis and conclusion by the viewer. And because it emphasizes free association over conventional cinematic language, it attracted painters who were visual artists first and filmmakers second. (Although dada preceded surrealism, they coexisted in the 1920s to such an extent that the two words are often used interchangeably to describe works that demonstrate these characteristics.)

In France, the major filmmakers working in these movements included the American-born Man Ray (*Emak-Bakia*, 1926); Jean Epstein, whose *The Fall of the House of Usher* (1928), inspired by one of Edgar Allan Poe's most famous tales, uses dreamy, impressionistic visual effects (slow motion, out-of-focus shots, multiple exposures, and distortions); René Clair (*Entr'acte*, 1924); Fernand Léger (*Ballet mécanique*, 1924); and Germaine

Surrealism on film

Inspired by Edgar Allan Poe's famous story, Jean Epstein's *The Fall of the House of Usher* (1928) remains captivating with its complex psychological themes, haunting exteriors and interiors, and overall dreamlike quality. In this image, Madeleine Usher (Marguerite Gance) returns from the tomb in which she was buried alive by her brother, Sir Roderick Usher (Jean Debucourt), who dies from fright when she falls upon him.

Dulac, one of the cinema's first female artists, whose *The Seashell and the Clergyman* (1928) is one of the two acknowledged masterpieces of surrealist cinema.

The other masterpiece is *An Andalusian Dog* (1929), created by two Spanish artists working in Paris: painter Salvador Dalí and filmmaker Luis Buñuel. Here, the logic is that of a dream. Its visual effects include an opening sequence in which we see a razor slitting a woman's eyeball (for an image of this famous shot, see Chapter 3, p. 79). While Dalí soon returned to painting his surrealist masterpieces (including his version of Leonardo's *Mona Lisa* with his own face replacing hers), Buñuel became one of the very few major directors to continue making surrealist feature movies, including *Viridiana* (1961), *Belle de Jour* (1967), and *The Discreet Charm of the Bourgeoisie* (1972).

The second type of French Avant-Garde filmmaking in the 1920s consists of psychological studies that emphasize naturalism, the idea that an individual's fate is determined by heredity and environment, not free will. This form becomes very powerful in a film such as *Rien que les heures* (1926), by the Brazilian-born Alberto Cavalcanti. A multilayered study of Paris over the course of a day, the film employs cinematic effects, including

Turning of *The Wheel*

The movies have always been fascinated by trains, but Abel Gance's *The Wheel* (1923) is obsessed with them. Its extraordinary mise-en-scène is a world surrounded by locomotives, tracks, smoke, and railroad workers. This highly melodramatic story contains elements that remind us of classical tragedy, and its sweeping vision of life is matched by a vividly avant-garde style, creating an unforgettable milestone in French cinema.

bold wipes, freeze-frames, double exposures, and split screens. It also reflects the influence of Soviet Montage in its juxtapositions and linkages of shots, some through contrast, others through irony, and still others unrelated. The overall impression of this film, which fits into a small, impressive category of films known as "city symphonies," is that of a mosaic: the images relate only when they are considered in connection to the whole picture. Also impressive are Dimitri Kirsanoff's *Ménilmontant* (1926) and Marcel L'Herbier's *L'Argent* (1928).

All of the films discussed so far in this section in one way or another emphasize visual form for its own sake, have a comparatively short duration, and for the most part were made independently of the French film industry. There was, however, another type of French Avant-Garde filmmaking of the 1920s—narrative, often feature-length movies far more ambitious in their scope, length, and overall visual effect. These include Abel Gance's *The Wheel* (1923), which embodies naturalistic philosophy and reflects Griffith's editing style, and *Napoléon* (1927), an almost 6-hour epic of astonishing cinematic beauty and power; Jean Cocteau's *The Blood of a Poet* (1930); Jean Vigo's *À propos de Nice* (1930); René Clair's *An Italian Straw Hat* (1928); and the strangely

powerful films of Danish-born Carl Theodor Dreyer, particularly his formalist masterpiece *The Passion of Joan of Arc* (1928). All these films, especially the short ones often screened in film history courses, offer an excellent introduction to the diverse art of the French silent movie in the 1920s.

1924–1930: The Soviet Montage Movement

The Soviet Montage movement represents, with the German Expressionist film movement, one of the twin high points of cinematic experimentation, innovation, and achievement in the years between the end of World War I in 1918 and the coming of sound in 1927. After the Bolshevik (Communist) Revolution of October 1917, led by Vladimir Ilyich Lenin, the challenge was to reunify a shattered nation. Lenin famously proclaimed that cinema would be the most important of the arts in this effort and valued the movies' power to both attract and indoctrinate audiences. He nationalized the film industry and established a national film school to train filmmakers to make propaganda films in a documentary style. Between 1917 and 1929, the Soviet government supported the kind of artistic experimentation and expression that is most effectively seen in the work of four directors: Dziga Vertov, Lev Kuleshov, Sergei Eisenstein, and Vsevolod I. Pudovkin. What they all share in varying degrees is a belief in the power of montage (they adopted the French word for "editing") to fragment and reassemble footage so as to manipulate the viewer's perception and understanding.

Vertov was the first great theorist and practitioner of the cinema of propaganda in documentary form. In 1922, the year of Robert J. Flaherty's *Nanook of the North*, Vertov launched *kino-pravda* (literally, "film truth"). He was influenced by the spirit of Flaherty and the Lumières, which focused on everyday experiences, as well as by the avant-garde pursuit of innovation. Vertov is best known today for *The Man with the Movie Camera* (1929).

Kuleshov, a legendary teacher who was influenced by the continuity editing in Griffith's *Intolerance* (1916), built significantly on Griffith's ideas. As a result, he became less interested in how editing helps to advance the narrative than in how it can create nonliteral meaning. He was thus more interested in discontinuity rather than continuity. Among his many feature-length films is

A day in the life of the Russians

Dziga Vertov's *The Man with the Movie Camera* (1929) is about how the Russians live and how movies are made. On first viewing, it does not seem to distinguish between the two. In this image, we see the real subject: the man with the movie camera. As a record of human life, it is the prototypical movie. Vertov shows us how to frame reality and movement: through the human eye and the camera eye, or through windows and shutters. But to confound us, he also shows us—through such devices as the freeze-frame, split screen, stop-action, slow motion, and fast motion—how the cinematographer and editor can transform the movements of life into something that is unpredictable. He proves that the camera has a life of its own while also reminding us of the editor, who is putting all of this footage together. Reality may be in the control of the artist, his camera, and its tricks, but it is also defined by the editor's presentation and ultimately the viewer's perception.

The Extraordinary Adventures of Mr. West in the Land of the Bolsheviks (1924).

Pudovkin took a third approach to montage, one based on the idea that a film was not shot, but rather built up from its footage. This style is reflected in his film *Mother* (1926), which uses extensive crosscutting of images, such as a sequence of shots showing a prison riot intercut with shots of ice breaking up on a river (a reference to Griffith's *Way Down East* [1920]). Because Pudovkin's approach emphasized the continuity of the film, where the shots are connected like the links in a chain, it is called *linkage*.

In the first two decades after the birth of the movies, two pioneering geniuses tower above all other filmmakers: D. W. Griffith and Sergei Eisenstein. While they share several notable characteristics—chiefly, inventing new modes of cinematic expression and producing epic historical movies—they are very different artists. Griffith was an American, a capitalist in his entrepreneurial production activities, and a Southern sentimentalist at heart. Unlike Eisenstein, he was self-taught (there were no film schools in the United States until the 1930s); he was not an intellectual, and he was influenced primarily by English literature and theater, in which he worked as an actor and director before turning to film. He did not write theory, but rather produced movies that exemplified his concepts.

By contrast, Eisenstein, a Russian Orthodox Christian, was also a Marxist intellectual whose propaganda movies were financed by the Soviet government. He studied to be an engineer but after the 1917 revolution joined an avant-garde theater group, where he was shaped

Eisenstein's battle spectacle *Alexander Nevsky*

Sergei Eisenstein's *Alexander Nevsky* (1938) stands out among Eisenstein's other movies, concerned chiefly with the class wars, for its emphasis on nationalism and patriotism. Focusing on Alexander Nevsky, a Russian prince who defended Russia's northwest territories against invading Teutonic hordes in the thirteenth century, the movie's parallels to contemporary events (i.e., the threat of invasion of Russia by Nazi Germany) were unmistakable. But the movie is far more than a political parable. The movie's set piece—the "Battle on the Ice" sequence, choreographed to Sergei Prokofiev's stirring score—has influenced many other movie battle scenes (e.g., battles in the Star Wars saga), particularly in its massing of forces, brutal warfare, and defining costumes. Noteworthy is Eisenstein's reversal of traditional iconography: throughout, as in this image, the bad guys (the Teutons) are in white while the Russian forces are in black.

by many powerful influences, including the theory and practice of world-famous directors Konstantin Stanislavsky and Vsevolod Meyerhold, by Marx and Freud, and by contemporary German, Russian, and American movies, including those of Griffith. From these varied sources, he developed his own theories of how an aesthetic experience can influence a viewer's psychological and emotional reactions. Unlike Griffith, Eisenstein was a modernist with a commitment to making cinema an art independent from the other forms of creative expression. His films, few in number, are stirring achievements: *Strike* (1925), *The Battleship Potemkin* (1925), *October* (*Ten Days That Shook the World*) (1928), *Alexander Nevsky* (1938; codirected by Dmitri Vasilyev), *Ivan the Terrible, Parts I and II* (1944, 1958), and *Que Viva México* (1930–32, uncompleted and unreleased).

Eisenstein regarded film editing as a creative process that functioned according to the dialectic of Karl Marx as well as the editing concepts of Griffith and Kuleshov. In theory, Eisenstein viewed the process of historical change as a perpetual conflict of opposing forces, in which a primary force (thesis) collides with a counterforce (antithesis) to produce a third force (synthesis), a new contradiction that is more than the sum of its parts and will become the basis of a new conflict.

In filmmaking practice, one shot (thesis) collides with another shot of opposing content (antithesis) to produce a new idea (synthesis). The result emphasizes a dynamic juxtaposition of individual shots that calls attention to each of these shots while forcing the viewer to reach conclusions about the interplay between them. This "montage of attractions," as Eisenstein called it, presents arbitrarily chosen images (some of them independent of the action) to create the maximum psychological impact. Thus conditioned, viewers would have in their consciousness the elements that would lead them to the overall concept that the director wanted to communicate. Artfully handled, of course, this is manipulation of the highest order, propaganda created to serve the Soviet state. The purest, most powerful example of this approach to filmmaking is *Battleship Potemkin* (1925).

Eisenstein's *Battleship Potemkin* is one of the fundamental landmarks of cinema. Indeed, it has become so popular from screenings in film-studies courses that, over the years, its ability to surprise has diminished. Nevertheless, it is essential to know why this movie

is important to film history. It depicts two events—the 1905 workers' mutiny on the *Potemkin* and the subsequent slaughter of ordinary citizens on the Odessa Steps. Through its dramatic reenactment of those events, the movie presents a successful example of revolution against oppression. Overall, the film's classic five-part structure emphasizes the need for unity in such struggles. But most people remember the "Odessa Steps" sequence, even though its impact may lessen when seen out of context, as it so often is. The sequence, set in Odessa on the wide steps leading from the town to the harbor, depicts czarist troops brutally killing ordinary citizens who are celebrating the successful mutiny on the *Potemkin*. Indeed, although the mass is the protagonist, it is the individual faces that we remember. The movie's brutal form (jump cuts and montage editing) perfectly matches the brutality of the massacre. Many directors have been influenced by Eisenstein's theory of montage; some pay homage to the "Odessa Steps" sequence, and others spoof it.

Battleship Potemkin is a great film not only because of its individual elements—the depth of Eisenstein's humanity, the historical and social significance of its story,

The beginnings of a revolution

In the first part of *Battleship Potemkin* (1925), Sergei Eisenstein steadily builds a case for the crew members' discontent with their lot—a discontent that will lead to violent revolt. Among other things, the sailors are unhappy with the ship's food. In this image, they examine a slab of the rotten meat they are forced to eat: "We've had enough rotten meat. It's not fit for pigs." Although the meat is crawling with maggots, the ship's doctor tells them that it will be edible if they just wash it off.

the formal perfection of its rhythm and editing, and its worldwide influence—but also because of the synergy by which each of these elements is enhanced by the others.

1927–1947: Classical Hollywood Style in Hollywood's Golden Age

The golden age of Hollywood was the most powerful and prolific period of film history yet. It is notable for the transition from silent to sound production, consolidation of the studio system, exploitation of familiar genres, imposition of the Motion Picture Production Code, changes in the look of movies, and the economic success of feature-length narrative films. Yet it was less a movement than a force, for in this period, the movies became inextricably linked with the development of American culture and society. From this point forward, the mov-

ies defined America, and America defined itself through the movies. (The formidable technological and organizational challenges that enabled these achievements are covered in Chapter 11.)

None of this could have been achieved without the efficiency of the studio system, which standardized the way movies were produced. It provided a top-down organization with management controlling everything, especially the employees, who regardless of their status were treated as employees, not artists, and whose careers were subject to the strict terms of their contracts. The transition to sound began in 1926 with the production of some short as well as feature films with recorded sound, and earlier experimental "talkies" were well known back to 1900. But once audiences saw Al Jolson—who in his prime was known as "the world's greatest entertainer"—in Alan Crosland's *The Jazz Singer* (1927), with its synchronized music score and a few sequences

Populism and popcorn

Frank Capra's *Mr. Deeds Goes to Town* (1936), *Mr. Smith Goes to Washington* (1939), and *Meet John Doe* (1941) are often described as a populist trilogy. Indeed, they are emblematic of populism in their belief that ordinary people have the right and power to struggle against the privileged elite. *Mr. Smith Goes to Washington* offers a sentimental vision of America, filled with stereotypes. Yet it was very successful with the American public, which was dissatisfied with Washington at the end of the Great Depression. In this image, Smith (James Stewart) finishes his filibuster before the U.S. Senate by pleading with his fellow senators to stand up and fight the corruption that is preventing the realization of his dream to finance a national camp for boys. Considering the national situation, this is a small issue indeed. And while it is almost impossible to imagine a similar incident paralyzing Washington today, it gives hope that the common man still has a voice in the direction of our country.

"Wait a minute. You ain't heard nothin' yet!"

While these are not the first words we hear Jack Robin (Al Jolson) speak in *The Jazz Singer* (1927; director Alan Crosland), they are the most memorable. Imagine the excitement of the 1927 audience hearing—for the first time—actors speaking in a movie. This is the melodramatic story of a young Jewish boy, Jakie Rabinowitz, who does not want to follow in his father's footsteps and become a cantor; instead, he becomes Jack Robin, a famous "jazz singer" in Broadway shows. It's a classic show-business movie, and Jolson, the country's biggest star in the 1920s, gracefully sings, whistles (image), and dances his way through it. His performance of several songs in blackface makeup may lead us today to make assumptions about Jolson's attitudes about race. Those songs are misleading, however, because Jolson was a prominent leader in the fight against show-biz segregation and was influential in promoting the careers of African American actors, singers, songwriters, and writers.

Screwball comedy

The genre of screwball comedy was popular during the Great Depression in the 1930s because it offered an escape from reality. It continues to exist today (in movies such as Peter Bogdanovich's *She's Funny That Way* (2014) and Joel and Ethan Coen's *Hail Caesar!* (2016), but without the wit or sting of the original. Its principal characteristics include stories of mistaken identity, often involving a person of the working class who accidentally (or not so accidentally) meets with someone from the upper class and, contrary to all expectations, becomes romantically involved; rapid, witty dialogue; and farcical, even fantastic, rags-to-riches plot situations. Mitchell Leisen's *Easy Living* (1937) easily fits the bill. Its script by Preston Sturges, a master of the genre, begins when tycoon John Ball (Edward Arnold), who resents his wife's buying a new sable coat, throws it from his penthouse roof. It lands on Mary Smith (Jean Arthur), an office worker who is riding on the top of a Fifth Avenue double-decker bus (behind her, the man in the turban is a classic bit of screwball incongruity). Seeing the coat, people assume she is rich, and she quickly learns to enjoy that illusion as she is enticed into a world of glamour and falls improbably in love with John Ball Jr. (Ray Milland).

Censorship threatens the release of *Baby Face*

The censors would have found plenty to dislike in Alfred E. Green's *Baby Face* (1933). It's the story of Lily Powers (Barbara Stanwyck), a Depression-era gold digger who sleeps her way to the top, both figuratively and literally, of a Manhattan skyscraper where she works. At each new floor, she finds a powerful new lover and, as a result, gets a better job. Eventually, she's in deeper than she thinks when one of her lovers murders another. Because the Motion Picture Production Code was not yet fully in power, the studio tried to get away with this version, but the New York State Censorship Board rejected it, so it trimmed some scenes and added a new ending that conformed with the code's principle that movies should endorse morality, not exploit it for entertainment purposes.

of synchronized sound, they wanted more. Its appeal was probably due less to the few moments of sound than to Jolson's exciting screen persona and his unexpected vocal ad-libbing. The first all-talking film was a routine gangster melodrama, Bryan Foy's *The Lights of New York* (1928).

Once the conversion to sound was completed in 1930, weekly attendance at the movies and box-office receipts had increased by 50 percent, again proving the Hollywood principle that profits derive from giving the public what it wants. Between 1927 and 1941 (when film production was reduced sharply due to wartime considerations), Hollywood produced more than 10,000 movies, an average of 744 each year (compared to 349 produced in 2013). The genres dominated production: screwball comedies, musicals, gangster movies, historical epics, melodramas, horror movies, Westerns, and biographies. Many of these movies were forgettable, but others are some of Hollywood's most important, influential, and memorable creations.

The moguls ran a tight, highly profitable business within their fortress-like studio walls. But outside there were calls for censorship, which, if not answered, threatened those profits. During the early 1920s, after several years of relatively frank portrayals of sex and violence on-screen (while the industry also suffered a wave of scandals), Hollywood faced a credible threat of censorship from state governments and boycotts from Catholic and other religious groups.

In 1922, in response to these pressures, Hollywood producers formed a regulatory agency called the Motion Picture Producers and Distributors of America (MPPDA, later the Motion Picture Association of America, or MPAA), headed by Will Hays. Originally conceived of as a public-relations entity to offset bad publicity and deflect negative attention away from Hollywood, the

The golden age at its popular best:
Gone with the Wind

Many people think of *Gone with the Wind* (1939; director Victor Fleming) as *the* enduring symbol of the golden age of Hollywood. Its romantic story is told against the sweep of the Civil War, its cast is formidable, its mise-en-scène and music are memorable, and it was the first movie to dominate the Oscars. Furthermore, it has won every award imaginable, and while it isn't a great movie in purely cinematic terms, it is a great crowd-pleaser, as attested to by its periodic theatrical revivals and television screenings. It also reflects the highest possible production values for its time—the studio system at its best—a tribute to the extraordinary commitment of its producer, David O. Selznick, who maintained tight, demoralizing control over every aspect of production. For example, the process of casting Scarlett O'Hara, which was not typical of Hollywood at the time (or at any time), involved a 2-year process in which Selznick tested nearly twenty-five major Hollywood and Broadway actors. Ironically, this quintessentially American role went to Vivien Leigh (*left*), a British actress virtually unknown in the American film industry.

Hays Office (as the agency was commonly known) in 1930 adopted the Motion Picture Production Code, a detailed set of guidelines concerning acceptable and unacceptable subject matter. Nudity, adultery, homosexuality, gratuitous or unpunished violence, and religious blasphemy were among the many types of content that the code strongly discouraged. Perhaps even more significant, the code explicitly stated that art can influence, for the worse, the morality of those who consume it (an idea that Hollywood has been reconsidering ever since).

Adherence to the Motion Picture Production Code remained fundamentally voluntary until the summer of 1934, when Joseph Breen, a prominent Catholic layman, was appointed head of the Production Code Administration (PCA), the enforcement arm of the MPPDA. After July 1, 1934, all films would have to receive an

MPPDA seal of approval before being released. For at least 20 years, the Breen Office rigidly controlled the general character and the particular details of Hollywood storytelling. After a period of practical irrelevance, the code was officially replaced in 1968, when the MPAA adopted the rating system that remains in use today.

Movies produced during Hollywood's golden age were made to be entertaining and successful at the box office, and the result was a period of stylistic conformity, not innovation. If an idea worked once, it usually worked again in a string of similar movies. The idea was to get the public out of the house and into the theater, give people what they wanted (entertainment, primarily), and thus help them forget the Depression and the anxieties caused by the events leading up to World War II. The values stressed in these movies were heroism, fidelity, family life, citizenship, community, and, of course, fun. Movies with important ideas were most often softened with comic touches and happy endings. So despite the large output, it is hard to find more than a few movies in Hollywood's golden age that stretched cinematic conventions, challenged prevailing social concepts, or provoked new ways of looking at the world. Hollywood during the golden age was not Europe, with its passion for the avantgarde, the revolutionary, or the film as art; few of those factors were part of the predominant American movie culture before World War II.

In the realm of cinematic style, narrative and editing conventions adapted to the challenges of sound production. Significant innovations were made in design, cinematography, lighting, acting, and editing, some related to sound, others not. Black-and-white film remained the industry standard through the early 1950s despite some interesting feature movies in Technicolor, which would become the new industry standard. Other technological advancements during the golden age included improvements in lighting, makeup, and film stock. While the predominant cinematographic style of the 1930s was soft-focus, the new lighting and film stock made it easier to achieve greater depth of focus, which created the illusion of perspective.

With the release of *Citizen Kane* in 1941, some 46 years after the invention of motion pictures, everything changed. Orson Welles's film revolutionized the medium and has since been considered the most important movie ever made. *Citizen Kane* is noteworthy for many reasons, but its reputation is due to Welles's genius as an artist and his vision of a new kind of cinema. He was twenty-four when he began the project, his first movie. While the story of newspaper magnate Charles Foster Kane rests firmly in the biopic genre, Welles tells it with a complex plot consisting of nine sequences (each using a different tone and style), five of which are flashbacks. Including the omniscient camera, the movie has seven narrators—some of them unreliable—who, taken together, present a modern psychological portrait of a megalomaniac. Released just 7 months before the United States declared war in December 1941, this was a radical film for Hollywood. And while the movie is open to various interpretations (the Freudian interpretation of young Charlie's relationship to his mother remains influential), *Citizen Kane* carries a strong antifascist message. It warns against Kane's arrogant abuse of the First Amendment right of freedom of speech and press, one of the many evils that Americans, reading their own newspapers, associated with Hitler.

Citizen Kane was also radical in its handling of the prevailing cinematic language of its time. We see this in the astonishing complexity and speed of the narrative. It may not seem so radical today, but that is only because it influenced the structure and pace of nearly every significant movie that came after it. In the other elements of cinematic form, Welles was equally innovative. The movie's stark design is heavily influenced by German Expressionism, as seen in the size, height, and depth of the rooms and other spaces at Xanadu. Through deep-space composition, lighting, deep-focus cinematography, and long takes, cinematographer Gregg Toland achieved the highest degree of cinematic realism yet seen. In contrast to the prevailing soft look of 1930s movies, *Citizen Kane* has a hard finish. The omniscient, probing, and usually moving camera, emphasizing its voyeuristic role, goes directly to the heart of each scene. The editing is mainly conventional, most often taking place within the long takes (and thus within the camera). Welles avoids such avant-garde techniques as Soviet Montage, for example, unless he wants to call attention to the editing, as he does in the "News on the March" sequence and the pans and swipes that create the passing of time during the famous breakfast-table sequence. Before going to Hollywood, Welles revolutionized American radio broadcasting, and his sound design for *Kane* creates an aural realism equivalent to the movie's visual realism. He frequently uses overlapping sound, which, like the deep-space composition, bombards us with a lightning mix of information that challenges us to choose what to listen to (just as in

Cinematic innovation in *Citizen Kane*

Citizen Kane (1941; director Orson Welles) is marked by brilliant innovations that changed cinematic language forever. Among these is deep-focus cinematography, pioneered by Gregg Toland, which permits action on all three planes of the image. Here, the action is focused both on the foreground and background. As Signor Matiste (Fortunio Bononova, *standing second from left*) becomes increasingly frustrated in his efforts to train the voice of Susan Alexander Kane (Dorothy Comingore), her husband, Charles Foster Kane (Orson Welles), standing in the background, registers his impressions of the rehearsal. Husband, wife, and vocal coach are all participating in a long take, making cutting between them unnecessary. However, Kane will soon make it clear—however small he may look in this image—that he, not Matiste, is in charge of his wife's singing career. She, of course, has nothing to say about it. This is only one of Kane's egotistical mistakes that help to ruin the couple's careers and marriage.

real life). The film is also much louder than the typical movie of the time, which is another innovation, and the bravado of its dialogue, sound effects, and music puts it in your ears as well as in your face. Bernard Herrmann's musical score was spare, modernist, and completely ahead of its time. In the film's acting, Welles called on his stage and radio experiences to break another Hollywood convention. Actors did not normally rehearse their lines except in private or for a few minutes with the director before shooting, but Welles rehearsed his cast for a month before shooting began, so his ensemble of actors could handle long passages of dialogue in the movie's distinctive long takes. And the performances, including Welles as Kane, are unforgettable.

Citizen Kane has been enormously influential on filmmakers around the world. Martin Scorsese said that Welles influenced more young people to become film directors than anyone else in film history. References to its unique style have been quoted in dozens of other films, but Welles's overall style has never been fully imitated. Even after repeated viewings, its tantalizing story, courageous political stance, provocative ambiguity, and razzle-dazzle style continue to exert their hold.

1942–1951: Italian Neorealism

With German Expressionism, the Soviet Montage Movement, and the French New Wave movements, Italian Neorealism stands as one of the most vital movements in the history of world cinema. Developed during World War II, neorealism rose to prominence after the war and then flourished for a relatively short period before ending abruptly.

Benito Mussolini, the Fascist dictator who ruled Italy from 1922 to 1943, believed, as did Lenin, in the propaganda power of film. To revive Italy's lackluster film industry, he instituted government subsidies and control, banned American movies, established a national film school, and constructed vast new studios. Although the Italian movies produced during his regime were commercially successful (audiences had no choices), they were artistically inferior to what the French were producing before the war. After Mussolini was driven from power in 1943 and executed in 1945, an opportunity arose to revitalize Italian cinema.

In 1942, Cesare Zavattini, a prolific Marxist screenwriter, launched what came to be known as the neorealist movement, influenced its style and ideology, and led a group of young filmmakers to make film history. The group was also influenced by French poetic realism, a movement that consisted of filmmakers seeking freedom in the increasingly repressive French society of the 1930s, and by two contemporary Italian films: Luchino Visconti's *Ossessione* (1943) and Roberto Rossellini's *Rome, Open City* (1945). Rossellini's film most clearly exhibits every characteristic of neorealism and became the standard for the films that followed.

In cinema, as well as the other visual arts, realism is often an elusive concept. It is nothing more or less than the depiction of subjects as they appear to the artist in everyday life, without adornment or interpretation. In postwar period neorealism, this definition adhered, but the movement was revolutionary because it deliberately broke with the Fascist past and adopted an ideology that reflects Marxist, Christian, and humanist values. Neorealist filmmakers placed the highest value on the lives of ordinary working people; decried such postwar conditions as widespread unemployment, poverty, child labor, government corruption, and inadequate housing (the results of Fascist rule); and focused on the struggle for a decent life in the postwar world. Politically, neorealism is antiauthoritarian, skeptical of the Catholic Church, antibureaucratic, and socialist. But overall, because it has no inherent political purpose, it is traditionally regarded more as a style than an ideology.

Stylistically, the characteristics of neorealism are specific. Despite the lavish production facilities available at the large studios that Mussolini built (or perhaps because of them), the neorealists sought simplicity in their working methods. They used actual locations rather than studio sites and hired nonprofessional actors. Their films had a documentary visual style that included shooting in the streets with natural light and

An early influence on neorealism

Luchino Visconti's *Ossessione* (1943) represents a transition between the lackluster Italian cinema of the pre–World War II period and the brief but significant flowering of neorealism. It reflects the older traditions in several ways: it uses professional actors, is based on an American novel, and is known mainly for its torrid love story. Soon after the two lovers—Giovanna (Clara Calamai), an unhappily married woman, and Gino (Massimo Girotti), a drifter—first meet, they become obsessively involved with one another. *Ossessione* foreshadows neorealism in its depiction of the daily routines of ordinary people, its focus on rural Italy, and its consistent use of long shots to preserve real time and emphasize how the setting constrains the characters from becoming independent. Mostly, though, its austere realism, in form and content, influenced the neorealist filmmakers. The film was remade in the United States twice, both times as *The Postman Always Rings Twice* (1946, director Tay Garnett; 1981, director Bob Rafelson).

lightweight cameras, using long takes to preserve real time, and employing deep-space cinematography to maintain the look of the actual spaces where shooting occurred. All of these characteristics broke with the prevailing cinematic conventions in Italy.

Zavattini was primarily a screenwriter, but he was also responsible for pioneering a kind of documentary film, *Love in the City* (1953). In that film, he and several other young filmmakers (Michelangelo Antonioni, Federico Fellini, Carlo Lizzani, and Dino Risi, each of whom became a prominent director) worked with nonprofessional actors who played themselves in dramatizing an aspect of their lives. This approach, a sort of staged documentary, would later influence the development of *cinéma vérité* in France, free cinema in England, and direct cinema in the United States.

The most indispensable neorealist films are Vittorio De Sica's *Shoeshine* (1946), *The Bicycle Thieves* (1948; also known as *The Bicycle Thief*), and *Umberto D.* (1952), which marks the end of the movement; Cesare Zavattini wrote the screenplays for all of these.

The Bicycle Thieves, the movement's masterpiece, is set in Rome two years after the end of the war. It recounts three consecutive days in the life of Antonio Ricci (Lamberto Maggiorani), a laborer, Maria (Lianella Carell), his wife, and Bruno (Enzo Staiola), his son, who looks about eight years old but nonetheless works twelve hours a day at a gas station. The story is simple but powerful. Antonio is out of work but, at the beginning of the movie, is offered a job (hanging movie posters) on the condition that he has a bicycle. Because his bicycle is in a pawnshop, his wife takes the family linen to the pawnshop so that he can reclaim his bicycle and take the job. On his first morning at work, the bicycle is stolen. His friends help him search for it, but they have no luck. When Antonio spots the thief, the Mafia protects that man. Social forces such as the church and fortunetellers cannot help him. Faced with a practical dilemma, he too becomes a bicycle thief (hence the movie's title) and is caught and publicly humiliated. At the end of the film, Antonio is in exactly the same dilemma as when the film began. This, then, is the story of a good man caught in a seemingly hopeless world, told with insightful observation and compassion. Its ending, true to the neorealist credo, is ambiguous.

In this film the stylistic characteristics of neorealism—the long takes, the actual locations, the spare dialogue, and so on—allow De Sica to show reality without

The Bicycle Thieves: a neorealist masterpiece

A 3-day chronicle comprises the plot of *The Bicycle Thieves* (1948; director Vittorio De Sica), which tells the story of Antonio Ricci's (Lamberto Maggiorani) desperate search for his dignity. Bruno (Enzo Staiola), his son, is the one person who stands by him. Through hardship after hardship, their shared bond of love and faith is challenged but never broken. Bruno gives his father the courage to survive one heartbreaking moment after another, and although the movie ends ambiguously, there is no question that father and son will remain friends. In this image, we see Bruno waving good-bye to his father as they both begin their workday. When director De Sica cast Staiola, an unknown boy from the streets, in this part, he found a natural actor who gave the world an unforgettable performance.

necessarily interpreting it. Nonetheless, he took complete control over the setting, cinematography, lighting, acting, and sound. Even though it is a sound film, much of its power comes from its relative silence, particularly its lack of voices. Like many films made before the coming of sound, *The Bicycle Thieves* demonstrates the intensity of silent acting.

One definition of a "classic" movie is that it can mean different things to different people at different times in their lives. *The Bicycle Thieves* is a classic and powerful film because of the director's spare style, humanist treatment of the story, and willingness to trust his viewers to make up their own mind about what it means.

Although neorealist films were innovative, they were not popular with Italians, who preferred the more upbeat American movies. Consequently, they were not successful at the box office (economic success was not one of the movement's primary goals). Critics, furthermore, said the films gave a false, even sentimental, portrayal of Italian society, one inconsistent with a country eager for prosperity and change. The government discouraged the neorealists' interest in social problems by not subsidizing them. Instead, it supported domestic films that focused on the new prosperity of the postwar society and implemented taxes and quotas on foreign movies.

By 1952 the Italian Neorealism movement was finished, yet it had an enormous impact on later Italian and world cinema. In fact, a handful of neorealist films helped rekindle greater awareness among filmmakers worldwide of the need to observe real life and to abandon, insofar as possible, the make-believe world of the movie studio. The movement also helped launch the careers of many great Italian directors, including De Sica, Rossellini, Visconti, Fellini, Antonioni, and Pietro Germi. Neorealism also influenced Italian directors who were not directly involved, including Pier Paolo Pasolini, Bernardo Bertolucci, Ermanno Olmi, and Paolo and Vittorio Taviani. Filmmakers as different as Satyajit Ray in India and Martin Scorsese in the United States regarded neorealism as the principal inspiration in beginning their careers. Today you'll see its influence in such different movies as Jean-Pierre and Luc Dardenne's *L'Enfant* (2005), John Carney's *Once* (2006), and even Matt Reeves's *Cloverfield* (2008).

1959–1964: French New Wave

After World War II, France, which had been occupied by the Nazis between 1940 and 1944, faced a unique set of problems, both foreign and domestic. Abroad, it was engaged in two wars with French-controlled territories: the French Indochina War (1946–54), which ended in a divided but independent Vietnam, and the Algerian War of Independence (1954–62), which led to Algeria's independence from France. At home, President Charles de Gaulle's government faced many challenges in dealing with myriad social, political, racial, ethnic, and cultural differences produced in part by the twin forces of collaboration and resistance during the Nazi occupation. Everywhere, calls for change were coming from students, artists, intellectuals, and philosophers— particularly the existentialists, who called for a new world in which individuals would be more responsible for their actions. The French New Wave was born within this broad context.

The originators of the New Wave were influenced by several movements. The first was the French cinema itself, including the 1930s cinematic style known as *poetic realism*. The term applied to movies that treated everyday life with a moody sensitivity to mise-en-scène and to the more contemporary films of Jean-Pierre Melville. The second influence was the philosophy of Jean-Paul Sartre, the leading figure in French philosophy in the postwar period. Sartre believed that contemporary artists should rebel against the constraints of society, traditional morality, and religious faith; should accept personal responsibility for their actions; and should thus be free to create their own world. His existentialist views helped shape the new French cinema's depiction of modern human beings, while his Marxist views helped form its interpretations of society and history. Finally, the movement learned much from film critic and director Alexandre Astruc. He declared that a filmmaker should use the camera as personally as the novelist uses a pen, thus inspiring the idea of the movie director as auteur.

Other influences on the French New Wave include Italian Neorealism, the contemporaneous British Free Cinema (discussed on pp. 386–387), and contemporary developments in the French documentary film. While the Italians and the British offered models of how to make narrative films that told real stories about real people, *cinéma vérité* evolved in France in the early 1960s as a documentary style (the name, which means "film truth," pays homage to Dziga Vertov's *kino-pravda* work in the Soviet Montage movement). Among other things, this style advocated using the lightweight, portable filmmaking equipment that enhanced a filmmaker's mobility and flexibility. Stylistically, its films had a rough, intimate look that often reflected the informality of the filmmaking process. Filmmakers appeared onscreen, cameras jiggled, framing was often informal, scenes were generally unscripted, and continuity was provided primarily through lots of close-ups and sound tracks that continued under the shots. Later, such stylistic innovations would characterize many New Wave movies.

Film theorist André Bazin, known as the father of the New Wave, synthesized these concepts into the coherent model on which the New Wave was established. This interaction of intellect and creativity recalls the origins of several movements you've already encountered: the German, Soviet, and French film movements of the 1920s. Bazin cofounded *Cahiers du cinéma,* which

1

2

French New Wave: beginnings

Among the first New Wave movies were François Truffaut's *The 400 Blows* (1959) and Jean-Luc Godard's *Breathless* (1960). Truffaut's protagonist, Antoine Doinel (Jean-Pierre Léaud), is a boy in his early teens who, as we see him here [1], has just escaped from a juvenile detention center; Godard's Michel Poiccard (Jean-Paul Belmondo) is a man in his early thirties who is preparing to steal a car and will shortly murder a policeman [2]. Antoine is just a boy prankster facing an unknown future, but Michel is a dangerous criminal whom the police will soon recognize and shoot in cold blood as he attempts to flee capture. Noteworthy is that Truffaut wrote the original treatment of *Breathless* and, after his great success with *The 400 Blows*, made a gift of it to Godard, suggesting that he submit it as the idea for his own first film.

became the leading French film journal of the time, and in his capacity as editor, he became the intellectual and spiritual mentor of the New Wave. His followers included *Cahiers'* contributors, many of whom would become directors: Jean-Luc Godard, François Truffaut, Claude Chabrol, Jacques Rivette, and Eric Rohmer. Others went directly into filmmaking: Chris Marker, Alain Resnais, Agnès Varda, and Louis Malle. (There were other major directors in postwar France who were not directly involved in the New Wave movement, including Jean Cocteau, Robert Bresson, Jean Renoir, Jacques Tati, Jacques Becker, and Max Ophüls.)

Bazin's central tenets were realism, mise-en-scène, and authorship (the director's unique style). For him, the most distinctive nature of a movie was its form rather than its content. Accordingly, he encouraged his followers to see as many films as possible, looking particularly at the relationship between the director and the material. In viewing these films, great and otherwise, the young critics and would-be filmmakers developed a particular fascination with those Hollywood films that seemed to prove what Bazin, following Astruc, was saying

about the director-as-author. They recognized that most directors of Hollywood films had little say over most aspects of production, but they believed that through his style, particularly the handling of mise-en-scène, a great director could undermine studio control and transform even the most insignificant Western or detective story into a work of art.

Obviously, the New Wave was based on a theory that advocated a change in filmmaking practices. Truffaut's 1954 *Cahiers* essay "A Certain Tendency of the French Cinema" elaborated on the auteur concept and started a critical controversy that has not yet abated.[12] The issue remains: Is it the director or the entire collaborative team, including the director, that makes a movie? Truffaut idolized directors who made highly personal statements in their films—directors such as Jean Renoir, Jean Cocteau, and Max Ophüls in France, and Orson Welles, Alfred Hitchcock, Howard Hawks, Fritz Lang, John Ford, Nicholas Ray, and Anthony Mann in Hollywood—so his answer was clear: the director was the primary "author" of the work. In another influential *Cahiers* essay, "The Evolution of the Language of Cinema," Bazin

12. See François Truffaut, "A Certain Tendency of the French Cinema," in *Movies and Methods: An Anthology*, ed. Bill Nichols, 2 vols. (Berkeley: University of California Press, 1976), I, pp. 224–237.

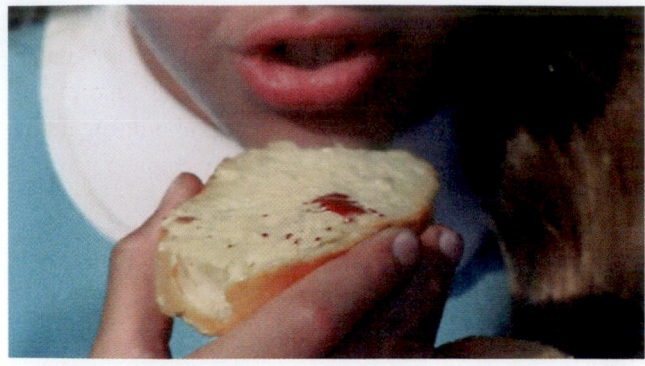

Hitchcock's influence on the New Wave

Alfred Hitchcock's movies were greatly admired by New Wave directors. Claude Chabrol, who carefully studied the movies of the master of suspense and surprise, is noted also for movies that combine romance with gory murders. In *The Butcher* (1970), thought by many to be his masterpiece, a group of schoolchildren accompany Hélène (Stéphane Audran), their teacher, to see a magnificent cave that contains prehistoric drawings. Afterward—in the image here—as they enjoy their picnic lunch, blood drips onto one girl's bread from a fresh corpse on a cliff above. When Hélène sees the body, she suspects that it is yet another woman who has been victimized by the local butcher, a man with whom the teacher has a platonic relationship. After that, the suspense—whose effect Chabrol learned well from Hitchcock—becomes almost unbearable.

Time and mortality in the New Wave

Agnès Varda, one of the few women in the New Wave movement, was a unique force in shaping it. Her experiments in the handling of cinematic time influenced such contemporaries as Jean-Luc Godard and Alain Resnais. And her concern with the cinematic perception of women is beautifully realized in *Cleo from 5 to 7* (1962). It follows 2 hours in the life of Cléo (Corinne Marchand), a pop singer who wanders aimlessly around Paris while waiting for the results of a biopsy. Her story is told in near–real time, as she grapples with such issues as the meaning of friendship, her work, and mortality. Just before going to the hospital to meet her doctor—fearing that she has cancer—Cléo drops her purse; picking up the pieces, she interprets her broken mirror as an omen of death. To call attention to Cléo's ordeal of killing time, Varda titles each episode and indicates its precise running time (here, translated into English): "Chapter 11—CLÉO from 6:04 to 6:12."

described mise-en-scène by stressing that everything we see on the screen has been put there by the director for a reason.[13]

The New Wave directors excelled at demonstrating that cinematic form is more important than content; their films were self-reflexive, focusing attention on them *as* movies and diverting our attention away from their narratives. In this, they manipulate our perceptions and keep an aesthetic and psychological distance between us and their movies. The style, substance, and achievements of the French New Wave directors had an invigorating effect on world cinema, and their movies remain very popular. Among their most important films are Jean-Luc Godard's *Breathless* (1960), François Truffaut's *The 400 Blows* (1959), Claude Chabrol's *The Butcher* (1970), Jacques Rivette's *Celine and Julie Go Boating* (1974), Eric Rohmer's *My Night at Maud's* (1969), Chris Marker's *La Jetée* (1962), Alain Resnais's *Last Year at Marienbad* (1961), Agnès Varda's *Cleo from 5 to 7* (1962), and Louis Malle's *Murmur of the Heart* (1971). Although

the movement was finished by 1964, many of these directors continued to make films.

If one movie symbolizes the fresh, innovative spirit of the New Wave, it is Godard's *Breathless* (1960). This work offers a comprehensive catalog of the movement's stylistic traits: rapid action, use of handheld cameras, unusual camera angles, elliptical editing, direct address to the camera, acting that borders on the improvisational, anarchic politics, and emphasis on the importance of sound, especially words. It is not any one of these techniques that defines the filmmaker's style, but rather the imagination and energy with which he uses them. *Breathless*, a movie that asserts Godard's personality and ideology, virtually defines what is meant by an auteur film. It tells a conventional crime story in an unconventional manner, rejecting the traditional cinematic values of unity and continuity in favor of discontinuity and contrast. Godard called his work a cinema of "reinvention," meaning that he generally kept all kinds of cinematic language in mind as he created his own. Consequently, by employing the iris-out, Godard not only offers homage to D. W. Griffith but also reminds modern audiences of a seldom-used visual device. Dedicating the film to Monogram Pictures (one of Hollywood's "B" or "Poverty Row" studios), Godard evokes the Hollywood film noir through allusions, direct and indirect, to tough films with tough leading men. He also pays homage to French film director Jean-Pierre Melville, a major influence on the New Wave, by casting him in the movie and patterning the role of his leading male character on the model in Melville's *Bob le flambeur* (1956). Finally, Godard includes allusions to writers, composers, and painters. Through this broad range of intertextual reference, or pastiche (making one artwork by mixing elements from others), Godard audaciously links his low-budget film noir with the works of some of the greatest artists of all time.

Most important, though, is Godard's editing, which is central to the telling of this narrative. Here, working in the radical tradition started by Eisenstein and his contemporaries—collision between and among images—Godard consciously and deliberately manipulates the images with such editing techniques as jump cuts and nondiegetic inserts. Thus he deliberately avoids such devices as crosscutting, which traditional directors would have used in cutting between the good guys and bad guys in the film's chase scenes, as well as the familiar sequence used to set up a scene—an establishing shot, long shot, medium shot, and close-up, generally in that order. The restless rhythm of the editing is perfectly suited to the restless mood of the story and the indecisiveness of the movie's two major characters.

While the term *New Wave* began with the French, its spirit soon spread internationally. These efforts were significantly bolstered in many of the countries discussed later by the establishment of state-supported filmmaking schools and film societies as well as the availability of lightweight filmmaking equipment. In the United States, the New Wave influence was noticeable early on—in Arthur Penn's *Bonnie and Clyde* (1967) and recently in Wes Anderson's *The Royal Tenenbaums* (2001) and Michel Gondry's *Eternal Sunshine of the Spotless Mind* (2004), to cite but three examples.

Many of the techniques pioneered by the French New Wave filmmakers have become commonplace, especially in today's independent cinema. Godard's films

from the early 1960s still look very modern, and the unusually stylized treatment of time and subjectivity in a film like Alain Resnais's *Last Year at Marienbad* remains cutting-edge to this day, confusing and alienating many viewers used to traditional cinematic conventions.

1947–Present: Movements and Developments in International Cinema

World War II, fought mainly in Europe and Asia but involving virtually every country in the world, was the most destructive war in history. Between 40 million and 50 million people were killed, and millions of others fled from their homes or countries. The war destroyed many historic cities, shattered economies, and left the specter of the Holocaust to redefine the concept of a civilized world. It was impossible for many countries to return to normal, even though the victory over Fascism held the promise of establishing a new and more just society.

How did filmmakers react to the war? They all knew that whatever they did with their movies, the international landscape had changed utterly and that they must acknowledge the horrors, postwar challenges, and hopes for the future. For some filmmakers, it was an opportunity to express their nation's identity through what we call a *national cinema*. While this term is used generally to describe the films identified by and associated with a specific country—for example, through financing, language, or culture—it remains a subject of debate among film scholars and critics.

In the following pages, we differentiate between two kinds of countries. First are those that resumed filmmaking pretty much as usual after the war, albeit with a different perspective, audience, and set of responsibilities (e.g., Canada, Australia, New Zealand, Ireland, Italy, Sweden, Spain, Russia and the Soviet Union, Hungary, the former Czechoslovakia and former Yugoslavia, Romania, Bulgaria, and many countries in Central and Latin America, Asia, Africa, and the Middle East). The second type of country includes those that established the new wave movements we discuss in this section: Great Britain, Denmark, Germany, Japan, and China. Today, new cinemas are also emerging in Albania, Bosnia, Slovenia, Serbia, Hungary, Estonia, Turkey, and the Czech Republic. (We emphasize the new wave movements because they represent pockets of resistance to dominant filmmaking traditions and have revitalized the cinemas of their respective countries with a distinctive stylistic effect.)

In making this simple distinction and in choosing to discuss the new wave movements, we do not overlook the profound achievements of such British and European directors as Ingmar Bergman, Andrzej Wajda, Michelangelo Antonioni, Satyajit Ray, David Lean, or Federico Fellini, to name only a few. The work of those artists significantly altered the psychological and imaginative landscape of postwar filmmaking. Nor do we overlook more recent directors—such as Jane Campion, Pedro Almodóvar, Abbas Kiarostami, or Ousmane Sembène—whose films, although they don't fall within a definable movement or trend, are widely recognized as modern masterpieces.

Like the original new wave of directors in France, each of the movements described next attempted to (1) make a clean break with the cinematic past, (2) inject new vitality into filmmaking, and (3) explore cinema as a subject in itself.

England and the Free Cinema Movement

The British Free Cinema movement developed between 1956 and 1959. Like Dziga Vertov and the Italian Neorealists, these British directors rejected prevailing cinematic conventions; in so doing, they also rejected an obstinately class-bound society, turned their cameras on ordinary people and everyday life, and proclaimed their freedom to make films without worrying about the demands of producers and distributors or other commercial considerations.

Because the films of the Free Cinema movement were entirely the expression of the people who made them, they serve as another manifestation of the growing postwar movement in Europe toward a new cinema of social realism. Its primary effect was a small but impressive body of documentary films, including Lindsay Anderson's *Every Day Except Christmas* (1957), an affectionate look at the people who make the Covent Garden market such a tradition; Karel Reisz's *We Are the Lambeth Boys*

Victim: the first major movie about gay rights

The British Free Cinema dealt courageously with controversial issues of class, race, gender, and sexual orientation. Basil Dearden's *Victim* (1961) was the first commercial British film to show that homosexuality existed at every level of contemporary society. At the time, homosexual acts between consenting adults were illegal in Great Britain, and gays suffered widespread discrimination and blackmail. In *Victim*, Dirk Bogarde gave a moving performance as Melville Farr, a distinguished lawyer who is exposed by a blackmailing ring for having had an emotional, but nonsexual, gay affair before he married. In this image, he sees the photograph that triggered the blackmail. Outraged by the widespread injustices against homosexuals, he agrees to help the police by giving evidence in court, knowing that sensational newspaper publicity could ruin his career. Bogarde, then one of England's major stars, was lauded for his personal courage in helping to break a social barrier, and *Victim* was instrumental in changing the social and legal climate. In 1967, Great Britain legalized homosexual acts between consenting adults.

(1958), an attempt to understand working-class youth; and Tony Richardson and Karel Reisz's *Momma Don't Allow* (1955), an admiring view of the emerging British pop culture in the mid-1950s.

After the war, the British class system began its slow disintegration, and Anderson understood the inherent challenges facing the country, as well as the role that movies might play in the transition, when he defined his approach to filmmaking: "I want to make people—ordinary people, not just Top People—feel their dignity and their importance, so that they can act from these principles. Only on such principles can confident and healthy action be based."[14]

This sentiment and Free Cinema movies helped to inspire the British New Cinema of the 1960s, an almost unique situation in which the documentary form was

14. Lindsay Anderson, qtd. in Richard M. Barsam, *Nonfiction Film: A Critical History,* rev. and exp. ed. (Bloomington: Indiana University Press, 1992), p. 252.

the catalyst for a revived spirit in narrative filmmaking. Memorable socialist-realist films were outspoken on the subjects of gender, race, and economic disparities among the classes, including Jack Clayton's *Room at the Top* (1959), Karel Reisz's *Saturday Night and Sunday Morning* (1960), Basil Dearden's *Victim* (1961), Tony Richardson's *The Loneliness of the Long Distance Runner* (1962), Lindsay Anderson's *if . . .* (1968), Joseph Losey's *The Servant* (1963), Richard Lester's *A Hard Day's Night* (1964), and Ken Loach's *Kes* (1969).

Denmark and the Dogme 95 Movement

Postwar Danish cinema is noted primarily for the Dogme 95 movement. It was founded in 1995 by three directors, including Lars von Trier, the one best known outside Denmark. The movement was based on the Dogme 95 manifesto of ten rules (known as "The Vow of Chastity"), with which participating directors were required to affirm their compliance. These are

1. Shooting must be done on location. Props and sets must not be brought in (if a particular prop is necessary for the story, a location must be chosen where this prop is to be found).

2. The sound must never be produced apart from the images or vice versa. (Music must not be used unless it occurs where the scene is being shot.)

3. The camera must be handheld. Any movement or immobility attainable in the hand is permitted. (The film must not take place where the camera is standing; shooting must take place where the film takes place.)

4. The film must be in color. Special lighting is not acceptable. (If there is too little light for exposure the scene must be cut or a single lamp be attached to the camera.)

5. Optical work and filters are forbidden.

6. The film must not contain superficial action. (Murders, weapons, etc. must not occur.)

7. Temporal and geographical alienation are forbidden. (That is to say that the film takes place here and now.)

Breaking the rules in *Breaking the Waves*

The Dogme rules are rigid, but Lars von Trier's *Breaking the Waves* (1996) demonstrates that a director can subvert them to facilitate production. Although the cinematographer used the requisite handheld camera, many of the scenes were shot not in real locations, but in studio settings. The story takes place in the past, not the here and now; and contrary to Dogme rules, the movie contains nondiegetic music. Furthermore, von Trier takes full credit for his role as director. Nonetheless, a major reason for seeing it is the astonishing performance by Emily Watson as Bess, a simple, childlike woman. When her husband, seriously injured in an oil-rig accident, fears that their sex life has ended, he encourages her to have sexual relations with other men. However, she believes, from voices that she hears, that what she is doing is God's wish. These voices—if indeed she hears them—often come to her in a deserted church.

8. Genre movies are not acceptable.

9. The film format must be Academy 35mm.

10. The director must not be credited.[15]

This statement of principles brought considerable attention to the country's cinema with such movies as von Trier's *The Idiots* (1998), *Breaking the Waves* (1996), *Dancer in the Dark* (2000), *Dogville* (2003), and *The Five Obstructions* (2003). These rules were rigid, and directors often broke their vows, as seen in such Dogme films as Harmony Korine's *Julien Donkey-Boy* (1999), Lone Scherfig's *Italian for Beginners* (2000), Martin Rengel's *Joy Ride* (2001), and Susanne Bier's *Open Hearts* (2002). The Dogme movement—clearly as bold, if not as significant, as the French New Wave—influenced some avant-garde directors in Europe and the United States. Its emphasis on freedom is relevant to filmmakers with access to digital video, home computers, and advanced editing software.

15. www.dogme95.dk/the_vow/vow.html (accessed March 24, 2015).

Germany and Austria

Following World War II and until 1990 (when it was re-unified as the Federal Republic of Germany), Germany was split into western and eastern parts. In West Germany, the Federal Republic reestablished independent film production, even though German audiences preferred Hollywood movies. In East Germany, film production remained under Soviet control, and little of significance was produced, except in the work of Kurt Maetzig, whose films helped Germans on both sides of the Berlin Wall to understand the Nazi past. In many feature films and documentaries, he dealt with Fascism, anti-Semitism, and the complicity of German corporations with the Nazi government. He founded East Germany's main film studio, which operated under the ideological dictates of the Communist Party, and he made films about life under that regime. He also made the most popular film of the postwar period—*Marriage in the Shadows* (1947)—as well as some that were banned, including *The Rabbit Is Me* (1965), a blunt criticism of the East German judicial system.

In 1962 a movement called *das neue Kino* (the New German Cinema) was born, and it flourished until the 1980s. Its founders, a group of young writers and filmmakers, recognized that any attempt to revive the German cinema must deal with two large issues: the Nazi period and the brutal break that it made in the German cultural tradition; and the reemergence of postwar Germany as a divided country whose western part was known, like Japan at the same time, as an "economic miracle." This group also knew the Italian, French, and British New Cinemas that preceded them and had a genuine affection for established genres in Hollywood, particularly melodrama. Like all serious radical groups, it issued a manifesto:

> The collapse of the conventional German film finally removes the economic basis for a mode of filmmaking whose attitude and practice we reject. With it the new film has a chance to come to life. . . .
>
> We declare our intention to create the new German feature film.
>
> This new film needs new freedoms. Freedom from the conventions of the established industry. Freedom from the outside influence of commercial partners. Freedom from the control of special interest groups.

Das neue Kino and Hollywood
German New Wave filmmakers had a genuine affection for Hollywood genres, including film noir. In Wim Wenders's *The American Friend* (1977), a crime thriller and neo-noir (shot in color), the title refers to the character of Tom Ripley, played by the American actor Dennis Hopper, shown here. Also appearing in the movie are two distinctly American movie directors: Nicholas Ray (who directed Hopper in *Rebel without a Cause* [1955]) and Samuel Fuller (*Pickup on South Street* [1953]). Although the film was shot mostly in Germany, some scenes were photographed in New York City.

> We have concrete intellectual, formal, and economic conceptions about the production of the new German film. We are as a collective prepared to take economic risks.
>
> The old film is dead. We believe in the new one.[16]

This 1962 document (known as the Oberhausen Manifesto) fused economic, aesthetic, and political goals. It sought to create a new cinema free from historical antecedents, one that could criticize bourgeois German society and expose viewers to new modes of looking at movies. A short list of the early work of the most significant directors includes Volker Schlöndorff's *Young Torless* (1966); Alexander Kluge's *Artists under the Big Top: Perplexed* (1968); and Margarethe von Trotta's *The German Sisters/Marianne and Juliane* (1981; von Trotta is perhaps the most important of a large group of female directors). Also included are Rainer Werner Fassbinder's *The Marriage of Maria Braun* (1979), *Fear of Fear* (1975), and *Berlin Alexanderplatz* (1980—a television series, released theatrically in a 15½-hour version, the longest narrative movie ever made); Wim Wenders's *The Goalie's Anxiety at the Penalty Kick* (1972), *The American Friend* (1977), and *Paris, Texas* (1984); and Werner

---

16. For the full text and list of signatories, see www.oberhausener-manifest.com/en/ (accessed June 15, 2015).

Herzog's *Even Dwarfs Started Small* (1970), *Aguirre: The Wrath of God* (1972), *Heart of Glass* (1976), and *Nosferatu the Vampire* (1979). Ultimately, the movement sparked a renaissance in German filmmaking by encouraging the production of quality films that created considerable excitement in the international cinema community. Its bold treatments of such contemporary issues as sexuality, immigration, and national identity have significantly influenced filmmakers worldwide.

The history of Austrian cinema includes a rich legacy from various film artists, such as Ernst Lubitsch and Billy Wilder, who emigrated during the 1930s and enriched the cinemas of Great Britain, France, and the United States. In the twenty-first century, a young generation of filmmakers has begun to create its own legacy with films that are uniquely Austrian in subject and style. These include Michael Haneke, arguably the best-known and most important Austrian filmmaker, with such films as *Funny Games* (1997; U.S. remake in 2008), *The Piano Teacher* (2001), *The White Ribbon* (2009), and *Amour* (2012); as well as Ulrich Seidl, *Import/Export* (2007) and his 2012 trilogy, *Paradise: Love, Paradise: Faith,* and *Paradise: Hope*; Jessica Hausner, *Lonely Rita* (2001), *Hotel* (2004), and *Lourdes* (2009); and Jan Schütte, *Love Comes Lately* (2007).

Japan

The movies were popular in Japan as early as 1896, a year after they were invented in the West. The Japanese film industry flourished, albeit with a highly stylized form of filmmaking that owed a great deal to Japanese literary and theatrical traditions as well as something to Western cinematic traditions, until World War II.

When the war ended in 1945, much of the country lay in ruins and was under occupation by the Allied powers. As the film industry began to revive, it was strongly influenced by such Hollywood masters as John Ford, Howard Hawks, and Orson Welles. However, filmmakers were limited, both by the occupying powers and by a film industry lacking money, to making films that extolled the freedoms made possible by democracy, particularly the emancipation of women. The three Japanese directors most familiar in the West are Akira Kurosawa, Kenji Mizoguchi, and Yasujirô Ozu. Mizoguchi and Ozu began their directing careers in the 1920s, but it was not until 1950 that Kurosawa launched the golden age of Japanese filmmaking with *Rashomon*.

To Western viewers, Akira Kurosawa is the most recognizable Japanese director, both for the quality of his work and because he, among his contemporaries, was most familiar with the conventions of Hollywood filmmaking, especially the work of John Ford. However, aside from familiar cinematic technique, his films are thoroughly Japanese in their fatalistic attitude toward life and death. He initiated the postwar rebirth of Japanese cinema with *Rashomon* (1950), which tells a single story—the rape of a woman—from four different points of view. Kurosawa shows us that we all remember and perceive differently and that truth is relative to those telling their stories. With this profound statement on the power of cinema, he produced a body of work that

Kurosawa's *Ran*: "a scroll of hell"

Ran, Kurosawa's adaptation of Shakespeare's *King Lear*, pushes the play to extremes. The word *ran* literally means "turmoil" or "chaos" and suggests rebellion, riot, or war. Kurosawa's *ran* is full of blood, violence, suffering, and death, qualities depicted in twelfth- and thirteenth-century Japanese scrolls known as "scrolls of hell," the term Kurosawa used to describe the movie itself. The director has transformed King Lear's three daughters into the three sons of powerful warlord Hidetora Ichimonji. Lady Kaede, the wife of Taro, one of the sons, is a lethal schemer who wants her husband to become leader of the clan. She fails, however, and at the end, she is confronted by a clan loyalist, who tells her, "Vixen . . . you have destroyed the house of Ichimonji, now you should know the shallowness and stupidity of a woman's wisdom." But Kaede has the last word: "It is not shallow or stupid. I wanted to see this castle burn and the House of Ichimonji ruined by the long grudge of my family. I wanted to see all this." We do not see Kaede beheaded, but in this spectacular image, her spattered blood is running down the wall. A maid crouches to the left and the assailant stands at the right; Kaede's body is on the floor. The image resembles a Japanese scroll; overall, it is framed by pots of flowers in the middle ground; in the background, the gruesome composition is framed by sliding doors. Ironically, the dripping blood recalls various abstract modern paintings.

Painterly composition in Mizoguchi's *Sansho the Bailiff*

Nothing could be further from the color and chaos of Kurosawa's *Ran* than the calm compositions of Kenji Mizoguchi's *Sansho the Bailiff*. After her husband is banished to a distant province, an aristocratic woman named Tamaki (Kinuyo Tanaka), her lone servant, and her children are forced to wander from place to place. In this image, the wife (*center right*), who cannot find shelter elsewhere, builds a structure of branches and reeds under the spreading limbs of a tree as the servant and children help her. The black-and-white composition of this image shows why Mizoguchi is revered as a master of mise-en-scène. The tree is theatrically perfect, as is the light through the upper branches of the tree, on the mother and daughter, and on the grasses at the right and left of the image. This pictorially pleasing image gives no hint of what's to come: the children are sold into slavery, and Tamaki is exiled to an island where she is forced to become a prostitute. Despite the loss of her daughter and her other hardships, Tamaki perseveres; finally, blind and alone, she is reunited with her son. Overall, the movie demonstrates Mizoguchi's interest in issues of freedom and women's place in society.

is notable for its interest in Japanese tradition, especially the samurai culture of medieval Japan, and for its spectacle, action, and sumptuous design. As John Wayne represented John Ford's idea of the ideal hero, so did Toshirô Mifune for Kurosawa, who used him in 16 of his films. In addition to *Rashomon*, there are many other masterpieces among Kurosawa's thirty films: *Ikiru* (1952), *Seven Samurai* (1954), *Throne of Blood* (1957), his version of Shakespeare's *Macbeth*, *Yojimbo* (1961), *Kagemusha* (1980), and *Ran* (1985), his stylized version

of Shakespeare's *King Lear*. In creating these works, Kurosawa was a classic auteur, involved in every phase of filmmaking.

If Kurosawa is the master of the samurai as well as contemporary social problem films, then Kenji Mizoguchi, a sublime artist, is the master of mise-en-scène, pictorial values, the long shot, and the moving camera. His stories are about place as much as anything else, and his films, no less than Kurosawa's, have had worldwide influence. Although they are much less known in the

Unique camera placement in Ozu's *Tokyo Story*

Set in postwar Japan, this unforgettable movie tells a familiar and touching story about Shukichi (Chishu Ryu, *left*) and Tomi Hirayama (Chieko Higashiyama, *middle*), two elderly parents who visit their children in Tokyo only to find that they are in the children's way. However, Noriko (Setsuko Hara, *right*), the couple's widowed daughter-in-law, who is less busy, cheerfully takes charge of entertaining them. In this image, their first meeting, the three are traditionally seated on the floor, where the low placement of Ozu's static camera (*behind and to the left of* Noriko) gives us Noriko's perspective. The image, with its deep-space composition, permits us to see the rooms behind this group. While it's a simple story, and Ozu observes it with calm detachment, its ending reminds us of the oneness of humanity and helped to make this film an international success.

***In the Realm of the Senses*: sex and violence**

When Nagisa Oshima's most provocative movie, *In the Realm of the Senses* (1976), was released, it was banned (or cut) in many parts of the world. It explores various sexual activities, including the power dynamics between a man and a woman obsessed with one another, and ends in one of the most disturbingly violent incidents in movie history. This image, a comparatively tame moment, depicts eroticism in eating, where actor Tatsuya Fuji is playfully fed a rare mushroom by his lover. The overall movie is based on a true story involving death-obsessed eroticism and is widely thought to be pornography.

United States than they deserve to be, that may be so because they were less influenced by Western filmmaking conventions than Kurosawa's were. Unlike Kurosawa, he had a flourishing career before the war. Mizoguchi's films are highly regarded for their treatment of women. Indeed, his major concerns are women's social, psychological, and economic positions (or lack of them), the differences between women and men, male-female relations, and the idea that a man can be saved by a woman's love. These themes characterize his greatest postwar movies: *The Life of Oharu* (1952), *Ugetsu* (1953), *Sansho the Bailiff* (1954), and *Street of Shame* (1956).

Of these three directors, the films of Yasujirô Ozu are considered by the international film community as the most Japanese in their modes of expression and values. Like Mizoguchi, he began his career long before World War II. His best films are concerned not with the traditional world of the samurai but with contemporary family life; indeed, the values of the lower-middle-class families who are the staple of his movies represent a microcosm of postwar society. And since most of them take place within the family home, their look is influenced by Japanese domestic customs and architecture. Because the Japanese often sit on the floor and thus make eye contact with others at that level, Ozu placed his camera similarly, pulling Western audiences immediately into a different world. His compositions are very formal, and his camera seldom moved; his editing consisted primarily of cuts rather than, say, fades or dissolves. Unlike Kurosawa, he did not seek to create Western-style continuity. Furthermore, his distinctive style included the use of offscreen space, meaning that his compositions force our eyes to consider the world outside the frame and, as a result, heighten our sense of a movie's reality. Like Kurosawa, he was an auteur, infusing his movies with a distinct style unlike any other. While that style might at first seem austere or rigid, the subject of his films is anything but. Many Western viewers find them difficult to watch and understand due to the differences in culture. Notable among his fifty-four films are *Late Spring* (1949), *Early Summer* (1951), *The Flavor of Green Tea over Rice* (1952), *Tokyo Story* (1953), *Early Spring* (1956), *Floating Weeds* (1959), and *An Autumn Afternoon* (1962).

Between the 1950s and 1970s, there arose an extreme new movement called Nubero Bagu. Also known as the Japanese New Wave, Nubero Bagu was significantly influenced by the French New Wave in its emphasis on upsetting cinematic and social conventions. Its representative directors were Hiroshi Teshigahara, Yasuzo Masumura, and Nagisa Oshima, among others, and their movies are full of brutality and nihilism. Oshima is, perhaps, the best known of the group, a provocative filmmaker whose work is often compared to that of Jean-Luc Godard. His movies include *Cruel Story of Youth* (1960), full of violent passion, *In the Realm of the Senses* (1976), a disturbing exploration of human sexuality, and *Merry Christmas, Mr. Lawrence* (1983), a film about intercultural communication in a Japanese prisoner-of-war camp that established Oshima's international reputation as a director who could also communicate across cultures.

Also well known in the United States is the work of the experimental filmmaker Nobuhiko Obayashi, who is best known for *House* (1977). This stylistically bizarre horror film demonstrates a strong familiarity with French, British, and Italian cinema of the 1960s as well as Japanese film history and silent film tradition. Although a short-lived movement, the Japanese New Wave—along with the postwar filmmakers of China—influenced the style and content of the New American Cinema (discussed on pp. 399–403).

China

After World War II, film production resumed in the People's Republic of China (often referred to as mainland China) as well as in two distinct political entities: Taiwan (the Republic of China), which asserts its independence from the People's Republic, and Hong Kong (a British colony until 1997, when it was transferred by treaty to the People's Republic). The People's Republic, a vast country with the world's largest population, is ostensibly Communist. Taiwan, an island off the southern coast of China, has a democratic government that desires independence even in the face of mainland China's threats of reunification. And Hong Kong, a small island near China's south coast, is—by terms of the treaty that reunified it with the People's Republic—a limited democracy

with considerable sovereignty compared to the other regions of China. The tripartite Chinese film industry is thus clearly affected by these circumstances of history, ideology, and geography.

The People's Republic Postwar government-subsidized filmmaking here has reflected the shifting ideological climate that developed after the 1949 Communist Revolution. Since 1976, with the death of Party Chairman Mao Zedong and Premier Zhou Enlai, filmmakers have focused less on party doctrines and become more concerned with individuals, and the Chinese film industry has become more oriented to the Western market. The most important directors are Chen Kaige, Yimou Zhang, and Tian Zhuangzhuang, each of whom has managed, within a repressive society, to make films about traditionally taboo subjects. Among their best-known movies are Chen's *Farewell My Concubine* (1993), about an extramarital love triangle; Yimou's *Raise the Red Lantern* (1991), which, among other subjects, is concerned with the struggle for women's rights; and Tian's *The Horse Thief* (1986), a brilliant study of China's ethnic minorities.

But the Chinese movies that are most popular and influential outside China—the action movies inspired by

***Farewell My Concubine*: sex and politics**
The Beijing Opera, one of China's major cultural treasures, forms the backdrop for two major contemporary Chinese movies, including Hark Tsui's *Peking Opera Blues* (1986). Chen Kaige's *Farewell My Concubine* (1993) tells the lengthy, complicated story of two of the opera's male actors, whose happiness together onstage and off is threatened by a prostitute. The turbulence of this personal story is mirrored by the political upheavals of the period from the 1920s to Mao's Cultural Revolution. The movie was banned in China not because of its treatment of politics, but because of its homosexual subject matter. The Beijing Opera is known for its lavish productions, exotic costumes, and stylized makeup as well as for its ancient tradition of using males to play the female roles.

various martial arts—are produced in Hong Kong and, to a lesser extent, Taiwan. Director Jia Zhangke found a way to build on this subject, taking the style of the classic martial arts movie (*wuxia*) and applying it to a study of one of the social problems growing out of the country's transformation into a global economic power: the growth of rebellious one-on-one violence. Even in a society that strictly censors its movies, he was able to speak out, perhaps because the problem was making newspaper headlines and thus was widely familiar. In *A Touch of Sin* (2013), his sixth feature, he recounts stories of four ordinary Chinese, one of them a furious mine worker, who under extreme circumstances goes on a shooting rampage against his boss. It's as bloody as it can get, and a departure from the director's previous work, but a signal that Chinese cinema may be opening up.

Hong Kong The Hong Kong martial-arts action movies stem from a venerable tradition in Chinese film history that, from the 1920s to the 1970s, shifted between two basic styles: wuxia (or wushu) and kung fu. Both of them combine, to varying degrees, these disparate elements: an intricate, sometimes incomprehensible, melodramatic plot; philosophical codes of honor based on mystical beliefs; spectacular violence; brilliantly choreographed fight sequences; the conflict between cops and gangsters; speeding vehicles; and lavish production values. Their formal characteristics include spectacular studio settings and natural locations, saturated colors, moody lighting, constant motion (slow and fast), disjointed editing techniques, and extensive computer manipulation of images and motion.

Between the late 1970s and early 1980s, a New Wave of Hong Kong cinema emerged in the work of such directors as Ann Hui, Yim Ho, Hark Tsui, Allen Fong, Patrick Tam, Clifford Choi, Dennis Yu, and others. Although many of these artists were trained in U.S. or U.K. film schools, they made movies that dealt with local experiences in a distinctly individual style. Remarkably, they worked in both mainstream cinema and television. This movement also stimulated change in the film industries of the People's Republic and Taiwan. Important early titles are Yim Ho's *The Extras* (1978), Ann Hui's *Vietnam Trilogy* (1980–81), Hark Tsui's *The Butterfly Murders* (1979), Patrick Tam's *A Spectrum of Multiple Stars: Wang Chuanru* [*sic*] (1975), Alex Cheung's *The First Step: Facing Death* (1977), and Allen Fong's *Father and Son* (1981).

Bands of bloody brothers

A Better Tomorrow (1986), directed by John Woo, is considered a classic example of Hong Kong cinema: violent action depicted in brilliantly choreographed scenes. The image here, from the movie's spectacular conclusion, exemplifies Woo's style: bright colors, gymnastic feats, dozens of blazing guns, exploding firestorms, blood galore, overwrought male bonding, and a certain sly humor that suggests a surreal world. Woo was influenced by such action directors as Sergio Leone and Sam Peckinpah (see *The Wild Bunch*, p. 402) and in turn had wide influence on both Chinese and American directors, including Quentin Tarantino, Robert Rodriguez, and the Wachowskis.

During this time, the film culture in Hong Kong expanded to include popular film clubs and academic programs in film studies and filmmaking. However, the strong personal style of the New Wave movies clashed with the prevailing commercial nature of the island's cinema; by 1985, the New Wave spirit had become diluted, and the movement was absorbed into the mainstream cinema. Important titles from this period include Hark Tsui's *Peking Opera Blues* (1986), Allen Fong's *Just Like Weather* (1986), Ringo Lam's *City on Fire* (1987), John Woo's *A Better Tomorrow* (1986), and Kar-Wai Wong's *Ashes of Time* (1994). Superstar performers like Bruce Lee, Jackie Chan (also a writer and director), Yun-Fat Chow, and Jet Li were an equally vital component of the success of these movies, one reason that they all went to Hollywood. Hong Kong directors who have worked in Hollywood include John Woo and Sammo Hung.

While the Hong Kong New Wave was short-lived, it stimulated cinematic innovations throughout China, encouraged the movement of directors between television and mainstream cinema, introduced new genres, and tackled formerly taboo subjects. The influence between Hong Kong and Hollywood has gone both ways. The Chinese have learned from such action directors as Sam Peckinpah and Sergio Leone and then influenced

Flying warriors in _Crouching Tiger, Hidden Dragon_

The films of Taiwan-born Ang Lee are known for their diversity (comedies, melodramas, traditional Chinese martial action), their ability to provoke discussion (e.g., _Brokeback Mountain_ [2005]), and their almost universal acclaim. _Crouching Tiger, Hidden Dragon_ (2000) has it all: a traditional intrigue-filled story about a legendary sword, magnificent exterior and interior settings, beautiful costumes, a love story, and astonishing swordplay. It is a fantastic feat of movie magic, distinguished by the exquisite choreography and special effects that give the illusion of its principal characters in flight. In this image, two female principals, Jade Fox (Cheng Pei-pei) and Jen (Zhang Ziyi), engage in a deadly battle.

such Hollywood directors as Quentin Tarantino (_Reservoir Dogs_, 1992, and the Kill Bill movies, 2003–4), Robert Rodriguez (_Desperado_, 1995), Sam Raimi (_A Simple Plan_, 1998), the Wachowskis (The Matrix trilogy, 1999–2003), Brett Ratner (the Rush Hour films, 1998–2007), and Rob Minkoff (_The Forbidden Kingdom,_ 2008). Action choreographer Yuen Woo-ping played a major role in many of these movies.

Taiwan By following European models, particularly the Italian Neorealism movement, postwar Taiwanese cinema developed independently of Hong Kong and the People's Republic. In contrast to the action movies of earlier decades, it was concerned with realistic depictions of ordinary people. Excellent examples are Hsiao-hsien Hou's _A City of Sadness_ (1989) and _Flight of the Red Balloon_ (2007), Edward Yang's _Taipei Story_ (1985), Tsai Ming-liang's _Vive l'amour_ (1994), and Stan Lai's _The Peach Blossom Land_ (1992). The first films of Ang Lee, the most familiar Taiwanese director—_The Wedding Banquet_ (1993) and _Eat Drink Man Woman_ (1994)—were so successful in the West that Lee went to Hollywood, where he showed an affinity for Western lit-

erature and themes and made, among other films, _Sense and Sensibility_ (1995), _The Ice Storm_ (1997), _Brokeback Mountain_ (2005), and _Lust, Caution_ (2007). In between, he returned to Taiwan to make _Crouching Tiger, Hidden Dragon_ (2000), a spectacularly beautiful martial-arts action movie in the venerable Chinese tradition.

Postwar Chinese filmmaking was too diverse, aesthetically and politically, to represent a unified movement such as the French New Wave, but its movies—particularly the Hong Kong action movies—have spoken in a distinct visual language across cultural and linguistic barriers and have had a dynamic effect on filmmaking worldwide, especially in the United States.

India

Despite the worldwide success of _Slumdog Millionaire_ (2008), an Anglo-Indian production, and the fact that the Indian film industry—producing more than 1,200 feature movies and an even larger number of documentaries every year—is the world's largest, Indian films are little known in the United States except in cities with a large Indian population. Indeed, India ranks first in annual film production, followed by Hollywood and China.

India, a vast country with some sixteen official languages, has a regional cinema that speaks to its many different audiences in social, political, cinematic, and linguistic terms it can understand. Thus a social protest film made in Chennai, in the South, might never be seen by those who live in Mumbai. These audiences not only speak a different dialect but seemingly prefer the lavish musicals made by Bollywood, as the Mumbai film industry is known. When Indian films are screened theatrically in the United States, the audiences are typically Indians, who understand the culture in which the movie was made and the language spoken in it. For others who want to learn more about this vast, diverse body of filmmaking, there are annual Indian (and South Asian) film festivals in such U.S. cities as New York, Boston, Chicago, and San Francisco. In these settings, the films are likely to be dubbed into English or have English subtitles.

The one exception to this description is director Satyajit Ray, the dominating figure in Indian cinema as it is known in the West. He was always unique among Indian filmmakers and, to the moviegoing public in the West, the only Indian director whose name they recognize. In that respect, he very much resembles Akira Kurosawa; both were instinctive filmmakers who made powerful and personal films with recurring themes. Ray and Kurosawa, two of the most individually unique filmmakers the world has ever produced, greatly admired each other's work. Of Ray, Kurosawa said, "Not to have seen the cinema of Ray means existing in the world without seeing the Sun or the Moon."

Ray was a Bengali, born in the Indian state of West Bengal, the capital of which is Kolkata (Calcutta). The principal influences on his cinematic style come from the literature and art of Bengali culture as well as from four great filmmakers: Vittorio De Sica, Akira Kurosawa, Jean Renoir, and John Ford. This helps to explain why his films are very Indian in content but the least Indian in their cinematic form.

Ray's most formative influence was Italian Neorealism, *The Bicycle Thieves* (1949) in particular. It convinced him to make a film about everyday Indian life exactly as De Sica had made his; the characteristics of this approach are discussed earlier in this chapter. The result was not one but three films, a trilogy known as the Apu trilogy for the name of its central character: *Pather Panchali* (*Song of the Little Road*, 1955), *Aparajito* (*The Unvanquished*,

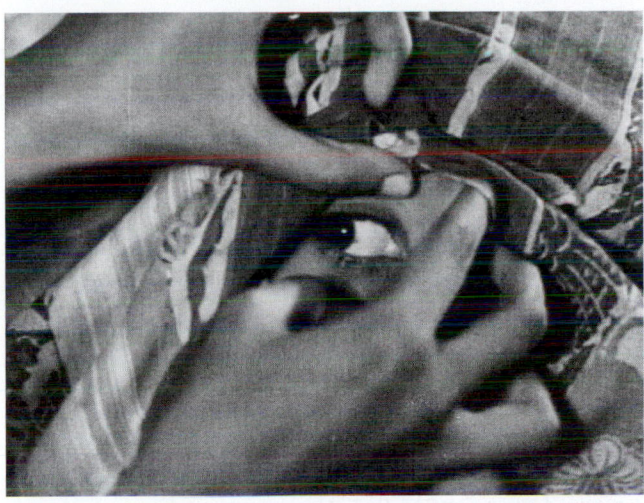

The eye as symbol of consciousness in *Pather Panchali*

Director Satyajit Ray is known for his attention to detail in the lives of ordinary people and for the subtle, detached angle at which he views them in his movies. His Apu trilogy, of which *Pather Panchali* is the first, recounts a series of small but significant episodes in the life of Apu, who lives with his impoverished family in a Bengali village. The trilogy spans the years from his childhood through his early twenties, but here he is a boy of six or seven. Near the beginning of the movie, Apu's sister Durga tries to awaken him so that he can get ready for school. She shakes him, but he does not budge. But then, poking her fingers through a hole in his blanket, she tenderly pries open a closed eye. We would be wrong to think that Ray will henceforth see things from Apu's point of view, for we are seeing the opening of Apu's consciousness of the world around him. He is a curious boy, delighted by everything he sees and hears—traveling entertainers, a freight train, a pond—and he also learns about life and death when realizing that his father is incapable of supporting the family and by witnessing the death of his aged aunt. Careful, connected observation characterizes both Apu and his creator.

1956), and *Apar Sansar* (*The World of Apu*, 1959). As a chronicle of a family, and in particular Apu's growth from a boy to a man, they are unparalleled in their humanistic insight and wonder at the natural world. (Note: Both Indian and English titles are given because they are cited in variant ways.) For these reasons, as well as for their cinematography and acting, the three films were recognized worldwide as landmarks of modern cinema. Ray, a true auteur, wrote, produced, and directed all three; he even scored the music.

In all, Ray made some thirty-four films, most of which were successful both in India and worldwide. Besides the Apu trilogy, his films include *Jalsaghar* (*The Music Room*, 1958), *Devi* (*The Goddess*, 1960), *Charulata* (*The*

Lonely Wife, 1964), *Shatranj-ke-Khilari* (*The Chess Players*, 1977), *Ghare-Baire* (*The Home and the World*, 1984), and *Agantuk* (*The Stranger*, 1992).

Ray's work represented the beginnings of a "new Indian cinema," or Parallel Cinema, meaning that it exists alongside the mainstream commercial industry. Leading this movement were Ritwik Ghatak and Mrinal Sen—like Ray, Bengalis; but unlike Ray, Marxists. Western audiences are familiar with the work of these directors, primarily because of their political views. Ghatak, in particular, influenced several young Marxist directors. Ghatak's most distinctive works are *Ajantrik* (*Pathetic Fallacy*, 1958) and *Jukti Takko Aar Gappo* (*Reason, Debate and Story*, 1974). Sen, the most prolific and experimental of the two, is best known for *Bhuvan Shome* (*Mr. Shome*, 1969), *Parasuram* (*Man with the Axe*, 1978), *Kharji* (*The Case Is Closed*, 1982), *Khandaar* (*The Ruins*, 1983), and *Antareen* (*The Confined*, 1993). Shyam Benegal's reputation as the most commercially successful director in the Parallel Cinema is largely due to his quartet of socially conscious films: *Ankur* (*The Seedling*, 1973), *Nishant* (*Night's End*, 1975), *Manthan* (*The Churning*, 1976), and *Bhumika* (*The Role*, 1977). He created a large body of documentaries, including two biographies: *Satyajit Ray, Filmmaker* (1985) and *Nehru* (1985).

The twenty regional cinemas of India—separate industries in virtually every major state that make movies in their own language—are marked by a vibrant diversity of aesthetic styles and political commitments. In the 1980s, for example, there was a resurgence of the Malayalam cinema of the state of Kerala, including films that appealed to an international audience, particularly Shaji N. Karun's *Piravi* (1989) and Rajiv Anchal's *Guru* (1997). Similar commercial success, both inside and outside India, has been made by some Tamil and Oriya films as well as by such commercial Hindi directors as Mira Nair, Nagesh Kukunoor, Nandita Das, and Sudhir Mishra. Bollywood has developed a new genre called Mumbai noir, urban films by such directors as Anurag Kashyap (*Black Friday*, 2004) and Deva Katta (*Prasthanam*, 2010). Finally, with such films as Homi Adajania's *Being Cyrus* (2005) and Sooni Taraporevala's *Little Zizou* (2009), the English-language cinema continues to be a part of India's multilanguage film industry. Indeed, Kashyap's two-part *Gangs of Wasseypur* (2010), a crime thriller about the Indian mafias' control of the coal industry, is, with its bold and murderous plot, the "Godfather" of the country's movies.

Contemporary Middle Eastern and North African Cinema

From its beginnings, cinema has been a part of the culture of many Middle Eastern and North African countries. But recent widespread civil unrest, revolution, and repression in these countries have had a negative impact on artistic freedom. This, as well as heavy restrictions and censorship by the governments of some of these countries—especially Iran—has not stopped the creation of serious movies, a large number of which were directed by women. Western films are often banned in these countries, leaving room for the development of a cinema rich in social, cultural, and political themes.

For the countries of Algeria, Egypt, Iraq, Iran, Israel, Lebanon, and Palestine, we have compiled a short list of contemporary films to introduce you to the work of directors who have earned a place in world cinema. Other Middle Eastern and North African countries—Bahrain, Jordan, Kuwait, Libya, Morocco, Oman, Saudi Arabia, Somalia, Sudan, Syria, Tunisia, Western Sahara, and Yemen—produce a comparatively smaller output of films that, in turn, are less well known in the West. Many excellent books are available to help you learn more about the films of all these countries.

Algeria *Days of Glory* (2006; director Rachid Bouchareb), *Masquerades* (2008; director Lyès Salem), and *Outside the Law* (2010; director Rachid Bouchareb).

Egypt *Sleepless Nights* (2003; director Hani Khalifa), *The Yacoubian Building* (2006; director Marwan Hamed), *Scheherazade, Tell Me a Story* (2009; director Yousry Nasrallah), *Asmaa* (2011; director Amr Salama), and *Yomeddine* (2018, director Abu Bakr Shawky).

Iraq *Muhammad and Jane* (2003; director Usama Alshaibi), *Jani Gal* (2007; director Jamil Rostami), and *Son of Babylon* (2009; director Mohamed Al Daradji).

Iran *Offside* (2006; director Jafar Panahi), *Persepolis* (2007; directors Vincent Paronnaud and Marjane Satrapi), *Women without Men* (2009; directors Shirin Neshat and Shoja Azari), *Circumstance* (2011; director Maryam Keshavarz), *A Separation* (2011; director Asghar Farhadi), *Like Someone in Love* (2012; director Abbas Kiarostami), *This Is Not a Film* (2012; directors Jafar Panahi and Mojtaba Mirtahmasb), and *The Salesman* (2016; director Asghar Farhadi). Mania Akbari, an Iranian filmmaker, has been self-exiled in London since 2012, when the Iranian government severely tightened the restrictions on artists. Her distinctive, feminist view of Iranian society in movies where women's and family's issues are inextricably linked include *10 + 4* (2007), a sort of sequel to Abbas Kiarostami's *Ten* (2002), in which she starred; *One. Two. One* (2011); *In My Country Men Have Breasts* (2012); and *I Slept with My Mother, My Father, My Brother and My Sister in a Country Called Iran* (2012).

Israel *Meduzot* (2007; directors Shira Geffen and Etgar Keret), *The Band's Visit* (2001; director Eran Kolirin), *Footnote* (2011; director Joseph Cedar), and *Foxtrot* (2017, director Samuel Maoz).

Lebanon *Stray Bullet* (2010; director Georges Hachem), *Where Do We Go Now?* (2011; director Nadine Labaki), and *A Play Entitled Sehnsucht* (2011; director Roy Badran).

Palestine *Chronicle of a Disappearance* (1996; director Elia Suleiman), *A Ticket to Jerusalem* (2002; director Rashid Masharawi), and *Slingshot Hip Hop* (2008; director Jackie Reem Salloum).

Latin American Filmmaking

Many countries in Latin America—primarily Argentina, Brazil, Cuba, and Mexico—have produced movies since the silent era, when traveling exhibitions of work by the Lumière brothers and others captivated audiences there as elsewhere around the world. Today cinema is vibrant in those countries as well as in Chile, Costa Rica, Peru, and Venezuela. Historically, their subject matter was largely political and largely controlled by dictators and religious groups. But since the 1960s, directors have been able to turn to more personal stories concerning ordinary life and such previously taboo subjects as sex and sexual identity. While the sociopolitical foundations of these movies make them more influential within Latin America than in other countries, they are successful with audiences in theaters and at international festivals. We'll take a brief look at filmmaking in the four countries first mentioned.

Argentina A historical pattern emerges in Argentina that is applicable to filmmaking in almost every Latin American country: a pre-sound era consisting of experiments with cinematic technique and subject matter, fol-

lowed by a golden age of popular filmmaking that lapses into the state-funded production of sociopolitical films. In Argentina, that's not saying much in aesthetic terms, because the two major influences on the industry were the Catholic Church and the dictator Juan Perón and his wife Evita. The Argentine film industry made conventional crime dramas, comedies, and adaptations of literary classics, all still under the watchful eye of the church and state. The turmoil of the Perón years yielded little of cinematic quality, and the international community did not begin to pay attention until *The Hour of the Furnaces* (1968), a film by Octavio Getino and Fernando Solanas about the country's struggle for freedom from neocolonialism and violence. Along with Patricio Guzmán's *The Battle of Chile* (1975–79), Getino's movie established a template for future radical, revolutionary filmmaking across Latin America. Leopoldo Torre Nilsson's *The Revolution of the Seven Madmen* (1973) was also highly regarded by foreign audiences.

A tentative "New Cinema" was born in the 1960s and 1970s. After democracy was established in 1983, Argentine filmmakers began making serious movies about the country's turbulent past, including Jeanine Meerapfel's *The Friend* (1988), to name but one. Today, the movies in Argentina tackle a broader range of subjects—family dramas, love stories, and crime dramas. *The Secret in Their Eyes* (2009; director Juan José Campanella) won the Oscar for Best Foreign Language Film.

Brazil Here, the cinema developed to the point where its most unique actress, Carmen Miranda, appeared in Hollywood movies to great acclaim. Its success continued into the 1960s, when *Cinema Novo* ("New Cinema") was born in the spirit of Italian Neorealism and the French New Wave. The movement was deeply influenced by the political and aesthetic theories of director Glauber Rocha, whose most important movie is *Black God, White Devil* (1964). Its advocates included directors such as Carlos Diegues (*Bye Bye Brazil*, 1979) and Nelson Pereira dos Santos (*Memoirs of Prison*, 1984). Production of documentaries and experimental films flourished, as did the importance of female directors such as Carla Camurati, whose *Carlota Joaquina, Princess of Brazil* (1995), an offbeat look at Brazilian history, was a great success there and abroad.

Through the years, Brazilian cinema has been largely state supported, which accounts for its somewhat uneven history. When there's money, there are films, many of them good; but when the money dries up, so does creativity. Nonetheless, Brazilian cinema has gained international recognition as well as an Oscar nomination for Best Foreign Language Film for *The Given Word* (1962; director Anselmo Duarte). In the years when state funding dried up, independent filmmakers tackled such problems as poverty and hunger—never very popular with the masses. When the support returned, it encouraged entrepreneurial filmmakers to produce movies with questionable value and importance to the country's film history. Today there is a revival of serious filmmaking, as seen in such works as *City of God* (2002; codirectors Fernando Meirelles and Kátia Lund) and Fernando Coimbra's *The Wolf at the Door* (2013).

Cuba Although the Cuban cinema was a significant industry, producing its own movies but relying heavily on Hollywood imports, it changed profoundly with the 1959 revolution led by Fidel Castro. Consistent with its Marxist principles—and adhering to Lenin's familiar remark, "cinema, for us, is the most important of the arts"—the Cuban government, in one of its first moves, established the Cuban Institute for Cinematographic Art and Industry (ICAIC) to encourage, improve, and support filmmaking at all levels.

Alfred Guevera, the father of modern Cuban cinema, headed the organization until 1980, when ideological differences between the Castro government and the ICAIC forced his ouster. (He returned later in a lesser capacity.) State funding has its price, and Cuban cinema suffered until it was revitalized by a movement known ironically as Imperfect Cinema. This experimental effort affected all aspects of Cuban filmmaking as long as it valued ideological content over aesthetic form. The party line remained dominant. But the movement's films were colorful, provocative, and very popular with the Cuban people, particularly those who supported the revolution and remained in the country. The movement died out in the mid-1970s. The end of this effort, coupled with the government's sharp reduction of production subsidies, had a negative effect on both the levels and quality of the Cuban cinema. It has been revitalized somewhat by international coproductions, especially with Mexico and Spain.

The 1959 revolution created a vast diaspora of disaffected Cubans (including many filmmakers) who emigrated to the United States and Latin American countries. There, they were free to make films critical of the Castro regime, and while these efforts did not have much impact in Cuba, some are well-known worldwide. These movies include Orlando Jiménez Leal's *The Other Cuba* (1983), *Amigos* (1986; director Iván Acosta), *Lejanía* (1985; director Jesús Diaz), and *Honey for Oshún* (2001; director Humberto Solás). Leal's *Improper Conduct* (1984; codirected by Néstor Almendros, one of the world's great cinematographers) focuses on the regime's imprisonment and mistreatment of dissidents and undesirables, particularly homosexuals. Other films on the plight of LGBT Cubans include *Strawberry and Chocolate* (1993; directors Tomás Gutiérrez Alea and Juan Carlos Tabío), which was nominated for an Oscar as Best Foreign Language Film. It's important to note that many talented Cuban exiles—writers, directors, cinematographers, and actors—have remained away from Cuba and enriched the international film world.

Other notable Cuban films—again more popular outside and than inside the country—are Tomás Gutiérrez Alea's *Memories of Underdevelopment* (1968), a brilliant film about a man who remains in Cuba rather than follow his family and friends into exile; Humberto Solás's *Lucía* (1969); and Miguel Coyula's *Memories of Overdevelopment* (2010). This movie, playing on Alea's film, concerns a man who leaves underdeveloped Cuba only to be confronted by the challenges in an overdeveloped United States.

Mexico Like other Latin American countries, Mexico had an early cinema as well as a golden age. It was dominated by film stars, such as Cantinflas and Dolores del Rio, who were also popular in the United States, and was brought to the world's attention when the great Russian director Sergei Eisenstein began to make *Que Viva Mexico* there in 1931. He attempted an epic account of Mexico's history, but for various reasons it remained unfinished. Equally important, this film left a large Marxist influence on subsequent Mexican cinema. The country's films dominated the Latin American market during the 1940s, bringing attention to the early work of directors Emilio Fernández and Luis Buñuel, but this presence weakened in the 1960s and 1970s. Mexican directors had not yet found a voice for their national cinema, and audiences were distracted by popular American movies. But as we have seen, there was a fresh burst of innovative filmmaking after World War II in countries across the globe. In Mexico, the New Mexican Cinema was founded with the help of government support.

The success of this movement is seen in Arturo Ripstein's *No One Writes to the Colonel* (1999), based on a novel by Gabriel García Márquez; Alfonso Arau's *Like Water for Chocolate* (1992); Alfonso Cuarón's *Y Tu Mamá También* (2001); Guillermo del Toro's *The Devil's Backbone* (2001) and *Pan's Labyrinth* (2006); and Alejandro González Iñárritu's *Amores Perros* (2000), which not only introduced the popular actor Gael García Bernal but was also nominated for an Oscar as Best Foreign Language Film. Iñárritu was nominated as Best Director for *Babel* (2005) and is the first Mexican director to be in the running for that award. In 2015, his *Birdman,* or (*The Unexpected Virtue of Ignorance*), won nine Oscars, including Best Director and Best Picture. Iñárritu, Cuarón, and del Toro have moved easily into the international filmmaking world. They have won major awards—as did Luis Buñuel, who worked primarily in Spain and France and was notable for his biting surrealist comedies such as *The Discreet Charm of the Bourgeoisie* (1972).

Gabriel Figueroa, a cinematographer, was another prominent Mexican film artist to achieve international fame. A superb artist, he shot dozens of important movies, including Emilio Fernández's *La Perla* (1947), Buñuel's *Los Olvidados* (1950) and *Simon of the Desert* (1965), and John Huston's *The Night of the Iguana* (1964) and *Under the Volcano* (1984). Many other Mexican film artists have also worked in Hollywood: they include cinematographers Rodrigo Prieto and Emmanuel Lubezki (who shot *Gravity* and several Terrence Malick movies), and actors Selma Hayek, Anthony Quinn, and Katy Jurado, among many others. Today Mexico continues to produce important movies with a social consciousness, including José Luis Valle's *Workers* (2013) and Amat Escalante's *Heli* (2013).

Finally, let's look briefly at films from other Latin American countries—Bolivia, Chile, Colombia, Haiti, Paraguay, and Peru. Widely varied in type and quality, these movies have achieved regional success and are beginning to be noticed worldwide. Many are concerned with local political issues, others with entertainment. A movie that is concerned with both is *Gloria* (2013; director Sebastián Lelio), about a middle-aged divorcée looking for some stability and love in a large Chilean city. Paulina Garcia plays the lead, who—even though she is attractive, has a good job, and is very independent—is eager to meet a man she can trust. The man who wins her heart turns out to be a rat—a lying, henpecked married man looking for some excitement. She bounces back from his deceit, though not without damage, and once more heads for the bar. We see her there, dancing to the Rolling Stones version of Van Morrison's "Gloria," sung in Italian by Umberto Tozzi. Just when you might begin to feel sorry for her, she changes the ball game. We can't make any assumptions about this mysterious, enigmatic person. And the actress is a marvel to watch.

The globalization of economies means the globalization of industries such as filmmaking. One result of this change is that great directors have influence both inside and outside their countries. They are truly international directors, and the list of those working today includes, among others, Bernardo Bertolucci (Italy), Nuri Bilge Ceylan (Turkey), Park Chan-wook (South Korea), Alfonso Cuarón (Mexico), Jean-Luc Godard (France), Michael Haneke (Germany), Roman Polanski (Poland, France), Steven Spielberg (USA), Quentin Tarantino (USA), and Béla Tarr (Hungary).

1965–1995: The New American Cinema

Twenty years after the end of World War II, the United States began to face political, cultural, and social challenges that were unprecedented in its history. It was now the most powerful and influential country in the world, yet it was locked with the Soviet Union in a "Cold War." The next 40 years would be marked by anti-Communist vehemence; the Korean War; the beginnings of the feminist, gay/lesbian/transgender, and environmental movements; the Vietnam War; and resolute antiwar and civil rights movements. There was also an unusually high level of violence, including the assassinations of President John F. Kennedy in 1963 and Senator Robert F. Kennedy and Dr. Martin Luther King, Jr., in 1968; the killing of four Kent State University students, who were protesting the Vietnam War, by the Ohio National Guard in 1970; assassination attempts on Presidents Gerald Ford and Ronald Reagan and Pope John Paul II; and terrorist attacks on the World Trade Center in 1993 and an Oklahoma City courthouse in 1995. Other major events included the U.S. landing on the Moon, the beginnings of a vibrant popular music culture, the Watergate crisis, and the resignation in disgrace in 1974 of President Richard M. Nixon. The 1980s saw the emergence of the AIDS virus, and in 1991 the Soviet Union collapsed.

Against such a fast-moving, turbulent background, it is not surprising that a New American Cinema emerged. The "new" Hollywood encompasses too many transitions from the "old" Hollywood to be simply called a movement. In describing the changes that affected the American film industry—and the resulting ripples that spread throughout the international film community— the term *phenomenon* is both more accurate and appropriate. These changes were hastened by the collapse of the old studio system, which was replaced by scattered enterprises known as "independent filmmakers." This event had both negative and positive implications.

The negative factors included declining audiences, caused in part by competition from television; the escalating costs of producing films independently rather than in the studios, where the permanent physical and human support structure was very cost-effective; and the forced retirement or relocation of studio personnel. However, these were outweighed by the positive factors. The new Hollywood adapted conventions of classical genres to conform to new modes of expression and meet audience expectations, abandoned the code for a new rating system, and did more shooting on location; the result was a more authentic look for the movies.

Furthermore, though the studios retained their names and kept their production facilities open to ensure the smoothness of the established preproduction/production/postproduction matrix, they have changed ownership frequently over the years. Movies are now made in complex deals involving the studios and independent production companies headed by individual producers, many of whom invested capital in their own work. The "star machine" collapsed as well, ushering in decades of new talent whose careers, which once would have been meticulously planned and monitored, were now subject to market forces. Marketing of movies remained a precise tool, carefully adapted to meet the needs of new audiences.

A positive effect of this transition was the increase in audience members who, because of college film-study classes and an overall greater awareness of film, had a better understanding of cinematic conventions than their parents and were attracted to films by a new breed of American directors, also trained in university film schools. With the old labor-dominated system gone,

***Stranger Than Paradise*: a milestone in the New American Cinema**

Jim Jarmusch's *Stranger Than Paradise* (1984) did more than any other movie to define the New American Cinema. It tells a distinctly American story; it was made in a fresh, easy style clearly influenced by American movies as well as the new waves in European and Asian cinema; and it was produced by a film-school graduate using funds from various sources, both American and foreign. Although unusual in production, form, and content, this art film was surprisingly successful at the box office. It is a distinctly marginal effort, but in winning the Cannes Film Festival prize for best first feature, it encouraged independent filmmakers and the reception of their work. *Stranger Than Paradise* was shot in a series of long takes, which are structured into three stages of a journey undertaken by three offbeat travelers. They are Willie (John Lurie), a hipster living in New York City; his cousin Eva (Eszter Balint), who comes from Hungary to visit him and their aunt in Ohio; and Willie's friend Eddie (Richard Edson). Eva's visit to New York is the first stage; the second, which takes place a year later, recounts a trip that Willie and Eddie make to Cleveland to visit Eva and the aunt; and the third stage follows them to the "paradise" of Florida. Their travels through the bleak landscape, shot in washed-out black and white, ultimately show that they are going nowhere, but they have a good time, and so do we. Here, we see the trio in Florida—(*left to right*) Eddie, Eva, and Willie—putting on their new sunglasses so they can look like "real tourists."

producers could hire artists from anywhere in the world, and American production was greatly enhanced by their contributions. Finally, to seal the death of the "old" Hollywood, New York and other cities in the United States and Canada emerged as thriving centers of film production.

Unlike the French New Wave, the New American Cinema was not born in theory but rather out of the more practical need to adapt to the values of its time. However, like the French New Wave, the prevailing spirit was innovation. But with so many auteurs, some from the old Hollywood and some from film schools, no single defining style emerged. Indeed, there was a range of styles, resulting in personal, highly self-reflexive films; edgy, experimental, low-budget movies; movies that paid homage to great European directors; and, of course, those that still adhered to the conventions of the golden age. Thus diversity and quality are the only links among such directors as Woody Allen, Robert Altman, Tim Burton, John Cassavetes, Joel and Ethan Coen, Francis Ford Coppola, Brian De Palma, Clint Eastwood, George Roy Hill, Jim Jarmusch, Diane Keaton, Stanley Kubrick, Spike Lee, Sidney Lumet, David Lynch, Terrence Malick, Gordon Parks, Sam Peckinpah, Roman Polanski, John Sayles, Paul Schrader, Martin Scorsese, Steven Spielberg, and Gus Van Sant. Typical of Hollywood, males outnumber females. But that ratio is changing. In a reversal of the Hollywood tradition, female as well as African American, Hispanic, and Asian directors have begun to write and direct movies.

Their guiding principle was not to discard cinematic conventions, but adapt them to the new audience. In terms of content, the most noticeable changes were in the predominance of sex and violence and in the nature of the protagonists, both male and female. To quote film historians Bruce F. Mast and Gerald Kawin, "In most cases, the protagonists . . . were social misfits, deviates, or outlaws; the villains were the legal, respectable defenders of society. The old bad guys became the good guys; the old good guys, the bad guys."[17] In a further twist of traditional gender roles, the female protagonists in two of the most distinctive movies of the period, Arthur Penn's *Bonnie and Clyde* (1967) and Roman Polanski's *Chinatown* (1974)—both insightful analyses of America in the 1930s—were as evil as the men, if not more so. Although sex and violence still dominate U.S. movies, there is a large, appreciative audience for films that tackle the other serious issues that once were mainly the province of foreign movies that played only in small "art houses."

Regarding form, the strongest influences were such contemporary directors as Ingmar Bergman, Michelangelo Antonioni, Orson Welles, Jean-Luc Godard, and François Truffaut. Plots became more complex in structure and embodied new storytelling techniques. For example, Penn's *Bonnie and Clyde* (1967) tells the story of

Femmes fatales in the New American Cinema

Faye Dunaway stars in two of the most important movies of the New American Cinema: Arthur Penn's *Bonnie and Clyde* (1967) and Roman Polanski's *Chinatown* (1974). As Bonnie Parker [1], she participates fully in a bank robbery with two other members of the fearless, violent Barrow gang: (*left to right*) Buck Barrow (Gene Hackman) and Clyde Barrow (Warren Beatty). In *Chinatown*, she plays Evelyn Mulwray [2], the neurotic, scheming liar who tries to outwit J. J. Gittes (Jack Nicholson, *pictured left*). In both cases, thanks in part to the rising feminist movement, these characters are at least the equals of their male counterparts. But Dunaway is also beautiful and seductive, preserving the role of the classic film noir femme fatale.

two notorious bank robbers that could have been taken from a 1930s Hollywood model. The audience easily read it as a comic/tragic parable of violent, amoral dissent against an authoritarian social order. Its style reflects not only the director's experience as a Hollywood veteran but also the dynamic of Eisenstein's montage and the surprise of Kurosawa's slow-motion violence.

Stories became palpably more sexual and violent in such movies as Penn's *Bonnie and Clyde* (1967), Dennis Hopper's *Easy Rider* (1969), Peter Bogdanovich's *The*

17. Mast and Kawin, *A Short History of the Movies*, 11th ed., p. 517.

The Wild Bunch: blood bath and beyond[18]

The New American Cinema ushered in a wave of movies as famous for good stories and superb filmmaking as they were for sex and violence. Director Sam Peckinpah, nicknamed "Bloody Sam," is noted for a string of graphically violent movies, including *The Wild Bunch* (1969), *Straw Dogs* (1971), and *Bring Me the Head of Alfredo Garcia* (1974). His brand of stylized violence reflects the influence of Arthur Penn's *Bonnie and Clyde* (1967) and in turn influenced many Hong Kong action movies as well as a host of American directors whose films include violent action—Martin Scorsese, Brian De Palma, and Francis Ford Coppola. At the conclusion of *The Wild Bunch*, the American gang of the title attempts to claim one of its men from Mapache, a Mexican rebel leader; when Mapache kills the man, he provokes one of the bloodiest battles in movie history. In an impressively choreographed gunfight between the rebel army and the gang members, most of the characters are killed, including the gang's leader, Pike (William Holden). While manning a vicious machine gun, Pike is struck by a bullet fired by a boy and dies in blood-drenched action.

Last Picture Show (1969), Sam Peckinpah's *The Wild Bunch* (1969), Bob Rafelson's *Five Easy Pieces* (1970), and Terrence Malick's *Badlands* (1973). Continuity editing remained the norm, but there was an increased use of such techniques as jump cuts, split screens, slow and fast motion, simulated "grainy" documentary footage, and a mixture of color and black-and-white footage. Stanley Kubrick's *2001: A Space Odyssey* (1968) used very long takes and an absence of editing that calls attention to itself to introduce us to outer space, where time shifts in unfamiliar ways.

Cinematography also adapted as more films were shot on location rather than on soundstages, and the old Hollywood ideal of visual perfection gave way to a depiction of recognizable actuality. A new generation of cinematographers—including Néstor Almendros, John Alonzo, Conrad Hall, Geoffrey Unsworth, Haskell Wexler, Gordon Willis, and Vilmos Zsigmond, to name but a few—brought a familiarity with European techniques in framing, lighting, camera movement, shot duration, and, especially, an experimental approach to color. Under the particular influence of such directors as Coppola and Lucas, there was also major experimentation with sound design, multichannel sound recording and reproduction, including the Dolby Digital system. Orchestral-type scores gave way to popular music, whose sounds and lyrics often more directly underscore a movie's action. Finally, for actors there was a seismic shift from the stables of highly groomed stars of the studio system to a large influx of new actors and a definite reliance on naturalistic acting styles.

In addition to these new directions in the narrative film, important advances took place in documentary film—notably in direct cinema, essentially an American adaptation of *cinéma vérité* (by such filmmakers as Robert Drew, Albert and David Maysles, and

18. "Blood Bath and Beyond" is the title of A. O. Scott's review in the *New York Times* of Quentin Tarantino's *Kill Bill: Vol. 1* (October 10, 2003).

1

2

Documentary and experimental films as pure cinema

Both Albert and David Maysles's *Grey Gardens* (1975) [1] and Stan Brakhage's *Dog Star Man* (1962–64) [2] stand out in their respective fields—documentary and experimental films—as superb examples of cinematic form. *Grey Gardens* is a candid, intimate, and often funny look into the lives of two extraordinary women who live together: Mrs. Edith Beale ("Big Edie") and her unmarried daughter, Edith ("Little Edie"). The filmmakers (directors-as-editors) let the film's content shape its form. The women constantly bicker and disagree with one another, so the editing pattern, which juxtaposes the women with each other—the younger woman with the older—creates a line between them and their views of the past and the present. The audience is left to put the pieces together and decide the nature of this power struggle. *Dog Star Man*, like *Grey Gardens*, does not fit a categorical mold, although it is considered a classic experimental film. Stan Brakhage's techniques include superimposing four sequences at once—a kind of visual juxtaposition similar to that used by the director-editors of *Grey Gardens* in creating multiple meanings—and cutting into the frame to add new material to it. Both movies are pure cinema: work that explores the meaning and experiments with potential of the medium, challenging our perceptions. Films such as these help us understand that the work of Stanley Kubrick, another maverick director, is also pure cinema. They involve, to quote the title of one of Brakhage's films, "the act of seeing with our own eyes."

D. A. Pennebaker)—and in experimental films by such artists as Andy Warhol, Ken Jacobs, Bruce Baillie, Carolee Schneemann, Stan Brakhage, and Hollis Frampton. Of late, feature-length animated films have thrived as never before. All of these efforts have had a liberating influence on mainstream filmmaking.

In the arena of industry economics and practices, American cinema saw many new independent producers, a new financing system by which actors independently arranged their contracts and compensation, a new rating system, and the ability of consumers to rent, buy, or stream movies for home screenings. Combined, these had an impact on production, distribution, exhibition, and profits.

The New American Cinema is significant for these many changes, both large and small, that have transformed the complete structure of the American film industry. Such redefinition and reorganization constitutes a new era, comparable in many ways to the golden age. It is dependent on tradition, eager for innovation, adapts to new audiences, and always keeps its eye on the bottom line.

Film history presents an impressive record of achievement, ranging from the first modest efforts to record images on film to the sophisticated movies of today. Even as photography has remained the basis of cinema, in a little more than 100 years film artists, technicians, and businesspeople have proved themselves flexible enough to meet, with innovative responses, each challenge facing the medium.

When audiences demanded movies with stories as complex as those in the novel and theater, the industry developed the full-length narrative film. When the public wanted to hear actors speak as they did on the stage, the industry was transformed with sound recording. And so it goes with other innovations: color film stock, images with greater width and depth, genres to please virtually any audience, and a star system that created every conceivable type of actor. At the same time, major improvements were made in the techniques of cinematography, editing, special effects, acting, and sound recording as well as in new cameras, lenses, film stocks, lighting equipment, and editing devices.

Today's artists continue to create new techniques, technologies, and cinematic conventions. They work not just in Hollywood, London, Paris, or Berlin but also in Calcutta, Tokyo, Hong Kong, and Moscow—indeed, in virtually every country and culture in the world. The result—a cinematic language that is universally understood—enables the films of Satyajit Ray, Ingmar Bergman, Steven Soderbergh, Michelangelo Antonioni, or Andrei Tarkovsky to reach an international audience.

The historical development of film is a dynamic process that has created a constantly evolving art form. As you will see in Chapter 11, the systems of production have kept pace with this aesthetic evolution. In this short history of the movies, we emphasize the films that explore every aspect of this language and in many cases are regarded as cinematic masterpieces. However, not all movies are masterpieces. Like novelists, painters, or composers, film artists can produce work that is mediocre. But despite their weaknesses, such films please vast audiences and produce the profits that make the film industry a vital part of the world's economy. The history of the movies reveals, among many other things, that art and commerce can coexist.

Looking at *Citizen Kane* and Its Place in Film History

When you finish this chapter, you will be familiar with the major trends in form and content shaping film history worldwide. In looking at some of the movies that have made this possible, you will know what made them important. And you may also come across the fact that, for many years, Orson Welles's *Citizen Kane* (1941) was considered "the best movie of all time." That conclusion represents the views of hundreds of international filmmakers, critics, and scholars and is one measure of its global influence. How can that be, when the movie is so *old*? When you may never have heard of it? There are obviously many things we want you to learn from this book, and one of them is to evaluate a movie not by its age but rather by its quality within the cinematic art

as a whole (in other words, film history). There is something judgmental about *old* that has little place in a discussion of art.

Citizen Kane is important to your study of the movies because, within the borders of film history—1895 to the present—it marks a major turning point between the films produced before it and those produced after. To say that Welles revolutionized moviemaking is no understatement. Since the 1950s, when his movie became familiar worldwide, dozens of young people have said that they became filmmakers because of Welles's approach in *Citizen Kane*. The movie's influence can be measured not necessarily by the specific cinematic effects in the films that followed (although that is often quite apparent), but rather by how it transformed people's overall thinking about making movies. Thus we began to talk favorably about the Wellesian aspects of certain films, whether that influence is in the cinematography, sound recording, or editing.

But you can't know this about *Citizen Kane*, and you certainly can't understand it, unless you've seen a few of its predecessor films and become familiar with their cinematic conventions. To do this, give yourself an enjoyable crash course by looking at *You Can't Take It with You* (1938; director Frank Capra), *Stagecoach* (1939; director John Ford), *Rebecca* (1940; director Alfred Hitchcock), and *The Maltese Falcon* (1941; director John Huston). Then, in that context, watch *Citizen Kane*.

Although most critics loved it, the movie was so unpopular with contemporary audiences that it virtually disappeared until the early 1950s, when the French New Wave filmmakers discovered it and declared it a masterpiece. For those contemporary audiences, what set *Citizen Kane* apart from the movies that they knew? Let's answer by describing it in light of the elements of cinematic form we emphasize: narrative, mise-en-scène, cinematography, acting, editing, and sound.

The movie's story, while in the familiar biography genre, is not told in a conventional manner. Instead of a chronological plot that follows Charles Foster Kane from his impoverished youth to his status as one of the world's richest and most powerful men, it begins with his death and works its way backward and forward in his life through a series of interviews with people who knew him. This approach was so influential for French director Jean-Luc Godard that it could have been the source of his memorable remark: "A story should have a beginning, a middle and an end, but not necessarily in that order." Welles's handling of cinematic time broke the mold—indeed, many people were confused by this and walked out. But today it is commonplace for a movie to cut seamlessly between past, present, and future, and not necessarily in that order—a legacy from *Citizen Kane*.

Its mise-en-scène owes far more to the theater than to the movies, using an art form that Welles helped revolutionize before going to Hollywood to make his first movie. A major difference between looking at movies and looking at theater is that, in the former, audiences are accustomed to the frequent use of close-ups; in the latter, they see two or more people on the stage most of the time. But Welles also wanted depth in his sets, and so he used deep-focus cinematography to capture a pictorial depth that effectively allowed actors to move around the set whenever and however they wanted. This way of shooting also opens up the power of the long take to record this movement in depth and enables the actors to produce an entire scene uninterrupted by editing. Previous directors had used deep-focus cinematography in a limited way to achieve limited results, but Welles's achievement overshadowed all of those efforts. No longer would audiences see actors working chiefly in the foreground; now they moved easily from foreground to background. Today, picturing depth (including the increasing use of 3-D technology) surprises no one; indeed, we expect it, because it's how the human eye sees naturally. Despite some experiments, no directors before Welles used deep-space composition and deep-focus cinematography in such sustained creative brilliance as Welles. That, too, is another reason for the importance of *Citizen Kane*.

In his editing and sound, Welles also broke away from Hollywood conventions. He shot the film in the usual Hollywood way (nonchronologically), but instead of editing it into a chronological format, he devised an elaborate flashback structure that posed great challenges for editing the footage and establishing rhythm. For the sound, he called on his vast radio experience to emphasize the immediacy and spontaneity of every scene. Except for Bernard Herrmann's musical score, most sounds come from the world of the story. Although the prevailing convention in Hollywood in 1940 was to rerecord in the studio virtually all sound that had first been recorded on the set, Welles insisted on direct sound recording made on the set. He was certainly not the first to do this, but the design of the setting itself—allowing for hidden microphones to catch every sound—helped considerably to make it work smoothly. The sound includes single and overlapping voices, music, and ambient sounds. He also uses sounds to help transitions from shot to shot and scene to scene, to define the *space* and the characters' placement within the mise-en-scène, and, when it is synchronous with the action, to help to represent *time*.

Welles's innovations had their roots, but not their equivalents, in previous film history. He built on the work of others, extending, refining, and redefining techniques. He is one of cinema's greatest directors because he had the vision to do something differently and the talent to inspire collaborators to experiment and help him realize that vision. While countless directors adopted and refined those innovations, they claim him as their master, and many others say it was his example that encouraged them to become filmmakers. His innovations in *Citizen Kane* had their influence almost immediately in changing the look, sound, and overall effect of Hollywood movies. And though it lacks many of the features audiences expect today—color, widescreen, 3-D, fast-paced action, violence, and sex—many of its aspects make it a classic. These include a timeless story of egomania, greed, and cruelty; brilliant use of the flashback to tell that story; and an unforgettable look. Today, more than 75 years after its release, *Citizen Kane* is the one movie you must know if you are to understand film history. Is it the best movie in the history of cinema? That's up to you to decide. But one thing is certain: it's the movie that changed the movies forever.

ANALYZING FILM HISTORY

From this short history of the movies, we can reach several conclusions. First, the movies—in their formal qualities, modes of expression, technologies, and audiences—have changed radically in the course of little more than a hundred years. Second, in many cases, the artists, technicians, and businesspeople responsible for these changes adapted or perfected the achievements of previous filmmakers to reach the next level of development. Third, working in different countries and cultures, they produced an art that spoke to a diverse audience in a cinematic language that was universally understood. While there are obviously other common threads unifying the complex course of film history, these should encourage you—when you become excited about a particular movie—to learn more about its place in film history

(if it's an older film) or to be alert to a contemporary movie's explicit or implicit connection to other eras of film history and/or particular movies in that history. As you continue to look at movies, whether in class or on your own, you will see the rewards of appreciating, say, a 1927 masterpiece for what it is, where it came from, and how it influenced subsequent film history rather than thinking of it merely as an "old" movie. Likewise, you will also be able to appreciate the latest release for what it is, identifying how those who made it were influenced by past masters as well as what they contributed that seems new. With this approach, you'll understand that there are no "old" or "new" movies, just a continuum of innovation and tradition composed of those movies that we treasure and others that we'd rather forget.

SCREENING CHECKLIST: FILM HISTORY

✔ As you study a particular film, explore its historical context. What year was it made? Who was likely to have seen it? What elements of the historical context are reflected in the film itself?

✔ What is the film's aesthetic context? Is it part of a film movement or a reaction to the prevailing tradition of the period? How does it measure up to the ideals of the movement? How does it compare or contrast with the era's mainstream aesthetic?

✔ Consider the history of the filmmakers who created the movie. Does the director have a recognizable style or pattern of subjects? How does this film fit into that pattern? How has the cinematographer approached the subject, and is it different from past work? How does the costume design reflect both the period depicted on-screen and the era when the film was made?

✔ Does the film depict a notable moment in history, like the Great Depression, Watergate, or 9/11? Learn as much as you can about the historical context. What does the film portray of these eras? What does it leave out? Does it seem "accurate"? If not, in what way?

✔ Does the film seem notable for its innovations in cinematic language or technology? Have you seen antecedents to it in other films? Have you seen its influence on films that followed? Who created the innovation (the director, the sound designer, etc.)?

✔ Does the film deal with a topic, such as gay rights, differently than the films that preceded or followed it? Can you trace how the presentation of its subject on film has changed over time?

Questions for Review

1. What is meant by the term *film history*? Why is a knowledge of it invaluable in looking at movies and analyzing them?

2. What are the four traditional approaches to film history? What are the specific concerns of each?

3. What stylistic movements made cinematic innovations that, as a result, changed the course of film history?

4. The simplest approach to film history is to divide it into the eras of silent and sound production. What was the general state of filmmaking in each of these periods, and how and why does that explain the way movies were made?

5. What (a) was the state of moviemaking in the golden age of the American studio system in the late 1930s, and (b) what film(s) besides Orson Welles's *Citizen Kane* (1941) had a profound effect on filmmakers following its release? What effect(s) did they have?

6. What are the principal differences between the following sets of stylistic movements: (a) German Expressionism and Soviet Montage; (b) the classical Hollywood style and the New American Cinema; and (c) Italian Neorealism and the French New Wave?

7. The term *New Wave* is used to describe many film movements after World War II. What are several of these movements, and what general stylistic characteristics do they have in common?

8. Who, in your understanding, are three of the most innovative and influential directors in film history? What are their contributions?

9. Of the historic events occurring since the invention of the movies, which were most influential in providing subject matter for the movies? Discuss at least two events, and identify two movies for each event.

10. From the "prehistory" of the movies, what are the key technological innovations that made the movies possible? Who were three important inventors or innovators, what did they accomplish, and in what countries did they work?

Wonder Woman (2017). Patty Jenkins, director. Pictured: Gal Gadot and Patty Jenkins.

HOW THE MOVIES ARE MADE

Money, Methods, and Materials: The Whole Equation

The art of the movies—the primary concern of this book—is inseparable from its business practices, filmmaking technologies, and production systems. In his novel *The Last Tycoon*, F. Scott Fitzgerald attempted to explain how Hollywood works:

> You can take Hollywood for granted like I did, or you can dismiss it with the contempt we reserve for what we don't understand. It can be understood too, but only dimly and in flashes. Not half a dozen men have ever been able to keep the whole equation of pictures in their heads.[1]

In fact, however, that equation is simple: moviemaking is, above all, a moneymaking enterprise.[2]

In the movie industry, costs and profits can be measured in hundreds of millions of dollars. Today's feature films can cost anywhere from around $5 million (e.g., *Get Out*, 2017; director Jordan Peele) to $300 million (*Justice League*, 2017; director Zack Snyder). A 2016 Film L.A. sampling of the highest-grossing films of that year found the average budget to be $75.4 million. An additional 50 percent of those costs is then applied to marketing and distribution for the film, so a $75 million movie must earn around $113 million before it generates any profit. Thus the individuals and financial institutions that invest in the production of films, and the producers and studios they invest in, care first about money (ensuring the safety and potential return of their investments) and second—often a distant second—about art. They focus on movies as commodities. For that reason, they often consider release dates, distribution, and marketing as more important than the products themselves. In view of this reality, it is all the more impressive, then, that the movie industry produces a small number of films each year that can be appreciated, analyzed, and interpreted as genuine works of art rather than simply as commercial products to be consumed.

Why do films cost so much? It's like everything else: labor and materials. Today's films (particularly blockbuster films) require hundreds of people at all levels of the actual production who are trained to use highly advanced digital technology. The next time you look at the rolling credits at the end of an action movie, you'll see dozens of job titles that did not exist before digital filmmaking. And the more Hollywood gives the audience, the more the audience wants, so when the industry adds such features as screening in the 3-D or IMAX formats, it is generating audience excitement but also increasing ticket prices.

Because movie production involves a much more complicated and costly process than do most other artistic endeavors, very few decisions are made lightly. Unlike some arts—painting, for example—in which the materials and the process are relatively inexpensive, every decision in filmmaking has significant financial ramifications. Painters may paint over pictures many times without incurring steep costs, so their decisions can be dictated almost entirely by artistic inspiration. Movies, in contrast, involve a constant tug-of-war between artistic vision and profitability.

A great movie generally requires two key ingredients: a good script and a director's inspiration, vision, intelli-

1. F. Scott Fitzgerald, *The Last Tycoon: An Unfinished Novel* (New York: Scribner's, 1941), p. 3.
2. David Thomson takes a nonfiction approach to defining the equation in *The Whole Equation: A History of Hollywood* (New York: Knopf, 2005).

gence, and supervision (but not necessarily control) of all aspects of the film's production. Because the director plays the paramount role in the production process and in most cases has final authority over the result, we ordinarily cite a film in this way: Greta Gerwig's *Lady Bird* (2017). But although movie history began with staunchly individual filmmakers, movies have been carried forward through the years by teamwork. From the moment the raw film stock is purchased through its exposure, processing, editing, and projection, filmmakers depend on a variety of artists, technologies, technicians, and craftspeople. And no matter how clear filmmakers' ideas may be at the start, their work will change considerably, thanks to technology and teamwork, between its early stages and the final version released to the public.

Many movie directors—working under such pressures as producers' schedules and budgets—have been known for taking their power all too seriously. They are difficult on the set, throw tantrums, scream at and even physically assault members of the cast and crew, and rag at the front office. Still, moviemaking is essentially a collaborative activity. Even then, as film scholar Jon Lewis observes, "What ends up on the screen is not only a miracle of persistence and inspiration but also the result of certain practical concessions to the limitations of the studio system."[3]

Film production is complicated by the cost-effective, standard practice of shooting movies out of chronological order. This means that the production crew shoots the film not in the order of what we see on the screen, but in an order that allows the most efficient use of human and financial resources. During production, a script supervisor stays as close to the director as possible, for this person is an invaluable source of information about the shooting. The script supervisor records all details of continuity from shot to shot; he or she ascertains that costumes, positioning and orientation of objects, and placement and movement of actors are consistent in each successive shot and, indeed, in all parts of the film.

Overall, the pattern of production includes securing and developing a story with audience appeal; breaking the story into units that can be shot most profitably; shooting; establishing through editing the order in which events will appear on-screen; and then adding the sound, music, and special effects that help finish the movie. The use of a video assist camera permits a director to review each take immediately after shooting, when it is much easier to match details from shot to shot.

The process once took place in the vast, factory-like studios that dominated Hollywood and other major film-production centers around the world. Today it happens in the self-contained worlds of individual production units, which often operate in leased studio facilities.

The differences between these two modes of production are, in a sense, reflected in movies' production credits. In older films, all the (brief) production credits generally appear at the beginning, and the names of the leading actors are sometimes repeated in (and constitute) the closing credits. Today opening credits vary widely, but closing credits are lengthy and often include hundreds of names, accounting for virtually everyone who worked on the film or had something to do with it (e.g., caterers, animal handlers, accountants). Collective-bargaining agreements between producers and various labor unions—representing every person who works on a union production—impose clear definitions of all crew members' responsibilities as well as the size and placement of their screen credits. These credits properly and legally acknowledge people's contributions to films. Because nonunion crews make many independent films, these conventions of the division of labor and screen credit do not necessarily apply to independent films. Often on such films, crew members may be relatively inexperienced, not yet qualified for union membership, or unwilling to play several roles in return for the experience and screen credit. Government agencies and volunteer individuals or organizations may also be credited for their contributions.

This chapter introduces readers to the history of motion-picture technologies and production systems, showing that Hollywood is very much a product of its past. Today's Hollywood reflects how well the industry has adapted to the challenges of changing content, technologies, audiences, and exhibition opportunities. It remains one of the world's largest industries, and the impact of American movies is felt around the globe. Today Hollywood faces major challenges, most of which will be decided almost entirely on the relationship between costs and profits, the only equation.

To understand certain aesthetic judgments made by film producers, directors, and their collaborators, you should be familiar with the fundamentals of how a movie is made—in particular, with the two filmmaking technologies (film and digital) and the three phases of the moviemaking process (preproduction, production, and postproduction).

Film and Digital Technologies: An Overview

Here, we cover the two major technologies used in filmmaking at a time when the film industry has nearly completed the conversion from film to digital technology. This conversion initially created significant opposition, but the economic and logistic advantages of digital cinematography and projection made the newer technology impossible—and impractical—for most of the motion-picture industry to resist. Even though *film stock* and *film projectors* may not be familiar items to some readers—and, indeed, may one day be obsolete—we believe it is useful to describe briefly what is involved in film and digital technologies, both of which are still currently in use.

Looking at movies is more about what is on the screen than the technology that is unique to this art form. And since that technology is far less complicated than you might think, knowing something about it should further enhance your understanding of how movies are made. Motion-picture technology—and the production systems it serves—has developed in a simple, straight line from the early 1890s until recently.

Film Technology

When we refer to film technology, we mean that film stock is the medium on which the image is recorded. Film is an **analog** medium in which the camera (1) creates an image by recording through a camera lens the original light given off by the subject, and (2) stores this image on a roll of negative film stock. That stock, coated with an emulsion containing silver crystals, yields an image that closely resembles what the human eye sees. We call it *analog* because the image is analogous, or proportional, to the input. Put another way, once the film is processed (or "developed"), the negative image (on the negative stock) becomes a positive image (on positive stock); the first image is analogous to the second.

Unlike the newer technologies, film involves a mechanical system that moves this film stock through several machines: a camera, a processor, and a projector. These three machines bring images to the screen in three distinct stages, and light plays a vital role throughout.

In the first stage, **shooting**, the camera exposes film to light, allowing that radiant energy to burn a negative image onto each frame. These single, discrete images are shot at a standard (for theatrical movies, anyway) 24 frames per second. In the second stage, **processing**, the negative is developed into a positive "work print" that the film editor can cut. When the edit is completed, the edited work print is then used as a guide to create a matching edited version of the original negative, a process called "conforming the negative." This conformed negative is used to create a final positive film print for screening. (These days, even those relatively rare movies that are still shot on film stock get edited digitally; the negative is digitized into high-resolution, positive digital files for editing and eventually, also for the creation of theatrical prints, whether the final prints are digital or film.) In the third stage, **projecting**, the final print is run through a projector, which shoots through the film a beam of light intense enough to project a large image on the movie screen. (This account greatly condenses the entire process to emphasize, at this point, only the cycle of light is common to all three stages.)

Projecting a strip of exposed frames at the same speed—traditionally 16 frames per second (fps) for silent film, 24 fps for sound—creates the illusion of movement. Silent cameras and projectors were often hand-cranked, and so the actual speed of the camera, which then had to be matched by the projectionist, might vary from 12 to 24 fps. Cameras and projectors used for making and exhibiting professional films are powered by electric motors that ensure perfect movement of the film (Figure 11.1). As digital technology replaces this mechanical process (Figure 11.2), it is changing the equipment and media on which the images are captured, processed, and projected. But the role of light remains the same essential component.

A movie film's **format** is the gauge, or width, of the film stock and its perforations (measured in millimeters) and the size and shape of the image frame as seen on the screen (Figure 11.3). Formats extend from Super 8mm through 70mm and beyond into such specialized formats as IMAX (ten times bigger than a conventional

Figure 11.1 | THE MOTION-PICTURE CAMERA

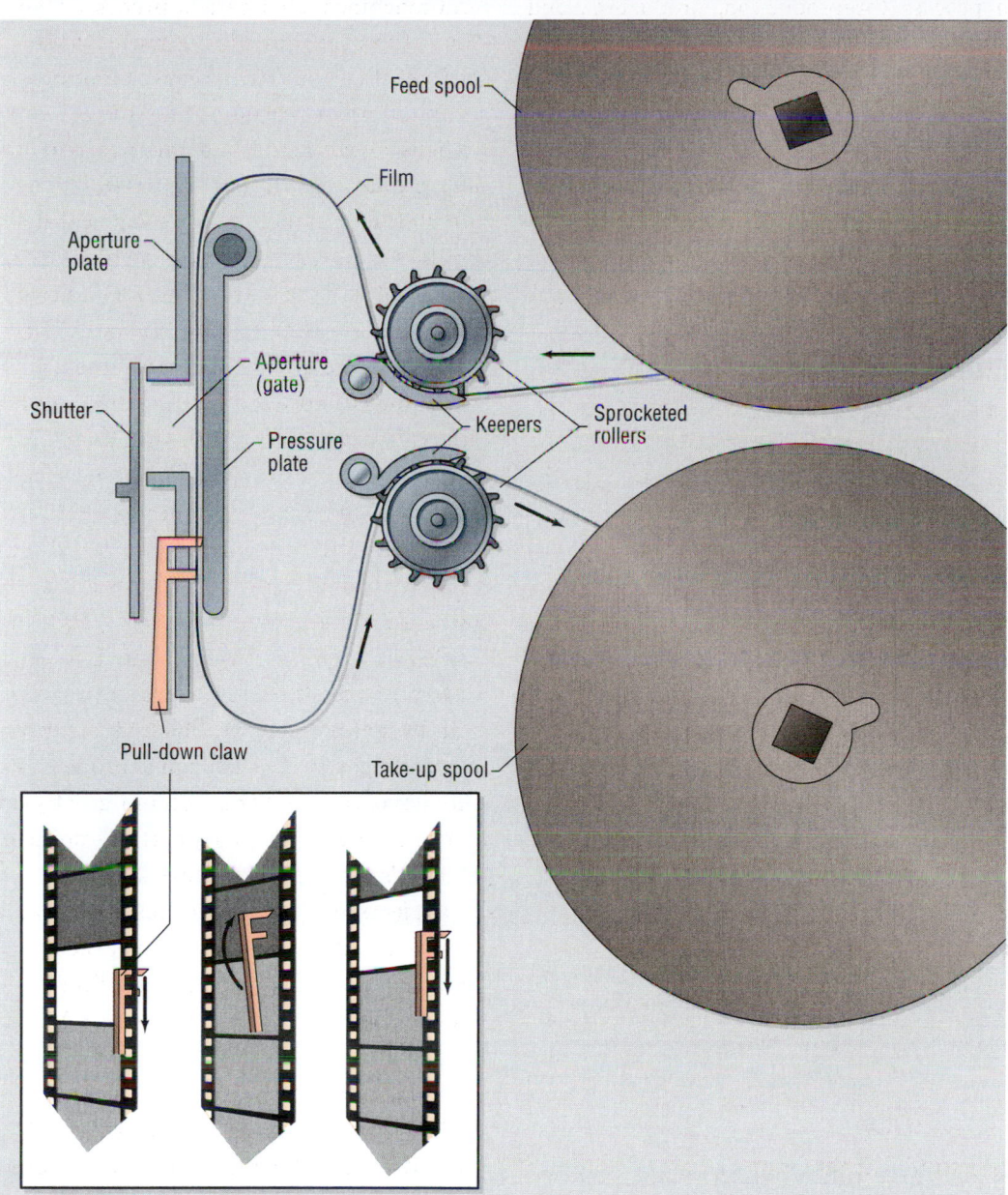

The motion-picture camera moves unexposed film from one storage area, called the **feed spool** (or, in professional cameras today, the portion of the magazine that stores unexposed film), along the **sprocketed rollers**. The rollers control the speed of the film as it moves through the camera and toward the lens, which focuses the image on the film as it is exposed. The **aperture** (or gate) is essentially the window through which each frame of film is exposed. The **shutter**—a mechanism that shields the film from light while each frame is moved into place—is synchronized with the motion of the **pull-down claw**, a mechanism used in both cameras and projectors to advance the film frame by frame. The pull-down claw holds each frame still for the fraction of a second that the shutter allows the aperture to be open so that the film can be exposed. The **take-up spool** (or, again, the portion of the magazine that stores exposed film) winds the film after it has been exposed.

Figure 11.2 | THE DIGITAL MOVIE CAMERA

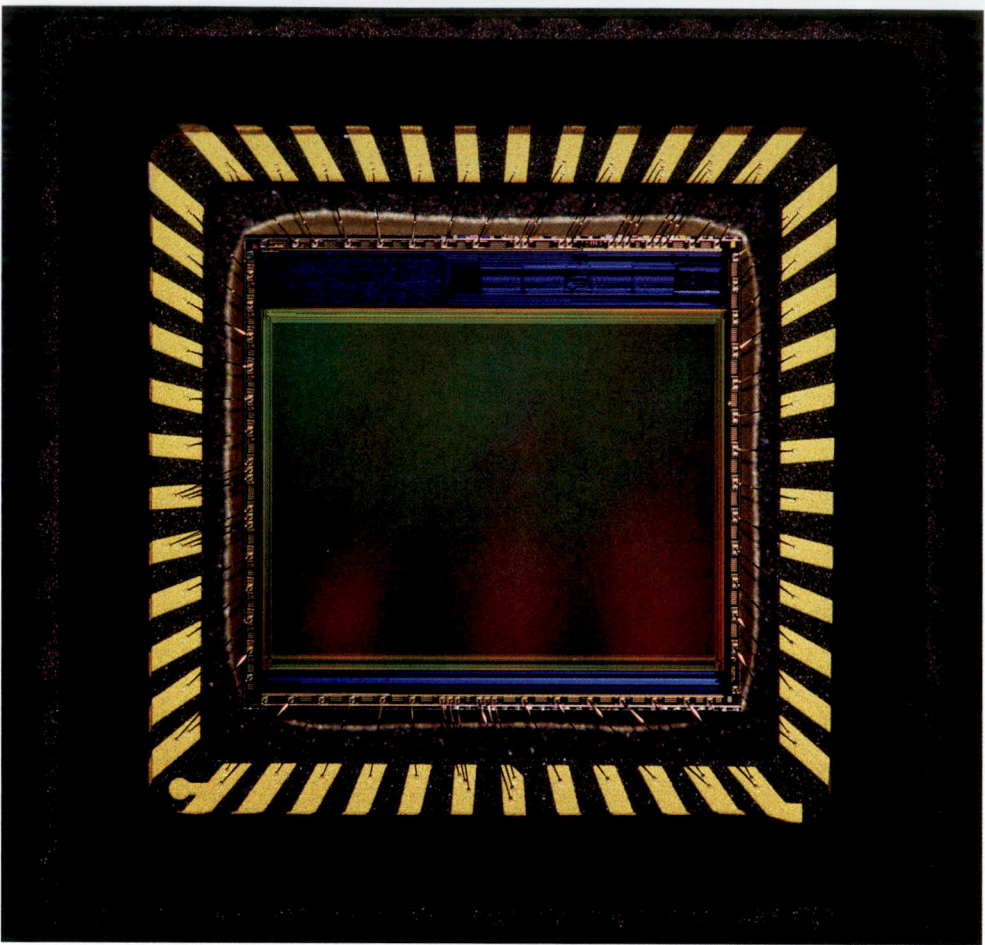

In a digital camera, the light that makes the image is captured by an electronic sensor. The size and configuration of the sensor and its associated electronics determine the resolution, depth of field, and tonal color values possible in the final film.

35mm frame and three times bigger than a standard 70mm frame). The format chosen depends on the type of film being made, the financing available to support the project, and the overall visual look that the filmmaker wants to achieve. For example, a wide-release narrative feature with a relatively healthy budget (such as Wes Anderson's *Moonrise Kingdom* [2012]) that seeks a certain stylistic look might be shot in 16mm, while a documentary designed for the big screen (such as Luc Jacquet's *March of the Penguins* [2005]) might shoot on the expensive 70mm or IMAX format. The **film-stock length** is the number of feet (or meters) or the number of reels being used in a particular film. The **film-stock**

speed (or *exposure index*) indicates the degree to which the film is light-sensitive. This speed ranges from very fast, at which the film requires little light, to very slow, at which it requires a lot of light. Film is also categorized into black-and-white and color stock.

In traditional film production, cinematographers control the photographic image in many ways: with their choice of stock; the amount and color of the lighting of each shot, the **exposure** (the length of time that the film is exposed to light), and the opening of the lens aperture (this regulates the amount of light that passes through the lens onto the surface of the film); the **resolution** (the capacity of the camera lens, film stock, and process-

Figure 11.3 | STANDARD FILM GAUGES

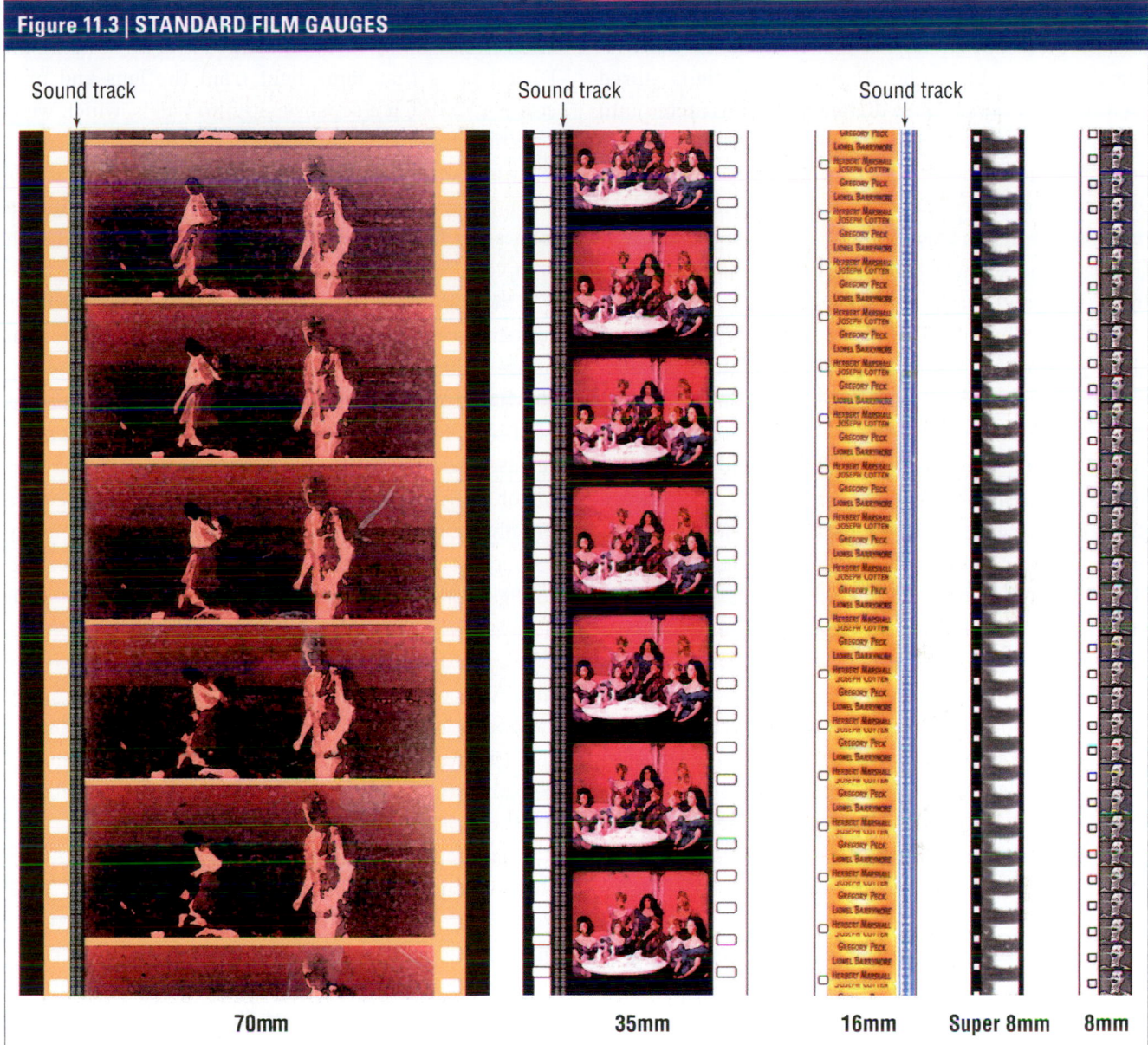

Sound track   Sound track   Sound track

70mm   **35mm**   **16mm**   **Super 8mm**   **8mm**

The most common variations on standard motion-picture film gauges. Digital technology does not use film, so the size and shape of the image is determined by the sensor, a central component in determining visual qualities. (See the following section, "Digital Technology.")

ing to provide fine detail in an image); the instructions provided to the processing laboratory, including special effects; and in the postproduction effort, through possible involvement in the editing process.

Professional motion-picture photography using film is a complex, time-consuming, and expensive process, but many filmmakers think it's worth it because it is the only way they can achieve the rich "look" that we traditionally associate with the movies. However, as we will discuss next, film and digital images are now virtually indistinguishable—just one factor spurring the momentum of making feature movies in digital technology.

Digital Technology

Digital technology involves an electronic process that creates its images through a numbered system of pixels (which we can think of as the binary numbers 0 and 1).

Unlike the analog images, digital images do not have a physical relationship to the original. Indeed, they are not exactly images but rather thousands of digits stored on a memory card. These digits are reconstructed into visual images each time the movie is edited or shown and, unlike film stock, can be manipulated endlessly. For example, filmmakers can make many alternate versions of any scene in searching for the perfect arrangement or timing of shots. They can also adjust and manipulate the light, color, and quality of the image.

Digital technology, like film technology, is used in all three stages of filmmaking: preproduction, production, and postproduction. And there are many significant similarities between the film and digital processes. When making conventional theatrical motion pictures, both systems shoot single, discrete images at a standard 24 frames per second. Every camera uses a lens, an aperture, shutter speed, frame rate, and so on—whether it shoots film or digital. The essential difference comes down to how the light is captured as an image. Digital uses a sensor, which transfers light as data onto a memory chip; film uses silver nitrate particles embedded on celluloid. In shooting a movie, digital cameras have different sizes of sensors recording the image and transferring it into electronic signals (see Figure 11.2). Instead of using different sizes of film gauges to determine the resolution and other visual performance/quality factors (such as depth of field, color retention, etc.), a digital camera uses the sensor for this work. In both film and digital processes, it all boils down to the size of the little square that the camera is focusing light onto. The bigger the gauge or sensor, the more information can be recorded with each frame.

Film versus Digital Technology

Before we proceed, let's summarize the strengths and weaknesses of both technologies. Film stock is a physical thing; digital is virtual representation. Film stock runs through a mechanical device and is subjected to a chemical reaction when light from the lens strikes silver-nitrate crystals on the stock, which must be kept locked away from light and must be processed by a lab and ed-

ited on a work print (which allows the editor to see only one version of any scene or sequence at any one time). Digital takes that same light from the lens and processes it through a sensor chip into pixels, which were traditionally put on various types of tape but increasingly are now recorded directly onto a memory card or a computer hard drive. It doesn't have to go through a laboratory for processing and can be manipulated with complete freedom on the computer.

These advantages have led to a nearly complete film-to-digital conversion in every stage of the commercial movie industry. In 2015, almost 90 percent of the top 100 U.S.-grossing films were shot digitally[4]; 100 percent of those films are edited and otherwise prepared for release digitally. In 2014, Paramount became the first major Hollywood studio to supply its films to theaters in only a digital format. By the middle of 2016, roughly 98 percent of the world's movie theaters had converted to digital projection systems.[5] However, there is small but significant opposition on the creative side from directors and cinematographers, in particular, who say they will continue to shoot on film. And the industry cannot afford to neglect people like Paul Thomas Anderson, Quentin Tarantino, or Christopher Nolan, who are dedicated to film's particular aesthetic: its film grain, its depth of color and shadow, even its imperfections.

That opposition created a problem, because Fuji stopped manufacturing motion-picture film in 2013. Eastman Kodak is now the only major company producing it. Faced with rapidly falling sales, Kodak was ready to follow Fuji. In 2014, a coalition of studios found a solution and made a deal with Kodak to ensure that the company will continue manufacturing motion-picture film for the next several years. Studios will buy a guaranteed quantity of that film and make it available to directors who wish to use it. The finished film, transferred to digital media and edited digitally, will be screened in theaters using digital projection. This arrangement preserves, in what we see, the visual quality of motion-picture film stock that many prefer.

Another strength of digital technology is that it uses less light than film technology and involves no processing. Overall, digital is much more versatile, easier, and (be-

4. https://stephenfollows.com/film-vs-digital/

5. David Hancock, "The Global Digital Conversion of Cinemas is Almost Over." IHS Technology (May 3, 2016). http://technology.ihs.com/577835/the
-global-digital-conversion-of-cinema-is-almost-over (accessed January 15, 2018).

yond the initial investment in new equipment) cheaper to work with than film. Film is fragile and disintegrates over time; digital copies are easily duplicated and virtually indestructible under normal conditions. Archival copies of both film and digital movies are costly.

Digital distribution and projection represents major cost savings for both distributors and theaters. Prior to digital distribution, hundreds—sometimes thousands—of new film prints, each costing around $1200, had to be made to even begin a theatrical release. Because a print deteriorates as it runs through a projector, additional prints would be needed as the film worked its way to smaller cities and second-tier markets. Print costs for a movie distributed to 25,000 screens (out of the 40,000 total in the United States) would cost the distributor $30 million, a price that does not include the cost of shipping the bulky, heavy cans that contain the prints. By contrast, securely downloading a digital copy of a film to a theater's computer system costs virtually nothing.

Digitally equipped theaters are able to offer programming beyond feature films, including recorded or simulcast presentations of sports, entertainment, and cultural events. Even independent movies that might not otherwise seem profitable can be more or less subsidized for short runs in a multiplex. With digital distribution, a blockbuster movie can be released and screened simultaneously in all areas of the United States, even around the world. Such instantaneous, widespread exposure might curtail pirating, where an illicit copy of a film is made surreptitiously inside a theater by a thief using a camcorder and then duplicated to produce cheap copies that are sold on the streets or offered online for download. However, the industry also fears that digital exhibition will foster the theft and subsequent pirating of the digital release prints themselves.

Of course, thanks to bigger, better, and cheaper flatscreen TVs, an increasing number of viewers now have their own relatively high-quality and large-format digital venues at home and access to thousands of streaming film titles, many of which are available immediately without an intervening theatrical release. In response, some moviemakers and many movie theaters seem to be intent on creating and exhibiting content designed for the theater experience. More and more theaters feature IMAX or similar large-format screen (and sound) systems designed to maximize the immersive experience of watching a blockbuster spectacle in ways that are impossible (so far) to re-create in anyone's living room.

How a Movie Is Made

The making of a movie, whether by a studio or an independent producer (as we'll discuss later) and whether it is shot on film or a digital medium, proceeds through three basic phases: preproduction, production, and postproduction.

Preproduction

The first stage, **preproduction**, consists of planning and preparation. It takes as long as necessary to get the job done—on average, a year or two. Initially, filmmakers develop an idea or obtain a script they wish to produce. They may secure from a publisher the rights to a successful novel or buy a writer's "pitch" for a story.

The opening segment of the late Robert Altman's *The Player* (1992) provides a comic view of the start of a studio executive's typical day. The executive, Griffin Mill (Tim Robbins), has the responsibility of listening to initial pitches from writers and recommending to his boss the ones he likes. Moving blithely through a world of business politics, intrigue, and power games, he hears from people with and without appointments, losers, hangers-on, hacks, and even experienced authors. Everyone he meets wants to be a screenwriter, and everyone wants to cast Julia Roberts. The pitches are mostly desperate attempts to make a new movie out of two previously successful ones: one scriptwriter, who cannot even agree with her partner on what they're talking about, summarizes a proposal as *"Out of Africa* meets *Pretty Woman."* The final pitch before the opening credits end, about a political thriller, serves as a transition to the thriller at the heart of Altman's film. One of Hollywood's most inventive and successful independent directors, Altman clearly knew the territory well enough to satirize it.

Once the rights to producing a story have been contracted and purchased, the producers can spend months arranging the financing for a production. How easily they accomplish this, and the funds that they secure, depends largely on the film they offer to their backers and its projected financial returns. As we'll see, a director may spend another month or more discussing the script with the screenwriter and the key people responsible for design, photography, music, and sound. Another 2 or 3 months may be spent rewriting the script.

Throughout the preproduction period, the producers continually estimate and reestimate the budget. The final budget, which should cover all foreseeable expenses, also reflects their marketing strategy. As one example, the producers of *Inception* (2010) allocated a production budget of $160 million and an advertising budget of $100 million, a shrewd calculation considering the movie was a major box-office success and was also nominated for an Academy Award for Best Picture.

During this process of previsualization, before the cameras start to roll, the director and the chief collaborators decide how they want the film to look, sound, and move. At least 2 to 3 weeks more can be devoted to organizational issues and details such as scheduling studio space and scouting locations, obtaining permissions to use those locations, and arranging for the design and construction of sets, costumes, and properties. Just before shooting begins, another 2 weeks will probably be devoted to rehearsals with the cast and crew.

Up to this point, likely almost a year has elapsed— assuming all has gone smoothly. Though the entire process of making a movie may seem straightforward, this description does not take into account the inevitable delays, the continuing difficulties in pulling together the financial package, and the countless details that must be attended to. For example, a film made at the peak of the Hollywood studio system would have been carefully planned, budgeted, and supervised by the producer in the front office, whether it was shot in a studio or on location. Daily reports to and from the set ensured that everyone knew, to the minute and to the dollar, the progress and the cost.

Orson Welles extensively composed and planned the shots of his first film, *Citizen Kane* (1941). It was photographed entirely in the RKO studio and miraculously (considering Welles's later reputation as a spendthrift independent director) was completed in less than a year and almost within the allotted budget. By contrast, Francis Ford Coppola, already a highly experienced director by the time he made *Apocalypse Now* (1979), began without a clear plan of what he wanted to achieve, worked as an independent producer with financing from United Artists, and shot the film in a foreign country under very difficult conditions. Ultimately, 115 hours of film

were exposed for every hour actually used. During the 4 years it took to complete the film, Coppola spent more than twice his original budget.

In making a film, meticulous preparation is everything, and key people take the time to think out alternatives and choose the one that seems best for the film. Thorough planning does not stifle further creativity or improvisation during production but rather encourages it, because planning makes the alternatives clear. Director Sidney Lumet emphasizes the logistics:

> Someone once asked me what making a movie was like. I said it was like making a mosaic. Each setup is like a tiny tile [a *setup*, the basic component of a film's production, consists of one camera position and everything associated with it]. You color it, shape it, polish it as best you can. You'll do six or seven hundred of these, maybe a thousand. (There can easily be that many setups in a movie.) Then you literally paste them together and hope it's what you set out to do. But if you expect the final mosaic to look like anything, you'd better know what you're going for as you work on each tiny tile.[6]

Production

Production, the actual shooting, can last 6 weeks to several months or more. Although the producer and director continue to work closely together, the director ordinarily takes charge during the shooting. The director's principal activities during this period are conducting blocking and lighting rehearsals on the set with stand-ins, followed by rehearsals with the cast; supervising the compilation of the records that indicate what is being shot each day and informing cast and crew members of their assignments; placing and, for each subsequent shot, replacing cameras, lights, microphones, and other equipment; shooting each shot as many times as necessary until the director is satisfied and calls "print"; reviewing the results of each day's shooting (called *rushes* or *dailies*) with key creative personnel and cast; and reshooting as necessary.

Every director works differently. Ordinarily, however, the director further breaks down the shooting script into manageable sections and then sets a goal of shooting

6. Sidney Lumet, *Making Movies* (New York: Knopf, 1995), p. 58.

a specified number of pages a day (typically, three pages is a full day's work). This process depends on the number of setups involved. Most directors try to shoot between fifteen and twenty setups a day when they're in the studio, where everything can be controlled; for exterior shooting, the number of setups varies. In any event, everyone involved in the production works a full day—usually from about 8:00 a.m. to about 6:00 p.m. (depending on their jobs and contracts), 5 days a week, with overtime when necessary. When complicated makeup and costuming are required, the actors may be asked to report for work early enough to finish that preparation before the crew is due to report. After each day's shooting, or as soon as the processing laboratory can deliver them, the director and others review the rushes. (Movies shot digitally or with a video assist camera can be reviewed immediately, allowing retakes to be made with the same setup or a different one.)

At a recent movie shoot in a Manhattan store, which was closed for the day to give the crew maximum access, any observer would have seen why it takes longer than might be expected to complete even the simplest shot. By actual count, forty crew members were there to support the director and four actors, who were ready to work. After the first setup was blocked, rehearsed, and lit, the director made three takes. This process took 3 hours. However, the rest of the day's schedule was abandoned because the lighting that had been brought in for the shoot failed. Why? The gaffer, the chief electrician, had neglected to ensure that the store's electrical capacity could support it. By the time generators were located and trucked to the site, 2 hours had been lost. Of course, any one of a dozen problems—human and technical—could have kept the director and crew from meeting their schedule.

During production, the number of people required to film a particular shot depends on the needs of that shot or, more precisely, on the overall scene in which the shot occurs. Many factors determine the size of the crew for any shot or scene, including the use of studio or exterior locations, day or night shooting, shooting on an uncrowded exterior location or a crowded city street, camera and lighting setups, and the extent of movement by the camera and the actors. For example, a scene that involves two people in a simple interior setting, with a basic camera and lighting setup, may require a minimal crew, while a scene involving many people in an exterior setting, with several camera positions and carefully choreographed movement, normally requires a large crew. The creation of artificial weather (rain, wind, or snow) and the use of animals or crowds are all expensive efforts that require additional personnel. Shooting on exterior locations is usually more expensive than shooting in a studio because it involves transportation and food, sometimes requires hotel accommodations, and depends largely on the weather.

To better understand what's involved in shooting, let's look briefly at the production of Robert Zemeckis's *Cast Away* (2000). The movie features Tom Hanks as Chuck Noland, a FedEx systems engineer based in Memphis, Tennessee. While he is en route from Moscow to the Far East, his plane crashes in the ocean. Chuck, the only survivor, washes ashore on a desert island. After sustaining himself physically, emotionally, and spiritually for 4 years, Chuck builds a raft and attempts to return to civilization. Overwhelmed by the elements and near death, he is picked up by a freighter and returned to Memphis, where he faces yet another emotional challenge.

In making *Cast Away*, the production crew faced daunting physical and logistical problems. Their largest challenge was to make the most efficient use of human, financial, and physical resources. The film, which cost $85 million to produce, was shot on soundstages in Hollywood as well as on actual locations in Texas, Tennessee, Russia, and the Fiji island of Monuriki in the South Pacific. The task of planning the overall production schedule was relatively routine, however. Although the largest part of the film's three-part structure is set on Monuriki and features only one actor (Hanks), the cast actually includes nearly sixty other actors. The credits list another 123 members of the production crew, most of them involved in creating the visual and special effects.

When shooting on Monuriki, the crew had to endure real winds, storms, and floods. When nature did not cooperate with their shooting schedule, they had to create their own bad weather. Furthermore, their work depended on the tides and available sunlight (Chuck would not have had artificial light on the island). The airplane crash was simulated in Hollywood, where considerable shooting was done underwater, and the scenes of Chuck's attempted escape by raft were shot on the ocean as well as in the perilous surf off another Fiji island. After 1 month's shooting on Monuriki, capturing footage that established Chuck's overall challenge, the crew took a yearlong hiatus while Hanks lost the 50 pounds he had gained to portray Chuck in the early part of the film. This change helped create the illusion that Chuck had spent 4 years on the island. Meeting these challenges as successfully as the filmmakers did (while maintaining visual consistency within the footage) was central to maintaining the film's verisimilitude.

Postproduction

When the shooting on a film has been completed, **postproduction** begins. Postproduction consists of three phases: editing, finishing, and bringing the film to the public (marketing and distribution).

In brief, editing consists of assembling the visual images and sound recordings, adding the musical score and sound effects, integrating the special effects, assembling the sound tracks, and doing any necessary dubbing. Finishing consists of mixing the many tracks of sound into one unified composite sound track and color grading the edited images to create the visual look of the film and maintain consistency of brightness and color from shot to shot. Bringing the film to the public consists of determining the marketing and advertising strategies and budgets, setting the release date and number of theaters, finalizing distribution rights and ancillary rights, and finally exhibiting the film.

In your study of movies, keep in mind that the art of the movies has been influenced not only by changes in technology and cinematic conventions but also by changes in the production process. Thus the Hollywood studio-system process that created F. W. Murnau's *Sunrise: A Song of Two Humans* (1927) was very different from the independent production process that created Greta Gerwig's *Lady Bird* (2017). The history of Hollywood production systems can be easily understood as comprising three basic periods: the studio system, the independent system, and a system today that manages to combine them. Let's look more closely at each of them.

The Studio System

Organization before 1931

The studio system's roots go back to the first decade of the twentieth century and the pioneering attempts of men such as Thomas Edison, Carl Laemmle, Thomas H. Ince, and D. W. Griffith to make, distribute, and exhibit movies. In 1905, Laemmle began to distribute and exhibit films, but by 1909 his efforts were threatened by the Motion Picture Patents Company (MPPC—not to be confused with the Motion Picture Production Code), a protective trade association (or trust) controlled by Edison, which sought both to control the motion-picture industry completely and to eliminate competition by charging licensing fees on production and projection equipment. However, widespread resistance to the MPPC encouraged competition and laid the groundwork for both the studio and independent systems of production. The U.S. government broke the MPPC monopoly in 1915.

Between 1907 and 1913, a large number of movie production companies in New York and New Jersey migrated to various spots in warmer climates, including Florida, Texas, and New Mexico. But eventually the main companies settled in southern California, in and around Hollywood. They did so to take advantage of the year-round good weather, the beautiful and varied scenery, the abundant light for outdoor shooting, and the geographic distance from the greedy MPPC. Soon these companies had a critical mass of both capital and talent on which to build an industry. By 1915, more than 60 percent of the American film industry, employing approximately 15,000 workers, was located in Hollywood.

The early studios relied on a system dominated by a central producer, a person in charge of the well-organized mass production system that was necessary for producing feature films. This system of central production began in 1912 and was the dominant practice by 1914. At his Hollywood studio, Inceville, Thomas H. Ince was the first studio head to insist that the authority and responsibilities of the producer, as executive head of a movie production, were distinctly different from those of the director.

Before 1931, typical Hollywood studios were dominated by central producers such as Irving Thalberg at Metro-Goldwyn-Mayer, Adolph Zukor at Paramount, and Harry and Jack Warner at Warner Bros. These men—known as moguls, a reference to the powerful Muslim Mongol (or Mogul) conquerors of India—controlled the overall and day-to-day operations of their studios. Executives in New York, generally called the "New York office," controlled the studios financially; various personnel at the studios handled the myriad details of producing films. Central producers, such as Thalberg, supervised a team of associate supervisors (not yet called producers), each with an area of specialization such as sophisticated comedies, Westerns, and so on. The associate supervisors handled the day-to-day operations of film production, but the central producer retained total control.

By the late 1920s, the film industry had come to see that the central-producer system encouraged quantity over quality and that less-than-stellar movies did not draw audiences into theaters. As a result, the industry sought a new system, one that would value both profits and aesthetic value.

Organization after 1931

In 1931, the film industry adopted the producer-unit system, an organizational structure that typically included a general manager, executive manager, production manager, studio manager, and individual production supervisors.[7] Each studio had its own configuration, determined by the New York office. The producer-unit system as it functioned at MGM in the 1930s illustrates the structure. (Figure 11.4 indicates the basic form and responsibilities of the producer-unit system. Note that the titles of these team members are generic; the actual titles varied with each studio.)

The general manager, Irving Thalberg, who had been supervising MGM's production since 1924, continued this work in the new unit. At the time, MGM's annual output was some fifty films. Reporting directly to Thalberg was a staff of ten individual unit production supervisors, each of them responsible for roughly six to eight films per year; the actual number varied widely based on the scope and shooting schedules of different productions. Each producer, who usually received screen credit with that title, was able to handle various types of movies. Such flexibility also enabled the general manager to assign these producers according to need, not specialization. This producer-unit management system (and its variations) helped create an industry that fa-

vored standardization, within which workers were always striving for the ideal relationship between cost and quality.

The system produced movies that had a predictable technical quality, often at the cost of stylistic sameness, or what we call the studio "look." It resulted in an overall output that inevitably—since hundreds of films were produced each year—valued profitability above all else. Yet although it could be stifling, standardization allowed for creative innovation, usually under carefully controlled circumstances. To help ensure such creativity, unit producers received varied assignments.

Hunt Stromberg and Bernard Hyman were two of Thalberg's individual unit production supervisors. In 1936, a busy year for MGM, the studio released six movies for which Stromberg received screen credit as producer: two musicals, two romantic comedies, and two Thin Man movies. Hyman also produced four equally diverse films that year.

Although Hyman regularly produced fewer films each year than Stromberg, both were members of Thalberg's inner group. Reliable if not particularly imaginative (exactly what Thalberg liked in his subordinates), these producers made movies that enhanced MGM's reputation for producing quality films, kept its major stars in the public eye, and satisfied the studio's stockholders. That's what the studio system was all about. Finally, these producers were forerunners of what today we call a *line producer*, the person responsible for supervising the daily operations of a film production.

The Hollywood studio system established the collaborative mode of production that dominated American filmmaking during its golden age while influencing the mode of film production worldwide. The studio system also established an industrial model of production through which American filmmaking became one of the most prolific and lucrative enterprises in the world. Furthermore, although its rigidity ultimately led to its demise after some 40 years, the system contained within itself the seeds—in the form of the independent producers that would replace it—to sustain American film production until the present day.

---

7. The material in this section was drawn from David Bordwell, Janet Staiger, and Kristin Thompson, *The Classical Hollywood Cinema: Film Style and Mode of Production to 1960* (New York: Columbia University Press, 1985), pts. 2 and 5; Thomas Schatz, *The Genius of the System: Hollywood Filmmaking in the Studio Era* (1988; repr., New York: Holt, 1996), pts. 2 and 3; Joel Finler, *The Hollywood Story*, 3rd ed. (New York: Wallflower, 2003), pt. 2; and Douglas Gomery, *The Hollywood Studio System: A History* (London: British Film Institute, 2005).

Figure 11.4 | PRODUCER-UNIT SYSTEM AT MGM

General Manager
Irving Thalberg

Thalberg supervised the overall production of some fifty films each year: his responsibilities included selecting the property, developing the script (either by himself or in collaboration with writers), selecting the actors and key production people, editing the film, and supervising marketing. Thus, without ever leaving his office to visit the set, he could be intimately involved in every phase of every production at the studio. He generally received screen credit as "producer."

Executive Manager

Responsible for the studio's financial and legal affairs as well as daily operations.

Production Manager

Responsible for all preproduction and postproduction work; key liaison among the general manager, studio manager, and individual production supervisors.

Studio Manager

Responsible for the support departments (research, writing, design, casting, cinematography, marketing research, etc.) representing almost 300 different professions and trades.

Individual Unit Production Supervisors

Ten men (e.g., Hunt Stromberg and Bernard Hyman) were each responsible for planning and producing six to eight films per year. Films were assigned by the general manager and production manager. These ten were often called *associate* or *assistant producers* and sometimes given screen credit as such. Each producer was sufficiently flexible to be able to handle various types of movies.

Organization during the Golden Age

By the mid-1930s, Hollywood was divided into four kinds of film production companies: majors, minors, "B" studios, and independent producers (Table 11.1).[8] The five major studios—Paramount, MGM, Warner Bros., 20th Century Fox, and RKO—were all vertically integrated companies, meaning that they followed a top-down hierarchy of control, vesting ultimate managerial authority in their corporate officers and boards of directors. These managers were in turn responsible to those who financed them: wealthy individuals (e.g., Cornelius Vanderbilt Whitney or Joseph P. Kennedy), financial institutions (e.g., Chase National Bank in New York or Bank of America in California), corporations related to or dependent on the film industry (e.g., RCA, manufacturers of sound equipment used in movie production), and stockholders (including studio executives and ordinary people who purchased shares on the stock market). Controlling film production through their studios and, equally important, film distribution (the marketing and promotion of a film) and exhibition (the actual showing of a motion picture in a commercial theater) through

8. See David A. Cook, *A History of Narrative Film*, 5th ed. (New York: Norton, 2004), pp. 239–255.

Table 11.1 | STRUCTURE OF THE STUDIO SYSTEM UNTIL 1950

Major Studios	Minor Studios	Most Significant "B" (Poverty Row) Studios	Most Significant Independent Producers
1. Paramount	1. Universal Studios	1. Republic Pictures	1. Samuel Goldwyn Productions
2. Metro-Goldwyn-Mayer	2. Columbia Pictures	2. Monogram Productions	2. David O. Selznick Productions
3. Warner Bros.	3. United Artists	3. Grand National Films	3. Walt Disney Studios
4. 20th Century Fox		4. Producers Releasing Corporation	
5. RKO		5. Eagle-Lion Films	

their ownership of film exchanges and theater chains, the majors produced "A" pictures, meaning those featured at the top of the double bill (ordinarily, for the price of a single admission, moviegoers enjoyed almost 4 hours of entertainment: two feature films, a cartoon, a short subject, and a newsreel).

The three minor studios—Universal, Columbia, and United Artists—also produced "A" pictures, but they were less similar than the majors. Universal and Columbia owned their own production facilities but no theaters, and thus depended on the majors to show their films. By contrast, United Artists (UA)—founded in 1919 by Mary Pickford, Charles Chaplin, Douglas Fairbanks, and D. W. Griffith—was considered a studio even though it was essentially a distribution company established by these artists to give them greater control over how their movies were distributed and marketed. During the 1930s, however, UA was distributing the work of many other outstanding producers, directors, and actors. Although UA declined during the 1940s, it was revived in the 1950s and today is part of MGM.

The five B studios (sometimes called the *poverty row studios* because of their relatively small budgets) were Republic Pictures, Monogram Productions, Grand National Films, Producers Releasing Corporation, and Eagle-Lion Films. Their B movies filled in the bottom half of double bills.

The most important independent producers in the 1930s, when independent production was still a relatively unfamiliar idea, were Hollywood titans Samuel Goldwyn, David O. Selznick, and Walt Disney. Each producer owned his own studio but released pictures through his own distribution company, one of the majors, or United Artists. Disney produced his classic animated films, such as *Pinocchio* (1940), at the Walt Disney studios and released them through his own distribution company, Buena Vista Productions. Goldwyn produced such major pictures as William Wyler's *The Best Years of Our Lives* (1946), which he released through RKO. In 1936, Selznick left MGM to establish Selznick International Pictures. In 1940, three of his films—Victor Fleming's *Gone with the Wind* (1939), Alfred Hitchcock's *Rebecca* (1940), and Gregory Ratoff's *Intermezzo* (1939)—together earned some $10 million in net profits, more than all the films of any of the majors, each of which produced roughly fifty-two films that year. Although he released his films through the major studios, including MGM, Selznick's prestige pictures and remarkable profits established the independent producer as a dominant force in Hollywood for the next 60 years and beyond.

The **producer** guides the entire process of making the movie, from its initial planning to its release. This person is chiefly responsible for the organizational and financial aspects of the production, from arranging the financing to deciding how the money is spent. The studio system was dominated by producers who, in turn, depended on directors who were under studio contract to direct a specific number of films in each contract period.

The work of the **director** is to determine and realize on the screen an artistic vision of the screenplay; cast the actors and direct their performances; work closely with the production designers in creating the look of the film, including the choice of locations; oversee the work of the cinematographer and other key production personnel; and in most cases, supervise all postproduction activity, including the editing. Although some studio system directors—Alfred Hitchcock, John Ford, and Vincente

Minnelli, for example—could be involved completely from preproduction through postproduction, most were expected to receive a script one day and begin filming shortly thereafter. They were seasoned professionals capable of working quickly and were conversant enough with various genres to be able to handle almost any assignment.

The career of Edmund Goulding, who directed thirty-eight movies, clearly exemplifies the work of a contract director. After starting in silent films in 1925 and directing several films at Paramount Pictures, Goulding made an auspicious start as a director at MGM with *Grand Hotel* (1932), an all-star blockbuster. He followed that with *Blondie of the Follies* (1932), a comedy featuring Marion Davies; the melodrama *Riptide* (1934), starring Norma Shearer; and *The Flame Within* (1935), also a melodrama. From MGM, Goulding moved to Warner Bros. There, as a contract director, he made *That Certain Woman* (1937), *Dark Victory* (1939), and *The Old Maid* (1939), all starring Bette Davis; *The Dawn Patrol* (1938), a World War I action film; *'Til We Meet Again* (1940), a wartime romance; and *The Constant Nymph* (1943), a romantic drama.

After World War II, Goulding moved to 20th Century Fox, where the declining quality of the movies he was assigned truly reflects the challenges facing a contract director. Starting with *The Razor's Edge* (1946; a quasi-philosophical movie nominated for an Oscar as Best Picture of 1946) and *Nightmare Alley* (1947), a melodramatic film noir, he went on to direct *We're Not Married!* (1952), an episodic comedy featuring Marilyn Monroe; *Teenage Rebel* (1956), a drama; and for his last film, *Mardi Gras* (1958), a teenage musical starring Pat Boone. Goulding made the most of the challenges inherent in such variety. He was also popular with actors and noted for his screenwriting, which accounts for some of the gaps between pictures (most contract directors were expected to make three or four movies per year). Goulding was also noteworthy as an openly gay man who successfully pursued his career at a time when most Hollywood gays and lesbians remained in the closet.[9]

The actual, physical studios, called "dream factories" by anthropologist Hortense Powdermaker, were complex operations.[10] If you were fortunate enough to get past a studio's high walls and through its guarded gates, you would find yourself in a vast industrial complex. MGM, for example, the largest studio, covered 117 acres, over which 10 miles of paved streets linked 137 buildings. There were 29 soundstages—huge air-conditioned and soundproofed production facilities, the largest of which had a floor area of nearly an acre. The studio was a self-contained community with its own police and fire services, hospital, film library, school for child actors, railway siding, industrial section capable of manufacturing anything that might be needed for making a movie, and a vast backlot containing sets representing every possible period and architecture. In the average year, MGM produced 50 full-length feature pictures and 100 shorts. Depending on the level of production, the workforce consisted of 4000 to 5000 people. The other major studios had smaller but similar operations.

The Decline of the Studio System

Fostered by aggressive competition and free trade, the studio system grew to maturity in the 1930s, reached a pinnacle of artistic achievement and industrial productivity in the 1940s, and then declined at the beginning of the 1950s. We can see this trajectory clearly by looking at the actual number of films produced and released by American studios during that downward swing. As Table 11.2 indicates, the average number of films annually produced and released in the United States from 1936 to 1940 was 495; from 1941 to 1945, the war years, that number fell to 426; in the immediate postwar period, 1946–1950, it fell even further, to 370. In 1951, the total number of U.S. films was 391, the highest it would be until 1990, when 440 films were released. In looking at these data, remember that the total film releases in any one year usually reflect two kinds of production: those begun in that year and those begun earlier. In any case, one thing is clear: total Hollywood production between 1936 and 1951 fell by 25 percent.

By the mid-1930s, in fact, the system had reached a turning point because of three intertwined factors.

---

9. See William J. Mann, *Behind the Screen: How Gays and Lesbians Shaped Hollywood, 1910–1969* (New York: Viking, 2001).

10. See Hortense Powdermaker, *Hollywood, the Dream Factory: An Anthropologist Looks at the Movie-Makers* (Boston: Little, Brown, 1950).

Table 11.2 | FEATURE FILMS PRODUCED AND RELEASED IN THE UNITED STATES, 1936–1951	
Year	**Number of Feature Films Released**
1936	522
1937	538
1938	455
1939	483
1940	477
1941	492
1942	488
1943	397
1944	401
1945	350
1946	378
1947	369
1948	366
1949	356
1950	383
1951	391

Note: These figures do not include foreign films released in the United States.

Source: Joel Finler, *The Hollywood Story* (New York: Crown, 1988), p. 280.

First, the studios were victims of their own success. The two most creative production heads—Darryl F. Zanuck, who dominated production at 20th Century Fox from 1933 until 1956, and Irving Thalberg, who supervised production at MGM from 1923 until his death in 1936—had built such highly efficient operations that their studios could function exceptionally well, both stylistically and financially, without the sort of micromanaging that characterized David O. Selznick's style at Selznick International Pictures. In a very real sense, these central producers and others had made themselves almost superfluous.

Second, several actions taken by the federal government signaled that the studios' old ways of doing business would have to change. President Franklin D. Roosevelt's plan for the economic revitalization of key industries—the 1933 National Industrial Recovery Act—

had a major impact on Hollywood. On the one hand, it sustained certain practices that enabled the studios to control the marketing and distribution of films to their own advantage; on the other, it fostered the growth of the labor unions, perennially unpopular with the studio heads, by mandating more thoroughgoing division of labor and job specialization than Hollywood had yet experienced. In 1938, however, the federal government began trying to break the vertical structure of the major studios—to separate their interlocking ownership of production, distribution, and exhibition—an effort that finally succeeded in 1948.

Third, the studios began to reorganize their management into the producer-unit system. Each studio had its own variation on this general model, each with strengths and weaknesses. Although the resulting competition among the units increased the overall quality of Hollywood movies, the rise of the unit producer served as a transition between the dying studio system and the emergence of the independent producer.

Three additional factors further undercut the studio system. The first was a shift in the relations between top management and creative personnel that loosened the studios' hold on the system. From the mid-1930s on, actors, directors, and producers sought better individual contracts with the studios—contracts that would give them and their agents higher salaries and more control over scripts, casting, production schedules, and working conditions. For example, in the early 1950s actor James Stewart had an agreement whereby he would waive his usual salary for appearing in two films (then $200,000 per picture) in exchange for 50 percent of the net profits. Equally significant, these profits would extend through the economic life of the film, whether it was shown on a theater screen, broadcast on television, or distributed via other formats.

The second factor was World War II, which severely restricted the studios' regular, for-profit operations (they were also making movies that supported government initiatives, such as films instructing people how to cope with food rationing or encouraging them to buy war bonds). As noted already, the production of feature films fell precipitously during the war. Because many studio employees (management and labor alike) were in the armed services and film stock was being rationed to ensure the supply needed by armed-services photographers, there were fewer people and materials to make films. Thus, even though audiences went to the movies in record numbers, fewer films were available for them to see.

The third blow to the studio system was the rise of television, to which Hollywood reacted slowly. When the federal government made the studios divest themselves of their theater holdings, it also blocked their plans to replicate this dual ownership of production and distribution facilities by purchasing television stations. At first, the major studios were not interested in television production, leaving it to the minors and to such pioneering independents as Desilu Productions (Desi Arnaz and Lucille Ball, producers). By 1955, though, the majors were reorganizing and retooling what remained of their studios to begin producing films for television. Some efforts were more successful than others, but even more profitable was the sale both of their real estate—on which the studios were built—for development and of the valuable films in their vaults for television broadcasting. Universal Studios had the best of both worlds, continuing to use part of its vast property at the head of the San Fernando Valley for film and television production and devoting the rest to a lucrative theme park dedicated to showing how movies are made.

The Independent System

Through the 1930s and 1940s, the independent system of production—sometimes called the *package-unit system*—coexisted with the studio system, as it continues to do with a much different set of studios. The package-unit system, controlled by a producer unaffiliated with a studio (independents such as Samuel Goldwyn, David O. Selznick, Walt Disney, and others), is a personalized concept of film production that differs significantly from the industrial model of the studio system. Based outside the studios but heavily dependent on them for human and technical resources, the package-unit system governs the creation, distribution, and exhibition of a movie (known as the *package*). The independent producer does what a movie producer has always done: chooses the right stories, directors, and actors to produce quality films.

Depending on many factors, the producer may also choose to be involved in creative responsibilities, ranging from developing the property, revising the screenplay, assembling the key members of the production team, supervising the actual production (including the editing), and marketing and distributing the finished product. Consider the career of Sam Spiegel, one of the most successful independent producers; his movies included John Huston's *The African Queen* (1951), Elia Kazan's *On the Waterfront* (1954), David Lean's *The Bridge on the River Kwai* (1957) and *Lawrence of Arabia* (1962), Joseph L. Mankiewicz's *Suddenly, Last Summer* (1959), and Elia Kazan's *The Last Tycoon* (1976), inspired by the life of his fellow producer Irving Thalberg. Spiegel controlled the money and thus the production. Although that attitude may seem arrogant, it makes excellent business sense to a producer responsible for films like Spiegel's, which were characterized by high costs, high artistic caliber, and high profits.

The producer's team may include an **executive producer**, **line producer**, and **associate** or **assistant producers**. These variations on the overall title of producer reflect the changes that have occurred since the studio system collapsed and, in different ways, reinvented itself. By the nature of film production, titles must be flexible enough to indicate greater or fewer responsibilities than those listed here. Unlike the members of the craft unions—cinematographers or editors, for example—whose obligations are clearly defined by collective bargaining agreements, producers tend to create responsibilities for themselves that match their individual strengths and experiences.

At the same time, the comparative freedom of independent filmmaking brings new benefits. Creative innovation is both encouraged and rewarded; actors, writers, and directors determine for themselves not only the amounts of compensation but also the ways in which they receive it; and though the overall number of movies produced each year has decreased, the quality of independently produced films has increased considerably from year to year. Whereas the producer helps transform an idea into a finished motion picture, the director visualizes the script and guides all members of the production team, as well as the actors, in bringing that vision to the screen.

The director sets and maintains the defining visual quality of the film, including the settings, costumes, action, and lighting. Those elements produce the total visual impact of the movie's image, its look and feel. When a film earns a profit or wins the Oscar for Best Picture, the producer takes a large share of the credit and accepts the award (true under the studio system also), but the director usually bears artistic responsibility for the success or failure of a movie. When a film loses money, the director often gets most of the blame.

Because creativity at this high level resists rigid categorization, we cannot always neatly separate the responsibilities of the producer and the director. Sometimes one person bears both titles; at other times the director or the screenwriter may have initiated the project and later joined forces with the producer to bring it to the screen. But whatever the arrangement, both the producer and the director are involved completely in all three stages of production.

A quick snapshot of a few differences between the studio and independent systems will give you an idea of how moviemaking has changed. At first, each studio's facilities and personnel were permanent and capable of producing any kind of picture, and the studio owned its own theaters, guaranteeing a market for its product. Now, by contrast, an independent producer makes one film at a time, relying on rented facilities and equipment and a creative staff assembled for that one film. Even figuring for those cost-saving elements, the expenses can be staggering.

Moviemaking entails various kinds of "costs." In both the old and the new American film industry, the total cost of a film is what it takes to complete the postproduction work and produce the release negative as well as one or two positive prints for advance screening purposes. But this "total cost" does not include the cost of marketing or of additional prints for distribution, so it is useful only for the special purposes of industry accounting practices. You will generally see this figure referred to as the negative cost of a movie, where *negative* refers to the costs of producing the release negative.

Contemporary filmmakers have found creative ways to reduce costs and increase profits. For example, in making *Minority Report* (2002), producer Steven Spielberg and his star Tom Cruise agreed to receive only minimal fees up front rather than their usual large salaries—a practice that Spielberg began with Tom Hanks in *Saving Private Ryan* (1998) and is now standard in the film industry. According to a clause in their contracts, Spielberg and Cruise were each guaranteed 17.5 percent of the studio's first-dollar gross profit, meaning that 35 cents of each dollar earned on the film went to them. The movie reportedly cost more than $100 million to make, and earned approximately $358 million in worldwide box office return and sales of 4 million DVDs, promotional products, and movie rights. Thus, it is conservatively estimated that each man earned $55 million. As in any other industry, costs and revenues are controlled by supply and demand. As costs increase for making the kind of blockbuster films that return sizable revenues, producers make fewer films, forcing people who work in the industry to become financially creative in negotiating the contracts that preserve their jobs.

Labor and Unions

Before the industry was centralized in Hollywood, movie production was marked by conflicts between management and labor. Strikes led to the formation of guilds and unions, which led to the division of labor; that development, as much as anything, led a hodgepodge of relatively small studios to prosper and grow into one of the world's largest industries. In 1926, the major studios and unions stabilized their relations through the landmark Studio Basic Agreement, which provided the foundation for future collective bargaining in the industry.[11]

Workers in the industry formed labor unions for the standard reasons: they sought worker representation, equity in pay and working conditions, safety standards, and job security. For example, the Screen Actors Guild, established in 1933, is the nation's premier labor union representing actors. In the 1940s, it fought the attempt of the studio system to break long-term engagement contracts; today, it faces new challenges in protecting artists' rights amid the movie industry's conversion to digital production. In addition, because of the uniquely collaborative nature of their jobs, industry workers needed a system that guaranteed public recognition of their efforts. Contracts between the labor unions and the studios covered the workers' inclusion in screen credits. Executive managers often had similar contracts.

In any manufacturing enterprise, division of labor refers to breaking down each step in that process so that each worker or group of workers can be assigned to and responsible for a specialized task. Although this system

---

11. An excellent account of the power of labor unions in Hollywood, including the pervasive presence of organized crime, is Connie Bruck's *When Hollywood Had a King: The Reign of Lew Wasserman, Who Leveraged Talent into Power and Influence* (New York: Random House, 2003).

was designed to increase efficiency in producing steel, cars, and the like, it was applied very successfully in the film industry. Indeed, Hollywood has often been compared to Detroit. Both of these major industrial centers are engaged in the mass production of commodities. Detroit's output is more standardized, though manufacturer and model differentiate the automobiles that roll off the assembly line.

Like automobile manufacturers, each studio during the studio era specialized in certain kinds of films in its own distinctive style (e.g., MGM excelled in musicals; Warner Bros., in films of social realism); but unlike the Detroit product, each film was a unique creative accomplishment, even if it fit predictably within a particular genre such as film noir. For the most part, each studio had its own creative personnel under contract, though studios frequently borrowed talent from each other on a picture-by-picture basis. Once a studio's executive management—board of directors, chairman, president, and production moguls—determined what kinds of films would most appeal to its known share of the audience, the studio's general manager (here titles varied among studios) developed projects and selected scripts and creative personnel consistent with that choice.

In Hollywood, the activities in the three phases of making a movie—preproduction, production, and postproduction—are carried out by two major forces: management and labor. Management selects the property, develops the script, chooses the actors, and assigns the key production people; but the actual work of making the film is the responsibility of labor (artists, craftspeople, and technicians belonging to labor unions). Members of management receive the highest salaries; the salaries of labor depend on the kind and level of skills necessary for each job. Such a division of labor across the broad, collaborative effort in creating a film shapes the unavoidable interaction between the work rules set by union contracts and the standards set by professional organizations.

Professional Organizations and Standardization

Beyond the labor unions, other organizations are devoted to workers in the motion-picture industry, including the American Society of Cinematographers (founded in 1918; chartered in 1919), the Society of Motion Picture

and Television Engineers (1916), and the American Cinema Editors (1950), which set and maintain standards in their respective professions.

These organizations engage in the activities of a traditional professional organization: conducting research related to equipment and production procedures; standardizing that equipment and those procedures; meeting, publishing, and consulting with manufacturers in the development of new technologies; promulgating professional codes of conduct; and recognizing outstanding achievement with awards. Although they do not represent their membership in collective bargaining, as do labor unions, they voice opinions on matters relevant to the workplace.

Membership in these societies has its distinctions. For example, members of the American Cinema Editors are nominated and elected on the basis of their professional achievements and commitment to the craft of editing. Membership entitles them to place "ACE" after their name in a movie's credits.

In 1927, the industry established the Academy of Motion Picture Arts and Sciences, which seeks, among its stated objectives, to improve the artistic quality of films, provide a common forum for the various branches and crafts of the industry, and encourage cooperation in technical research. Since ancient times, an *academy* has been defined as a society of learned persons organized to advance science, art, literature, music, or some other cultural or intellectual area of endeavor. Although profits, not artistic merit, are the basic measure of success in the movie industry, using the word *academy* to describe the activities of this new organization suited early moviemakers' strong need for social acceptance and respectability.

A masterful stroke of public relations, the Academy is privately funded from within the industry and is perhaps best known to the public for its annual presentation of the Academy Awards of Merit, or Oscars, as they are commonly known. Membership in the Academy is by invitation only. Now numbering around 5800, members fall into sixteen categories: actors, art directors, cinematographers, directors, documentary, executives, film editors, makeup artists and hairstylists, music, producers, public relations, short films and feature animation, sound, visual effects, members-at-large, and writers. Members in each category make the Oscar nominations and vote to determine the winners. All voting members are also eligible to vote for the Best Picture nominees.

Currently, Academy members award Oscars for the "best" in these twenty-four categories: Actor in a Leading Role, Actor in a Supporting Role, Actress in a Leading Role, Actress in a Supporting Role, Animated Feature, Animated Short Film, Art Direction, Cinematography, Costume Design, Director, Documentary Feature, Documentary Short Subject, Film Editing, Foreign Language Film, Live Action Short Film, Makeup and Hairstyling, Original Score, Original Song, Picture, Sound Editing, Sound Mixing, Visual Effects, Writing—Adapted Screenplay, and Writing—Original Screenplay. In addition, the Academy has the option to present honorary awards, scientific and technical awards, special-achievement awards, and the Jean Hersholt Humanitarian Award and Irving G. Thalberg Memorial Award. Various attempts to add the following new categories have not been approved: Casting, Stunt Coordination, and Title Design.

Financing in the Industry

The pattern for financing the production of motion pictures, much like the establishment of labor practices, developed in the industry's early years. Within the two decades after the invention of the movies, there were two major shifts: first from individual owners of small production companies (e.g., Edison and Griffith) to medium-sized firms and then to the large corporations that not only sold stock but also relied heavily on the infusion of major capital from the investment community. Because prudent investors have traditionally considered producing films to be a risky business, the motion-picture industry recognized that it would need efficient management, timely production practices, and profitable results to attract the capital necessary to sustain it. As Hollywood grew, its production practices became more and more standardized. Today, producers aggressively seek the support of a newer breed of investors.

From the beginning, however, the vertical organizational structure of the studios was challenged by independent producers. Although the studios dominated the distribution and exhibition of films (at least until 1948, when the federal government broke that monopoly), the independents did have access to many movie theaters and could compete successfully for the outside financing they required. The early success of independent producers—such as David O. Selznick in gaining the financing for such major undertakings as *Gone with the Wind* (1939)—demonstrates their individual strengths as well as the viability and possible profitability of their alternative approach to the studio system.

No rule governs the arranging of financing. Money may come from the studio, the producer, the investment community, or (most probably) a combination of these. Nor does one timetable exist for securing money. By studying the production credits of films (known as the billing block), you can see just how many organizations may back a project.

For example, Figure 11.5 lists the opening credits of Bill Condon's *Gods and Monsters* (1998) in the order of their appearance on the screen. Universal Studios released the film, which involved the financial as well as creative input of six entities: Lionsgate Films, Showtime, Flashpoint, BBC Films, Regent Entertainment, and Gregg Fienberg. Separate title screens identify two line producers, three co-executive producers, two executive producers, and two more executive producers. Finally, a "Produced By" screen credit lists three more names. Each person receiving credit as a producer was affiliated with one of the six entities listed at the beginning of the film and may also have had some creative responsibility beyond her or his financial and organizational concerns.

With twelve people listed as producers at one title or another on *Gods and Monsters*, you might wonder about the hierarchy among these names, who the *actual* producers are, and what they do. You would not be alone in feeling confused. Apparently, the Producers Guild of America (e.g., the producers' union) saw that confusion and, in 2012, adopted the "producers' mark," a designation (p.g.a.) that appears on the screen following the names of those producers receiving the "produced by" credit in motion pictures. This mark signifies that those persons have met the guild's standard of undertaking "a majority of producing duties on a motion picture" so that, should their movie win the Academy Award for Best Picture, each would receive an Oscar statuette.[12]

Some producers will have enough start-up financing to ensure that the preproduction phase can proceed

12. See Ben Schott, "Assembling the Billing Block," *New York Times* (February 24, 2013), Sunday Review section. www.nytimes.com/interactive /2013/02/24/opinion/sunday/ben-schott-movies-billingblocks.html (accessed September 22, 2014).

Figure 11.5 | PRODUCERS' CREDITS ON *GODS AND MONSTERS*

UNIVERSAL

[Title superimposed over company logo]

LIONSGATE FILMS
SHOWTIME and FLASHPOINT
in association with
BBC FILMS
Present

A
REGENT ENTERTAINMENT
PRODUCTION

in association with
GREGG FIENBERG

A
BILL CONDON
FILM

Next, separate titles list the principal members of the cast, film title, and major members of the production crew.

LINE PRODUCERS
JOHN SCHOUWEILER
&
LISA LEVY

CO-EXECUTIVE PRODUCERS
VALORIE MASSALAS
SAM IRVIN
SPENCER PROFFER

EXECUTIVE PRODUCERS
CLIVE BARKER
&
STEPHEN P. JARCHOW

EXECUTIVE PRODUCERS
DAVID FORREST
&
BEAU ROGERS

PRODUCED BY
PAUL COLICHMAN
GREGG FIENBERG
MARK R. HARRIS

with key people on the payroll; others will not be able to secure the necessary funds until they present investors with a detailed account of anticipated audiences and projected profits. Whether a movie is produced independently (in which case it is usually established as an independent corporation) or by one of the studios (in which case it is a distinct project among many), financial and logistic control is essential to making progress and ultimately completing the actual work of production as well as to holding down costs. Initial budgets are subject to constant modification, so budgeting, accounting, and auditing are as important as they would be in any costly industrial undertaking.

In the old studio system, the general manager, in consultation with the director and key members of the production team, determined the budget for a film, which consisted of two basic categories: direct costs and indirect costs. Direct costs included everything from art direction and cinematography to insurance. Indirect costs, usually 20 percent of the direct costs, covered the studio's overall contribution to "overhead" (such items as making release prints from the negative, marketing, advertising, and distribution). Table 11.3 shows the summary budget for Michael Curtiz's *Casablanca* (1942), including a line-item accounting for each major expense. Direct costs were 73 percent of the total budget.

Today, in the independent system, budgeting is done differently. Usually the producer or a member of the producer's team prepares the budget with the assistant director. The total cost of producing the completed movie generally breaks down into a ratio of 30 percent to 70 percent between above-the-line costs (the costs of the preproduction stage, producer, director, cast, screenwriter, and literary property from which the script was developed) and below-the-line costs (the costs of the production and postproduction stages and the crew).[13] Categorizing costs according to where they are incurred in the three stages of production is a change from the studio-system method.

Costs also vary depending on whether union or nonunion labor is being used. In some cases, producers have little flexibility in this regard, but usually their hiring of personnel is open to negotiation within industry standards. Finally, we must always remember that no matter what approach is taken to making movies, movie-industry accounting practices traditionally have been as creative as, if not more creative than, the movies themselves.

Marketing and Distribution

After screening a movie's answer print (the first combined print of the film, incorporating picture, sound, and special effects) for executives of the production company as well as for family, friends, and advisers, the producer may show it to audiences at previews. Members of preview audiences are invited because they represent the demographics of the audience for which the film is intended (e.g., female teenagers).

After the preview screening, preview viewers are asked to complete detailed questionnaires to gauge their reactions. At the same time, the producer may also have chosen a smaller focus group from this audience and will meet with them personally after the screening to get their reactions firsthand. After analyzing both the questionnaires and the responses of the focus group, the person in charge of the final cut—either the producer or the director—may make changes in the film.

Although this procedure is presumably more "scientific" than that employed in previous years by the studios, it reflects the same belief in designing a film by the numbers. Since most major movies are intended as entertainment for the largest, broadest audience possible, the strategy makes business sense. Films intended to appeal to smaller, more homogeneous audiences must attract them through publicity generated by media coverage, festival screenings and awards, and audience word of mouth.

The mode of production determines how the activities in this final phase of postproduction are accomplished. Under the studio system, in the days of vertical integration, each studio or its parent company controlled production, distribution, and exhibition. Independent producers, however, have never followed any single path in distributing films. A small producer without a distribution network has various options, which include renting the film to a studio (such as Paramount) or to a producing organization (such as United Artists or Miramax) that will distribute it. These larger firms can also arrange for the film to be advertised and exhibited.

Deciding how and where to advertise, distribute, and show a film is, like the filmmaking process itself, the work of professionals. During the final weeks of postproduction, the people responsible for promotion and marketing make a number of weighty decisions. They determine the release date (essential for planning and carrying out the advertising and other publicity necessary to build an audience) and the number of screens

---

13. An excellent source of information on current budgeting practices is Deke Simon with Michael Wiese, *Film and Video Budgets*, 4th ed. (Studio City, CA: Michael Wiese Productions, 2006).

Table 11.3 | SUMMARY BUDGET FOR *CASABLANCA*

	Subtotals	Totals	Grand Totals
DIRECT COSTS			**$638,222**
Story		$67,281	
Story	$20,000		
Continuity and treatment (writers, secretaries, and script changes)	$47,281		
Direction		$83,237	
Director: Michael Curtiz	$73,400		
Assistant Director: Lee Katz	$9,837		
Producer: Hal Wallis		$52,000	
Cinematography		$11,273	
Camera operators and assistants	$10,873		
Camera rental and expenses	$400		
Cast		$217,603	
Cast salaries: talent under contract to studio, including Humphrey Bogart, Sydney Greenstreet, Paul Henreid, and others	$69,867		
Cast salaries: outside talent, including Ingrid Bergman, Claude Rains, Dooley Wilson, Peter Lorre, and others	$91,717		
Talent (extras, bits, etc.)	$56,019		
Musicians (musical score, arrangers, etc.)		$28,000	
Sound expenses		$2,200	
Sound operating salaries		$8,000	
Art department		$8,846	
Wardrobe expenses		$22,320	
Makeup, hairdressers, etc.		$9,100	
Electricians		$20,755	
Editors' salaries		$4,630	
Special effects		$7,475	
Negative film stock		$8,000	
Developing and printing		$10,500	
Property labor		$10,150	
Construction of sets		$18,000	
Standby labor		$15,350	
Striking (dismantling sets and storing props)		$7,000	
Property rental and expenses		$6,300	
Electrical rental and expenses		$750	
Location expenses		$1,252	
Catering		$1,200	

	Subtotals	Totals	Grand Totals
Auto rental expenses and travel		$5,000	
Insurance		$2,800	
Miscellaneous expenses		$3,350	
Trailer (preview)		$2,000	
Stills		$850	
Publicity		$3,000	
INDIRECT COSTS			**$239,778**
General studio overhead (35%)		$223,822	
Depreciation (2.5%)		$15,956	
GRAND TOTAL COST (release negative)			**$878,000**

Source: Adapted from Joel Finler, *The Hollywood Story* (New York: Crown, 1988), p. 39.

on which the film will make its debut. At the same time, they finalize domestic and foreign distribution rights and ancillary rights, contract with firms who make DVDs, schedule screenings on airlines and cruise ships, and, for certain kinds of films, arrange marketing tie-ins with fast-food chains, toy manufacturers, and so on.

The model for distributing and exhibiting a movie depends on the product itself. For example, there are exclusive and limited releases (a first-run showing in major cities, often used to gauge public response before a wider release), key-city releases (a second-tier release that further measures public response), and wide and saturated releases on hundreds or thousands of screens in the major markets as good reviews and word of mouth build public awareness and demand. In addition, based on the mode of release, there are complex formulas for establishing the rental cost of a print (or digital download), ticket prices, length of run, up-front guarantees, and box office grosses. The latter do not reflect what a theater or studio earns, but rather what the public spends to see a film. What part of a movie's gross goes to the producers, investors, and those (directors, writers, actors, etc.) who have a share of the gross included in their contracts remains one of Hollywood's most mysterious dealings.

In a further attempt to create new revenue streams for studios and new viewing options for consumers, Hollywood is planning to bring movies to homes at the same time (or close to it) that they are released in the-aters. Such distribution practices are not yet proven to be economically or technically feasible and, in any event, are likely to throw the current method of theatrical distribution into turmoil. For example, on-demand streaming services like Netflix and Amazon Prime Video have already begun to change when, how, and where we look at movies.

Some or all of this activity is responsive to the voluntary movie rating system administered by the Motion Picture Association of America (MPAA), the trade association of the industry. Because the rating helps determine the marketing of a film and thus the potential size of its audience, it is very important. But ratings should also tell parents all they need to know to make wise choices about what their children see, and that's where they fall short, especially with the PG-13 ratings. Such films have increasing amounts of violence, profanity, and nudity, factors that are often played down by the rating system. Since movies rated PG-13 appeal to a teenage audience—especially boys, whose attendance is vital to their success at the box office—the rating language has become less useful (Table 11.4).

Once initial marketing and distribution decisions have been made, all that remains is to show the film to the public, analyze the reviews in the media and the box office receipts of the first weekend, and make whatever changes are necessary in the distribution, advertising, and exhibition strategies to ensure that the movie will reach its targeted audience.

Table 11.4 | MPAA MOVIE-RATING SYSTEM

Rating Category	Explanation
G: General Audience	Nothing that would offend parents for viewing by children.
PG: Parental Guidance Suggested	Parents urged to give "parental guidance." May contain some material parents might not like for their young children.
PG-13: Parents Strongly Cautioned	Parents are urged to be cautious. Some material may be inappropriate for preteenagers.
R: Restricted	Contains some adult material. Parents are urged to learn more about the film before taking their young children with them.
NC-17: No One 17 and under Admitted	Clearly adult. Children are not admitted.

Source: From www.mpaa.org/film-ratings/ (accessed August 2014).

Production in Hollywood Today

The production system in Hollywood today is an amalgam of (1) a studio system that differs radically from that of the golden age described earlier and (2) independent production companies, many of which are "small picture" or "prestige" (non-genre) divisions of the larger studios. The term *studio system* no longer means what it once did: a group of vertically integrated, meticulously organized factories that employ large numbers of contract employees in the creative arts and crafts. Today there is no "system," and the studios exist to make and release movies, one at a time. In addition, now that almost every studio has its own prestige "indie" division, very few producers are truly independent.

As Table 11.5 shows, there are currently six major studios in the United States, as well as four independent producers that are referred to in Hollywood as *mini-majors*. The best known of these mini-majors are Lionsgate and Lantern Entertainment (formerly The Weinstein Company). There are, in addition, many other independent producers too numerous to list. In terms of numbers of films and earning power, the mini-majors and other independents have become more important than the major studios. Altogether in 2016 (the latest year for which definitive information is available), these three groups released 718 theatrical movies that grossed $11.4 bil-lion in the U.S. market. Of that total number of films, 139 were produced by the major studios (19 percent) and 579 (81 percent) by the independents, some of which are subsidiaries of the majors. These figures alone show how dramatically production has changed in Hollywood.[14]

Because they dominate the international market, the major studios continue to define movie production in the United States. When one of the smaller studios has a larger corporate owner, the parent firm is usually the distributor. In addition, countless independent producers must distribute their movies through the "big six" studios if they want the largest possible audience and the maximum profits on their investments.[15]

To get a better sense of how this arrangement works today, consider Table 11.6, which shows how the nine Oscar nominees for Best Picture of 2016 were produced and released. All nine involved multiple coproduction deals, and three were released by major studios: *Arrival*, *Fences*, and *Hidden Figures*. In one way or another, the major studios kept control of the box office.

Today, with its reorganization into a production system dominated by independent producers and its ongoing conversion to digital technology, Hollywood is in a strong position to face the future. But television is attracting new audiences with programs of content that rival Hollywood in sophistication, violence, and previously untouched subjects. The traditional networks and cable companies have been joined in such production by Netflix and Amazon. In addition, new delivery systems have

14. Data from https://www.mpaa.org/wp-content/uploads/2017/03/MPAA-Theatrical-Market-Statistics-2016_Final-1.pdf (accessed January 15, 2018).

15. Benjamin M. Compaine and Douglas Gomery, *Who Owns the Media: Competition and Concentration in the Mass Media Industry*, 3rd ed. (Mahwah, N.J.: Erlbaum, 2000), p. 373.

Table 11.5 | HOLLYWOOD STUDIOS AND INDEPENDENT PRODUCTION COMPANIES TODAY

Major Studio	Owner	Independent Production Companies Owned by Studio
20th Century Fox	21st Century Fox	Blue Sky Studios, Fox Searchlight Pictures
Columbia Pictures	Sony	Screen Gems, Sony Pictures Animation, Sony Pictures Classics
Paramount Pictures	Viacom	
Universal Pictures	Comcast	DreamWorks Animation, Focus Features, Illumination Entertainment, Working Title Films
Walt Disney Pictures	The Walt Disney Company	Disneynature, DisneyToon Studios, Lucasfilm, Marvel Studios, Pixar, Walt Disney Animation Studios
Warner Bros. Pictures	Time Warner	New Line Cinema, Warner Bros. Animation
Mini-Major Production Companies		
Lionsgate Films	Lionsgate	Summit Entertainment
Open Road Films	Tang Media Partners	
STXfilms	STX Entertainment	
The Weinstein Company	Bob Weinstein	Dimension Films

Table 11.6 | PRODUCTION AND DISTRIBUTION DATA FOR THE 2016 OSCAR NOMINEES FOR BEST PICTURE

Title	Producers*	Number of Coproduction Companies	U.S. Distributors
Arrival	Shawn Levy, Dan Levine, Aaron Ryder, David Linde	3	Paramount Pictures
Fences	Todd Black, Scott Rudin, Denzel Washington	5	Paramount Pictures
Hacksaw Ridge	Bill Mechanic, David Permut, Terry Benedict, Paul Currie, Bruce Davey, Brian Oliver, William D. Johnson	5	Summit Entertainment
Hell or High Water	Sidney Kimmel, Peter Berg, Carla Hacken, Julie Yorn	4	CBS Films
Hidden Figures	Donna Gigliotti, Peter Chernin, Jenno Topping, Pharrell Williams, Theodore Melfi	3	20th Century Fox
La La Land	Fred Berger, Jordan Horowitz, Gary Gilbert, Marc Platt	6	Summit Entertainment
Lion	Iain Canning, Angie Fielder, Emile Sherman	5	The Weinstein Company
Manchester by the Sea	Matt Damon, Kimberly Steward, Chris Moore, Kevin J. Walsh, Lauren Beck	7	Roadside Attractions, Amazon Studios
Moonlight	Adele Romanski, Dede Gardner, Jeremy Kleiner	3	A24

*Names recognized by the Academy of Motion Picture Arts and Sciences for legal and award purposes.

been developed for both movie and television content, including streaming video and renting movies on demand. These systems are sure to negatively affect DVD and Blu-ray sales. While formats remain the same, it's still an open question whether 3-D movies are here to stay. In 2010, *Avatar* (2009; director James Cameron), *Toy Story 3* (2010; director Lee Unkrich), and *Alice in Wonderland* (2010; director Tim Burton) helped 3-D movies capture 21 percent of box office sales in North America. By 2016, revenue drawn by 3-D movies had shrunk to just 14 percent of total ticket sales. When 3-D was first introduced, some industry analysts predicted the technology might be applied to almost all industry output. Today, 3-D is primarily reserved for major animated children's films and big-budget science-fiction and action spectacles.[16]

As the following discussion shows, Hollywood is also facing other challenges: new sources of production and distribution, the importance of movie franchises to the whole equation, new movie content, shifting demographics in audiences, and new delivery systems.

Audience Demographics

While Hollywood is aggressively planning its future in various ways, it must also be able to attract a broad audience globally as well as in the United States. The 2016 U.S. box office of $11.4 billion was up 2 percent over that of 2015; 3-D box office was down 8 percent from the previous year. More women (52 percent) than men went to the movies, and the overall demographic composition was 59 percent white, 20 percent Hispanic, 12 percent African American, and 9 percent composed of Asian Americans and others. The largest share of the audience was in two groups: 18- to 24-year-olds and 25- to 39-year-olds, with shrinking figures in the 40- to 49-year-old age group. Of the five top-grossing films of 2016, three of the more family-friendly features attracted more female audience members, while two more action-oriented films, *Rogue One: A Star Wars Story* and *Captain America: Civil War*, attracted primarily male audience members. Figures such as these play an incalculable role in planning and making movies.

Franchises

A franchise offers a fertile if not always fresh source of content. Literally, a movie franchise involves the licensing of an original work to others, such as the licensing of J. K. Rowling's fantasy novels to Warner Bros. studios, which then produced a series of (so far) seven Harry Potter films and two Fantastic Beasts movies. Fifteen of the twenty-five top-grossing films of 2017 in the United States were in this category, as indicated in bold in the

list below. Of the ten non-franchise films on this list, two are remakes (*Beauty and the Beast* and *It*), and one is a sequel (*Jumanji: Welcome to the Jungle*). Only seven are entirely self-contained stories.

1. ***Star Wars: The Last Jedi***
2. *Beauty and the Beast*
3. ***Wonder Woman***
4. ***Guardians of the Galaxy Vol. 2***
5. ***Spider-Man: Homecoming***
6. *It*
7. ***Thor: Ragnarok***
8. ***Despicable Me 3***
9. ***Logan***
10. ***The Fate of the Furious***
11. ***Justice League***
12. *Dunkirk*
13. *Coco*
14. ***The LEGO Batman Movie***
15. *Get Out*
16. *The Boss Baby*
17. ***Pirates of the Caribbean: Dead Men Tell No Tales***
18. *Jumanji: Welcome to the Jungle*
19. ***Kong: Skull Island***
20. ***Cars 3***
21. ***War for the Planet of the Apes***
22. *Split*
23. ***Transformers: The Last Knight***
24. *Wonder*
25. *Girls Trip*

The movie franchise is almost as old as the movies themselves. When a movie featuring a certain type of character or story is successful, Hollywood seeks to repeat that success with as many sequels as the market will bear. For example, when the first Tarzan film attracted a

---

16. https://www.hollywoodreporter.com/behind-screen/is-golden-age-3d-officially-1025843 (accessed January 15, 2018).

large audience in 1918, a sequel was rushed into production and came out the same year. Three additional Tarzan films were released in the next three years. And it's not over yet; the most recent Tarzan film (*Tarzan of the Jungle*; director David Yates) was released in 2016.

Among the most long-lasting and successful of Hollywood franchises, both live action and animation, are the Star Wars, Harry Potter, and Lord of the Rings movies, as well as those featuring (in various guises, settings, and plots) characters such as James Bond, Sherlock Holmes, Batman, Shrek, Wolverine, Captain Jack Sparrow, various vampires and zombies (in the Twilight and Resident Evil series), the indestructible policeman John McClane of the Die Hard films, and animals such as Lassie and Beethoven. Movie franchises tap into the same audience preferences that propel TV franchises such as *Game of Thrones* and *Stranger Things*. Viewers enjoy following the development of a particular story and cast of characters over a long course of time.

One such franchise is the X-Men series from 20th Century Fox, which is based around the titular Marvel Comics characters. At this writing, the series includes *X-Men* (2000), *X2* (2003; both directed by Bryan Singer), *X-Men: The Last Stand* (2006; director Brett Ratner), *X-Men: Origins: Wolverine* (2009; director Gavin Hood), *X-Men: First Class* (2011; director Matthew Vaughn), *The Wolverine* (2013; director James Mangold); *X-Men: Days of Future Past* (2014; director Bryan Singer), *Deadpool* (2016; director Tim Miller), *X-Men: Apocalypse* (2016; director Bryan Singer), *Logan* (2017; director James Mangold), and *The New Mutants* (2018; director Josh Boone).

In the wake of the success of Twentieth Century Fox's X-Men series, Marvel Entertainment (formerly Marvel Comics) launched a franchise based on character rights the company still retained. The franchise, known as the Marvel Cinematic Universe, is composed of multiple film series that take place in the same narrative and cinematic world. Individual trilogies exist for characters such as Iron Man, Captain America, and Thor, yet these characters often appear in one another's films, the stories of which maintain a shared narrative continuity. The Marvel Cinematic Universe is the highest-grossing franchise in history. Seventeen films have been released as of 2017, as have multiple television series; seven more films are currently in development. Disney took control of the project following its acquisition of Marvel in 2009.

Other studios have attempted to follow Marvel's example, notably Warner Bros., owner of the rights to Marvel's rival, DC Comics. A "DC Cinematic Universe" was launched with Zack Snyder's *Man of Steel* (2013). The studio has had varying levels of success with follow-ups: Zack Snyder's *Batman v Superman: Dawn of Justice* (2016), David Ayer's *Suicide Squad* (2016), Patty Jenkins's *Wonder Woman* (2017), and Snyder's *Justice League* (2017). In addition, Warner Bros. is currently coproducing a different "universe" of films alongside Legendary Pictures; dubbed the "MonsterVerse," the films revolve around the famous movie monsters Godzilla and King Kong. Installments include Gareth Edwards's *Godzilla* (2014), Jordan Vogt-Roberts's *Kong: Skull Island* (2016), and the upcoming *Godzilla: King of the Monsters* (2019). Plans are currently in place for the fourth film to pit Godzilla and Kong against each other.

Universal's "Dark Universe" represents a less successful franchise effort. The studio attempted to develop an entire expanded series of films, each of which would feature a monster from the studio's acclaimed horror franchises from the 1930s and 1940s. However, the franchise's inaugural release, Alex Kurtzman's *The Mummy* (2017), was critically panned and lost money, leaving the future of this particular "universe" uncertain.

The animated series Despicable Me, which includes a film trilogy as well as the spin-off film *Minions* (2015), is another notable contemporary franchise. All four films have been tremendous box office successes, with *Despicable Me 3* (2017) and *Minions* each grossing more than $1 billion worldwide. The four films combined have earned more money than any other animated film franchise in history.

James Cameron's 3-D science-fiction spectacle *Avatar* (2009) is the best-selling movie in history, but it has yet to launch a franchise. But fear not: Cameron plans four successive Avatar movies to be released between 2020 and 2025. Its producers can only predict box office numbers at this point, but much is riding on this project's success.

LGBT Movies

Recent years have seen an increased prominence for LGBT cinema, as attitudes about queer, genderqueer, and transgender individuals continue to change around the globe. Although Todd Haynes's critically acclaimed film *Carol* (2015), a romance about two women in 1950s New York, was denied nominations for Best Picture and Best Director at the 88th Academy Awards (to some controversy), the next year saw *Moonlight* (2016; director Barry Jenkins), a rare film dealing with homosexuality and black masculinity, achieve a surprise win for Best Picture, making it the first LGBT-themed film to win the prestigious award.

Other noteworthy films of the past few years include Tom Hooper's *The Danish Girl* (2015), about transgender artist Lili Elbe, Park Chan-wook's erotic thriller *The Handmaiden* (2016), Robin Campillo's 2017 AIDS drama *BPM (Beats per Minute)*, and the romantic dramas *Call Me by Your Name* (2017; director Luca Guadagnino) and *God's Own Country* (2017; director Francis Lee).

African American Movies

In the first decade of the new century, an increasing number of African American movies were released. Their stories, cast, and crew reflect a continuingly growing diversity of race, gender, and background.

The blockbuster franchises featuring black stories and characters include Michael Bay's Bad Boys films (1995, 2003), Barry Sonnenfeld's Men in Black series (1997, 2002), Brett Ratner's Rush Hour franchise (1998, 2001, 2007), and the nine films in Tyler Perry's Madea franchise (2005–13).

Other notable films in this period were Jim Sheridan's *Get Rich or Die Tryin'* (2008), Lee Daniels's *Precious* (2009) as well as *The Butler* and *The Paperboy* (both 2012), Tate Taylor's *The Help* (2011), Joshua Bee Alafia's *Let's Stay Together* (2011), Quentin Tarantino's *Django Unchained* (2012), Tim Story's *Think Like a Man* (2012), Benh Zeitlin's *Beasts of the Southern Wild* (2012), Steve McQueen's *12 Years a Slave* (2013), Ryan Coogler's *Fruitvale Station* (2013), *Creed* (2015), and *Black Panther* (2018), Justin Chadwick's *Mandela: Long Walk to Freedom* (2013), Ava DuVernay's *Selma* (2014), and F. Gary Gray's *Straight Outta Compton* (2015).

Following criticisms of the lack of diversity in the filmmakers and films nominated for the 87th and 88th Academy Awards, Hollywood has seen increased recognition for films starring and/or made by African Americans over the past several years. At the 89th Academy Awards, the Academy of Motion Picture Arts and Sciences nominated such films as *Fences* (2016; director Denzel Washington), *Hidden Figures* (2016; director

Theodore Melfi), *Loving* (2016; director Jeff Nichols), and *Moonlight* (2016; director Barry Jenkins) for various awards; *Moonlight* became the first film with an all-black cast to win the Oscar for Best Picture.

F. Gary Gray's *The Fate of the Furious* (2017) and Ryan Coogler's *Black Panther* (2018) have brought African American directors into the blockbuster franchise field. *A Wrinkle in Time* (2018) made Ava DuVernay the first woman of color to direct a feature film with a budget of more than $100 million.

Foreign Influences on Hollywood Films

Of the $38.6 billion global box office in 2017, 71 percent came from foreign audiences, among which China was the largest. Hollywood faces a great challenge to make movies that will continue to sell to these audiences. Studios try to enhance the appeal of their movies in various ways by collaborating with local producers, hiring more foreign actors in blockbusters, rewriting scripts to enhance a story's global appeal, and concentrating on producing action movies that are the most successful.

Toward this end, we have recently seen a surge of multinational productions in which the United States shares financing with China, Germany, Britain, or France. These movies, which are truly international in story and casting as well as financing and distribution, include blockbusters like *Transformers: Age of Extinction* (2014; director Michael Bay), *The Great Wall* (2017; director Zhang Yimou) and *Kong: Skull Island* (2017), and prestige dramas such as *Lion* (2016; director Garth Davis) and *Dunkirk* (2017). These examples and other multinational productions are engineered to appeal to global audiences.

Looking at the Future of the Film Industry

Among the major U.S. industries—including manufacturing, banking, chemicals, mining, utilities, and health care—one of the most resilient is the entertainment industry (particularly the movies). Since the founding of this industry in the early years of the twentieth century, film studios have opened and closed, and creative talent has come and gone. But the production of movies has never stopped, although it slowed considerably during World War II. Unlike the car manufacturing or banking industries, the movies have avoided large-scale government surveillance, takeovers, and bailouts. Hollywood realized early in the 1930s that self-regulation through various but relatively ineffective ratings systems was better than government censorship, no matter what it was called. Because the movie industry is continually adapting to new technological and market forces, because it enjoys a high rate of consumer satisfaction, and because its profits (despite its voodoo accounting methods) please its investors, it remains a significant part of the U.S. industrial economy.

We know that today's movie industry is more concerned with explosions. Moviegoers are seeing more digital demolition per movie than ever before. But director Steven Spielberg recently warned that the failure of six or so $250 million movies would cause an implosion—a violent inward collapse—that could alter the industry forever. Director George Lucas agreed that the film industry is going through a period of extraordinary turmoil, and he predicted a virtual trifecta of doom: fewer films would be released and they would stay in theaters longer (about a year), and ticket prices would be much higher. Books appeared with titles like *Do the Movies Have a Future?* (2012) and *Film after Film: Or, What Became of 21st Century Cinema?* (2012).

People have been predicting the death of the film industry for as long as it has existed. Of all the major industries, it is probably the one most vulnerable to the ups and downs created by technological changes, particularly the rapid development of alternative digital means of getting the movie to the viewer; available financing for production; and unpredictable customer tastes. When sound came in, industry analysts predicted that theater owners would go broke in refitting their theaters with new projectors and sound systems; they were wrong. The advent of color caused die-hard traditionalists to argue that movies were supposed to be made in black and white. Depending on your preferences, they may have been right; depending on the creative opportunities afforded by shooting on color film stock (as a contrast to black and white), they were completely correct. When television came in, analysts predicted that people would stay home to watch movies on television and shun the theaters; they were partly right and partly wrong. The tales of gloom and doom go on.

So what happened to all these predictions? While a significant number of blockbusters failed, the studios continued to make them and to be unfazed by such colossal wrecks as Josh Trank's *Fantastic Four* (2015), Gore Verbinski's *A Cure for Wellness* (2016), and Guy Ritchie's *King Arthur: Legend of the Sword* (2017). There always have been, and always will be, big-budget stumbles. The studios know that the blockbuster strategy works. And, as for digital technology, the fast-paced conversion continues without any studio or theater chains going bankrupt or out of business. The cinema, in this country and around the world, is neither dying nor dead. Hollywood is sticking with the two strategies that work most effectively—producing blockbusters and movies that are part of a successful franchise. But it is also producing the kind of carefully budgeted, star-driven movie that many say isn't being made anymore, such as David Mackenzie's *Hell or High Water* (2017), as well as a healthy list of **art house** movies, such as Darren Aronofsky's *Mother!* (2017). A film critic for the *Wall Street Journal* says, "The future for films of quality is breaking good."[17] Large capital investments are ensuring a steady digital conversion. Enrollments in film production schools have never been higher, and we are seeing a growing list of new directors including Sean Baker, Ryan Coogler, Ava DuVernay, Greta Gerwig, Barry Jenkins, and Dee Rees.

Statistics support this careful, optimistic outlook.[18] In 2016 (the last year for which authoritative figures are available), U.S. box office income was up, thanks to increased ticket prices, while admissions remained steady. More than two-thirds of the population went to the movies at least once in that year. Attendance was higher for most age groups, and 25- to 39-year-olds, the most active movie-viewing demographic, accounted for 24 percent of tickets sold.

Because the movie industry is driven by the box office numbers, the following analysis of the twenty-five top-grossing movies of 2017 (see the list of movies on p. 436) will provide a good idea of what U.S. audiences were seeing.

17. Joe Morgenstern, "In Defense of the Movies," *Wall Street Journal* (September 20, 2013), sec. D1, p. 1.

18. https://www.mpaa.org/wp-content/uploads/2017/03/MPAA-Theatrical-Market-Statistics-2016_Final-1.pdf (accessed January 16, 2018).

❭ Overall, twenty (80 percent) of these twenty-five movies were live-action features; five were animated features.

- Thirteen movies (52 percent) were in the action/adventure genre.
- Thirteen (52 percent) were in the action/adventure genre with some secondary overlap in one or more of the following genres: comedy, drama, fantasy, sci-fi, mystery, and crime.
- One (4 percent) was a comedy.
- One (4 percent) was a drama.
- One (4 percent) was a history film.
- Three (12 percent) were horror movies.

❭ Percentages of total by rating:
- One (4 percent) was rated G.
- Six (24 percent) were rated PG.
- Fourteen (56 percent) were rated PG-13.
- Four (16 percent) were rated R.

❭ Fifteen (60 percent) of the total twenty-five movies were part of a franchise series.

❭ Seven (12 percent) of the total twenty-five movies were based on a comic book.

The movies in this list offer plenty of good entertainment for all ages. But there are other movies in all genres, from all parts of the world, that help us to track other trends in contemporary film production. For example, the annual international poll conducted by *Sight & Sound*, the international film magazine, produced the following list of the best films of 2017 (with director and countries of production):

❭ *Get Out* (Jordan Peele; USA and Japan)

❭ *Twin Peaks: The Return* (David Lynch; U.S.)

❭ *Call Me by Your Name* (Luca Guadagnino; Italy, France, Brazil, and U.S.)

❭ *Zama* (Lucrecia Martel; Argentina and others)

❭ *Western* (Valeska Grisebach; Germany, Bulgaria, and Austria)

❭ *Faces Places* (JR/Agnès Varda; France)

❭ *Good Time* (Benny Safdie/Josh Safdie; U.S.)

❭ *Loveless* (Andrey Zvyagintsev; Russia, France, Germany, and Belgium)

❭ *Dunkirk* (Christopher Nolan; U.K., Netherlands, France, and USA) tied with *The Florida Project* (Sean Baker; USA)

❭ *A Ghost Story* (David Lowery; USA)

❭ *Lady Macbeth* (William Oldroyd; U.K.) tied with *120 BPM* (Robin Campillo; France) and *You Were Never Really Here* (Lynne Ramsay; U.K., France, and USA)

❭ *God's Own Country* (Francis Lee; U.K.)

❭ *Personal Shopper* (Olivier Assayas; France, Germany, Czech Republic, and Belgium) tied with *The Shape of Water* (Guillermo del Toro; USA and Canada) and *Strong Island* (Yance Ford; USA and Denmark)

❭ *I Am Not Your Negro* (Raoul Peck; Switzerland, France, Belgium, and USA) tied with *Lady Bird* (Greta Gerwig; USA), *Let the Sunshine In* (Claire Denis; France and Belgium), *Moonlight* (Barry Jenkins; USA), *Mother!* (Darren Aronofsky; USA), and *Mudbound* (Dee Rees; USA)

❭ *The Other Side of Hope* (Aki Kaurismäki; Finland, and Germany) tied with *Silence* (Martin Scorsese; USA, Mexico, and Taiwan)

By comparing this list of favorites, based on an international poll, with the list of the twenty-five top-grossing movies in the United States, you will see that there is only a small amount of overlap: only *Get Out* and *Dunkirk* were both international favorites and among the U.S. top-grossing films. Many critically acclaimed films are theatrically distributed in limited areas and never reach large audiences. In the past, discerning movie lovers outside of large cities might never see or even hear about these important and worthy films. But, thanks to the Internet, viewers now have new ways to read about, research, and watch these and other high-quality movies. In addition to online DVD and Blu-ray sales and major video streaming and disc rental companies such as Netflix, curated sites and services such as FilmStruck and Kanopy offer large catalogs of new releases, as well as classic and cult films, to anyone willing to pay the subscription fee.

ANALYZING HOW THE MOVIES ARE MADE

Understanding and appreciating what can, and has been, achieved in a particular movie is closely linked to understanding the technology and production systems that existed at the time it was made. Major—sometimes revolutionary—advances in technology and production systems (the how and where movies are made) have generally been made when a director or producer asks for a stylistic effect for which neither technique nor technology currently exist. Sometimes, the response is "That's impossible" or "That's not the way we do things here." Fortunately, though, such requests throw down challenges to the artists and technicians working on the movie. For example, even though Orson Welles had never made a movie before *Citizen Kane*, he knew what he wanted and was sufficiently enthusiastic and persuasive to convince his crew to improve existing technologies (e.g., in deep-focus cinematography) or invent new ones (e.g., in sound recording). The result, of course, radically changed the prevailing conventions of moviemaking. But even *Citizen Kane*, revolutionary as it was, has its weaknesses. Take, for example, the special effects used throughout the movie. Although the effects represent the state of the art in 1940, they are not seamlessly integrated into the images and so, in contrast to what we see today, are clumsy. Understanding what could (and could not) be achieved at a particular time in film history helps us to understand the current state of film art and the opportunities (and limitations) available to filmmakers. Keeping this perspective is vital today as we watch the film industry making its first steps toward what most experts agree will be an almost total conversion to digital technologies. Yesterday's movies are being digitally remastered to restore the visual depth and sparkle of the original 35mm prints, and while those movies today that are being shot digitally do not necessarily improve the image, they are challenging our visual perception and thus the way we look at movies.

SCREENING CHECKLIST: HOW THE MOVIES ARE MADE

✔ In studying a particular movie, learn as much as you can about the prevailing cinematic conventions and state of the filmmaking art at the time it was made. In particular, do some research on the major creative personnel to determine if any of them are known for particular innovations. For example, if you are studying the influence of F. W. Murnau's *Sunrise: A Song of Two Humans* (1927) on Hollywood conventions, it's important to know his key role in the development of the German Expressionist film as well as his pioneering use of the moving camera.

✔ Movies made during the height of the studio system in Hollywood and those made in the independent system that followed are often quite similar in their look. However, the studio system had some space for mavericks, the independent system relies heavily on traditional methods of moviemaking, and the production system in place today is very much a hybrid of the two. In studying a movie, try to determine how much the production system affected its production. You might, for example, examine such related aspects as design, lighting, and cinematography.

✔ Today we have six major studios (all carryovers from the golden age) as well as four "mini-major" production companies. Take a close look at a movie by one studio that was produced near the beginning of that studio's history, and then compare it to another made more recently. From this comparative viewing, what can you say about how and to what extent that studio has changed from its beginnings?

✔ An interesting way to gain insight into the production of an independent movie is to examine its financing, particularly the nature and investment of each producer and/or production company. This and other related information can be found in such publications as the *Wall Street Journal*, *Variety*, and the *Hollywood Reporter* as well as online at IMDbPro (https://www.pro.imdb.com). From this information, you can see the hierarchy of financial influences behind the film and pose questions about how they might have affected the movie's content and form.

✔ The conversion to digital technology is a key factor in the overall future of the production, distribution, and exhibition systems of the international film industry. As such, a study of the challenges, costs, and implications of just one of these areas is an excellent subject for your further study, perhaps even a term paper. One way to look at this phenomenon is in the context of the conversion to sound in the late 1920s and early 1930s.

Questions for Review

1. What are the key technological milestones that laid the foundation for the invention of the movies?
2. How do the two filmmaking technologies—film and digital—differ from each other?
3. What are the strengths and weaknesses of film and digital technology?
4. Why are some filmmakers less than enthusiastic about digital technology?
5. What are the challenges and benefits involved in converting the film industry to digital technology in the areas of production, distribution, and exhibition?
6. How was the studio system organized in the golden age, and what factors contributed to its decline?
7. In what major ways does the independent system differ from the studio system?
8. What are the principal activities in each of the three basic phases of making a movie: preproduction, production, and postproduction?
9. How is a movie financed, and why are today's movies so expensive to make?
10. How are movies marketed and distributed? Have these aspects changed between the studio and independent systems?
11. Who were three major Hollywood producers (choose from both the studio and independent systems), and what are the similarities among them?

GLOSSARY

A

AC See **assistant cameraperson**.

ADR See **automatic dialogue replacement**.

additive color systems In early filmmaking, techniques used to add color to black-and-white images, including hand-coloring, stenciling, tinting, and toning. Compare **subtractive color systems**.

aerial-view shot See **bird's-eye-view shot**.

alienation effect Also known as *distancing effect*. A psychological distance between audience and stage for which, according to German playwright Bertolt Brecht, every aspect of a theatrical production should strive, by limiting the audience's identification with characters and events.

ambient sound Sound that seems to the viewer to emanate from the ambience (background) of the setting or environment being filmed. Ambient sound is almost always added or enhanced during postproduction.

American shot See **medium long shot**.

amplitude The degree of motion of air (or other medium) within a sound wave. The greater the amplitude of the sound wave, the harder it strikes the eardrum, and thus the louder the sound. Compare **loudness**.

analog When shot using film stock, film is an analog medium in which the camera creates an image by recording through a camera lens the original light given off by the subject and stores this image on a roll of negative film stock. Opposite of **digital**.

animated film Drawings or other graphical images placed in a series photography–like sequence to portray movement. Before computer graphics technology, the basic type of animated film was created through drawing.

animatic A video that is produced by sequencing storyboard images and adding sound; it is used during previsualization to help filmmakers envision how planned shots will function in an edited sequence.

animatronics A mechanized puppet programmed or remotely controlled by computers or humans. Existing before digital special effects, it is used to create human figures or animals that do not exist and action that is too risky for real actors or animals or too fantastic to be possible in real life.

antagonist The character, creature, or force that obstructs or resists the protagonist's pursuit of her or his goal. Compare **protagonist**.

antihero An outwardly unsympathetic protagonist pursuing a morally objectionable or otherwise undesirable goal.

antirealism A treatment that is against or the opposite of realism. However, realism and antirealism (like realism and fantasy) are not strict polarities. Compare **realism**.

aperture The opening in an iris through which light passes to fall upon the camera film or sensor. See **iris**.

archival material Preexisting images or sound that is incorporated into a documentary film. This material can be any media captured previously and by different sources, including radio broadcasts, news footage, historical photographs, official documents, and home movies.

art director The person responsible for transforming the production designer's vision into a reality on the screen, assessing the staging requirements for a production, and arranging for and supervising the work of members of the art department.

art house A movie theater featuring independent or foreign movies that appeal to small, discerning audiences. While the term is somewhat outdated, it frequently appears in industry business publications.

aspect ratio The relationship between the frame's two dimensions: the width of the image related to its height.

assistant cameraperson (AC) Member of the camera crew who assists the camera operator. The *first AC* oversees everything having to do with the camera, lenses, supporting equipment, and the material on which the movie is being shot. The *second AC* prepares the slate that is used to identify each scene as it is being filmed, files camera reports, and is responsible for moving the camera to each new setup.

associate (or assistant) producer Person charged with carrying out specific responsibilities assigned by the producer, executive producer, or line producer.

associative editing Also known as *intellectual editing*. An editing technique in which contrasting or incongruent images are inserted into a scene or sequence to create juxtapositions that imply a thematic relationship between the content of the paired images.

asynchronous sound Sound that comes from a source apparent in the image but is not precisely matched temporally with the actions occurring in that image.

auteurism A **film theory** based on the idea that the director is the sole "author" of a movie. The application of auteurism frequently takes two forms: a judgment of the whole body of a film director's work (not individual films) based on style, and a classification of great directors based on a hierarchy of directorial styles.

automatic dialogue replacement (ADR) Also known as *looping*. A postproduction process that is used to replace dialogue compromised by intrusive sounds or other on-set recording problems. Actors perform new dialogue in a recording studio while watching looped (repeating) footage of the moment in question.

avant-garde film See **experimental film**.

axis of action An imaginary line connecting two interacting figures in a scene that defines the 180-degree space within which the camera can record shots of those figures. See **180-degree rule**.

B

backlight Also known as *rim light*. Lighting positioned behind the subject and the camera, used to create highlights on the subject as a means of separating it from the background. When the subject is positioned directly between the backlight and the camera, the subject is thrown into silhouette. Using shadows to eliminate recognizable surface detail abstracts the character, which can make him or her (or it) more frightening or impressive, depending on the context of the story at that moment.

backlighting A technique that depicts the subject as a silhouette by using a backlight as the sole light source.

backstory A fictional history behind the cinematic narrative that is presented on-screen. Elements of the backstory can be hinted at in a movie, presented through narration, or not revealed at all.

best boy First assistant electrician to the gaffer on a movie production set.

bird's-eye-view shot Also known as *aerial-view shot*. An extreme high angle shot that is typically taken from a crane, drone, or aircraft.

bit player An actor who holds a small speaking part.

Black Maria The first movie studio—a relatively small shack in which Thomas Edison and his staff began making movies. The Black Maria had a retractable roof and was built on a large turntable that allowed it to be turned to face the sun.

blimp A soundproofed enclosure somewhat larger than a camera, in which the camera may be mounted to prevent its sounds from reaching the microphone.

blockbuster A movie that, whatever its cost, has exceptionally large box office receipts.

blocking The actual physical relationships among figures and settings. Also, the process during rehearsal of establishing those relationships.

boom A pole-like mechanical device used to position the microphone outside the camera frame, but as close as possible to speaking actors.

b-roll Documentary footage of subjects in action and events as they unfold.

C

cameo A small but significant role often played by a famous actor.

camera angle The level and height of the camera in relation to the subject being photographed.

camera crew Technicians that make up two separate groups: one concerned with the camera, and the other concerned with electricity and lighting.

camera obscura Literally, "dark chamber." A box (or a room where a viewer stands), in which light entering (originally through a tiny hole, later through a lens) on one side of it projects an image from the outside onto the opposite side or wall.

camera operator The member of the production crew who operates the camera under the supervision of the director of photography.

casting The process of choosing and hiring actors for a movie.

catalyst See **inciting incident**.

causality The relationship between cause and effect. Compare **narrative**.

celluloid roll film Also known as *motion-picture film* or *raw film stock*. A material for filming that consists of long strips of perforated cellulose acetate on which a rapid succession of frames can be recorded. One side of the strip is layered with an emulsion consisting of light-sensitive crystals and dyes, and the other side is covered with a backing that reduces reflections. Each side of the strip is perforated with sprocket holes that facilitate the movement of the stock through the sprocket wheels of the camera, the processor, and the projector.

character An essential element of film narrative; any of the beings who play functional roles within the plot, either acting or being acted on. Characters can be flat or round; major, minor, or marginal; protagonists or antagonists.

characterization The process of developing a character in a movie. Characterization is the collaborative result of the creative efforts of the actor, the screenwriter, and the director.

character role An actor's part that represents a distinctive character type (sometimes a stereotype).

chiaroscuro The use of deep gradations and subtle variations of lights and darks within an image.

chronophotographic gun See **revolver photographique**.

cinéma vérité See **direct cinema**.

cinematic conventions Accepted systems, methods, or customs by which movies communicate. Cinematic conventions are flexible; they are not "rules."

cinematic language The systems, methods, or conventions by which the movies communicate with the viewer.

cinematic time The passage of time within a movie, as conveyed and manipulated by editing. Compare **real time**.

cinematography The process of lighting, framing, and capturing moving Images on film stock or a digital medium.

classical cutting Editing decisions made for dramatic emphasis.

climax The highest point of conflict in a conventional narrative; the moment of the protagonist's ultimate attempt to attain the goal by overcoming the final obstacle. Compare **crisis**.

closed frame An approach to framing a shot that implies that neither characters nor objects may enter or leave the frame, rendering them hemmed in and constrained. Compare to **open frame**.

close-up (CU) A shot that often shows a part of the body filling the frame—traditionally a face, but possibly a hand, eye, or mouth.

codec A computer program that encodes and decodes data captured by a digital camera. Codecs compress information into manageably sized files for editing and viewing.

color As related to sound, see **quality**.

color grading In postproduction, the process of altering and enhancing the color of a motion picture (or video or still image) using electronic, photochemical, or digital techniques.

colorization The use of digital technology to "paint" colors on movies meant to be seen in black and white; a process similar to hand-tinting.

color temperature The variations of light wavelengths emitted by different light sources. These wavelengths register as different colors when captured on film or digital video.

composition The organization, distribution, balance, and general relationship of stationary objects and figures—as well as of light, shade, line, and color—within the frame.

compositional stress Mood or meaning created by intentionally framing subjects and objects in a way that denies viewer expectations of balanced composition.

computer-generated imagery (CGI) The application of computer graphics to create images, backgrounds, animated characters, and special effects.

content The subject of an artwork. Compare **form**.

content curve A concept that considers and applies the interplay between the information presented in a shot and the time needed for a viewer to comprehend that information.

continuity editing A style of editing that seeks to achieve logic, smoothness, sequential flow, and the temporal and spatial orientation of viewers to what they see on the screen. Compare **discontinuity editing**.

costumes The clothing worn by an actor in a movie; sometimes called *wardrobe*.

cover shot See **master shot**.

coverage The use of a variety of shots of a scene—taken from multiple angles, distances, and perspectives—to provide the director and editor a greater choice of editing options during postproduction.

crane shot A **shot** that is created by movement of a camera mounted on an elevating arm (crane) that in turn is mounted on a vehicle that, if shooting requires it, can move on its own power or be pushed along tracks.

crisis A critical turning point in a story when the protagonist must engage a seemingly insurmountable obstacle.

crosscutting Also called *parallel editing*. Editing that cuts between two or more lines of action, often implied to be occurring at the same time but in different locations.

CU See **close-up**.

cut 1. the act of an editor selecting an in point and an out point of a shot as part of the editing process; 2. a direct change from one shot to another as a result of cutting; that is, the precise point at which shot A ends and shot B begins; 3. an edited version of a scene or film, as in a "rough cut".

cutting In a process that predated digital editing, editors used scissors or a devise known as a splicer to cut shots out of a roll of film before joining them together with glue to form a continuous whole. Also, a general term for the editing process.

cutting on action Also known as *match-on-action cut*. A continuity editing technique that smooths the transition between shots portraying a single action from different camera angles. The editor ends the first shot in the middle of a continuing action and begins the subsequent shot at approximately the same point in the matching action.

D

dailies Also known as *rushes*. Usually, synchronized picture/sound work prints of a day's shooting that can be studied by the director, editor, and other crew members before the next day's shooting begins.

decor The color and textures of the interior decoration, furniture, draperies, and curtains.

deep-focus cinematography The process of rendering the figures on all planes (background, middle ground, and foreground) of a deep-space composition in focus.

deep-space composition An approach to composition within the frame that places significant visual and narrative information on two or more of the three planes of depth (foreground, middleground, and background) in such a way that not only emphasizes depth, but also conveys information, mood and meaning. Deep-space composition is often, though not always, shot with deep-focus cinematography.

depth of field The portion of the space in front of a camera and its lens in which objects are in apparent sharp focus.

design The process by which the look of the settings, props, lighting, and actors is determined. Set design, decor, prop selection, lighting setup, costuming, makeup, and hairstyle design all play a role in shaping the overall design.

dialogue The lip-synchronous speech of characters who are either visible on-screen or speaking offscreen, say from another part of the room that is not visible or from an adjacent room.

diegesis (adj. diegetic) The total compilation of a story—events, characters, objects, settings, and sounds—that form the world in which the story occurs. Compare **story**.

diegetic element An element—event, character, object, setting, and sound—that helps form the world in which the story occurs. Compare **nondiegetic element**.

diegetic sound Sound that originates from a source within a film's world. Compare **nondiegetic sound**.

digital An electronic process that creates its images through a numbered system of pixels (which can be thought of as the binary numbers 0 and 1) that are stored on a memory card or a computer hard drive. Opposite of **analog**.

digital animation Also known as *computer animation*. Animation that employs computer software to create the images used in the animation process (as opposed to analog techniques that rely on stop-motion photography, hand-drawn cells, etc.).

digital imaging technician (DIT) Working in collaboration with the cinematographer, during production the DIT is responsible for managing media capture that will result in the highest image quality.

direct address narration A form of narration in which an on-screen character looks and speaks directly to the audience.

direct cinema A documentary filmmaking movement originating in the late 1950's and early 1960's that pioneered an observational approach to nonfiction filmmaking. See **observational documentary**.

director The person who determines and realizes on the screen an artistic vision of the screenplay; casts the actors and directs their performances; works closely with the production design in creating the look of the film, including the choice of locations; oversees the work of the cinematographer and other key production personnel; and in most cases, supervises all postproduction activity, especially editing.

discontinuity editing A style of editing (less widely used than continuity editing, and often but not exclusively used in experimental films) that joins shots A and B in ways that upset the viewer's expectations and cause momentary disorientation or confusion. The juxtaposition of shots in films edited for discontinuity can often seem abrupt and unmotivated, but the meanings that arise from such discordant editing often transcend the meanings of the individual shots that have been joined together. Compare **continuity editing**.

dissolve Also known as *lap dissolve*. A transitional device in which shot B, superimposed, gradually appears over shot A and begins to replace it at midpoint in the transition. Dissolves sometimes imply a passage of time, or a relationship between the people, objects, or events depicted in the scenes connected by the transition.

distancing effect See **alienation effect**.

documentary film A film that purports to be nonfictional. Documentary films take many forms, including instructional, persuasive, and propaganda. Compare **narrative film**.

dolly A wheeled support for a camera that allows the camera to move smoothly and noiselessly during moving camera shots. Dollies often run on tracks.

dolly in Slow movement of the camera toward a subject, making the subject appear larger and more significant. Such gradual intensification is commonly used at moments of a character's realization or decision or as a point-of-view shot to indicate the reason for the character's realization. See also **zoom in**.

dolly out Movement of the camera away from a subject. See **slow disclosure**.

dolly shot Also known as *tracking shot*. A shot taken by a camera fixed to a wheeled support called a dolly.

double-system recording The standard technique of recording film sound on a medium separate from the picture. This technique allows for both maximum quality control of the medium and the many aspects of manipulating sound during postproduction editing, mixing, and synchronization.

dubbing See **rerecording**.

duration A quantity of time. In any movie, we can identify three specific kinds of duration: story duration (the time that the entire narrative arc—whether or not explicitly presented on-screen—is implied to have taken), plot duration (the time that the events explicitly shown on-screen are implied to have taken), and screen duration (the actual time elapsed while presenting the movie's plot; that is, the movie's running time).

Dutch-angle shot Also known as a *Dutch tilt* or *oblique-angle shot*. A **shot** in which the camera is tilted from its normal horizontal and vertical positions so that it is no longer straight, giving the viewer the impression that the world in the frame is out of balance.

E

ECU See **extreme close-up**.

editing The process by which the editor combines and coordinates individual shots into a cinematic whole; the basic creative force of cinema.

ellipsis In filmmaking, generally an omission of time—the time that separates one shot from another—to create dramatic or comedic impact.

ELS See **extreme long shot**.

ensemble acting An approach to acting that emphasizes the interaction of actors, not the individual actor. In ensemble acting, a group of actors work together continually in a single shot. Typically experienced in the theater, ensemble acting is used less in the movies because it requires rehearsal time that is usually denied to screen actors.

establishing shot A shot whose purpose is to briefly establish the viewer's sense of the setting of a scene, and the relationship of figures in that scene to the environment around them. Extreme long shots of exterior locations sometimes function as establishing shots, as do long shots that establish the relative placement of characters within a setting. See **master shot**.

executive producer Person responsible for supervising one or more producers, who in turn are responsible for individual movies.

experimental film Also known as *avant-garde film*, a term implying a position in the vanguard, out in front of traditional films. Experimental films are usually about unfamiliar, unorthodox, or obscure subject matter and ordinarily made by independent (even underground) filmmakers, not studios, often with innovative techniques that call attention to, question, and even challenge their own artifice.

explicit meaning Everything that a movie presents on its surface. Compare **implicit meaning**.

exposition The images, action, and dialogue necessary to give the audience the background of the characters and the nature of their situation, laying the foundation for the rest of the narrative.

expository documentary An approach to documentary filmmaking that uses formal elements, a script prepared in advance, and an authoritative narrator to explain subject matter to the viewer. Compare **observational documentary, poetic documentary, participatory documentary, performative documentary**, and **reflexive documentary**.

exposure Exposing the recording medium (film or digital) in a camera to light in order to produce a latent image on it, the quality of which is determined primarily by the source and amount of light. The cinematographer can further control that image by the choice of lens and film stock, use of filters, and the aperture that regulates the amount of light passing through the lens. Normally, it is desirable to have images that are clear and well defined, but sometimes the story requires images that are overexposed (very light) or underexposed (dark or dense).

exposure index See **film-stock speed**.

external sound A form of diegetic sound that comes from a place within the world of the story, which we and the characters in the scene hear but do not see. Compare **internal sound**.

extra An actor who usually appears in a nonspeaking or a crowd role and receives no screen credit.

extreme close-up (ECU, XCU) A very close shot of a particular detail, such as a person's eye, a ring on a finger, or a face of a watch.

extreme long shot (ELS, XLS) A shot that is typically photographed far enough away from the subject that the subject is too small to be recognized, except through the context we see, which usually includes a wide view of the location as well as general background information. When it is used to provide such informative context, the extreme long shot is also referred to as an *establishing shot*.

eye-level shot An angle in which the camera is positioned at the eye level of the subject; the standard camera angle used for most shots. If the camera is functioning as narrator, the eye level angle functions as a neutral view of the action on screen. If the shot represents the point of view of a character, the eye level is a natural angle to represent how and what that character sees. Camera angles take on a wider range of expressive meetings as soon as the filmmakers deviate from this "normal and neutral" viewpoint.

eye room Space placed on the side of the frame in which a subject is looking. The implied significance of the character's gaze helps stabilize what would otherwise be considered an imbalanced composition. Also known as *looking room*.

eyeline match cut An editing transition that shows us what a particular character is looking at. The cut joins two shots: the character's face, with his or her eyes clearly visible, then whatever the character is looking at. When the second shot is of another character looking back at the character in the first shot, the resulting reciprocal eyeline match cut and the cuts that follow establish the two characters' proximity and interaction, even if only one character is visible on-screen at any one time.

F

factual documentary A documentary film that usually presents people, places, or processes in a straightforward way meant to entertain and instruct without unduly influencing audiences. Compare **instructional documentary, persuasive documentary**, and **propaganda documentary**.

fade A transitional devise in which the first shot *fades out* (gets progressively darker) until the screen is entirely black. After a moment, the succeeding shot *fades in* (becomes increasingly exposed). Fades often imply a passage of time. Compare **dissolve**.

familiar image Any image that a director periodically repeats in a movie (with or without variations) to help inform or stabilize the narrative.

fast motion Cinematographic technique that accelerates action on-screen. It is achieved by filming the action at a rate *less* than the normal 24 frames per second (fps). When the shot is then played back at the standard 24 fps, cinematic time proceeds at a more rapid rate than the real action that took place in front of the camera. Compare **slow motion**.

featured role See **major role**.

feed spool The storage area for unexposed film in the movie camera.

fiction film See **narrative film**.

fidelity The faithfulness or unfaithfulness of a sound to its source.

figure Any significant thing—person, animal, or object—that moves on the screen.

figure movement The movement of a character, animal, or object used as an element of mise-en-scène.

fill light Lighting, positioned at the opposite side of the camera from the key light, that can fill in the shadows created by the brighter key light. Fill light may also come from a reflector board.

film criticism Evaluating a film's artistic merit and appeal to the public. Film criticism takes two basic forms: reviews written for the general audience and appearing in popular media, and essays published in academic journals for a scholarly audience. Compare **film theory**.

film speed See **film-stock speed**.

film stock Celluloid used to record movies. Different film stocks capture light, color, contrast, and depth of field in different ways, so cinematographers exercise the care when selecting a film stock. Compare **codec**.

film-stock length The number of feet (or meters) of film stock, or the number of reels used in a particular film.

film-stock speed Also known as *film speed* or *exposure index*. The rate at which film must move through the camera to correctly capture an image. Very fast film requires little light to capture and fix the image, whereas very slow film requires a lot of light.

film theory Evaluating movies from a particular intellectual or ideological perspective. Compare **film criticism**.

first AC See **assistant cameraperson**.

first-person narration Narration by an actual character in the movie. Compare **third-person narration** and **voice-over narration**.

flashback The interruption of chronological plot time with a shot or series of shots depicting an event that has happened earlier in the story.

flash-forward A device for presenting the anticipation of the camera, a character, the audience, or all three. In a flash forward, the action cuts from the narrative present to a future time, when, for example, the omniscient camera either reveals directly or a character imagines from his or her point of view what is going to happen. Compare **flashback**.

flat character A relatively uncomplicated character exhibiting few distinct traits. Flat characters do not change significantly as the story progresses.

floodlight A lamp that produces soft (diffuse) light. Compare **focusable spotlight**.

focal length The distance from the optical center of a lens to the focal point—the film plane that the cameraperson wants to keep in focus—when the lens is focused at infinity.

focusable spotlight A lamp that produces hard, mirror-like light that can be directed to precise locations. Compare **floodlight**.

Foley sound A sound belonging to a special category of sound effects, invented in the 1930s by Jack Foley, a sound technician at Universal Studios. Technicians known as Foley artists create these sounds in specially equipped studios, where they use a variety of props and other equipment to simulate sounds such as footsteps in the mud, jingling car keys, or cutlery hitting a plate.

form The means by which a subject is expressed. The form for poetry is words; for drama, it is speech and action; for movies, it is pictures and sound; and so on. Compare **content**.

formal analysis Film analysis that examines how a **scene** or **sequence** uses formal elements—narrative, mise-en-scène, cinematography, editing, sound, and so on—to convey the story, mood, and meaning.

formalism An approach to style and storytelling that values conspicuously expressive form over the unobtrusive form associated with realism.

format When referring to film stock, also called *gauge*, the dimensions of the film stock and its perforations, and the size and shape of the image frame as seen on the screen. Formats extend from Super 8mm through 70mm (and beyond into such specialized formats as IMAX), but they are generally limited to three standard gauges: Super 8mm, 16mm, and 35mm. In reference to digital cinematography, format may refer to a specific codec or digital sensor.

fragmentation The breaking up of stories, scenes, events and actions into multiple shots that provide a diversity of compositions and combinations with which to convey meaning.

frame 1. A still photograph that when recorded in rapid succession with other still photographs creates a motion picture; 2) the borders of a motion picture, within which formal elements are composed.

framing The process by which the cinematographer determines what will appear within the borders of the moving image (the frame) during a shot.

freeze-frame Also known as *stop-frame* or *hold-frame*. A still image within a movie created by repetitive printing in the laboratory of the same frame, so that it can be seen without movement for whatever length of time the filmmaker desires.

frequency The speed with which a sound is produced (the number of sound waves produced per second). The speed of sound remains fairly constant when it passes through air, but it varies in different media and in the same medium at different temperatures. Compare **pitch**.

frontal light Light aimed at the subject from the same angle as the camera. Frontal light eliminates shadows on the subject's face, thus flattening the appearance of facial features.

full-body shot See **long shot**.

fusil photographique A form of the chronophotographic gun—a single, portable camera capable of taking twelve continuous images. See **revolver photographique**.

FX See **special effects**.

G

gaffer The chief electrician on a movie production set.

gauge See **format**.

generic transformation The process by which a particular **genre** is adapted to meet the expectations of a changing society.

genre The categorization of narrative films by form, content, or both. Examples of genres include musical, science fiction, horror, and western.

German expressionism In cinema, an approach to film style that uses distorted settings, oblique angles, artificial and exaggerated lighting, and highly stylized performances to present the world on screen as a projection of a character's subjective perception.

goal A narratively significant objective pursued by the protagonist.

graphic match cut A match cut in which the similarity between shots A and B is in the shape and form of the figures pictured in each shot; the shape, color, or texture of the two figures matches across the edit, providing continuity.

grip All-around handyperson on a movie production set, most often working with the camera and electrical crews.

group point of view A point of view captured by a shot that shows what a group of characters would see at their level. Compare **omniscient point of view** and **single-character point of view**.

H

Halloween lighting Also known as *bottom lighting*. Lighting directed at a subject from below, a direction that casts dramatic shadows on vertical surfaces and distorts facial features by reversing the normal placement of illumination and shadows.

handheld camera An approach to operating the moving camera in which the operator holds the camera (as opposed to mounting the camera on a tripod, dolly, or Steadicam). The relatively unstable frame typical of handheld camera is often used to invoke distressed states of mind or documentary realism.

hard light Light that shines directly on the subject. Compare **soft light**.

harmonic content The wavelengths that make up a sound. Compare **quality**.

headroom The amount of space above the top of the subject's head in the composition of a frame.

high-angle shot Also known as *down shot*. A shot that is made with the camera above the action; it typically implies the observer's sense of superiority to the subject being photographed. Compare **low-angle shot**.

high-key lighting Lighting that produces an image with very little contrast between darks and lights. It's even, flat illumination expresses virtually no opinion about the subject being photographed. Compare **low-key lighting**.

hold-frame See **freeze-frame**.

I

ideological meaning Meaning expressed by a film that reflects beliefs on the part of filmmakers, characters, or the time and place of the movie's setting. Ideological meaning is the product of social, political, economic, religious, philosophical, psychological, and sexual forces that shape the filmmakers' perspectives.

implicit meaning An association, connection, or inference that a viewer makes based on the given (explicit) meaning conveyed by the story and form of a film. Lying below the surface of explicit meaning, implicit meaning is closest to our everyday sense of the word *meaning*. Compare **explicit meaning**.

implied proximity The apparent distance between the camera (and thus the viewer) and the subject of a shot. This implied spatial relationship can influence how viewers interpret the significance of the character, object, or action on screen.

improvisation Actors' extemporization; that is, delivering lines based loosely on the written script or without the preparation that comes with studying a script before rehearsing it. Or "playing through" a moment; that is, making up lines to keep **scenes** going when actors forget their written lines, stumble on lines, or have some other mishap.

inciting incident Also known as the **catalyst**. The narrative event that presents the protagonist with a goal that sets the rest of the narrative in motion.

insert/insert shot A shot containing visual detail (an object or figure not from the scene) that is inserted between one shot and another to establish a story point or to provide additional information or dramatic emphasis. For example, shot A might be an establishing shot of a room (giving us the place); shot B, the insert, might be a close-up of a clock photographed on a wall (giving us the time); and shot C would logically return us to the room.

insert titles/intertitles Words (printed or handwritten) inserted into the body of a film, such as "The day after" or "Saturday morning"; in common usage today, but used extensively in silent movies.

instructional documentary A documentary film that seeks to educate viewers about common interests, rather than persuade them with particular ideas. Compare **factual documentary**, **persuasive documentary**, and **propaganda documentary**.

intellectual editing See **associative editing**.

intercutting The insertion of shots into a scene in a way that interrupts the narrative. Examples of intercutting include flashbacks, flash-forwards, shots depicting a character's thoughts, shots depicting events from earlier or later in the plot, and associative editing that inserts shots to create symbolic or thematic meaning through juxtaposition.

interior monologue A variation on the mental, subjective point of view of an individual character that allows us to see the character and hear his or her thoughts in their own voice, even though the character's lips don't move.

internal sound A form of diegetic sound in which we hear the thoughts of a character we see on-screen but other characters cannot hear them. Compare **external sound**.

interview A component of documentary filmmaking, traditionally shot with the person being interviewed speaking to an off-camera interviewer.

iris An adjustable diaphragm that controls the amount of light passing through the lens of a camera. See **aperture**.

iris-in Iris shot that begins with a small circle and expands to a partial or full image.

iris-out Iris shot that begins with a large circle and contracts to a smaller circle or total blackness.

iris shot Optical wipe effect in which the wipe line is a circle; named after the iris of a camera.

J

jump cut The removal of a portion of a continuous shot, resulting in an instantaneous advance in the action—a sudden, perhaps illogical, often disorienting ellipsis.

K

key light The primary source of illumination in a shot. Positioned to one side of the camera, it creates deep shadows, which are modified by the fill light.

kinesis The aspect of composition that takes into account everything that moves on the screen.

Kinetograph The first motion-picture camera.

Kinetoscope A peephole viewer, an early motion-picture device.

Kuleshov effect The discovery of Lev Kuleshov, a Soviet film theorist, that two shots need not have any actual relationship to each other for viewers to perceive a spatial relationship. For example, the placement of one shot of a person's reaction (a look of shock) after a shot of an action by another person (falling down a flight of stairs) immediately creates the perception that the two are occupying the same space.

L

lap dissolve See **dissolve**.

leading role See **major role**.

lead room Open compositional space on the opposite side of the frame from that of a character whose lateral screen movement is tracked by a moving camera. This method is necessary to balance the composition because the implied lateral movement of a character carries compositional weight.

lens The piece of transparent material in a camera that focuses the image on the film or digital processor. Lenses are classified by focal length. See **short-focal-length lens**, **middle-focal-length lens**, **long-focal-length lens**, and **zoom-lens**;

lighting ratio The relationship and balance between illumination and shadow—the balance between key light and fill light. If the ratio is high, shadows are deep, and the result is called *low-key lighting*. If the ratio is low, shadows are faint or nonexistent and illumination is even, and the result is called *high-key lighting*.

line of action See **180-degree rule**.

line producer The person, usually involved from preproduction through postproduction, who is responsible for the day-to-day management of the production operation.

loader The loader is the member of the camera crew that feeds film stock into magazines to be loaded into a camera. Compare **Digital Imaging Technician**.

long-focal-length lens Also known as *telephoto lens*. A lens that flattens the space and depth of an image and thus distorts perspectival relations. Compare **middle-focal-length lens**, **short-focal-length lens**, and **zoom lens**.

long shot (LS) A shot that presents background and subject information in equal measure and is as much about setting and situations as any particular character. Long shots show the full human body and some of its surroundings. Long shots that establish the relative placement of characters within a setting can function as establishing shots.

long take Also known as *sequence shot*. An uninterrupted shot that lasts significantly longer than a conventional shot. Long takes may be as short as 1 minute or as long as an entire feature film. There are two basic approaches to the long take: 1. those that exploit the mobile frame; and 2. those that hold the viewer in a state of relative stasis.

looping See **Automatic Dialogue Replacement (ADR)**.

loudness The volume or intensity of a sound, which is defined by its amplitude. Loudness is described as either loud or soft.

low-angle shot Also known as *low shot*. A shot that is made with the camera below the action; it typically places the observer in a position of inferiority. Compare **high-angle shot**.

low-key lighting Lighting that creates strong contrasts; sharp dark shadows, and an overall gloomy atmosphere. Compare **high-key lighting**.

low shot See **low-angle shot**.

M

magic lantern A device predating motion pictures that projected still images painted or printed on transparent plates.

main role See **major role**.

major character One of the main characters in a movie. Major characters make most things happen or have most things happen to them. Compare **marginal character** and **minor character**.

major role Also known as *main role, featured role*, or *leading role*. A role that is a principal agent in helping to move the plot forward. Whether movie stars or newcomers, actors playing major roles appear in many scenes and—ordinarily, but not always—receive screen credit preceding the title. Compare **minor role**.

makeup artist A person responsible for using makeup to enhance or alter an actor's appearance.

marginal character A minor character that lacks both definition and screen time.

mask An opaque sheet of metal, paper, or plastic (with, for example, a circular cutout, known as an iris) that is placed in front of the camera and admits light through that circle to a specific area of the frame to create a frame within a frame.

master scene technique A method of capturing footage to construct a scene in which the action is photographed multiple times with a variety of different shot types and angles. This approach allows the editor to construct the scene using the particular viewpoint that is best suited for each dramatic moment.

master shot A wide angle shot that covers the action of a scene in one continuous take. See **coverage** and **master scene technique**.

match cut A cut that preserves continuity between two shots. Several kinds of match cuts exist, including eyeline match cut, graphic match cut, and match-on-action cut.

match-on-action cut Also called *cutting on action*. A match cut that shows us the continuation of a character's or object's motion through space without actually showing the entire action. This is a fairly routine editorial technique for economizing a movie's presentation of movement.

mechanical effect A special effect created mechanically by an object or event on the set and in front of the camera. Also known as *practical effect*. Compare **optical effect** and **visual effect**.

mediation An agent, structure, or other formal element, whether human or technological, that transfers something, such as information in the case of movies, from one place to another.

medium close-up (MCU) A shot that shows a character from the middle of the chest to the top of the head. A medium close-up provides a view of the face that catches minor changes in expression, as well as some detail about the character's posture.

medium long shot (MLS) Also known as the *plan Américain*, or *American shot*. A shot that shows a character from the knees up and includes most of a person's body.

medium shot (MS) A shot framed to show the human body from the waist up.

method acting Also known simply as the *Method*. A naturalistic acting style, loosely adapted from the ideas of Russian director Konstantin Stanislavsky by American directors Elia Kazan and Lee Strasberg, that encourages actors to speak, move, and gesture not in a traditional stage manner, but in the same way they would in their own lives. An ideal technique for representing convincing human behavior, method acting is used more frequently on the stage than on the screen.

middle-focal-length lens Also known as *normal lens*. A lens that does not distort perspectival relations. Compare **long-focal-length lens, short-focal-length lens**, and **zoom lens**.

minor character A supporting character in a movie. Minor characters have fewer traits than major characters, so we know less about them. They also may be so lacking in definition and screen time that they can be considered marginal characters.

minor role Also known as *supporting role*. A role that helps move the plot forward—and thus may be as important as a major role—but is played by an actor who does not appear in as many scenes as the featured actors do. Compare **major role**.

mise-en-scène The composition, or *staging*, of all of the elements within the frame, including setting, costumes and makeup, actors, lighting, and figure movement.

mixing The process of adjusting relative volume of multiple sound tracks, and then combining those tracks onto one composite sound track that is synchronous with the picture.

mobile framing A technique that uses a moving camera to capture multiple viewpoints, compositions, and actions within a single shot.

montage Another term for editing, from the French verb *monter* ("to assemble or put together"). Montage may also function as a noun to refer generally to an edited assembly of images or sounds.

montage editing An approach to editing pioneered by theorists and filmmakers in the former Soviet Union who posited and proved that the juxtaposition of images can create new meaning not present in any single shot by itself.

montage sequence An integrated series of shots that rapidly depicts multiple related events occurring over time. Not to be confused with *montage editing*, montage sequences are used to condense time when an accumulation of actions is necessary to the narrative, but developing each individual action would consume too much of the movie's duration.

motion capture Also known as *mocap, motion tracking,* or *performance capture.* A process in which the movements of objects or actors dressed in special suits are recorded as data that computers subsequently use to render the motion of CGI characters on-screen.

motion-picture film See **celluloid roll film**.

motif A recurring visual, sound, or narrative element that imparts meaning or significance.

movie star A phenomenon, generally associated with Hollywood, comprising the actor, the characters played by that actor, an image created by the studio to coincide with the kind of roles associated with the actor, and a reflection of the social and cultural history of the period in which that image was created.

moving frame The result of the dynamic functions of the frame around a motion-picture image that contains moving action, but also can move and thus change its viewpoint.

N

narration The act of telling the story of the film. The primary source of a movie's narration is the camera, which narrates the story by showing us the events of the narrative on-screen. When the word *narration* is used to refer more narrowly to *spoken* narration, the reference is to the commentary spoken by either an offscreen or on-screen voice. When that commentary is not spoken by one of the characters in the movie, it is omniscient narration; when spoken by a character within the movie, it is first-person narration.

narrative A cinematic structure in which content is selected and arranged in a cause-and-effect sequence of events occurring over time. Compare **plot** and **story**.

narrative film Also known as *fiction film.* A movie that tells a story—with characters, places, and events—that is conceived in the mind of the film's creator. Stories in narrative films may be wholly imaginary or based on true occurrences and may be realistic, unrealistic, or both. Compare **documentary film**.

narrator Who or what that tells the story of a film. The primary narrator in cinema is the camera, which narrates the film by showing us events in the movie's narrative. When referring to the more specific action of voice narration, the narrator may be either a character in the movie (first-person narrator) or a person who is not a character (omniscient narrator).

negative When referring to shooting on film stock, a negative photographic image on transparent material that makes possible the reproduction of the image.

negative space Intentional empty space within a composition that creates an expectation that something will arrive to fill the empty space and restore compositional balance. The technique is often used to generate suspense in narrative contexts featuring the imminent arrival of an anticipated character or force.

nondiegetic element Something that we see and hear on the screen that comes from outside the world of the story, such as background music, titles and credits, and voice-over narration. Compare **diegetic element**.

nondiegetic sound Sound that originates from a source outside a film's world. Compare **diegetic sound**.

nonsimultaneous sound Sound that has previously been established in the movie and replays for some narrative or expressive purpose. Nonsimultaneous sounds often occur when a character has a mental flashback to an earlier voice that recalls a conversation or to an earlier sound that identifies a place, event, or other significant element of the narrative. Compare **simultaneous sound**.

normal lens See **middle-focal-length lens**.

normal world In a narrative screenplay, the state of the character and setting before the inciting incident.

O

oblique-angle shot See **Dutch-angle shot**.

observational documentary An approach to documentary filmmaking that seeks to immerse viewers in an experience as close as is cinematically possible to witnessing events as an invisible observer. Observational documentaries typically rely entirely on b-roll and eliminate as many other signs of mediation as possible. Compare **expository documentary**, **poetic documentary**, **participatory documentary**, **performative documentary**, and **reflexive documentary**.

obstacles Events, circumstances, and actions that impede a protagonist's pursuit of the goal. Obstacles often originate from an antagonist and are central to a narrative conflict.

offscreen sound A form of sound, either diegetic or nondiegetic, that derives from a source we do not see. When diegetic, it consists of sound effects, music, or vocals that emanate from the world of the story. When nondiegetic, it takes the form of a musical score or narration by someone who is not a character in the story. Compare **on-screen sound**.

offscreen space Cinematic space that exists outside the frame. Compare **on-screen space**.

omniscient Providing a third-person view of all aspects of a movie's action or characters. Compare **restricted**.

omniscient point of view The most common point of view portrayed in movies. An omniscient POV allows the camera to travel freely within the world of the film, showing us the narrative's events from a godlike, unlimited perspective that no single character in the film could possibly have. Compare **group** point of view and **single-character** point of view.

on location Shooting in an actual interior or exterior location away from the studio. Compare **set**.

180-degree rule Also known as the *180-degree system.* The fundamental means by which filmmakers maintain consistent screen direction, orienting the viewer and ensuring a sense of the cinematic space in which the action occurs. The system depends on three factors working together in any scene: the action in a scene must move along a hypothetical line that keeps the action on a single side of the camera, the camera must shoot consistently on one side of that line, and everyone on the production set—particularly the director, cinematographer, editor, and actors—must understand and adhere to this system.

on-screen sound A form of diegetic sound that emanates from a source that we both see and hear. On-screen sound may be internal or external. Compare **offscreen sound**.

on-screen space Cinematic space that exists inside the frame. Compare **offscreen space**.

open frame A frame around a motion-picture image that, theoretically, characters and objects can enter and leave. Compare **closed frame**.

optical effect An effect created manipulating an image captured on celluloid in the camera during production and/or during film stock processing after the negative has been exposed. Compare **mechanical effect** and **visual effect**.

option contract During the classical Hollywood era, an actor's standard 7-year contract was reviewed every 6 months. If the actor had made progress in being assigned roles and demonstrating box-office appeal, the studio picked up the option to employ that actor for the next 6 months with a raise; if not, the studio dropped the option and the actor was out of a job.

order The arrangement of plot events into a logical sequence or hierarchy. Across an entire narrative or in a brief section of it, the filmmaker can use one or more methods to arrange its plot: chronological order, cause-and-effect order, logical order, and so on.

outtake Material that is not used in either the rough cut or the final cut, but is nevertheless cataloged and saved.

overhead A diagram of a set as seen from above that is used as part of the previsualization process to plan blocking and camera positions.

overlapping action The repetition of parts or all of an action using multiple shots.

overlapping sound Also known as a *sound bridge*. Sound that carries over from one shot to the next before the sound of the second shot begins.

P

pace The speed at which a multi-shot sequence occurs. The pace of a scene or sequence is accomplished by using shots of the same general duration. Compare to **rhythm**.

pan shot The horizontal movement of a camera mounted on the gyroscopic head of a stationary tripod; like the tilt shot, the pan shot is a simple movement with dynamic possibilities for creating meaning.

parallel editing Also called *crosscutting*. The cutting back and forth between two or more lines of action that occur simultaneously. Compare **intercutting** and **split screen**.

participatory documentary An approach to nonfiction filmmaking in which the filmmaker interacts with the subjects and situations being recorded and thus becomes part of the film. Compare **expository documentary**, **observational documentary**, **poetic documentary**, **performative documentary**, and **reflexive documentary**.

performance capture See **motion capture**.

performative documentary An approach to nonfiction filmmaking related to the participatory documentary. The filmmaker's interaction with the subject matter is deeply personal and often emotional. In a performative documentary, the filmmaker's experience is central to the way viewers engage and understand the subject matter. Compare **expository documentary**, **observational documentary**, **poetic documentary**, **participatory documentary**, and **reflexive documentary**.

persuasive documentary A documentary film concerned with presenting a particular perspective on social issues or with corporate and governmental injustice. Compare **documentary**, **instructional documentary**, and **propaganda documentary**.

photography Literally, "writing with light." Technically, the recording of static images through a chemical interaction caused by light rays striking a sensitized surface.

pitch The level of a sound, which is defined by its frequency. Pitch is described as either high or low.

pixel A combination of the words *picture* and *element*; the smallest unit of visual information in a digital image.

plan Américain See **medium long shot**.

plane Any of three theoretical areas—foreground, middle ground, and background—within the implied depth of the frame.

plot The specific actions and events that filmmakers select, and the order in which they arrange those events and actions to effectively convey on-screen the movie's narrative to a viewer. Compare **narrative** and **story**.

plot duration The elapsed time of the events within a story that a film chooses to tell. Compare **screen duration** and **story duration**.

plot point Significant events that turn the narrative in a new direction.

poetic documentary An expressive approach to nonfiction filmmaking that provides a subjective and often impressionistic interpretation of a subject by an emphasis on conveying mood and generating ideas, rather than developing a realistic observational experience or communicating an information-driven explanation. Compare **expository documentary**, **observational documentary**, **participatory documentary**, **performative documentary**, and **reflexive documentary**.

point of view (POV) The position from which a film presents the actions of the **story**; not only the relation of the narrator(s) to the story, but also the camera's act of seeing and hearing. The two fundamental types of cinematic point of view are omniscient and restricted.

point of view (POV) shot: a shot that represents what a character is looking at. POV shots may be framed to present a literal spatial perspective, or how the character sees *and* feels about the object of her gaze. For example, a POV shot of a relatively distant but significant subject may be framed as a close up. Compare **point-of-view editing**.

point-of-view editing The process of editing different shots together so that the resulting sequence makes us aware of the perspective or POV of a particular character or group of characters. Most frequently, it starts with an objective shot of a character looking toward something outside the frame and then cuts to a shot of the object, person, or action that the character is supposed to be looking at.

postproduction The third stage of the production process, consisting of editing, preparing the final print, and bringing the film to the public (marketing and distribution). Postproduction is preceded by preproduction and production.

POV See **point of view**.

practical effect See **mechanical effect**.

preproduction The initial planning and preparation stage of the production process. Preproduction is followed by production and postproduction.

previsualization A process used by filmmakers to aid in visualizing each individual shot and help achieve a unified approach to shot compositions and editing. Previsualization can include **storyboards**, **overheads**, and **animatics**.

prime lens A lens that has a fixed focal length. The short-focal-length, middle-focal-length, and long-focal-length lenses are all prime lenses; the zoom lens is in its own category.

processing The second stage of creating motion pictures, in which a laboratory technician washes exposed film that contains a negative image with processing chemicals. Processing is preceded by shooting and followed by projecting.

process shot Live shooting against a background that is front- or rear-projected on a translucent screen.

producer The person who guides the entire process of making the movie from its initial planning to its release, and is chiefly responsible for the organizational and financial aspects of the production, from arranging the financing to deciding how the money is spent.

production The second stage of the production process—the actual **shooting**. Production is preceded by preproduction and followed by postproduction.

production designer A person who works closely with the director, art director, and director of photography in visualizing the movie that will appear on the screen. The production designer is both an artist and an executive and is responsible for the overall design concept (the *look* of the movie—its individual sets, locations, furnishings, props, and costumes) and for supervising the heads of the many departments (art, costume design and construction, hairstyling, makeup, wardrobe, location, and so on) that create that look.

production value The amount of human and physical resources devoted to the image, including the style of lighting. Production value helps determine the overall style of a film.

projecting The third stage of creating motion pictures, in which edited film is run through a projector that shoots through the film a beam of light intense enough to project a large image on the movie-theater screen. Projecting is preceded by shooting and processing.

propaganda documentary A documentary film that systematically disseminates deceptive or distorted information. Compare **factual documentary**, **instructional documentary**, and **persuasive documentary**.

properties Also known as *props*. Any object handled by actors on-screen. Compare with **set dressing**.

prop master The member of the production design crew responsible for selecting and maintaining props and for ensuring that props are properly prepared and placed prior to shooting.

prosthetics Synthetic materials attached to an actor's face or body to change the actor's appearance.

protagonist The primary character whose pursuit of the goal provides the structural foundation of a movie's story. Compare **antagonist**.

pull-down claw Within the movie camera and projector, the mechanism that controls the intermittent cycle of shooting and projecting individual frames and advances the film frame by frame.

pull focus The act of adjusting focus within a shot to maintain focus on a moving actor or object, or on a static object or actor recorded by a moving camera. Compare **rack focus**.

Q

quality When referring to sound, also known as *timbre, texture,* or *color*. The complexity of a sound, which is defined by its harmonic content. De-scribed as simple or complex, quality is the characteristic that distinguishes a sound from others of the same pitch and loudness. In lighting, quality refers to the degree to which light is diffused between the source and the subject, and its effect on the interplay between illumination and shadow.

R

rack focus A change of the point of focus from one subject to another within the same shot. Rack focus guides our attention to a new, clearly focused point of interest while blurring the previous subject in the shot.

raw film stock See **celluloid roll film**.

realism In cinematic terms, an approach to narrative filmmaking that employs naturalistic performances and dialogue; modest, unembellished sets and settings; wide-angle compositions and other unobtrusive framing; and story lines that portray the everyday lives of "ordinary" people. Compare **antirealism** and **formalism**.

real time The actual time during which something takes place. In real time, screen duration and plot duration are exactly the same. Many directors use real time within films to create uninterrupted "reality" on the screen, but they rarely use it for entire films. Compare **cinematic time**, **stretch relationship**, and **summary relationship**.

reenactment A staged re-creation of actions and events used in a nonfiction film when authentic documentary footage is unavailable or impossible to obtain. Reenactments are typically filmed and presented in ways that make clear their status as fabricated representations of real events.

reflector board A piece of lighting equipment, but not really a lighting instrument because it does not rely on bulbs to produce illumination. Essentially, a reflector board is a double-sided board that pivots in a *U*-shaped holder. One side is a hard, smooth surface that reflects hard light, and the other side is a soft, textured surface that reflects softer fill light.

reflexive documentary An approach to documentary filmmaking that explores and sometimes critiques the documentary form itself. The documentary production process becomes part of the experience in ways that may challenge viewer expectations of nonfiction filmmaking conventions. Compare **expository documentary**, **observational documentary**, **poetic documentary**, **participatory documentary**, and **performative documentary**.

reframing A movement of the camera that adjusts or alters the composition or point of view of a shot.

repetition The number of times that a story element recurs in a plot. Repetition signals that a particular event has noteworthy meaning or significance.

resolution The concluding narrative events that follow the climax and celebrate, or otherwise reflect upon, story outcomes. Also, the capacity of the camera lens, film stock, and digital sensors to provide fine detail in an image.

restricted Providing a view from the perspective of a single character. Compare **omniscient**.

restricted narration Reveals information to the audience only as a specific character learns of it.

reverse-angle shot A shot in which the angle of shooting is opposite that of the preceding shot.

revolver photographique Also known as *chronophotographic gun*. A cylinder-shaped camera that creates exposures automatically, at short intervals, on different segments of a revolving plate.

rhythm In cinematic terms, the practice of changing the pace, either gradually or suddenly, during a scene or sequence. Compare to **pace**.

rising action The development of the action of the narrative toward a climax.

rough-draft screenplay Also known as *scenario*. The step after a treatment, the rough-draft screenplay results from discussions, development, and transformation of an outline in sessions known as *story conferences*.

round character A complex character possessing numerous, subtle, repressed, or contradictory traits. Round characters often develop over the course of a story.

rule of thirds A principle of composition that breaks the frame into three equal vertical sections, and three equal horizontal sections, resulting in a grid. This grid acts as a guide which filmmakers use to balance visual elements in the frame in terms of three: top, middle, bottom; left, center, right; foreground, middleground, and background. Typically, for every visual element placed in one section, there will be a corresponding element in the opposite section to counter-balance the composition.

rushes See **dailies**.

S

scale The size and placement of a particular object or a part of a scene in relation to the rest—a relationship determined by the type of shot used and the placement of the camera.

scenario See **rough-draft screenplay**.

scene A complete unit of plot action taking place in a continuous time frame in a single location.

scope The overall range of a story.

score music Nondiegetic music that is typically composed and recorded specifically for use in a particular film and is used to convey or enhance meaning and emotion.

screen direction The direction of a figure's or object's movement on the screen.

screen duration The amount of time that it has taken to present the movie's plot on-screen; that is, the movie's running time. Compare **plot duration** and **story duration**.

screen test A filming undertaken by an actor to audition for a particular role.

script supervisor The member of the crew responsible for ensuring continuity throughout the filming.

second AC See **assistant cameraperson**.

separation A framing and editing technique that uses eyelines and juxtaposition to draw viewers into a participatory cycle that creates intensified relationships between alternating subjects seen separately on-screen.

sequence A series of edited shots characterized by inherent unity of theme and purpose.

sequence shot See **long take**.

series photography The use of a series of still photographs to record the phases of an action.

set A constructed space used as the setting for a particular shot in a movie. Sets must be constructed both to look authentic and to photograph well. Compare **on location**.

set decorator A person in charge of the countless details that go into furnishing and decorating a set.

set dressing Objects and applications used to create the look of the environment in which the filmed action takes place. Set dressing may include curtains, paint, carpets, and any object visible in the area, such as furniture, books, knickknacks, and other objects or decorations. Compare **prop**.

setting The time and space in which a story takes place.

setup One camera position and everything associated with it. Whereas the shot is the basic building block of the film, the setup is the basic component of the film's production.

shooting Capturing images on a motion picture camera. In reference to shooting on film stock, the first stage of photographing motion pictures in which images are recorded on previously unexposed film as it moves through the camera.

shooting angle The level and height of the camera in relation to the subject being photographed. The five basic camera angles produce eye-level shots, high-angle shots, low-angle shots, Dutch-angle shots, and bird's-eye-view shots.

shooting script A guide and reference point for all members of the **production** unit in which the details of each shot are listed and can thus be followed during filming.

short-focal-length lens Also known as *wide-angle lens*. A lens that creates the illusion of depth within a frame, although with some distortion at the edges of the frame. Compare **long-focal-length lens**, **middle-focal-length lens**, and **zoom lens**.

shot 1. In an edited film, an unbroken span of action captured by an uninterrupted run of the camera that lasts until it is replaced by another shot by means of a cut or other transition. 2. During the pre-production and production process: a specific arrangement of elements to be captured in a particular composition from a predetermined camera position. Compare to **setup** and **take**.

shot/reverse shot One of the most prevalent and familiar of all editing patterns, in which the camera is repeatedly crosscutting between **shots** of different characters, usually in a conversation or confrontation. When used in continuity editing, the shots are typically framed over each character's shoulder to preserve screen direction.

shutter A camera device that shields the film from light at the aperture during the film-movement portion of the intermittent cycle of shooting.

simultaneous sound Sound that is diegetic and occurs on-screen. Compare **nonsimultaneous sound**.

single-character point of view A point of view that is captured by a shot made with the camera close to the line of sight of one character (or surveillance camera), showing what that character would be seeing of the action. Compare **group point of view** and **omniscient point of view**.

slate A device used to identify the scene, shot, and take on camera and on sound recordings before action is called. The slate creates an audio or digital mark used to synchronized picture and sound.

slow motion Cinematographic technique that decelerates action on-screen. It is achieved by filming the action at a rate *greater* than the normal 24 frames per second (fps). When the shot is then played back at the standard 24 fps, cinematic time proceeds at a slower rate than the real action that took place in front of the camera. Compare **fast motion**.

slow disclosure A technique that uses camera movement to allow new information into the frame that expands or changes the viewer's initial interpretation of the subject or situation.

soft light Light that is scattered or diffused so that it does not follow a direct path between the light source and the subject. Compare **hard light**.

sound Transmitted vibrations received by the ear and thus heard by the recipient. In cinematic terms, the expressive use of auditory elements, such as dialogue, music, ambience, and effects.

sound bridge See **overlapping sound**.

sound crew The group that physically generates and controls a movie's sound, manipulating its properties to produce the effects that the director desires.

sound design A state-of-the-art concept, pioneered by director Francis Ford Coppola and film editor Walter Murch, combining the crafts of editing and mixing and, like them, involving both theoretical and practical issues. In essence, sound design represents advocacy for movie sound, to counter some people's tendency to favor the movie image.

sound effect A sound artificially created for the sound track that has a definite function in telling the story.

soundstage A windowless, soundproofed, professional shooting environment that is usually several stories high and can cover an acre or more of floor space.

sound track In the sound editing process, a single track consisting of recordings of a specific type of sound, such as a character's dialogue, sound effects, ambient sound, music, and so on. These individual sound tracks are layered during the sound editing process, and mixed during the finishing stages of post-production. Compare **sound mix**.

source light See **key light**.

special effects (FX, SPFX) A general term reserved for technology used to create images that would be too dangerous, too expensive, or simply impossible to achieve with traditional cinematographic approaches. In the film industry, the current specific use of the term refers to effects generated on set that can be photographed by the camera. See **mechanical effect**; compare **visual effect**.

speed See **film-stock speed**.

SPFX See **special effects**.

split screen A method that breaks the screen into multiple frames and images. Split screen typically conveys multiple simultaneous actions, but may convey nonsimultaneous action or present multiple viewpoints of the same action.

sprocketed rollers Devices that control the speed of unexposed film as it moves through the camera, printer, or projector.

staging See **mise-en-scène**.

stakes In a conventional narrative, that which is at risk due to the protagonist's pursuit of the goal.

stand-in An actor who looks reasonably like a particular movie star or an actor playing a major role—in height, weight, coloring, and so on—and substitutes for that actor during the tedious process of preparing setups or taking light readings.

Stanislavsky system A system of acting, developed by Russian theater director Konstantin Stanislavsky in the late nineteenth century, that encourages students to strive for realism, both social and psychological, and to bring their past experiences and emotions to their roles. This system influenced the development of method acting in the United States.

Steadicam A camera suspended from an articulated arm that is attached to a vest strapped to the cameraperson's body, permitting the operator to remain steady during "handheld" shots. The Steadicam removes jumpiness and is now used for smooth, fast, and extended camera movement.

stock See **film stock**.

stop-frame See **freeze-frame**.

stop-motion cinematography A technique that allows the camera operator to stop and start the camera to facilitate changing the subject while the camera is not shooting. Frequently used for Claymation and other forms of physical animation.

story In a movie, all the events we see or hear on the screen, as well as all the events that are implicit or infer to have happened but are not explicitly presented. Compare **diegesis**, **narrative**, and **plot**.

storyboard A shot-by-shot breakdown that combines sketches or photographs of how each shot is to look and written descriptions of the other elements that are to go with each shot, including dialogue, sound, and music.

story conference One of any number of sessions during which the **treatment** is discussed, developed, and transformed from an outline into a rough-draft screenplay.

story duration The implied amount of time taken by the entire narrative arc of a movie's story—whether or not explicitly presented on-screen. Compare **plot duration** and **screen duration**.

stream of consciousness A literary style that gained prominence in the 1920s in the hands of such writers as Marcel Proust, Virginia Woolf, James Joyce, and Dorothy Richardson and which attempted to capture the unedited flow of experience through the mind.

stretch relationship A time relationship in which screen duration is longer than plot duration. Compare **real time** and **summary relationship**.

stunt-person A performer who doubles for another actor in scenes requiring special skills or involving hazardous actions, such as crashing cars, jumping from high places, swimming, or riding (or falling off) horses.

subplot A subordinate sequence of action in a narrative, usually relevant to and enriching the plot.

subtractive color system Adopted in the 1930s, this technique involved shooting three separate black-and-white negatives through three light filters, each representing a primary color (red, green, blue). Certain color components were subtracted or removed from each of the three emulsion layers, creating a positive image in natural color. Compare **additive color systems**.

summary relationship A time relationship in which screen duration is shorter than plot duration. Compare **real time** and **stretch relationship**.

supporting role See **minor role**.

surprise A taking unawares that is potentially shocking. Compare **suspense**.

suspense The anxiety brought on by partial uncertainty—the end is certain, but the means are not. Compare **surprise**.

swish pan A type of transition between two or more shots made by moving the camera so rapidly that it blurs the moment of transition.

symmetry In cinema, a balanced composition in which one side of the frame virtually mirrors the other.

synopsis A condensed description of a film's essential narrative ideas and structure. Compare *treatment*.

T

take On a film production, one of sometimes multiple recordings of a pre-determined shot. Multiple takes of a shot may be taken to remedy mistakes or to provide the editor with varied performances, blocking, or camera movements.

take-up spool In a movie camera that shoots film stock, a device that winds the film stock inside the camera after it has been exposed.

telephoto lens See **long-focal-length lens**.

text and graphics An element of documentary filmmaking that includes statistics, graphs, maps and text. Text is commonly used to identify interview subjects, dates, and locations presented on screen.

texture As related to sound, see **quality**.

theme A shared, public idea, such as a metaphor, an adage, a myth, a familiar conflict, or personality type.

third-person narration Narration delivered from outside the diegesis by a narrator who is not a character in the movie. Compare **first-person narration** and **voice-over narration**.

30-degree rule A general principle of continuity editing that states that the camera position in relation to the subject should shift at least 30 degrees between successive shots of the same subject. The guideline is designed to avoid a jarring spatial effect that makes the subject's image appear to "jump" forward or backward.

three-point system Also known as *three point lighting*. Perhaps the best-known lighting convention in feature filmmaking, a system that uses three sources of light—key light, fill light, and backlight—each aimed from a different direction and position in relation to the subject. The three-point system allows filmmakers to control the ratio between illumination and shadow.

three-shot A shot in which three characters appear; ordinarily, a medium shot or medium long shot.

three-shot salvo An intentional disregard of the 30-degree rule that uses multiple (typically three) increasingly closer or wider framings of the same subject, shot from the same camera position or angle, which are then edited together in rapid succession. This discontinuous editing technique is typically used to add significance or emphasis to a character reaction or point of view.

tilt shot The vertical movement of a camera mounted on the gyroscopic head of a stationary tripod. Like the pan shot, the tilt shot is a simple movement with dynamic possibilities for creating meaning.

timbre As related to sound, see **quality**.

tonality In cinematography, the range of tones from pure white to darkest black.

top lighting Light cast on a subject from above.

tracking shot See **dolly shot**.

treatment An extended prose outline of the action that relates a film's basic narrative progression. Compare **synopsis**.

two-shot A shot in which two characters appear; ordinarily a medium shot or medium long shot.

typecasting The casting of actors because of their looks or "type" rather than for their acting talent or experience.

V

variable-focal-length lens See **zoom lens**.

verisimilitude A convincing appearance of truth. Movies are verisimilar when they convince you that the things on the screen—people, places, and so on, no matter how fantastic or antirealistic—are "really there."

video assist camera In cameras that shoot film stock, a tiny device mounted in the viewing system that enables filmmakers to view the framed shot on a video monitor.

viewfinder On a camera, the little window that the cameraperson looks through when taking a picture; the viewfinder's frame indicates the boundaries of the camera's point of view.

visual effect An effect created and integrated using computers in postproduction. Compare **mechanical effect** and **optical effect**.

voice-over narration Narration heard concurrently and over a scene but not synchronized to any character who may be talking on-screen. It can come from many sources, including a third person, who is not a character, to bring us up to date; a first-person narrator commenting on the action; or in a nonfiction film, a commentator. Compare **first-person narration** and **third-person narration**.

W

walk-on A role even smaller than a cameo, reserved for a highly recognizable actor or personality.

wardrobe The clothing worn by an actor in a movie; also the term that designates the department in a studio in which clothing is made and stored. See **costumes**.

wide-angle lens See **short-focal-length lens**.

widescreen aspect ratio Any aspect ratio wider than 1.33:1, the standard ratio until the early 1950s.

wipe A transitional device between shots in which shot B wipes across shot A, either vertically or horizontally, to replace it. Although (or because) the device reminds us of early eras in filmmaking, directors continue to use it.

workflow The term for the collective editing stages completed as part of the postproduction process, including rough cut, fine cut, picture lock, finishing, and delivery.

X

XCU See **extreme close-up**.

XLS See **extreme long shot**.

Z

zoom in A shot in which the image is magnified by movement of the camera's lens only, without the camera itself moving. This magnification is the essential difference from the dolly in.

zoom lens Also known as *variable-focal-length lens*. A lens that is moved toward and away from the subject being photographed, has a continuously variable focal length, and helps reframe a shot within the take. A zoom lens permits the camera operator during shooting to shift between wide-angle and telephoto lenses without changing the focus or aperture settings. Compare **long-focal-length lens**, **middle-focal-length lens**, and **short-focal-length lens**. See also **prime lens**.

zoopraxiscope An early device for exhibiting moving pictures—a revolving disk with photographs arranged around the center.

PERMISSIONS ACKNOWLEDGEMENTS

Frontmatter

P. vii (top): © Walt Disney Co./courtesy Everett/Everett Collection; **(bottom):** Photo Courtesy of Fox Searchlight Pictures; **p. viii:** © Cohen Media Group/courtesy Everett Collection; **p. ix (top):** © Fox Searchlight/Courtesy Everett Collection; **(bottom):** © Walt Disney Co./courtesy Everett/Everett Collection; **p. x:** © Sony Pictures/Courtesy Everett Collection; **p. xi (top):** © Focus Features/courtesy Everett Collect/Everett Collection; **p. xi (bottom):** ©TriStar Pictures/Courtesy Everett Collection; **p. xii:** ©Warner Bros/courtesy Everett Collection; **p. xiii:** Movie Poster Image Art/Getty Images; **p. xiv:** © Warner Bros./courtesy Everett Collection.

Chapter 1

p. 1: © Walt Disney Co./courtesy Everett / Everett Collection; **p. 2 [1]:** Brokeback Mountain © 2017, Focus Features, River Road Entertainment, and Alberta Film Entertainment; **[2]:** Get Out © 2017, Blumhouse Productions and Monkeypaw Productions; **p. 4:** The Last of Us © 2013, Sony Entertainment and Naughty Dog; **p. 5 (bottom):** Chennai Express © 2013 Red Chillies Entertainment; **(top):** Christian Vorhofer/image BROKER/REX/Shutterstock; **p. 7 (all):** Sweeney Todd © 2007 Dreamworks Pictures; **p. 8:** Juno © 2007 Dancing Elk Productions/FOX; **p. 9 (both):** Juno © 2007 Dancing Elk Productions/FOX; **pp. 10–13 (all):** Juno © 2007 Dancing Elk Productions/FOX; **p. 14:** Back to the Future © 1985 Universal Pictures; **pp. 15–20 (all):** Juno © 2007 Dancing Elk Productions/FOX; **p. 22 [1]:** Way Down East © 1920 D.W. Griffith Productions; **[2]:** The Miracle of Morgan's Creek © 1944 Paramount Pictures; **[3]:** Rosemary's Baby © 1968 William Castle Productions; **[4]:** Knocked Up © 2012 Apatow Productions; **[5]:** Waitress © 2007 Fox Searchlight Pictures; **[6]:** Obvious Child © 2014 Rooks Nest Entertainment; **p. 23 [1]:** Star Wars: A New Hope: Episode IV © 1977, Lucasfilm Ltd.; **[2]:** The Hunger Games, © 2012 Lions Gate/Color Force; **p. 24:** Star Wars: The Last Jedi © 2017, Lucasfilm, Ram Bergman Productions, and Walt Disney Pictures; **p. 25 [1]:** Star Wars: A New Hope: Episode IV, 1977, Lucasfilm Ltd.; **[2]:** Rogue One: A Star Wars Movie © 2016, Lucasfilm Ltd.; **p. 26:** Star Wars: The Last Jedi © 2017, Lucasfilm, Ram Bergman Productions, and Walt Disney Pictures; **p. 27: (top)** Star Wars: The Last Jedi © 2017, Lucasfilm, Ram Bergman Productions, and Walt Disney Pictures; **(bottom):** Star Wars: The Force Awakens © 2015, Lucasfilm, Bad Robot, Truenorth productions, and Walt Disney Pictures.

Chapter 2

p. 32: Photo Courtesy of Fox Searchlight Pictures; **p. 33 (both):** Juno © 2007 Dancing Elk Productions/FOX; **p. 34 [1]:** Erich Lessing / Art Resource, NY; **[2–3]:** Alamy Stock Photo, **p. 35:** Anomalisa © 2015, Harmonius Claptrap and Snoot Entertainment; **p. 36 (both):** Bonnie and Clyde © 1967, Warner Brothers/Seven Arts; **p. 37 (both):** Way Down East © 1920 D.W. Griffith Productions; **p. 38 (all):** The Silence of the Lambs (1991), Strong Heart/Demme Productions; **p. 39 (all):** The New World © 2005, First Foot Films, Sarah Green Film;

p. 41 (all): The Grapes of Wrath © 1940, Twentieth Century Fox; **p. 42 (all):** Atonement © 2007, Working Title Films and Studio Canal; **p. 44:** The Gold Rush © 1925, Charles Chaplin Pictures; **p. 45 (all):** The Gold Rush © 1925 Charles Chaplin Pictures; **p. 46 (1a, b):** Boyhood © 2014, IFC Films; **[2]:** Victoria (II), MonkeyBoy; **[3]:** Happy Death Day © 2017, Blumhouse Productions; **[4]:** Dunkirk © 2017, Syncopy; **[5]:** Wonder Woman © 2017, RatPac-Dune Entertainment, DC Films, Atlas Entertainment; **p. 47:** City of God © 2002, O2 Films and VideoFilmes; **p. 48 (all):** Killer © 1989, Film Workshop; **p. 50 (all):** The Matrix © 1999 Warner Bros. Pictures; **p. 51 (both):** © 1895 Lumiere; **p. 52 (top):** Beasts of the Southern Wild © 2012, Cinereach; **[1]:** Two Days, One Night © 2014, Les films du Fleuve; **[2]:** Cloverfield © 2008, Paramount Pictures; **p. 53 [1]:** classicpaintings/Alamy Stock; **[2]:** Philadelphia Museum of Art, Pennsylvania, PA, USA / The Louise and Walter Arensberg Collection © 1950 / Bridgeman Images; **p. 54:** The Shape of Water © 2017, Bull Productions; **p. 56:** Jane Eyre © 2011 Focus Features; **pp. 57–59 (all):** Donnie Darko © 2001, Pandora Cinema.

Chapter 3

p. 63: ©Cohen Media Group/courtesy Everett Collection; **p. 65 (all):** Star Wars: Episode IV A New Hope © 1977, Lucasfilm Ltd. Production, Twentieth Century Fox; **p. 66 (all):** Slacker © 1991, Orion Classics; **p. 68 [1–2]:** Twin Peaks © 1990-91, Lynch/Frost Productions and Propaganda Films; **[3]:** Isle of Dogs © 2018, Indian paintbrush; **p. 69:** Nanook of the North © 1922, Pathé Exchange; **p. 70 (top):** Dina © 2017, Cinereach; **(bottom):** Triumph of The Will © 1935 Reichsparteitag-Film; **p. 71 [1]:** Fast, Cheap, and Out of Control © 1997, American Playhouse; **[2]:** Thin Blue Line © 1988, American Playhouse, **[3]:** Wormwood © 2017, Fourth Floor Productions and Moxie Pictures; **p. 72:** 13th © 2016, Kandoo Films; **p. 73 (both):** Grey Gardens © 1975, Portrait Films; **p. 74 [1]:** Supersize Me © 2004, The Con; **[2]:** Tarnation © 2003; **(top right):** The Act of Killing © 2012, Final cut for Real; **p. 75 (all):** Tribulation 99: Alien Anomalies under America © 1992, Other Cinema; **p. 78:** Ballet mécanique © 1924, Synchro-Ciné; **p. 79 (all):** An Andalusian Dog © 1929, Luis Bunuel; **p. 80:** Removed © 1995 Naomi Uman; **p. 81 [1]:** Borat © 2006, Four by Two; **[2]:** Under the Skin © 2013, Studio Canal; **p. 82 (both):** Symbiopsychotaxiplasm © 1968, Take One Productions; **p. 83 [1]:** Mean Streets © 1973, Taplin-Perry-Scorsese productions; **[2]:** Goodfellas © 1990, Warner Bros. Pictures; **[3]:** The Wolf of Wall Street © 2013, Paramount Pictures; **p. 85:** 2001 A Space Odyssey © 1968, Metro-Goldwyn-Mayer; **p. 87 [1]:** Iron Man 2 © 2010, Paramount Pictures; **[2]:** Under the Skin © 2013, BFI and Film4; **[3]:** Hitchcock © 2012, Fox Searchlight Picture; **p. 88:** The Godfather © 1972, Paramount Pictures and Alfran Productions; **p. 89:** White Heat © 1949, Warner Bros. Pictures; **p. 91 [1]:** Double Indemnity © 1944, Paramount Pictures; **[2]:** Sunset Boulevard © 1950, Paramount Pictures; **p. 92 [1]:** Brick © 2005, Bergman Lustig Productions; **[2]:** Fargo © 1996, PolyGram Filmed Entertainment; **[3]:** Insomnia © 2002, Alcon Entertainment; **p. 93 [1]:** Close Encounters of the Third Kind, 1977, Columbia Pictures Corporation; **[2]:** War of the Worlds © 1953, 2005, Paramount Pictures; **p. 94:** Interstellar © 2014, Legendary

Pictures; **p. 95 [1]:** Train to Busan, 2016, Next Entertainment World; **[2]:** The Conjuring, 2013, Warner Bros. Pictures; **p. 96 [1]:** Suspiria © 1977, Seda Spettacoli; **[2]:** Get Out © 2017, Blumhouse Productions and Monkeypaw Productions; **p. 97:** Bride of Frankenstein © 1935, Universal Pictures; **p. 98 (both):** Butch Cassidy and the Sundance Kid © 1969, Campanile productions; **p. 99 [1]:** Unforgiven © 1992, James Productions; **[2]:** Dead Man © 1995, Pandora Films; **p. 100:** My Darling Clementine © 1946, Twentieth Centure Fox Film; **p. 101 [1]:** The Broadway Melody © 1929, Metro-Goldwyn-Mayer; **p. 102 [1]:** Pitch Perfect © 2012, Brownstone Productions and Gold Circle Films; **[2]:** La La Land © 2016, Summit Entertainment, Black Label Media, and TIK Films; **p. 104 [1]:** Dracula © 1931, Universal Pictures; **[2]:** The Twilight Saga: Eclipse © 2010, Summit Entertainment; **(bottom right):** The Blair Witch Project © 1999, Haxan Films; **p. 105:** Guardians of the Galaxy © 2014, Walt Disney Studios Motion Pictures; **p. 106 [1]:** Tower © 2016, Go-Valley, Killer Impact, and Meredith Vieira Productions; **[2]:** Motion Painting No. 1 © 1947 Oskar Fischinger; **[3]:** The Comb © 1991, Channel Four, Koninck Studios, and La Sept; **p. 107:** Persepolis © 2007, The Kennedy/Marshall Company; **p. 109:** The Polar Express © 2004, Warner Bros. Pictures; **pp. 110–111 (all):** The Lego Movie © 2014, Warner Bros.

Chapter 4

p. 115: © Fox Searchlight/Courtesy Everett Collection; **p. 117 (all):** Notorious © 1946, RKO Radio Pictures; **p. 118:** Stranger than Fiction © 2006, Mandate Pictures; **p. 119 [1]:** The Royal Tenenbaums © 2001, Touchstone Pictures; **[2]:** The Spectacular Now © 2013, Andrew Lauren Productions and 21 Laps Entertainment; **[3]:** Deadpool © 2016, Marvel Entertainment; **p. 120:** Black Swan © 2010, Cross Creek Productions; **p. 121 (both):** Precious © 2009, Lee Daniels Entertainment; **p. 122:** District 9 © 2009, QUED International and WingNut Films; **p. 123:** Rocky © 1976, Chartoff-Winkler Productions; **p. 125:** The Big Lebowski © 1998, Working Title Films; **p. 126 (both):** The Grand Budapest Hotel © 2014, American Empirical Pictures and Indian Paintbrush; **p. 127 (all):** 127 Hours © 2010, Pathé; **p. 130 [1]:** Howl © 2010, Werc Werk Works; **[2]:** Kill Your Darlings © 2013, Killer Films; **p. 132 (all):** The Social Network © 2010, Relativity Media; **p. 134 [1]:** Great Expectations © 1946, Cineguild; **[2]:** Great Expectations © 1998, Art Linson Productions; **p. 135 (top):** Citizen Kane © 1941, Mercury Productions; **(bottom):** Memento © 2000, Summit Entertainment; **p. 136 (both):** Whiplash © 2014, Bold Films and Blumhouse Productions; **p. 137:** Game of Thrones © 2011, Television 360; **p. 138 (both):** Raging Bull © 1980, Charkoff-Winkler Productions; **p. 139 (left):** Timecode © 2000, Screen Gems; **(right):** Birdman © 2014, Regency Enterprises; **p. 141 (both):** Psycho © 1960, Shamley Productions; **p. 142:** Blade Runner © 1982, The Ladd Company; **p. 143:** Room © 2015, Telefilm Canada and Filmnation Entertainment; **pp. 145–149 (all):** Stagecoach © 1939, Walter Wanger Productions.

Chapter 5

p. 153: ©Walt Disney Co./courtesy Everett/Everett Collection; **p. 154:** Selma © 2014, Pathé Plan B Entertainment; **p. 155 [1]:** Moonrise Kingdom © 2012, American Empirical Pictures, Indian Paintbrush; **[2]:** Children of Men © 2006, Strike Entertainment, Hit and Run Productions; **p. 156:** Trolls © 2016, DreamWorks Animation; **p. 157 [1–2]:** Pan's Labyrinth © 2006, Estudios Picasso, Tequila Gang, Esperanto Filmoj; **[3]:** Andor Bujdoso/Alamy Stock Photo; **[4]:** Museo Nacional del Prado / Art Resource, NYImage Reference; **p. 158 (top):** The Social Network © 2010 Columbia Pictures, **(bottom):** Ex Machina © 2014, Flim4, DNA Films, **p. 159: (top left):** Cabiria © 1914, Itala Film; **[1–2]:** Arrival © 2016, Xenolinguistics, Lava Bear Films, FIlmNation Entertainment; **p. 160 (all):** Okja © 2017, Plan B Entertainment, Kate Street Picture Company,

Lewis Pictures; **(bottom):** The Leopard © 1963, Titanus; **p. 161 [1]:** The Get Down © 2016, Bazmark Films; **[2]:** Stranger Things © 2016, 21 Laps Entertainment; **p. 162:** Silver Screen Collection/Getty Images; **p. 163 [1]:** Monster © 2003, Denver & Delilah Films, K/W Productions; **[2]:** Mad Max: Fury Road © 2015, Village Roadshow Pictures, RatPac-Dune Entertainment, Kennedy Miller Productions; **[3–4]:** Young Adult © 2011, Mandate pictures, Denver & Delilah Films, Mr. Mudd; **p. 164 [1]:** The Private Lives of Elizabeth and Essex © 1939, Warner Bros. Pictures; **[2]:** Hatfield House, Hertfordshire, UK / Bridgeman Images; **(right):** Alice in Wonderland © 2010, Walt Disney Pictures, Roth Films; **p. 165 (top left):** No Country for Old Men © 2007, Scott Rudin Productions, Mike Zoss Productions; **(bottom right) [1–2]:** The Dark Knight © 2008, Warner Bros., Legendary Entertainment; **p. 166 [1–3]:** City of God © 2002, 02 Filmes, VideoFilmes; **p. 167 (left) [1]:** The Sweet Smell of Success © 1957, Norma Productions, Curtleigh Productions; **(left) [2]:** Ja Manhattan © 1979, Jack Rollins & Charles H. Joffe Productions; **(right) [1–2]:** Citizen Kane © 1941, RKO Radio Pictures, Mercury Productions; **p. 168 [1]:** Scarlett Empress © 1934, Paramount Pictures; **(bottom right):** John Wick © 2014, Thunder Road Pictures; **p. 169 (left) [1]:** THX1138 © 1971, American Zoetrope, Warner Bros.; **[2]:** Arrival © 2016, Xenolinguistics, Lava Bear Films, FIlmNation Entertainment; **(right) [1]:** Citizen Kane © 1941, RKO Radio Pictures, Mercury Productions; **[2]:** Don't breathe © 2016, Screen Gems, Stage 6 Films, Ghost House Pictures; **p. 170 (top left):** Bride of Frankenstein © 1935, Universal Pictures; **(bottom left):** The Godfather © 1972, Paramount Pictures, Alfran Productions; **(top right):** Laura © 1944, 20th Century Fox; **p. 171 (top) [1–2]:** The Night of the Hunter © 1955, Paul Gregory Productions; **(bottom right):** AF archive/Alamy Stock Photo; **p. 172 (top) [1–2]:** The Best Years of Our Lives, 1946, The Samuel Goldwyn Company; **p. 173 [1–2]:** Hidden Figures © 2016, Fox 2000 Pictures, Chernin Entertainment/Levantine Films; **p. 174 (top left):** The Shining © 1980, Warner Bros., Hawk Films; **(top right):** Ratcatcher © 1999, Pathé Pictures, BBC Films; **(bottom left) [1–2]:** Run Lola Run © 1998, X-Filme Creative Pool, WDR, Arte; **p. 175 (top):** The Return of the King © 2003, Wingnut Films, The Saul Zaentz Company; **(bottom left):** Notorious © 1946, Vanguard Films; **p. 176 (top left):** Citizen Kane © 1941, RKO Radio Pictures, Mercury Productions; **(bottom left):** The Little Foxes © 1941, Samuel Goldwyn Productions; **(bottom right):** Crouching Tiger, Hidden Dragon © 2000, Columbia Pictures Film Production Asia, Good Machine International; **p. 177 [1]:** Gravity © 2013, Heyday Films, Esperanto Filmoj; **[2]:** Royal Wedding © 1951, MGM, Loew's; **[3]:** Forrest Gump © 1994, Wendy Finerman Productions; **p. 178 (top):** The Bicycle Thieves © 1948, Produzioni De Sica; **(bottom):** Georges Méliès' The Eclipse Star-Film 1907; **p. 179 [1–4]:** The Cabinet of Dr. Caligari © 1920, Decla-Bioscop AG; **p. 180 [1]:** Bride of Frankenstein © 1935, Universal Pictures; **[2]:** The Third Man © 1949, London Film Productions; **[3]:** The Night of the Hunter © 1955, Paul Gregory Productions; **[4]:** Edward Scissorhands © 1990, Twentieth Century Fox; **[5]:** Twin Peaks: The Return © 2017, Lynch/Frost Productions, Propaganda Films; **p. 182:** Sleepy Hollow © 1999, Mandalay Pictures, Scott Rudin Pictures, American Zoetrope, Tim Burton Productions; **p. 183 [1–2]:** Sleepy Hollow © 1999, Mandalay Pictures, Scott Rudin Pictures, American Zoetrope, Tim Burton Productions; **[3]:** Black Sunday © 1997, Paramount Pictures, Robert Evans Company; **pp. 183 (left), 184–185 (all):** Sleepy Hollow © 1999, Mandalay Pictures, Scott Rudin Pictures, American Zoetrope, Tim Burton Productions.

Chapter 6

p. 187: © Sony Pictures/Courtesy Everett Collection; **p. 189:** The Social Network © 2010, Relativity Media, Scott Rudin Productions, Michael De Luca Productions, Trigger Street Productions; **p. 190:** In Cold Blood © 1967, Pax Enterprises, Inc.; **p. 191 [1]:** Pi © 1998, Protozoa Pictures;

[2]: Carol © 2015, Number 9 Films, film4, Killer Films; **p. 193 [1]:** Stage-coach © 1939, Walter Wanger Productions; **[2]:** The Searchers © 1956, C.V. Whitney Pictures; **[3–4]:** Mad Max: Fury Road © 2015, Village Roadshow Pictures, Kennedy Miller Mitchell, RatPac-Dune Entertainment; **p. 194 (top left):** The Seventh Seal © 1957, Svensk Filmindustri (SF); **(bottom left) [1]:** A Girl Walks Home Alone at Night © 2014, Logan Pictures, Spectre Vision; **[2]:** Ida © 2013, Opus Film, Phoenix Film Investments, Canal+ Polska; **p. 195:** High Noon © 1952, Stanley Kramer Productions; **p. 196 [1]:** The Great Train Robbery © 1903, Warner Bros.; **[2]:** Way Down East © 1920, D.W. Griffith Productions; **[3]:** Black Pirate © 1926, The Elton Corporation, Technicolor Motion Picture Corporation; **[4]:** Gone with the Wind © 1939, Selznick International Pictures, Metro-Goldwyn-Mayer; **p. 197 (bottom):** Barry Lyndon © 1975, Hawk Films; **(top):** Tangerine © 2015, Duplass Brothers Productions; **p. 198 (both):** Fantastic Beasts © 2016, Heyday Films; **(bottom):** My Darling Clementine © 1946, Twentieth Century Fox Film Corporation; **p. 199 (left):** Dave Monahan, **(right) [1–2]:** Me and Earl and the Dying Girl © 2015, Indian Paintbrush; **p. 200 (top):** Requiem for a Dream © 2000, Thousand Words, Protozoa Pictures; **(right):** Sunset Boulevard © 1951, Paramount Pictures; **(left):** Barry Lyndon © 1975, Hawk Films; **p. 201 (both):** Hurt Locker © 2008, Voltage Pictures, Grosvenor Park Media; **p. 202 (top left) [1–2]:** The Devil's Backbone © 2001, Canal+ España, **(bottom right):** Cameraperson © 2016, Big Mouth Productions, Fork Films; **p. 203 (all):** The Grand Budapest Hotel © 2014, Indian Paintbrush; **p. 204:** The Graduate © 1967, Mike Nichols/Lawrence Turman Productions; **p. 206 (all):** The King's Speech © 2010, UK Film Council, See-Saw Films; **p. 208 [1–2]:** Gold Diggers of 1933 © 1933, Warner Bros.; **[3]:** Citizen Kane © 1941, Mercury Productions; **p. 209 [1]:** Jackie © 2016, LD Entertainment, Wild Bunch; **[2]:** Jackie © 2016, LD Entertainment, Wild Bunch; **p. 210 (left) [1]:** Love Me Tonight © 1932 Paramount Pictures; **[2]:** North by Northwest © 1959, Metro-Goldwyn-Mayer; **(right) [1]:** Do the Right Thing © 1989, 40 Acres and a Mule Filmworks, **[2]:** The Shining © 1980, The Producer Circle Company, Peregrine Productions, Hawk Films; **p. 211 (top left):** The Bride of Frankenstein © 1935, Universal Pictures; **(bottom right) [1–2]:** Lion © 2016, The Weinstein Company; **p. 212 (all):** M © 1931, Nero-Film; **p. 214 (top both):** Citizen Kane © 1941, Mercury Productions; **(bottom):** picture-alliance / Newscom; **p. 216 (all):** Touch of Evil © 1958, Universal Pictures; **p. 217 (both):** The Shining © 1980, The Producer Circle Company, Peregrine Productions, Hawk Films; **p. 218 (left):** ©DreamWorks/Courtesy Everett Collection; **p. 218 (right):** Russian Ark © 2002, Seville Pictures; **p. 219 [1–6]:** Chinatown © 1974, Paramount-Penthouse; **p. 221 (top left):** Mother! © 2017, Protozoa Pictures; **(bottom right) [1–2]:** The Lower Depths © 1957, Toho Studios; **p. 222 (all):** The Bad Batch © 2016, Annapurna Pictures, VICE Films; **p. 223 (both):** Silence of the Lambs © 1991, Strong Heart/Demme Production; **p. 224 (all):** The Birds © 1963, Alfred J. Hitchcock Productions; **p. 225 [1]:** A Clockwork Orange © 1971, Hawk Films, Polaris Productions; **[2]:** 21 Jump Street © 2012, Original Film; **p. 226 [1]:** The Revenant © 2015, Regency Enterprises, RatPac Entertainment; **[2]:** Visitors © 2013, Cinedigm; **p. 227:** Birth © 2004, New Line Cinema; **p. 228:** Swiss Army Man © 2016, Tadmor, Astrakan Films AB; **p. 229: (top)** Blade Runner 2049 © 2017, Warner Bros; **(bottom):** Metropolis © 1927, Ufa; **p. 230 (both):** The Hobbit © 2012, WingNut Films, New Line Cinema, Metro-Goldwyn-Mayer; **p. 231 (all):** Moonlight © 2016, A24, Plan B Entertainment; **pp. 232–233 (all):** Moonlight © 2016, A24, Plan B Entertainment.

Chapter 7

p. 235: ©Focus Features/courtesy Everett Collect / Everett Collection; **p. 236:** The Quiet American © 2002, Miramax; **p. 239:** I'm Not There © 2007, Endgame Entertainment; **p. 240 [1]:** We Need to Talk About Kevin © 2011, BBC Films; **[2]:** Only Lovers Left Alive © 2013, Recorded Picture Company; **[3]:** Doctor Strange © 2016, Marvel Studios; **[4]:** Okja © 2017, Plan B Entertainment; **p. 244:** Broken Blossoms, 1919, D.W. Griffith Productions; **p. 245:** Singin' in the Rain © 1952, Metro-Goldwyn-Mayer; **p. 248:** The Philadelphia Story © 1940, Metro-Goldwyn-Mayer; **p. 249 [1]:** A Place in the Sun © 1951, Paramount Pictures; **[2]:** Who's Afraid of Virginia Woolf? © 1966, Warner Bros; **p. 251 [1]:** On the Waterfront © 1954, Horizon Pictures; **[2]:** East of Eden © 1955, Warner Bros.; **p. 252:** Iron Man © 2008, Paramount Pictures and Marvel Enterprises; **p. 253 [1]:** The Letter © 1940, Warner Bros; **[2]:** The Beguiled © 2017, American Zoetrope; **p. 255 (left) [1]:** The Big Trail © 1930, Fox Film Corporation; **(left) [2]:** The Shootist © 1976, Paramount Pictures; **(right) [1]:** Starman © 1984, Columbia Pictures Corporation, Industrial Light & Magic (ILM), and Delphi II Productions; **(right) [2]:** True Grit © 2010, Skydance Productions; **p. 256:** The Social Network © 2010, Relativity Media; **p. 258:** The Bank Dick © 1940, Universal Pictures; **p. 259:** The Maltese Falcon © 1941, Warner Bros.; **p. 261 (top left) [1]:** Tinker Tailor Soldier Spy © 1979; BBC; **[2]:** Tinker Tailor Soldier Spy © 2011, StudioCanal; **(bottom right):** Henry V © 1944, Two Cities Films; **p. 262:** The Man from London © 2007, TT Filmulmuhely; **p. 263 [1]:** Knocked Up © 2007, Apatow Productions; **[2]:** Edward Scissorhands © 1990, Twentieth Century Fox; **p. 265:** Taxi Driver © 1976, Columbia Pictures; **p. 266 (both):** Citizen Kane © 1941, Mercury Productions; **p. 267:** Citizen Kane © 1941, Mercury Productions; **p. 268 (all):** Citizen Kane © 1941, Mercury Productions; **p. 269 (all):** Citizen Kane © 1941, Mercury Productions; **p. 270:** Boyhood © 2014, IFC Productions; **p. 271 (top):** The Passion of Joan of Arc © 1928, Société générale des films; **(bottom):** Morocco © 1930, Paramount Pictures; **p. 273 [1]:** Throne of Blood © 1957, Toho Studios; **[2]:** The Piano © 1993, CiBy 2000 and Jan Chapman Productions; **p. 274:** 12 Years a Slave © 2013, Summit Entertainment; **p. 275:** My Week with Marilyn © 2011, The Weinstein Company; **p. 276: (all):** Blue Valentine © 2010, Hunting Lane Films.

Chapter 8

p. 281: © TriStar Pictures/Courtesy Everett Colle/Everett Collection; **p. 283:** Step © 2017, Epiphany Story Lab; **p. 284 [1]:** Popperfoto/Getty Images; **[2]:** Photofest; **p. 285:** Annie Hall © 1977, Jack Rollins & Charles H. Joffe Productions; **p. 286 (all):** Loving © 2016, Raindog Films and Big Beach Films; **p. 287:** T2: Trainspotting © 2017, FIlm4, Creative Scotland; **p. 288 [1]:** 500 Days of Summer © 2009, Dune Entertainment; **[2]:** Annie Hall © 1977, Jack Rollins & Charles H. Joffe Productions; **p. 290 (all):** Requiem for a Dream © 2000, Thousand Words, Protozoa Pictures; **p. 291 (all):** Requiem for a Dream © 2000, Thousand Words, Protozoa Pictures; **p. 292 [1–2]:** Lucy © 2014, EuropaCorp; **p. 293:** Star Wars: The Force Awakens © 2015, Lucasfilm Ltd., Bad Robot Productions; **p. 294 (left) [1]:** Lawrence of Arabia © 1962, Horizon Pictures; **[2]:** Lawrence of Arabia © 1962, Horizon Pictures; **(right) [1–3]:** Shaun of the Dead © 2004, StudioCanal, Working Title Films; **p. 295 (both):** Citizen Kane © 1941, Mercury Productions; **p. 296 [2]:** Butch Cassidy and the Sundance Kid © 1969, Newman-Foreman Company; **p. 298 (all):** Natural Born Killers © 1994, Regency Enterprises; **p. 299 (top left):** Dr. Strangelove or: How I learned to Stop Worrying and Love the Bomb © 1964, Hawk Films; **(top right) [1–2]:** The Good, The Bad, and the Ugly © 1966, Produzioni Europee Associati (PEA); **p. 301 (all):** Casablanca © 1942, Warner Bros., First National Pictures; **p. 302 (all):** Breathless © 1960, Les Productions Georges de Beauregard; **p. 303 [1–3]:** Election © 1999, MTV Films, Bona Fide Productions; **p. 305 (all):** Billy Lynn's Long Half Time Walk

INDEX